Wögala raus.   Wos mog denn dai doi klana Maus?   Wos mog er klaner? Sög ers ner.

Thös mir doi Sauterla hergöben.   Dös Gaila is mei Leib und Löben.

en her?   Wen doi Latern klener wär: Mei Sach is wül recht schoi Madàm.

TOYS, TRIFLES & TRINKETS

BASE-METAL MINIATURES FROM LONDON 1200 TO 1800

Copyright © 2005 Museum of London

First published in 2005

Unicorn Press
76 Great Suffolk Street
London SE1 OBL

unicornpress@btinternet.com

ISBN: 0 906 290 74 0

All rights reserved

No part of the contents of this book may be reproduced, stored in a retrieval system, or transmitted in any form or by any means, electronic, mechanical, photocopying, recording, or otherwise, without the written permission of Museum of London and Unicorn Press.

Designed by Helen Swansbourne
Printed and bound by Compass Press Limited

Front cover: Detail from *Retour d'un pèlerinage à Saint Antoine*, c. 1550 by Pieter Aertsen [1508–1575] showing a trinket stall with pilgrim souvenirs, baubles and toys. It is possible that some of the base-metal toys included in this book were sold on stalls of this kind. See plate XV, p. 368. Oil on panel, 110 x 170 cm. Musées royaux des Beaux-Arts de Belgique, Brussels

Back cover: Detail from *Het Straatje*, 1655–60 by Jan Vermeer [1632–1675] showing children playing on the pavement outside their home in Delft. See plate XII, p. 364. Oil on canvas, 54.3 x 44 cm. Rijksmuseum, Amsterdam

Endpapers: *Der Nürnbergisch Kindlesmark*, 1797 by Johann Georg Trautner [1750–1812]. Etching, 28.9 x 34.5 cm. Germanisches Nationalmuseum, Nuremberg. Inscriptions below each trinket stall from left to right and top to bottom are as follows:

> I'd like such a little angel.
> I am not selling this basket for that amount of money.
> I want this little carriage over there.
> What would you like, darling?
> What would you like son? Just say it.
>
> If only this little carriage was mine!
> Would you hand me that knife?
> Here is the money for your pliers.
> Would you give me that bag?
> I want this horse more than anything else in the world.
>
> I'd like one of these, mummy!
> And I'd like this little drum.
> What shall I give you?
> If only your lantern was smaller!
> My things are quite beautiful, madam.
>
> I shall have two roasted herrings.
> Roasted almonds, aren't they?
> Miss, take this candle.
> This needlework table would not be bad.
> I quite like this copper bow.

Title page: Detail of pewterer Robert Peircy's trade card, c. 1750. Trustees of the British Museum, Heal Collection

Contents page: *York Water Gate and the Adelphi by Moonlight*, c. 1850 by Henry Pether [1828–1865]. See plate XII, p. 357. Oil on canvas, 58.7 x 84.1 cm. Museum of London, Acc. no. 60.50

Drawings by Nick Griffiths: pp. 28, 49, 61, 112, 117, 119, 126, 127, 199, 200, 206, 351 & 393

TOYS, TRIFLES & TRINKETS

BASE-METAL MINIATURES FROM LONDON 1200 TO 1800

Hazel Forsyth with Geoff Egan

MUSEUM OF LONDON

UNICORN PRESS
LONDON

Contents

Acknowledgements 6

Preface 7

Abbreviations 8

Conventions used in the text 9

Note to readers 9

PART I 10

Introduction

The origins of the Museum of London's base-metal toy collection 12

Mudlarks and the Thames foreshore 14

Toys on the foreshore 20

Archaeological contexts for early base-metal toys (GE) 26

Toys, trifles or trinkets? 32

Markets and consumers 40

Metallurgy and manufacture 52

Trends in dating and production (GE) 58

PART II 74

Catalogue

1 **Arms & armour** 76
Armour 78
Artillery 79
Edged weapons 86
Firearms 87

2 **Cooking vessels & utensils** 106
Bowls 110
Cauldrons 111
Dripping pans 116
Frying pans 119
Gridirons 124
Pot hangers 127
Skillet 128
Spit 130

3 **Cutlery** 132
Forks 134
Knives 135
Spoons 136

4 **Figurines** (GE) 140
Equestrian figures 144
Female figures 152
Male figures 158

5 **Fixtures, furnishings & other household items** 178
Candlesticks 181
Hearth furniture & grates 184
Mirrors & mirror frames 189
Picture 191
Tray 192
Voider 192

6 **Furniture** 194
Bird cages 197
Buffets, cup boards or cupboards 198
Chairs 213
Chests 218
Cradle 234
Stool 234

7 Shies 238

8 Tableware 242
   Basins, dishes, plates & saucers 245
   Drinking & serving vessels 275
   Porringers 296

9 Tools 310
   Handsaw 312
   Shears 313
   Scissors 313

10 Transport (GE) 314
   Carriages & coaches 316
   Ships 323
   Anchors 324

11 Twirlers 332

12 Watches 336

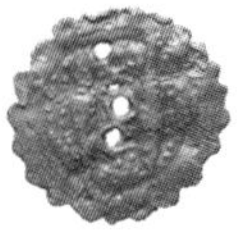

13 Whirligigs 386

14 Windmills 392

15 Miscellaneous 398

PART III 408

Appendix I 410
Microstructure and composition of pewter miniatures from medieval London
Meg Chuping Wang

Appendix II 424
Elemental analyses of six tin-lead toy watches from London
Dafydd Griffiths

Appendix III 436
Pewter toymakers from the Worshipful Company of Pewterers' records and other sources

Appendix IV 441
The maker/s I(D)Q
Geoff Egan & Hazel Forsyth

Bibliography 443

Concordance 457

Index 472

Acknowledgements

For their advice and help I would like to thank Silke Ackerman, Vivienne Aldous, the late Janet Arnold, David Beasley, Peter Briers, Valentine & Roderick Butler, Victor Chinnery, Ann Eatwell, David Edge, Anne Donnelley, Ian Eaves, Firth & Janine Fairbank, Penelope Fussell, Jan Gadd, Dr Loreen Giese, Philippa Glanville, Dana Goodburn-Brown, Christopher Green, Nick Hall, Charles Hull, Philip Lankester, Santina Levy, Ian McIntyre, Keith Miller, Gustav Milne, James Mosely, Anthony North, Graeme Rimer, Dr Ann Saunders, Peter Saunders, the late Brian Spencer, David Starley, Anthony Steiner, Judith Stephenson, Beverly Straube, Peter Tandy, Professor Joan Thirsk, David Thompson, Peter Thornton, Jenny Tiramani, H.J.E. van Beuningen, Karen Watts, Michael Webber, Sir George White and Dr Annemarieke Willemsen.

I would like to thank Lyn Thompson of Dolls' House Parade, Chislehurst, Kent, for her advice and help on the current market, and I should like to express particular gratitude to Dr Ron Homer, Archivist of the Worshipful Company of Pewterers, for reading bits of the text and for his helpful advice and comments. Particular thanks must also go to Jonathan Horne of Jonathan Horne Antiques, London, for mounting the exhibition *Playthings from the Past* at his gallery, which together with the accompanying publication (Egan 1996) paved the way for the Pilson Collection to be made over to the Museum of London.

The staff of the Corporation of London Record Office and the Guildhall Library have been very kind, and I would like to offer my thanks to the Worshipful Company of Clockmakers, the Worshipful Company of Drapers, the Worshipful Company of Haberdashers, the Worshipful Company of Goldsmiths, the Worshipful Company of Mercers and the Worshipful Company of Pewterers.

Within the Museum of London, I have been grateful for the support of John Clark, Beverley Cook, Meriel Jeater, Rose Johnson, Jacqueline Pearce, Kate Starling, Hedley Swain and Alex Werner. Particular thanks must go to John Chase and Richard Stroud for their photography, Johan Hermans for helping with Dutch translations and Jenny Hall for her innumerable kindnesses. I would also like to thank Sally Brooks for her help and useful comments, and I am especially indebted to Mark Kilfoyle, and Roz Sherris who has formatted the text, produced the concordance and has generally done a fantastic job in turning my typescript into a book. Special thanks is also extended to Mr S. Shemmell for the generous gift of four toy watches, and to a number of members of the Society of Thames Mudlarks who have also donated toys and miniatures to the Museum's collection. Their names are recorded with gratitude: Mr J. Auld, Mr K. Bellringer, Mr F. Fairbank, Mr R. Hooper, Mr T. Letch, Mr A.G. Pilson, Messrs R. & I. Smith.

Thanks are due to all the contributors to the catalogue, Nick Griffiths for his illustrations, Dr Dafydd Griffiths and Meg Wang for their analytical work, Geoff Egan for his archaeological expertise and perspective, and Helen Swansbourne, who has done a marvellous job on the design. Last, but by no means least, I would like to thank my family who have encouraged and supported me throughout.

Preface

'Men deal with life, as children with their play,
Who first misuse, then cast their toys away.'[1]

This book is the first comprehensive study of an intriguing but relatively neglected subject: base-metal (lead-alloy and copper-alloy) toys and miniatures mass-produced between approximately 1200 and 1800.

Based on the Museum of London's collection, which is unrivalled for its size, diversity and quality, the book is divided into three parts. Part I begins with an account of the origins of the collection and provides an overview of the social and cultural context in which the toys were manufactured and marketed. Other themes in this section include a brief discussion of children's playthings, trends in dating and production as well as a consideration of the various meanings of the word 'toy' and information on the makers and their milieu.

The second and main part is a catalogue of the Museum's collection. In the catalogue the material has been arranged into 15 sections by subject and these are presented in an alphabetical sequence apart from the unidentified items, which are placed in the miscellaneous category at the end. Each section has a discursive piece at the beginning which attempts to place the finds in their cultural context and, where possible, the surviving toys and miniatures are compared with their full-scale counterparts. The last part contains various appendices on metallurgy, together with a list of 17th- and 18th-century London pewterers engaged in the production of toys from the records of the Worshipful Company of Pewterers, the Sun Insurance Company and other sources. A short assessment of the work of the maker/s I(D)Q is also considered in this section.

All of the toys and miniatures in this book have been recovered from the ground, and every item listed in the catalogue was found in the capital or the wider metropolitan area. More base-metal toys of medieval and early modern date have been recovered from London than any other place in the British Isles, a phenomenon due to the commercial and economic prosperity of the capital, its dominance of trade and manufacture, the cultural and social mores of its inhabitants, and above all to extensive archaeology and the unparalleled deposits of the Thames foreshore. Where possible, references have been made to similar objects from other parts of the country, as well as to those found in Continental collections. Literary, documentary and pictorial sources have been used throughout, and the various types of evidence are discussed in detail below.

Abbreviations

Acc. no.	Accession number	JPS	*Journal of the Pewter Society*
BM	British Museum	L	Length
Burl. Mag.	*Burlington Magazine*	LTR	London Topographical Record
Cat. no.	Catalogue number	MC	Mayor's Court
City	City of London	MoL/Museum	Museum of London
CLRO	Corporation of London Record Office	MoLAS	Museum of London Archaeological Service
Com. Ser.	Common Serjeants Book	MS/S	Manuscript/s
Commissioners	Crown Estate Commissioners	NACF	National Art Collections Fund
Conn.	*Connoisseur*	OC	Orphans Court
Cott.	H.H. Cotterell, *Old Pewter: Its Makers and Marks* (London, 1929; repr. 1963)	OED	Oxford English Dictionary
		PA	Potential acquisition
		Pers. comm.	Personal communication
D	Design	PLA	Port of London Authority
Diam	Diameter	PRO	Public Record Office
Doc.	Documents	RA	Royal Armouries
Dpt	Depth	Sec.	Section
EETS	Early English Text Society	Soc.	Society
EHR	*Economic History Review*	Soc. TM	Society of Thames Mudlarks
Enq. no.	Museum of London enquiry number	T	Type
		Th	Thickness
Exch.	Exchequer Documents	V&A	Victoria & Albert Museum
Furn. Hist. Soc.	Furniture History Society	W	Width
GL	Guildhall Library	WCP	Worshipful Company of Pewterers
H	Height	[ ]	Archaeological context number
Inv.	Inventory	< >	Archaeological find number

Conventions used in the text

The subject sections in the catalogue have been allotted a unique number which corresponds to their alphabetical sequence (see preface). Against each entry, the first number indicates the section and the second denotes a particular item within that section. When two or more items are of the same design they have been grouped together under one entry, and the accession number sequence follows the Museum's convention of placing the earliest accessioned items first. Otherwise every object has been given a separate number in the catalogue series. Illustrations are numbered consecutively. Tables are enumerated within each chapter or section. Where there are multiple objects of the same design, the best example, indicated with an asterisk, has been selected for photography. Where catalogue entries have the same dimensions, only one set of measurements is given.

The Museum of London was established in 1975 by the merger of the Guildhall Museum and the London Museum and the object-numbering or accession systems of the three museums are summarised as follows. The Guildhall Museum used a running number system. Each number referred to a single object or occasionally a group of objects; in the latter case, the group number was subdivided by the addition of a lower-case letter suffix (e.g. 8031a). The London Museum initially used a letter prefix followed by a running number, with 'A' denoting permanent acquisitions (e.g. A13941). But in 1927, this was changed to a two-digit prefix indicating the year the object was acquired, and a full stop followed by a number for the overall accession, i.e. year.accession number (e.g. 79.262). Multiple objects within one accession were indicated by a running sequence of numbers after a slash, i.e. year.accession number/object number (e.g. 82.147/22). The Museum of London adopted the London Museum style (e.g. 98.2/100). In 2000, the year prefix was changed to four digits.

Toys recovered from archaeological contexts have a two or three letter site code followed by the year (two digits) of excavation, the context (layer) number and the find/accession number (e.g. ABO98 [388] <1992>.

To protect the anonymity of individual owners of base-metal toys in London and elsewhere, the term 'Private Collection' has been used. Over the last 30 years thousands of finds have been brought into the Museum for identification. Those which were not acquired were recorded on special 'object identification sheets'. In recent years, the system of recording includes individual object cards, and each item is given a unique enquiry number. Occasionally this enquiry number has been cited in a catalogue entry (e.g. 2076/1).

Note to readers

Contributions to the text by Geoff Egan are indicated by the initials GE. The ongoing debate about the attribution of early base-metal miniatures as playthings for children or novelties for adults is reflected in the viewpoints of the two authors.

Unless stated otherwise, all of the catalogued objects have come from the Thames foreshore. Occasionally records have been kept of the general find spot and when this is known the provenance is noted. The term 'City' with an initial capital letter denotes the area subject to the jurisdiction of the Corporation of London, and 'London' means the whole metropolitan area of 1,554 square kilometres within the Museum of London's collecting remit.

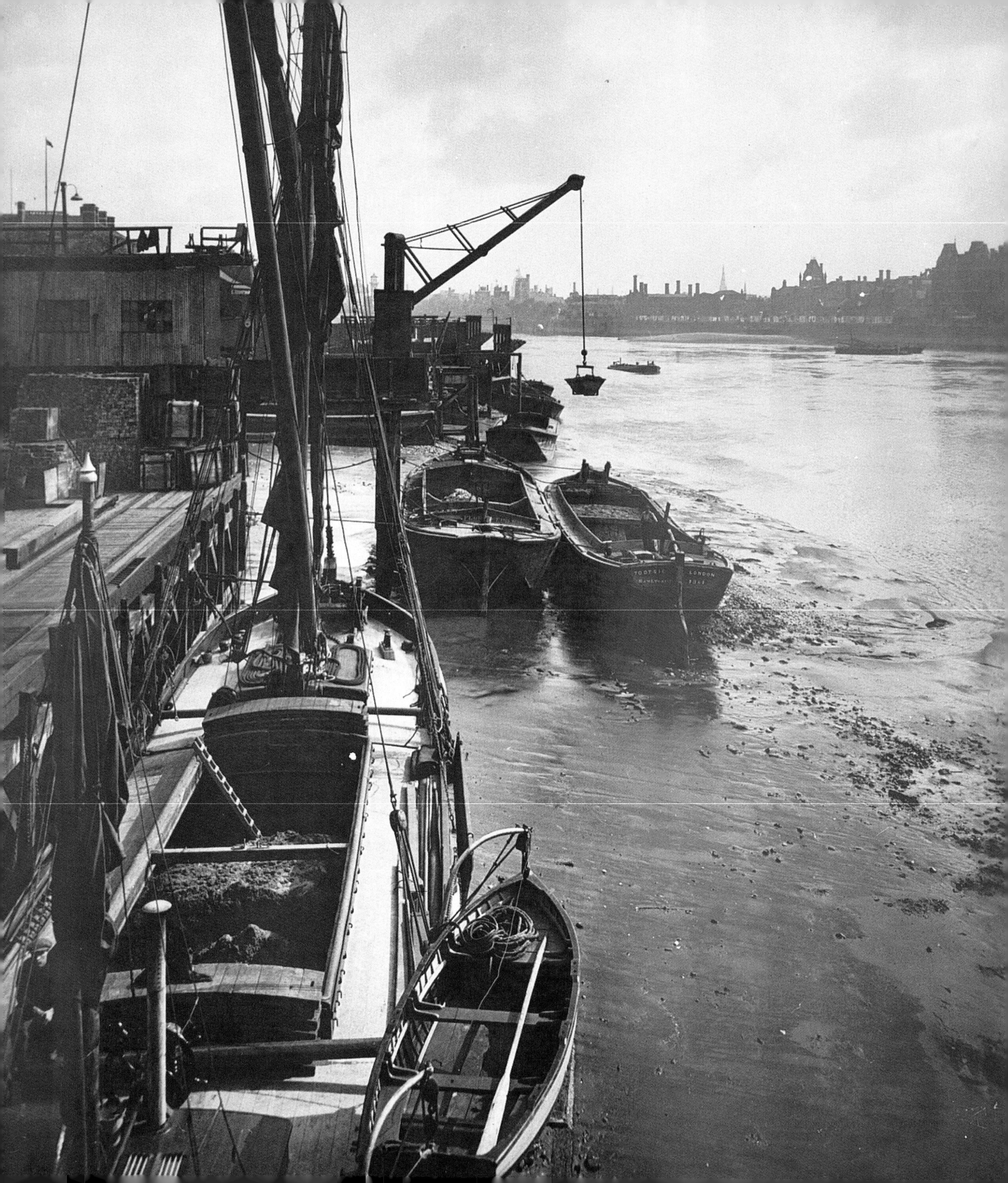

PART I
Introduction

Fig. 1. Looking east from Vauxhall Bridge towards Lambeth at low tide. The sailing barge in the foreground is unloading a cargo of building materials at Bridge Wharf and the hydraulic crane is discharging gravel from a dumb barge and lighter. When this photograph was taken London was the greatest port in the world and there were 10,000 lighters and 1,000 sailing barges on the Thames. Large stretches of the foreshore were consolidated to create level 'barge beds' which enabled the vessels to load and discharge their cargoes effectively.
Photograph by George Reid, late 1920s – early 1930s
Museum of London, Acc. no. IN8891

'As I came up she opened her arms, and dropped on the grass before me a toy-engine with three wheels missing, a doll without arms, a humming-top with no peg, a paint-box with no brushes, and one cube of paint, a clockwork windmill, wanting two sails, four lead soldiers badly chipped, and a toy gun without a trigger.

She said: "You can have these. I don't want them." On the way home Uncle Frank said: "What's the matter, cock? Got the toothache?" I said "No," and laughed...

If the waste patch behind the potting-shed of a big house at Greenwich is ever dug up by its new owner, he will find, about a foot below the surface, some half-dozen broken toys.'[2]

The origins of the Museum of London's base-metal toy collection

THE COLLECTIONS OF THE MUSEUM OF LONDON and those of its precursors the Guildhall and London Museums, have been assembled to promote understanding and appreciation of the history of London and of its society and culture.[3] Like most museum collections, however, serendipity and chance have had as big a part to play as policy, and many items have been acquired in a piecemeal and *ad hoc* fashion. The first base-metal toys and miniatures were acquired in the late 19th and early 20th centuries from private collectors and dealers, and in the 1950s a few chance finds by London navvies during the post-war re-development of the City were added to the Guildhall Museum's collection. During the last 30 years the toy collection has grown exponentially following the invention of the metal detector, official recognition and monitoring of the activities of professional and hobby mudlarks on the Thames foreshore, and latterly through a massive and intensive programme of archaeological investigation. The following sections examine the various sources of evidence that have contributed to the growth of the toy collection since the 1970s.

English galleon recovered from Billingsgate foreshore in 1981
Acc. no. 91.61/1, Cat. no. 10.16

Mudlarks and the Thames foreshore

'…*yt is to bee noted that as there is everye daye twoo ebbes and two floddes, so is there also everye Mooneth twoo courses of greate tyddes and scant tydes…*'[4]

In Halsbury's *Laws of England*, the foreshore is defined as 'the whole of the shore that is from time to time exposed by the receding tide'.[5] For the river Thames with a tidal fall of as much as seven metres, this means over 100 kilometres of foreshore between Teddington and the outer estuary. Hydrologists have calculated that an area of 1,200,000 square metres of foreshore is exposed at every low tide and this 'most extensive and valuable archaeological site'[6] in London has become an extraordinarily rich hunting ground for treasure hunters and those 'commonly known by the name of "mud-larks", from being compelled, in order to obtain the articles they seek, to wade … through the mud left on the shore by the retiring tide'.[7] The anaerobic conditions of the foreshore mud has ensured the preservation of metals and organic materials which would have otherwise perished, and most of the toys in this volume have been recovered from this source.

The first person to recognize the historical value and significance of foreshore finds, and to comment specifically on toys, was Ivor Nöel Hume who worked for the Guildhall Museum as an archaeologist in the immediate post-war period. His book *Treasure in the Thames* published in 1955 includes an evocative description of children's toys which is worth quoting in full:

> Some are broken and thrown away for that reason, while others are complete save for wear occasioned by their long sojourn in the river. Their discovery evokes the echo of childish tears shed more than three centuries ago. Toys were neither so varied nor so plentiful as they are in this modern age, but, strange as it may seem, their basic forms have changed little.[8]

Hume noted that most of the objects littering the surface of the foreshore had already been removed by the mudlarks 'who foraged *en masse*' after the Second World War, and he suggested that although it was possible that further items would be drawn to the surface by tidal action it was simply not worth digging for them. Any attempt to do so, he argued, would cause serious if not irreparable damage to the foreshore, and many of the potentially productive sites were inaccessible anyway because they were covered by barge beds.[9] The book ends with a heartfelt plea that the finds of the river are not for private collectors, but 'for local museums who can … preserve for the nation the Treasure that still lies in the Thames'.

The foreshore was left relatively untouched by mudlarks until the early 1970s when 'treasure hunting' with the metal detector became a widespread and popular pastime. Soon holes were dug to retrieve the finds, and in an effort to protect the fragile foreshore environment and ensure that any antiquities were recorded and protected, the Port of London Authority (PLA), the Crown Estate Commissioners (the Commissioners) and the Museum of London introduced a licensing arrangement in 1979 which has operated with minor changes ever since.[10] Under the terms of the licence 'every object found by the holder, its exact location and details of the circumstances of its finding must be reported as quickly as possible to the Museum'. The PLA and the Commissioners reserve their rights of ownership in any objects found, but there is a tacit understanding that mudlarks can retain their finds if they choose to do so. Those wishing to dispose of their finds, however, are required to offer first refusal to the Museum. If the finds are acquired as a 'purchase' the finder is given an *ex gratia* payment which is based on a mutually agreed valuation.

Under the terms of their licence, mudlarks can search the whole foreshore between Teddington and the Thames Barrier, apart from the areas adjacent to the Palace of Westminster and its gardens, the Tower of London, parts of the foreshore at Lambeth and the Bridewell Estate foreshore in Wapping. Other areas of particular archaeological importance or designated as an ancient monument are also restricted and occasionally access is temporarily prohibited for environmental or safety reasons. But while much of the 100 kilometres of foreshore is theoretically accessible for search, and the odd toy has been recovered from Kew in the west to Greenwich and Dartford in the east, most of the mudlarking activity is concentrated in the areas closest to, or within, the jurisdiction of the City and the opposing Southwark shore. Until relatively recently this area of approximately 6km from Vauxhall to Wapping was a hive of activity and one of the most commercially important sectors of the river. Quays, landing stages, slipways and stairs lined the banks, dutiable cargoes were unloaded and vessels thronged the wharves. Barge beds or 'hards' of compacted sediment, re-used masonry or chalk were constructed on the foreshore between the river walls and timber revetments, to provide a smooth surface for the barges and lighters to settle at low water for loading and unloading, and the foreshore was punctuated with buoys, bollards and mooring posts. Warehouses, houses

Chest end panel, porringer and side panel from a carriage
Acc. nos. 98.2/70, 98.2/244 & 80.536/2, Cat. nos. 6.68, 8.155 & 10.1

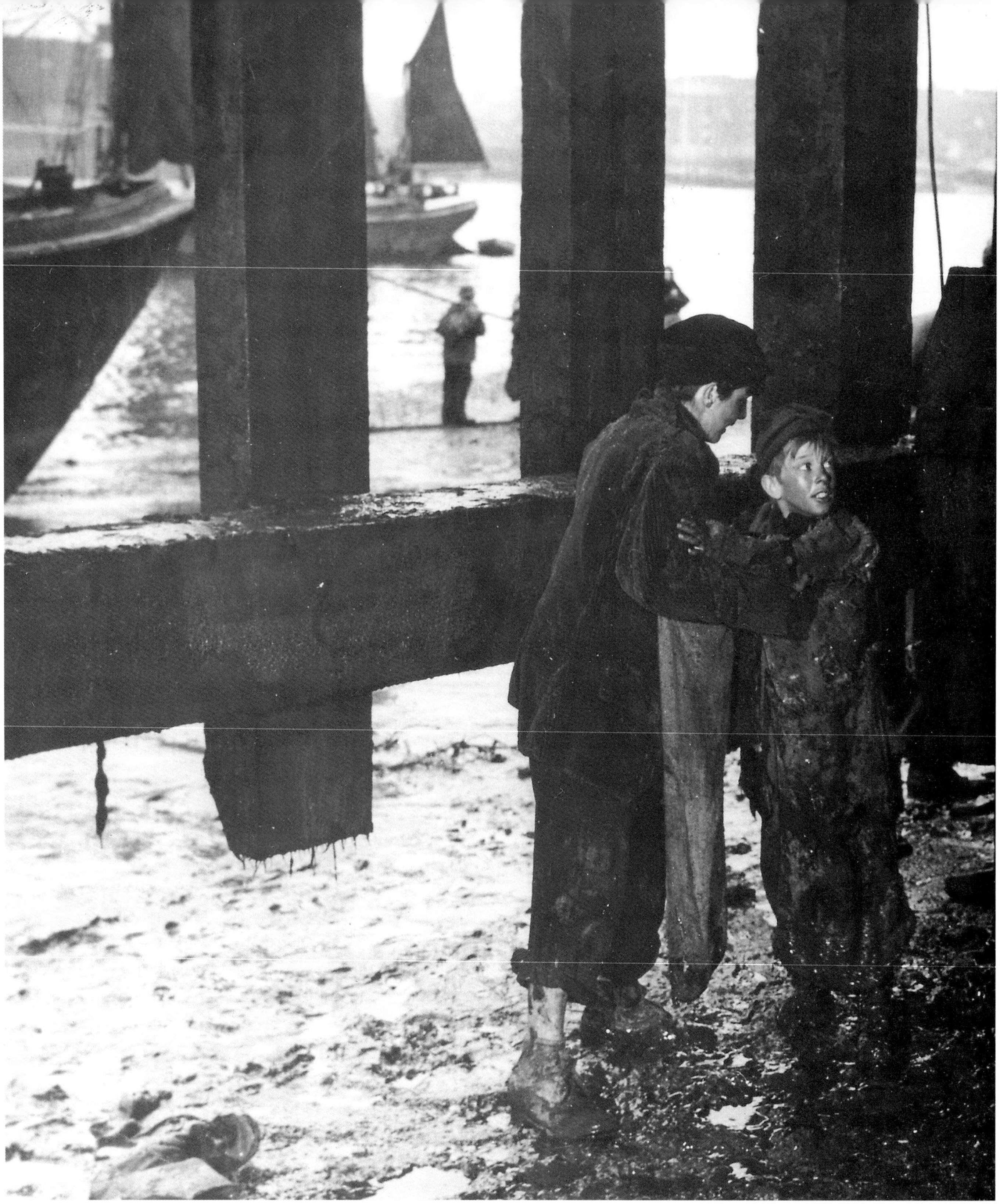

and tenements jostled for space and to gain much needed land the river was narrowed by revetments of timber and masonry, backfilled with rubbish and capped by gravel or stone. From the late 10th to early 16th centuries, piecemeal but continuous reclamation into the Thames produced a strip of land between 50 to 100 metres deep in places along the north bank,[11] and by 1632 contemporaries noted that 'for divers yeares then past' the river had 'beene straightned, lessened, and stopped' and the 'shoares and soyle' had been used for 'makeinge of howses, tenements, Docks and wharffes thereupon to the great hurte and prejudice of the Crown'.[12] Spasmodic encroachment and embanking over the next 400 years has had a marked impact on the regime of the Thames, affecting the width, profile and matrix of the foreshore as well as the artefacts within it.

The mudlark's permit stipulates that the exact find spot of every object should be noted and reported, but in practice the recording of site details is at best patchy. This deficiency is partly due to the lack of an Ordnance Survey map or detailed survey, to the variable structure and ever changing profile and gradient of the foreshore, and to the physical and practical problems of finds retrieval. The tidal pattern offers a narrow window of opportunity for excavation, and the deposits lowest on the foreshore are often only accessible for 20 minutes before the tide returns. Even the highest areas can only be dug for 3–4 hours which leaves little time to create a grid reference for each find (see Concordance). As a result the finds spots tend to be non-specific and the locations supplied to the Museum are usually those by which the area is generally known. Most of the toys have been found between Blackfriars Bridge to just downstream of London Bridge on the north and south sides, with particular concentrations in Queenhithe Dock, Southwark Bridge (north) and Custom House Quay. Dockhead and Limekiln Dock to the east have also yielded a number of toys mostly of 18th-century date.

Even though it is tempting to ascribe particular significance to these areas because they have produced the greatest number of finds, the composition of the sediments, the area of the foreshore exposed at low tide, rates of aggradation and degradation, as well as the personal skills, inclinations and favoured spots of the mudlarks have all affected the distribution pattern and rates of recovery and survival. There are no clusters of toys of a particular type and date to suggest part of a consignment or the proximity of a workshop, and all that can be said with any degree of confidence is that toys have been found in virtually every area of the foreshore where mudlarks have been active.

As the archaeology and environment of the foreshore is so fragile and susceptible to any disturbance, mudlarks may only dig holes and leave them unfilled for 24 hours. In practice this means that the depth of any excavation rarely exceeds two metres. The substrate of the foreshore is extremely variable, and this has an obvious effect on the

Fig. 2. In 1861, the wretched lives of Thames mudlarks attracted the attention of the social commentator Henry Mayhew, who wrote 'that they may be seen of all ages from mere childhood to positive decrepitude crawling among the barges at various wharfs along the river' searching for cordage, nails, coals and rags to sell. Today, mudlarks frequent the foreshore from choice and for the pleasure of finding small trifles from the past.
Photographic still from *The Mudlark*, 20th Century-Fox, 1951
Courtesy of the British Film Institute

rapidity and ease with which a mudlark can dig a hole and the depth achieved. In some areas the foreshore is extremely soft and muddy, in others, the sediments have been compacted to the consistency of concrete. Rates of aggradation and degradation also vary from place to place and the foreshore is in a continual state of flux according to the state of the tide, the velocity of the river currents, seasonal changes to the river regime, erosion, dredging, river traffic and many other factors. Some areas have been extensively worked because the sediments are easily accessible, but other parts of the foreshore are overlaid with barge beds so that potentially rich archaeological deposits remain undisturbed.

By the early 1990s the Museum had recorded and acquired hundreds of artefacts from the foreshore, and had built up the largest collection of medieval and early modern base-metal toys in the public domain. But there was an even bigger collection in private hands which had been assembled with enthusiasm, diligence and determination by A.G. Pilson, a founder member of the Society of Thames Mudlarks. With considerable perspicacity Mr Pilson recognized the significance of these objects, and while other mudlarks in the 1970s and 80s focused on the more immediately desirable or marketable daggers and pilgrim badges, Pilson made a conscious effort to search and recover every unconsidered trifle, toy and miniature on the foreshore whether it was damaged, fragmentary, or indeed recognizable. It was only when a considerable quantity of these fragments had been assembled that distinct objects and distinguishing features began to emerge. Previously unidentified panels were recognized as part of a chest or chair, a squashed disc became a porringer, a mangled piece of openwork became part of a carriage and so on. The importance and historic value of Mr Pilson's collection grew with its size, and before long he was known by fellow mudlarks as the man to whom such finds should be brought. Pilson began to acquire pieces from mudlarks and dealers and within a few years he had 'cornered the market' so that it was simply not worth any of his colleagues bothering to collect these items for themselves.

Every time Mr Pilson and his associate Mr Smith found a toy or unrecognizable fragments of base metal, the finds were brought into the Museum. Each item was recorded and sometimes a particularly interesting piece was acquired. By the 1980s Mr Pilson's collection was unparalleled and Brian Spencer, then Keeper of Medieval Antiquities, offered to house the ever-expanding collection for security and research purposes. The attention of Museum archaeologist and finds specialist Geoff Egan was drawn to the collection, and he began to make a serious study of these objects, following on from the prescient and seminal work of Ivor Nöel Hume.[13] A spate of articles and papers on the subject culminated in an exhibition in 1996 at Jonathan Horne Antiques[14]

Fig. 3. This photograph gives some indication of the thriving commercial activity on the Thames during the early 20th century. The spars, rigging and sails of the barges alongside Greenmoor Wharf almost obliterate the dome of St Paul's. The wharf was used as Southwark Corporation's rubbish depot and the barges and lighters were loaded with refuse for land reclamation projects in Kent and Essex. In the medieval period most of the City's rubbish was dumped behind timber revetments on the north shore, and many of the early base-metal toys in this collection were probably deposited in these tips.
Photograph by George Reid, 1920s–30s
Museum of London, Acc. no. IN9448

and the accompanying booklet compiled by Geoff Egan, *Playthings from the Past: Lead alloy miniature artefacts c. 1330–1800*, presented a synthesis of the major types of toys recovered from the foreshore over the last thirty years.[15] This publication, described by the author as a 'preview', did much to stimulate interest in the subject in this country and abroad,[16] and base-metal toys and miniatures now feature in most exhibitions on the material culture of medieval and early modern England.

In January 1998 Mr Pilson offered his entire collection to the Museum and this was acquired with the generous support of the Heritage Lottery Fund (HLF) and the National Art Collections Fund (NACF). A condition of HLF funding was that the Museum should publish a full catalogue of *The Pilson Collection*, and this book is the result. Although *The Pilson Collection* forms the nucleus of this volume, the opportunity has been taken to assess and evaluate all of the Museum's collection of base-metal toys and miniatures, including those retrieved during the course of archaeological investigation.

Toys on the foreshore

'August 5 – Rowland fell into the Thames over head and ears about noon or somewhat after.' John Dee, 1582 [17]

Until the early 1970s it was widely believed that the foreshore deposits were of little archaeological significance. But excavations of the Saxon and medieval waterfront[18] and recent work conducted by the Thames Archaeological Survey have shown that stratified archaeological layers and features are present over large stretches of the foreshore. The mudlarks have long held to this view and date a find by its general context and the depth of sediment from which it was recovered. But sequences of foreshore deposits do not necessarily develop identically on adjacent sites, or even on the upper and lower parts of the same foreshore, and accurate dating is really only possible with systematic three-dimensional recording of all finds.

Since many factors have affected the distribution and deposition of foreshore finds, it cannot be assumed that artefacts found in a particular spot today were actually left in that area in the past. The migration of objects in the river and within the foreshore sediments is hugely variable, and the factors that determine the manner in which a specific object behaves in the water are based on its mass and shape as well as the state of the tide and the degree of turbulence and velocity of the current at the point of deposition. Recent hydrological surveys of the Thames have shown that there is always a greater accumulation of rubbish on the inside of a meander, but the densities and types of refuse are affected by the direction of the prevailing wind, bankside vegetation and the composition of the foreshore substrate.[19] The surveys also show that the velocity of the river is generally highest in the centre of the stream, slackening off towards the shore, so that if the toys were left behind by children playing on the foreshore or discarded in rubbish from riverside properties, they were probably embedded fairly rapidly. Over the years, however, the profile of the river bed and foreshore has been dramatically altered by natural erosion, dredging, embanking and other encroachment, and it is noticeable that the areas most affected by these changes are those where the majority of toys have been found. Old London Bridge with its massive starlings (the only bridge over the Thames until 1729), and the building of its replacement in 1831, also had a significant impact on the river

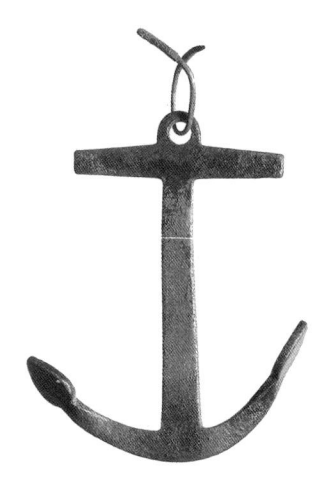

Anchor
Acc. no. 98.2/694, Cat. no. 10.21

regime, rates of scouring and shoaling and the shape and composition of the adjacent foreshore.[20]

It is natural to assume, and it is certainly the view of mudlarks, that toys are found on the foreshore because children used the waterfront as a playground. Children do play, and probably always have played, in unsuitable places in their quest for adventure, and for a child living in a riverside property or neighbouring tenement, the river traffic, commercial activity and muddy foreshore must have had a magnetic appeal. This supposition is supported by many early accounts of accidents and drowning in the Thames because a child leant too far over the quayside, or toppled into the river from

Fig. 4. Downstream from new London Bridge, a group of fisherman wait for the tide to turn while a little boy plays with his wooden boat. The piers of old London Bridge can be seen in the distance. The 19 arches and large starlings supporting old London Bridge had a significant impact on tidal flow and the composition and profile of the foreshore.
View of New London Bridge from Billingsgate, 1833. Etching by Edward W. Cooke [1811–1880]
Guildhall Library Print Room

a boat or slippery steps.[21] In 1485 for example, six-year-old William Granger of Stepney almost drowned after he fell out of a moored boat, and his 'miraculous' recovery was attributed to his father's vow to take a four-pound candle to the shrine of Henry VI at Windsor.[22] The accident-prone son of the mathematician and astrologer John Dee also narrowly escaped drowning in 1582 when he plunged head over heels into the Thames. Despite these recorded incidents, however, no direct evidence has come to light to suggest that the waterfront was actually used as a playground in the medieval and early modern periods, although there are early 19th- century illustrations of little boys playing with their toy boats on the Billingsgate and Vauxhall foreshores (fig. 4), and photographs of older children enjoying the river in the 1930s (fig. 5).

Even if we suppose that a few local children used the foreshore as a playground in earlier periods, very few of the toys in this volume are likely to have been owned by children living in riverside tenements. Moreover, the environment was fraught with dangers and large stretches of the City and Southwark waterfronts would have been inaccessible or entirely unsuited as a playground. It is really only in the last 50 years with the decline of commercial trade that the waterfront has a benign aspect with beach-like areas exposed at low tide, and looking at the quiet and pleasant scene today it is difficult to imagine that it was any different in the past. For centuries though, the occupants of riverside properties complained that the sluggish river flow above London Bridge had encouraged the build-up of effluent and refuse, and eventually tolls had to be levied on the vessels supplying hay and rushes to the City because the material found its way into the water and blocked up the quays and docks to the hindrance of shipping and commercial activity.[23] Coroners' records also underline the hazards of working on or near the river, and there are many cases of water carriers being swept away and drowned, people losing their footing to be crushed by boats and cargoes, or suffering the dreadful fate of drowning in one of the many laystalls that lined the foreshore. So dirty and dangerous were the conditions that it is difficult to conceive that any caring parent would allow their offspring to go anywhere near the foreshore, even if the street urchins ventured to do so with their homemade and makeshift playthings. In the 1860s, the social commentator Henry Mayhew describes the desperately dangerous and wretched working conditions of the child mudlarks of the Thames, who were obliged through force of circumstance to wade through mud and effluent to find scraps of metal and rope to sell.[24] These children were on the foreshore because they had no other choice.

How then might the toys have ended up on the foreshore? One possibility is that they were lost overboard from a passenger boat. Until well into the 17th century, transport by river was the cheapest and most convenient way to cross from the north and south banks

Fig. 5. For these local children seated on a cobbled causeway under Southwark Bridge, the sights and sounds of the river offered limitless entertainment. To the right are Borax Wharf, Southwark Wharf, Bridge Wharf and Ceylon Wharf with the Dutch auxiliary coaster, *Stella,* alongside. Cannon Street Railway Bridge can be seen in the distance. Play on the foreshore itself was usually restricted by the river authorities and some wharves were closed to the public.
Photograph by George Reid, *c.* 1930
Museum of London, Acc. no. IN9462

TOYS ON THE FORESHORE • *23*

24 • TOYS, TRIFLES & TRINKETS

Fig. 6. The small dock next to the Two Brewers tavern in Limehouse was used to repair barges and lighters. A large expanse of foreshore was exposed at low tide and local children probably used the dock as a playground. Several 18th-century toys have been recovered from this area.
The Two Brewers Limehouse, 1889 by Richard Henry Nibbs [1816–1893]
Brown wash drawing, 17 x 24.6 cm
Museum of London, Acc. no. 68.138/2

or from the City to Westminster and vice versa, and Londoners and visitors to the capital hired small craft which darted 'quickly hither and thither … according to the whims of those inside.'[25] Many personal items must have been lost while stepping from a bobbing boat on to slippery stairs, particularly in rough weather. Adults probably snagged their cloaks, lost buttons, cufflinks, jewellery, weapons and other items, and it is conceivable that child passengers dropped a doll or a cherished toy overboard. Did the string of a violently twirled whirligig break at a critical moment catapulting the disc into the mud? Was a windmill, held aloft to catch the breeze, forced apart by a sudden gust of wind? Was a toy boat whisked away in the current? It is even possible that the odd toy was lost because the owner threw the object into the Thames by mistake. The essayist and journalist Joseph Addison saw his friend 'Will Honeycomb squirt away his watch a

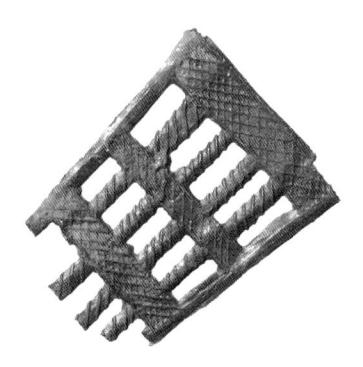

Windmill sail
Acc. no. 98.2/109, Cat. no. 14.3

ABOVE: Fig. 7. In 1934, at the suggestion of King George V, an artificial beach was constructed on the Tower foreshore for the free use of the children of London. Over the next six years this 15-metre-wide stretch of sand was enjoyed by half a million people and gave particular pleasure to the children of Stepney and Poplar. The beach was used as a public amenity until 1971.
Photograph by Henry Grant, 1952
Museum of London, Acc. no. HG1391/5

RIGHT: Fig. 8. In this detail from *The City from Bankside*, 1828–30, a tiny girl is left to amuse herself on the quayside while large blocks of stone are being lifted overhead. See plate XIV, pp. 366-7

considerable way into the Thames thinking it was the pebble he had just picked up from the grand walk,'[26] and although absentmindness of this order must have been exceptional, perhaps a few toys were lost in a similar fashion.

Accidental loss hardly accounts for the range and variety of miniatures found on the foreshore, however, and the most likely explanation of their presence in this area is that they were gathered up in the rubbish collected from households around the City. For much of the period covered by this book, the waterfront was used by Londoners as a convenient refuse tip, and despite the efforts of the City authorities to prohibit the 'dumping of rubbish, earth, gravel and dung into the Thames ... for saving the body of the river, and preserving the quays, such as Douuegate, Quenhethe, and castle Baynard ... and also for avoiding the filthiness that is increasing in the water and upon the banks', a good deal of illicit and surreptitious tipping went on.[27] City rubbish was also deliberately dumped behind timber and masonry revetments for land reclamation purposes, and over time many of these structures collapsed or were extended, repaired and removed. As a consequence, the foreshore contains a mixture of sealed and re-deposited refuse and over the years the action of the river, commercial activity and dredging has brought some of these finds to the surface.

Like a coal seam or any exploited natural resouce, the archaeological deposits of the foreshore are finite, and in the last couple of years the number of finds brought into the Museum of London by mudlarks has diminished. Although some areas of the foreshore have been intensively 'worked', significant areas remain and constant erosion and other changes to the waterfront may expose finds which were inaccessible before.

Archaeological contexts for early base-metal toys (GE)

In addition to the finds recovered from the Thames, an increasing number of base-metal toys and miniatures have been found during the course of archaeological excavations over the last couple of decades. The reasons for this increase include improved methods of recording and recovery (including the use of metal detectors), greater awareness and appreciation of post-medieval archaeology, and more extensive and systematic site excavation. Yet of the 200,000 registered finds in the Museum of London's archaeological archive, the largest in Britain, only some 30 base-metal toys and fragments have been recognized. These finds constitute the merest fraction of the total base-metal toy corpus, but because they have come from securely dated contexts, they provide corroborative and invaluable dating evidence. With greater awareness and improved techniques of excavation, it is probable that more base-metal toys and miniatures will be recovered and recognized in the future.

All of the base-metal miniatures and toys in the Museum of London's collections have come from the soil of London. The majority are, perhaps unjustly, termed 'chance finds'. This is in order to differentiate them from those found in the course of formal archaeological investigations. The advent in the mid-1970s of the metal detector transformed the numbers recovered by members of the public of these generally very small metal items, which are often of a colour similar to that of the ground in which they lie. From this point onwards toys were an occasional but regular feature of assemblages found on the Thames foreshore that were brought in to the Museum for recording and comment by curatorial staff. It remained a mystery why this distinct category never turned up on archaeological sites with deposits of the same character and date as the foreshore, while a small but steady stream continued to emerge from the individuals searching on the other side of the river wall. In fact no toy was recovered from the sites until the early 1980s, when detectors were first used in the course of archaeological fieldwork by volunteers – in London these were from the local Society of Thames Mudlarks (i.e. the group which had been working the foreshore for some time). It gradually became clear not only that the detector was the essential tool for the retrieval of such items, but also that it was at its most effective in the hands of a limited number of virtuoso practitioners, several of whom had been through a kind of Darwinian selection process via the rigours of their efforts on the foreshore.[28]

It apparently remains the case to date, with the exception of a single toy watch found in the course of sieving a pond deposit for environmental material, that all the metal toys recovered during routine archaeological work at formal excavations in London have been pinpointed by detectors in the hands of the Mudlark Society volunteers (or by the member of this group who came to be employed full-time in the late 1980s and early 1990s by the Museum as a site detectorist). Sieving is undoubtedly a more rigorous recovery technique than detecting, not least because it is applicable to non-metal finds, but it is very labour-intensive and so resources almost invariably dictate that it cannot be used as extensively as might be hoped during urban rescue work. These fundamental parameters should be borne in mind while considering what follows.

The greatest number of items in the same categories as those discussed elsewhere in this volume to be recovered from formal archaeological sequences so far came from the Abbots Lane site (ABO92) in Bermondsey, where foreshore and similar riverine deposits from the late 15th century to *c.* 1700 were investigated (the Museum's detectorist, Alan Gammon, being employed here for the duration of the main fieldwork). Thirteen playthings of diverse categories, mainly if not all from the two centuries indicated, were recovered.[29] Excavation within a cofferdam of the actual foreshore at the Vintry site (VHA89) in the centre of the City river frontage produced three post-medieval items and a medieval one came from the inland part of the investigation (together the next largest number), followed by three at the JAC96 site (also on the Bermondsey waterfront). Next are the extensive city waterfront sites at Swan Lane and Billingsgate watching brief, which together yielded a handful of medieval playthings through the sustained efforts of many volunteers over several months. This emphasized the scarcity of medieval miniatures and toys within the full range of finds recovered. The great majority of the toys from the sites are of post-medieval date. The relatively few finds recovered in these circumstances are significant in that they have provided checks in the form of fixed points for many of the other toys in the Museum's collections, via the normal means of assigning chronology to the sequences excavated through coin and pottery dating, sometimes supplemented by dendrochronology. It is fair to say that overall this has largely been a process of confirmation of the educated guesswork that had previously been applied to many of the listed items. In the limited instances where intrinsic dating was available for objects, like some of the pieces by the maker/s I(D)Q, there was agreement. There are also some anomalies, such as the 18th-century dating assigned a fragment of a buffet from the Fleet Valley site (Cat. no. 6.7). This kind of

28 • TOYS, TRIFLES & TRINKETS

discrepancy may be a function of the presumably still very tiny portion of the overall range of playthings produced through the centuries considered that has so far been recorded. Alternatively, a few playthings might have been kept in a family long-term. There must be many more versions that have not yet been recovered or recognized even for successful lines, and so the time span covered by any one is probably still not fully charted. More broadly, it was encouraging to have a first basic indication of the rarity or frequency of occurrence of playthings amongst the wider assemblages recovered once an effective method of retrieval had been introduced.

Beyond London only a very few toys have been recovered, though the numbers are growing as fragments come to be recognized for what they are and the detector is more

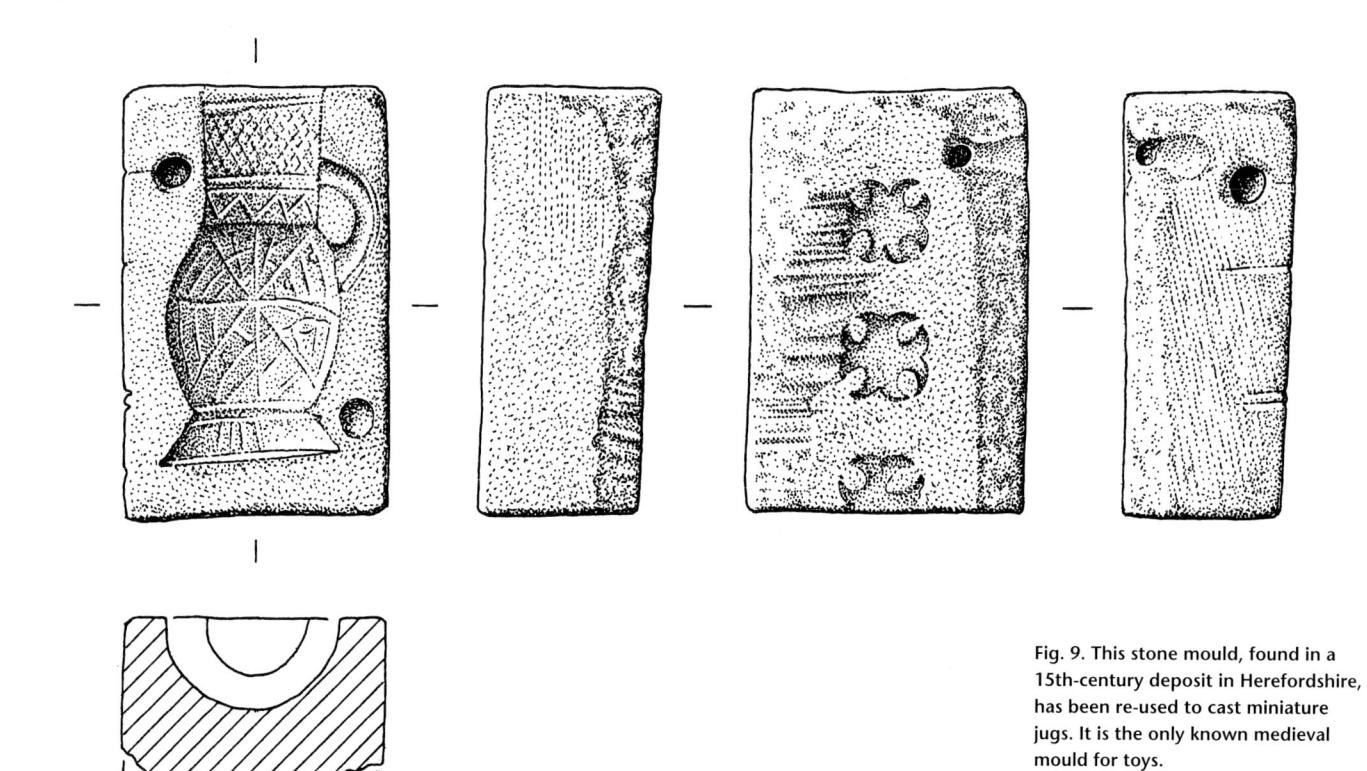

Fig. 9. This stone mould, found in a 15th-century deposit in Herefordshire, has been re-used to cast miniature jugs. It is the only known medieval mould for toys.
Hereford Museum

regularly employed. One of the IDQ products, a fragment of an arc-topped chest, is known from Salisbury, where the river also produced a lead-alloy tripod cauldron, jug and a miniature spoon (the last may be a pendant).[30] There is also a medieval jug from York Cathedral.[31] A stone mould for jugs found at Hereford (fig. 9) is of particular significance, not only as the sole medieval example of this production requisite known anywhere for playthings, but the fact that it comes from a city far from the economic foreground in the national league table at the time suggests that most urban settlements of a certain size would have had a critical mass of potential customers with spare cash for cheaply produced playthings.

Rural finds are very few, but these do show that the phenomenon was not entirely urban. For example, a miniature jug was found at Sigglesthorne, Yorkshire,[32] and part of a copper-alloy candleholder has been identified from Buckinghamshire.[33] Again the sparsity may to some extent be a problem of recognition. There is an emphasis in fields on recovery of post-medieval shy-type toys and copper-alloy handguns and cannon (the last two perhaps the most widespread of all toy categories), all of which are relatively robust, a factor that may have helped these (in preference to playthings with thinner components) survive different soils and agricultural chemicals. A category that has only turned up in an urban area once (in the form of a fragment from west London) but is fairly widespread across the country is the crude, lead-alloy version of a horn book. Some of these seem to date from the late 17th century. They not infrequently include mistakes such as reversed or omitted letters in their alphabets, and so they must have catered for children in families where literacy was not developed – this may explain their primarily rural distribution.

On the Continent, the archaeological picture is still patchy in some areas, such as France and parts of Germany (nothing at all seems to be known from Iberia), but it is much fuller in other areas, notably the Low Countries. There is an overall tendency towards earlier dating for several categories between the 13th and 15th centuries than is currently attested in England.[34] Whether this represents genuine cultural differences or there will be a convergence of views as more information is collated remains to be seen. The culture of lead-alloy miniatures appears to continue across the Continent to Denmark, where there are a few objects comparable to those listed in this volume in the Copenhagen City Museum, but none has so far been noted into the Baltic Sea area, where they seem to be replaced by wooden playthings comprising a different repertoire, as exemplified in the collections of the Stockholm City Museum.[35] Eastwards, lead-alloy objects are not common but hints of an essentially similar range to England's seem to be emerging across Germany and up to the Alps. Italy, whose material culture was for some of the period under consideration the most advanced and sophisticated in Europe, seems long to have remained aloof from recognizing medieval or later excavated toys of the kind discussed here, though the process has begun.[36] Nevertheless, the close comparisons between a few items listed below and some in a well-known collection in Naples, recently republished as Roman,[37] suggest they are in fact there in some numbers but some are unrecognized amongst earlier material.

So far, the earliest toys recognized in the colonial world of America appear to be from the 18th century (e.g. a boat of tree bark at Williamsburg).[38] There are also claims of miniature cannon like those published in this volume among the treasure-hunting fraternity in the United States, but no documented instance has been traced yet. Providing children destined for a long and tedious, not to say hazardous, journey to a new life in the colonies with playthings of some kind to distract them, would seem only common sense for their parents, but seemingly no toy has yet been noted from formal excavation from deposits assigned to the 17th century.[39] It is probably only a matter of time before the first toy from the 1600s is recognized somewhere in North America. Recent archaeological work in 19th-century New York has produced the first sizeable assemblages in the USA to include a range of children's toys and other items such as tableware. It is notable (given a slightly different emphasis on the numbers perceived) that these finds have been hailed in much the same way as those in this present work from the 13th and early 14th centuries: as a turning point when provision of specific children's material culture brought them from a bleak early life of preparation for productive work, to enjoy for the first time the kind of childhood almost universally recognized today: 'for the first time toys and other things [were] made and marketed for middle-class children, with the thought that these objects would help teach them appropriate adult roles. It is from this period that archaeologists first find a profusion of children's toys and other items.'[40]

Archaeology tends to highlight commonplace, mass-produced goods of materials that survive in the particular soil conditions where excavation takes place. It is perhaps initially surprising that pewterware should be so prominent in the surviving cannon. This has its own logic, however, when the readiness of lead/tin to take fine detail and its low melting temperature (making for relatively cheap production) are considered, and the poor survival of many of the other materials used is also taken into account. This is against the background of England being one of the few countries where the two basic metals needed to make the appropriate alloys occur naturally. What has come through to today certainly makes up only a very incomplete picture, mainly of one branch of a very varied series of industries. The silver toys of the aristocracy and the very rich only exceptionally escaped recycling in the melting pot to be lost in the ground, just as the cheapest ones of organic materials either decayed or are inherently unrecognizable.[41] It is telling that just two items from the catalogue, both plates (Cat. nos. 98.2/262 & 98.2/264), have a precise parallel traced among above-ground survivals. Some of the toys from the ground are most unusual survivals from a lower part of the social spectrum (but by no means the lowest), probably where children regularly played outside in the street (or perhaps beside the river), and these represent a different milieu from that represented by many museum collections of other material of comparable date. They are the more remarkable for this.

Plate
Acc. no. 98.2/262, Cat. no. 8.57

Plate
Acc. no. 98.2/264, Cat. no. 8.66

Toys, trifles or trinkets?

'I believe from these childish toys and gilded baubles, I shall pick up a comfortable maintenance. For really, as it is a triffling age, so nothing but triffles are valued in it ...' [42]

The word 'toy', as the compilers of the Oxford English Dictionary (OED) have noted, has a complex and uncertain etymology. Although the first recognized use of the word appears in a text by Robert of Brunne in 1303, it does not occur regularly in literature or documents until the 16th century. Quite why, as the OED writers have commented, it 'should [virtually] disappear for two centuries, and then should all at once burst into view with a wide sense-development' is unclear,[43] but perhaps the word gained currency in the 16th century because more people could afford to buy and import a vast range of luxuries, fripperies and trifles to adorn their home and person.[44]

Throughout the 1500s the word 'toy' – variously spelt as 'toye' or 'toie' – was predominately used to denote an idle fancy, an ornament or thing of little worth, and in Cotgrave's *Dictionary of the French and English Tongues* published in 1611 and revised with a supplement in 1673, it is defined as 'all kinds of superfluous trifles used, or usually bought by women', a 'trinket' and 'a paltry object' of no value. Interestingly, it is the French equivalent *babiole* which is accompanied by the English definition 'a trifle, whimwham, gugaw' (gewgaw), as well as 'a small toy for a child to play withal'. During the 17th century the term trifle was adopted by the Pewterers' Company to describe small wares or items of little value, but confusingly, trifle was also the name given to a pewter alloy of intermediate standard between fine metal and lay metal. The workers in this alloy were known as triflers, but it is clear from contemporary records and surviving products that they actually made a wide variety of wares of different sizes.[45] The ambiguous double sense of the word was demonstrated when the Company met to determine the sizes of 'tryffeleres' wares in 1612–13.[46] No children's toys or trinkets or even especially small items of little value are listed, and the wares range in size from children's beakers to large-capacity ewers and measuring pots. To add to the confusion, according to the various standards set down by the Company for producing a range of pewter wares, 'all Childrens Pewter Toys' were to be made from the lower-quality ley metal rather than trifling metal.[47]

TOYS, TRIFLES OR TRINKETS? • 33

Fig. 10. John Jackson sold a wide range of trifles and knick-knacks from his shop in Cheapside as well as 'all sorts of Toys for Children'. Some of these toys were made from pewter, and two of the plates in the collection (Cat. no. 8.45) bear Jackson's touchmark.
Trustees of the British Museum Heal Collection

JOHN JACKSON at the Unicorn th' Corner of Woodstreet, Cheapside, London,

Selleth all sorts of Knives, Combs, Scissors, Razors, Canes, Whips, and Spurs, Umbrelloes, Buttons for Sleeves, fine Buckles for Shoes and Girdles; fine Snuſh-boxes and Tobaco-boxes, Tables, Cheſt-boards; fine French Necklaces, Pendants, fine Seals, Pocket-books, Letter-caſes, Needle-books, Coffee-Mills, Purſes, Watch-chains for Men and Women, Eſſence-bottles, Powder-flasks, Shot-bags, Ink-horns, Water-gilt Buttons for Cloaths, and other ſorts of Metal-buttons; fine Steel Work, Silver Toys, Lignum Vitæ and Ivory Toys; Tunbride Ware, and all ſorts of Toys for Children; Stone Pendants, and Ear-rings, and Stone Rings, in Silver and Gold, with other Curioſities for Gentlemen and Ladies, at reaſonable Rates. By Wholeſail or Retail.

All ſorts of Fine Snuſh.

Because the word toy had various meanings depending on the context of use, contemporaries often used the prefix 'child' or 'children' to make it clear that they were referring to an object made expressly for play rather than a mere toy or trinket for adult amusement. So the phrase 'all sorts of children's toys' often appears in trade bills of the 17th and 18th centuries, and inventories include references to 'toyes for children' and 'knacks for children'[48] or 'child's buwbbles'[49] and other similar phrases. Occasionally words are combined for added clarification and there are references to 'toys and gewgaws'; 'toyes and trifles'; 'tricks and toies'. It is only when the word 'toy' is used on its own that it is often difficult to know what was meant. Sometimes of course the context provides the clue, so that when toys are listed in the inventory of a dining room or in a women's closet, one can be fairly certain that they were trinkets or ornaments rather than a child's plaything.[50] But what of the reference to 'a toy room' in the inventory of Luke Lee,[51] and to 'toyes in boxes' such as those imported into London on the ship *Trinitie Bull* on 13 November 1481, which were to be delivered to the merchant Frank Mathew.[52] Were these children's toys or adult conceits?

It is equally difficult to know whether the products sold by 'toysellers' or 'toymen' included children's toys amongst their usual range of luxury goods, knick-knacks and trinkets.[53] Some did sell 'toys for children' such as John Jackson of the Unicorn in Cheapside (fig. 10),[54] John Sotro of the Acorn in St Paul's Churchyard and the aptly named Coles Child of the Blew Boar on London Bridge, all of whom made a point of advertising the fact in their trade bills.[55] Unlike most toymen who sold silver playthings,[56] Child sold 'all sorts of English and Dutch toys' in addition to pill and nest boxes, babies, marbles, alleys, children's trumpets and, most importantly from the point of view of this publication, 'lead … toys of all sorts'.[57] In the 16th and 17th centuries 'toys of all sorts' were also part of the stock-in-trade of haberdashers of small wares. Specific references to these articles are extremely rare, but the surviving records do provide some information about the base-metal toy trade in London. For instance, in 1647 James Burton's shop in St Michael Crooked Lane included 'a parcell of broken, leadden toyes' and in 1660 the appraised goods of one City haberdasher included 'a pcell [parcel] of Iron & brasse toyes'.[58] While it is unclear whether these were children's toys, there is little doubt about the entries appended to the schedule of goods of the haberdasher Gregory Day, which were appraised on 22 March 1633. Unfortunately the materials are rarely specified, but the lists covering six pages of double columns include dozens of 'babies' (dolls) of various kinds, hobby horses, children's trumpets, fiddles and drums, as well as 'ten dozen horses on wheeles at 16s per dozen', 'froggen sticks' at 2s 6d per dozen, 'sixteene coaches' at 4s 8d, and in the shop at the back, '2 doz & ? of toyes in boxes' valued

Milkmaid
Acc. no. 98.2/439, Cat. no. 4.23

at 4s 2d[59] and '1 doz of toyes in boxes' at 2s.[60] Toys of various types were also sold in provincial towns and cities and the inventory of the stock-in-trade of Mr Howells, a haberdasher of small wares in Norwich,[61] included 'One Great Box wth 4 dozen of henns and chickens & peacocks and other toyes' valued at 12 shillings; many different types of 'babyes'; boxes with 'fruit dishes', 'horses' and 'mice' and 'broken toyes'; '15 horses with Coaches' at 2s 6d; 'leaden Looking glasses' at 10d per dozen; four and a half dozen 'milke Mayds at 1s 6d'[62] as well as 25 dozen leaden toyes at 3s 1d. Unfortunately the 'leaden toyes' are not individually itemised.

Most of the toys and miniatures considered in this publication, however, were probably sold by pewterers rather than haberdashers and toymen, and yet apart from a handful of references in trade bills and Company records, little is known about the marketing of these wares. Some pewterers probably sold toys and miniatures as a sideline, such as Francis Piggott of the Golden Dish in Paternoster Row, who made 'all sorts of pewter toys' in addition to a wide range of full-scale wares, while others undoubtedly employed or relied on hawkers and chapmen to distribute their products around the capital and beyond.[63] The extent of the retail and marketing trade in base-metal toys is shown by one Exeter tinman who had 'a Great Variety of London, Bristol and Dutch toys' when his stock was advertised for sale in the *Exeter Flying Post* in February and March 1767.[64]

However, none of the sampled inventories of 16th- and 17th-century London pewterers examined by the author includes toys among the shop or warehouse goods,[65] and while it is conceivable that very small parcels of toys might have been overlooked or even disregarded by the appraisers, large quantities would surely have been noted and itemized. In contrast to the paucity of London evidence, a number of inventories survive in the Netherlands which include 'poppengoedsvormen' (literally moulds for doll's paraphernalia) and in 1611, some 30 of these moulds were included in the appraised stock of Rotterdam pewterer, Leendert Jansz Pot.[66] So far no sources have come to light to suggest that pewterers were specialist retailers of toys and miniatures in England before the early 18th century, and the *c.* 1750 trade bill of Robert Peircy of Whitecross Street provides the first concrete evidence for exclusive trade in pewter toys which were sold wholesale and retail (fig. 81, p. 408). By the 1770s, however, there were apparently enough pewter toymakers to form a specialist branch of the trade, although it is unclear whether they sold toys exclusively.[67] The large touchmark of one of the self-identified toymakers would suggest that he made full-scale items as well as miniatures.[68]

Some of the best places to buy toys, trifles and trinkets throughout the medieval and early modern period were fairs, and toy booths and trinket stalls are quite often shown in contemporary depictions of market and fair grounds, including the one chosen for the cover of this book. Many of these images were produced to accompany emblematic and moralistic texts on the follies of adult life (fig. 43, p. 187),[69] but others, such as those issued by the German town of Nuremberg (still renowned for its toy fairs) were essentially broadsheet advertisements (figs 12 & 13).[70] The best English example, depicted on a fan design of *c.* 1730, includes a toy booth as part of the attractions and amusements of Bartholomew Fair (fig. 37, p. 148 & plate V, p. 165) and shows a female

Fig. 11. In this Dutch street scene showing children's games, three girls have set up a table display of doll's toys and miniature household items around a tree.
Probably 17th century, not signed or dated
Bodleian Library, University of Oxford,
Douce Print E.2.1 (315)

toy seller surrounded by various baubles including toy watches and base-metal toy plates and dishes.

Documentary and literary evidence for the retail of toys in English fairs and markets is comparatively thin, and most of the references are either incidental or used for satirical and ironic purpose. For instance, the anonymous writer of *The Puisnes Walks About London*, published in *c.* 1605 said that he 'gap'd as yongsters still/Gape on toyes, in Bartilmew faire',[71] and a Royalist pamphlet published on 24 August 1649 urges

38 • TOYS, TRIFLES & TRINKETS

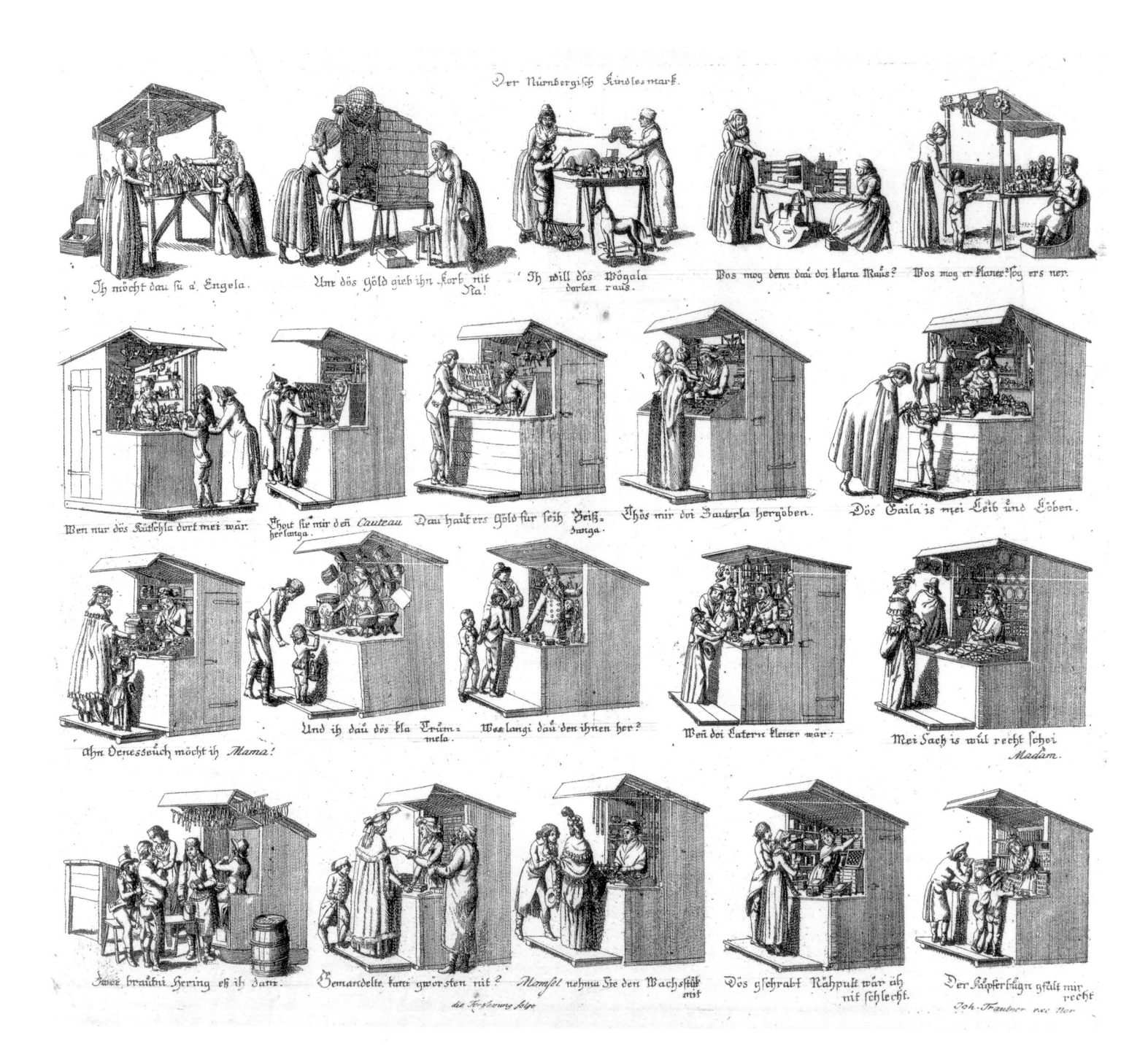

TOYS, TRIFLES OR TRINKETS? • 39

OPPOSITE: **Fig. 12. The Nuremberg toy fair is the oldest, specialist toy market in the world and attracts thousands of exhibitors and visitors each year. A series of popular prints has been produced to advertise the fair and this 1797 broadsheet advertisement showing various stalls is one of the earliest. Many kinds of children's toys are offered for sale alongside assorted knick-knacks and snacks.**
Johann Georg Trautner [1750–1812]
Etching, 28.9 x 34.5 cm
Germanisches Nationalmuseum, Nuremberg

BELOW: **Fig. 13. Detail of two stalls from the Nuremberg toy fair, 1797 by Johann Georg Trautner.
The inscriptions from left to right are: 'If only this little carriage was mine' and 'If only your lantern was smaller.'**
Germanisches Nationalmuseum, Nuremberg

Londoners to go a 'fairing' before political circumstances prevent them from doing so, for the writer says:

This Bartholomew will be the last, I fear …
You Independents buy no trifling matters
Hobby-horses, babies, dishes, or platters.[72]

It is possible that the sale of pewter toys in London fairs declined after 1654, when the Pewterers Company felt that the 'kepinge of boothes in Smithfield or ther abouts at Barthollmetide or in Southwarke' was prejudicial to trade, and stipulated that freemen should either sell their wares from their shops, or in fairs beyond the jurisdiction of the City.[73] This regulation was probably difficult to enforce and a few years later, an anti-papal tract, produced at the height of the Popish Plot affair, draws an analogy between the 'Toys and Baubbles, gaudy shews and Tricks of Legerdemain … Babies and Hobby Horses' of Bartholomew Fair and the 'wares', fancies and follies of the Church of Rome.[74] Unfortunately these and other similar references say little about specific types of toys and their constituent materials, and nothing is known in detail about toy booth stock in the medieval and early modern periods.

Markets and consumers

'certain toys and fancy ornaments [always] preserve a healthy vogue'[75]

Although the value of the domestic toy market rose by 6.7% to £1.76 billion in 2000, the health of the British toy industry has declined significantly over the last couple of decades, and most business analysts would classify the trade as a very marginal industry.[76] Yet as recently as the 1970s the price-earnings ratio of toy shares was higher than that of any other industrial sector,[77] and in the late 1960s the toy manufacturers Lesney (makers of the Matchbox Series of diecast model vehicles) had a greater capital value on the stock market than the engineering giant Vickers.[78] In the 19th century, the scale of the metal toy trade was such that *Chamber's Journal* in 1877 noted that:

> Pewter toys are made in London in very large quantities. At one establishment a ton of metal is consumed each month in the production of Lilliputian tea, coffee and dinner sets. English taste may be gathered from the fact that the number of tea-sets made is nearly thirty times larger than either of the other two. Twenty-three separate articles make up a set, and of these (two and a half million) are made yearly by one house alone. Metal is provided from miscellaneous goods, such as old candlesticks, tea-pots, pots and pans, bought from 'marine' store dealers by the hundred-weight; and when melted, is formed into the regular shapes by different processes of casting in moulds. One girl can make 2,500 small tea-cups in a day. Putting together the four separate pieces of gun metal [mould] she fills it with the molten metal, dips its mouth into cold water, takes it to pieces, and turns out a cup that only wants trimming, the tea sets being thirty times more numerous than either of the other two.

The scant references to base-metal toys before 1800 could imply that the trade was negligible and of little consequence in the medieval and early modern periods, and yet the sheer quantity and range of surviving toys indicates that the domestic and international toy market, although slight in relation to the base-metal industry as a whole, was probably more important to manufacturers and consumers than documentary or pictorial sources would suggest. But without adequate documentation, we can neither measure the relative importance of the base-metal toy trade nor determine the size of the market and the scale of production. We do not know whether the mid-12th-century toys, the earliest known in England, were really the first examples of their type, and we cannot tell whether the relative abundance of late 16th- and 17th-century items are simply an accident of survival, or whether they reflect a sudden growth in the toy market and a concomitant increase in consumer demand.[79]

The downturn in the current toy market has been partly attributed to the declining birth rate, and it is quite likely that fluctuations in the child and adult populations in the past had a similar impact on toy manufacture and trade. The phenomenal growth of London from about 55,000 inhabitants in 1500 to roughly one million by 1800 must have had a bearing on scales of production. But what percentage of the population were consumers of toys? It would have been difficult at the time, and is impossible now, to assess the relative importance of toys in the marketplace. Were more toys produced because there were more people around to buy them? Demographic analysis of the late 16th- to mid-18th-century metropolis has shown that nearly a quarter of marriages were childless,[80] and the very high rates of infant and child mortality meant that only three out of five of those born would survive to the age of 15.[81] The number of surviving children per family throughout this period was rarely more than two.[82] Specific analysis of the social structure of London households from the 1692, 1694 and 1698 poll tax returns have shown that there were children in just 8,576 (33.2%) of City households. Although there were relatively few children across the City, there does seem to have been a definite link between the numbers of children per household and the relative wealth of the occupants. Those with the highest mean number of children tended to live in the affluent and mercantile sectors of the City around Cornhill, and these people would have been able to afford to buy base-metal toys and trifles for themselves and their offspring.[83]

The general rise in London's population was matched by the rising price of consumer goods and though there were peaks and troughs in the rate of inflation, many short-term reversals and periods of severe hardship, the real value of wages and the levels of disposable income increased in the period covered by this book.[84] By the late 17th century a much wider range of consumer goods had become available at lower prices, but even though Londoners were considerably better off than the rest of their countrymen, many would still have had to cut their cloth to suit their purse. Since relatively little is known about patterns of consumption in the medieval and early modern periods, however, it is uncertain whether fluctuations in the domestic economy had an adverse effect on the toy market and consumer expenditure of non-essential items.

It is also unclear whether the massive expansion of trade and commerce from the late 15th century had an effect on London's share of the international toy market. Apart from a few references to 'boxes of toyes' in customs accounts and other lists of dutiable cargoes, the only specified children's toys were 'babyes' or 'poppets' (dolls) imported from Germany and the Low Countries.[85] Doll imports grew steadily from the late 15th century and by 1559, some £178 3s 4d worth of 'babies' were included in the list of 'certain necessary and unnecessary Wares brought into the Port of London'.[86] Not surprisingly, 'babies' and toys in general were among the group of commodities regarded as frivolous. But since these trifles continued to be in great demand, the more astute political economists argued that if Londoners could not do without fripperies and luxuries, the only way to stem the tide of imports, improve the balance of payments and protect and encourage domestic industries, was to manufacture these items within the realm. By 1563 an Act was passed 'for the avoyding of dyvers forreyne wares made by handye craftsmen beyonde the seas', and although foreign fripperies and large numbers of 'babies' and other 'toyes' continued to be imported, it is possible that the various schemes for economic revival and the general growth of English non-ferrous metal manufactures at this time helped to stimulate domestic toy production.[87]

Current assessments of the toy industry have shown that the toy market is highly susceptible to seasonal factors, with around 55–60% of all toy sales taking place during winter months and particularly in the weeks immediately preceding Christmas.[88] The custom of giving presents to children at Christmas is comparatively recent, however,[89] and there is no evidence that English children were given toys to celebrate particular festivals or holy days, or enjoyed the edible treats and toys which were given to their Dutch peers on 5 December, the eve of the Feast of St Nicholas (plate IX, p. 353). There are references in parish churchwardens' accounts to the extraordinary custom of appointing a boy-bishop on 6 December, a practice largely discontinued after the Reformation, but no gifts to these children or their retinues apart from the rather ambiguous entry of 9s 6d for a 'tin pair of candlesticks and a ship of tin at Christmas'.[90] It is likely that the Dutch community in London maintained their festive traditions on 5 December, but whether this had a noticeable effect on domestic toy sales in the winter months is unknown. A survey of Dutch inhabitants undertaken in 1617 showed that there were 882 children and servants out of a community of 1,572 and although some parents probably purchased toys from London retailers, others might have preferred to buy directly from their homeland. Seasonal fluctuations in the level of demand for toys was probably less marked than it is today, and output was probably sustained throughout the year to ensure that there were sufficient toys to sell at the major fairs. No

Buffet
Acc. no. 94.43, Cat. no. 6.5

Mounted knight
Acc. no. 98.2/406, Cat. no. 4.4

Male figure: game hawker
Acc. no. 88.9/35, Cat. no. 4.37

doubt some toymakers tried to anticipate demand by producing specific types of object for particular events and special occasions, and it is just possible that the late 16th-century warships (p. 323) were made to celebrate the success of the English forces against the Spanish Armada.[91] A number of toy buffets and chests incorporate the arms of the City of London and Drapers' Company and these items may have been specially commissioned for the members of the Livery (pp. 205–6 & 223).

While some toymakers might have focused too narrowly on particular types or designs which had been successful in the past, the more enterprising and commercially-minded makers probably tried to keep abreast of cultural trends by updating their toys. The extent to which 'product development' took place is, however, unknown. The maker Hux seems to have made several types of watch with different designs in a range of sizes, but we do not know whether one type replaced another or whether they were made contemporaneously.[92] A number of the toys seem to have been adapted, and one of the mounted knights (p. 147) has a trimmed helmet which was probably done to 'keep in line with changing fashions in armour',[93] perhaps because it was easier to make this small modification than to go to the extra trouble and expense of updating the mould.[94] It is quite likely that some toymakers tried to entice custom and boost their sales by adopting various marketing strategies and promotional ploys, and these might have been rather similar to those employed by the toysellers in the Lowther Arcade in the 19th century.[95] In this toy emporium, the novelist George Augustus Sala notes that 'there are certain toys and fancy ornaments that always … preserve a healthy vogue, and command a ready sale … although their nominal nomenclatures are sometimes altered to suit the exigencies of fashion. Thus we are enticed to purchase Uncle Buncle's Noah's Ark, Peter Parley's rubber balls, or Jenny Lind's Doll's mansion'.[96] It is also possible that a similar commercial ploy lay behind, or gave stimulus to, the production of the 'Cries of London' miniatures (pp. 157 & 171), which seem to be the first examples of figurative 'characterisation' within the base-metal toy corpus.

Some makers might have dominated the market in a particular period because their products were better than their competitors', or because they offered a range of toys which had a broader market appeal. A number of 18th-century commentators on trade and manufacture pointed out that the English propensity to specialize gave them a distinct manufacturing advantage 'over many Foreign Nations' who were 'obliged to employ the same hand in every branch of the trade', for as Robert Campbell argued in the *London Tradesman*, published in 1747: 'it is impossible to expect that a man employed in such an infinite variety can finish his work to any perfection, at least, not so much as he who is constantly employed in one thing.'[97] Perhaps the increasing tendency towards specialisation and sub-contracting also extended to the manufacture of base-metal toys.

Despite the Pewterers' Company stipulation in 1503/4 that the makers of all pewter 'Ley Metell wrought within the Cite of London ... shall marke [their] wares with sevall marke of their owne,'[98] only a tiny percentage of the toys have any kind of identifying mark. These marks mostly take the form of single or double letters (see below) although the maker/s I(D)Q use a triad of intials which could suggest a husband and wife, or father and son partnership. Only the products of the late 17th-century makers John Jackson and Charles Rack bear a genuine touchmark in accordance with Company regulations. Unfortunately nothing is known about individual manufacturers of base-metal toys in the medieval period, and only four of the makers of post-medieval toys in the collection have been identified. The earliest group of inscribed toys, dating from the mid-16th to early 17th century, incorporate the letters EL[Z] or RC, but since these letters are prominently placed, repeated and combined with the City of London and Drapers' Company arms they may have had some other purpose. The significance of these marks has been discussed elsewhere (pp. 204–5). Makers' initials begin to appear fairly consistently on base-metal toys from the early 17th century, and 110 items in the collection are marked with the initials or surnames of some 30 makers who seem to have been active from *c.* 1640 to *c.* 1740 (see Appendix III).

A few of these inscribed pieces are accompanied by a date, and a couple of the 18th-century watches include the maker's surname, or are just inscribed 'LONDON'. The first dated pieces known are those by the maker/s I(D)Q which seem to have been produced between 1636 and 1646 (see Appendix IV). Apart from the I(D)Q products, only one other maker, AF, is known to have added a date to some of his wares. Since the dates do not seem to have a commemorative or national significance, it is very difficult to know why some toymakers chose to date their toys, and we can only speculate as to the possible motive. Some might have been dated for whimsical reasons, or because the full-scale prototype was invariably dated or hallmarked and the toymaker wished to follow wider fashion. But it is also possible that the toys were dated for the purposes of quality control. If this assumption is correct, the moulds must have been changed, or literally updated on an annual basis, and this introduces the wider question of the extent to which the pressure for change came from the makers or their customers. It seems reasonable to assume that most of the dated toys were made in the year inscribed upon them and, from the customers' perspective, a dated piece would indicate a new range, reflecting current fashion. Since it is unlikely that anyone would want an 'out-of-date' miniature, it is possible that some toymakers changed the date on their products as a

Watch case lid panel, dated 1646 and inscribed I D over Q
Acc. no. 98.2/623, Cat. no. 12.2

convenient marketing ploy to entice custom and boost their sales. This also raises the interesting question as to whether the moulds were altered or changed to coinicide with the New Year celebrations on 1 January, or when the legal year began in England on 25 March.[99] Whenever the dates were changed, however, the toymakers must have been fairly confident that they could shift their stock before the end of the year, since they would presumably not want to have out-of-date material on their hands. Perhaps this is why only a few makers chose to mark their wares in this way.

More dishes, plates, porringers and watches are inscribed than any other category of toy and there are a number of reasons for this. First, these categories constitute the largest statistical groupings within the corpus, so the relative number of inscriptions is accordingly high. Second, their full-scale counterparts were often inscribed with the maker's or owner's initials or (in the case of watches) signature and place of manufacture. Thirdly, since a number of makers seem to have specialized in a particular branch of the toy trade, it was obviously essential that an individual maker's work could be identified for quality control and to protect his or her commercial interests in the face of acute competition. It is of course possible that the same mark was shared by two or more pewterers in the same workshop, and it is also conceivable that moulds were passed around or sold on to other makers who may have made subtle adaptations to the matrix for individualistic and aesthetic reasons. The exchange of moulds seems to have been commonplace in the Low Countries, and the 30 toy moulds included among the appraised goods of Rotterdam pewterer Leendert Jansz Pot were sold off after his death in 1611.[100]

Generally, the marking of toys throughout the early modern period seems to have been undertaken in a rather arbitrary and haphazard fashion. While some makers evidently preferred anonymity, possibly because they hoped to circumvent regulations, others seem to have been particularly assiduous in ensuring that their wares could be identified. Whatever the case, the absence of comment in contemporary records suggests that the Pewterers' Company was not overly concerned that these small trifles were largely left unmarked, even though there were clearly occasions when a positive attribution would have been helpful. When John Strickland was summoned before the Court in 1718 for 'his toy porringers at 3 gr' worse than lay, he denied the charge and claimed that they 'were made by Mr Hux'. The Court decided to dismiss the case since Mr Hux was not present to affirm or refute the charge, and because the wares were 'untouched'.[101] The general lack of marks also perhaps suggests that base-metal toys from the Netherlands, Germany and France were either so distinct that they were not easily mistaken for English products, or the competition was so slight as to be hardly worth insisting that toys manufactured in this country needed to be identified. The fact that some marks are applied upside down or back to front, however, suggests that some makers were not concerned about their image or the quality of their work.

Several lead-alloy toys have been found by the maker/s I(D)Q both in London and on the Continent, and since many of these items are dated, there must have been a certain amount of cross-Channel trade during the 1630s and 1640s in these wares.

Table 1

Mark	Object/s	Quantity	Date
EA	Dish	1	
AB	Plate	1	
	Porringers	3	
	Watches	2	
BEESLEY [Francis]	Watch	1	
IB	Watch	1	
IC	Dish	1	
RC	Buffets	3	
AE	Dish	1	
[T]F	Dish	1	
AF	Dish	1	
	Frame	1	
	Porringer	1	
	Miscellaneous panel	1	1668
D [G]	Porringer	1	
	Miscellaneous panel	1	1639
IG	Watch	1	
[...] H	Watch	1	
H	Candlestick	1	
	Miscellaneous panel	1	
	Chaise	1	
	Ship	1	
AH	Porringer	1	1640
GH	Buzz wheel	1	
Richard H[eath]	Watch mould	1	
HUX [William]	Watches	9	
I I [John Jackson]	Plates	2	
RK [KR]	Chests	2	
WL	Plate	1	

Mark	Object/s	Quantity	Date
DQ*	Ewer	1	
	Plate	1	
	Spoons	6	
IDQ	Chair	1	1640
ID over Q	Bell	1	
	Dish	1	
	Miscellaneous panels	4	1640/1646
	Plates	2	
	Porringers	12	
	Tableware	7	
	Watches	3	
I over DQ	Miscellaneous panel	1	
IQ	Candlestick	1	
	Dishes	3	
	Figurine	1	
	Plate	1	
	Spoon	1	
R	Chests	3	
R [...]	Buffet	1	
BR	Dish	1	
CR [Charles Rack]	Plates	3	
CT	Chests	3	
R [T]	Chest	1	
EL[Z]	Buffets	7	
IZ	Plate	1	

All of the DQ pieces have a bar across the downstroke of the D, but none of the IQ products has this feature. If the bar was used as a contraction for IDQ, one would expect the IQ products to be marked in a similar fashion. DQ and IQ marks are also used on toys which have a sufficiently large surface area to accommodate the IDQ triad, so the fact that there are toys with DQ and IQ suggests that these toys were designed and made by individual members of the partnership or dynasty. Three objects have been found in England (now in private collections) with other marks: RI on the butt of a musket, and Randall and RR on two watches.

One of the most intriguing and yet difficult questions to consider is for whom these toys were made. Did the base-metal toy market cater primarily for children, or were these objects also enjoyed by adults as amusing trifles and trinkets? Were these toys made exclusively for a rich clientele, or were they affordable to many? Unfortunately hardly any of the available sources provide any information about the consumers of base-metal toys, and most of the records are insufficiently detailed to enable us to ascertain how these toys were actually used and enjoyed. The first specific reference so far known from English sources is a rather enigmatic entry in the 1562 Wardrobe Accounts of Elizabeth I to 'one Baby of pewter' for Ippolyta the Tartarian. This toy was presumably similar to the figurines discussed on page 152, but although as Janet Arnold notes Ippolyta 'seems to have been a child, perhaps a midget, she is described as "our woman" in the warrants.'[102] If Ippolyta was a dwarf or a midget, was she given a doll because contemporaries thought of her as a child? Fortunately, Continental evidence for the usage of base-metal toys is less ambiguous and far more comprehensive. In 1572, for example, the five- and ten-year-old princesses of Saxony were given a magnificently equipped model kitchen replete with tin vessels and utensils, which included '71 dishes, 140 plates (40 of which were for meat), 36 spoons and 28 egg cups'.[103] Similar gifts were given to the six-year-old dauphin (later Louis XIII) who, according to the journal compiled by his physician Héroard in 1607, received 'un petit ménage', a box of assorted pewter toys (which included a tiny chalice and censer, a cock and a female figure) and several pots and pans (presumably of copper alloy) to cook with. These toys were taken 'to the chamber of the queen where he made a fire, and put there his little stew pot in which he put lamb, pork, beef and cabbages'.[104] Even if the merest morsels of these ingredients went into the one pot, it must have much larger than the miniature cooking pots with sooted bases in this collection, but the reference is interesting because it does show that base-metal toys were actually used.

Although these references show that wealthy children were given expensive presents which included base-metal toy vessels and utensils, miniatures were also collected by adults to display in cabinets or *Wunderkammer*. By the mid-16th century special scale-model buildings and Baby Houses were constructed for adults who could afford to indulge their passion for miniatures.[105] The taste for collecting was pursued with extraordinary vigour on the Continent and one of the first recorded Baby Houses was commissioned by Duke Albrecht V of Bavaria for his daughter. This Baby House was so lavish that it was never played with but was displayed with the rest of the Duke's eclectic collection of 3,500 items in a series of cabinets for the privileged few to admire.[106] Although the majority of Baby Houses were very much the preserve of the rich, and were kept for private delectation as display pieces, Anna Köferlin, an enterprising and resourceful citizen of Nuremberg, 'put together with industry and much effort' a Baby House with the express intention of providing instruction in the art of household management. This

OPPOSITE: **Fig. 14. Anna Köferlin's Baby House was exhibited to the citizens and children of Nuremberg and the attraction was advertised by a broadsheet pamphlet with a woodcut of the façade on the front cover. The inscription from top to bottom reads: 'In my beginning I consider my end/ To God alone the glory, 1631'. The image is accompanied by a verse which makes it clear that Anna hoped the attraction would instruct children in the art of household management. The initials HK above a beetle probably allude to Anna's husband Hans Köferlin (Käferlein = small beetle in German).**
Illustration reproduced from original in the Germanisches Nationalmuseum, Nuremberg

PRINCIPIO RESPICE FINEM

MDC SOLI DEO GLORIA XXXI

Baby House was exhibited to the public in 1631 and a broadsheet advertisement was produced by its owner with an accompanying poem which encouraged children to 'look at it and learn well ahead how you shall live in days to come' (fig. 14).[107]

Such was the fascination for miniatures of all sorts that vast sums were expended to create exquisitely equipped Baby Houses, and there is some evidence that affluent German, Dutch and Flemish citizens strove to out-do each other in their enthusiasm for collecting miniatures of various kinds, and no doubt some toymakers catered specifically for this rich adult clientele. The same is true today. Current estimates of the turnover of the doll's house trade in the United Kingdom suggest that the business is worth between £25–£50 million, and 85% of the revenue generated through specialized shops and fairs is from adults who are prepared to spend significant sums on their hobby. Retail sales of doll's house and other miniatures in the United States is currently worth about $112 million per annum and in 1996 a survey of 1,200 readers of the *Dollhouse Miniatures* magazine (which has a circulation of 45,098) showed that some people were prepared to spend an average of $506 per year on their collections.[108]

It is noticeable that all of the surviving Baby Houses contain objects which were made in similar ways and with identical materials to their full-scale counterparts, and a wide range of skilled craftsmen were employed in their creation. The production of miniatures, as the German lexicographer Johann Heinrich Zedler remarked in 1741, was extensive, for 'there is probably no trade where the things usually made in full size are not also fashioned in very small models, with the cities of Augsburg and Nuremberg in particular being ahead of the others in this respect'.[109] The only base-metal articles in surviving Baby Houses, however, are copper-alloy kitchen utensils and pewter plate, and yet, of course, the range of extant base-metal miniatures represented in this collection and found abroad shows that, unlike other craftsmen, the pewterers seem to have been making miniatures of just about every item which could conceivably be required for a well-equipped home. It is possible that an extensive range of objects was made in base metals because it was difficult to obtain miniature items in the correct materials in England. If so, this does not explain why items replicating full-scale objects of wood, textiles, ceramics and other materials have been found in lead alloy on the Continent where the tradition of the Baby House, Nuremberg kitchen and *Wunderkammer* was well established. Whether lead-alloy miniatures were collected in preference to, or as an alternative to, miniatures in silver or other materials is unknown. Most of the base-metal miniatures in this volume are made to scales which would tend to preclude their use in a Baby House, and virtually all of the items in this collection are highly decorated, whether their full-scale counterparts were ornamented or not. By contrast, equivalent items in surviving Baby Houses are plain. The reasons for this difference are unknown, but it is possible that the miniatures in this book were not intended for a Baby House, and English makers might have chosen to decorate their wares for capricious or aesthetic reasons or because consumers preferred highly ornamented miniatures whether the patterns were appropriate or not.

Present-day evidence suggests that 'childhood' is becoming 'increasingly shorter as children become sophisticated consumers in their own right and grow out of their toys earlier than ever before'.[110] Market analysis has also shown that older children have erratic and fickle tastes, and are particularly susceptible to the vagaries of fashion and peer-group pressure, so that one type of toy is hugely popular for a short period and then dropped in favour of another. The most successful toys (apart from the soft, cuddly toys which are the most popular of all) are those which incorporate innovative technologies, and six of the current 15 bestsellers are interactive products. Innovative and interactive toys were also popular in the past, and it is significant that many seem to have been made contemporaneously with their highly fashionable, leading-edge technology full-scale counterparts: the toy guns and the toy watches are notable examples. This suggests that some toys and miniatures were made for their novelty appeal at a time when the full-scale object was extremely expensive and had barely begun to make its mark in contemporary society. Were these children's toys or adult conceits?

Musket
Acc. no. A10429, Cat. no. 1.34

Metallurgy and manufacture

'our pewterers, who in times past employed the use of pewter only upon dishes, pots, and a few other trifles for service here at home ... are grown unto such exquisite cunning that they can in manner imitate by infusion any form or fashion of cup, dish, salt bowl, or goblet, which is made by goldsmiths' craft'[111]

All of the toys and miniatures in this book have been cast from alloys of tin, lead, copper and zinc. The vast majority are made from a tin-lead (pewter) composition and the remainder are almost pure tin, or alloys of copper-tin (bronze) or copper-zinc (brass). The generic terms 'lead alloy' or 'copper alloy' have been used in preference to 'pewter', 'bronze' and 'brass' because it is impossible to determine the composition of the alloys without instrumental analysis, and the external appearance of base-metal artefacts recovered from the soil also varies considerably depending upon burial conditions and the degree of corrosion.[112] Almost all of the toys considered here have been recovered from the waterlogged environment of the Thames foreshore, and although the anaerobic conditions are largely beneficial to preservation of metals, it has been shown that sulphate-reducing bacteria in the sediments can generate distinct corrosion products so that it can be 'difficult to distinguish between copper alloys and lead alloys, even under a microscope'.[113] Most of the lead-alloy toys in the collection have a smooth dull grey black appearance, but a few have a thin layer of gold-green sulphide corrosion which not only mimics copper alloy but can even be mistaken for gilding. The copper alloys are also affected by sulphide corrosion, and many have pitted, crazed and 'bubbly' gold-coloured uniform or patchy brown-black corrosion. Subsequent treatment and storage have also affected the appearance of the metals.

Throughout the period covered by this book, there was no fixed recipe for pewter, bronze or brass, and contemporaries often used terms in a misleading and loose fashion. The terms 'latten' and 'brass' were frequently interchanged, and some writers used the word 'brass' to mean a true brass as well as bronze or copper. Similar ambiguities arise with the term 'pewter' since it was used to describe various compositions of tin and copper as well as tin and lead. Because the nomenclature was so fluid and 'many persons, not knowing the right alloys, nor yet the mixtures or the right rules of the trade, do work and make … things not in due manner', the Pewterers' Company tried to establish standards for particular combinations of metal.[114] The first, in an Ordinance of 1348, stipulated that 'all manner of vessels of pewter such as esquelles [porringers], saltcellars, platters, chargers, pichers square and cruetz squared and chrismatories, and other things that are made square or ribbed, shall be of fine pewter with the proportions of copper to tin, as much as of its own nature, it will take. And all other things … to be wrought of tin alloyed with lead in reasonable proportions. And the proportions of the alloy are to one hundredweight of tin 22 lb of lead.' In essence, there were two standards or qualities of pewter: fine metal wares of tin with a little copper, and ley metal wares of tin with as much as 30% lead. To confuse matters further, an intermediate or 'triffling' standard emerged in the 17th century.

The Company's efforts to maintain particular standards for certain types of wares were continually hampered by pewterers who either disregarded or tried to circumvent trade practices. Those caught producing substandard wares were taken to task, however, and as the Company records show, toymakers were not exempt from quality control. Time and again, toymakers were reprimanded for their 'bad Mettle'; Francis Lea, for instance, appeared before the Court on 15 September 1668/9 for selling 'Toy Pestell and Mortars and other toyes at five grains below the standard quality'.[115] He was fined 10s. One of the most interesting cases of substandard toy production is highlighted by the long-running campaign between the Company and William Hux between 1703 and 1715.[116] What is so interesting about the Hux dispute is not just that he was using 'bad metall', but that he was also using a combination of two different alloys or standards of pewter to make his toy watches. The cases were made from fine metal and the dial plates from lay metal. While the Company was prepared to accept or overlook the fact that the toy watches were made from two standards of alloy, the issue of quality was too important to ignore. The production of poor metal toys continued to give cause for concern throughout the 18th century, and in 1770 the toymaker William Wightman complained to the Court of the Pewterers' Company 'that toymakers in general made their toys of very bad metal and that as a consequence of this he alone was not able to keep his wares up to the Standard and sell at the same price with the rest of the persons in that Branch'. Wightman asked for the 'Directions of the Court in that respect as he was desirous of making his wares of good metal and yet could not afford to be a loser by his trade'.[117] Although Wightman's complaint was 'referred to the Committee appointed for preventing the making and selling of bad metal for them to report their opinion at the next Court', the matter seems to have dropped for there are no further references to the complaint in the Company records. Two years later, however, the *Table of the*

Assays of Metal was published, which stipulated that 'All Children's Pewter Toys' were to be made from lay metal with an alloy ratio of approximately three parts tin to lead, and this was defined for the purposes of assay as 198 grains heavier than fine tin.[118] This reference is the first specified standard for pewter toys known, and it is tempting to conclude that it was included in the Table because the Company was not only fully aware of malpractice, but was under some pressure to reassert its control over the manufacture of these trifles. Perhaps Wightman's complaint was heeded after all.

Until now, none of the base-metal toys of medieval or early modern date had been analysed to see if it corresponded to the standards set down by the Pewterers' Company. This publication has provided us with an ideal opportunity to analyse a few of the toys to see what alloy compositions were used. Although the sample groups are extremely small,[119] the analysis was undertaken to address specific questions. The largest sample of 17 toys, representing a broad spectrum of dates and subject categories, was taken from the main corpus of foreshore finds (Appendix I). These were analysed with a Scanning Electron Microscope (SEM) and Electron Microprobe Analysis (EMPA) to see whether there was a discernable difference in the composition of the toys over time and across the range of subject categories. We also wanted to see whether the toys were made from lay metal, and whether they conformed to the standard. The results, discussed in full in the Appendix, showed that three types of alloy were used. Four items were 94.2–99.3% tin with negligible amounts of lead, 11 were made from a lay-metal composition (with a tin to lead ratio of 3:1), and two substandard toys are 48.9% and 52.9% lead. Though the two substandard items are both from the late 17th–18th century, there does not seem to be any correlation between metal quality and date in the rest of the sample group.

Because antimony was used as a hardening agent instead of copper in Continental pewter from the mid-15th century but 'did not become significant in [England] before the end of the 17th or early 18th century,'[120] we wanted to analyse the toys to see if any trace of this metal could be detected in the hope that it would give a clue as to whether the toys were of Continental or domestic manufacture. Antimony is present as a trace element in some medieval objects manufactured in England. A number of pieces by the mid-17th century maker/s I(D)Q, were included in the sample group because I(D)Q toys are the only recognized toys by the same maker/s to have been found in London, Amsterdam and Paris. None of the toys contains antimony and since more I(D)Q toys have been found in this country than in Amsterdam or Paris, it is tempting to conclude that they were made here, perhaps by an immigrant craftsman, while those found abroad were London exports (see Appendix IV for fuller discussion of I(D)Q). However,

Watch
Acc. no. 2001.15/2, Cat. no. 12.47

until more toys have been sampled in this country and abroad, no firm conclusions can be drawn. Moreover, it is entirely possible that toymakers did not need to use antimony as a hardening agent.

The second sample set of six toy watches and components by the makers Hux and Beasley were analysed to see if the compositions varied according to type, whether two qualities of pewter were used to make the dial and case, and whether the compositions matched the descriptions in the records of the Pewterers' Company (discussed in the 'Watch' section). The results of this analysis are described in Appendix II.[121]

It takes an effort of the imagination to visualize the lead-alloy toys as they would have appeared in their freshly manufactured state. Those with high tin contents would have looked much like silver, and even the lay metal toys would have had a bright shiny appearance. Athough English pewterers were strictly forbidden to paint and gild their wares in '[e]xept it be a Tryfell to geue awaye' to a friend 'and well proved to be geven awaye', one of the Hux watches seems to have been deliberately silvered (see Cat. no. 12.47 & Appendix II) and many items seem to have been painted or treated with other coatings to improve their appearance or to emphasize a particular feature. A number of the late 17th- and 18th-century toys have traces of red, orangey yellow and white pigment and it is possible that many more were originally painted or treated with other coatings, even though these are no longer visible to the naked eye.[122] By the 18th century there is some evidence that pewter toys were painted by the retailer and a bright yellow-gold colour was achieved by applying a heated and strained mixture of honey, saffron, gum water and vinegar.[123] A translucent bluish lacquer was also used.[124] Analysis of the pigments of 63 toys in the collection, however, has shown that the primary colourant was vermilion, although patches of red ochre and white calcite deposits were also detected.[125]

The toymakers undoubtedly experimented and varied the composition of the alloys according to the types of object they were making, and the successful casting of a new range probably required a certain amount of trial and error before the right proportion was achieved. For some items, such as the Type 8 watches (p. 371), the metallurgical properties of particular alloy compositions were fundamental to a successful casting, and different combinations of alloy were used in one object to achieve the desired level of detail and strength. Sometimes a deliberate composition was used because the toy had to withstand active or even violent use, and for this reason all of the pistols and cannon are made from copper alloys. For other types of toy, the precise blend of alloy was probably far less critical and this might have contributed to the tendency of toymakers to produce substandard 'bad metal' products. The copper-alloy toys constitute a tiny percentage of the total because the material is much more difficult to produce and it is impossible to achieve the same level of detailed and intricate moulding.[126] By contrast, the tin-lead objects are easy to cast because the alloys have a low melting point, and the ductile properties of the metal mean that a wide range of intricate shapes and decorative mouldings can be produced quickly and cheaply. The flat or shallow forms were cast from simple two-part moulds, which could be used repeatedly, and the hollow items were slush cast. The slush-cast process was a quick and cheap way of producing several objects from the same mould without the complication of a 'core' of sand or wax. The method is particularly suited for small castings because the moment that the molten metal comes into contact with the mould, it begins to solidify and contract. Once sufficient time has elapsed for a thin skin to form on the matrix, the toymaker could invert the mould so that the excess or slushy liquid metal in the centre could be drained off. After a further cooling period, the two parts of the mould were opened to reveal the finished piece. It is significant that all of the hollow toys in the sample analysis were made from tin-rich alloys rather than lay metal which reflects the fact that tin is better suited to the slush cast process.[127]

Modern experiments in casting replica lead-alloy secular and pilgrim badges show that a single object can be manufactured in less than a minute, and thousands of items can be produced in one day. The evidence from the toy watch mould (fig. 74, p. 351), which has different matrices on each side, shows that two or more patterns and designs could be produced simultaneously, and it is possible that a whole series of interlocking moulds were assembled for batch production. Toys might also have been produced with other small lead-alloy objects, and the only other toy mould known in England, now in the collections of Hereford Museum (fig. 9, p. 28), has matrices for mounts on one side and a toy jug on the other.[128] It is not known whether these objects were manufactured at the same time, but the fact that the mould has been cut down through one of the mounts suggests that it was probably re-used at a later date to cast lead-alloy toy jugs, which could indicate that the pewterer was diversifying to keep pace with changing fashion and demand.

Although some of the toys were cast in one piece and required only a minimal amount of tidying up to remove flashes and extraneous pieces of metal, other toys needed to be finished on a lathe and more complex shapes had to be 'cold worked' into three-dimensional form by folding and soldering. The toys requiring the most labour intensive production were the watches and pistols which had to be assembled from separately cast components. Most of the toys have been well finished, but there are a few examples with solder damage, or flashes and misruns where the metal has either oozed out of the mould seams or failed to fill the matrix properly. A few of the copper alloys show signs of thermal stress and some of the lead alloys have poorly defined mouldings which could be due to the alloy composition, temperature fluctuations in the casting process, a worn mould or poor workmanship. It is also possible that some of the crudely made items were cast by children. In the 1940s for example, it was quite common to melt down a broken lead soldier and recast it in a mould made from garden clay. My father used one of my grandmother's saucepans for the purpose, and the new soldier was then painted to match the others. If this creative method of repair or replacement was widespread among boys of my father's generation, even allowing for the exigencies of the wartime situation, it is quite likely that young boys did similar things in earlier periods, and this could explain why some of the early flat soldiers have such crudely defined mouldings.

It is axiomatic that a cast product is only as good as the mould from which it was made, and because alloy compositions and the technical accomplishments of the makers also varied considerably, toys of different qualities were produced. The two toy moulds from London and Hereford are both made from fine-grained stone, but the differences in the quality of the carving is quite marked. A number of makers have tried very hard to copy the shapes and characteristic textures and decoration of full-scale objects and have done their best to imitate contemporary fashion, while others seem to have been content with a vague approximation and have used a limited stock of motifs. The work of some makers stands out because they have found a unique style and have stuck to it, so that all of their products are decorated in a similar fashion whether the motifs are really appropriate to the object or not. This is particularly noticeable in the high-quality wares of the maker/s I(D)Q whose toys are easily identified because virtually every piece has the same combination of motifs. Presumably this individual style and 'exclusive range' was adopted for commercial as well as aesthetic reasons.

Although there is very little documentary evidence about early modern pewter toy manufacture in London, the surviving records do indicate that there was a network of makers engaged in this particular branch of the industry from at least the 1660s. An unbroken chain of 18 masters and apprentices can be traced from the 1630s to the late 18th century, most, if not all, of whom were makers of pewter toys and other wares (see Appendix III).

Trends in dating and production (GE)

The medieval period

Twenty-five years ago only a handful of miniature playthings from the Middle Ages, as extensively represented in this present work, were in museum collections in this country. There was not and still is not one in the British Museum, for example. Only one of these items had actually been definitively recognized for what it was.[129] The barrier to recognition was threefold. Firstly, medieval playthings are by no means common as they tend to be made of materials – thin lead alloys and organics – that only survive well in the ground in special conditions in particular soils. In practical terms in Britain, this usually means waterlogged riverbeds or similar, constantly wet areas. Secondly, retrieval of such small objects, often of a similar colour to the soil that has preserved them, is not at all easy just by eye. The final barrier was a series of difficulties which conspired to prevent medieval children's playthings actually being recognized as such. In the 1960s, the influential French social historian Philippe Ariès advanced the view that in the medieval period children were treated as untrained economic producers for the family.[130] The youngest members were to be brought as soon as possible into the family's efforts to make a living, and this imperative denied them the opportunities for frivolities like play – in a word, childhood as we understand it today in society at large. There was a concomitant reluctance to put a great emotional investment into individual children in an age of very high infant mortality. These ideas, though virtually baseless as it has subsequently emerged from a number of detailed studies of contemporary sources,[131] had a profound effect on the attitudes of a generation of students and researchers at the time the first of the playthings in this volume were being recovered and puzzled over. Against the grain, the finders and curators at the Museum of London, to which these and other finds were routinely reported, quickly formed the opinion that medieval toys did indeed exist. The process of sifting out which of various candidate categories and fragments of potential playthings really were for children's play continues today, but it was soon clear to those involved in this process that not only was this phenomenon a reality, but that medieval toys survived in some numbers. When faced, particularly in the early days, with an isolated, single example of a category like standing bowls – or 'flat cups' (p. 294) – it was difficult to be confident there was not some other interpretation of the object. As the picture gradually filled out, it emerged that this was just the kind of prestige vessel that would have been available in toy form while the actual objects were briefly in fashion. Confidence was bolstered by reference to the growing range of other medieval tableware miniatures that were gradually bridging gaps to form chronological series. This probably began in the 13th century and it merges at the late end with aboveground survivals from the 18th century. Over some of the more fully represented periods it had become a seamless progression, covering in all about half a millennium. The first identification of any particular category was the hardest step, and some of the suggestions made have proved erroneous, but the majority appear to be vindicated. All of this would not have been quite so problematic in the Low Countries, where local early toys had been discussed as such in print at least a generation earlier[132] and so the basic idea needed little assimilation when there, too, a range of new discoveries began to emerge with the use of the metal detector.

The best of the latest work on medieval childhood now fully acknowledges playthings in the sense used in this volume as a reality.[133] There remain others who are either sceptical or simply uninformed from archaeological sources.[134] There is still a way to go in persuading some commentators that lead-alloy playthings were produced more for a mass market than the privileged treasures of a rich elite.[135] Of course, those without any spare money would not have been able to afford such trifles, but within towns there would have been many families for whom the occasional indulgence of a few pence on their children would have been readily expended. There are, inevitably, still great areas in this subject that remain unknown. The near absence of recognized medieval playthings made of organic materials is a notable lacuna. Wooden toy ships have been excavated in Dublin, the earliest of Viking form and dating from the 11th–12th century. A gap in the British Isles to the early 17th century before coming to the next-latest one[136] is a reminder of the patchiness of the record so far established. This may be underlined by a wooden horse dated to the Anglo-Norman period, also from Dublin excavations, which remains isolated as a category.[137] Just why no reliably identified find of any kind of animal and only one multiply produced bird of medieval date (fig. 35) has yet been forthcoming is a remarkable feature of the English corpus. This is the more extraordinary as it is such a stark contrast with multiple late-medieval Continental finds from several major towns from the Netherlands, across to Scandinavia and Russia, and through to Hungary, of horses (both riderless and ridden) and occasional birds and other animals, made of wood or more frequently of pottery.[138] At present not one verified wooden medieval plaything has been found in London. So far, the capital has produced just a single toy made from organic materials, a rough human figure, carved with a bearded face, and analogous in form to a peg doll, making ingenious use of the natural shape of a red deer antler. It was excavated as part of the investigation of Guildhall Yard and is closely dated to the late 12th century.[139] From the same site and of similar date is the figure of a bird, cut from lead sheeting and with some details added by scratching.[140] What characterizes both of these two, earliest post-Roman London finds of playthings (presuming they have indeed been correctly identified) is an awareness at the start of the potential of simple figures of living beings for play. They are also both one-off productions, presumably made by individuals related or at least known to the children who played with them. At this stage, there is no evidence for the multiple production that is characteristic of goods made for the market stall, to be purchased for children unknown to the producer. All this fits with the wider picture that, despite extensive research, no intentionally made toy has been recognized in mainland Britain from the Saxon period.[141] A very few miniature objects found in pagan children's and young people's graves may have been placed there as symbols of the life they failed to fulfil, and there are occasional geological or other curiosities of the kind that may have fascinated a child and been possessions favoured enough to be put in the graves with their owners (such items are arguably toys in one sense).

Returning to the mainstream of toys from the later Middle Ages, as represented by mass-produced lead-alloy finds in the Museum of London's collections, two main strands are immediately obvious – mounted knights for the boys and tableware for the girls. These categories both have educational overtones, pointing the way the child was expected to develop. The boys' martial playthings are more aggressive and outward-looking than the smart but everyday domestic items produced for their sisters – an accurate reflection of the aspirational norms of medieval society. It has occasionally been suggested that small spindle whorls were educational toys for girls.[142] This may be true, but they may as an alternative simply have been for the production of fine thread. Girls would probably have found no more difficulty using larger whorls, and if there is any accuracy in the notion that some of them were encouraged to make a contribution to the household's economic efforts, this is the most likely context, as the extended usage of the term 'spinster' implies.

The knights begin with a hollow-cast example from *c.* 1300 (Cat. no. 4.1), using the technique of manufacture established for pilgrims' souvenir *ampullae* for holding holy water. This accomplished, attractive toy is closely datable from several aspects of the arms and armour. Accurate delineation of the latest contemporary developments in the riders' armour and the horses' trappings seems to have been important in these playthings, just as they are as in many latter-day counterparts. This continues to hold

Fig. 15. This detail showing two men with their puppet knights was accompanied by an image of King Solomon, and a Latin legend underlining the futility of those who waste their time in vain pursuits and wasteful play. It is possible that the three-dimensional figurines (pp. 152 & 158–60) were manipulated in a similar fashion to the puppets shown here.
Redrawn from a copy of *c.* 1170 manuscript (now lost) entitled *Hortus Deliciarum* by Herrad von Landsberg of Strasbourg, now in the Bibliothèque nationale de France, Paris

true through the 14th and 15th centuries, with differing methods of manufacture resulting in less fully three-dimensional figures than the earliest one, up to a version known only from a lower fragment, in which the armour skirt is of fluted gothic style assignable to the early 16th century (Cat. no. 4.5). The three examples recovered of one 14th-century version of the mounted knight attest to the great popularity these playthings must have enjoyed. Although the numbers of toy knights retrieved is small, the series in the collection is remarkable – the more so because its existence was unknown just 20 years ago. Still unknown in England are larger-scale copper-alloy mounted knights with lances and set on wheels (possibly the earliest post-Roman wheeled toys). Several of these survive on the Continent and a pair is shown in an early 16th-century depiction of the Emperor Maximilian's childhood, where he is learning knightly skills from them. Despite a number of variations on the lead/tin toys just described having been excavated in towns in the Low Countries and France,[143] there is so far no precise parallel for any of those from London. The evidence of these martial toys, at this stage at least, emphasizes different producers in England and on the Continent. The apparent abrupt end of the toy mounted knight (until its resurrection

62 • TOYS, TRIFLES & TRINKETS

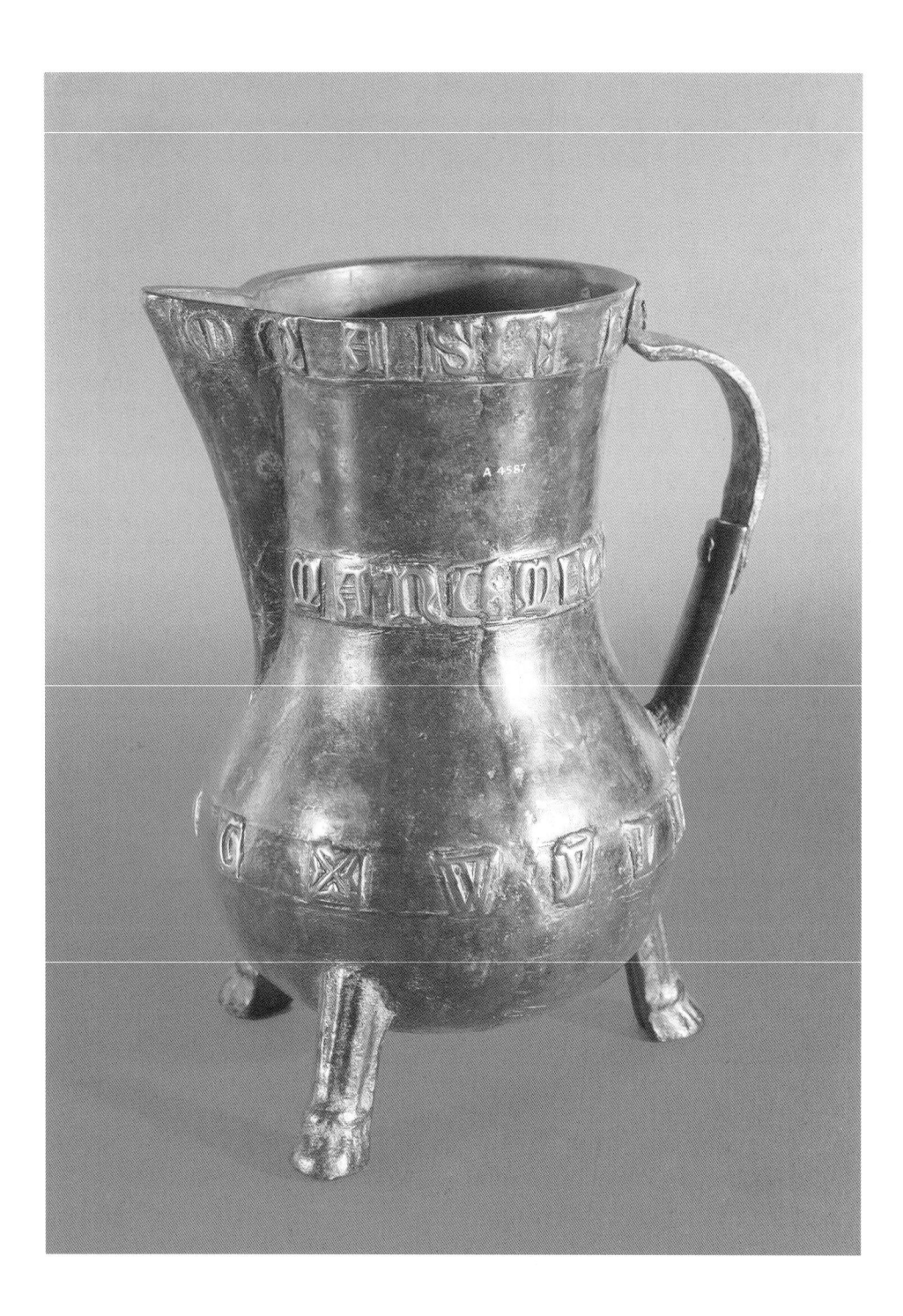

Fig. 16. Many miniature jugs and ewers copy full-scale vessels in ceramic and metal. This full-sized cast bronze ewer, *c.* 1400, does not seem to have a toy equivalent, although it is quite possible that miniature versions were available in the medieval period which have not survived. H. 300mm.
The miniatures below copy full-scale vessels of ceramic and metal.
Museum of London, Acc. no. A4587
Miniatures, Acc. nos. 98.2/162 & 8193, Cat. nos. 8.114 & 8.119

as a historical figure in the 18th century – this later manifestation is not present in the collection) is an appropriate point to regard as the end of this strand of over two centuries' duration in the medieval tradition. The seemingly peaceable standing male figure (Cat. nos 4.26 etc.) – destined to be another enduringly popular plaything – appears to have taken over this place in the repertoire of popular playthings.

The miniature jugs, many decorated with what can be seen as versions of the ceramic trailing on their full-sized counterparts (fig. 16), cover a similar time span. Just as the mounted knight was the most advanced contemporary fighting machine, the jug was not simply one of the containers for drink, but the centrepiece of most family meal tables – a decidedly prestigious vessel. Regional variations may emerge with further study from the tableware they are based on, but there are indications from similar versions in London and on the Continent that some of these toys are likely to have been traded across the sea (just like some of their full-scale counterparts).

As with the knights, fashions in tableware changed radically in the 16th century, with metal vessels (if possible precious ones rather than pewterware) replacing the traditional ceramic ones for the most part by the Reformation. Again, this change is reflected in the miniatures, though possibly as a function of the greater number of jugs recovered, it does not appear to have been as abrupt when compared with the picture suggested by the limited finds of knights. Miniatures in the form of metalware domestic vessels (including some categories for which no full-sized versions are known) were around from the 14th century onwards, becoming predominant in the early 16th century. The repertoire of miniature tableware expanded towards the end of the Middle Ages, with standing bowls or flat cups (Cat. nos. 8.129 etc.), and the first just before 1500 of what was to become the overwhelmingly predominant category in lead alloy – the plate. Kitchenware, for the preparation rather than consumption of food, such fish griddles (Cat. nos. 2.28 etc.), is one of those categories where the dating assigned to miniatures is significantly earlier in the Low Countries than in England. As with the places of manufacture and extent of any early trade in toys, it will take many more, well stratified finds to tease out and chart the main trends.

In addition to the two main categories, a few completely different lines in playthings from the medieval period are in the Museum's collection. A miniature bird (fig. 35, p. 143), perhaps a fledgling, excavated from a deposit assigned to the late 13th–early 14th century, is a very well-made, realistically three-dimensional plaything (this interpretation has been questioned, though it seems somewhat more reliable now that a parallel has been identified in the Netherlands).[144] This toy originally had a hollow body capable of swivelling back and forth when the tail was pushed, so that the tongue (fixed to a horizontal, internal bar joined with the base) appeared to go in and out – a remarkably sophisticated plaything at such an early date.

Four lead-alloy hollow heads, each just over the size of a large thimble, can now be assigned to the 14th century. These could be finger puppets of some kind. One head is perhaps Christ as Man of Sorrows, one appears grotesque and the two others, which are identical to each other, may depict a caricatured Jewish man's head (fig. 34, p. 142).[145] This all leads to the suggestion that these could be characters from a biblical or morality play with Christ, Judas Iscariot and perhaps King Herod. There are many other lead-alloy miniatures from the late medieval period that over decades of intensive study have now been definitively identified as pilgrims' souvenirs or heraldic and other badges of allegiance, but which initially looked like toys. Overall, there are doubtless some items that remain wrongly classified among this vast range, particularly where only fragments are known. It is salutary to look with all this in mind, for example, at miniature shrines and a windmill (with revolving sails), a series of tiny axes, a miniature scabbard, a shoe and a pendant jug, in addition to several two-dimensional standing secular figures that are currently classified as brooches.[146] There is clearly still plenty of scope for error.

The range of medieval toys now known, though impressive, as has already been observed is doubtless far from complete. The most significant factors at this stage are probably the soil conditions that have determined survival or decay over the centuries up to the point when retrieval might occur. The absence from London of any identified medieval wooden toy otherwise looks suspect from the viewpoint of plain common sense, the more so when the miniature ships and suggested toy horse of this material found in Dublin (see above) are considered. It is not so surprising that cloth playthings like rag dolls and figures made of straw and other plant materials[147] have not survived in the soil. While the current absence from the medieval repertoire of a particular material can, perhaps, be accounted for through this archaeological logic – the strength of which may not be as compelling to the non-professional as it is to archaeologists themselves – the absence at any time of entire categories of subject matter (particularly any which appears today an obvious plaything, like marbles in urban contexts) is even harder to explain. One can only return to the need for more appropriate assemblages, which may add to the range now becoming known.

The post-medieval period

There is no strict division of a distinct medieval tradition in toymaking as represented in the collection from a later one. It is possible to focus on the change from knights to standing male figures, the cessation of ceramic jugs as models for playthings, and (less certainly) the development of copper-alloy playthings that were intended to withstand heating or even gunpowder (cauldrons, cannon and firearms – the precise period of manufacture for the latter two is not yet certainly defined in this country). Furniture, in the form of elaborate chairs and simple three-legged stools (Cat. no. 6.89), as well as the first chests with openwork, late gothic tracery also seems to appear around 1500 in England (though earlier dating for similar trinkets has been claimed on the Continent. The same is true of the earliest food-preparation kitchen utensils, such as ladles and fish griddles). All this would imply that the 16th century was, in this country at least, a major turning point. What was happening in toys largely followed the varied changes to material culture in the adult world around this time. It is perhaps more profitable, while noting the significant changes in the 1500s, to chart the many individual strands in the constantly adapting toy business which took place throughout its history.

Overall, the greatest conservatism among the toys that have come down is evident in plates. A significant proportion of these retained the central rose motif, which began in the late 1400s, through all the changes in design on full-sized versions over half a millennium (the same rose design is still available on Nuremberg toys today). Others followed contemporary fashions. At the other end of the scale, that most prestigious possession, the watch, appears to have retained a particular cachet (from when it first became available as a toy in the mid-17th century) that meant small changes in fashion, such as the case's design and materials, were faithfully represented by the more accomplished toymakers.

The first female figures from the 16th century, presumably companion pieces to the contemporary male ones, appear in the developed form of the highly detailed, hollow-cast standing women. Both toys were produced in several versions, some more realistically modelled than others. Those with looped hands could have been walked between two children on strings. Although these are seemingly completely unknown on the Continent, there is a very strong tradition of essentially similar ceramic female figurines from France to Hungary, with a significant production focus in Nuremberg.[148] Increasing diversity characterizes the toys available from the 1500s onwards.[149] The hollow male figures continued into the 1630s and 1640s with IQ's characterful version (fig. 40, p. 169), but there is, strangely, no evidence for equivalent females in the 17th century. There

Female figure
Acc. no. 98.2/433, Cat. no. 4.13

are human flats of both sexes, one- or two-sided, most originally on stands as first exemplified by the hollow-cast male figures. While some flats were perhaps simply cheaper versions of the attractive three-dimensional playthings, in the 17th century the repertoire extended to include a range of street traders among other characters, perhaps along with theatrical entertainers (these are particularly difficult to date). Military figures made an apparent comeback with solid-cast early 17th-century pikemen, but it is not until the end of the 17th century or early in the 18th that flat soldiers – infantry, musicians and mounted officers – seem to have attained the start of the popularity that was such a marked feature of the toy trade in the 19th and early 20th centuries.[150]

Transport toys, both for land and sea, arguably came in during the late 16th century. Wheeled, openwork coaches seem to have been immediately popular (despite their flimsiness) with a series of different versions perhaps over the course of a century. On the other hand, demand for flat warships, which could not easily be propelled across a floor, may have only matched that for the former sporadically – perhaps at times of national pride in the navy, as with the defeat of the Spanish Armada, which could perhaps account for the pair of late 16th-century versions.[151] Any similarly immediate reason for the analogous, late 17th-century version is open to speculation. The man-in-chaise toy, of which three versions are known, includes some with the presumed maker's initial. It looks as if the phenomenon of product-marking in this way, and with dates, came to the fore at points in the post-1600 period, when there was commercial constraint in the developing toy business. The copying by rival makers of successful lines

Three-masted ship
Acc. no. 98.2/432, Cat. no. 10.17

Chaise and driver
Acc. no. 98.2/395, Cat. no. 10.13

at such times would have been particularly irksome. I(D)Q's careful indication of his products, several of which (like his watches, in at least two versions) seem to be innovative in the 1630s and 1640s, is echoed by initials of other makers on plates at the same time. The political troubles of the period may mean that the market for trinkets was in decline.

Toy shies (Cat. nos. 7.1–7.5), identified by their robustness, as they were intended to have missiles thrown at them, seem to be a relatively late phenomenon. A shy cock from Pre Construct Archaeology's NHU98 site to the east of the City of London is from a deposit assigned to *c.* 1730–80. In contrast to many categories included in this volume, several have been found in rural areas. Their crudeness means most are not inherently datable. They include the only post-medieval bird figures considered in the catalogue.

Whirligigs are alone in the collection as playthings that were adapted from other objects,[152] or from any scrap that gave an adequate area of sheet-like lead. The few indications of dating suggest those listed all may be from the late 16th century or later. If there were trade-manufactured versions from this period, they have yet to be recognized.

Whirligig
Acc. no. 98.2/714, Cat. no. 13.5

1. Cowper 1872, 'Hope' (1782), p. 145, line 127.
2. Burke 1924, pp. 56–7. I am most grateful to Alex Werner for this reference.
3. Museum of London Act 2 June 1965 and 26 March 1986, sec. 3c.
4. Digges 1568/9.
5. Halsbury 1985.
6. Webber 1999.
7. Mayhew 1861, vol. 2, p. 155.
8. Hume, 1955, p. 168.
9. Hume, 1955, pp. 248–9.
10. The PLA licence permits surface searching, but members of the Society of Thames Mudlarks are granted the additional privilege of digging.
11. Schofield & Dyson 1980, p. 50.
12. Statute 8 Charles I, 1632, Exchequer Documents O, series 3, vol. 12, 66b – 8 May: 'The decree in the case of Attorney General v. Philpott'.
13. Hume 1955 & 1970, pp. 313–21.
14. Egan 1988a, 1988b & 1998, pp. 281–3.
15. Egan 1996.
16. Willemsen 1994, 1998 & 2000; Wustenhoff 1999, pp. 16–17; Woolgar 1999, pp. 101–2 and fig. 37; Karel 2001.
17. Rowland, the small and rather accident-prone son of Dr. Dee, survived the experience. See Bodleian Library, Oxford, MSS Ashmole 487 & 488.
18. Milne 1982 (excavation period 1974–6).
19. Thames Water, the PLA, Environment Agency and the Tidy Britain Group, 1996.
20. Rodwell Jones 1931.
21. Orme 2001, p. 100 for other accidents involving water, and Hanawalt 1986, pp. 1–22. See also Milne 2003, pp. 100–2.
22. Spencer 1978, p. 243.
23. PRO Calendar of Close Rolls, London Rolls Series, (1369–74). See also Sharpe 1898, bk A, p. 218.
24. Mayhew 1861, vol. 2, pp. 155–8.
25. Magno 1562; repr. 1983, p. 143.
26. *The Spectator*, no. 77, Tuesday, 29 May 1711.
27. Riley 1868, pp. 298–9.
28. This is how all the toys found in the course of formal archaeological excavations up to the mid 1980s were recovered. See Egan 1985/6 and 1998, nos. 930–2.
29. Egan forthcoming a. The individual items are noted as comparanda at appropriate points in the catalogue entries.
30. Egan 2001, pp. 105–6 & 177, nos. 173–5.

31 Staff of York Archaeological Trust, pers. comm.

32 Didsbury 1989; see Egan 1997, p. 415, fig. 3.

33 Egan forthcoming c.

34 Willemsen 1998.

35 Bi Skaarup and Ingrid Dylén Tackmann, pers. comm.

36 Garau & Zagari 1997, pp. 396–9, fig. 4.

37 Barbera 1991.

38 Hume 1973, p. 23.

39 Beverley Straube confirms that there is none so far from the first permanent English settlement in America at Jamestown, despite the extensive and very varied finds assemblages recovered from the earliest deposits at the site. Pers. comm.

40 Cantwell & di Zarega Wall 2001, p. 207. Brown 1996, p. 13, suggests that toys of wood and ivory were being made in New York in the late 1760s.

41 Brown 1996, p. 59.

42 Dodsley 1756.

43 There are a few references in the 14th and 15th centuries: see 'toi' in the *Middle English Dictionary* published by the University of Michigan Press, 1996.

44 Sir Thomas Smith's *Discourse of the Common Weal of this Realm of England* (1549) discusses the contemporary enthusiasm for luxuries which the author claimed could be 'cleaned spared'.

45 Ron Homer, pers. comm., 18 June 2002. I would like to thank Dr Homer for his advice and helpful comments.

46 27 January 1612–13.

47 Previous writers, notably Hatcher & Barker 1974, p. 224, have stated that in the 16th century 'a third, and lower, standard of pewter was permitted for the making of trifles – toys, buttons, salts, candlesticks etc.' Ley or lay metal was certainly used in this period for making small wares 'trifles', but the first references to trifling wares by the Pewterers' Company seem to occur in the following century. The first specific reference to pewter children's toys in the *Tables of Assay* is dated 22 January 1772.

48 CLRO OC 360, 24 January 1666.

49 CLRO MC1/228/101, September 1660.

50 CLRO Com. Ser. fol. 95b, box 4, 1587: 18 February 1679, Joseph Floyd, Mercer: 'a prele [parcel] of toys over chimney piece'. A few inventories in the Netherlands, however, do refer to base- and precious-metal children's toys in various rooms around the house. Pieter Ouseel and Betarix Ernest's household goods included a 'doll's copper kettle' as well as a set of partly damaged 'children's poppegoet in silver'. For full details see Willemsen 1998, p. 292. I am grateful to the author for pointing out these sources.

51 CLRO OI Com. Ser. bk 405 52B/79, April 1630.

52 PRO, E 122/194/25: Petty Customs Account 1480–1, no. 33: 1 box with toys valued at £7. 3s 4d.

53 The terms 'toyman', 'toymaker' and 'toyseller' appear in London inventories and other sources from the 1660s onwards.

54 Jackson had a shop on the corner of Wood Street and Cheapside in 1699.

55 Sotro was a goldsmith and his 'Childrens Toys' which were sold 'Wholesale & Retail' were almost certainly made from silver.

56 The whole business of the silver toy trade falls outside the scope of this publication, but the subject has been fully addressed in Houart 1981 and Poliakoff 1986.

57 Child's shop, the Blew Boar, was demolished when the houses on the bridge were removed in 1760, and he then moved to 123–4 Upper Thames Street. Heal Collection, 1756.

58 CLRO MC1/74/B38, September 1647, and MC1/228/118, September 1660.

59 The appraisers of the inventory have put '2 doz & ? toyes in boxes at XXs p doz'. The 's' must be an error to judge from the total. Presumably they meant to put 'd' instead.

60 CLRO MC1/56/190, 22 March 1633.

61 I am greatly indebted to Philippa Glanville for drawing my attention to this inventory which was appraised on 15 March 1681. Norfolk Record Office, ANW 23/1/114

62 It is possible that the 'milke Mayds' were similar to that described in Cat. no. 4.23.

63 Spufford 1984, pp. 57 & 89. See also Hornsby 1989, pp. 21–7.

64 I am particularly indebted to Dr Homer for this reference, pers. comm. The advertisements appeared in the issue of 20–27 February 1767 and in subsequent issues to 13–20 March. Webber's stock included 'a great variety of PEWTER, BRASS, COPPER and TIN WARES'.

65 CLRO Com. Ser. bks, vols 1–4 (1586–1713).

66 Willemsen 1998, p. 190–1 and pers. comm. I am most grateful to the author for drawing this reference to my attention. The fact that the moulds were described as 'poppengoedsvormen' would suggest, however, that they were made to a much larger scale than the sorts of toys and miniatures described in this volume.

67 GL MS 7090, 18 October, 1770, Ron Homer, pers. comm.

68 William Wightman, Cott. no. 5139. See Appendix III.

69 Engraving from Jacob Cats, *Houwelijck* (1625). See similar images in Cats' *Spiegel van den ouden ende nieuwen tijdt* (1632). Rijksmuseum Library, Amsterdam

70 An etching of *Der Nürnbergisch Kindlesmark* by Johann Georg Trautner, 1797. Germanisches Nationalmuseum, Nuremberg.

71 British Library, MS Harleian 3910, fol. 36.6; repr. in Wright & Halliwell 1841–3.

72 *A Pedler in Haste with an Horn* (London, 1649).

73 GL MS 7090/5, 17 August 1654.

74 *The Pope's Harbinger, by way of Diversion* (London, 1680).

75 Sala 1859.

76 Mintel, June 2001.

77 Government Statistical Service, *Report on the Census of Production*, 1982: Toys and Sports Goods, Table 4.

78 *Toys International*, September–October 1968, p. 32.

79 See discussion under 'anchors' for references to model ships in Ireland which date to the Viking period.

80 Brodsky 1986, pp. 134–7.

81 Finlay 1979, pp. 26–8.

82 Schwarz 1992, p. 133 .

83 Spence 2000, p. 65, table 4.1; p. 91, fig. 4.14; and p. 93.

84 Rappaport 1983, pp. 107–52; Phelps Brown & Hopkins 1956.

85 *The Overseas Trade of London Exchequer Customs Accounts 1480–1*, Cobb, H.S., ed. (London Record Society, 1990), no. 24; see also Willan 1962, pp. 6 & 48.

86 PRO SP 12/8, no 31: 'The Particular Value of certain necessary and unnecessary Wares brought into the Port of London in the second year of the Queen Majesty's reign, the overquantity whereof most lamentably spoileth the realm yearly'.

87 Burt 1995, pp. 23–45.

88 Mintel, June 2001.

89 There are cases and references to the giving of gifts at Christmas but these take the form of clothing, food and other perquisites for servants: see 7 Henry V letter book 1, fol. 238 in Riley 1868, p. 670. Toys were given to children at Christmas on the Continent, however, and in 1572 the three children of August Elector of Saxony were 'given a hunt and many household things' from the Mayor of Leipzig: see Theodor Distel *Speilsachen für die Kinder des Kurfürsten August von Sachsen*; cited in von Wilckens 1978, p. 48 and note 190.

90 GL. MS 4071/1, fols. 44a & 52a.

91 Egan 1988 b.

92 Since the toys are just marked HUX, we do not known whether these were made by William Hux or his son Thomas. A 'Mr Hux' (William) also seems to have been making toy porringers, if the accusations of fellow pewterer, John Strickland were correct. See Appendix III and GL MS 7090/9, 10 April 1718.

93 Egan 1996, p. 3.

94 It is unclear whether some of the repairs and adaptations were done by the retailers or consumers. Most of the whirligigs seem to have been made from coins or scrap metal.

95 For further information on the Lowther Arcade, see Stokes 1971.

96 Sala 1859.

97 Campbell 1747; repr. 1969, p. 142.

98 Welch 1902, vol. 1, p. 96, 19 Henry VII, cap. 6, 1503/4.

99 Although the Gregorian Calendar was used on the Continent from 1582, the Julian Calendar was used in England until 1752.

100 Willemsen 1998, pp. 190–1 and pers. comm. I am grateful to the author for this reference.

101 GL MS 7090/9, 10 April 1718.

102 PRO LC5/33m, fols. 10, 11m warrant dated 20 October 1562. Ippolyta the Tartarian was in the service of Elizabeth I: see Arnold 1988, p. 107.

103 Boesch 1900.

104 Heroard 1989.

105 The Baby House of Duke Albrecht V of Bavaria, *c.* 1550–79, is the earliest known example.

106 Bazin 1967, p. 72.

107 Von Wilckens 1978, pp. 14–16.

108 United States Census of Manufactures, July 1994, and information from the Miniatures Industry Association of America (MIAA).

109 Zedler 1741.

110 Mintel, June 2001.

111 Harrison 1577, bk 3, ch. 16.

112 I am conscious that the adoption of the term 'lead alloy' may antagonize those concerned with the pewter trade, since fine pewter has no lead at all, and lay metal is usually 60% tin to lead. The term has been used, however, for the reasons outlined above, and because it is a convention in museum and archaeological circles.

113 For a detailed discussion of these corrosion products, see Duncan & Ganiaris 1987.

114 22 Edward III 1348, letter book F, fol. 155 in Riley 1868, p. 242. See also Homer 1975, pp. 5–8

115 Cott. no. 2882.

116 See pp. 343–5 and Appendix III.

117 GL MS 7090, 18 October 1770. I am greatly indebted to Ron Homer for this reference, pers comm.

118 The original manuscript is held in the Guildhall Library, but has been transcribed in full in *JPS* 4 (3) (Spring 1984).

119 Some 80 pieces were originally selected for analysis, but unfortunately it was only possible to analyse a fraction prior to publication.

120 Homer 1975, p. 7.

121 A group of seven toys from Abbots Lane, Southwark, from closely dated contexts were analysed for a separate publication: see D. Dungworth in Egan forthcoming a. Apart from the lead whirligig or buzz wheel, the other toys were all made from poor-quality metal with a high lead to tin ratio.

122 Welch 1902, vol. 2, p. 248: Court Minutes for 29 August 1564–5.

123 Crouch 1725, p. 116, notes the import ban on painted toys which could suggest that domestic producers were making similar items and needed protection from foreign competition.

124 Hughes 1973, p. 133.

125 I am grateful to Dr Gregory Dale Smith of Brookhaven National Laboratory, New York, and Dr Tracey Chaplin, Department of Chemistry University College London, for their work on this material.

126 It is quite possible that the copper-alloy toys were actually manufactured by pewterers, since at some point before 1551 the pewterers took over the guild of coppersmiths. Many provisional pewterers also worked in brass and bronze. See R. Homer in *JPS* 13 (Spring 2000), p. 11 and Hatcher & Barker 1974, p. 241, note 3.

127 The late Arthur Trotman, former Head of Conservation at the Museum of London, made a copy of a 13th-century mould and demonstrated 'that the slush technique could be successfully performed only with pure tin and considerable dexterity'. See Spencer 1998, p. 12.

128 Hereford Museum, inv. no. 1987–107. I am grateful to Judith Stevenson for making this object accessible.

129 King 1973, p. 5, tentatively assigned to the 14th century. This is the ewer published here (Cat. no. 8.119) which was included in the Guildhall Museum catalogue in 1908, p. 305, no. 74, plate 93, no. 2.

130 Ariès 1960.

131 See, for example, Willemsen 1998.

132 See, for example, Verster 1958. This English version of a Dutch book for pewter collectors had little impact on acceptance of the notion in the UK as all the objects it discussed were from the other side of the North Sea.

133 Orme 1995 and 2001, pp. 4–5, 172–4, figs 62–4 & 167–76. Both publications drew on the Pilson collection for illustrative material. Several recent Continental works (apart from Willemsen 1998) such as Riché & Bidon 1994 and Falk 1995 are fully aware of the point and have useful illustrations.

134 eg. Hanawalt 1993, whose document-based survey of childhood in medieval London does not mention the word 'toy', presumably because no local documentary reference has been traced.

135 Woolgar 1999, pp. 101–2, referring to 'children of the wealthy' and plate 37, showing the earliest mounted knight of those listed in this catalogue.

136 Lang 1988, pp. 79–80; Christensen 1988, pp. 19–21, figs 8–9; Heal 1992.

137 Lang 1988, p. 34, fig. 54. Brown 1996, p. 11, states that Noah's Arks were popular from the early 17th century, but does not cite a source for this information. Even if these playthings were mainly of wood, it is remarkable that there was apparently no response from pewter manufacturers.

138 Willemsen 1998 gives a good idea of the range produced.

139 Bateman 2000, p. 57.

140 Egan 1998, no. 930. The parallel was kindly drawn to my attention by Annemarieke Willemsen, pers. comm.

141 Crawford 1999, pp. 141–4.

142 Two examples from Salisbury – Egan 2001, p. 106 & fig. 38, nos. 177–8 – if correctly interpreted seem (at just over 3.5g each) to be the smallest noted in this country.

143 *Der Weisskünig in dem Jahrbuch der Kunsthistorischen Sammhungen* 6, Vienna 1888.

144 Egan 1988, no. 930. The parallel was kindly drawn to my attention by Annemarieke Willemsen, pers. comm.

145 Egan 1997, p. 414 was written when the first 'Jewish head' was thought to be significantly earlier. A similar find from a closely dated deposit at the MBC98 site now permits this revision to be put forward. See 'Man of Sorrows' (Spencer 1998, no. 180b) and grotesque head (Egan 1998, pp. 281–2, no. 931).

146 Spencer 1998, nos. 165a–b & 292a–b; nos. 299ff; no. 303; no. 325j; no. 3251. Compare nos. 297d–298d.

147 See Crawford, S., 1999, p. 141.

148 Grönke & Weinlich, 1998.

149 Brown 1996, pp. 15–17, makes a similar point for the 18th and 19th centuries.

150 Brown 1996, pp. 1 & 58 for the 18th and late 19th centuries.

151 Egan 1988a, though the discovery of a comparable plaything in the Netherlands now makes this seem unlikely. See ships under 'Transport'.

152 Brown 1996, pp. 1–40 suggests a significant number of home-made adaptations for one-off toys were current right up to the early 20th century. This is not the picture that is presented by the excavated material catalogued in this volume. Perhaps the adaptations tended to be too flimsy for survival below ground.

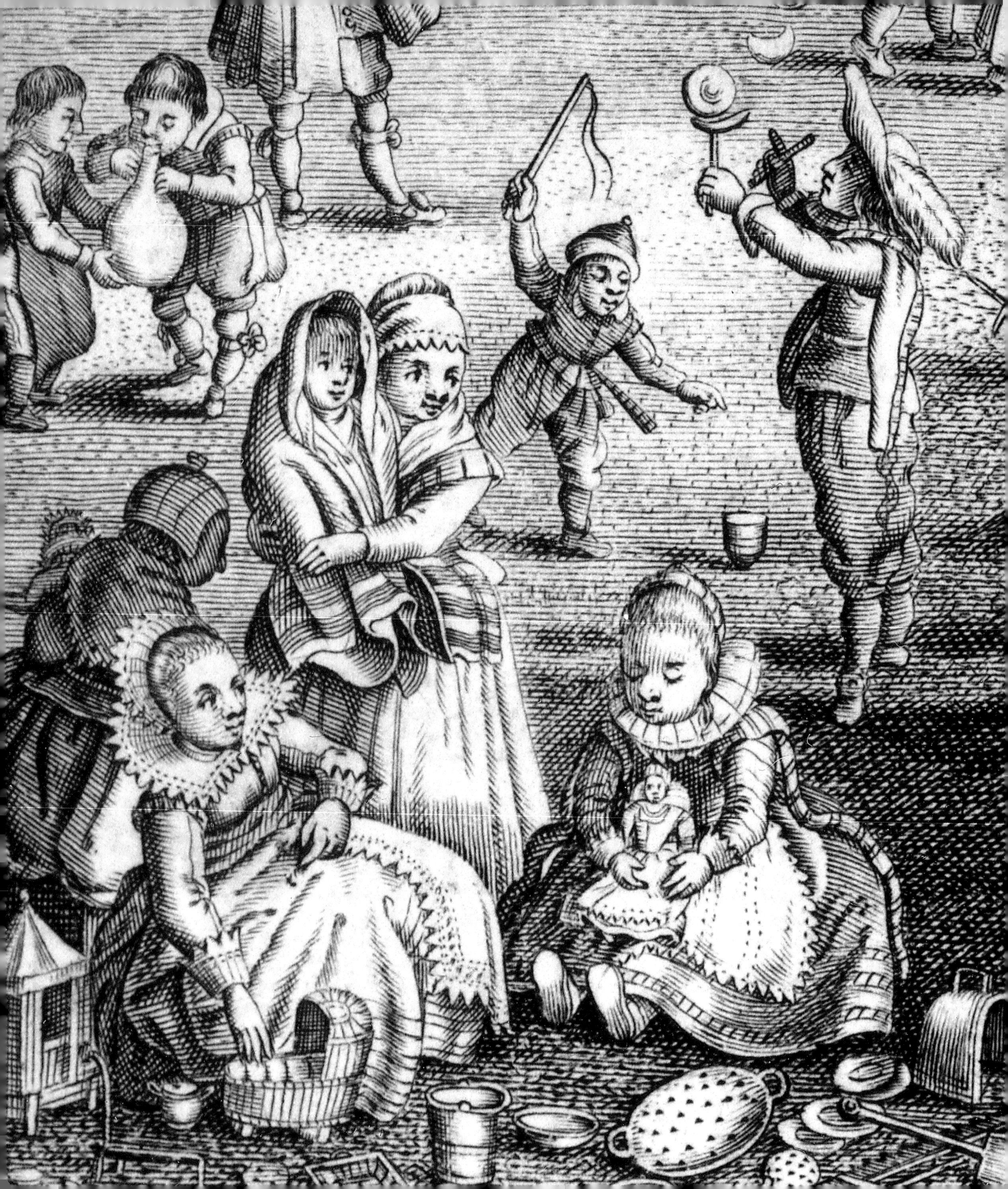

PART II
Catalogue

Fig. 17. Detail from an engraving by Experiens Silleman [1611–1653] which accompanies the poem 'Kinder-spel' by Jacob Cats, 1625. See fig. 43, p. 187

Unless otherwise stated all of the finds have come from the Thames foreshore. Additional provenance details have been added when the information is known.

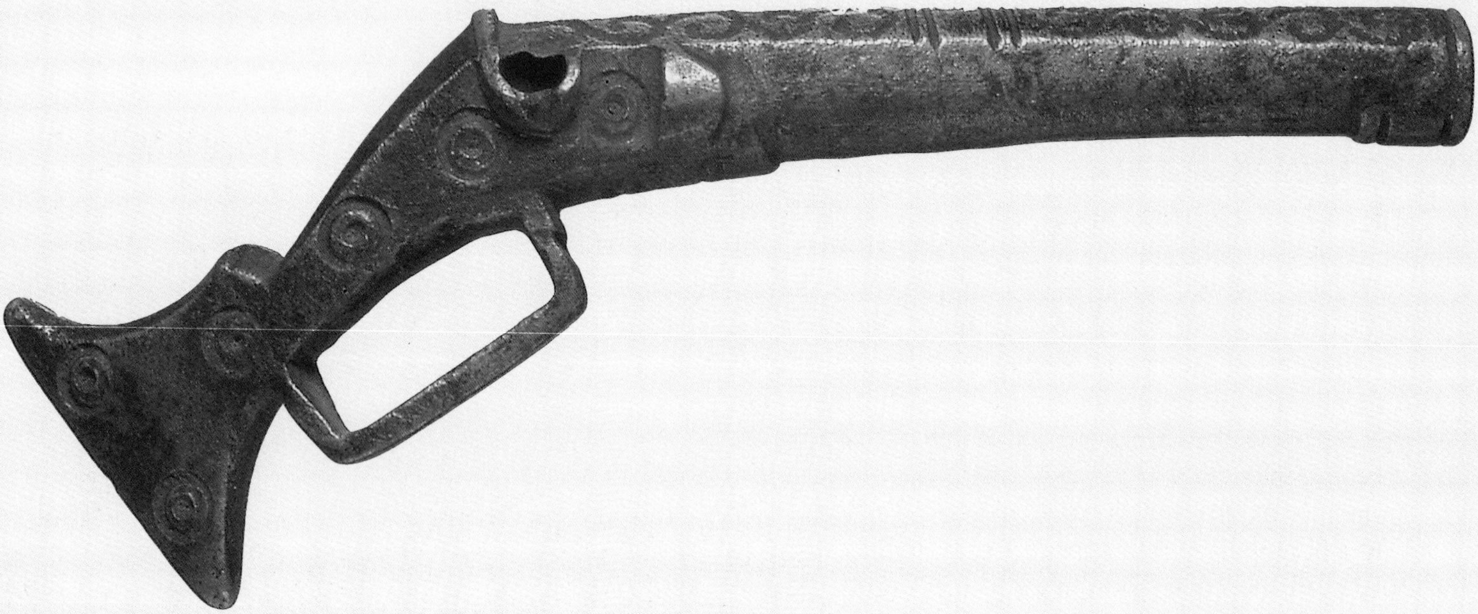

1 Arms & armour

'Great care must be taken in the Casting of Pieces of Ordnance, that they be equal every way in proportion of Metals ... otherwise your Piece will fail ...'[1]

Miniature weapons were evidently produced in large numbers throughout the early modern period, but only a few of the highly crafted scale-model replicas and some of the more durable examples of cheap mass-production have survived. The items discussed in this section represent the cheapest end of toy and miniature arms and armour production.

Firearms, ordnance and other pieces of artillery constitute the bulk of finds, not because they were necessarily more popular than other types of weapon, but because the majority were made to be fired and were therefore cast in copper alloys to withstand firing pressures. The comparative strength and durability of their material has ensured a better level of preservation and a concomitantly higher survival rate than those objects made from lead alloys, which are not only weaker and liable to fragment but also deteriorate rapidly in the soil.

Hardly any comparable material has been found during excavations on the Continent, although a few late 16th- and early 17th-century toy pistols have been found on colonial sites in America.[2] Most of the examples described here were probably manufactured in England although documentary evidence for production is lacking. The material has been divided into the following categories: armour, artillery, edged weapons and firearms, and each section is accompanied by a short introduction.

Armour

A large number of high-quality miniature armours in steel and other materials survive in collections throughout the world, but the only item in this category from London soil is a lead-alloy helmet of morion style.[3]

TYPE 1, DESIGN 1

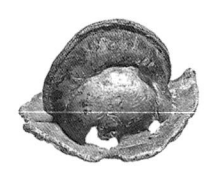

1.1 Morion

Accession number: 98.2/402
Material: Lead alloy
Condition: Complete; slight damage
Dimensions: H 16mm; W 25 x 20 mm
Description: An open helmet or hat of combed morion style with narrow brim and fore and aft peak. The contours are rounded and the comb has a reeded edge.
Date: Late 16th – early 17th century
Provenance: Dockhead
Comments: Similar-shaped morions were made in Nuremberg in the 1580s and were worn by foot soldiers during the second half of the 17th century. But since the shape was adopted for civilian use and textile versions were made for fashionable gentlemen in this period, it is possible that the toy is not a 'helmet' but a 'hat'. See, for example, a felt hat covered with embroidered black velvet c. 1600 (the gift of the Prince of Schwarzburg in 1877) in the collections of the Germanisches Nationalmuseum, Nuremberg. A small hollow-cast male figure in clothing of the period 1580–1610 in the collections of the Musée de Cluny has a similar head covering.
Comparandum: See Wallace Collection Catalogues, vol. 1, A116 & A117

Artillery

Artillery rammers

'Instruments by which great guns are charged, and clensed in its much shooting'[4]

These copper-alloy rods with a disc at each end resemble a specific kind of artillery combination tool first recorded in English inventories from the end of the 15th century. The full-scale tool, commonly known as a rammer, has a cylindrical block at one end to drive home the wadding and charge, and a fleece sponge at the other to clean the gun before and after firing. Both ends are the same diameter as the bore of the gun for which they were made. The toy rammers have discs of different diameters and although the smallest end could have been used for many of the guns in the collection, the diameter of the largest disc suggests that they were really designed for guns with a much greater calibre, which have not survived. The largest disc gets no further than the muzzle ring on the largest gun (Cat. no. 1.3) and while Acc. no. 98.2/654 is a reasonable fit for the second largest calibre cannon in the collection, the rammer will not go beyond the chamber.

TYPE 1, DESIGN 1

1.2 Artillery rammer

Accession number: 98.2/653*; 98.2/654
Material: Copper alloy
Condition: Complete
Dimensions: 98.2/653: L 82mm; Diam 3.5 x 5 mm; 8 x 7 mm
　　　　　　98.2/654: L 79mm; Diam 5mm; 8mm
Description: Double-ended artillery rammer with polygonal-sectioned shafts and flat discs at each end. Both shafts have been filed and 98.2/653 has been crudely made.
Date: Probably late 16th – early 17th century

Cannon

'These Great Guns, either for land or sea service, haue seuerall names according to their largenesse, and the weight of the ballor bullet they shott …'[5]

Although cannon were employed by English forces from the 14th century, it was not until the early 1500s that miniature firing guns began to make their appearance, and because they were popular and attracted the interest of adults and children alike, toy cannon and artillery models of various kinds began to be made in significant numbers. The earliest surviving examples are scale-model guns, which were either commissioned as a gift or presentation piece or produced in royal arsenals as a prototype for didactic and experimental purposes. But the vast majority of artillery miniatures were cheaply produced, stylized copies of contemporary or historic guns, which seem to have be made for the mass-market from the end of the 16th century.

All of the toy cannon in the collection are muzzle-loaders and the majority have a cascabel button, breech chamber, vent, trunnions and circumferential mouldings to represent base, reinforce, trunnion and muzzle rings of a full-scale gun. Some, however, lack trunnions and were supported by a pair of integrally cast basal lugs beneath the reinforce field and chase.[6] Although this feature is not found on full-scale cannon, similar shaped lugs were sometimes used to mount pistols to a stock during the 18th and 19th centuries, and it is possible that the toymaker copied this method of attachment so that these guns could be mounted on to a stock, block or an adapted truck rather than a carriage.[7]

Approximately 85% of the toy cannon are hollow-cast in a two-part mould from copper alloys and although a superficial glance suggests that the majority could be fired, close examination shows that some are imperfectly cast and others have thin and weak barrels which are incapable of withstanding the force of an explosion. It is possible that two classes of miniature gun were produced to satisfy contemporary demand: toy cannon that could be fired and toy cannon intended for imaginative play rather than active use. To an untrained eye, however, one class of toy cannon looks much like the other and if the temptation to fire a gun became overwhelming, it is conceivable that inferior-quality toys could have been unwittingly used with potentially tragic results.

Although several of the guns in the collection could have been successfully fired and might have seen regular use, four cannon with exploded barrels provide dramatic evidence of a misfiring. The fractured metal on these guns suggests that they were blocked at the muzzle with mud, grease, water or shot lodged in the bore, but it is also possible that the wrong powder was used and the guns were overcharged, contributing to an expansion of gas and a build-up of pressure which exceeded the tensile strength of the barrel. Most of the cannon have small vents, which would have retained the force of the explosion, but others have large touch holes, creating a lot of smoke and a flash back.

It is possible that the guns were acquired with loading and firing instructions but if so, no documentary evidence has survived, and although modern calculations based on the length of the barrel and the bore diameter suggest that the guns could accommodate from 0.28g (0.01oz) to approximately 2.84g (0.1oz) of black powder depending on their size, without experiment it is really impossible to calculate how much powder was needed to charge the guns, and probably a successful firing was more a matter of luck than judgment. No doubt a combination of trial and error improved the success rate, although if the error was serious this could have put an abrupt stop to the experiment. The larger-calibre guns are potentially lethal in unskilled hands and a misfiring or explosion could have resulted in a serious or even fatal blast injury.

Children probably had little difficulty in obtaining a suitable propellant for their toy guns because black powder was readily available and inventories of the late 16th and 17th centuries suggest that most London households had a musket or two. A small quantity of black material (possibly powder) has been found in the breech of one of the guns, but since the composition and chemical balance of the ingredients will have altered and the sulphur and nitre has almost certainly leached out into the surrounding waterlogged sediments during the years of burial, trace analysis is futile.[8] Pistol shot, buck and birdshot was also in plentiful supply and these could have been used for the medium- to large-calibre guns, while home-made projectiles were probably manufactured for the smaller pieces.[9] The velocity, range and penetration of the projectiles would have varied considerably, and while it is difficult to calculate the range of many of the guns, the largest were as powerful as a pocket pistol and were probably capable of shooting a projectile over a considerable distance. The unwary gunner could have been caught out by the recoil of some of these guns, in some cases up to two to three pounds, and unless the carriages were firmly secured the force of recoil could have caused the guns to leap backwards or flip upwards and over to one side, which might explain why so few of the carriages have survived!

Once the guns had been loaded with powder and shot, they must have been fitted with some sort of fuse, which was probably a slow match (hemp impregnated in a saltpetre solution) or if this was too thick, individual strands from a slow match. It is possible that some daring individuals might have resorted to a quick match (which incorporates gunpowder) or even some sort of taper or heated wire. The sensible gunner would have touched off the fuse from the end of a long stick to increase the safety margin. Wadding materials have not been detected and since they are not strictly necessary for miniatures at this scale, they might not have been used.

A couple of cannon have lead in the breech and although the precise purpose is unknown, it has been suggested that this was deliberately added to plug the breech face to bring the charge and ball forwards into

Table 1.1

Type	Acc. no.	Length	Width	Material	Bore	B/length	Weight	Exploded
1	2000.59	100mm	–	Cu/Pb	10.0mm	82mm	116.58g	Yes
2	98.2/640	52mm	10mm	Cu	5.0mm	41mm	13.71g	No
2	98.2/642	52mm	10mm	Cu	5.0mm	41mm	13.56g	No
3	98.2/643	65mm	23mm	Cu	5.0mm	55mm	27.29g	No
4	98.2/636	42mm	19mm	Cu	3.5mm	–	11.61g	No
5/ D1	98.2/638	75mm	25mm	Cu	7.5mm	67mm	42.43g	No
5/ D2	98.2/648	42mm	–	Cu	9.0mm	42mm	14.51g	Yes
6/ D1	98.2/645	75mm	16mm	Cu	7.5mm	67mm	44.16g	No
6/ D1	98.2/647	75mm	–	Cu	7.5mm	67mm	6.79g	Yes
6/ D2	98.2/644	88mm	7mm	Cu	8.5mm	70mm	56.78g	No
7	98.2/634	53mm	16mm	Pb	4.5mm	45mm	37.12g	No
8	98.2/646	50mm	12mm	Pb	5.5mm	51mm	17.00g	No
9	83.422/2	38mm	11mm	Pb	–	–	12.30g	No
10	98.2/639	34mm	12mm	Cu	2.5mm	26mm	3.70g	No
11	98.2/641	47mm	20mm	Cu	4.5mm	37mm	2.05g	No
12	A1152	60mm	28mm	Cu	7.0mm	49mm	58.00g	No

the correct position below and in front of the vent.[10] This would have reduced the amount of powder need to fire the gun, and the additional weight at the breech end might have enhanced the firing capacity and improved the arc of trajectory. The plug was probably created by pouring molten metal down the barrel and the uneven grainy surface tends to confirm this supposition. The plug on Acc. no. 98.2/644 has an angled profile from the vent to the muzzle and this might have been caused by filing out extraneous metal to provide an open channel from the vent to the firing chamber.[11]

As Table 1.1 shows, Types 7, 8 and 9 are made from lead alloy. The London pieces bear only a superficial resemblance to a full-scale gun, but more convincingly moulded examples in lead alloy have been recovered in other parts of the country.[12] None of these guns could have withstood an explosive force. It is just conceivable that Cat. no. 1.12 might be an early version of a modern toy spring-action gun.

Despite their abundance and wide distribution, hardly any toy cannon have been recovered during excavations and the only examples from securely dated contexts have been found in 17th-century deposits in the Netherlands and from 18th-century contexts in America.[13] All of the English examples have been recovered by chance, and although as a group, toy cannon constitute the most common toy find outside London, very few have been found in the capital. The 19 guns catalogued below do seem to reflect the full range of standard types, however, and the majority have features that imitate evolutionary developments in artillery dating from the 17th to the late 18th century. Precise dating is generally impossible because any potentially diagnostic features are too stylized and there is also the distinct probability that some of the apparently 'early' pieces are later versions produced in a 'historic' style (Type 9 is a possible example). Fourteen distinct forms have been identified.

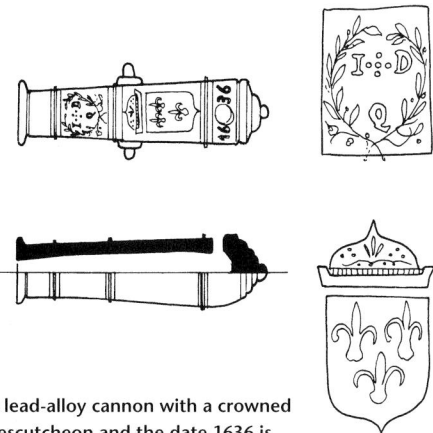

Fig. 18. This lead-alloy cannon with a crowned fleur-de-lys escutcheon and the date 1636 is the earliest known product of the maker/s I(D)Q. Found in Amsterdam in 2002. L 48mm
Private Collection

TYPE 1, DESIGN 1

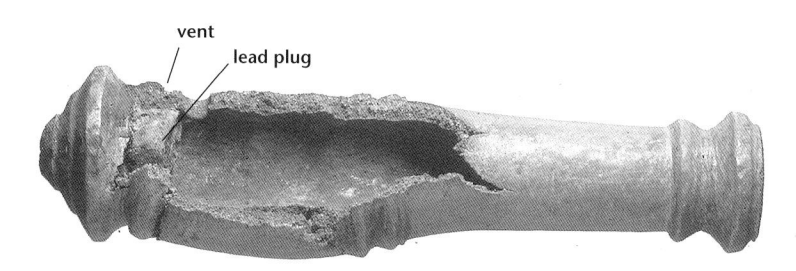

1.3 Cannon

Accession number: 2000.59
Material: Copper alloy; lead
Condition: Exploded
Dimensions: L 100mm; L (bore) *c.* 82mm; Diam (bore) 10mm; Th 3mm
Weight: 116.58g
Description: This gun, of exceptional length and size, has a pronounced base ring, tapering cascabel mouldings and a single reinforce defined by a double ring and fillet. The chase tapers to the muzzle, which has pronounced mouldings. One small circular trunnion has survived and the vent has been drilled. An explosion has ripped out a large section of the barrel and there are several fractures exposing the chamber and a semi-circular plug of lead, which is jammed into the breech behind the severed vent hole. The cascabel button has been imperfectly cast.
Date: This cannon is similar to a piece from 1630–50.
Provenance: Bull Wharf
Comments: The blast damage suggests that this gun was probably blocked at the muzzle and the size and calibre is such that gun could accommodate pistol shot or goose and swan shot with pistol size balls. The cannon is as powerful as a pocket pistol with a recoil of a few pounds.
Comparanda: RA XIX.29–33, English, dated 1639 in Blackmore 1976, p. 66, cat. no. 41. See also Christie's *Antique Arms and Armour,* Wed. 19 September 1990, lot 114.

82 • TOYS, TRIFLES & TRINKETS

TYPE 2, DESIGN 1

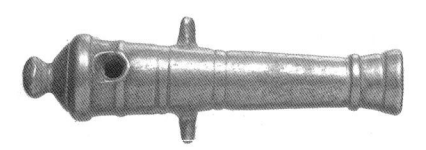

1.4 Cannon

Accession number 98.2/640*; 98.2/642
Material: Copper alloy
Condition: Some damage, cause uncertain
Dimensions: L 52mm; L (bore) c. 41mm; W (across trunnions) 10mm; Diam (bore) 5mm
Weight: 98.2/640: 13.71g. 98.2/642: 13.56g
Description: Cast in one piece with a tapering cascabel and flaring button. The base, vent and muzzle rings are in relief, while the first and second reinforce rings are incuse. The chase tapers towards the muzzle, which flares out from the ring. There is an irregular hole through the upper face of the chase (98.2/642) where the wall is extremely thin and weak. The vent hole (98.2/640 has a very large aperture) have been integrally cast and the trunnions are of circular section.
Date: Possibly late 17th or early 18th century
Comments Although the mouldings on 98.2/640 are a little more crisp, the guns are identical and were probably cast from the same mould.

TYPE 3, DESIGN 1

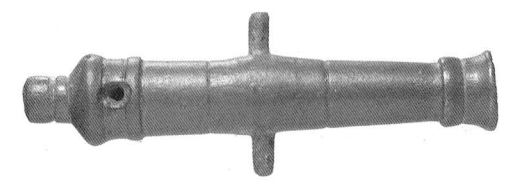

1.5 Cannon

Accession number: 98.2/643
Material: Copper alloy
Condition: Complete
Dimensions: L 65mm; L (bore) 55mm; W (across trunnions) 23mm; Diam (bore) 5mm
Weight: 27.29g
Description: Cast in one piece with a thickened base ring, plain tapering breech and incised cylindrical cascabel button. The vent field is no wider than the diameter of the vent and the first and second reinforce rings are incuse. The gun tapers slightly towards the muzzle, which is reinforced with a wide flaring bevelled flange around the bore. The muzzle ring is incuse and the tiny trunnions are of circular section.
Date: Late 17th – early 18th century, but not normal gun shape

TYPE 4, DESIGN 1

1.6 Cannon

Accession number: 98.2/636
Material: Copper alloy; lead
Condition: Complete
Dimensions: L 42mm; L (bore) 3.5mm; W (across trunnions) 19mm
Calibre: Shot Diam approximately 3mm
Weight: 11.61g
Description: Cast in one piece with thickened base ring, ridged cascabel and mushroom shaped button. The vent hole is tiny and the vent field corresponds to the diameter of the vent. Both the first and second reinforce rings are in relief and these are positioned either side of the trunnions which are little more than pointed pins. The gently tapering chase terminates in a thickened and flaring muzzle with a relief muzzle ring. A ball is lodged in the mouth of the gun.
Date: Typical cannon shape of the first half of the 18th century

TYPE 5, DESIGN 1

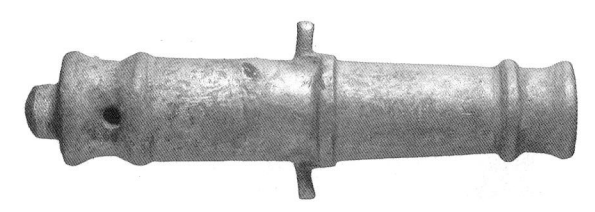

1.7 Cannon

Accession number: 98.2/638
Material: Copper alloy
Condition: Complete
Dimensions: L 75mm; L (bore) 67mm; W (across trunnions) 25mm; Diam (bore) 7.5mm
Weight: 42.43g
Description: Cast in one piece with a pronounced base ring, flat breech and domed cascabel. The vent hole butts on to the first reinforce ring and the second reinforce ring merges with tiny trunnions of square section. The chase is slightly tapered and terminates in a pronounced muzzle ring. There is a thickened, but plain muzzle moulding. The surface is slightly pitted and the metal seems to have a very high zinc content. Traces of black powder mixed with mud from the foreshore were found in the breech.
Date: Probably first half of the 18th century

Comments: This gun is very similar to T5, D2 below, although the mouldings have a different profile and the trunnions are longer.

TYPE 5, DESIGN 2

1.8 Cannon

Accession number: 98.2/648
Material: Copper alloy
Condition: Exploded
Dimensions: L 42mm; Diam (bore) 9mm
Weight: 14.51g
Description: Cast in one piece and destroyed by an explosion. Only part of the second reinforce, one minuscule trunnion, and the chase and muzzle survive. Inside is a distinct ridge, which marks the position of the second reinforce ring, although it is not aligned directly with it.
Date: Probably first half of the 18th century
Comments: Very similar to T6 below

TYPE 6, DESIGN 1

1.9 Cannon

Accession number: 98.2/645*; 98.2/647
Material: Copper alloy
Condition: 98.2/645: complete. 98.2/647: exploded
Dimensions: L 75mm; L (bore) 67mm; Diam (bore) c. 7.5mm
Weight: 98.2/645: 44.16g. 98.2/647: 36.79g
Description: Cast in one piece with a pronounced base ring, flat breech and circular cascabel with a cone-shaped terminal. The vent field has a concave profile and central vent seems to have been drilled. The first and second reinforce and muzzle rings are pronounced and the gun tapers evenly to the muzzle. There are two vertically aligned, integrally cast lugs with triangular sheered points underneath the first reinforce field and the chase. The barrel, from the first reinforce to the muzzle ring (98.2/647) has ruptured, and the resulting damage is indicative of pressure build-up at the muzzle.

Date: Probably 18th century, although lugs are not found on full-scale cannon
Comments: The lugs are, however, identical to those on mounted pistols, and the damage was almost certainly caused by removing the cannon from a stock of some kind.

TYPE 6, DESIGN 2

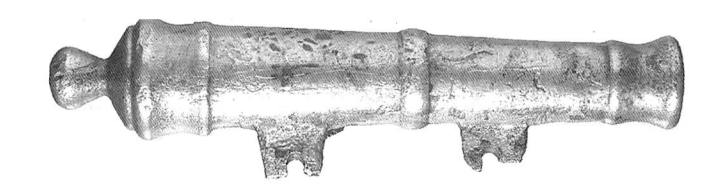

1.10 Cannon

Accession number: 98.2/644
Material: Copper alloy
Condition: Virtually complete
Dimensions: L 88mm; L (bore) c. 70mm; Diam (bore) 8.5mm
Weight: 56.78g
Description: Cast in one piece with pronounced base ring and tapering breech. The cascabel is an inverted and rounded cone and the vent hole is large (drilled?) and occupies the width of the vent field. Both the first, second reinforce rings and muzzle ring are in relief and the gun tapers gently to flare out at the muzzle. Underneath are two vertically aligned lugs in the first reinforce field and chase field. Both are broken at the tip.
Date: Very crude, possibly 18th century, but not like any known cannon
Provenance: London, 1986 (originally photographed with a separate ball, although this has not been traced)
Comments: The proportionally large vent would have helped pressure release in the chamber, thereby helping to reduce the strain on the barrel, which is fairly weak.

TYPE 7, DESIGN 1

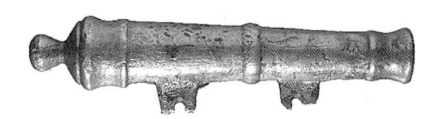

1.11 Cannon

Accession number: 98.2/634
Material: Lead alloy
Condition: Some damage
Dimensions: L 53mm; L (bore) 45mm; Diam (bore) 4.5mm
Weight: 37.12g
Description: An extremely crude gun which has been cast in one piece. There is a misshapen cascabel and vent hole but the gently tapering barrel is otherwise completely smooth and plain with no mouldings. There are two areas of damage on the underside.
Date: Possibly 18th century

TYPE 8, DESIGN 1

1.12 Cannon

Accession number: 98.2/646
Material: Lead alloy
Condition: Almost complete, some damage
Dimensions: L 50mm; L (bore) 51mm; Diam (bore) 5.5mm
Weight: 17g
Description: Cast in two pieces with a rough polygonal-sectioned 'vent field' and knob to represent the vent. The breech is ridged and there is a hole where the cascabel should be. The barrel is smooth and plain apart from two ridges with two lateral knobs to crudely represent the position of trunnions. There is a faint muzzle ring and muzzle moulding.
Provenance: Bankside, June 1983
Comments: Possibly an early version of a spring-action gun.
Date: Possibly 18th century

TYPE 9, DESIGN 1

1.13 Cannon

Accession number: 83.422/2
Material: Lead alloy
Condition: Virtually complete
Dimensions: L 38mm; Diam (bore) 1mm
Weight: 12.30g
Description: Solid and cast in one piece. This gun is very crude and the barrel has widely spaced rings from end to end and a flaring muzzle. The cascabel is sharply pointed and only one trunnion survives. The tiny bore is slightly recessed.
Date: Possibly 18th century
Comments: Although this gun has hoop-type mouldings, the presence of the cascabel suggests that it was manufactured in the post-medieval period.

TYPE 10, DESIGN 1

1.14 Cannon

Accession number: 98.2/639
Material: Copper alloy
Condition: Complete; some damage
Dimensions: L 34mm; L (bore) 26mm; W (across trunnions) 12mm; Diam (bore) c. 2.5mm
Weight: 3.70g
Description: Cast in two pieces with an elongated cylindrical-shaped cascabel. The vent field is concave and the barrel is plain, smooth and straight sided, flaring out from the muzzle ring. The tiny trunnions are circular in section.
Date: Nothing like a real gun, and therefore very difficult to date – perhaps 18th century

TYPE 11, DESIGN 1

1.15 Cannon

Accession number: 98.2/641
Material: Copper alloy
Condition: Complete
Dimensions: L 47mm; L (bore) 37mm; W (across trunnions) 20mm; Diam (bore) 4.5mm
Weight: 12.05g
Description: Cast in one piece, with a prominent base ring, curved tapering breech and round knop cascabel. The vent field is concave and the vent fairly large. There is a thickened first reinforce ring but the barrel is otherwise completely plain and smooth. The flaring muzzle has a bevelled flange around the bore. The trunnions are quite long and circular in section.
Date: Possibly 18th century

TYPE 12, DESIGN 1

1.16 Cannon

Accession number: A1152
Material: Copper alloy
Condition: Complete
Dimensions: L 60mm; L (bore) 49mm; W (across trunnions) 28mm; Diam (bore) 7mm
Weight: 58g
Description: Cast in one piece with a pronounced base ring, tapering breech and large spherical cascabel. The vent field corresponds to the diameter of the vent hole and there are first reinforce, trunnion and muzzle rings. Very wide trunnion ring and square-sectioned trunnions.
Date: Probably 18th century

Gun carriage

Despite the fact that miniature cannon are found in greater numbers throughout the country than any other category of toy, hardly any miniature gun carriages have been recovered. While one might expect wooden truck or block carriages to have disintegrated and rotted away, it is surprising that the more robust copper-alloy field carriages also seem to have perished, but perhaps constituent parts or fragments lie unidentified within archaeological archives, or heavy use destroyed the carriages beyond recognition and recovery.

The only carriage recovered from London soil has stylistic features which suggest an 18th-century date, and this field piece accommodates guns with narrow, circular-sectioned trunnions approximately 17mm across. Two of the guns[14] within the corpus actually fit the carriage, but although the swivel action and balance is good, the scale is somewhat at odds with the proportions and position of a real gun on a field carriage of this type, and the breech is entirely unsupported. The omission of the breast transom was clearly designed to introduce flexibility into the design, enabling the brackets to be sprung apart so that the trunnions can be located in their respective holes, and this is why the carriage will only support a smallish gun of *c.* 50mm in length. One of the wheels and the wire are modern replacements.

TYPE 1, DESIGN 1

1.17 Gun carriage

Accession number: 98.2/659
Material: Copper alloy; iron
Condition: Virtually complete
Dimensions: H *c.* 23mm; L 64mm; W (axle) *c.* 45mm
Description: This three-dimensional field carriage is made from 1mm-thick copper-alloy sheet, and each piece has been cut and roughly filed. The two cheeks or brackets curve outwards towards the trail, which has a recurving terminal. There are breech and trail transoms only and these are riveted into the cheeks and reinforced with solder. The toymaker has simplified the usual method of trunnion attachment to the bracket, and instead of a trunnion plate and cap square, there are holes in each cheek through which the trunnions are fed. Each bracket has a notch, which slips over the wheel axle to lock them in place. Both ends of the axle are narrowed and pierced, and the central shaft has one bevelled edge to which the recurving profiles of the bracket notches are secured. The narrow ends of the axle poke through the axle holes and the wheels are retained by coiled wire threaded through the piercings on each side. The wheels are crudely cut with three spokes.
Date: Probably 18th century

Edged weapons

Hardly any toy edged weapons and accessories have been recovered from London soil and finds throughout the rest of the country are extremely rare.[15] The few items and fragments that have been recognized and recorded are all made from lead alloys and if these are in any way typical, the fragility of the material has undoubtedly contributed to their absence in the archaeological record.

The scale of these objects is hugely variable, from the tiny rondel dagger found in Salisbury to the larger swords and guards, which would comfortably fit in a child's hand. Some are extremely well modelled, if a little at variance with the full-scale article, while others are so crude that it is difficult to distinguish any diagnostic features at all.

Scabbards

TYPE 1, DESIGN 1

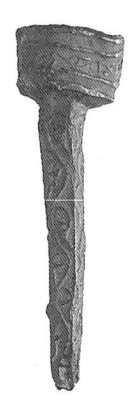

1.18 Scabbard

Accession number: 98.2/174
Material: Lead alloy
Condition: Complete but damaged
Dimensions: L 49mm; W 15mm
Description: A hollow, three-dimensional scabbard, cast in one piece. The scabbard is divided into two sections: the expanded upper part is asymmetrical with a curving front and straight back to accommodate the hilt, while the lower sheath is of tapering square section to cover the blade. The entire surface is covered with a linear pattern of foliate scrolling suggestive of tooled leatherwork on dagger sheaths of the 14th to 16th centuries.
Date: Probably late medieval
Comments: The shape suggests that the scabbard was designed for a dagger, but whether it actually held one is uncertain because the interior is blocked.
Comparandum: Museum of London, 14th-century leather scabbard from Finsbury Circus, Acc. no. A2351

Swords

TYPE 1, DESIGN 1

1.19 Sword hilt

Accession number: 2001.20/12
Material: Lead alloy
Condition: Incomplete
Dimensions: H 25mm; L 62mm
Description: The hilt of a sword or rapier with an ovoid-shaped pommel and round pommel button. The pommel has moulding to suggest fluting and the elongated and slightly ovoid grip has a knobbed surface to indicate a wire binding. The guard is very large and straight and the top of the blade is offset to one side.
Date: Probably 16th century

TYPE 2, DESIGN 1

1.20 Sword guard

Accession number: 2001.20/7
Material: Lead alloy
Condition: Some damage
Dimensions: H 33mm; W 50mm
Description: A crudely cast dagger or sword guard with a rectangular slot for the hilt tang, straight quillons decorated with star motif terminals, a side ring and what appears to be a truncated *pas d'âne*, although this is in the wrong position.
Date: Probably 16th–early 17th century
Provenance: Queenhithe
Comments: It is possible that the guard was originally attached to a wooden dagger or sword, which has long since perished. One other similar-sized weapon is known in England. Found in a field near Chelmsford, Essex, the style of the hilt with extended ring guards and decorative 'escutcheon' (possibly representing the arms of Castile) matches a late 15th-century sword in the Instituto del Conde de Valencia de Don Juan; see Oakeshott, R. Ewart, *The Sword in the Age of Chivalry* (London, 1964), plates 39c and 43c. The find is remarkable for its size and possible attribution. It is difficult to understand why a late 15th-century Spanish weapon has ended up in Essex, although many 17th-century textiles woven in Colchester were marketed in Iberia.

TYPE 3, DESIGN 1

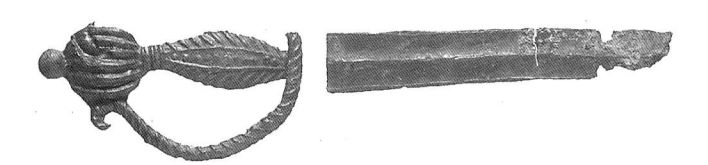

1.21 Sword

Accession number: 98.2/660
Material: Lead alloy
Condition: Two parts; incomplete
Dimensions: L (hilt) 36mm; L (blade) 47mm
Description: A three-dimensional sword, cast in one piece with matching detail on both sides, but now broken with top of blade and part of hilt and the down-turned quillon missing. The large spherical pommel has vertical ribbing and is surmounted by a round tang button. There is a narrow ovoid-shaped grip decorated with a beaded fillet flanked by diagonal hatching. Part of the cable-decorated knuckle-guard with recurving terminal survives together with the lower section of the double-edged, 'hollow ground' diamond section blade.
Date: Swords of this type were produced from 1660 to the very early 1700s.

Fig. 19. Stamped with the letters R[I] this is the only toy musket known with a maker's mark (as yet unidentified). Found on the Billingsgate foreshore
Private Collection

Firearms

Even though the invention of the matchlock action marked a significant turning point in the evolution and development of the handgun, it was not until the wheel lock appeared at the beginning of the 16th century that the primitive, unwieldy and inaccurate medieval firearm was transformed into a weapon of import and value. For the first time handguns were equipped with a mechanical self-ignition device which meant that they could be held in both hands while they were aimed and fired, and the consequent improvement in reliability, effectiveness and accuracy increased the popularity of firearms to such an extent that by the 1530s contemporaries started to prefer the handgun over the long-bow. Within a few years statutes were passed which entitled 'lords, knights, esquires, and gentlemen, and the inhabitants of every city… to have and keep in every of their houses such hand-gun or hand-guns, of the length of one whole yard'[16] and by the end of the century, fowling pieces, shotguns and other types of handguns were widely used for hunting and military purposes.

As firearms became increasingly popular, gunsmiths and toymakers started to produce a range of miniature and toy handguns for the amusement and entertainment of wealthy clients, collectors and children. The earliest miniature firearms were exquisite working replicas of contemporary guns, which were greatly prized for their novelty and entertainment value.[17] But within a few years the popularity of handguns was such, that basic versions started to be made for the mass-market, and the miniature firearms discussed in this section are of this type.[18]

The toy firearms, in contrast to the perfectly made and expensive scale-models, were cheaply produced for the mass-market, and the available evidence suggests that they were either hollow-cast in copper alloy, or flat-cast in lead alloy. The firing guns in the collection are all muzzle-loaders and these comprise 18 muskets and ten pistols. The pistols are generally made to a larger scale because they were fitted with a modified form of matchlock, and although only one gun has a complete mechanism, the others have matching drill holes, which suggests that they were fitted with the same type of action. Several rammers have been found and a number of guns show dramatic signs of use because they have exploded barrels.

Detailed analysis of these early toy firearms is unnecessary because little new evidence has come to light since Howard Blackmore's seminal study on Elizabethan toy guns was published in 1989,[19] and although more guns have been recovered throughout England during the last decade, none is strikingly different from the basic types that Blackmore has identified. The only significant find is a musket with the letters R [I] on the butt, recovered from Billingsgate spoil, which is the only inscribed example known.[20]

The absence of miniature firearms from securely dated archaeological contexts and a corresponding lack of evidence in contemporary literature and documents means that attribution and dating is heavily reliant upon stylistic features. But while it is probable that the toy guns were made contemporaneously with their full-scale counterparts, it is possible that the same basic shapes were made over an extended period, and some of the toy guns might have been made to reflect an earlier form no longer in current use.[21] None of the copper- or lead-alloy handguns of the types represented here has been found on the Continent, and while it is tempting to think that toy guns might have been a uniquely English product, their apparent absence in Europe is not necessarily a reliable indicator of contemporary centres of production and distribution.

Fig. 20. The toy muskets all have fishtail-shaped butts like their full-scale counterparts and many are stamped with ring and dot motifs to imitate the bone, ivory and mother-of-pearl inlays on western European gun stocks of the late 16th and early 17th centuries. This 1630–40 matchlock musket with powder flask bears the arms of the Haberdashers' Company and the initials OC.
Museum of London, Acc. nos. 76.131 & C2327

Muskets

'the largest fire arme that is managed by a single person both for charging and discharging of the hand by resting the butt end of it to the right shoulder'[22]

These hollow-cast guns all have the distinctive shaped 'fishtail' butt found on standard English muskets from 1600–40, and are decorated with integrally cast scrolling patterns and punched ring and dot motifs in loose imitation of inlaid, engraved or etched work on a full-scale gun. The muskets have certain basic features in common, but none has come from the same mould, and out of a sample of 18 guns six broad types have been identified. As the table shows the sizes range from 67mm to 130mm.

The guns all have integrally cast rudimentary pans for the priming powder, and the majority have a curious square-shaped bulge in front, which, as Blackmore has pointed out, might have 'served some purpose in holding the match ready for firing.'[23] Although there seems to be little correlation between the overall size of the musket and the calibre and thickness of the barrel walls, all of the guns have a hollow bore to the chamber and so technically even the smallest could be fired with individual grains of birdshot with a diameter of *c.* 1mm (0.04 inches). The largest muskets could accommodate 3mm (0.12 inches) diameter birdshot or a similar-sized projectile and for effective firing these guns would have needed about 0.57g (0.02oz) of black powder. Two of the muskets in the collection have split barrels, but in both cases the walls are extremely thin and in one case it is difficult to tell whether the damage is due to wear and tear, corrosion or an explosion. The touch holes also vary considerably in size and profile, and while some are little bigger than a pinhead, others are extremely large, which would have caused some sort of flashback if they were fired. The disproportionately large angular trigger guard, a feature introduced but not widely employed on full-scale guns during the 16th century, is almost large enough to accommodate a child's index finger, but it is extremely unlikely that these guns were actually held and fired because the risk of injury is too great.

The muskets have no pipes for the rammer and only a handful have vestigial mouldings to indicate the position of front and back ramrod pipes on a full-scale gun. For this reason, the musket rammers seem to have been 'stored' or screwed within the barrel and this is probably why the extant rammers have a thread section at the button end. Several muskets have riffled muzzles which was presumably done to secure the rammer rather than improve the ballistic capability of the gun. The only musket which has actually been found with a threaded rammer, however, is not tapped at the muzzle, and as the

Table 1.2

Type	Design	Length	Bore length	Calibre	Decorated stock	Decorated barrel	Grooves	Weight
1	1	130mm	96mm	5mm	Yes	Yes	2	57. 45g
1	2	91mm	62mm	4mm	Yes	Yes	2	33. 26g
2	1	90mm	58mm	4mm	Yes	Yes	4	32. 96g
2	2	67mm	59mm	4mm	Yes	Yes	4	15. 96g
3	1	90mm	57mm	3mm	Yes	Yes	–	23. 74g
4	1	125mm	88mm	5mm	No	Yes	4	40. 30g
4	2	99mm	88mm	5mm	No	Yes	4	35. 60g
4	3	71mm	45mm	3mm	No	Yes	4	14. 43g
5	1	87mm	56mm	4mm	No	No	2	22. 01g
5	2	67mm	38mm	3mm	No	No	4	11. 86g
5	3	77mm	3mm	4mm	No	No	4	16. 71g
5	4	77mm	43mm	3mm	No	No	4	16. 41g
5	5	112mm	71mm	3mm	No	No	6	35. 49g
5	6	78mm	45mm	3mm	No	No	–	19. 37g
6	1	70mm	40mm	2mm	No	No	6	16. 00g
6	2	113mm	77mm	3mm	No	No	8	38. 82g
6	3	68mm	40mm	–	No	No	2	10. 29g

diameter of the rammer button is much greater than the bore of the gun, it could not have served a functional purpose. The relevance of the thread is an intriguing puzzle, and until more guns are found with rammers the precise function of this feature will remain uncertain.

Although the toy handguns seem to imitate muskets of the first half of the 17th century, it is possible, although perhaps not very likely, that they were made over a longer period.

TYPE 1

The top flats of these musket barrels have a central wavy line flanked by scrolling and there are transverse mouldings underneath the stock, which seem to represent front and back ramrod pipes. The butts are decorated with ring and dot ornament.

TYPE 1, DESIGN 1

1.22 Musket

Accession number: 79.262
Material: Copper alloy
Condition: Complete but bent with exploded barrel
Dimensions: L *c.* 130mm; L (bore) 96mm; Diam (bore) 5mm
Weight: 57.45g
Description: Cast in one piece with fishtail-shaped butt, faceted barrel, open circular pan and large angular trigger guard. There is a pronounced ridge at the breech, two pairs of transverse grooves midway down the barrel and a muzzle ring. The top flats of the barrel are decorated with a medial wavy line flanked by scrolling and the linear pattern is interrupted by the transverse grooves. The rounded fore-end of the stock has two transverse grooves near the muzzle and there is another pair to the right of the trigger guard, and although these were probably designed to represent the front and back ramrod pipes, the ramrod itself (now missing) was originally screwed into the muzzle because this has an internal thread. The barrel has a large longitudinal gash and has been ripped open by the force of an explosion. There is a tiny vent, and to the right of the pan, a rectangular-shaped wedge with grooves on either side. The stock is decorated with ring and dot punches, five on the vent side and six on the other.

Date: 1600–40
Provenance: Three Cranes Wharf
Comments: This gun has been imperfectly cast with partially punched ring and dot on the butt and scratch marks on the other side and there are a few irregular dots on one of the side flats of the barrel near the muzzle. It is difficult to tell whether the explosion was caused by blockage at the breech or the muzzle, although the extent of damage seems to indicate the latter.

TYPE 1, DESIGN 2

1.23 Musket

Accession number: A13941
Material: Copper alloy
Condition: Complete but bent
Dimensions: L 91mm; L (bore) 62mm; Diam (bore) 4mm
Weight: 33.26g
Description: Cast in one piece with fishtail butt, faceted barrel, open circular pan and angular trigger guard. There is a pronounced ridge at the breech which curves round to form the pan, two pairs of transverse grooves midway down the barrel and a muzzle ring. The rounded fore-end of the stock has two transverse grooves near the muzzle and another pair to the right of the trigger guard, and these mouldings were possibly designed to represent the front and back ramrod pipes, even though the ramrod (now missing) originally screwed into the threaded muzzle. The top flats of the barrel are decorated with a central wavy line flanked by scrolling and the linear pattern is interrupted by the transverse grooves. The stock has a rounded fore-end and the faceted butt is decorated with ring and dot ornament; six on each side; with an additional ring and dot underneath. There is a wedge-shaped raised moulding to the right of the pan, which is unusually pronounced.
Date: 1600–40
Provenance: King William Street

TYPE 2

The barrels on these muskets are decorated with opposing wavy lines and transverse grooves and the butt has ring and dot ornament.

TYPE 2, DESIGN 1

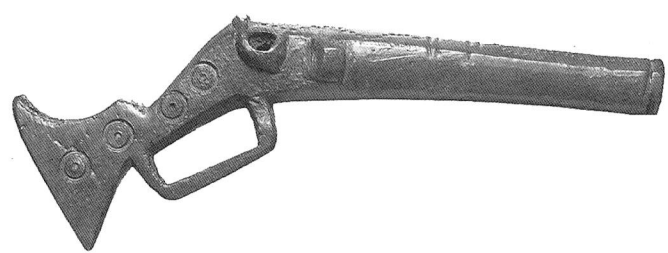

1.24 Musket

Accession number: 78.45
Material: Copper alloy
Condition: Complete
Dimensions: L 90mm; L (bore) 58mm; Diam (bore) 4mm
Weight: 32.96g
Description: Cast in one piece with fishtail butt, unevenly faceted barrel, open circular pan and angular trigger guard. There is a pronounced ridge at the breech, two pairs of transverse grooves midway down the barrel and a muzzle ring. The top flats of the barrel are decorated with opposing wavy lines, which stop and start either side of the transverse grooves. The stock has a rounded fore-end and the unevenly faceted butt is decorated with ring and dot ornament, four on each side. The vent is quite large and there is a rectangular wedge to the right of the pan. The muzzle has internal threading and the ramrod is missing.
Date: 1600–40
Provenance: City ditch by St Giles Churchyard
Comparandum: A similar example was recovered from a Billingsgate spoil tip in Dagenham with ring and dot punched decoration and stamped with the letters R[I] (see fig. 19), the only toy musket known with a maker's mark. L 91mm; Diam (bore) 5mm. Private Collection

92 • TOYS, TRIFLES & TRINKETS

TYPE 2, DESIGN 2

1.25 Musket

Accession number: 7740
Material: Copper alloy
Condition: Butt and rear end of trigger guard missing;
Dimensions: L 67mm; L (bore) 59mm; Diam (bore) 4mm
Weight: 15.96g
Description: Cast in one piece with unevenly faceted barrel, open circular pan and angular trigger guard (part missing). There is a pronounced ridge at the breech, two pairs of transverse grooves midway down the barrel and a muzzle ring. The top flats of the barrel are decorated with opposing wavy lines, which stop and start either side of the transverse grooves. The stock has a rounded fore-end and the unevenly faceted butt is decorated with ring and dot ornament. The vent is tiny and there is a square-shaped wedge to the right of the pan. The muzzle has internal threading and the ramrod is missing.
Date: 1600–40

TYPE 3

These muskets have opposing wavy lines on the barrel flats and ring and dot ornament on the stock.

TYPE 3, DESIGN 1

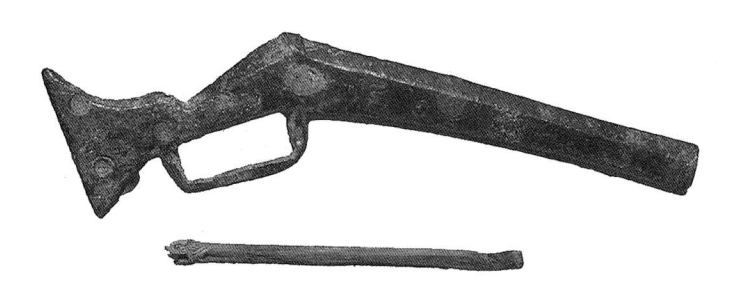

1.26 Musket

Accession number: A10374
Material: Copper alloy; wood
Condition: Complete
Dimensions: L 90mm; L (bore) 57mm; Diam (bore) 3mm
Weight: 23.74g
Description: Cast in one piece with fishtail butt, faceted barrel, open circular pan and angular trigger guard. There is a pronounced ridge at the breech which curves round to form the pan and the top flats of the barrel are decorated with opposing wavy lines. The stock has a rounded fore-end and the faceted butt is decorated with ring and dot ornament; five on each side. The vent is small and there is a square-shaped bulge to the right of the pan. The muzzle does not appear to be internally threaded and a spindle of wood was jammed into the barrel.
Date: 1600–40
Provenance: Westminster

TYPE 4

The barrel flats are decorated with opposing wavy lines and transverse grooves. The stock is plain but there are raised mouldings to represent the front and back ramrod pipes.

TYPE 4, DESIGN 1

1.27 Musket

Accession number: 98.2/651
Material: Copper alloy
Condition: Complete; slight damage at the breech and muzzle
Dimensions: L 125mm; L (bore) 88mm; Diam (bore) 5mm
Weight: 40.30g
Description: Cast in one piece with fishtail butt, faceted barrel, open circular pan and trapezoid-shaped trigger guard. There is a pronounced ridge at the breech which curves round to form the pan and the top flats of the barrel are decorated with opposing wavy lines and a two pairs of transverse grooves. The plain stock has a rounded fore-end and there are two raised mouldings to represent the front and back ramrod pipes, although the ramrod (now missing) originally screwed into the tapped muzzle. There is a square low relief moulding to the right of the large vent and deep pan. The wall of the breech is very thin and there are holes between the pan and raised moulding.
Date: 1600–40

TYPE 4, DESIGN 2

1.28 Musket

Accession number: A6479
Material: Copper alloy
Condition: Almost complete; butt and part of trigger guard missing
Dimensions: L 99mm; L (bore) 88mm; Diam (bore) 5mm
Weight: 35.60g
Description: Cast in one piece with faceted barrel, open circular pan and angular trigger guard (part missing). There is a pronounced ridge at the breech which curves round to form the pan. The top flats of the barrel are decorated with large dots arranged in opposing open wavy lines, and there are two pairs of transverse grooves and a muzzle ring. The plain stock has a rounded fore-end and there are two relief mouldings to represent the front and back ramrod pipes. The muzzle seems to be untapped and there is a square low relief moulding to the right of the small vent and deep pan.
Date: 1600–40
Provenance: London Wall

TYPE 4, DESIGN 3

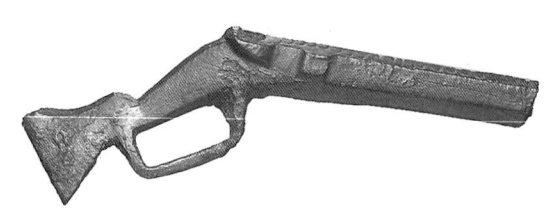

1.29 Musket

Accession number: 11697
Material: Copper alloy
Condition: Complete; slight damage
Dimensions: L 71mm; L (bore) 45mm; Diam (bore) 3mm
Weight: 14.43g
Description: Cast in one piece with fishtail butt, faceted barrel, open circular pan and angular trigger guard. There is a pronounced ridge at the breech which curves round to form the pan. The top flats of the barrel are decorated with large dots arranged in opposing open wavy lines and there are four transverse grooves at midpoint with a muzzle ring. The plain stock has a rounded fore-end and there is a square moulding to the right of the pan. The slightly damaged muzzle shows no sign of internal threading.
Date: 1600–40
Provenance: South Place Chapel
Comparandum: Similar example in the Salisbury Museum

TYPE 5

These muskets have a plain stock and, apart from a pair of transverse grooves, the barrel is also plain.

TYPE 5, DESIGN 1

1.30 Musket

Accession number: A22903
Material: Copper alloy
Condition: Complete
Dimensions: L 87mm; L (bore) 56mm; Diam (bore) 4mm
Weight: 22.01g
Description: Cast in one piece with fishtail butt, faceted barrel, open circular pan and angular trigger guard. There is a pronounced ridge at the breech which curves round to form the pan. The plain barrel has two pairs of transverse grooves at midpoint and a muzzle ring. The plain stock has a rounded fore-end and there is a square moulding to the right of the pan. The muzzle has internal threading.
Date: 1600–40
Provenance: Great Smith Street, Westminster

TYPE 5, DESIGN 2

1.31 Musket

Accession number: A9454
Material: Copper alloy
Condition: Complete with rammer; barrel exploded
Dimensions: gun: L 67mm; L (bore) 38mm; L (rammer, including button) 47mm; Diam (bore) 3mm
Weight: 16g (gun 11.86g; rammer 4.14g)

Description: Cast in one piece with fishtail butt, faceted barrel and angular trigger guard. There is a pronounced ridge at the breech which curves round to form a pan-shaped wedge with pinhole vent. The plain barrel has a longitudinal split from the breech to the muzzle and there are two pairs of transverse grooves and a muzzle ring. The plain stock has a rounded fore-end and although the muzzle does not appear to be tapped, the gun was found with a rammer in the barrel. The rammer has a large button and a roughly faceted tapering shank.

Date: 1600–40

Provenance: London

Comments: The wall of the barrel is extremely thin and it is difficult to tell whether the damage is the result of an explosion or corrosion. The diameter of the rammer button exceeds the diameter of the bore and so was clearly made for show rather than use.

TYPE 5, DESIGN 3

1.32 Musket

Accession number: A2459
Material: Copper alloy
Condition: Complete
Dimensions: L 77mm; L (bore) 43mm; Diam (bore) 4mm
Weight: 16.71g
Description: Cast in one piece with fishtail butt, plain faceted barrel and angular trigger guard. There is a pronounced ridge at the breech which curves round to form a wedge-shaped pan. The stock is plain and barrel has a pair of widely spaced transverse grooves and a muzzle ring. The vent is fairly large, there is a bulge to the right of the pan and the muzzle is untapped.

Date: 1600–40

Provenance: London

TYPE 5, DESIGN 4

1.33 Musket

Accession number: 98.2/650
Material: Copper alloy
Condition: Complete
Dimensions: L 77mm; L (bore) 43mm; Diam (bore) 3mm
Weight: 16.41g
Description: Cast in one piece with fishtail butt, plain faceted barrel and angular trigger guard. There is a pronounced ridge at the breech which curves round to form the pan. The stock is plain and barrel has a pair of widely spaced transverse grooves and a muzzle ring. The conical-shaped pan is angled into the breech and there is a very large vent and a wedge-shaped bulge to the right. The muzzle is untapped.

Date: 1600–40

TYPE 5, DESIGN 5

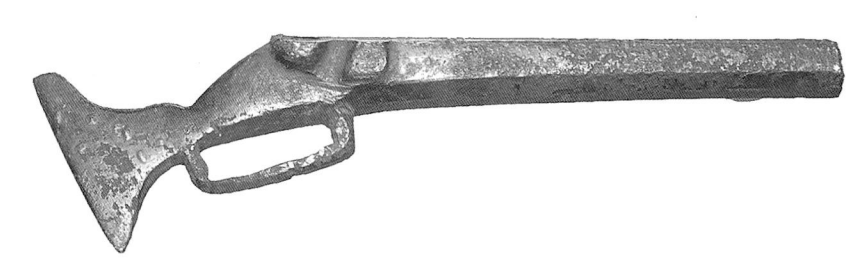

1.34 Musket

Accession number: A10429
Material: Copper alloy
Condition: Complete
Dimensions: L 112mm; L (bore) 71mm; Diam (bore) 3mm
Weight: 35.49g
Description: Cast in one piece with fishtail butt, plain faceted barrel and angular trigger guard. There is a pronounced ridge at the breech which curves round to form a wedge-shaped pan. The stock is plain and barrel has three pairs of widely spaced transverse grooves. The conical-shaped pan is angled into the breech and there is a large vent. There is a wedge-shaped bulge to the right of the pan. The muzzle is not tapped and the ramrod is missing.

Date: 1600–40

Provenance: Westminster

TYPE 5, DESIGN 6

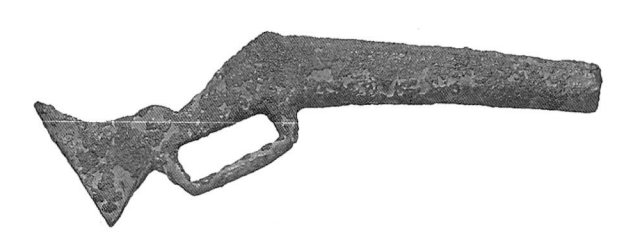

1.35 Musket

Accession number: 7746
Material: Copper alloy
Condition: Complete but extremely corroded
Dimensions: L 78mm; L (bore)45mm (?); Diam (bore) 3mm
Weight: 19.37g
Description: Cast in one piece with fishtail butt, faceted barrel and angular trigger guard. There is a pronounced ridge at the breech which curves round to form a wedge-shaped pan and there is a bulge to the right. The whole surface is corroded and the barrel is blocked.
Date: 1600–40
Provenance: City of London

TYPE 6

These muskets have a circular uncovered pan but there is no wedge moulding.

TYPE 6, DESIGN 1

1.36 Musket

Accession number: 7738
Material: Copper alloy
Condition: Complete
Dimensions: L 70mm; L (bore) 40mm (?); Diam (bore) 2mm
Weight: 16g
Description: Cast in one piece with fishtail butt, plain faceted barrel and angular trigger guard. There is a pronounced ridge at the breech which curves round to form the pan. The stock is plain and barrel has three pair of widely spaced transverse grooves, one at the breech, one midway and one at the muzzle. The conical-shaped pan is angled into the breech and there is a pinhole vent. There is no wedge-shaped bulge to the right of the pan. The muzzle is not tapped and the ramrod is missing.
Date: 1600–40
Provenance: Brook's Wharf

TYPE 6, DESIGN 2

1.37 Musket

Accession number: 80.271/38
Material: Copper alloy
Condition: Complete

Dimensions: L 113mm; L (bore) 77mm; Diam (bore) 3mm
Weight: 38.82g
Description: Cast in one piece with fishtail butt, plain faceted barrel and angular trigger guard. There is a pronounced ridge at the breech which curves round to form a wedge-shaped pan. The stock is plain and barrel has four pairs of widely spaced transverse grooves. The conical-shaped pan is angled into the breech and there is a large vent. There is no wedge-shaped bulge to the right of the pan. The muzzle is not tapped and the ramrod is missing.
Date: 1600–40
Provenance: London

TYPE 6, DESIGN 3

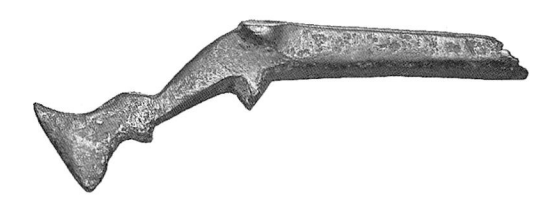

1.38 Musket

Accession number: 21642
Material: Copper alloy
Condition: Almost complete; trigger guard and end of barrel missing
Dimensions: L 68mm; L (bore) 40mm
Weight: 10.29g
Description: Cast in one piece with fishtail butt, plain faceted barrel and trigger guard (part only). There is a pronounced ridge at the breech which curves round to form a solid pan-shaped wedge with a rough-edged vent at the top. The stock is plain and incomplete barrel has a pair of transverse grooves. There is no wedge-shaped bulge to the right of the pan.
Date: 1600–40

Petronels

Unlike the other firearms in the collection, these guns are made from lead alloy and they are the only two known. The guns are convincing imitations of the standard cavalry petronel or arquebus, a light form of handgun with a characteristic curving butt which was fired from the chest. Petronels were common during the first half of the 17th century, and although they were usually fitted with a wheel-lock, the toymaker has produced a stylized matchlock or snaphance mechanism probably because this was an easier action to replicate in miniature form.

TYPE 1, DESIGN 1

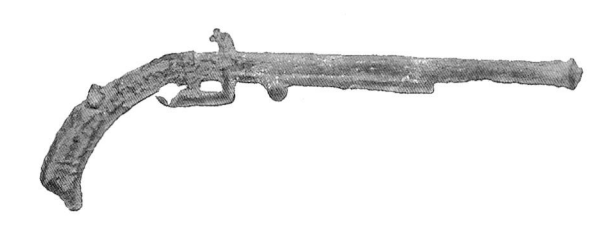

1.39 Petronel

Accession number: 98.2/655*; 98.2/661
Material: Lead alloy
Condition: 98.2/655: complete. 98.2/661: part of butt and back of trigger guard missing
Dimensions: 98.2/655: L 75mm
Description: Two flat petronels, probably cast from the same mould. These crudely made pistols have been cast in one piece with identical mouldings on each side. They have a long circular barrel, integral ramrod, angular trigger guard, downward-curving straight-edged butt and a hook or wall-mount. The lock mouldings suggest a matchlock or snaphance mechanism.
Date: 1600–30
Provenance: Southwark Bridge, north side
Comparandum: Mann 1962, vol. 2, pp. 522–3, A1116

Pistols

'a small gun discharged with one hand of which there are severall sorts'[24]

Unlike the rather basic toy musket discussed above, the copper-alloy pistols are composed of ten separate elements which include the separately cast lock components and the rammer. The main body of the pistol was hollow-cast in one piece and then the stock was drilled in three places to accommodate a modified form of matchlock action. The most complete surviving locks include a double cock or serpentine, cock pin, trigger and trigger spring which pivot on three screws attached to the stock.[25] The cock plates have a lateral hole at the tip to take the jaw screw (Acc. nos. O2455 & 7745), and the screw underneath the stock serves the double function of securing the rammer as well as the trigger spring. Excessive use of the guns would have inevitably weakened the lock and damaged the mechanism, and this is probably why hardly any pistols have been found with a complete action. Almost all of the pistols have tiny pinholes on the plain side of the stock, and since these match the position of the lock screws they were presumably caused by over-enthusiastic drilling.

The presence of the lock and the hollow bore to the breech suggests that these toys were capable of being fired and several have exploded barrels. Even though the pistols seem to have been made in two basic sizes and the weights vary, the calibres are fairly uniform and most can accommodate small birdshot of approximately .12 diameter to the inch. Most of the pistols have wide uncovered pans, but these have different profiles. The sizes of the touch holes also vary considerably.

Presumably when the gun had been loaded and primed, a strand of smouldering match fibre was attached to the serpentine and the powder was ignited when the trigger lever lowered the match over the pan. It is possible that the trigger lever was rigged with string so that the gun could be fired from a safe distance to reduce the risk of injury.

All of the pistols have integrally cast front ramrod pipes with a corresponding hole in the stock to take the tip, but hardly any ramrods survive and only one has been found with a gun.[26] The presence of the ramrod pipe moulding on the pistols might indicate that they were manufactured after *c.* 1620 when rammers were typically held at the fore-end with a short tubular pipe.[27]

The overall profiles of the pistols are extremely similar and the shape of the stock and barrels are modelled on French, German, and to a lesser extent English wheel-lock, flintlock and snaphance pistols of the late 16th and early 17th centuries with their characteristic long tapering curving butts and faceted ovoid pommels.[28] Dated examples of the so-called lemon-butted pistols range from 1610 to the 1630s, as Claude Blair notes in his *Pistols of the World,* and it is likely that the toy versions were produced at this time.[29] A debased version of a matchlock mechanism was fitted to the toy guns rather than the standard wheel-lock because it was the easiest action to adapt and reproduce cheaply. Unlike the muskets, most of the decoration is confined to the three barrel flats and this consists of simple designs of pellet scrolling and single or paired transverse grooves or raised strap mouldings to represent engraved ornament on the genuine article. Only one gun is undecorated.

Table 1.3

Type	Design	Acc. no.	Length	Bore length	Calibre	Weight
1	1	O2455	118mm	73mm	3 x 4 mm	43.25g +
1	2	7745	118mm	71mm	4mm	42.47g +
1	3	7739; A10489	112mm	76mm	4mm	58.84g +; 45.75g
1	4	7744	112mm	74mm	4mm	45.31g
2	1	A18742	119mm	76mm	4.5 x 5 mm	49.83g
3	1	A10751	100mm*	70mm	3mm	42.85g
4	1	7743	117mm	73mm	3mm	48.75g
5	1	98.2/652	109mm	79mm‡	4mm	56.70g
6	1	A2457	109mm	67mm	3mm	34.82g

* pommel missing
‡ different to length of barrel – bore extends further back into breech
+ part of lock mechanism extant

TYPE 1, DESIGN 1

1.40 Pistol

Accession number: O2455
Material: Copper alloy
Condition: Almost complete
Dimensions: L 118mm; L (bore) 73mm; W (bore) 3 x 4 mm
Description: A multi-component three-dimensional pistol. The stock, barrel, pan and ramrod pipe have been cast in one piece and there are four holes in the stock; three for the lock mechanism and one for the ramrod. The plain stock has a rounded fore-end and long tapering butt, which terminates in a plain hexagonally fluted ovoid pommel. The butt is rounded on the upper face and faceted below. There is an incomplete lock mechanism on one side and this consists of the lower part of one serpentine cock (the pin and second cock are missing), the trigger and part of the trigger spring and these pivot on three rivets plugged into the stock. There is a transverse groove at the breech, two transverse mouldings across the barrel and a simple muzzle ring. The barrel is faceted and decorated with a linear, curving pattern of stamped dots. There is a thin ramrod pipe and corresponding hole in the stock, but the ramrod itself is missing. The lower right rivet serves the double function of securing the rammer as well as trigger spring. There is a pinhole on the plain side of the stock, which corresponds with the drilled hole for the left trigger rivet.
Date: 1620–40
Provenance: Unknown, but part of the Layton Collection in the Museum of London

TYPE 1, DESIGN 2

1.41 Pistol

Accession number: 7745
Material: Copper alloy
Condition: Some damage; part of lock extant
Dimensions: L 118mm; L (bore) 71mm; Diam (bore) 4mm
Description: A different mould, but otherwise virtually identical to Acc. no. O2455 above. The muzzle, ramrod pipe and pan are damaged and there is a jagged hole in the barrel. All of the lock rivets have survived (two complete) and the tip of the rammer is jammed into the stock. The surface is pitted and discoloured and the ovoid pommel has octagonal facets.
Date: 1620–40
Provenance: City of London (one of four found: see Acc. nos. 7743–6)
Comments: Damage possibly due to minor explosion

100 • TOYS, TRIFLES & TRINKETS

TYPE 1, DESIGN 3

1.42 Pistol

Accession number: 7739*; A10489
Material: Copper alloy
Condition: 7739: part of mechanism extant
  A10489: no mechanism
Dimensions: L 112mm; L (bore) 76mm; Diam (bore) 4mm
Weight: 7739: 58.84g. A10489: 45.75g
Description: Two multi-component three-dimensional pistols cast from an identical mould. The stock, barrel, ramrod pipe and pan have been cast in one piece and there are four holes in the stock on one side; three for the lock mechanism (partially complete on Acc. no. 7739) and ramrod (both missing). The vents are large and the pan (broken off on A10489) has a square-dished profile with bevelled edges. The fore-ends are rounded and the faceted barrels are decorated with a criss-cross pattern of dots. There are deep grooves at the breech, a pair of transverse mouldings along the barrel and simple muzzle rings. The long tapering butts are faceted and terminate in ovoid octagonally faceted pommels. Although A10489 is in better overall condition, there is no lock mechanism and only the broken-off stump of one rivet survives, whereas Acc. no. 7739 retains part of the lock, and this consists of one large serpentine cock; part of the trigger and three rivets. There is a tiny pinhole on the plain side of the stock, which aligns with the drilled hole of the trigger rivet. In addition, there is a small jagged hole at the breech and another underneath to the left of the trigger spring rivet.
Date: 1620–40
Provenance: 7739: Bunhill Row, 1866. A10489: Millbank Street, 1913

TYPE 1, DESIGN 4

1.43 Pistol

Accession number: 7744
Material: Copper alloy
Condition: No mechanism
Dimensions: L 112mm; L (bore) 74mm; Diam (bore) 4mm
Description: Very similar to Acc. no. A10489 above. There is no lock mechanism and the ovoid pommel has octagonal facets. The surface is pitted and damaged.
Date: 1620–40
Provenance: London

TYPE 2, DESIGN 1

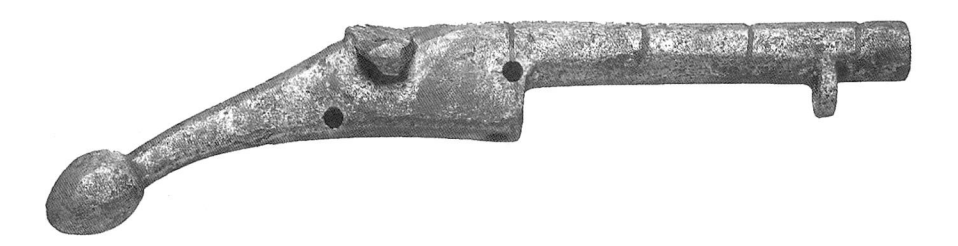

1.44 Pistol

Accession number: A18742
Material: Copper alloy
Condition: No mechanism
Dimensions: L 119mm; L (bore) 76mm; Diam (bore) 4.5 x 5 mm
Description: Part of a multi-component three-dimensional pistol. The stock, barrel, ramrod pipe and pan have been cast in one piece and there are four holes in the stock; three for the lock mechanism and one for the ramrod (both missing). The vent is large and the integrally cast pan has a square-dished profile with bevelled sides. A long tapering, slightly bent butt terminates in an octagonally fluted ovoid pommel. The fore-end of the stock is rounded and the faceted barrel has stamped decoration (now indistinct). There is a transverse groove at the breech and four transverse grooves along the barrel.
Date: 1620–40
Provenance: Old Queen Street, 1917

TYPE 3, DESIGN 1

1.45 Pistol

Accession number: A10751
Material: Copper alloy
Condition: Incomplete; pommel missing; no mechanism
Dimensions: L 100mm (no pommel); L (bore) 70mm; Diam (bore) 3mm
Description: Part of a multi-component three-dimensional pistol. The stock, barrel, ramrod pipe and pan have been cast in one piece and there are four holes in the stock on one side; three for the lock mechanism and one for the ramrod (both missing). The vent is tiny and the solid flat-topped square pan has a rounded, bevelled edged base. Both the fore-end and the long tapering butt have faceted profiles. The pommel has broken off. There is a deep transverse groove across the breech and the faceted barrel is decorated with a criss-cross linear design of crudely stamped interlaced circles. There are two pin-sized holes on the plain side of the stock which correspond with the larger rivet holes on the other side and these were presumably caused by the lathe during drilling. The muzzle is slightly angled.
Date: 1620–40
Provenance: Kingsway 1913

TYPE 4, DESIGN 1

1.46 Pistol

Accession number: 7743
Material: Copper alloy
Condition: No mechanism
Dimensions: L 117mm; L (bore) 73mm; Diam (bore) 3mm
Description: Part of a multi-component three-dimensional pistol. The stock, barrel, ramrod pipe and pan have been cast in one piece and there are four holes in the stock on one side; three for the lock mechanism and one for the ramrod (both missing). The gun is of octagonal section and the long, slightly curving tapering butt terminates in an octagonally fluted ovoid pommel. There is a deep transverse groove at the breech, two pairs of transverse mouldings on the barrel and a further pair at the muzzle. The barrel is decorated with a criss-cross linear design of crudely stamped interlaced circles (now indistinct) but similar to Acc. no. A10751. The vent is small and the fairly large solid square pan has a flat top and rounded, bevelled edged base. Two of the lock rivet holes have been drilled all the way through the stock.
Date: 1620–40
Provenance: London

TYPE 5, DESIGN 1

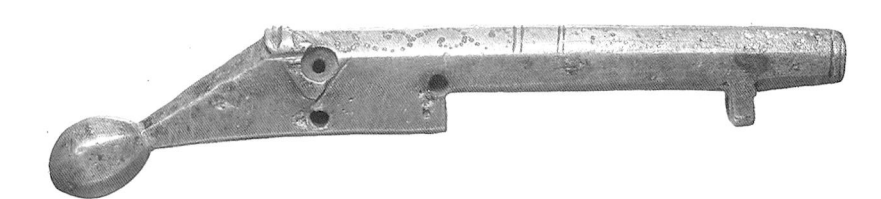

1.47 Pistol

Accession number: 98.2/652
Material: Copper alloy
Condition: No mechanism
Dimensions: L 109mm; L (bore) 79mm; Diam (bore) 4mm
Description: Part of a multi-component three-dimensional pistol. The stock, barrel and ramrod pipe have been cast in one piece and there are four holes in the stock on one side; three for the lock mechanism and one for the ramrod (both missing). The plain stock has a rounded fore-end and short tapering faceted butt which terminates in an octagonally faceted ovoid pommel. There is no pan and the vent hole is small and thickened on one side. The faceted barrel has a pair of transverse mouldings and is decorated with a punched wavy pattern flanked by scrolling. There is a muzzle ring and a deep transverse groove at the breech.
Date: 1620–40
Provenance: Brook's Wharf

TYPE 6, DESIGN 1

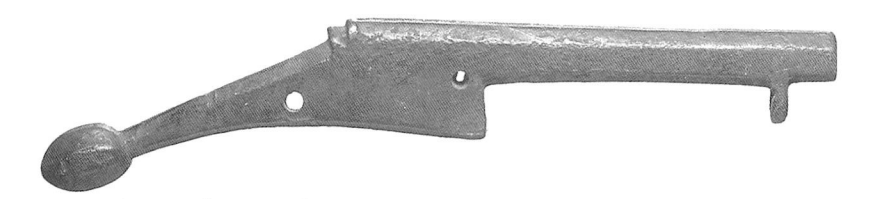

1.48 Pistol

Accession number: A2457
Material: Copper alloy
Condition: No mechanism
Dimensions: L 109mm; L (bore) 67mm; Diam (bore) 3mm
Description: Part of a multi-component three-dimensional pistol. The stock, barrel, pan and ramrod pipe have been cast in one piece and there are four holes in the stock on one side; three for the lock mechanism and one for the ramrod (both missing). The gun is of octagonal section and the long tapering butt terminates in an octagonally faceted ovoid pommel. There is a thin flat rectangular pan and the touch hole has an internally curving profile with the vent positioned to the right to facilitate firing. There is a transverse groove at the breech and the barrel is plain.
Date: 1620–40
Provenance: Lincoln's Inn, 1912, Hilton Price Collection

Rammers

Full-scale ramrods made in wood or other materials, were easily damaged or mislaid, and for this reason most of the early handguns in public and private collections have later replacements. Toy ramrods for handguns are also rare and only three have been found in London.

The toy ramrods have been cast in one piece in copper alloy and they have a tapering rod with a threaded section near the button. None of the ramrods slides into the apertures of the ramrod pipes on the surviving pistols, and the diameters of the buttons also exceed the bore of all the guns in the collection, which suggests that they were either a gimmick or made for different calibre weapons.

TYPE 1, DESIGN 1

1.49 Rammer

Accession number: 98.2/665
Material: Copper alloy
Condition: Complete
Dimensions: L 58mm; Diam (button) 7mm
Description: Cast in one piece with ovoid knop, circular button and tapering threaded shank
Provenance: Brook's Wharf

TYPE 1, DESIGN 2

1.50 Rammer

Accession number: 98.2/662
Material: Copper alloy
Condition: Complete
Dimensions: L 75mm; Diam (button) 6mm
Description: Cast in one piece with ovoid knop, circular button and tapering shank, which has been filed down and partially threaded at one end.
Provenance: Custom House Quay

1. *The Compleat Gunner* (London, 1672), ch. 2, p. 2.
2. Hume 1970, p. 314 & fig. 6.
3. Beard 1928 and Norman 1977 who pointed out that the majority of the surviving miniature armours were produced during the 19th century.
4. Holme 1688, bk 3, ch. 18, sec. 2d Firearms, no. 59.
5. Holme 1688, bk 3, ch. 18, sec. 2d Firearms, no. 54.
6. Acc. nos. 98.2/645; 98.2/647; 98.2/644; other lug guns have been recovered from Limekiln Dock, London; Hatfield Oak in Essex and the Medway.
7. I am extremely grateful to David Edge (Wallace Collection) for this information.
8. I am grateful to David Starley, at the Royal Armouries, Leeds for his advice on this point.
9. See Acc. no. 98.2/636.
10. This suggestion has been put forward by David Edge.
11. It is unlikely that the lead is a piece of shot.
12. Lead-alloy toy cannon have appeared as field finds in Colchester and Dorset.
13. Baart 1977, pp. 469 & 901. A lead-alloy gun with the initials IDQ and the date 1636 in a private collection was recovered from Amsterdam, and miniature cannon in lead and copper alloys have also been found on colonial sites in America. See fig. 18 & Hume 1970, p. 314.
14. Acc. nos. 98.2/640 & 98.2/642.
15. An almost complete and rather ill-proportioned rondel dagger of *c.* 15th-century date (with a curiously placed wrythen knop in the centre of the hilt and diamond-sectioned 'blade') was found in Salisbury (L 57mm). Another rondel dagger (L 50mm) and two similar-sized swords have been found in the Thames at Vintry and Billingsgate – now in private collections.
16. PRO Statute Henry VIII 1541.
17. The earliest surviving example of this kind is a 50mm-long Nuremberg piece of *c.* 1580 with a wheel-lock mechanism. Slightly larger 1630s miniature wheel-locks are signed by the Augsburg metalworker Michael Mann, and a few pieces of similar date bear the signature of the Turin gunsmith Walter Agnoletto. See Lindsay 1970 and Blackmore 1989.
18. As yet there is no firm dating evidence for the introduction of the toy handgun.
19. Blackmore 1989, p. 11.
20. Stamped with the maker's mark. L 91mm; Diam (bore) 5mm.
21. Blair 1968, cat. no. 745, p. 151, English late 16th or early 17th century. See V&A no. 1025–1870, L *c.* 90mm, made in imitation of a musket of *c.* 1600. See also Granscsay 1949, pp. 28–9.
22. Holme 1688, bk 3, ch. 18, sec. 2d Firearms C.
23. Blackmore 1989, p. 12.
24. Holme 1688, bk 3, ch. 18, sec. 2d Firearms B.
25. RA Leeds, Inventory no. XII–5235, which is virtually the same as MoL Acc. no. O2455 and another in a private collection with a more conventional serpentine-shaped cock. All of these guns were found on the Thames foreshore.
26. Acc. no. 7745.
27. Blair 1968, p. 23.
28. Examples of lemon-butt pistols: see Christie's 26 October 1994, lot 239 (early 17th century) and Christie's *The Armoury of Their Serene Highnesses the Princes zu Salm-Reifferscheidt-Dyck (Part I)* 15 April 1992, lot 269 (Nuremberg, late 16th century); V&A no. M.1082–1910 (German [Nuremberg?], early 17th century) and no. M.488–1927 (French [Alsace?], *c.* 1600); Metropolitan Museum, New York no. 19.53.14 (French, *c.* 1600). Other examples are held by the Historisches Museum, Dresden; Levens Hall, Westmoreland; and Pilgrims' Hall, Plymouth, Mass.
29. Blair 1968, p. 8.

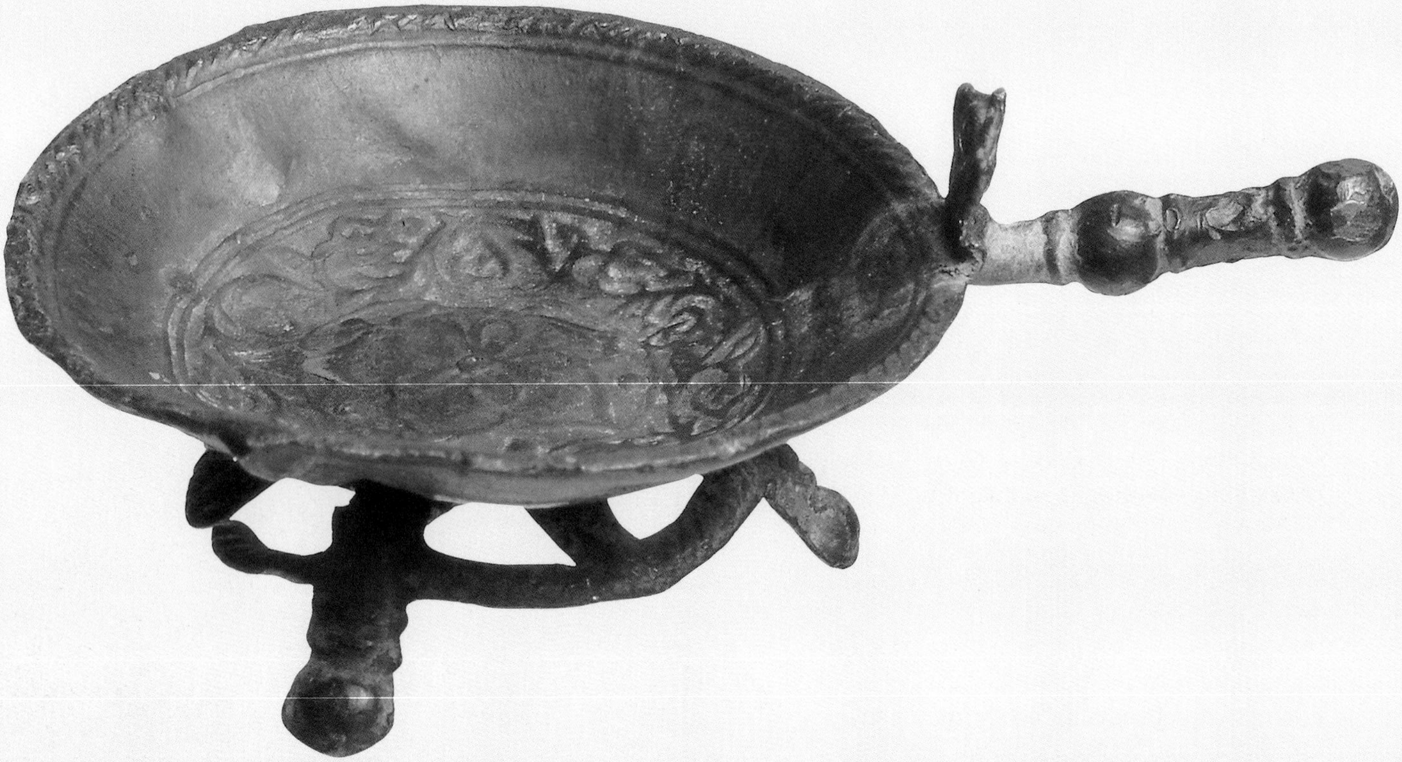

2 Cooking vessels & utensils

'such boiling and broiling, such roasting and toasting, such stewing and brewing, such baking, frying, mincing, cutting, carving, devouring and gorbellied gormondizing ...'[1]

Throughout the period covered by this book, most domestic cooking was done over an open fire. Few people possessed an oven or kitchen and records show that the majority of households lacked the elaborate equipment needed for roasting and baking. Despite the limitations of the hearth-based cuisine, however, meals were probably more varied and interesting than is generally supposed, and Londoners could always supplement their daily diet with a pie or roast from a cookshop or tavern. While most households had a cauldron, flesh hook, ladle, pot hanger, skillet and frying pan, inventories show that the kitchens belonging to wealthy citizens and those in inns, taverns and cookshops had a huge range of equipment at their disposal. A typical list of kitchen equipment compiled from London inventories of the 16th and 17th centuries includes a range, spits, jack, pot hangers, bellows, warming pans, chafing dishes, chopping knives, fish kettle, pestle and mortar, bowls, basting ladles and skimmers, gridirons, scales and weights, meat forks, toasting irons, graters, colanders, moulds, numerous iron and copper cooking pots and dripping, sauce and frying pans. While these inventories give a good indication of the quantity and variety of kitchen equipment, detailed descriptions of individual

Fig. 21. Base-metal miniatures seem to have been made in a wide variety of sizes. In this print by Jan Luyken [1649–1712] designed to accompany a moralistic verse, young girls arrange their doll-sized vessels and plate on a buffet. A trivet, fire tongs and bucket can be seen on the ground.
Het poppegoed, late 17th century
Rijksmuseum, Amsterdam

items are rarely recorded. Fortunately still-life and genre paintings provide some of the best evidence for the shapes, styles and materials of kitchen equipment but since these mostly depict the kitchens and pantries of Continental Europe, comparative analysis should be undertaken with caution.

In genre paintings, the kitchen and pantry are often depicted in exquisite detail, and pots and pans and other cooking utensils frequently occupy a central place in the composition. The sheer variety of vessel forms, and the luminescent and reflective qualities of their materials added to the aesthetic appeal of the image and helped to emphasize the status and affluence of the household. But while these conspicuous displays of material wealth provide important typological and dating evidence, surviving examples are few. Little survives because most

Table 2.1

Object	Types	Designs	Lead alloy	Copper alloy	Dates	Total
Bowls	4	4	9	–	1600–1750	9
Cauldrons	2	7	3	4	1300–1700	7
Dripping pans	2	5	8	–	1550–1650	8
Frying pans	8	11	13	–	1550–1700	13
Gridirons	1	4	5	–	1550–1750	5
Pot hangers	1	2	3	–	1550–1650	3
Skillet	1	1	–	1	1400–1600	1
Spit	1	1	1	–	1400–1600	1
Trivet[3]	1	1	1	–	1650–1700	1
Total	**21**	**36**	**43**	**5**		**48**

kitchen equipment was made from iron or copper alloys, and since the materials were too valuable to be discarded, when an item was damaged or broken, it was either repaired or melted down for recycling.[2] Any surviving miniature versions are therefore of particular interest and importance.

Most, if not all, of the cooking vessels and utensils shown in paintings or listed in documents were probably made in miniature form, and yet as Table 2.1 shows, only nine types of toy kitchenware have been found in London.[4] The range of items reflects the main types of kitchenwares although, as one might expect from their long period of use, the cauldrons have the widest date range. Many more base-metal kitchenware miniatures are known in Continental collections and these include items which reflect culinary traditions as well as the standard range of cooking vessels and utensils.[5]

Some of the cooking vessels seem to have been made from both tin and copper alloys. This suggests that the toymaker was not only concerned to reproduce a good imitation of the real thing, but also to make miniatures from similar materials to their full-scale counterparts. It is possible that market demand for functional toy cooking pots encouraged makers to produce wares in appropriate metals, and one copper-alloy cauldron shows signs of active use on or near a fire.[6] The copper alloys constitute only 11.6% of the total, but since the sample is so small it would be unwise to place too much emphasis on this figure. Within the range of extant toy cooking vessels and utensils, only the cauldrons seem to have been manufactured in two metals, but it is entirely possible that other forms were also available in different materials, as yet unrepresented.

Although the toymakers have tried to reflect the form of full-scale vessels, most of the miniatures have unrealistic decoration. The frying pans have beaded or rope-twist rims; the gridirons are covered in diagonal hatching and other kinds of decorative moulding; the pot hangers are smothered in chevrons, pellets and foliate scrolling, while the dripping pans have patterned bases and decorative rims. One can only conclude that the decoration added to the appeal of these utilitarian objects and presumably the ornate mouldings were not an obstacle to a child's imagination.

Bowls

Bowls are distinguished from dishes by their height to width ratio. The rims are wider than the base and the height measurements are at least a third, and usually considerably more, than the rim diameter. All of the miniature bowls from London have been cast in one piece with a simple foot ring and some have been lathe-turned.[7] The vessels are classified according to their shape and profile.

Bowls were common in the late medieval period,[8] but the relative proportion of bowls to other vessels begins to increase from the late 1500s and, by the mid 17th century, they are one of the most frequently represented forms in archaeological contexts.[9] Full-sized pewter bowls with foot rings are unknown, but there are many examples in tin-glazed earthenware and porcelain dating from the second half of the 17th century. The plainness of the miniatures suggests that they were probably intended to represent a pudding or flour basin, rather than an elaborate tea bowl or punch bowl.

TYPE 1, DESIGN 1

2.1 Bowl

Accession number: 98.2/203
Material: Lead alloy
Condition: Complete; slight damage
Dimensions: H 10mm; Diam (rim) *c.* 28mm; Diam (base) 14mm
Description: This bowl has a wide flanged rim and curving bowl which tapers in towards the foot ring.
Date: Possibly 17th century

TYPE 2, DESIGN 1

2.2 Bowl

Accession number: 79.319/4*; 98.2/199*; 98.2/201; 98.2/202; 98.2/205 (see also Cat. no. 8.67 – very distorted and crushed)
Material: Lead alloy
Condition: Complete; 98.2/205 compressed; very slight rim abrasion
Dimensions: Four sizes:

i) 79.319/4: H 10mm; Diam (rim) 24mm; Diam (base) 13mm
ii) 98.2/201: H 15mm; Diam (rim) 30mm; Diam (base) 18mm
iii) 98.2/199; 98.2/202: H 14mm; Diam (rim) 32mm; Diam (base) 15mm 
iv) 98.2/205: H 22mm; Diam (rim) *c.* 47mm; Diam (base) 20mm

Description: All plain with everted bevelled edged rims and a curving bowl which tapers in towards the foot ring. The base of 98.2/205 has been additionally turned and the lathe marks are visible underneath.
Date: Late 17th–18th century

TYPE 3, DESIGN 1

2.3 Bowl

Accession number: 98.2/204
Material: Lead alloy
Condition: Complete; slightly squashed
Dimensions: H *c.* 13mm; Diam (rim) *c.* 30mm; Diam (base) 17mm
Description: A wide bowl with smooth curving sides tapering towards the simple foot ring.
Date: 1725–35

TYPE 4, DESIGN 1

2.4 Bowl

Accession number: 98.2/200
Material: Lead alloy
Condition: Complete
Dimensions: H 13mm; Diam (rim) 28mm; Diam (base) 15mm
Description: This bowl has a plain rim and gently curving bowl tapering to the high foot ring.
Date: Similar in shape to bowls of 1725–35

Cauldrons

Without doubt the most important item of cooking equipment for centuries, cauldrons have been made in a variety of sizes in bronze, bell-metal, iron and occasionally sheet brass. The earliest forms were large open-necked round containers with a semi-circular rod handle for suspension. By the medieval period, the form assumes a squatter or spherical profile with a sharply bevelled rim and diametrically opposed lug handles. Used with or without a lid, the cauldron was either suspended above the fire on an adjustable pot hanger, or placed directly on the hearth surrounded by the hot ashes. Tripod feet provided stability and allowed the air to circulate freely underneath so that food could be cooked with minimal risk of burning or sticking.

The basic form has hardly altered because the functional purpose of the cauldron has changed so little over time, and although there are subtle differences in shape and decoration, accurate dating is extremely difficult, if not impossible. In general, however, the earliest examples tend to have longer legs because they were placed on the hearth and needed to be raised up as much as possible from the flames and intense heat. The legs are usually decorated with vertical reeding and invariably terminate in a claw foot.[10]

There are two types of cauldron in this corpus and the characteristics of each are discussed below. Both types were cast in one piece. Lead-alloy cauldrons have been found in some numbers during excavations in the Netherlands from 13th–16th-century contexts,[11] but the only securely dated example in this country is of copper alloy which dates to the 17th century.[12]

TYPE 1

These cauldrons have flaring rims and bulbous bodies with either rounded or angular lug handles and long legs of square or triangular section. The vessels range in height from 19mm to 60mm and all but Acc. no. 98.2/195 have sagging bases. The earliest dates to the 14th century and the latest to the end of the 17th century. Only one (Acc. no. 90.245) bears an inscription, and the choice of a religious rather than secular phrase is extremely unusual. Real cauldrons are rarely inscribed, and when they are, the inscription usually consists of the founder's name and a date. One vessel has traces of sooting.

TYPE 1, DESIGN 1

2.5 Cauldron

Accession number: 90.245
Material: Lead alloy
Condition: Complete but damaged and crushed
Dimensions: H *c.* 55mm; Diam (rim) 35mm
Description: A tripod cauldron with flaring rim and bulbous body widening towards the sagging base. Two opposing diamond sectioned handles with angular profiles run from the shoulder to just below the lip of the rim. Around the centre is a blundered inscription 'AVE MARIA GRA …' [Hail Mary Full of Grace …]
Some of the letters are inverted and each word is separated by a cross patée. The base of the vessel is decorated with cross-hatching and the basal edge of the body has a band of cross-hatched chevrons. Three small thin legs decorated with vertical ribs taper out towards the slightly thickened feet, and one of these has broken off.
Date: 14th century
Provenance: Thames Exchange spoil (Upper Thames Street) dumped at Beckton (TEX88[4002]); purchased by the Museum of London in 1990
Comments: A similar-sized pewter vase from the Steelyard also bears a central band with the inscription AVE MARIA GRACIA PLENA. H 64mm; Diam 45mm (see Mitchener 1986, p. 128, no. 327). See also a full-scale example presented to the Society of Antiquaries in 1801, inscribed William Angetel.

TYPE 1, DESIGN 2

2.6 Cauldron

Accession number: 98.2/196
Material: copper alloy (?) sooted, blackened; also contains some charred material
Condition: One leg missing
Dimensions: H 19mm; Diam (rim) 15mm; W 23mm
Description: A small cauldron with flaring bevelled rim, slightly waisted neck and long bulbous body widening towards the sagging base. There are two long, square sectioned legs (one broken off) with internally chamfered feet. The vessel has two diametrically opposed angular loop handles of rod section joining rim to shoulder.
Date: 15th–16th century
Provenance: London Bridge, south side

112 • TOYS, TRIFLES & TRINKETS

Fig. 22. In this anonymous engraving from *Kuchenmeisterei*, a best-selling cookery book by Johann Froschauer (Augsburg, 1507), the cook samples the contents of one cauldron while skimming the fat from another. Joints of meat roast on a mechanical spit and frying pans hang from a rack.
Reproduced from an original woodcut in the Sächsischen Landesbibliothek, Leipzig

COOKING VESSELS & UTENSILS • 113

TYPE 1, DESIGN 3

2.7 Cauldron

Accession number: 98.2/195
Material: Lead alloy
Condition: Almost complete; some damage
Dimensions: H 26mm; Diam (rim) 20 x 17 mm; Diam (base) 17 x 16 mm; W *c.* 29mm
Description: A cauldron with thin oval rim, short sloping neck, and cylindrical body with a flat base. There are two diametrically opposed sharply angular loop handles of diamond section, which stem just below the rim to the shoulder. The three widely splayed long legs are D-shaped and decorated with vertical ribbing.
Date: 14th–16th century
Provenance: London Bridge, north side
Comments: The flat base and squarish profile is unusual.

Fig. 23. This full-sized 14th-century bronze cauldron was found under the floor of an old house in Sumner Street, Blackfriars. 'Cauldrons', wrote the 15th-century French cook Chiquart in his treatise *Du Fait de Cuisine*, 'should be provided large, fair, and proper … for cooking large meats, and other medium ones … for making potages and doing other things necessary for cookery.'
Museum of London, Acc. no. A27445

TYPE 1, DESIGN 4

2.8 Cauldron

Accession number: 98.2/197
Material: Copper alloy
Condition: Almost complete; one leg missing
Dimensions: H 28mm; Diam (rim) 17 x 18 mm; W 30mm
Description: A crudely cast cauldron with wide flaring, bevelled rim, short neck carinated at the shoulder and spreading out to form a globular body with sagging base. There are two diametrically opposed loop handles of rod section, one with an angular profile and the other larger and curved. There are two long legs (one broken off leaving the stump) of facetted triangular section, which splay outwards at the foot. Both legs have collars.
Date: 15th–16th century

TYPE 1, DESIGN 5

2.9 Cauldron

Accession number: 7860
Material: Copper alloy – heavily sooted
Condition: Complete
Dimensions: H 60mm; Diam (rim) 37mm; W 48mm
Description: A tripod cauldron with flaring bevelled rim and bulbous body widening towards the base. There are two opposing rounded loop handles joining the rim to shoulder. The long, almost triangular sectioned legs have internally chamfered feet.
Date: 16th–17th century
Provenance: London Wall

TYPE 2

These cauldrons have very short tripod bun feet and are more crudely made in comparison with the Type 1 vessels.

TYPE 2, DESIGN 1

2.10 Cauldron

Accession number: 98.2/192
Material: Copper alloy
Condition: Almost complete; two legs missing
Dimensions: H 26mm; Diam (rim) 19.5mm; W 29mm
Description: This cauldron has a thickened rim, two diametrically opposed loop handles of rod section and a large globular body with sagging base. Only one short, stubby rectangular sectioned leg has survived, which curves outwards.
Date: Possibly 14th–15th century
Comments: Of continental style

TYPE 2, DESIGN 2

2.11 Cauldron

Accession number: 98.2/198
Material: Lead alloy
Condition: Complete; some damage to rim; slightly crushed.
Dimensions: H 27mm; Diam (rim) 23 x 17 mm; W 35mm
Description: A wide, thin slightly flaring rim, short tapering neck and long bulbous body with flat base and tripod bun feet. There are two diametrically opposed loop handles of diamond section and angular profile.
Date: Possibly 16th–17th century

Fig. 24. A full-sized 17th- to early 18th-century cauldron from the Sturton Foundry in South Petherton
Museum of London, Acc. no. 10119

Dripping pans

Dripping pans were laid across the hearth directly under the spits to collect the hot fat that dripped from the joint. According to Randle Holme in 1688, there were two basic types of oval or square shape with or without handles, and with one or two pouring lips, and these were made 'of potters earth or Iron'.[13] Some were partially raised by a pair of feet on one side so that the pan could be placed at an appropriate angle to the fire, and this slant helped the cook scoop up the fat for basting and minimized the risk of splashing. Single handles on metal vessels were usually reinforced with a bracket.[14]

The identification of the eight dripping

Fig. 25. Dripping pan handles were often reinforced with a bracket. This miniature (actual size H 35mm; L 46mm) from the Thames foreshore is the best example of the type known.
Private Collection

pans in this collection is largely based on an almost complete example in private hands which has a single pouring lip and bracket handle (fig. 25). Some of the pans have stubs for handle brackets and a single pouring lip, while others have a different body profile with one long bevelled edge. This suggests that the toymakers were producing at least two forms of dripping pan and since both types include examples with identical decoration, it is possible that they were produced in the same workshop.[15]

The dripping pans have been organized by decorative motif rather than form because many of the distinguishing features are missing or uncertain. The designs suggest a production date from the early to mid-17th century, which corresponds with the 1630–50 context of the only toy dripping pan recovered from excavations in this country.[16] Fourteen lead-alloy dripping pans with bracket handles and long narrow rectangular decorated pans have been found in the Netherlands dated to the 15th and 16th centuries, and it is possible, although perhaps not very likely, that Cat. nos. 15.27 and 15.28 (in the Miscellaneous section) are in fact dripping pans of this sort.

DESIGN 1

2.12 Dripping pan

Accession number: 98.2/578
Material: Lead alloy
Condition: Almost complete; handle missing
Dimensions: H 27mm; L 38mm
Description: A rectangular pan with bevelled sides and angular handle. The rim is beaded and the flat base decorated with a circle of ring and dot motifs and a plain and beaded circle enclosing a sexfoil double rose. Between each calyx point are pellets flanked by ring and dot. In the corners ring and dot motifs with radial lobes are tipped by a trefoil pattern of pellets.
Date: Early to mid-17th century
Provenance: Queenhithe Dock, March 1983
Comparanda: Two almost identical examples from the Thames in private collections

DESIGN 2

2.13 Dripping pan

Accession number: 98.2/575; 98.2/579; 98.2/600*
Material: Lead alloy
Condition: Handle missing
Dimensions: H 27mm; L 38mm
Description: A rectangular pan with integrally cast handle, bevelled sides, flat base and pouring lip at one end. The rim has a cable edge and the stubs of the handle and one bracket support survive. There is a rosette in the centre of the base with radiating lines each terminating in a cluster of pellets. The central motif is surrounded by a circle of rings and each corner has a ring and dot motif with radiating lines and clustered pellets at the tip.
Date: Early to mid-17th century
Provenance: Limekiln Dock
Comparandum: Toy dripping pan of 1630–50 with very similar decoration excavated from ABO92<654>[635]

DESIGN 3

2.14 Dripping pan

Accession number: 98.2/599

Material: Lead alloy

Condition: Most of handle missing

Dimensions: H 30mm; L 46mm

Description: A rectangular pan with bevelled sides, flat base and pouring lip at one end. Only the base of the handle has survived. The rim is beaded and the base has a cross-hatched ground with pellets at each intersection, a central rosette and a pattern of swirls and slashes in rococo style. The sides are also decorated with swirls, slashes and pellets.

Date: Early to mid-17th century

Comments: Either the same object, or another of the same design, was found by Mick Moran in August 1989 on the Rotherhithe foreshore (H 32mm; L 48mm) PA1868.

DESIGN 4

2.15 Dripping pan

Accession number: 98.2/598*; 98.2/601

Material: Lead alloy

Condition: Almost complete; no handle

Dimensions: H 25mm; L 38mm

Description: These rectangular pans have been cast from the same mould. The rectangular pans have bevelled sides and a pouring lip at one end. The rims are plain and one example (98.2/598) has a handle scar on one side. There is a cinquefoil double rose in the centre with calyx points between the outer row of petals, surrounded by two concentric circles and a linear frame which follows the outline of the pan. There are circles in each corner.

Date: Early to mid-17th century

Provenance: Southwark Bridge, south side, March 1983

DESIGN 5

2.16 Dripping pan

Accession number: 98.2/580

Material: Lead alloy

Condition: Almost complete; no handle

Dimensions: H 23mm; L 35mm

Description: A rectangular pan with bevelled sides, flat base and one straight edge. The rim is beaded and the base decorated with a stylized crown with a beaded oval cartouche in the centre containing a rosette. The crown is flanked on both sides with a large rosettes.

Date: Probably 18th century

Fig. 26. Dripping pan
Reproduced from Randle Holme, *The Academy of Armory* (Chester, 1688)

Frying pans

Fried food must have provided a welcome change from boiled, steamed and stewed meals, and wrought iron or copper frying pans have been an essential item of equipment from the Roman period onwards. The actual shape of the pan has scarcely altered during this time and most had an extended handle so that they could be held safely over an open fire. Pans of this type were still available in the early 1900s. By the late 17th century, however,[17] with the gradual adoption of the enclosed oven and level hot plate, a short-handled form evolved, and this corpus includes a miniature version with an integrally cast trivet, which is the only specimen known from London.

Although the ubiquitous circular long-handled frying pan is the standard form represented here, only three are complete. The pans have a flat base with straight bevelled sides and the handles are looped or pierced at the tip in imitation of the genuine article, which typically hung from a hook when not in use. Unlike a real pan, however, all the rims are either decorated with cable or beaded mouldings and one has a slight flange. Evidently the thin, weak handles were liable to snap off and most have broken at the point of greatest mechanical weakness: at the junction of the pan and handle. The apparent survival of pans as opposed to handles is not surprising since tiny thin strips of lead alloy are unlikely to have been recognized for what they are, and as a result have not been identified in archaeological assemblages or recovered from the foreshore. Moreover, the pan element is much more likely to have been kept as a serviceable bowl or platter, and at least one was converted to form a whirligig.[18] The pan profiles match the complete long-handled forms but because the original handle lengths are unknown, typological distinctions and classifications are based on specific mould variations rather than form.

The variety of mould designs amongst the long-handled pans is quite striking and although precise dating is impossible, it is quite likely that several designs were available at any one time. Evidence from the three complete examples suggests that they were all cast in one piece and with the exception of Type 1, which is plain, all have two fish in the pan.[19] These fish are arranged at 90° to the handle, mostly head to tail, but occasionally pointing in the same direction.[20] Most of the fish are surrounded by pellets that were presumably designed to represent sizzling bubbles of fat or perhaps herbs and berries, while others have finely hatched lines, indicating a liquid sauce, fish juices or a different cooking method such as poaching. Only one pan has fish without any other markings.[21]

Pictorial sources and contemporary recipes suggest that frying pans were used for many kinds of foods and yet the base-metal toy pans only seem to have been cast with fish, reflecting the fact that

Fig. 27. Detail from a woodcut showing a cook surrounded by the tools of her trade. A cauldron is suspended over the hearth from a pot hanger while a gridiron, frying pans and skillets hang from the wall.
From an anonymous volume, *Bambergischen halzgerichts und rechtlich Ordenung ...* (Bamberg, 1510)

fresh and dried fish were a staple element of the diet.[22] Until the Reformation fish were eaten on 153 days in the year; and thereafter on the obligatory Fish Days (held on two days a week before 1550 and on three days a week after 1563) or during Lent. Battered stockfish or dried cod and herrings were especially popular, but Londoners also enjoyed flounders, sturgeon, salmon, pike and a wide range of freshwater fish. The mould-makers have clearly made some effort to produce the salient features of a fish, and although some of the anatomical details are highly stylized, most are shown with gills and scales, and even pectoral, dorsal and anal fins. When fried, a whole fish tends to curl in the pan and some of the fish are authentically shown with curved bodies and tails. It is also evident that some attempt has been made to represent different species, and these are partly indicated by shape, size, the presence or absence of barbels and spines and other anatomical details. Significantly all of the frying pans are round which probably suggests a date no latter than the middle of the 18th century. Thereafter, in England at least, oval pans were generally used for frying fish.

TYPE 1, DESIGN 1

2.17 Frying pan

Accession number: Enq. no. 2076/1
Material: Lead alloy
Condition: Complete
Dimensions: L 67mm; L (handle) 38mm; Diam (rim) 29mm; Diam (base) 26mm; Dpt 5mm
Description: A complete frying pan, cast in one piece with wide, straight parallel handle, rounded and pierced end. The plain pan has straight sides. There are two very faint concentric circles underneath; possibly a casting fault, and the exterior base has traces of paint.
Date: Probably 17th century
Provenance: Butler's Wharf, 22 May 2000, now in a private collection
Comments: It has been suggested that the circles on the base were probably caused when the pan was removed from the mould.[23]
Comparandum: Norfolk Museums Service, excavated from a 1550–1700 context: see Margeson 1993, p. 219, no. 1792, fig. 168; cited in Egan 1996

TYPE 2, DESIGN 1

2.18 Frying pan

Accession number: 98.2/183; 98.2/185
Material: Lead alloy
Condition: 98.2/183: complete. 98.2/185: pan only
Dimensions: L 61mm; L (handle) 33mm; Diam (rim) *c.* 29mm; Diam (base) 19mm; Dpt 3mm
Description: The complete frying pan is cast in one piece. It has a long, straight, parallel-sided, flat handle terminating in a loop, and a shallow circular pan with straight sides, which tapers to a flat base. Both of the pan rims are beaded and they contain two fish in high relief, placed on their sides, head to tail across the pan at right angles to the handle. Both fish have prominent eyes and there is a suggestion of gills, but they are appear to be slightly different species: one has a smooth skin, with obvious pectoral, dorsal and anal fins, although these are of equal size and shown on both sides. The other has a fringe of lateral spines suggestive of a flat fish, with pectoral and prominent anal fins. Both of the tails touch the edges of the pan and curl up the sides. The fish are surrounded by an evenly spaced, fine stippling, suggestive of hot bubbling fat.
Date: Probably 17th century

TYPE 3, DESIGN 1

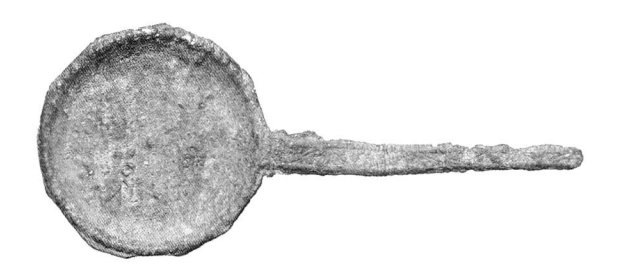

2.19 Frying pan

Accession number: 98.2/184; 98.2/191
Material: Lead alloy
Condition: 98.2/184: complete. 98.2/191: pan only
Dimensions: L 75mm; L (handle) 43mm; Diam (rim) 32mm; Diam (base) 24mm; Dpt 5mm
Description: The complete frying pan is cast in one piece with a flat handle, which tapers to the end. The shallow pans have a beaded rim with straight sides tapering to a flat base, containing two poorly moulded fish. A few pellets around the fish suggest bubbling fat.
Date: Probably 17th century

TYPE 4, DESIGN 1

2.20 Frying pan

Accession number: 98.2/190
Material: Lead alloy
Condition: Pan only
Dimensions: Diam (rim) 30mm; Diam (base) *c.* 21mm; Dpt 2mm
Description: A complete pan with rope-twist rim. The profile is extremely flat and it is difficult to know whether this is the result of burial and crushing. There are two fish, placed head to tail across the flat base, at right angles to the handle (the stub remains) and these are surrounded by large pellets, suggestive of hot bubbling fat. Both fish seem to be identical with the suggestion of scales and pectoral, dorsal and anal fins showing on both sides and of equal size. The tails cover the sides of the pan and the tips reach the rim.
Date: Probably 17th century
Comparandum: A whirligig (Cat. no. 13.5) made from a frying pan of this type

TYPE 4, DESIGN 2

2.21 Frying pan
Accession number: 98.2/188
Material: Lead alloy
Condition: Pan only; slight damage
Dimensions: Diam (rim) 29mm; Diam (base) 19mm; Dpt 3mm
Description: This pan has a small rim flange with decorative beading, and straight sides to a slightly convex, possibly distorted base. Two fish are placed head to tail across the pan, possibly at right angles to the handle (the rim is damaged in three places). The identical fish have fine scales, pectoral, dorsal and anal fins of equal size evident on both sides of the body and curling tails touching the sides of the pan. They are surrounded by pellets suggestive of hot bubbling fat.
Date: Probably 17th century
Comparandum: An identically moulded pan with handle stub in good condition from Custom House Quay (private collection)

TYPE 4, DESIGN 3

2.22 Frying pan
Accession number: 98.2/186
Material: Lead alloy
Condition: Pan only; completely flattened
Dimensions: Diam (rim) 19mm; Diam (base) 18mm; Dpt 5mm
Description: The circular pan has a beaded rim. There are two fish placed head to tail across the pan at right angles to the handle (notch in rim). One fish is larger and its tail touches the rim of the pan. Both have large eyes and crude detail, with a suggestion of scales and one fish has either anal fins or spines. The fish are surrounded by tiny pellets to indicate sizzling fat.
Date: Probably 17th century

TYPE 5, DESIGN 1

2.23 Frying pan
Accession number: 98.2/208
Material: Lead alloy
Condition: Pan only
Dimensions: Diam (rim) 32mm; Diam (base) 25mm; Dpt 4mm
Description: A very shallow pan with curving sides, flat base and rope-twist rim. There are two large fish placed head to tail across the pan, at right angles to the handle (stub extent). These have prominent heads, large scales, pectoral, dorsal and anal fins with spines and fin bones. The fish are slightly different and their tails touch the edge of the pan. Both are surrounded by large pellets to indicate sizzling fat.
Date: Probably 17th century
Comparandum: Another example, in poor condition, from the same mould recovered from Bull Wharf east (private collection)

TYPE 6, DESIGN 1

2.24 Frying pan

Accession number: 98.2/189
Material: Lead alloy
Condition: Pan only
Dimensions: Diam (rim) 27mm; Diam (base) 19mm; Dpt 4mm
Description: This circular pan has straight sides, a flat base and a beaded rim. Two fish pointing in the same direction are at right angles to the handle (stub extant). Both seem to be identical with scales and small curling tails. There are no fins and the base of the pan is unmarked.
Date: Probably 17th century

TYPE 7, DESIGN 1

2.25 Frying pan

Accession number: 78.219
Material: Lead alloy
Condition: Pan only; completely flattened; slight damage to rim
Dimensions: Diam (rim) 28mm; Diam (base) *c.* 19mm; Dpt *c.* 4mm
Description: A circular pan, now flattened, with a notched rim. Two fish placed head to tail across the pan at right angles to the handle (notch in rim). The fish, though different in shape and size, have prominent eyes, scales, dorsal and anal fins with spines. Although the tips of the tails touch the edge of the pan, the larger fish's tail curves downwards. Both are surrounded by fine lines suggestive of liquid or fish juices.
Date: Probably 17th century
Comparandum: Another from the same mould recovered from Custom House Quay (private collection)

TYPE 7, DESIGN 2

2.26 Frying pan

Accession number: 98.2/187
Material: Lead alloy
Condition: Pan only; completely flattened
Dimensions: Diam (rim) 28mm; Diam (base) *c.* 20mm; Dpt *c.* 4mm
Description: A circular pan, now flattened, with notched rim. There are two fish placed head to tail across the pan at right angles to the handle (notch in rim). The fish are slightly different: one has pectoral, dorsal and anal fins, the other has dorsal and anal fins. The tails touch the edge of the pan and the fish are surrounded by fine lines suggestive of liquid or fish juices.
Date: Probably 17th century

TYPE 8, DESIGN 1

2.27 Frying pan and trivet

Accession number: 98.2/182

Material: Lead alloy

Condition: Complete

Dimensions: Pan: Diam (rim) 30mm; Dpt *c.* 7mm. Trivet: Diam (top) 19mm; W 24mm

Description: A short-handled frying pan with a large deep curving bowl. The grip has a knop at each end, successfully imitating the turned wood handles on full-scale vessels. At the junction of the handle and pan there is a vertical tab, or 'splash guard' decorated on one side with ring and dot. The pan is also decorated with a rope-twist rim, plain border and two concentric circles enclosing foliate scrolling and a large five-petalled flower surrounded by pellets. It is soldered on to a round-topped trivet with shaped and splayed legs and bulbous feet. The casting is imperfect and there are gaps in the outer ring.[24] The exterior surface is decorated with diagonal hatching and there are cordons around the legs.

Date: Mid-17th century

Provenance: Tower foreshore

Comments: Separate round and square trivets have been found during excavations in the Netherlands: see Willemsen 1998, pp. 386–7, B104 & B105. This object was purchased with the assistance of NACF.

Comparandum: An almost identical example in the Musée national du Moyen Age, Paris (15 x 27 mm) dated to the 17th century[25]

Gridirons

From the medieval period, free-standing rectangular or square wrought iron grids were used on an open hearth for toasting bread and for broiling or grilling fish and smaller cuts of meat. A longish handle, occasionally reinforced with a bracket, extended from one side, and gridirons were supported on four short legs of equal length until the enclosed range was introduced at the very end of the 17th century. The grid was generally composed of seven bars, although the number varies in relation to the size of the frame. The handles and frame corners were sometimes embellished with scrolling, and occasionally the bars were formed into decorative openwork motifs.[26] Most of the toy gridirons are highly decorated and some of the bars have diagonal hatching or rope-twist mouldings.

There are four gridirons in the collection and although the designs and shapes are all different, they are each cast with fish. Some are extremely well made, while others are very crude and stylized, a disparity which not only reflects the skill of the mould-maker but perhaps also the retail price. Given the fact that gridirons were amongst the most common items of kitchen equipment until well into the 18th century, it is surprising that so few toy versions have survived in this country, but perhaps the openwork form made them particularly susceptible to damage and, like the frying pans, the handles would have taken most of the strain.[27] It is also significant that, like the frying pans, only fish are shown rather than other types of foods. Precise dating is impossible because there are no discernible changes to the shape of the genuine article until the early 18th century. Moreover, the toys are too fragmentary and stylized to make a direct comparison possible.[28] Since there are no circular gridirons within the sample, the toys were probably made during the 16th or early 17th century before the circular form became common. Square and rectangular lead-alloy toy gridirons with fish mouldings have been found in France and the Netherlands dating from the 15th to 17th centuries.[29]

COOKING VESSELS & UTENSILS • 125

DESIGN 1

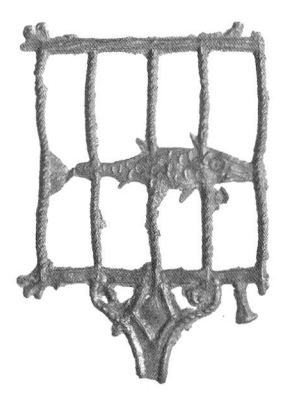

2.28 Gridiron

Accession number: 98.2/584
Material: Lead alloy
Condition: Almost complete; part of handle missing
Dimensions: H 47mm; W 34mm
Description: A square gridiron with three bars, short legs (one extant) and bracket scroll handle (incomplete). The bars are decorated with rope-twist, the grid corners terminate in a trefoil and the handle is ornamented with a lozenge. A large fish straddles the bars and the tail and mouth touch the outer frame. The fish is convincingly formed with prominent eye, mouth, scales and pectoral, dorsal and anal fins.
Date: 16th or early 17th century

DESIGN 2

2.29 Gridiron

Accession number: 98.2/585
Condition: Handle and part of grid missing
Dimensions: H 37mm; W 40mm
Description: Part of a square, five-bar gridiron with two recurving feet (?) (one or two feet probably missing). The grid supports two large fish, placed head to tail across and underneath the bars. Both fish extend beyond the outer frame, and although different, have clearly defined scales, eyes and spines.
Date: 16th or early 17th century
Comments: Part of another of the same design (Acc. no. A24766/30) was previously published as a badge.[30]

DESIGN 3

2.30 Gridiron

Accession number: 98.2/586
Material: Lead alloy
Condition: Part only
Dimensions: H 17mm; W 46mm
Description: Part of a five-bar(?) gridiron (outer bars missing) decorated with alternate plain and rope-twist bars within a frame of chevrons and pellets. A fish across the bars is finely cast with convincing detail: bony mouth, large eye, gills, scales, curving tail and eight fins or spines.
Date: 16th or early 17th century

DESIGN 4

2.31 Gridiron

Accession number: 98.2/587; 98.2/588*
Material: Lead alloy
Condition: Damaged
Dimensions: H 29mm; W 47mm
Description: Two sections from a six bar gridiron. There is a suggestion of pellet and scrolling decoration on the frame corners, but otherwise the bars are plain. There are two large fish placed head to tail across and extending beyond the grid. Both are extremely crude and the eyes are the only feature indicated.
Date: 16th or early 17th century
Provenance: Queenhithe

Fig. 28. In this busy kitchen, fish lie on a gridiron waiting to be cooked while fish and fowl roast on the spits.

Reproduced from Cristoforo da Messisburgo, *Libro novo* (Ferrare, 1549)

Pot hangers

For centuries various kinds of hangers have been used to support cooking pots over the fire. The adjustable ratchet hanger or trammel with saw-toothed bar came into common use from the early 17th century and three examples are represented here. The ratchet system allowed pots to be raised or lowered over the fire as required and this degree of flexibility made open-hearth cooking easier and safer.

On the whole, surviving full-scale adjustable hangers are plain and functional, but occasionally the wrought iron terminals are embellished with swirls and there are a few specimens with openwork decoration and even brass and copper inlays. The toy hangers have elaborate decoration and were probably made during the mid- to late 17th century. Similar examples in lead and copper alloys have been recovered from excavations in the Netherlands dating from the 15th to 17th centuries.[31]

TYPE 1, DESIGN 1

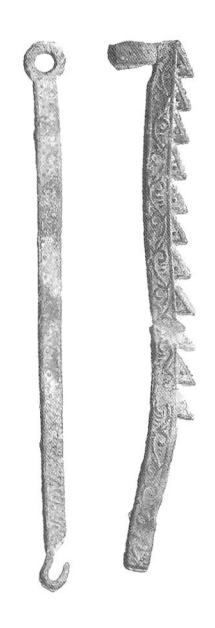

2.32 Pot hanger

Accession number: 86.239/23 & 86.239/24
Material: Lead alloy
Condition: Almost complete
Dimensions: Ratchet: L 69mm; W (bar) 3mm; W (incl. teeth) 6mm. Hanger: L 71mm; W 3mm
Description: A saw-toothed adjustable ratchet or trammel with 11 straight-sided teeth, hanger, curving hook and suspension loop. The curving ratchet hook is missing. Bars elaborately ornamented on both sides with foliate scrolling, chevrons, pellets and rope-twist.
Date: Probably mid- to late 17th century

Fig. 29. Large cooking pots suspended over the hearth could be raised or lowered over the heat by means of an adjustable pot hanger.
Reproduced from Randle Holme, *The Academy of Armory* (Chester, 1688)

Fig. 30. Detail showing a pot hanger, from the 15th-century manuscript *La Fleur des histoires*. See plate VI, p. 166

TYPE 1, DESIGN 2

2.33 Pot hanger

Accession number: 98.2/589
Material: Lead alloy
Condition: Ratchet bar only; slight damage
Dimensions: L 60mm; W (bar) 6mm; W (incl. teeth) 8mm
Description: Part of an adjustable ratchet or trammel with ten curving teeth. Decorated on one side only with a central design of cross-hatched diapers interspersed with pellets arranged in a triad.
Date: Probably mid- to late 17th century
Provenance: Thames Exchange, via Crayford Spoil Tips

Skillet

These small circular pots[32] with a short handle and tripod legs were used throughout the late medieval and early modern period until the flat hob grate of the 18th century rendered the rounded base and raised legs obsolete. Bronze or ceramic skillets were used like a modern saucepan for gentle boiling and simmering and the preparation of sauces. Since the vessels were slow to warm and retained their heat even when they were removed from the fire, the skillet was ideally suited for cooking custards and creamy mixtures and for any ingredients that needed to be heated gradually without burning or curdling. This is the only skillet in the collection and although the handle is missing, the form suggests manufacture between the late 15th and early 17th century.

TYPE 1, DESIGN 1

2.34 Skillet

Accession number: 98.2/194
Material: Copper alloy
Condition: Almost complete; handle missing
Dimensions: H 23mm; Diam (rim) 10mm; W 22mm
Description: Cast in one piece, with short tapering bevelled neck, sharply carinated shoulder and bulbous body with sagging base, supported by three long legs of triangular section with splayed and collared feet. The stubs of the open braced handle remain.
Date: Late 15th – early 17th century
Comparandum: Similar vessel attributed to the Bridall foundry, Exeter, in Butler & Green 2003, pp. 9 & 38

COOKING VESSELS & UTENSILS • *129*

Fig. 31. A full-sized copper-alloy skillet cast from the Sturton foundry in Somerset, with the date 1670, initials IPE and founder's mark and inscription on the handle THIS IS GOOD WARE TS. Skillets of this kind are unknown in miniature form.
Museum of London, Acc. no. 80.271/10

Spit

For roasting and broiling, meat was either held vertically over the fire from a hook, or skewered on a horizontal spit. If the hearth was wide enough, spit roasting was preferred because the meat cooked through quickly and several joints could be cooked at once. Each spit, supported by racks, was turned slowly to achieve a thorough even roasting. The simplest form, the so-called 'hand broach' of the type represented here, has one pointed end to pierce the meat and a crank handle to facilitate rotation. A flattened, slightly wider, middle section prevented the joint from swivelling around and for additional support the meat was usually held in place by adjustable forks.

Although the spit was such a principal item of kitchen equipment, only one complete toy version is known in this country.[33] So far, no fragments have been identified and yet toy spits must have been produced in their hundreds during the medieval and early modern period. Perhaps the bar or crank handle was too fragile to withstand heavy play, and the broken spits may have been so damaged that fragments have either been destroyed or remain unrecognized in archaeological assemblages.

This spit is shown with a suckling pig (?). The creature has been inaccurately positioned at the far end of the rod, which shows little understanding of the roasting process. A precise date is impossible, because the basic form of the spit remained unchanged until the middle of the 17th century when the crank handle was replaced by a wooden wheel.

TYPE 1, DESIGN 1

2.35 Spit

Accession number: 98.2/590
Material: Lead alloy
Condition: Complete
Dimensions: L 91mm; W 3mm
Description: A simple spit with thin, parallel-sided bar and bent end to serve as a crank. There is a crudely cast 'skewered' animal at the other end, and although the overall shape suggests a boar or hog with thick coarse hair, indicated by diagonal lines on the body, the scale suggests a suckling pig.
Date: 15th–17th century

1. Taylor 1630: 'Jack a Lent'.
2. Woodward 1985, particularly part 3, p. 183.
3. This trivet is actually attached to a short-handled frying pan. On the Continent, trivets have been found as separate items.
4. There is a toy mortar in the collections of the Cuming Museum: H 30mm; Diam 42mm, pewter, found Moorfields, 1865, Acc. no. C4457 (I am grateful to Sue Gosling for this information). The Court Minutes of the WCP include a reference to the manufacture of 'Toy Pestell and Mortars' on 15 September 1668/9.
5. Willemsen 1998, for examples of dripping pans p. 388, B110; spits p. 383, B91; gridirons p. 386, B106 & B107 and p. 393, B126; pot hanger p. 391, B119 and p. 393, B129; strainers p. 392, B125; hanging trivets p. 386, B104; round trivets p. 387, B105; and wafering irons p. 390, B116 – all from 15th–17th-century contexts.
6. T1, D3: Acc. no. 98.2/196.
7. A turned lead-alloy toy bowl was recovered from excavations on the site of the Millennium Footbridge (MFB98).
8. There is an example in the collections of the Worshipful Company of Pewterers (S1/130) of 14th-century date, and another recovered from excavations in Exeter: see Allan 1984, p. 345, fig. 192.
9. Pearce 1992, has shown in her analysis of Hampshire–Surrey Border wares that the relative proportion of bowls to other Border ware forms steadily increases from the late 16th century onwards, and by the mid-17th century the bowl is one of the most well represented forms. A similar pattern emerges within the tin-glazed earthenware industry.
10. Butler & Green 2003. I'm most grateful to Mr and Mrs Butler and Mr Green for their comments on this collection, and in particular the suggestion that the copper-alloy vessels were almost certainly cast by founders.
11. Willemsen 1998, p. 374, B63 & B64 – 25 examples.
12. PCA site from Temple Court (TCT99<19>[66]).
13. Holme 1688, bk 3, ch. 14.
14. Part of a dripping pan with curving profile, pouring lip and bracket handle can be seen in a stained-glass window, showing an medieval turnspit roasting a bird and smoking fish, in the V&A.
15. Similar examples are shown in Cats 1632, ch. 39, p. 118, entitled 'A Gatto che Lecca. Spiedo non gli fidate arrosto' (this dripping pan has a pouring lip and bracket handle) and ch. 12, p. 47 entitled 'Als morfige lieden kuys worden. fo schuerenfe de panne van achteren' (with a bracket handle and plain rectangular tray).
16. Abbot's Lane, Southwark, (ABO92<654>[635]).
17. In 1671 the Hallen's or Hollands were producing shorter-handled, lightweight frying pans at their brass battery works in Wandsworth, Surrey.
18. A T4, D1 frying pan has been converted into a whirligig: see Acc. no. 98.92/714, Cat. no. 13.5.
19. One pan recovered from the Thames and now in a private collection has three fish. (I am most grateful to Ron Homer for this information, pers. comm.)
20. T3, D1: Acc. nos. 98.92/184; 98.92/191; T6, D1: Acc. no. 98.92/189. There is a toy silver frying pan in the Westfries Museum, Hoorn, which has two fish facing in the same direction. This pan was probably made in Haarlem between 1704 and 1737 (L 90mm).
21. Ten plain lead-alloy frying pans have been excavated from various sites in the Netherlands, compared with just one (pan only) with fish. The contexts range from the late 14th to 17th centuries: see Willemsen 1998, p. 372, B56 & p. 378, B74.
22. The only exception to fish mouldings that the author has found is a long-handled silver frying pan in the Fries Museum, Leerwarden by Ipens Siccama (18th century (?); L 76mm). This pan rim has chevron chasing and there are seven raised discs in the base. The smooth discs were probably designed to represent fritters or possibly eggs.
23. Geoff Egan, pers. comm.
24. Egan 1996, p. 6.
25. Bruna 1997, p. 4, fig. 9.
26. Lindsay 1927, fig. 139 and p. 29.
27. A square gridiron with fish placed head to tail (41 x 35 mm) dated to the 17th century is in the collection of the Museé national du Moyen Age: see Bruna 1997, p. 4, cat. no. 10. Egan 1996 has drawn attention to other post-medieval toy gridirons in the collections of the Naples Museum, which are published as a classical find in Barbera 1991, p. 20, fig. 12.
28. Circular gridirons were particularly common during the 17th and 18th centuries and the absence of this form in the corpus perhaps points to an earlier date for these specimens.
29. Bruna 1997, p. 4, fig. 10 and Willemsen 1998, p. 387, B106, B107 & B126.
30. London Museum 1940, 'Miscellaneous Badges', p. 264 and pl. 72, no. 49.
31. Willemsen 1998, p. 391, B119 (eight of lead alloy) & p. 393, B129 (three of copper alloy).
32. These vessels are also described as posnets. See Butler & Green 2003, pp. 9–10, for discussion of terminological issues.
33. There is an almost identical spit (L 91mm) in the collections of the Museé national du Moyen Age, Paris dated to the 17th century: see Bruna 1997, p. 4, cat. no. 6. One spit and spit-dog of lead alloy has been excavated from Reimerswall in the Netherlands from a context *c.* 1530: see Willemsen 1998, p. 383, B91.

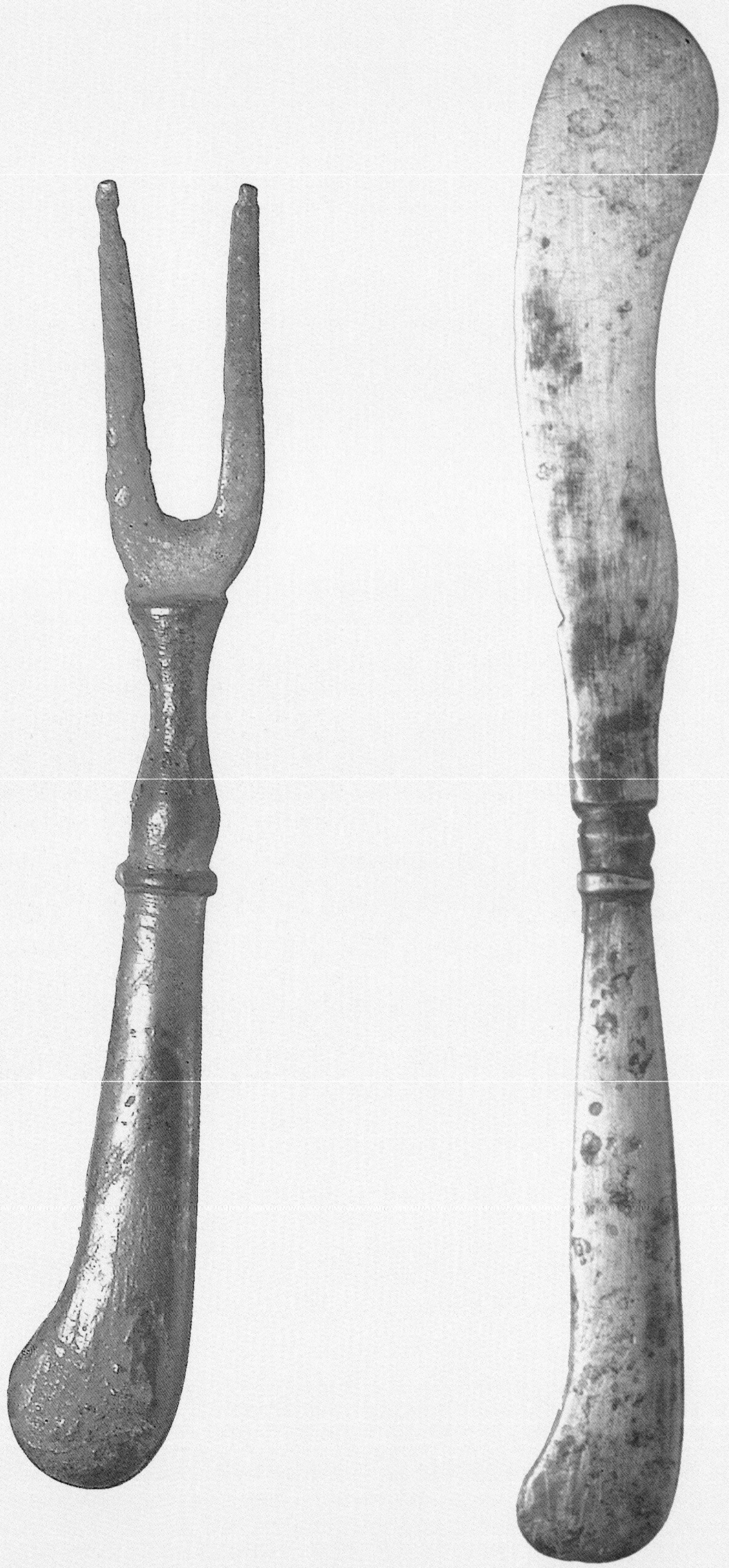

3 Cutlery

'The Italians ... do always at their meals use a little fork when they cut their meat...The reason for this their curiosity is because the Italian cannot endure by any means to have his dish touched by fingers, seeing that all men's fingers are not alike clean.' [1]

Although table knives and spoons were widely used from the Roman period onwards, base-metal miniatures are extremely scarce. There are 22 knives, spoons and forks in the collection, and each type is considered in detail below.

While the relative lack of forks can be explained by the late appearance of this implement in England, the complete absence of toy knives before the 18th century is extraordinary. Survival rates might have been affected by the fragile nature of these objects, which were no doubt highly susceptible to damage and breakage.

Forks

Large forks served a useful purpose in the kitchen, but it was not until the early 11th century that the habit of eating with a small table fork was introduced into southern Europe. By the 13th century the Italians were using tiny forks to eat sticky succades and sweetmeats and within a few years forks began to be used for general dining throughout Italy. Eating with a knife and fork in the Italian fashion was largely unknown in England and even when a few daring individuals adopted the practice at the end of the 16th century, the custom was scorned by most Englishmen who preferred to use their fingers and a sharp pointed knife. In 1611, the indefatigable traveller Thomas Coryat was ridiculed by his countrymen when he imitated 'the Italian fashion by this forked cutting of meate'[2] but within a few years the use of table forks was considered 'laudable … as they are sparing of napkins'.[3] Despite this change in attitude, forks were seldom used, and it was not until the third decade of the 17th century that the fork was adopted as a regular item of cutlery in England.

Hardly any base-metal toy forks appear to have survived and only four have been recovered from London soil. The earliest seems to date from the period when forks were finally accepted as an essential piece of cutlery in England, and as the use of the fork became more widespread there must have been a corresponding demand for miniature versions, which were probably sold as a knife and fork set by the toymaker. The forks of late 17th- and 18th-century date are considerably larger than the earliest piece in the collection, and these were probably used as doll's toys. It is possible that the copper-alloy fork was actually used by a child during play and, unlike the flimsy lead-alloy versions, would certainly have withstood heavy use. So far no base-metal toy forks have been recognized from excavations on the Continent apart from a toy toasting fork recovered from a late 16th- or early 17th-century context in the Netherlands.[4]

TYPE 1, DESIGN 1

3.1 Fork

Accession number: 98.2/569
Material: Lead alloy
Condition: Complete
Dimensions: L 35mm; L (handle) 15mm
Description: Cast in one piece with two long straight tines, long neck and faceted flaring handle, terminating in a knop or button
Date: 1670–90; probably 1670s

TYPE 2, DESIGN 1

3.2 Fork

Accession number: 98.2/561; 98.2/562*
Material: Lead alloy
Condition: Complete
Dimensions: 98.2/561: L 70mm. 98.2/562: L 67mm; L (handle) 29mm
Description: Two identical forks cast in one piece with two long straight tines, oval-sectioned, straight-sided flaring shoulder, circular bolster and flattened oval flaring handle with rounded end. The shoulder is decorated with a criss-cross pattern and the handle with stylized scrolling foliage, which was possibly designed to represent pique-work. Both forks having matching fronts and backs.
Date: c. 1690

TYPE 3, DESIGN 1

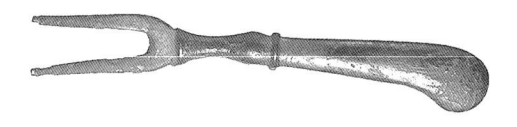

3.3 Fork

Accession number: 98.2/563
Material: Copper alloy
Condition: Complete
Dimensions: L 63mm; L (handle) 30mm
Description: Cast in one piece with two long slightly curving tines, baluster neck, ring bolster and pistol-grip handle
Date: c. 1740

Knives

Before forks came into common use during the 17th century, the table knife had to serve the dual function of cutting and skewering food. Since etiquette demanded that food should be conveyed to the mouth with the fingers, roasted and baked meats, fish and pies were generally jointed, carved and sliced into manageable portions that could be lifted directly from the serving platter to the trencher by hand or on the point of the knife. The chronological and evolutionary development of the table knife has been discussed in detail elsewhere, but from the early 1600s 'the shape of blade underwent various changes which seem to have been dictated by fashion rather than considerations of utility'.[5] From the mid-century a very broad curved 'scimitar' blade started to become fashionable and by the early 18th century the 'pistol-grip' handle was introduced.

Even though table knives were obviously essential implements and have been found in their thousands from archaeological excavations in the capital, no toy examples in base metals earlier than the mid-18th century seem to have survived, and none has been recognized or recorded elsewhere in the country. All of the knives in this collection are cast from copper alloy. It is possible that toy knives were originally sold as a knife and fork set, and like the 18th-century copper-alloy fork in the collection, they are all large enough to fit into a child's hand.

TYPE 1, DESIGN 1

3.4 Knife

Accession number: 98.2/566; 98.2/568*
Condition: Part of blade and handle
Material: Copper alloy
Dimensions: 98.2/566: L 40mm. 98.2/568: L 52mm
Description: Cast in one piece, possibly from the same mould. Only part of the blade survives, but enough to suggest a sabre shape (98.2/568) and both have a pronounced notch on the cutting edge towards the handle. The knives have a circular ribbed bolster and pistol-grip handle.
Date: 1760–80
Comments: The notched blade is not found on full-scale knives, although knives of this date do have a sharp heel at the base.

TYPE 2, DESIGN 1

3.5 Knife

Accession number: 98.2/564
Material: Copper alloy
Condition: Complete
Dimensions: L 72mm; L (blade) 38mm; L (handle) 34mm
Description: A complete knife cast in one piece with a sabre-shaped blade, knop and rib bolster and pistol-grip handle. The cutting edge at the base of the blade is notched.
Date: 1750–75

TYPE 3, DESIGN 1

3.6 Knife

Accession number: 98.2/565
Material: Copper alloy
Condition: Complete
Dimensions: L 71mm; L (blade) 40mm; L (handle) 31mm
Descriptions: Cast in one piece. The blade is sabre-shaped with a straight cutting edge, and the flattened oval-sectioned handle flares outwards and slightly downwards to the squared-off end. Both sides of the handle and the base of the blade are decorated with a random pattern of incised zig-zags.
Date: 1760–70
Provenance: Dockhead

Spoons

As pulpy semi-liquid foods or 'spoon-meats' constituted such an important part of the diet in the medieval and early modern periods, spoons were the principal eating utensil until well into the 17th century, and because they were indispensable they were made in a wide range of materials and fashioned to suit different tastes and pockets. Simple spoons made from cheap materials such as wood, horn and base metals were used by all strata of society for everyday needs, while those made from precious materials were usually reserved for special occasions or kept for show. The best-quality spoons made ideal presentation gifts, commemorative tokens and souvenirs and these were often suitably inscribed and cherished for their symbolic, sentimental or intrinsic value and handed down from one generation to the next, whereas the very cheap spoons were generally discarded once they were no longer serviceable and were either thrown away or recycled. Some of the base-metal spoons were evidently recast to suit contemporary fashion and, as Ron Homer has pointed out, 'many of the crude unmarked 17th-century spoons found in present-day collections undoubtedly originated in this way',[6] while others were melted down for other purposes.

Even though spoons are far more abundant than other types of toy cutlery, only seven complete examples have been recognized from London. No toy spoons of early medieval date have been recovered in England and although there are two spoons in the collection that might have been produced as early as the late 15th century, the majority have features that suggest manufacture from the late 16th to early 19th centuries.[7] Some are precise miniatures of contemporary forms, 'made plaine, but with wroughte shanks and heads with diverse devises',[8] but others (such as Type 9) have no obvious counterpart or are a confusing blend of shapes and styles which present considerable problems for dating and attribution. The presence of a large rosette moulding in over half the bowls, for example, has no full-scale equivalent. Was this motif included to imitate the type of silver chasing which was fashionable in precious metal spoon bowls in Scandinavia, Germany and the Netherlands during the late 16th and 17th centuries, and if so, does this suggest foreign manufacture?[9] Or was the rosette motif included to identify the work of a particular maker such as IQ or DQ (fig. 32) whose initials appear on some of the complete examples of this type?[10]

Specific evidence for toy spoon production in medieval and early modern England is extremely limited. A few pieces in the collection have characteristic English features and were probably produced in London, but others are closely modelled on Continental forms and one spoon, Type 4, has the distinctive shape of a particular style of spoon only found in the Netherlands, Germany and Norway during the 17th century.[11] If the ratio of English as opposed to foreign spoons in this small group is an accurate reflection of the contemporary toy market, a significant quantity of base-metal toy spoons were probably imported to satisfy domestic demand.

All of the spoons are cast in one piece in lead alloy or latten (a mixture of copper and zinc) and some might have been produced from the same mould or from the same workshop. The spoons seem to replicate plain, ordinary everyday eating implements as well as highly decorative ornamental types made from precious metals. Those of medieval and early post-medieval style are cast to a fairly uniform size of approximately 48mm; whereas the 18th-century and later spoons are extremely variable in size and quality. The biggest spoon in the collection, Acc. no. 98.2/559, is large enough to fit comfortably in a child's hand and was probably used for a 'doll's tea-party'.[12]

Fig. 32. Spoon: detail showing the inscription DQ
Acc. no. 98.2/550, Cat. no. 3.9

TYPE 1, DESIGN 1

3.7 Slip top spoon

Accession number: 98.2/549; 2001.20/3*
Material: Latten
Condition: Complete
Dimensions: 98.2/549: L 48mm; L (stem) 32mm; Diam (bowl) 14mm
   2001.20/3: L 50mm; L (stem) 35mm; Diam (bowl) 14mm
Description: Plain spoons with a deep fig-shaped bowl and thick diamond-sectioned stem with a 'slipped' or bevelled end
Date: Possibly late 15th, but probably late 16th or 17th century
Provenance: 2001.20/3 from Bull Wharf
Comments: Slip top spoons date from the late 15th century (1498 silver) to the 1680s in England and were also fairly common in the Netherlands and Germany during the 17th century.

TYPE 2, DESIGN 1

3.8 Spoon

Accession number: 98.2/547
Material: Lead alloy
Condition: Bowl and stub of handle
Dimensions: L 29mm; Diam (bowl) 24 x 18 mm
Description: A plain fig-shaped bowl with the stub of a triangular-sectioned stem
Date: Bowls of this shape were the standard form in England from 1400–1650.

TYPE 3, DESIGN 1

3.9 Spoon

Accession number: 98.2/550*; 98.2/551
Material: Lead alloy
Condition: Complete
Dimensions: 98.2/550: L 46mm. 98.2/551: L 45mm; L (stem) 31mm; Diam (bowl) 14mm
Inscription: 98.2/550: DQ. 98.2/551: IQ
Description: Two virtually identical spoons with deep rounded bowls with a single raised dot in the centre. Both stems are decorated, front and back, with closely placed diagonal mouldings to represent a 'wrythen' effect, and this extends to the terminal loop which has diagonal slashes on the front. The stem on 98.2/551 is a little thicker. Both have a rat's tail on the back of the bowl with initials on either side (as given above).
Date: Probably mid-17th century
Comments: Spoons with wrythen stems were made in the Low Countries during the 16th and 17th centuries. It is has been suggested that these spoons are ladles because they have loop terminals, but the short decorative stem would tend to suggest otherwise, since ladle stems are much longer and are invariably plain to facilitate cleaning. The Type 5 spoons below (see Cat. no. 3.11, Enq. no. 1659/1) also seem to have had loop terminals and these were obviously modelled on good-quality table spoons.

TYPE 4, DESIGN 1

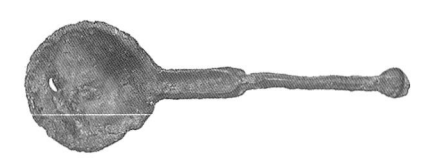

3.10 Ball-knopped spoon

Accession number: 98.2/548
Material: Lead alloy
Condition: Complete; worn and slightly damaged bowl
Dimensions: L 53mm; L (stem) 35mm; Diam (bowl) 17mm
Description: A shallow round bowl, with a partially thickened rim, joins a rod stem with a flattened rectangular base and ball knop. The back of the stem is decorated with chevrons at the base followed by beading.
Date: Mid- to late 17th century.
Provenance: Billingsgate, September 1984
Comments: The changing profile of the stem is a characteristic feature of spoons made in the second half of the 17th century in the Netherlands, Germany and, to a lesser extent, Norway. However, the decoration is normally on the front.

TYPE 5, DESIGN 1

3.11 Spoon

Accession number: Enq. no. 1659/1; 98.2/25; 98.2/552*; 98.2/553; 98.2/554
Material: Lead alloy
Condition: Enq. no. 1659/1: complete. 98.2/25; 98.2/552: almost complete. 98.2/553; 98.2/554: bowls with base of stem
Dimensions: L 50mm; Diam (bowl) 16 x 14 mm
Inscription: DQ
Description: The faces of the deep round bowls are decorated with a five-petalled double rose and the calyx points extend beyond and between the outer row of petals. Each rose is contained within a plain circle. All have a stem of triangular section and there is a short rat's tail on the back of the bowl which is inscribed on either side with the letters D and Q. The stem on Enq. no. 1659/1 has a double baluster divided by a central knop and there are diagonal slashes at each end to represent a spiral twist. The stem terminates with a loop and small knop. The balusters have slashed mouldings to suggest lobes or fluting. The stems are only decorated on the front.
Date: Probably mid-17th century.
Comments: The most complete example of this type Enq. no. 1659/1 was recovered from Bull Wharf (3/10/01) and is now in a private collection.
Comparanda: A spoon with a similar stem is illustrated in Gask 1938, fig. VI but the spoon has a fig-shaped bowl and a wrythen knop and has been dated to *c.* 1500. Other examples have been recovered from the Thames foreshore but the tips of the stems have broken off.

TYPE 6, DESIGN 1

3.12 Spoon

Accession number: 98.2/555; 98.2/556*; 98.2/557
Material: Lead alloy
Condition: Bowls only
Dimensions: Diam 16mm
Description: All with deep round bowls decorated with a four-petalled double rose with calyx points extending beyond and between the outer row and enclosed within a plain circle. Part of the rim has faint cable decoration.
Date: Probably mid 17th century

TYPE 7, DESIGN 1

3.13 Spoon

Accession number: 98.2/560
Material: Lead alloy
Condition: Bowl and part of stem only
Dimensions: L 29mm; Diam (bowl) 18 x 12 mm
Description: A pointed oval bowl with flattened rectangular-sectioned stem. The stem is decorated on the front with two parallel rows of beading and joins the bowl with a truncated strap. The back of the bowl is decorated with a triad of pellets just below the end of the stem.
Date: Probably 18th century

TYPE 8, DESIGN 1

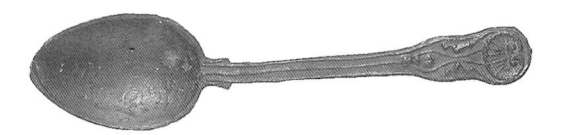

3.14 Spoon

Accession number: 98.2/559
Material: Lead alloy
Condition: Complete
Dimensions: L 69mm; L (stem) 45mm; Diam (bowl) 24 x 15 mm
Description: A pointed oval bowl with shouldered flat, splayed end stem. The stem is decorated on both sides with a debased classical column and the terminal is decorated with a scallop shell surrounded by mantling. The back is more simply decorated with longitudinal ribbing, which flares out to enclose a scallop shell. There is a truncated rat's tail on the back of the bowl, which is otherwise plain.
Date: Probably late 18th or early 19th century
Comments: Found in November 1984

TYPE 9, DESIGN 1

3.15 Spoon

Accession number: 98.2/558
Material: Lead alloy
Condition: Complete
Dimensions: L 26mm; L (stem) 18mm; Diam (bowl) 7 x 6 mm
Description: A tiny spoon with rounded oval bowl and a stem in the shape of an arrow. The flights are decorated with two rows of large pellets. The back is plain.
Date: Probably late 18th or 19th century
Comments: Found in March 1983

1   Fynes Moryson, *Itinerary* (London, 1617).
2   Coryat 1611, pp. 90–91.
3   Jonson 1616.
4   Baart *et al.* 1977, p. 466, cat. no. 885.
5   Hayward 1957, pp. 8–9.
6   Homer 1975, p. 3.
7   Willemsen 1998, p. 379, B79. Twenty-three examples have been recovered from 11 sites throughout the Low Countries from late 14th- to 17th-century contexts.
8   Holme 1688, p. 6.
9   Marquardt 1997, pp. 41 & 48, although here the decoration either covers the entire surface of the bowl or is confined to the area adjacent to the stem or around the bottom edge.
10 The rosette seems to be a favourite motif of this maker and all of the IQ and IDQ toys are highly decorative.
11 Jackson 1890, p. 139, figs 59–61; Marquardt 1997, p. 49, figs 126 & 129; p. 87, fig. 243; and p. 100, fig. 296.
12 Small-size infants' spoons or, as they were described in inventories, 'a little childs spoon' might have been used as playthings. See the lead-alloy spoon (L 99mm) described as a toy in Baart 1977, pp. 303–4, no. 578.

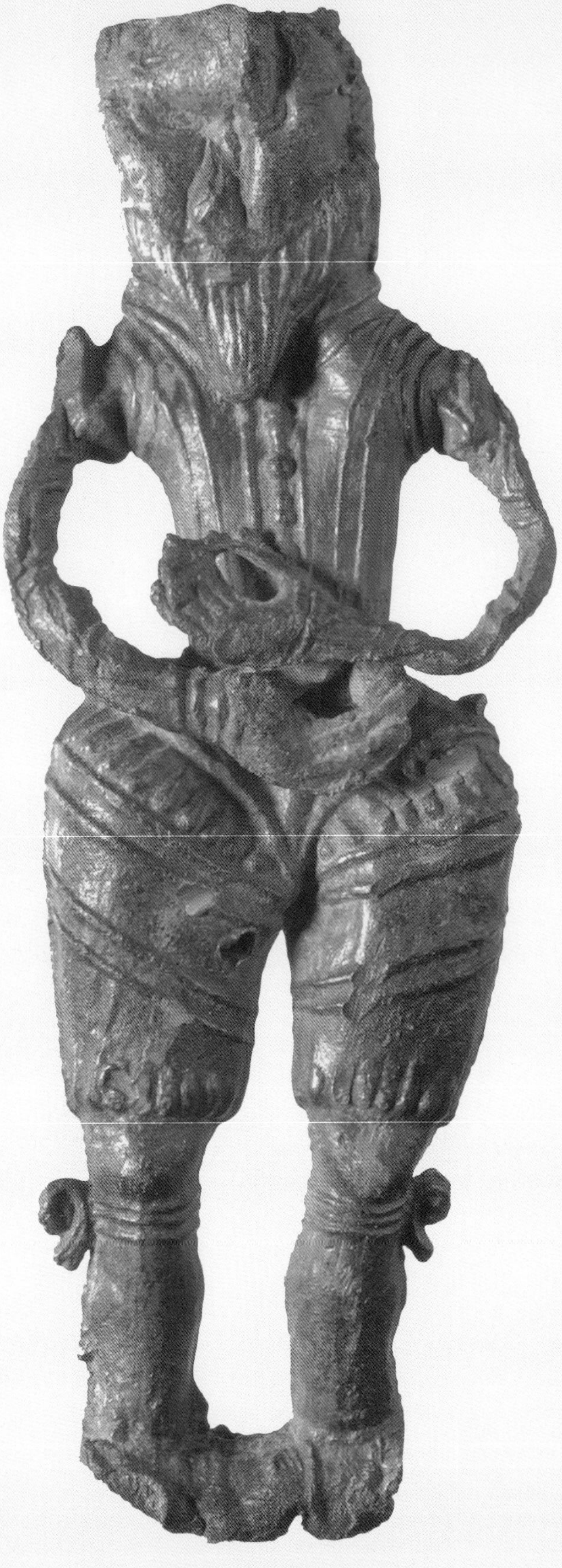

4 Figurines (GE)

'Each soldier was exactly like the rest; but one of them had been cast last of all, and there had not been enough tin to finish him; but he stood as firmly upon one leg as the others on their two...'[1]

Human figures have long been among the most obvious categories of playthings.[2] Both are known from the Roman period. The earliest post-Roman toy of this kind in England is a one-off peg-doll-like figure made from a red-deer antler and with a bearded face, dating from the late 12th century[3] – an isolated example of a tradition that is otherwise unrepresented here. There are a number of wooden figures, both men and women, of varied merit, from the late-medieval period on the Continent.[4] The complete absence of comparable items from England so far is surely an accident resulting from compounded factors of survival and retrieval in this country.

Apart from some enigmatic puppets' heads that may have fitted on wooden sticks (fig. 34, p. 142), the known lead-alloy figures for the medieval period – from the 14th to the early 16th century – are mounted knights (the absence of medieval female figurines is notable). The first two varieties represented, datable from about 1300 to the mid-14th century, are hollow-cast (see Cat. nos. 4.1–4.4).[5]

142 • TOYS, TRIFLES & TRINKETS

Details of the armour and weapons were kept up to date on subsequent versions of this toy. These are 'flats' or variations on this form, up to the time when the institution of chivalry itself ceased to be in the forefront of military affairs in the early 16th century, and toy knights fell out of favour, too.

From the late 16th century onwards individual standing human figures came to the fore in the repertoire of lead/tin playthings. As with many other goods, a successful toy went through several different versions, more or less competent according to the mould-maker. The best ones of the present category usually furnish considerable accurate detailing of the costume and any accessories. The

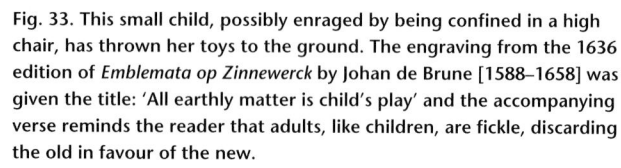

Fig. 33. This small child, possibly enraged by being confined in a high chair, has thrown her toys to the ground. The engraving from the 1636 edition of *Emblemata op Zinnewerck* by Johan de Brune [1588–1658] was given the title: 'All earthly matter is child's play' and the accompanying verse reminds the reader that adults, like children, are fickle, discarding the old in favour of the new.
Rijksmuseum, Amsterdam

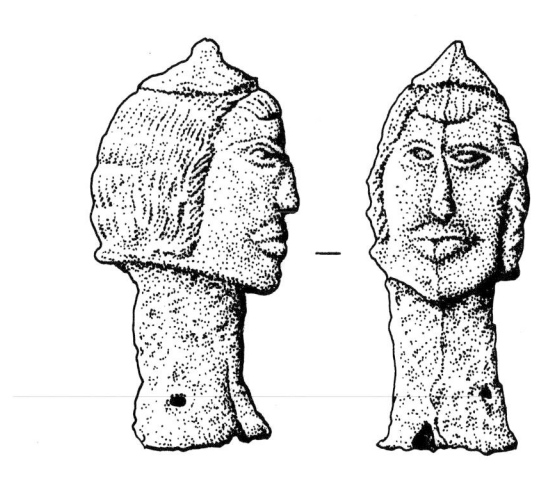

Fig. 34. Puppet head (?) with pointed Jewish hat, the *pileum cornutum*, possibly representing Judas Iscariot. Found at Billingsgate
Museum of London, Acc. no. 84.240/4

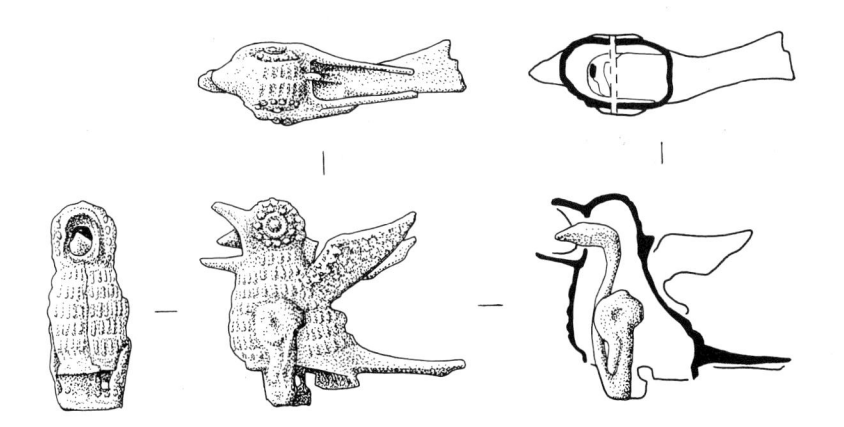

Fig. 35. A hollow-cast bird, possibly a fledgling, with moving parts which enabled the bird to bob and its tongue to go in and out. Found in 1983 from a late 13th- or early 14th-century deposit in the City Museum of London, Acc. no. BWB83[136]<285>

first of these were three-dimensional, hollow-cast females and males (not obviously military), Cat. nos. 4.13–4.17 and 4.26–4.30, probably based on expensive, carved wooden versions with accurately rendered textile clothing (fig. 38, p. 153). Several versions from a number of moulds are known, and both sexes also appear in very crude, flat versions (see Cat. no. 4.19) that have often turned up in rural areas in northern England. There are also several more accomplished flats, such as the female figurine Cat. no. 4.21. The three-dimensional male line seems to go on up to the version by IQ from the late 1630s or 1640s (Cat. nos. 4.31–4.32). Smaller, solid male figures from the early 17th century appear at present to be confined to militia, such as the pikeman Cat. no. 4.33. After the Restoration a new range of flats appears, both male and female, some of which seem to be based on the 'London Cries' tradition of interest in street hawkers.[6] Apart from a milkmaid, the game seller, and perhaps a singing-bird vendor (Cat. nos. 4.23, 4.37, 4.38, 4.42), identification is difficult, not least because the modellers appear not always to have focused on the defining wares as much as might have been expected (the same lack of immediate appeal can be claimed for the early 18th-century hunched male figure sitting in a chaise, of which three versions are known – see Transport, Cat. no. 10.13).

The series of soldier flats, which continues into the period of above-ground survivals by the end of the 1700s may begin in the late 17th century – possibly as early as the 1680s (Cat. no. 4.40). The collection includes some flats, including fragments, for which a close date is very difficult to assign – an eastern brigand (?), a possible Roman or Scotsman (Cat. nos. 4.39 & 4.47) and a couple of characterful heads, one male the other female.

A few of the items listed have been pierced, perhaps in attempts to hold them in place during play or display. This practice is manifest in various ways, ranging from the large holes in Cat. nos. 4.2 & 4.39 to the pinhole in Cat. no. 4.42. It also appears among the miniature vessels.

Animal figurines are very poorly represented throughout the period under consideration. This seems to be particularly noticeable in England, where the sole medieval representative of this category is a hollow-cast bird (fig. 35). This is uniquely sophisticated among the known toys from the Middle Ages in this country in that moving parts (in its original state) made it appear that the tongue was going in and out.[7] On the Continent, in contrast, there is a continuing tradition through the late medieval period and beyond particularly of ceramic horses (possibly to seat knights of other materials) and, less commonly, birds and other animals, from France right across to Russia and Hungary.[8]

Equestrian figures

There seems to be a development for medieval toy knights from the 14th to the 16th centuries.[9] The earliest examples are hollow-cast – a difficult technique – and later versions are folded, which was presumably easier to produce (Cat. no. 4.5). These early, medieval-tradition versions were followed by an apparent hiatus from the time when the institution of armoured, chivalric knighthood had declined in the mid-16th century, through to a revival in probably the late 17th century, when single- and (perhaps more commonly) double-sided soldier flats, both mounted and infantry, regained popularity for this basic boy's toy through to the present.

TYPE 1

Hollow-cast figurines.

TYPE 1, DESIGN 1

4.1 Mounted knight

Accession number: 98.2/404
Material: Lead alloy
Condition: Almost complete; the figure's left arm neatly cut off at the shoulder and any headwear missing; some reshaping since retrieval
Dimensions: H 53mm; L 40mm; W 16mm
Description: A free-standing, hollow-cast mounted knight. The panoply seems to include a mail hauberk with large, rounded scales (possibly curtailed at the lower end before loss) and long sleeves. He carries a sword upright in the right hand. Any helmet, along with whatever was in the left hand, is missing (there is a straight-edged opening where separate headgear may have been attached) but no sign of a sword belt, baldric or scabbard. The legs appear unprotected and the footwear has prick spurs. The face is not well registered but appears to be clean-shaven. Lines at the side and back of the head seem to represent wavy hair rather than a mail coif. The sword has a broad tapering, double-edged blade of lozenge section with a slightly rounded point; its short quillons incline towards the blade and the hilt terminates in a round pommel. The heavily built mount appears to be standing still. It has large ears with a full mane (including a prominent frontal fringe) and tail, and feathered fetlocks. The cross-hatched harness consists of a breast and crupper strap, and the saddle cloth is represented by two surviving wide bands and parts of a third, each with a series of slightly curving lines transversely.
Date: Late 13th– early 14th century; probably *c.* 1300 ('within ten years either side' according to the Royal Armouries when first found). The prick spurs and the absence of face or neck guards suggest a date up to the beginning of the 14th century, while the sword with its short grip, circular pommel and lozenge-sectioned blade seems to represent a type popular from the late 13th to late 15th century, although these generally have attenuated quillons.[10]
Provenance: Recovered from Billingsgate redevelopment spoil, 1983.
Comments: Without the helmet, confirmation of the close dating is difficult. This nevertheless seems to be the earliest three-dimensional toy knight known in England. Despite some infelicities, notably the head of the steed, this is a technically accomplished piece for the period, at the very beginning of a tradition of hollow-casting toy knights that lasts (with breaks) up to the present. The method of manufacture by hollow-casting is comparable with that of contemporary pilgrims' ampullae.[11] The object was acquired with the assistance of NACF.
Comparanda: The figure is broadly comparable with some 13th–14th-century lead-alloy knights found on the Continent.[12]

Fig. 36. In 1509 Matthäus Schwarz of Augsburg compiled an autobiographical costume book with 137 illustrated plates. This detail, perhaps a childhood memory, shows a little boy covered in spots and clearly unwell. The nurse fans him to keep him cool and tries to keep him amused with toy knights on horseback. See plate X, p. 362

TYPE 2

These hollow-cast figurines reflect developments in the military helmet between the late 13th and the mid-14th century, which have been traced by armour specialists, as well as in changing depictions of the knights attacking Thomas Becket on contemporary souvenir holy-water containers (also of lead alloy) from Canterbury and found in London. The flat-topped helmet is fashionable in the mid-13th century, possibly going out of favour in the late 13th century, and becoming conical or round-topped in the early 14th century.[13] Brooches in the form of a very similar knight and mount have also been found in London.[14] There are Continental finds of 'flat' versions of similar mounted knights from the Seine in Paris (now in the Musée de Cluny), another excavated from Amsterdam, and a third in the Meyers Collection, Brussels.[15] The similarities of design of Cat. nos. 4.2–4.4 suggest production in the same workshop.

TYPE 2, DESIGN 1

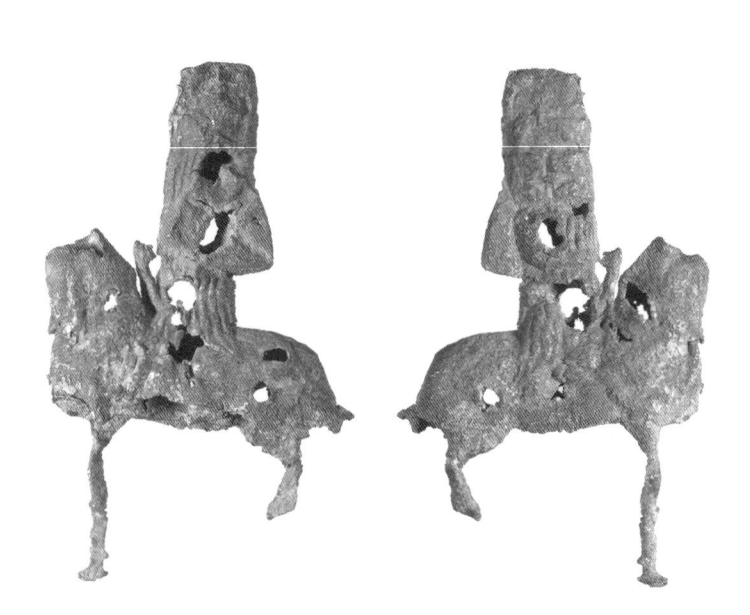

4.2 Mounted knight

Accession number: 98.2/405
Material: Lead alloy
Condition: Incomplete; corroded and crushed; two of the holes possibly result from having been nailed onto something
Dimensions: H 65mm; L 43mm; W 5mm
Description: Hollow-cast. The knight's panoply includes a flat-topped helm with eyesights, a square ailette, a small triangular shield and a pleated (perhaps padded), sleeveless surcoat (i.e. a military jupon) over a long-sleeved hauberk. The surcoat splits to hang either side of the high-cantled saddle and the rider's disproportionately small legs are not obviously protected apart from the piked footwear. A heraldic cross appears on both the shield and the ailette. Any sword or other weapons are missing. The horse is very damaged, with the head, tail and three legs missing. Since the rider's leg is set forward, the horse is being reined in – i.e. the ensemble is delineated moving quickly forward. Only a faint trace of the harness and trappings can be discerned.[16]
Date: Early 14th century
Comments: Parchment or leather ailettes, usually worn on both shoulders between 1300 and 1350, were emblazoned with the arms of the wearer.[17] The flat-topped great helm had appeared and the shield assumed a triangular shape with flat profile by the beginning of the 13th century.

TYPE 2, DESIGN 2

4.3 Mounted knight

Accession number: 98.2/407
Material: Lead alloy
Condition: Upper part of knight and horse's lower legs missing
Dimensions: H 42mm; W 52mm
Description: A hollow-cast mounted knight (top half of body missing) with calf-length pleated surcoat, piked footwear and unprotected legs. The horse has a strangely proportioned body, with very long ears, short head and wide neck. The harness includes a headstrap, cheekstrap, reins, girth strap, breastband and crupper strap and these are embellished with pendant trappings. A small hole (not visible when the plaything is upright) under the front legs probably served to let gases escape during manufacture.[18]
Date: Early 14th century

TYPE 2, DESIGN 3

4.4 Mounted knight

Accession number: 98.2/406
Material: Lead alloy
Condition: Upper part of knight only
Dimensions: H 33mm; W 22mm
Description: The upper part of a hollow-cast knight. The panoply includes the helm, which in this instance had been adapted prior to discarding by secondary cutting to make a conical top. The rider also has a pleated surcoat over a long-sleeved hauberk and a shield. The right hand probably held a sword (now missing). Both the ailette and shield bear a cross on a cross-hatched field. The cross-hatched saddle has a high pommel and cantle.[19]
Date: Possibly mid-14th century
Comparandum: An excavated fragment, perhaps of a similar toy from a different mould, comprising the horse's front legs and fore quarters with cross-hatched saddlecloth; the legs and feet of the rider are separated in this version from the steed as openwork.[20]

TYPE 3

Cast in three-part mould and then folded.

TYPE 3, DESIGN 1

4.5 Mounted knight

Accession number: 98.2/408; 98.2/409*
Material: Lead alloy
Condition: 98.2/408: upper part of horse and legs of rider only. 98.2/409: slightly more complete; horse's tail missing; legs only of rider
Dimensions: H 51mm; W 50mm
Description: Two identical mounted figures, cast from a mould of three parts as a basically inverted T-shaped product. Subsequent downward folding along the casting seam formed the spine of the horse and two matching, flattish sides. The horse's head and presumably the rider's missing body comprised a single sheet, detailed on both sides. Cast directly onto the horse's body is the lower half of the rider (rather small in comparison with his steed), who wears a fluted 'gothic' armour skirt (tonlet) with an undulating lower edge, breeches and stockings. The horse has a loose mane with feathered fetlocks and shod feet (with prominent nailing); the harness includes a headstall, chequered strap, noseband, reins, girth strap, strap for the stirrups, breastband, breechband and hip straps; the latter two bands are adorned with pendent roundels.[21]
Date: Tonlet skirt suggests a date of 1510–20.

Fig. 37. Souvenir fan design (detail) showing the attractions and diversions of St Bartholomew Fair about 1730. The fair was famed for its trinket stalls, and this detail is the only English depiction of a toy booth. A wide range of toys are offered for sale, including dolls, whistles, trumpets, hobby-horses, beads, windmills, rattles, bows and arrows, doll's furniture and toy watches. See plate V, p. 165

TYPE 4

Flat-cast, with detailing on one side only. There is one medieval example of this type, and three much later designs. Although rare survivals and pictorial representations of military dress and equipment give a good idea of provision and fashions at the time of the Civil War, the 18th century is in general not as well served. The late series of figures below may well start in the late 17th century. Both infantry and mounted troops are included. While it is likely that most of the items listed here represent English soldiers, there is a possibility that some could be intended for Continental troops for particular war games and set-piece restagings of actual events, particularly if the owners were grown-ups with military connections. A few of the figurines on foot are not readily distinguishable from hunters – though these seem an unlikely subject for a toy at such an early date.[22]

TYPE 4, DESIGN 1

4.6 Mounted figure

Accession number: 98.2/427
Material: Lead alloy
Condition: Fragment of front of mount
Dimensions: H 20mm; W 17mm
Description: Fragment consisting of the head, neck and shoulders of a horse, profile to left, with the rider's armoured leg having a long-necked rowel spur on the armoured shoe, which has an elongated point. A drawn sword pointing forwards and downwards is wielded by the armoured rider's gauntlet; the lower part of the blade may be tangled with a strap-like object (unless this is the horse's foreleg and the mould-cutter's inspiration lapsed at this point) – i.e. the rider may have been striking an adversary in front of him. If the fragment is part of a pilgrim badge for St George, this would be a dragon – a suitably remarkable encounter to draw the steed's attention. This item would be the earliest plaything to incorporate an adversary along with the main character.
Date: Probably 1470s–80s from details of the footwear
Comments: A pilgrim badge or plaything (?)

TYPE 4, DESIGN 2

4.7 Mounted soldier: dragoon (?)

Accession number: 98.2/413
Material: Lead alloy; red pigment
Condition: Almost complete; head and lower part of horse's feet missing
Dimensions: H 52mm; W 53mm
Description: A flat-cast mounted figure, profile to right, wearing a long-sleeved coat with deep upturned cuffs, breeches, thigh-length riding boots and rowel spurs. He holds a musket in the right hand and slung from the saddle pommel is a pouch, costrel or powder flask and a pistol in its holster. The saddle flap is decorated with diagonal hatching and the position of the horse's legs suggest movement.
Date: Probably 18th century

TYPE 4, DESIGN 3

4.8 Mounted figure: dragoon (?)

Accession number: 98.2/414
Material: Lead alloy; red pigment
Condition: Almost complete; upper half of rider and lower part of horse's foreleg missing
Dimensions: H 60mm; W 43mm
Description: The rider wears a cloak or full pleated coat with thigh-length riding boots. He holds a sword and there is an empty pistol holder suspended from the saddle. The horse, profile right, has reins but no other harness, and the legs are attached to a thin bar or stand with an additional reinforcing strut from the stirrup.
Date: Possibly 18th century

TYPE 5

Flat with mouldings on both sides.

TYPE 5, DESIGN 1

TYPE 5, DESIGN 2

4.9 Mounted British Light Dragoon

Accession number: 84.18
Material: Lead alloy; red pigment
Condition: Almost complete; rider's arm and horse's back legs missing
Dimensions: H 40mm; W 28mm
Description: The rider is seated on a cantering horse and wears a plumed, cocked hat, thigh-length jacket with buttoned front and belt, tight breeches to the knee and riding boots. The upper part of his right arm is bent back and the forearm is missing. The angle of the arm suggests that the figure was brandishing a sabre, the scabbard of which is shown hanging from his left hip. Pistol holsters and/or powder bags hang from the saddle in front of the rider on both sides. The horse's harness includes a headstall, noseband, reins, stirrup, breast and breech bands and the saddle cloth has a beaded border. Behind the rider is a saddle roll (?). Red paint survives on the saddle cloth on one face. [23]
Date: 17th century, possibly Civil War period
Comment: Only equestrian military figure assignable to this time

4.10 Mounted soldier

Accession number: 98.2/410
Material: Lead alloy; red pigment
Condition: Most of rider and front legs and tail of horse missing
Dimensions: H 38mm; W 46mm
Description: Only the rider's looped-up coat, turned-back cuff, hand and lower legs survive. He wears riding boots with spurs and holds a sword in his right hand and the scabbard hangs from his left hip. Mouldings suggestive of pistol holsters are visible on both sides of a blob of solder, which presumably made good a bubble hole from the casting. The large saddle cloth has foliation within its ornate border. The harness consists of a headstall, cheekstrap, noseband, reins, girth strap and crupper strap. The back legs are bent, suggesting movement, perhaps a canter. Red paint survives on the coat-tails. The missing part of the rider has been neatly cut off (to smooth a ragged break, perhaps), probably along with the tip of the sword. [24]
Date: Probably late 18th century

TYPE 5, DESIGN 3

4.11 Mounted figure: dragoon (?)

Accession number: 98.2/412
Material: Lead alloy; red pigment
Condition: Fragment only; much worn
Dimensions: H 33mm; W 28mm
Description: The rider seems to be equipped with a baldric, belt, sword and musket but the rest of his clothing is indistinct. Only the neck and withers of the horse survive and the harness includes the reins and a breastband.
Date: Possibly 18th century

TYPE 5, DESIGN 4

4.12 Mounted figure

Accession number: 98.2/411
Material: Lead alloy; red pigment
Condition: Almost complete; rider's head and lower part of horse's legs missing
Dimensions: H 32mm; W 29mm
Description: The rider is seated on a cantering horse and his posture and the moulding of his uniform suggest rapid movement. He wears an unbuttoned knee-length long-sleeved coat with shoulder epaulettes, tight-fitting breeches and riding boots. There is a gorget or lace ruff at his neck and he wears a sword belt and sash. Both hands clutch the reins and his sword hangs from the saddle on the left side. The horse's harness includes a headstall, cheekband, noseband, breastband and crupper strap and there is a large plain saddle cloth.
Date: Probably 18th or 19th century
Comments: Possibly depicts a fairly high ranking officer

Female figures

TYPE 1

At least four variants of mid- to late-16th-century, three-dimensional, hollow-cast standing women are represented in the listing below, though none has been recorded outside London. A comparable hollow figure of a different design is known, found in rural Norfolk; this is a headless fragment of a crudely cast lead female figure wearing a pleated skirt and padded sleeves, possibly late 16th-century (H 56mm; W 38mm).[25] A 'baby of pewter' noted in the possession of a woman (midget?) at the court of Elizabeth I in 1562 could be analogous.[26]

Similar ceramic figurines are attested across Europe.[27] This may be the form in which these popular toys came from the Continent to this country. A reference in 1568 notes the import to London of 'babies' valued for customs rates at almost one shilling and eight pence each on a ship from Bruges.[28] These very expensive ones must have been much more elaborate than those rated at six shillings and eight pence per gross in a handbook of customs duties in 1582 and 1609 (?),[29] which in turn are likely to have been superior to the present versions. In the complete absence of comparable pewter female figures or fragments from extensive investigations in the Low Countries, these distinctive pewter playthings may well, despite their Continental fashions, have been made in England.

The recurrent characteristics of the series are a full-length, hollow-cast figure, a tight French hood with central frontal jewel covering the hair; a heavily pleated, full-length skirt (covering the feet) open at the front to reveal an ornately patterned kirtle or apron with pendent tassel or sweetmeat bag; solid arms held out at the sides, with slashed and puffed shoulders and tight, full-length paned sleeves. The stance of Cat. no. 4.13 looks as if it was original. Only one hand (on Cat. no. 4.14) survives among all the females. The hands on some of the range of equivalent males (below) are, like this one, attached at the sides, while others have loops here, which in at least one instance look as if strings etc passing through have given some wear in this area. It is possible that slightly more expensive versions of both sexes were provided with loops so that they could, for example, be waddled across a tabletop between two players facing each other.

There are presumably companion pieces to the male figurines (Cat. nos. 4.26–4.30). These present ones would presumably have been for girls while the latter were for boys.

TYPE 1, DESIGN 1

4.13 Female figure

Accession number: 98.2/433
Material: Lead alloy
Condition: Almost complete; left hand and lower right arm missing; broken in two at the waist when found, now soldered together
Dimensions: H 81mm; W 36mm
Description: A hollow-cast, full-length, female figure with the arms held unnaturally out and stiffly down at the sides. Made from a three-part mould. The hair is covered by a heart-shaped French hood or caul with lines of pellets between vertical lines running from the nape of the neck to the top of the head, suggesting jewel ornaments. A central, V-shaped flap on the forehead possibly represents a *bongrace* (shade to protect the complexion) or jewel. The buttoned partlet has a V-neck with short, standing collar and the bodice is laced at the back. The bell-shaped, heavily pleated skirt opens at the front to reveal a kirtle or apron decorated with diagonally hatched horizontal bands around patterned (embroidered) panels. There are large, slashed puffs at the shoulder, and the horizontally banded, paned sleeves are tight-fitting down to the wrist. A chain or decorative cord hangs from the waist, terminating in either a pleated sweetbag or a tassel.
Date: Mid- to late 16th century (?)
Provenance: Thames foreshore, October 1983
Comments: It is unclear whether the upper garment is a partlet or a doublet and so it is impossible to determine whether the puffs on the shoulder are part of the sleeve or padded rolls on the shoulder of a

Fig. 38. In 1632, Jacob Cats [1577–1660] used this engraving of a toy stall to illustrate the emblem 'Schoon voor-doen is half verkocht' (Well set out is half sold). The accompanying verse instructs the reader in the arts of wooing.
Anonymous artist after Adriaen van de Venne published in *Spiegel van den ouden ende niieuwen tijdt*, Hague, 1632
Rijksmuseum, Amsterdam

doublet. It is also difficult to tell whether the standing collar is part of the partlet/doublet or the chemise underneath. The general style of dress, however, and in particular the shape of the sleeve, the style of the partlet and the horizontal bands on the kirtle/apron point to German and Swiss fashions around the area of Frankfurt, Cologne and Geneva during the mid- to late 16th century.[30] Acquired with the assistance of NACF

Comparanda: Those from different moulds listed below, and an almost complete example found at Bull Wharf[31]

TYPE 1, DESIGN 2

4.14 Female figure

Accession number: 90.2/131
Material: Lead alloy
Condition: Head and one arm missing; slightly crushed and damaged
Dimensions: H 60mm; W 27mm
Description: A full-length three-dimensional female figure, hollow cast in one piece. The arms (one missing) are solid. The V-necked partlet or doublet opens at the front and the bodice appears to be laced at the back. The conical pleated skirt opens at the front to reveal a kirtle ornamented with cross-hatched horizontal bands edged with pellets. A girdle hangs from the waist and terminates in a tassel (?). There are tight puffs at the shoulder and tight-fitting sleeves to the wrist. The surviving arm is extremely thin and curves round so that the hand joins the hip.
Date: Mid- to late 16th century
Comments: A cruder version of Cat. no. 4.13, but almost certainly from the same source and of similar date

TYPE 1, DESIGN 3

4.15 Female figure

Accession number: 80.244/9
Material: Lead alloy
Condition: Skirt only; damaged and crushed flat
Dimensions: H 45mm; W 35mm
Description: Part of a hollow-cast three-dimensional female figure. Now flattened, the originally bell-shaped, pleated skirt opens at the front to reveal a kirtle or apron decorated with diagonally hatched, horizontal bands interspersed with pellets and swirls. A chatelaine or girdle hangs from the waist, terminating in a pleated sweetbag or tassel.
Date: Mid- to late 16th century
Comments: Almost identical pattern to Cat. nos. 4.13 and 4.14, but from a different-sized mould

TYPE 1, DESIGN 4

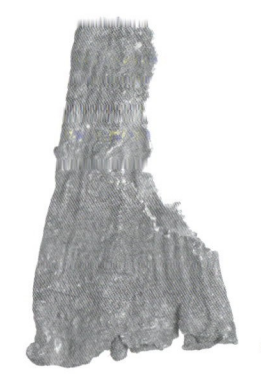

4.16 Female figure

Accession number: 81.35/3
Material: Lead alloy
Condition: Part of skirt only; damaged and crushed flat
Dimensions: H 47mm; W 30mm

Description: Part of a hollow-cast three-dimensional female figure. The now flattened, but cone-shaped pleated skirt opens at the front to reveal a kirtle or apron decorated with diagonally hatched horizontal bands interspersed with pellets and swirls. A chatelaine or girdle hangs from the waist and terminates in a pleated sweetbag or tassel.
Date: Mid- to late 16th century
Comments: Similar to Cat. no. 4.15, but from a different-sized mould

TYPE 1, DESIGN 5

4.17 Female figure

Accession number: 98.2/435
Material: Lead alloy
Condition: Head only
Dimensions: H 20mm; W 18mm
Description: Head of a hollow-cast three-dimensional female figure, possibly associated with Cat. no. 4.13. The slightly crested hair is pushed under a heart-shaped French hood (caul) adorned with curving lines and pellets. Circular moulding or hair ornament on the brow line.
Date: Mid- to late 16th century

TYPE 2

Two-sided flat figures.

TYPE 2, DESIGN 1

4.18 Female figure

Accession number: 98.2/436
Material: Lead alloy
Condition: Head only
Dimensions: H 16mm; W 14mm
Description: A relatively crude, two-sided female head, cast from a two-part mould, with earrings and combed or built-out hair (delineated by vertical lines at the back) possibly under a headdress.
Date: 16th century[32]
Provenance: Dockhead

TYPE 2, DESIGN 2

4.19 Female figure

Accession number: 98.2/391
Material: Lead alloy
Condition: Torso and arms only; poor and damaged
Dimensions: H 25mm; W 30mm
Description: An extremely crudely detailed, solid, two-sided female (?) torso with similar hatched ornament on the front and back. The short upper garment is decorated with diagonal lines and the arms are looped round so that the hands rest on the waist. The sex is inferred from a pair of pellets on the chest on one side.
Date: Late 16th–17th century
Provenance: Found by Southwark Bridge
Comparanda: This is the only fragment known from London or any other town comparable to an extensive series of flat figures otherwise from rural areas (mainly but not exclusively female). They have a marked concentration around Whitby in Yorkshire.[33] The roughness of these figures makes them extremely difficult to date accurately. They may be seen as much cheaper versions of the hollow three-dimensional figures, continuing probably from the late 16th into the mid- or late 17th century.

TYPE 2, DESIGN 3

4.20 Female figure

Accession number: 81.542/2
Material: Lead alloy
Condition: Lower half only; one foot missing
Dimensions: H 46mm; W 25mm
Description: The lower half of a flat, two-sided, full-length female figure with similar detailing on the back and front. There is a prominent radiating ornament (?) at the waist and her skirt is swagged, flounced and adorned with ribbons (?). There is a wide decorative band near the hem. Only one foot survives, the shoe having a pronounced heel and a broad strap or rectangular buckle.
Date: Probably 1820s
Comments: The foot points downwards – this stance appears to be original despite damage here. Along with the ornate dress, it suggests a dancing figure.

TYPE 3

One-sided flat figures.

TYPE 3, DESIGN 1

4.21 Female figure

Accession number: 82.353/1*; 98.2/437
Material: Lead alloy
Condition: 82.353/1: head, arms and torso only. 98.2/437: head only
Dimensions: H 42mm; W 34mm
Description: The upper part of a one-sided, flat-cast (originally full-length?) female figure with high, bushy hair parted in the centre. The high, stiffened, fan-shaped collar or ruff has a scalloped edge and the gown has a low, square décolletage. The bodice extends to a point below the natural waistline and there is a central panel of foliate decoration flanked by fine cross-hatching. The elaborately decorated sleeves taper to the wrist and the turned-back lace cuffs have a scalloped edge. The rich dress is embellished with beads or jewels, and the lady wears a necklace, chain (?) and earring. She holds an accessory in one hand, which could be the upper part of a folding fan.
Date: This accomplished figure represents an affluent lady of 1590–1610.[34] A square neckline and long stomacher were both fashionable then.[35]
Provenance: 98.2/437: Dockhead

TYPE 3, DESIGN 2

4.22 Female figure

Accession number: 81.231/2
Material: Lead alloy
Condition: Lower half and base only
Dimensions: H 37mm; W 24mm
Description: The lower part of a one-sided female figure on an elongated hexagonal flat base. Only the outer edge of the ankle-length skirt is visible and this is decorated with a pattern of crosses. The large, pleated apron and deep hem are represented by perfunctory lines. The lower part of the stomacher survives.
Date: Perhaps 1640s[36]

Fig. 39. Portrait of a girl with a doll by Johan van der Veer, 1591. Thousands of dolls ('babies') were imported into London during the 15th and 16th centuries. Some were expensively dressed like this doll in textile clothes which accurately reflect adult fashions.
Fries Museum, Leeuwarden, The Netherlands

TYPE 3, DESIGN 3

TYPE 3, DESIGN 4

TYPE 3, DESIGN 5

4.23 Milkmaid

Accession number: 98.2/439
Material: Lead alloy
Condition: Almost complete; base missing
Dimensions: H 43mm; W 36mm
Description: A one-sided flat figure depicting a milkmaid. She carries two pails on a yoke and both arms are outstretched to guide and support the buckets. Her hair is completely hidden by her hood and a flat-crowned, broad-brimmed hat. She wears a chemise with rolled-up sleeves and a tightly laced bodice. A pleated apron covers most of her ankle-length, flounced skirt and she wears pattens over her shoes. This figure seems to have been supported by a rod between her feet (a stub remains, probably once attached to a flat base).
Date: Probably late 17th century
Comments: Milkmaids traditionally danced in the streets of London on the First of May.[37] Apart from the hat, the costume is similar to that worn by a Dutch milkmaid in a painting dating to the the 1620s.[38]

4.24 Female figure

Accession number: 86.144/1
Material: Lead alloy
Condition: Almost complete; head missing; broken off at feet and end of left arm
Dimensions: H 56mm; W 33mm
Description: Part of a relatively simply detailed, one-sided, full-length female figure (head, hand and feet missing). The shoulders and arms are plain and there is a cuff around the wrist of the better preserved arm. She wears a stiff, low-cut straight bodice and the heavily pleated, ankle-length skirt is gathered at the waist. The right arm crosses the body and the left one (damaged) curves outwards at the elbow. She holds a long rod (?) or tube in her right hand.
Date: 17th century (?) or later (the long sleeves might suggest an early date in the 1600s)
Comments: The object in her hand could be a tape or yard,[39] but is perhaps more likely to be a flute of some sort.

4.25 Female figure

Accession number: 98.2/440
Material: Lead alloy; red paint (?)
Condition: Almost complete; arms missing
Dimensions: H 68mm; W 20mm
Description: A full-length, relatively crudely detailed, one-sided flat-cast female figure with flat-crowned, narrow-brimmed hat, laced bodice, exaggeratedly narrow waist and full, ankle-length pleated skirt decorated with hatched and wavy lines.
Date: 17th – mid-18th century

Male figures

TYPE 1

Three-dimensional hollow-cast figurines, which again are completely unknown in Britain outside London. At least four designs are present among the listed items. Cat. nos. 4.26 and 4.28 have looped arms, while Cat. no. 4.27 does not.

TYPE 1, DESIGN 1

4.26 Male figure

Accession number: 85.586*; 96.1; 98.2/368; 98.2/369; 98.2/370; 98.2/371; 98.2/373; 98.2/374; 98.2/375
Material: Lead alloy
Condition: 85.586: complete. 98.2/368: arms missing. 98.2/369; 98.2/370: heads missing. 98.2/371: lower half of body only. 96.1: hat, head and trunk. 98.2/373; 98.2/374: head and trunk. 98.2/375: left leg only

Dimensions: 98.2/368: H 79mm
 85.586 (complete): H 70mm (also 96.1; 98.2/369; 98.2/370; 98.2/371; 98.2/373; 98.2/374; 98.2/375)
Description: These full-length, hollow-cast male figures in doublet and trunk hose are made from two-part moulds. Although the designs are almost identical, the figures seem to have been produced in at least two sizes. The most complete (Acc. nos. 85.586 & 98.2/368; also 98.2/374) have a straight-edged aperture at the top of the head to which the separately cast hat was soldered (see Cat. nos. 4.50 and 1.1). The hat may be of morion form (Cat. no. 1.1). There is a little hair around the temples and the figures have a curled-up moustache and goatee beard. Faint vertical lines suggest hair on the back of the head. It is not clear whether the buttoned upper garment is meant to represent a doublet or a sleeveless jerkin with a doublet underneath. The prominent mouldings on the shoulder could be interpreted as either the wings of a jerkin or the pads on a doublet. This garment has a short skirt, which tapers to a point at the centre front and back. The vertical panels on the chest and back, and the horizontal and vertical mouldings on the arms, are clearly designed to represent the contemporary fashion for braided, paned, slashed and padded textiles or pinked leather. Only Acc. no. 85.586 has arms and hands, and these are bent across the body (as found). The tip of the thumb is joined to the index finger to form a loop, and there are tabs on each hip. There is a small codpiece and the pear-shaped breeches stop just above the knee. The breeches are decorated with short and long diagonal lines to suggest paning, and vertical mouldings at the bottom represent a pickadil edge (i.e. prominent fringe). Ribboned garters support the hose or stockings and the figures are apparently without feet. Instead, they are supported on a flat (85.586; 98.2/369; 98.2/370; 98.2/375) or perhaps curved base (85.586). Both 96.1 and 98.2/374 have a loop from the left shoulder to the neck. The ornate, incomplete stand on 98.2/371 is tripartite (originally cruciform?) with three points on each part.
Date: Style of clothing suggests a date of 1545–60 or later.
Comments: The clothing is probably Continental in origin, perhaps German, but the figures are likely to be English.

TYPE 1, DESIGN 2

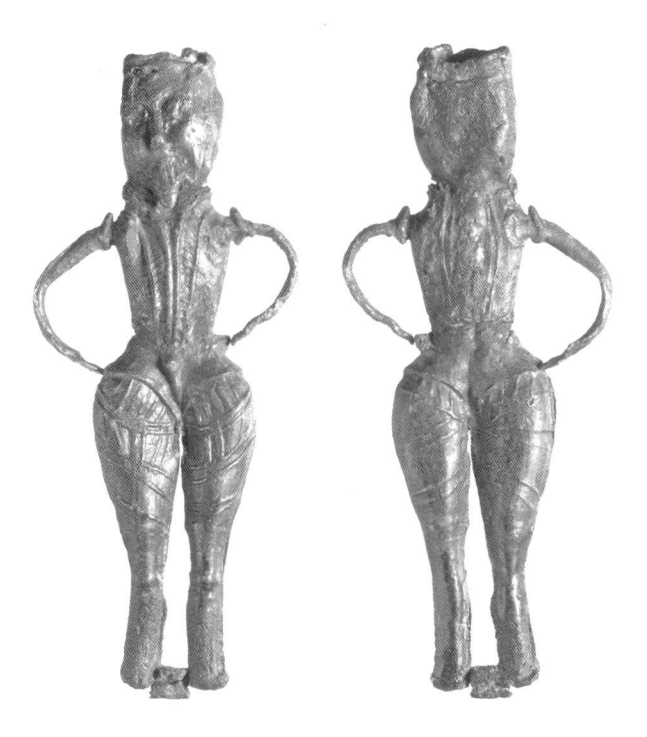

TYPE 1, DESIGN 3

4.27 Male figure

Accession number: 98.2/367
Material: Lead alloy
Condition: Almost complete; hat and part of stand missing
Dimensions: H 87mm; W 40mm
Description: A hollow-cast full-length male figure in doublet and trunk hose. There is a wide aperture at the top of the head to which a hat (now missing) was soldered. The face is slightly crushed and the figurine has a goatee beard without a moustache. There are no hair mouldings on the back of the head. The collar of the upper garment has a curved neck edge and centre front opening, flanked by panels of diagonal hatching and the semi-circular arm-hole mouldings on the back seem to indicate a sleeveless jerkin over a doublet. The jerkin skirt tapers to a long point at the centre front and back and there is a fairly prominent codpiece. The unrealistically thin, perfunctorily detailed arms curve round so that the 'hands' rest on the waist. The pear-shaped breeches are decorated with diagonal panels and vertical hatching to represent paned, slashed or braided textiles, and they are gathered just above the knee. There are no garters. The figure is truncated at the ankles. An arched plate between the ankles is presumably the distorted remains of a stand.
Date: 1550–60
Comments: A cruder version of Cat. no. 4.26, lacking hand loops. Acquired with the assistance of NACF

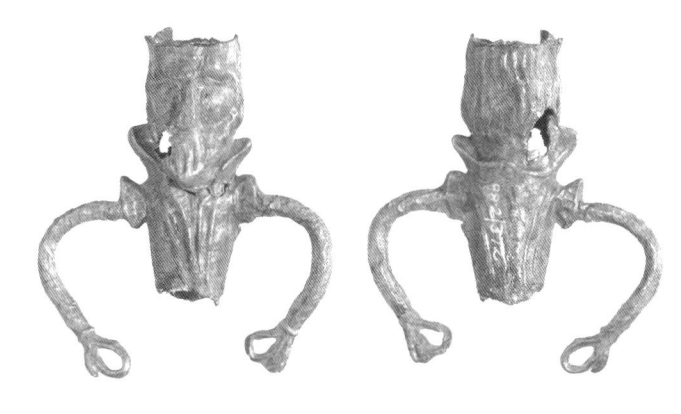

4.28 Male figure

Accession number: 98.2/372
Material: Lead alloy
Condition: Head, trunk and arms only (arms repositioned after discovery, and now restored to what is suggested to be their original configuration)
Dimensions: H 35mm; W 41mm
Description: Part of a hollow-cast male figure with straight-edged aperture at the top of the head to which a hat (now missing) was soldered. Only the upper part of the trunk survives. The figure has a pointed beard, with wavy hair mouldings on the back of the head. Since the upper garment has a high standing collar with a curving neck edge and open centre front, it probably represents a sleeveless jerkin over a doublet. The wings have mouldings suggestive of pickadil decoration. The arms, of flattened oval section, are thin and plain, terminating in crudely moulded loops.
Date: 1550–60
Comments: Similar to Cat. nos. 4.26 and 4.27. Possibly associated with trunk hose fragment Cat. no. 4.30

TYPE 1, DESIGN 4

4.29 Male figure

Accession number: 98.2/377
Material: Lead alloy
Condition: Flattened and damaged
Dimensions: H 22mm; W 18mm
Description: A head from a hollow-cast male figurine with straight-edged aperture at the top, to which a hat (now missing) was originally soldered. The figure has a thin, curling moustache and goatee beard, and linear mouldings on the back of the head represent hair.
Date: 1550–60
Comments: Seems to be a different mould from Cat. nos. 4.26–4.28

TYPE 1, DESIGN 5

4.30 Male figure

Accession number: 98.2/376
Material: Lead alloy
Condition: Fragment: leg (?)
Dimensions: H 32mm; W 15mm
Description: The left (?) upper leg from a hollow-cast full-length male figurine. Part of the pointed skirt survives and the tight-fitting, pear-shaped breeches taper to the knee. The bottom of the trunk hose is gathered in and there are mouldings to suggest a ribboned garter. The breeches are decorated with vertical ribbing composed of lines, diagonal hatching and pellets to suggest a paned, braided or padded garment. Vertical mouldings around the bottom hem seem to represent a pickadil edge. This fragment is more finely detailed than the preceding items, but there is enough in common to suggest they are all the same basic plaything.
Date: 1550–60

Plate I. A miniature lead-alloy tripod ewer alongside a full-sized version made in London-type ware in the mid-12th century.
Museum of London, Acc. no. C676, H 275mm
Miniature, Acc. no. 98.2/161, Cat. no. 8.113

Plate II. Silver-gilt pair-cased verge watch with pierced and engraved case and champlevé dial. Signed 'Rodet London', but possibly manufactured in Switzerland c. 1710. Shown alongside toy watch of similar date and style by HUX LONDON
Museum of London, Acc. no. 34.181/47, Diam 51.8mm
Miniature, Acc. no. 98.2/442, Cat. no. 12.43

TOYS, TRIFLES & TRINKETS • *163*

Plate III. A battered lead-alloy miniature cauldron without legs has a similar profile to this full-sized copper vessel made in the Sturton foundry, Somerset in the 17th or early 18th century.
Museum of London, Acc. no. 10119
Miniature, Acc. no. 98.2/198, Cat. no. 211

Plate IV. All of the toy muskets have the standard fishtail-shaped butts of their full-scale counterparts and date from the late 16th to mid-17th century. Several of the miniatures have exploded barrels indicating that they were actually fired.

Museum of London, matchlock musket, Acc. no. 76.131; powder flask, Acc. no. C2327
Miniature, Acc. no. A13941, Cat. no. 1.23

TOYS, TRIFLES & TRINKETS • *165*

Plate V. Detail from a fan design depicting one of the most popular London fairs, St Bartholomew's, held annually in Smithfield during August. Jostling for space alongside the booths selling snacks and drinks were the trinket stalls selling a wide range of knick-knacks and toys. Many of the base-metal miniatures in this collection were probably sold in fairs of this kind.

Coloured etching and aquatint, 355 x 535 mm
Museum of London, Acc. no. A6861

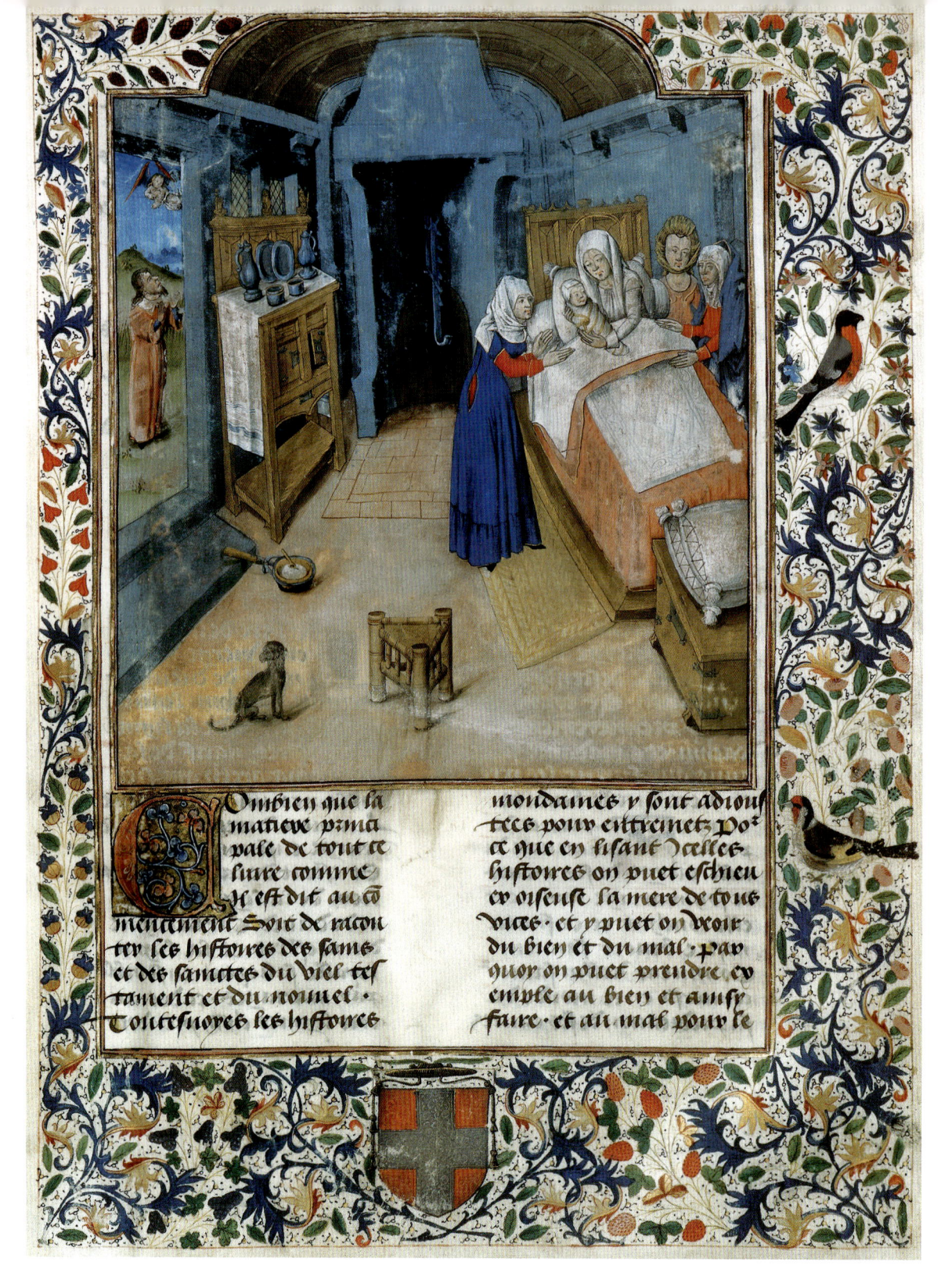

Plate VI. Many of the objects in this scene have miniature equivalents in base metal.
From the 15th-century manuscript *La Fleur des histoires* by Jean Mansel [c. 1400–c. 1474]
Bibliothèque nationale de France, Paris, MS français 297, fol. 1

Plate VII. The buffet depicted in the *Roman de Renaud de Montauban* in the late 15th century has a single-stage high back and arched canopy like some of the three-dimensional miniature cupboards from London.

Bibliothèque de l'Arsenal, MS 5073, fol.148; reproduced in Paul Lacroix, *Moeurs, Usages et Costumes au Moyen Age et à l'époque de la Renaissance* (Paris, 1873)

168 • TOYS, TRIFLES & TRINKETS

Plate VIII. A number of three-dimensional toy carriages not unlike the vehicle shown here have been found on the Thames foreshore. From *La Chasse des Dames*, after a miniature in the late 15th-century manuscript *Epîtres d'Ovide* Bibliothèque nationale de France, Paris, MS 7231; reproduced in Paul Lacroix, *Moeurs, Usages et Costumes au Moyen Age et à l'époque de la Renaissance* (Paris 1873)

FIGURINES • 169

TYPE 1, DESIGN 6

4.31 Male figure

Accession number: 2001.21/5
Material: Lead alloy
Condition: Fragment: damaged base with feet only
Dimensions: H 29mm; W 23mm
Inscription: IQ
Description: Oval, flat base with cross-hatching, retaining two shoes that are neatly laced with the letters IQ behind. The base is similar to a stand supporting a three-dimensional figure from the Netherlands, which also bears the mark of the maker I(D)Q (fig. 40).[40]
Date: Possibly 1640s
Comparandum: It is possible that this style of figure represents a transitional form between Cat. nos. 4.26–4.30 and a more substantial figurine wearing a combed morion in the Musée de Cluny in Paris.[41]

TYPE 1, DESIGN 7

4.32 Male figure

Accession number: 98.2/72
Material: Lead alloy
Condition: Fragment: base with feet only
Dimensions: H 30m; W 7mm
Inscription: 1644
Description: From a three-dimensional figure (now missing). Half-oval base with oblique hatching, lobe and pellet edge outside corded border and a pair of shoes (laced like those in the preceding item)
Date: 1644
Comments: Presumably a later version of Cat. no. 4.31 and (from the date) probably made by I(D)Q too

TYPE 2

This type comprises three-dimensional solid-castings.

TYPE 2, DESIGN 1

4.33 Male figure

Accession number: 98.2/400
Material: Lead alloy
Condition: Almost complete
Dimensions: H 42mm; W 24mm
Description: A full-length, solid figure in the form of a pikeman from a two-part mould. He wears the pikeman's armour of helmet, gorget, backplate, breastplate and tassets and stands in the recognizable drill position known as 'Order your Pike'.[42] The top part of the pike has broken off. Underneath his armour he wears what is presumably a buff coat, with knee-length breeches, stockings and heavy shoes and he stands on a small, flat rectangular base.
Date: c. 1630 – early 1640s[43]
Comments: During the period of the civil wars, the wearing of the pikeman's armour declined and there is no evidence for the manufacture of it in this country after the early 1640s. The detail is appropriately different on the front and back – an accomplished figure.

Fig. 40. Hollow-cast male figure by the maker IQ (initials on base). Found in Amsterdam
Private Collection

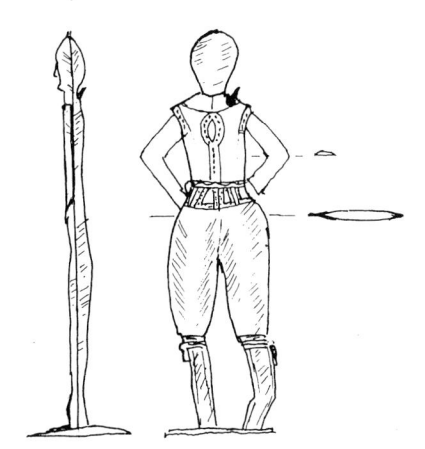

170 • TOYS, TRIFLES & TRINKETS

TYPE 2, DESIGN 2

4.34 Male figure

Accession number: 98.2/398
Material: Lead alloy
Condition: Almost complete; lower legs missing; possibly distorted
Dimensions: H 26mm; W 13mm
Description: A crude but detailed three-dimensional, solid figure wearing a pot helmet, backplate, breastplate, tassets and baggy breeches. The left hand rests on the waist and the right is bent upwards as though to support a staff weapon (now missing); the right leg is bent – perhaps this is distortion rather than an indication of animated movement (or even dancing).
Date: Early to mid-17th century (?)
Comments: Possibly a pikeman

TYPE 2, DESIGN 3

4.35 Male figure

Accession number: 98.2/399
Material: Lead alloy
Condition: Almost complete; legs and weapon missing
Dimensions: H 37mm; W 20mm
Description: A three-dimensional solid-cast soldier, possibly a pikeman. His head is turned to the left and he wears a breastplate (?) over a short apron-fronted buff coat and baggy breeches, which stop just above the knee. His left arm is bent upwards and the hand is angled to hold a staff weapon (now missing).
Date: Mid-17th century (?)
Provenance: Greenwich

TYPE 3

Flat figures, moulded on one side only.

TYPE 3, DESIGN 1

4.36 Male figure (?)

Accession number: 98.2/378
Material: Lead alloy
Condition: Face only
Dimensions: H 15mm; W 12mm
Description: A rough, male face with a moustache, goatee beard and bushy eyebrows. The hair on the top of the head seems to be set apart from the pate in a pair of almost horn-like excrescences.
Date: 16th century or later
Provenance: Dockhead
Comments: Possibly a fragment of a toy

TYPE 3, DESIGN 2

4.37 Male figure: game hawker

Accession number: 88.9/35*; 98.2/392

Material: Lead alloy; red pigment (the fullest survival of pigment on any of the excavated toys listed)

Condition: 88.9/35: complete. 98.2/392: lower leg and stand missing

Dimensions: H 75mm; W 32mm

Description: Figures in the form of a game hawker. Advancing to the right, he wears a flat-crowned, broad-brimmed hat, cravat, buttoned coat with turned-back cuffs, breeches, stockings and high vamped shoes. The stand is an elongated hexagon. He sports a moustache and his hair is shoulder-length. He carries a stick across his shoulder from which hangs a dressed rabbit in front (the part behind him is missing), and there is a dead duck in his left hand.

Date: Late 17th – early 18th century

Comments: These figures seem to be loosely modelled on the hawker 'Buy a Rabbet a Rabbet' in Marcellus Laroon's 'Cries of London' series, published in 1688.[44]

TYPE 3, DESIGN 3

4.38 Male figure

Accession number: 98.2/381

Material: Lead alloy; red pigment

Condition: Almost complete; lower limbs missing; worn and abraded surface

Dimensions: H 55mm; W 28mm

Description: Part of a relatively crude figure, with head three-quarters profile, advancing to the left in a fairly high-crowned, wide-brimmed hat, buttoned coat with back flaps and horizontally topped pocket, and breeches. The man carries a snugly fitting pack, possibly a woven basket, on his back. Although not identifiable from any published series, this may be another street seller analogous to the 'Cries of London' figures (see Cat. no. 4.37).

Date: Probably late 17th – early 18th century

TYPE 3, DESIGN 4

4.39 Male figure

Accession number: 98.2/383

Material: Lead alloy; traces of pigment (?)

Condition: Lower part of body only; damaged

Dimensions: H 54mm; W 33mm

Description: The lower part of a figure, possibly in highland or 'Roman' dress, with part of the jacket, kilt (?) etc. On the right is the lower part of an unidentified object (not obviously a bagpipe). There is a large, central hole, perhaps from a nail.

Date: Possibly 18th century or later

Comments: Perhaps to be dated after 1739 (when the Highland Regiment of Foot was formed) if in highland dress, or alternatively a theatrical character

172 • TOYS, TRIFLES & TRINKETS

TYPE 3, DESIGN 5

4.40 Male figure

Accession number: 98.2/384
Material: Lead alloy
Condition: Head, lower limbs and hands missing
Dimensions: H 44mm; W 30mm
Description: The torso of a soldier or huntsman with buttoned waistcoat, breeches, neck stock and open coat with turned-back, buttoned cuffs. He carries two bags (the military cartridge pouch became plainer through the 18th century), one on each hip suspended from straps crossed across the chest.
Date: Probably late 17th – early 18th century

TYPE 3, DESIGN 6

4.41 Male figure

Accession number: 98.2/379
Material: Lead alloy
Condition: Lower part of body; both feet missing; some damage
Dimensions: H 50mm; W 21mm
Description: The lower part of a male figure in civilian dress with long, tight-fitting breeches, which are gathered in at the knee. The detailing suggests decorative side seams and a series of gathers in the fabric.
Date: Late 18th century (?)

TYPE 3, DESIGN 7

4.42 Male figure

Accession number: 98.2/388
Material: Lead alloy
Condition: Torso only; central pinhole
Dimensions: H 27mm; W 30mm
Description: The torso of a man wearing a open-necked, buttoned, long-sleeved coat with turned-back cuffs and pointed, falling collar. He carries a long, rectangular item, which is marked with horizontal and vertical lines, under his right arm.
Date: Late 17th century (?)
Comments: The object carried could be a cage for birds – perhaps singing pets. Possibly another tradesman analogous to the 'London Cries' series (see Cat. no. 4.37; similar cages are shown for rodents in van de Venne's 1620s depictions of a rat catcher and a mouse-trap seller, but the rats are prominent – outside the cage in the former instance)[45]

TYPE 4

Flat, with mouldings on both sides.

TYPE 4, DESIGN 1

4.43 Male figure: military

Accession number: 98.2/380
Material: Lead alloy
Condition: Part only
Dimensions: H 28mm; W 38mm
Description: The trunk and arms from a figure in the uniform of a Yeoman of the Guard (?). The long-sleeved jacket has vertical ribbing interspersed with fine horizontal hatching to suggest braided textile. There are beaded circles or badges depicting, on the front, a crown over a slipped and entwined rose and thistle (emblems of England and Scotland), and on the back a different cipher perhaps intended for the monarch's initials. Yeomen today wear identical breast badges on the front and back of their scarlet coats. In 1709 the slipped thistle was added to the rose. The motif on the back is not known on actual Yeomen's uniforms; it might be the maker's attempt to represent AR for Queen Anne.
Date: 1709–14 (?)[46]

TYPE 4, DESIGN 2

4.44 Male figure: military

Accession number: 98.2/389
Material: Lead alloy; red pigment
Condition: Complete
Dimensions: H 42mm; W 16mm
Description: A profile figure of a guardsman in parade dress with tall conical cap, buttoned coat open and looped at the skirt, turned-back cuffs, waistcoat, breeches and gaiters. The soldier stands on a flat, rectangular base and he carries a musket and sword.
Date: Mid-18th century
Comments: Militiaman, possibly a musician. It was customary to wear the coat skirt looped back when on parade.

TYPE 4, DESIGN 3

4.45 Male figure: military
Accession number: 98.2/385
Material: Lead alloy
Condition: Trunk; one arm and upper legs
Dimensions: H 45mm; W 28mm
Description: Part of a full-length figure of an infantryman in parade uniform with different mouldings on the front and back. He wears a buttoned waistcoat and coat with open looped (?) back skirt, breeches and a baldric. There is a musket (?) in his left hand.
Date: Mid- to late 18th century
Comments: Probably a guardsman

TYPE 4, DESIGN 4

4.46 Male figure: military
Accession number: 98.2/387
Material: Lead alloy; red pigment
Condition: Lower torso and upper part of legs
Dimensions: H 38mm; W 23mm
Description: Part of a profile figure of a guardsman in parade uniform with buckled waistcoat, open coat with looped skirt, sword hanger and sword, buttoned breeches and baldric (?). The details are identical on the front and back (an unusual feature).
Date: Probably mid-18th century

TYPE 4, DESIGN 5

4.47 Male figure: pirate (?)

Accession number: 98.2/382
Material: Lead alloy; red pigment
Condition: Almost complete; head and legs missing
Dimensions: H 51mm; W 28mm
Description: Part of a two-sided flat figure with different detailing on the front and back. His exotic apparel consists of a short, open-necked jerkin with short skirt over a gathered chemise, which hangs loose at the elbows. Long, gathered pantaloon-style breeches are held up with a twisted and braided cummerbund fastened by a tasselled knot. A cutlass in a scabbard hangs from a hanger and three pistols are tucked into his belt. His left arm is bent upwards and the hand grasps a staff (?) or a rigging stay.
Date: Probably 18th century, possibly 19th century
Provenance: Limekiln Dock
Comments: This well-armed figure wears the clothing of a pirate or brigand – perhaps a theatrical piece.

TYPE 4, DESIGN 6

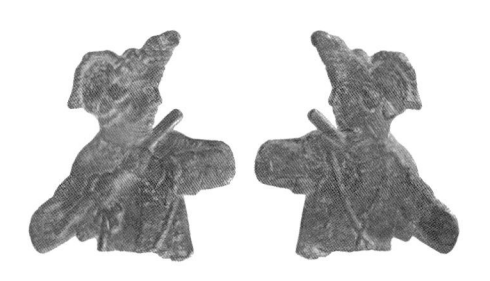

4.48 Male figure: flautist

Accession number: 98.2/386
Material: Lead alloy
Condition: Upper half only
Dimensions: H 31mm; W 30mm
Description: A military flautist in profile with hat, long tied wig, cravat and open coat with turned-back cuffs. His chemise billows out at the cuffs and there is a crossed shoulder strap and baldric (?) on his back. He holds a transverse pipe, perhaps a fife, to his lips.
Date: Late 17th – early 18th century

176 • TOYS, TRIFLES & TRINKETS

TYPE 4, DESIGN 7

4.49 Male figure: harlequin

Accession number: 98.2/390
Material: Lead alloy
Condition: Almost complete; part of both feet and one arm missing; (sword (?) etc missing from strap at hip)
Dimensions: H 72mm; W 31mm
Description: An animated, full-length figure with fine detailing on both front and back, depicting a rapidly turning, walking or dancing harlequin. He holds his high-crowned, broad-brimmed hat to his head, and wears the harlequin's costume of a lozenge-patterned (multi-coloured) suit with buttoned front, short jacket, belt and tight-fitting trousers. The falling ruff is larger than usual. The beard he wears is presumably the harlequin's traditional false one (there is no sign of the usual half mask). Harlequins conventionally carry a wooden sword or bat and pouch and they move with extravagant capers.
Date: 17th century or later
Comments: The haphazardly patched garments of the harlequin had changed from a random pattern to symmetrical aligned lozenges by the 17th century. Beyond this terminus post quem, dating is difficult for this traditional theatrical character.[47]

Accessories

TYPE 1, DESIGN 1

4.50 Conical hat

Accession number: 88.432/11*; 92.95/3
Material: Lead alloy
Condition: Both complete; 92.95/3 crushed; both slightly damaged
Dimensions: H 22mm; W *c.* 15mm
Description: Hollow-cast conical hats with high-pointed crowns and deep brims. The crown has vertical mouldings and the brim has two bands of chevrons and pellets, perhaps to suggest a pleated fabric, trimmed with braid or embroidery.
Date: 1560–1600 (?)[48]
Comments: Possibly associated with male figurines Cat. nos. 4.26 etc.

TYPE 2, DESIGN 1

4.51 Hat with brim

Accession number: 98.2/403
Material: Lead alloy
Condition: Complete
Dimensions: H 6mm; Diam 15mm
Description: An accurately delineated three-dimensional hat with broad brim, flat crown and plume
Date: Late 17th–18th century (?)
Provenance: Bull Wharf

1. Hans Christian Andersen, 'The Constant Tin Soldier', 1837.

2. The comments of a number of colleagues over the years, notably Kay Staniland and Valerie Cumming, is gratefully acknowledged. Consensus is still to be reached for some items. Most of the catalogue entries and specific references below to clothing in artistic representations were compiled by HF. The advice of Keith Miller (National Army Museum) on several points concerning the uniforms and equipment of the later military figures is gratefully acknowledged, as are several helpful comments by Jenny Tiramani.

3. MoL GYE92, Acc. no. <3942>.

4. See Willemsen 1998, pp. 88–90 for finds from the Netherlands; Gläser 1995, pp. 32–3 for finds in Germany.

5. Spencer 1998, pp. 11–12.

6. As originally suggested by HF.

7. Egan 1998, no. 931, assigned to the late 13th or early 14th century.

8. See Falk 1995, p. 40; Petényi 1994, p. 86, fig. 15 & pp. 100–101, figs 20–21; Moscow Museum 1995.

9. The following text incorporates several helpful comments, both on details and dating of the armour and on the various stances of rider and mount, from Karen Watts and others over a period of years of HM Royal Armouries.

10. Ward Perkins 1940, pp. 25–6; Oakeshott 1995.

11. Spencer 1998, p. 11.

12. See Willemsen 1998, p. 195; two falconers on horseback, published by Nickel 1966, pp. 172–3, may actually be two of the three legs of an ornate tripod candlestick.

13. Spencer 1998, pp. 53, 71 & 65.

14. Spencer 1998, pp. 296 & 299, nos. 296a & 296b. There is also a poorly modelled, green-glazed ceramic version (made in a mould) from the Kingston-ware production site – see Egan 1996, fig. 49; Egan 1997, fig. 2. This unattractive competitor to the metal playthings seems not to have been a commercial success.

15. See Gay 1887, I, pp. 62 & 69; Willemsen 1998, p. 397, B141; Baart 1988, p. 102.

16. Egan 1996, fig. 5.

17. Spencer 1998, p. 299.

18. Egan 1996, fig. 5.

19. Egan 1996, fig. 5.

20. MoL VHA89, Acc. no. <15>, dated from associated pottery to the 15th century, perhaps the first half – Jacqui Pearce, pers. comm.

21. Egan 1996, fig. 6 & cover. See also Willemsen 1998, p. 397, B143–4, with a total of five examples recorded.

22. Thanks to Keith Mitchell (National Army Museum) for comments on these items.

23. McKenzie, 1975, p. 31 and illustration p. 36, fig. 11.

24. Egan 1996, fig. 10.

25. Richard Gladdle, pers. comm., 22 June 1999 (Enq. no. 2034/14).

26. Arnold 1988, p. 106.

27. E.g. Hurst et al. 1986, pp. 98–9, fig. 45, no. 133 & pp. 235–6, fig. 122, no. 356; Grönke & Weinlich 1998; Petényi 1994, pp. 90 & 92 figs 17 & 19. See also the Raeren stoneware equestrian figurines, 1500–40, in the Museum of London's collection, illustrated and described in Gaimster 1997, pp. 228–30, cat. no. 78 and colour plate 15. It is possible that these figures were used as devotional objects rather than playthings.

28. Dietz 1972, p. 78 no. 491.

29. Willan 1962, p. 6: 'Book of Rates' (1609?), unpaginated.

30. De Bruyn 1581, plates 4 & 16 (British Library). A similar long, pleated dress is worn by a servant woman in the background of the Holbein portrait of Henry VIII and his family; see also Egan & Forsyth 1997, pp. 127–8.

31. E.g. Egan 1997, p. 416, fig. 5.

32. Egan & Forsyth 1997, pp. 227–8.

33. Egan 1996, fig. 9 right; see Egan 1999, pp. 192–3, fig. 14, no. 121 for the only known male, found at Reigate in Surrey.

34. See portrait attributed to Mark Gerhaerts the Younger, 1605–10.

35. See a 1595 portrait of Lady Eleanor Herbert, by an unknown artist, at Powys Castle.

36. See Wenceslaus Hollar's engraving of an English Gentlewoman.

37. Shesgreen 1990, pp. 120–1; Spencer 1998, pp. 308–11, figs 306c, 307 & 307a for late 14th–15th-century badges depicting milkmaids with garlands and churns.

38. Royalton-Kisch 1988, pp. 248–9 pl 54.

39. 'The Town Crier', anonymous, private collection, London, 17th century.

40. Willemsen 2000, p. 348, fig. 1, top right. We are most grateful to the private collection for permission to use their illustration.

41. Garratt 1971, pl 12.

42. This is the 1st, 25th and 32nd posture laid down in Jacob De Gheyn's manual *Exercise of Arms* published in 1607.

43. Blackmore 1990, p. 63.

44. Shesgreen 1990, pp. 110–11. Rabbit vendors operated during the autumn and winter months in London and sold undressed and dressed game. Most preferred to sell dressed animals to increase their profit margin.

45. Royalton-Kisch 1988, pp. 306–7, plates 83 & 83a.

46. Hennell 1904.

47. Sand 1915, p. 62.

48. Compare the headgear depicted in a portrait attributed to Corneille de Lyon (c. 1560, Louvre, Paris) and one with a felt base and silk pile (1560–1600; gift of the Prince of Schnarzburg, 1877; Germanisches Nationalmuseum, Nuremberg).

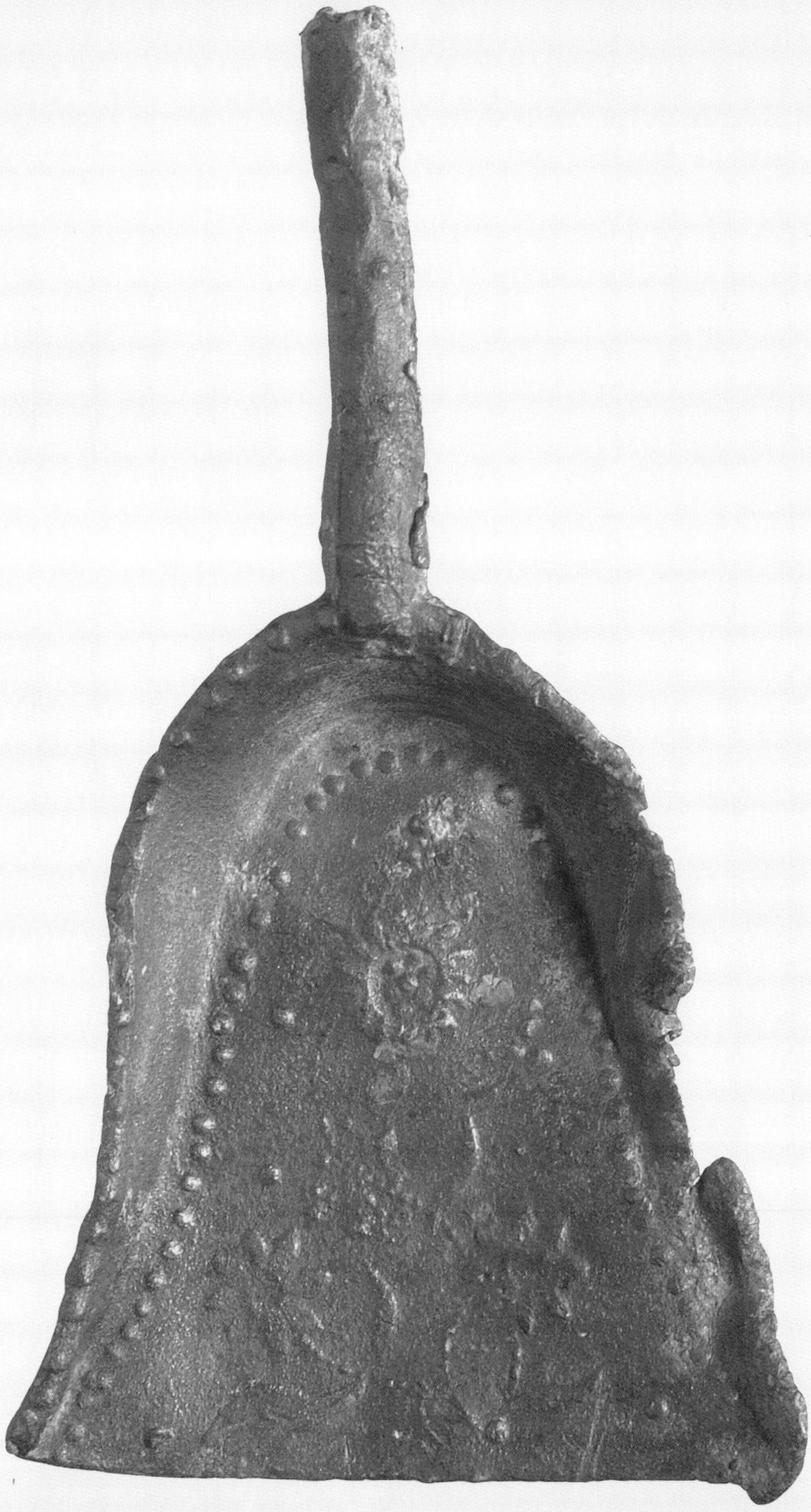

5 Fixtures, furnishings & other household items

'everything which belonged to a house and its management was reproduced in [small scale] and many went to such lengths of sumptuousness that the cost of such a plaything would run to 1,000 gulden or more'[1]

Base-metal miniatures of household items seem to have been made from the late medieval period, but the majority of examples in this section date from the late 17th to late 18th century when inventories show that Londoners were living 'in houses which were better lit, were hung with more attractive textiles and were furnished in a way which would have made both sitting and sleeping more of a pleasure.'[2] By the end of the 17th century even those with modest incomes could afford to buy mirrors, pictures, ornaments and other knick-knacks which would have been beyond their means a few years before, and it is likely that miniature versions were produced in ever increasing numbers to represent and reflect the array of furnishings available at this time.[3]

Some of the best evidence for miniature fixtures and furnishings comes from 16th- and 17th-century Low Countries genre prints showing children at play. Such pictures (figs 41 & 43, pp. 180 & 187) often show groups of little girls in the street or doorway with their dolls and an assortment of scaled-down

Fig. 41. Detail of an engraving of children's games by Experiens Silleman [1611–1653], accompanying the poem 'Kinder-spel' by Jacob Cats in *Houwelijck* (1625). See fig. 43, p. 187

domestic objects which typically include a cradle, canopied bed, mirror, foot warmer, curfew, tongs and other hearth furniture as well as a range of cooking pots and utensils.[4] Enough, in fact, to allow the children to play 'house' and imitate the daily tasks of adult life. Because these prints were often used to accompany moralistic manuals on marriage, the follies of adult behaviour and the nature and innocence of childhood,[5] the effectiveness of the symbolic and didactic message was largely predicated upon the artists' ability to illustrate as many games as possible within a single composition, and to represent those games and childhood passions as accurately as possible.

The genre prints and paintings of children at play suggest that household miniatures were not only popular, but were made in different sizes and materials. Quite often the relative sizes of the toys in a group are disproportionate; a chair is shown as large as a bed, and a curfew smaller than a colander. Whether the toys belonged to one child, or several children in the group is of course unclear, but playing with different-sized objects has rarely proved much of a bar to a child's imagination, and it probably did not matter greatly that some things were excessively large while others were small. It is possible that the artists increased the scale so that individual items could be identified clearly, but large miniatures of 16th- and 17th-century date have been recovered from archaeological contexts in the Low Countries, and there are a few 17th-century examples in ceramic and pewter in the collections of the Museum of London. The majority of household miniatures surviving from the medieval and early modern period however, including those discussed in this section, are considerably smaller than comparable items illustrated in the genre scenes.

The following section deals with a miscellaneous assortment of furnishings, fixtures and general household items which survive in small quantities and do not merit their own chapters.

Candlesticks

Base-metal candlesticks of pricket and socket form were used in domestic and ecclesiastical contexts throughout the medieval period. But it was not until the late 13th century that the socket candlestick really began to be favoured for domestic purposes. These candlesticks were generally supported on tripod feet and the sockets were typically cast with apertures to facilitate the removal of the spent candle. Candlesticks with identifiable national features started to make their appearance during the late 14th century and the 'first stabilized form to be produced in England' had an unpierced socket, tall columnar stem and a slightly dished conical spreading base which served as a drip pan (fig. 42, page 183).[6] By the end of the 17th century, socket candlesticks with a central knop and drip pan were the standard type, and as Randle Holme pointed out, 'it was left to workmen to adorne his worke the best he can to sett it the more splendidly forth: whithere by raised worke, corded, or twist worke, or by makeing the bottome and flower part round, square, Hexagon, or octagon like, with chased worke, &c.'[7]

Surviving full-size pewter candlesticks are rare in England before the 17th century, but several 'miniature' candle-holders in lead alloy have been recovered from late 13th- and 14th-century contexts.[8] The largest examples were loosely modelled on contemporary candlesticks of tripod-based form with a sufficiently capacious socket to hold a small candle, and those with religious iconography and French or Latin inscriptions were evidently manufactured as devotional souvenirs for the pilgrim trade.[9] But the smallest, just 12mm in height, with flat bases and crudely formed sockets are clearly too small for functional use and it is just possible that these were made expressly for the toy market.[10] No other examples of base-metal 'toy' candle-holders of medieval date have been found in England,[11] apart from a handful of copper-alloy and lead/tin 14th-, 15th- and 16th-century miniatures which might have been made for children's use.[12] The earliest toy candlestick in the collection dates from the mid-17th century, but toy lead-alloy pricket-style candlesticks have been recovered from 16th-century contexts in the Netherlands,[13] and a single lead-alloy toy socket candlestick from the Seine rather like the Type 1 candlestick described below, has been dated to the 15th century.[14] Lead-glazed earthenware socket candlesticks of 17th-century date in the Boijmans Museum, Rotterdam, are thought to have been made as doll's toys and the largest examples could hold a small candle.[15]

Most of the toy candlesticks represented here have stylistic features which enable fairly tight dating up to 1780, and it is clear that the toymakers changed their moulds frequently to keep up with contemporary fashion in candlestick and chamberstick design. There are no copper-alloy candlesticks in this collection, although a number of full-scale examples have survived in museum collections. No toy rushnips, sconces, snuffers or other kinds of lighting apparatus have been identified in base metal, although presumably many of these articles were also made in miniature form.

TYPE 1, DESIGN 1

5.1 Candlestick

Accession number: 98.2/539
Material: Lead alloy
Condition: Complete
Dimensions: H 53mm; Diam 27mm
Inscription: IQ
Description: A socket candlestick cast in one piece from a two part mould. The cylindrical hollow socket has a cordon around the rim and basal edge, and is decorated with 'shield' type mouldings around the circumference. The very slender solid baluster stem has foliate decoration and there is a double-reeded knop in the centre. The flat circular foot is covered in foliate ornament which incorporates a small cartouche inscribed IQ.
Date: Probably mid-17th century
Comments: Although the slender stem and general form is vaguely suggestive of Low Countries sticks of c. 1550, (see Caspall 1987, p. 79, fig. 136), the initials I Q on the base point to a mid-17th century production. The closest parallels of mid-17th-century date are French, but these candlesticks, like all candlesticks of this period are plain.
Comparandum: Lear Collection of Socket Candlesticks, Christie's sale, 15 December 1998, lot 37, 'from northwest Europe, probably 16th century'

182 • TOYS, TRIFLES & TRINKETS

TYPE 2, DESIGN 1

5.2 Candlestick

Accession number: 98.2/545
Material: Lead alloy
Condition: Complete
Dimensions: H 47mm; Diam (rim) 17mm; Diam (base) 30mm
Description: A socket candlestick probably cast in one piece. The 'socket', just 3mm deep, has a wide octagonal flange which is decorated with beading and pellets. The cylindrical stem has a tapering upper section, and there is an annular knop with cordons just below mid-point with a ball-shaped section below. The ball has an angular profile and joins a sharp-edged basal knop. The plain octagonal foot has a depressed edge with beading. There are pronounced ridges underneath the foot to provide stability.
Date: 1660–75
Provenance: Bankside, May 1978
Comments: Octagonal-based candlesticks with an octagonal socket flange were made in England from 1660–75.

TYPE 3, DESIGN 1

5.3 Candlestick

Accession number: 98.2/540
Material: Lead alloy
Condition: Complete
Dimensions: H 52mm; Diam (rim) 13mm; Diam (base) 38mm
Description: A hollow-cast socket candlestick, produced from a two-part mould. The plain, unpierced, cylindrical socket has a pronounced everted rim with beaded edge. There is a reeded band approximately half way down the slender, cylindrical stem, which is otherwise plain. The pedestal base expands to a slightly crested round foot, with twelve semi-circular lobes around the edge. Each lobe is decorated with radial relief slashing to represent gadrooning.
Date: 1740–55
Comments: This candlestick is a realistic copy of the so-called 'petal-based' candlesticks, a multi-lobed variety fashionable in England from 1740–55 (Caspall 1987, pp. 115–17).

TYPE 4, DESIGN 1

5.4 Candlestick

Accession number: 91.123/2*; NN21169
Material: Lead alloy
Condition: 91.123/2: complete
 NN21169: almost complete
Dimensions: H 40mm; Diam (base) 24mm; W (incl. handle) 43mm
Description: Hollow-cast from a two-part mould with an integrally cast, recurved strap-reeded handle (missing on NN21169). The long plain tubular stem tapers slightly to the foot and there are six round (now damaged) holes, three on each side. The piercings are directly opposed and are spaced at regular intervals along the vertical axis. The plain, round foot 'pan' is very slightly concave.
Date: Probably 1750–70
Comments: These sticks replicate chambersticks of the mid-to late 18th century which were cast with a hollow stem or socket to protect the bulk of the candle from the flame. The side apertures were used to push the candle up the stem and facilitate the removal of the molten tallow or wax. These sticks were usually equipped with a slide device, push-rod ejector or latch, but the toys lack similar features. The toys were probably made in the same workshop.
Comparanda: Other examples from London (now in private collections) found on the Thames foreshore at the Vintry in 1986 and St Katherine's Wharf in 1988

FIXTURES, FURNISHINGS & OTHER HOUSEHOLD ITEMS • 183

TYPE 5, DESIGN 1

5.5 Candlestick

Accession number: 98.2/542; 98.2/543*; 98.2/544
Material: Lead alloy
Condition: Complete. 98.2/544: base only
Dimensions: H 60mm; W (base) 28mm
Description: Socket candlesticks cast in a two- part mould. The most complete example (98.2/542) has a wide flat, square flange, with an unpierced, urn-shaped socket reposing on a square knop, and vertically fluted stem. The circular basal knop joins a pyramidal foot with five ledges. There is relief, slash decoration on the basal knop and the raised edge of the foot to represent gadrooning. The toys are very similar, but 98.2/542 & 98.2/543 have urn sockets of a slightly different size and profile; the latter with an additional cordon between the body and pedestal foot. There are casting flaws on each stick.
Date: These candlesticks are faithful copies of neo-classical style candlesticks in silver, brass and bronze produced in England from 1760–65 (Caspall 1987, pp. 123–31).
Provenance: 98.2/542: west London, August 1984

TYPE 6, DESIGN 1

5.6 Candlestick

Accession number: 98.2/541
Material: Lead alloy
Condition: Complete

Dimensions: H *c.* 61mm; Diam (base) 29 x 32 mm
Inscription: H
Description: A slightly distorted, hollow-cast socketed candlestick, made in a two-part mould. The unpierced, urn-shaped socket has a slightly everted rim with pronounced beading around the edge and there is a small square knop between the socket and square-sectioned fluted column. The column tapers to an ovoid pedestal base decorated with beading and radial ridges to imitate faceting. Underneath the foot is the letter H.
Date: Probably 1780s
Comments: Square-sectioned fluted columns were commonly combined with pyramidal bases, but there was a fashion for ovoid-faceted bases on candlesticks during the 1780s. At this period it was common practice for candlestick-makers to place their mark under the foot and the letter H on the toy candlestick might have been added to reflect this practice.

Fig. 42. Socket candlesticks of this type were made in France and England during the 14th century, but this is the only surviving example known. The earliest miniature candlestick in the collection, made by the maker/s I(D)Q, dates to the mid-17th century. Recovered from Queenhithe on the Thames foreshore. **H 100mm**
Museum of London, Acc. no. 78.238/1

Hearth furniture & grates

Once brick chimneys and wall flues started to be inserted into houses during the 13th century, the hearth moved from the centre to the sides of the room. The resulting multiplication of fireplaces meant that separate hearths could be used for cooking and heating, and this increased the demand for hearth furniture and different types of accessories. The gradual shift from firewood to sea-coal in late 16th century[16] also had a dramatic effect on the range, type and design of hearth furniture. Iron bar grates were introduced to facilitate combustion, pokers replaced fire forks to aerate the coals, and fire shovels were pierced so that the lumps of coal could be sifted. By the early 17th century, contemporary plans and inventories show that even the 'smallest houses in London possessed a chimney and several heated rooms, [a] luxury not found in other English towns',[17] and by 1700, most people had a range in the kitchen and grates in other rooms with their accompanying suite of iron backs, tongs, andirons, fire shovels, pokers and bellows.

Despite the ubiquitous use of hearth furniture in the early modern period, there are few extant examples of early date, and brass and silver specimens are exceedingly rare. Miniature versions are likewise scarce, and the majority of English examples in base metals date from the late 17th and 18th centuries. Although most types of hearth furniture were probably available in miniature form, only a limited range of items have survived in this country: there are no curfews, brushes, fire forks, creepers, fire backs or pokers, and andirons, bellows and tongs are only represented by single examples.[18] A slightly wider range of articles have been recovered from 15th- and 16th- century contexts in the Netherlands, however, and miniature hearth furniture is frequently included in Low Countries genre paintings of children at play.[19]

Andiron

To improve combustion, firewood was raised from the base of the hearth by wrought-iron andirons or firedogs. The earliest examples were double-ended and linked by a horizontal billet bar, but once the wall down-hearth was established, separate single-ended forms were placed at each end of the fireplace and the outward, visible face was often decorated and occasionally embellished with applied panels of brass or silver surmounted by an elaborate finial. With the widespread introduction of sea-coal, andirons were effectively redundant and 'sett on each side the chimney more for Ornament then profit',[20] although they continue to feature in most inventories until the end of the 18th century because they were either adapted to form a fire-basket, or used as a decorative prop for fire irons.

TYPE 1, DESIGN 1

5.7 Andiron

Accession number: 98.2/603
Material: Lead alloy
Condition: Almost complete
Dimensions: H 63mm; W 43mm
Description: The front section of a three-dimensional andiron with pierced scallop border surrounding a semi-circular base and centrally placed upright. The openwork base has a radial pattern ornamented with scrolling, pellets and herring-bone hatching. Between the base and upright is a decorative roundel with cable edging, scrolling and central boss. The upright is decorated with a symmetrical pattern of hatched foliate scrolls. The reverse is plain and there is a longitudinal casting seam with the stub of the billet bar, a loop and part of a possible hook.
Date: 16th or 17th century
Provenance: Southwark Bridge, north side, February 1985
Comments: The elaborate decoration coupled with the absence of hooks on the front suggest that this piece was probably designed as an andiron rather than a spit dog. It is possible that the hook fragment is part of the basket of a cresset which was occasionally placed at the top of an andiron.
Comparandum: V&A inv. no. M656-1905

Bellows

Hardly any medieval and or early modern bellows have survived although they are frequently mentioned in household inventories from the early 16th century. Plain, functional hand-bellows were made for everyday use 'to blow up fires for their more speedy Kindling'[21] while those with richly decorated boards covered with pierced or engraved metal plates, textiles, or embossed, moulded and gilded leather were generally acquired for ornamental purposes. The miniature version has elaborate moulded decoration which suggests that it was designed to represent an object of quality. It is the only example known.

TYPE 1, DESIGN 1

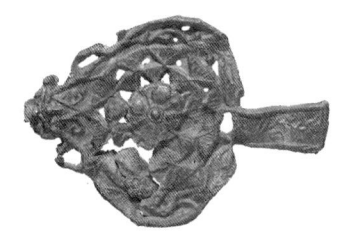

5.8 Bellows

Accession number: 86.416/1
Material: Lead alloy
Condition: One side only; damaged
Dimensions: L 42mm; W 29mm
Description: Almost complete side from a pair of bellows with openwork floral and geometric designs. There are two folded projections on the back and three slots around the edge which suggest that the bellows were originally made up from two or more sections. The nozzle tip has broken off and the rectangular handle, decorated with a foliate pattern, tapers slightly towards the board which is decorated with a central rosette within concentric circles of hatched triangles and foliate scrolling.
Date: Probably 17th century

Fire grates

Because sea-coal required an intense heat to combust, grates were devised to contain the fuel and to stop lumps of coal falling on to the hearth. The earliest examples seem to have been little more than a free-standing frame of closely packed wrought-iron bars, but gradually the grate became a decorative feature in its own right. During the 18th century the aperture of the fireplace was reduced to increase the draught and special framed or 'enclosed grates' were produced to fit them. From the mid-18th century the hob grate, flanked by hot plates, were especially popular, and the toy grates in this collection are of this type.

Toy grates were produced in their thousands for doll's houses during the 18th century, but only two have been identified from archaeological deposits in London.

TYPE 1, DESIGN 1

5.9 Fire grate

Accession number: 98.2/606
Material: Lead alloy
Condition: Complete
Dimensions: H 48mm; W 69mm
Description: A two-dimensional five-bar grate in rococo style with openwork scrolls, garlands and beading
Date: 18th century

TYPE 2, DESIGN 1

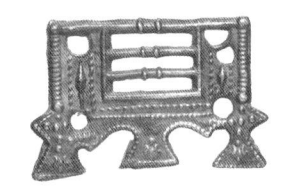

5.10 Fire grate

Accession number: 98.2/604
Material: Lead alloy
Condition: Complete panel
Dimensions: H 20mm; W 33mm
Description: The front of a hob-grate, with bracket feet and elaborately moulded decoration. There are several holes in the boxes which may have been attachment points for other panel sections.
Date: Probably 18th century
Provenance: Tower of London foreshore

186 • TOYS, TRIFLES & TRINKETS

Fire shovels

Despite the absence of extant examples from the medieval period, pictorial evidence suggests that the general shape of the fire shovel has scarcely altered over the years. From the late 16th century onwards, pierced pans were introduced to filter lumps of coal, and the elaborate moulded floral designs on the toy pans probably represent the functional and ornamental piercings on the genuine article. Toy fire shovels have been found in greater quantities than any other type of hearth furniture, and the range of styles and mould variations suggests that these objects were made in significant numbers throughout the 17th and 18th centuries.

TYPE 1, DESIGN 1

5.11 Fire shovel

Accession number: 96.62/2
Material: Lead alloy
Condition: Handle and parts of pan missing
Dimensions: H 28mm; W (pan) c. 30mm; Dpt 3mm
Description: Cast in one piece with a fairly shallow, bell-shaped flaring pan. The straight edge has cable decoration and the flat base is decorated with a two-handled vase of flowers including tulips.
Date: Possibly late 17th century

TYPE 1, DESIGN 2

5.12 Fire shovel

Accession number: 98.2/609
Material: Lead alloy
Condition: Handle missing; slight damage; completely flattened
Dimensions: H 32mm; W (pan) 30mm
Description: Cast in one piece with a fairly shallow flattened, long bell-shaped flaring pan. The plain rim has a thickened edge and the flat base is decorated with a vase of flowers incorporating a tulip.
Date: Possibly late 17th century
Provenance: Limekiln Dock

TYPE 1, DESIGN 3

5.13 Fire shovel

Accession number: 98.2/612
Material: Lead alloy
Condition: Complete (?)
Dimensions: H 60mm; L (handle) 24mm; W (pan) 33mm; Dpt 8mm
Description: Cast in one piece with a short slender handle and a broad bell shaped flaring pan. The curving rim and corresponding base outline are beaded and the flat ground is decorated with a sunflower and two smaller plants interspersed with pellets. The handle (possibly incomplete) is decorated with a waving line and opposing pellets. There is a short rats-tail at the junction of the handle, but the back is otherwise plain. The shovel walls are fairly deep with a bevelled profile.
Date: Late 17th or early 18th century

TYPE 1, DESIGN 4

5.14 Fire shovel

Accession number: 98.2/610
Material: Lead alloy
Condition: Handle missing; slight damage
Dimensions: H 38mm; W (pan) 29mm; Dpt 4mm
Description: Cast in one piece with a slender handle (only the stub remains) and a long shallow, bell-shaped flaring pan. The rim has a rope-twist edge and the flat base is decorated with a vase of flowers.
Date: Late 17th early 18th century

Fig. 43. European artists liked to depict the carefree world of the child at play to emphasize the burdensome reality of adult life. In his emblem book *Houwelijck* (1625), Jacob Cats uses children's games to indicate the transience of life and the folly of adult behaviour.
Engraving by Experiens Silleman [1611–1653]
Museum Boijmans Van Beuningen, Rotterdam

TYPE 1, DESIGN 5

5.15 Fire shovel

Accession number: 81.302/7
Material: Lead alloy
Condition: Handle and part of rim missing
Dimensions: H 31mm; W (pan) c. 27mm; Dpt 2mm
Description: Cast in one piece with a very slender handle (stub only) and a fairly long shallow, bell-shaped flaring pan. The curving rim and corresponding base outline are beaded and the flat ground is decorated with a flowing pattern of open scrolls.
Date: Late 17th or 18th century

TYPE 2, DESIGN 1

5.16 Fire shovel

Accession number: 98.2/607
Material: Lead alloy
Condition: Handle missing; slightly flattened
Dimensions: H 43mm; W (pan) 46mm; Dpt 4mm
Description: Cast in one piece with a very large bell-shaped flaring pan. There are two decorative ears or knops either side of the handle scar. The rim is beaded and the flat base decorated with a rococo style arrangement of rosettes, foliate tendrils and flowering plants.
Date: Probably 1730s
Provenance: From a culvert at the southeast end of Southwark Bridge, August 1982

TYPE 2, DESIGN 2

5.17 Fire shovel

Accession number: 98.2/608
Material: Lead alloy
Condition: Most of handle missing; slight damage
Dimensions: H 42mm; W (pan) c. 32mm; Dpt 4mm
Description: Cast in one piece with a slender handle of semi-circular section and a long, shallow bell-shaped flaring pan. There are two small ears or knops either side of the handle. The rim is beaded and the flat base decorated with a vase of flowers and leafy tendrils.
Date: Probably early 18th century

TYPE 2, DESIGN 3

5.18 Fire shovel

Accession number: 96.62/1
Material: Lead alloy
Condition: Handle and part of pan missing; completely flattened
Dimensions: H 32mm; W (pan) 31mm
Description: Cast in one piece with a bell-shaped flaring pan. Only one of the ears or knops has survived. The pan has a plain, thickened rim and the entire base is decorated with flowers, hatched leaves, foliate tendrils and a rosette.
Date: Probably early 18th century

TYPE 2, DESIGN 4

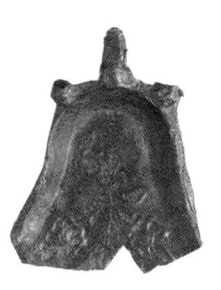

5.19 Fire shovel

Accession number: 98.2/611
Material: Lead alloy
Condition: Most of handle missing; slight damage to pan
Dimensions: H 33mm; W (pan) c. 27mm; Dpt 4mm
Description: Cast in one piece with a slender, flat handle (base only) and a fairly deep bell-shaped flaring pan. There are two

ears or knops either side of the handle. The rim is plain and the flat base is decorated with a vase of roses (?).
Date: Probably early 18th century

Tongs

Tongs were required to lift and manoeuvre smaller billets as well as lumps of coal, and they occur in most inventories from the 15th century onwards. Contemporaries seem to have made a distinction between the functional large plain kitchen or fire tongs, and the more decorative variety with a short-knobbed handle, bow-shaped hinge and straight tapering jaws which seems to have been reserved for 'ladyes chambers and seldom used there, but hung by the grate side more for shew and ornament, then use'.[22] The toy tongs represent the chamber form, which remained essentially unchanged over the centuries, although later examples tend to be more elaborate, smaller and less robust. This the only example of its kind so far recognized from excavations in England.

TYPE 1, DESIGN 1

5.20 Fire tongs

Accession number: 98.2/602
Material: Lead alloy
Condition: Complete
Dimensions: H 77mm; W 22mm
Description: A pair of three-dimensional fire tongs cast in one piece with mouldings on both sides. The long straight jaws broaden out to form a heart-shaped spring and there is a short handle of cylindrical section with central cordon and knop terminal. The tongs are decorated with diagonal hatching and the angles of the spring are embellished with shell-shaped fluting.
Date: 17th or 18th century

Mirrors & mirror frames

'these sorts of glasses are mostly used by lady's to look their faces in, and to see how to dress their heads, and sett their top knotts on their fore heads upright'[23]

Only one of the frames in the collection can be identified with certainty as a mirror because fragments of mica are retained between the front and back frames and within the central aperture. The toymaker has made good use of the transparent, reflective, lightweight properties of the mineral and because the crystalline structure of mica produces thin flexible sheets which are easily cut, the material is an ideal substitute for glass. Commercially viable mica for the Navy and other industrial purposes was imported by the Muscovy Company into England from Russia and Sweden, and flakes of the mineral were readily available in London during the second half of the 17th century when this toy mirror was probably made. The style and profile of the pierced 'cushion' frame, suggests a date from the 1660s to the 1690s, although the actual design does not reflect contemporary fashion.

Until 'large Looking-glass Plates, the like never made in England before, both for size and goodness'[24] started to be made in the London glass factory at Vauxhall in the 1670s, the Venetian and French glass houses had largely monopolized the manufacture of glass mirror plates in Europe. As the manufacture of plate glass technology improved, looking glasses became larger and larger. By the 1680s wealthy citizens started to use great expanses of mirror plate to lighten the interior, and mirrors were fitted above the mantle shelf and between the windows to reflect and maximize the light.

By the end of the century, inventories suggest that most households had looking glasses in the principal rooms and mirrors were no longer a luxury item.

There is no indication that the other frames in the collection held glass, mica or any other kind of reflective foil or coloured paper because there are no lugs or tabs for attachment, but the form and general style of the frames do suggest that they were intended as wall mirrors rather than picture frames. The smallest (Acc. nos. 98.2/592 & 98.2/593) have pierced frames of 'cushion' style which were probably made during the 1660s and 1670s. But Acc. no. 98.2/591 has cresting and a beaded aperture indicative of frames of the mid-17th to early 18th century, and Acc. no. 98.2/595 seems to be a stylized version of a pier-glass frame of the late 17th century.

TYPE 1, DESIGN 1

5.21 Mirror

Accession number: 98.2/594
Material: Lead alloy
Condition: Fairly complete; mica and parts of frame missing
Dimensions: H 55mm; H (aperture) 19mm; W 37mm; W (aperture) 12 mm; Dpt c. 3mm;
Description: A complex multi-component rectangular mirror frame with a mica insert between the front and back plates. The front frame is slightly larger with a convex profile and the long sides are embellished on the outer edge with protruding pellets. The frame is otherwise partly pierced to reveal tiny flashes of reflective mica, and is decorated with a geometric design of beaded chevrons and pellets. The rim of the aperture is thickened and beaded and there is a crude suspension loop at one end. The back plate has what appears to some sort of openwork cresting incorporating a suspension loop and the simple, narrow frame is cross-hatched and infilled by an interlace design.
Date: Probably second half of 17th century
Provenance: Southwark Bridge, north side, 1989
Comments: Unlike full-scale mirrors, this object has suspension loops at both ends. The purpose of the decorative openwork back panel is also a puzzle, although perhaps the toymaker opted for a pierced design to reduce the weight.

TYPE 2, DESIGN 1

5.22 Probable mirror frame

Accession number: 98.2/592
Material: Lead alloy
Condition: Complete
Dimensions: H 30mm; H (aperture) 13mm; W 26mm; W (aperture) 13 mm
Description: An openwork square frame with integral suspension loop. The frame has bevelled corners and the openwork design consists of eight equal-sized compartments, each filled with a scroll.
Date: Probably 1660–80

TYPE 2, DESIGN 2

5.23 Mirror frame

Accession number: 98.2/593
Material: Lead alloy
Condition: Complete
Dimensions: H 30mm; H (aperture) 13mm; W 28mm; W (aperture) 10 mm
Description: An openwork frame with cable and bevelled edging. The frame has bevelled corners and the openwork design consists of four compartments of trelliswork. Part of the frame has been improperly cast.
Date: Probably 1660–70

TYPE 2, DESIGN 3

5.24 Mirror frame

Accession number: 98.2/591
Material: Lead alloy
Condition: Almost complete; loose fragment and parts of frame decoration missing

FIXTURES, FURNISHINGS & OTHER HOUSEHOLD ITEMS • 191

Dimensions: H *c.* 55mm; H (aperture) 30mm; W 47mm; W (aperture) 22 mm

Description: An elaborate solid rectangular frame with integrally cast circular suspension loop. The corners are embellished with trefoils and there are diametrically opposed scrolled crests on each side. The outer edge is cabled, and the frame has a band of two lines with pellets at each corner and in the middle of each side so that they are aligned with the crests. There is a scalloped 'filigree' border around the aperture composed of overlapping ring and dots each surmounted by a pellet.

Date: Probably second half of the 17th century

TYPE 2, DESIGN 4

5.25 Mirror frame

Accession number: 98.2/595

Material: Lead alloy

Condition: Almost complete; part of frame missing

Dimensions: H 77mm; H (aperture) 51mm; W 44mm; W (aperture) 33 mm

Description: An openwork rectangular frame with integrally cast pierced pediment and circular suspension loop. The pediment is decorated with a chevron trellis design and the frame has a cross in each corner with circles between.

Date: Late 17th century

Picture

Although there was a thriving art market throughout Europe during the 17th century, it was not until the 1660s that there was marked increase in the ownership of paintings in London households. Toy pictures for doll's houses were evidently made to reflect the contemporary demand for works of art, and although hundreds must have been produced with a variety of scenes and images to represent current taste, this is the only example in base metal which has been recognized in this country. The toy picture, with moulded decoration to represent a still-life flower painting, is small enough to hang in the parlour or bed chamber of a doll's house, and the subject matter, frame profile and decoration suggest production between 1660 and 1680, when works of this kind in 'cushion' frames were very much in vogue. Still-life flower paintings depicting baskets crammed with lilies, tulips, anemones, hortensias, carnations or rare and exotic blooms seem to have been particularly popular during the 1660s, and Samuel Pepys was astonished by the virtuosity and verisimilitude of a 'little flower-pott' painting which he noted was 'the finest thing that ever I think I saw in my life – the drops of Dew hanging on the leaves, so as I was forced again and again to put my finger to it to feel whether my eyes were deceived or no.'[25] It is possible that the tulips in the toy 'still life' were included for their emblematic significance,[26] and the inclusion of the crown, a probable allusion to the Restoration of the Monarchy, suggests English manufacture. The initials A and F either side of the basket are almost certainly those of the toymaker. It is possible that the '3 doz tin pictures' at 2s in the stock of haberdasher Gregory Day (see p. 34) were of a similar nature to the pieces described here.[27]

TYPE 1, DESIGN 1

5.26 Picture

Accession number: 98.2/576

Material: Lead alloy

Condition: Almost complete; some damage and a loose fragment

Dimensions: H *c.* 37mm; W 48mm

Inscription: AF

Description: A rectangular integrally cast 'still life' flower picture and pierced 'cushion-style' frame in a landscape format. The frame is decorated with partly open tulip blooms suspended from a twisted rope, and the edges are defined by cabling. The slightly recessed picture on a cross-hatched ground, depicts a basket of flowers with a quatrefoil rose flanked by tulips, 'berries' and foliage. The basket is hatched and cross-hatched to resemble canework, and is surmounted by an arched crown with cross patée. In the bottom corners are the letters A and F. Part of the frame is pierced, and the entire surface is covered with floral scrolling incorporating rosettes and partly opened tulip blooms.

Date: Probably 1660–70

Tray

Richly decorated pierced and embossed silver trays or shallow baskets with two handles were produced during the third quarter of the 17th century as presentation pieces,[28] but it was not until the mid-18th century that the standard form of tray emerged.[29] The miniature tray in this collection has the shape and stylistic features of silver and papier-mâché trays of the early 19th century, and possibly dates from this period.[30]

TYPE 1, DESIGN 1

5.27 Tray

Accession number: 98.2/577
Material: Lead alloy
Condition: Almost complete; one handle missing
Dimensions: H 25mm; W (without handle) 37mm
Description: A completely flat rectangular tray with beaded rim and one integrally cast angular handle (the other missing). Each corner is rounded and the upper face is decorated with a large plant within an engrailed beaded 'stem' with branching flowering tendrils.
Date: Late 18th or early 19th century

Voider

During the 17th century, the term 'voider' or 'night basket' was used in England to describe shallow round or oval baskets of straw or osier twigs 'made white [and] very neatly made with a round foote and 3 or 4 eares or handles, some on the sides, others on the tope'.[31] These voiders had bevelled sloping sides, and were 'much used by nurses, and waiting women, to put either childrens, or their mistrises night and day cloaths in'. Luxury versions – in beadwork, tin-glazed earthenware and silver – were also made for a newborn's layette, as receptacles for christening presents or simply for display, and a number have survived in English, Continental and American collections dating from 1652 to the early 1680s.[32] The shallow, rectangular tray in this collection clearly represents a luxury voider of this kind, and while an English attribution is not impossible, the general shape and the presence of lug rather than loop handles tend to suggest a Continental origin or influence. The foliate relief and general decoration on the miniature is reasonably convincing, although as Geoff Egan has pointed out, 'the [central] rose motif probably owes more to the 17th-century tradition of decorating flat-vessel toys than to designs on actual christening trays'.[33]

TYPE 1, DESIGN 1

5.28 Voider

Accession number: 98.2/574
Material: Lead alloy
Condition: Complete; very slight damage and fragment of handle missing
Dimensions: H 32mm; W 36mm
Description: A shallow rectangular tray with bevelled sides and flat base. The rim is beaded and there are S-shaped scroll handles in the middle of the long axis. The sides are decorated with diametrically opposed bifurcated designs and there are concentric rings in each corner. There is a very large sexfoil double rose in the centre with calyx points extending beyond and between the outer row of petals. Concentric ring motifs fill the corners.
Date: Probably 1660s

1. Paul von Stetten, *Erlaüterung der in Kupfer … In historischen Briefen an ein Frauenzimmer* (Augsburg,1765)

2. Earle 1989, p. 300.

3. Willemsen 1998, p. 292, refers to the inventory of Adriana Bloys van Treslong (1647) which included '1 black deal case with all kinds of doll's apparatus, representing the household'.

4. It is difficult to know whether the children actually played with these toys in the street (although it is quite possible that they did) or whether the artist chose an outdoors setting because that was the only way to illustrate the mix of rough and tumble games with sedentary activities.

5. Cats 1618 includes Adriaen van de Venne's prints, *Children's games expounded as symbols and moral precepts* to which he added a didactic commentary.

6. Michaelis 1975, p. 42.

7. Holme 1688, bk 3, ch. 14, sec. 1b, no. 21.

8. Five from the Billingsgate foreshore recovered in 1984; one from Swan Lane, 1989; and one from Salisbury, 1987.

9. Spencer 1998, p. 5, fig. 3 and Kashden 1987, p. 46, fig. 1. This candlestick is now part of the Neish collection in the Pewter Museum, Stratford-upon-Avon. One of the Billingsgate candlesticks is inscribed with the names of the Three Wise Men.

10. Kashden 1987, p. 47, figs 3–5 (private collection).

11. A possible medieval socket candlestick in lead alloy found in Canterbury in March 1987 (now in a private collection) has the remains of what appears to be a tripod, pricket-style candle-holder base.

12. Egan, forthcoming a, no. 609, from a 16th-century context; Bangs 1995, 78 & 234, no. 40 which have been attributed to the 16th century with a possible West Country provenance. The Lear Collection of Socket Candlesticks, sold at Christies's 15 December 1998, also included several miniatures in lead and copper alloy, two of which were ascribed to the 14th century (see Bangs 1975, nos. 171 & 172).

13. Willemsen 1998, p. 375, B67, from Middelburg, Rotterdam and Sluis. It is also possible that the object described as a toy brazier from an early 14th-century context in the Amsterdam Historisch Museum (inv no. Ne-13) is actually a pricket candlestick with a broken-off spike. The 'bowl' or drip pan is decorated with circles and geometric patterns.

14. Bruna 1997, p. 4, fig. 8 (45 x 32 mm), now in the collections of the Musée national du Moyen Age, Paris.

15. Willemsen 1994, fig. 6.

16. There is some evidence that sea-coal was used in London homes during the 13th century: see Brimblecombe 1982.

17. Schofield 1995, p. 115.

18. There are several objects shaped like fire backs in the collection, but these seem to have the vestiges of bracket handles which suggests that they were intended as dripping pans.

19. Willemsen 1998: earthenware curfews p. 369, B51; tin-lead-alloy curfews, p. 389, B114 & p. 393, B127; tongs p. 379, B76; and shovel p. 392, B124. See also Baart 1977, p. 466, no. 886.

20. Holme 1688, bk 3, ch. 14, sec. 1f, no. 92.

21. Holme 1688, bk 3, ch. 14, sec. 1b, no. 29.

22. Holme 1688, bk 3, ch. 14, sec. 1b, no. 28.

23. Holme 1688, bk 3, ch. 14, sec. 1d, nos. 58–9.

24. *The Post Man*, 13 February 1700.

25. Samuel Pepys, *Diary,* 11 April 1669.

26. Taylor 1995.

27. CLRO MCI/56/190, 22 March, 1633.

28. Oman 1970, p. 47 & plate 45; Clayton 1971, no. 10.

29. Clayton 1971, p. 322; Dixon 1964.

30. Clayton 1971, nos. 699 & 698.

31. Holme 1688, bk 3, ch. 14, sec. 1f, no. 82. The term 'voider' was also used to describe a receptacle into which something was emptied, particularly after a meal.

32. Decorative art historians describe vessels of this form as 'layette baskets', although this term was not used in England much before the early 19th century. Beadwork examples: V&A no. T.69–1936 (English, dated 1659). Silver examples: Rijksmuseum, by Hans Coenradt Brechtel (date letter 1652) in den Blaauwen 1979, p. 116, no. 56; Museum of Fine Arts, Boston, by Adriaen gan Hoaecke (1666–7); Gilbert Collection, Somerset House (possibly English, *c.* 1670) in Schroder 1988, pp. 112–15, no. 25. Tin-glazed earthenware: Colonial Williamsburg Foundation (dated 1679) and City Museum, Liverpool (dated 1681).

33. Egan 1996, p. 12.

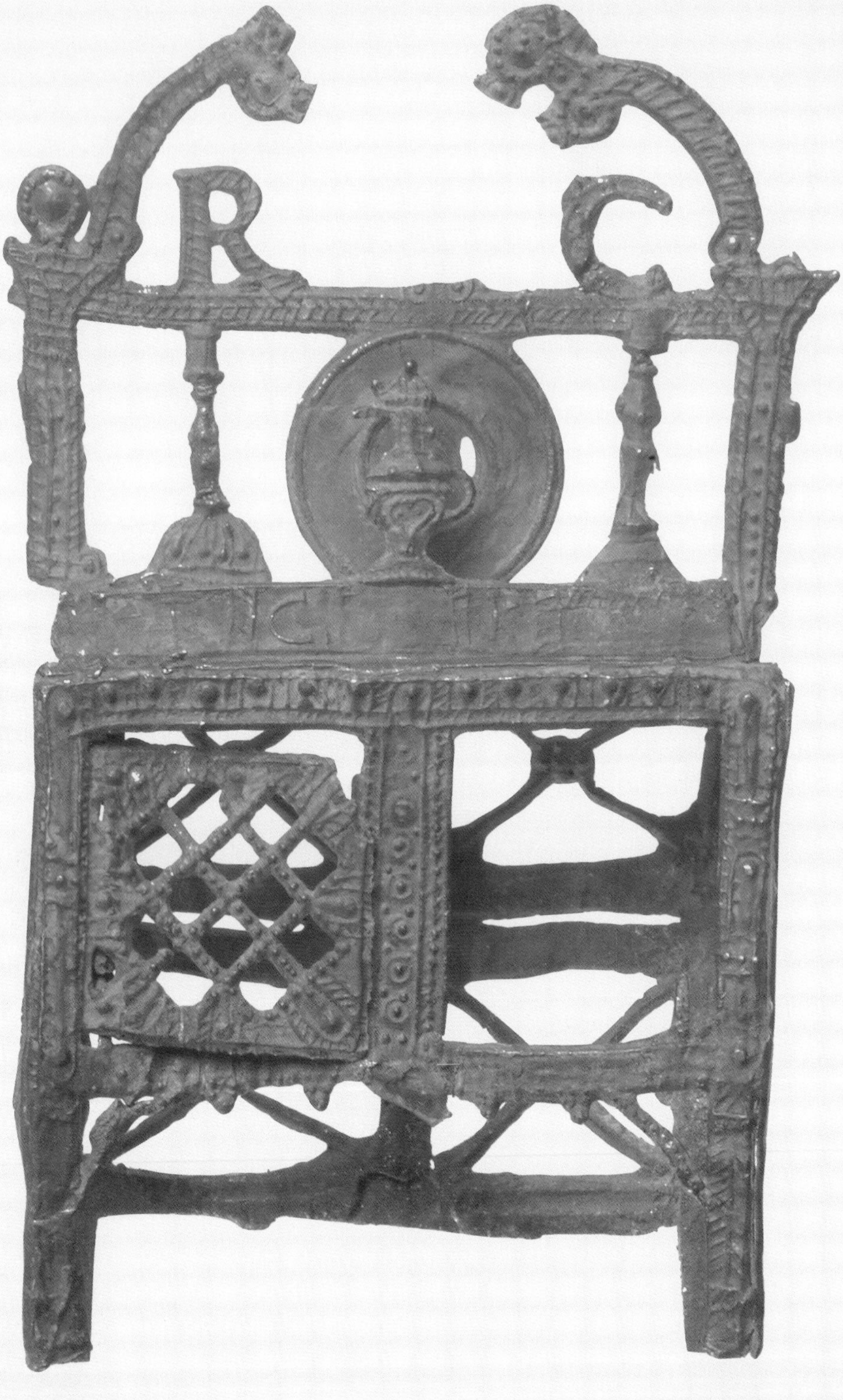
R
C

6 Furniture

'The furniture of our houses...exceedeth, and is grown in manner even to passing delicacy'[1]

Until a virtually complete toy buffet (cupboard) was discovered in March 1994, the enigmatic nature of many of the fragments included in this section posed considerable problems of identification and attribution. There were a few recognizable items, but in most cases it was not even clear whether the fragments were related to pieces of furniture at all, and for some, an element of doubt remains. Thus the discovery of an almost complete toy buffet was not only remarkable in itself, but provided much needed evidence which enabled us to re-evaluate all the toy furniture and analogous material.

Furniture has always had an aesthetic and cultural significance beyond its functional purpose, and throughout the late medieval and early modern period pieces were acquired to emphasize wealth, status and social aspiration. Specific forms were produced to reflect the tastes and cultural mores of the day, and by the end of the 16th century inventories show that most households had several pieces of furniture in each room. Unfortunately, however, very little early furniture has survived changing fashions and the vicissitudes of centuries, and some forms are only known from contemporary illustrations and descriptions. Chests are more numerous than any other category of English medieval furniture but as furniture historian Penelope Eames has cautioned, 'chance rather than a meaningful pattern has dictated what remains' and the survival rates of certain types should not be viewed as an indicator of their relative importance or popularity in the past.[2] The same argument should be applied to the toy furniture fragments. Some of the toys represent forms that have not survived, or are not known in full scale, while other common furniture types such as armoires, beds and benches do not appear to be represented in the toy corpus at all.[3]

There are 136 items of furniture and furniture components in the collection and the following types are represented:

Table 6.1

Bird cages	5
Buffets	44
Chairs	18
Chests	67
Cradle	1
Stool	1
Total	**136**

The toys appear to be modelled on furniture ranging in date from the 15th to the late 18th centuries, although the majority have stylistic and design features that point to a production date between *c.* 1500 and 1700. Five pieces bear dates from 1640 to 1646, and some are closely datable because they represent particular styles of furniture that were fashionable during a specific period. Others are virtually impossible to date, either because they are too fragmentary and stylized or because no comparable examples have survived in full scale. Dating is also difficult when the designs imitate styles that were in vogue over a long period. But the range of types and the considerable number of mould variations within each type do give an indication of the scale of production and the popularity of base-metal toy furniture in the early modern period. The best leave little to the imagination in the complexity of their construction, design and ornamentation, and some are so sophisticated and delicate that they were probably made as adult conceits. Others are extremely crude, such as the Type 3 buffets, but whether these were cheaper products, examples from an earlier phase of toy furniture manufacture or simply examples of inferior workmanship is unclear. A range of types of different quality and price may have been produced coevally, perhaps geared to a particular market; just as today, relatively cheap plastic, metal and wooden toys are manufactured for children whilst expensive highly crafted miniatures are made for adult collectors.

Most of the pieces were designed to be freestanding three-dimensional structures, and these were created from a single casting which was bent into shape and secured by solder, but a few seem to have been cast in a complex part mould. No discernible change in production technique or assembly method is apparent over time, and the pieces found on the Continent seem to have been made in exactly the same way. Although the tradition of toy furniture manufacture is strong in Europe and many exquisite wood and silver examples survive in private and national collections, extant examples in base metals are comparatively rare.[4] Most of the fragments in the corpus copy English forms and styles and seem to have been made in London, but it is possible that base-metal toy furniture manufacture had its origins in Europe and early examples might have found their way to England, inspiring domestic manufacture. As yet no documentary evidence has come to light on either side of the Channel to suggest a trade of this kind.

Bird cages

'the Bird-Fanciers in and about London are so numerous a Tribe, that there is a pretty good Demand for their Goods'[5]

As levels of disposable income increased in the 17th century, more and more people could afford to buy luxuries. A flourishing trade in song birds developed, and contemporary newspapers carried advertisements for 'choice singing Canary Birds' or 'Wistling Birds, of all sorts'. The demand for white and grey canaries from Germany, the Netherlands, Italy and the Canary Islands as well as parakeets and other exotic species from the West Indies was considerable, and the birds were housed in wire, wicker, wood and ceramic cages. The quality of the materials and complexity of design were a potent symbol of wealth and status,[6] and while the wealthiest bird fanciers could afford elaborate architectural cages for their show and breeding birds, most people preferred the simpler bell-shaped form favoured by the Dutch, which could be suspended from the ceiling or wall.[7]

The toy bird cages are of two kinds. The Type 1 cages were made from a flat casting which was subsequently folded and soldered into a freestanding, three-dimensional structure. These have a rectangular form with an integrally cast handle and seed pot, a little like the cage depicted in 'Buy a fine singing Bird' from Marcellus Laroon's *Cries of London* series published in the 1680s. The Type 2 lid fragments with suspension loops probably represent the openwork cylindrical cages of wood or brass, which are frequently depicted in Low Countries genre paintings of the 17th century. None of the distinctively shaped rush or wicker cages is represented within the toy corpus, although these were undoubtedly also made in miniature form.[8] The earliest known toy bird cage, excavated in Nieuwlande from an early 16th-century context, has a rectangular domed profile with a tiny metal bird inside.[9]

TYPE 1, DESIGN 1

6.1 Bird cage

Accession number: 98.2/596
Material: Lead alloy
Condition: Fairly complete; two sides and top and bottom plates
Dimensions: H 33mm; W 23mm; Dpt 13mm
Description: Part of a three-dimensional rectangular bird cage with solid base and lower sides, closely packed triangular-sectioned bars and solid top. On one side, an integrally cast handle is attached halfway up the bars and the plain panel below has the relief profile of a bird feeder. By contrast, the opposing panel has a tiny rectangular 'draw tray' with a scalloped border, surrounded by floral and foliate tendrils. Although the top and bottom plates are entirely covered with a diaper pattern with pellets at each intersection, the pattern is different.
Date: 17th–18th century
Comparandum: An identical bottom plate recovered from Butler's Wharf, August 2001

TYPE 1, DESIGN 2

6.2 Bird cage

Accession number: 98.2/597
Material: Lead alloy
Condition: Part only; flat
Dimensions: W 22mm; Dpt 12mm
Description: This fragment is now flat, but represents the lower section of a three-dimensional rectangular bird cage. The narrow side has the relief profile of a bird feeder just below the bars, but is otherwise plain. The long side is decorated with two lines of horizontal beading and there is a small rectangular 'drawer' at the top left with ring and dot motifs. To the right a line of inverted Vs with 'tied' tops are aligned with the bar stubs. The diaper pattern base with pellets at each intersection has a hatched ground and beaded edge.
Date: 17th–18th century
Comments: The V-shaped 'ties' might represent tied struts or bars.

TYPE 1, DESIGN 3

6.3 Bird cage

Accession number: 98.2/128
Material: Lead alloy
Condition: Part; probably top of the cage
Dimensions: H 13 mm; L 23mm
Description: One solid panel section from a three-dimensional bird cage, decorated with a diaper pattern, pellets at each intersection and beading on three sides. There is a wide band and ridge along one side and the stubs of the cage bars are extant.
Date: 17th–18th century
Comments: Probably a top panel

TYPE 2, DESIGN 1

6.4 Bird cage

Accession number: 98.2/614*; 98.2/615
Material: Lead alloy
Condition: 98.2/614 with suspension loop; both damaged
Dimensions: H c. 10mm; Diam 34mm
Description: Domed lids cast from the same mould with pierced top and integrally cast suspension loop. There are three or four rectangular slots around the edge for attachment and the lid is decorated with radial gadrooning and beading.
Date: 17th century
Comments: Probably the top of a cylindrical bird cage of the type depicted by Gerrit Dou [1613–1675] in *A Lady playing a Clavichord*, Dulwich Picture Gallery

Buffets, cup boards or cupboards

'Than emperialle thy Cuppeborde with Silver and gild fulle gay, thy Ewry borde with basons and lavour, watur hoot and cold, eche other to alay'[10]

For much of the medieval and early modern periods, the terms cup board and cupboard were used indiscriminately to describe several different kinds of furniture. Used in its original and literal sense, the cup board was simply a board or table used for the display of standing cups, flagons, bottles and other drinking vessels. But as the function of the cup board evolved and changed during the course of the 15th century, the words were combined to describe furniture with open shelves for display as well as furniture with enclosed spaces for storage. Since cupboards assumed many forms and were used for so many different purposes, contemporaries tried to distinguish one cupboard from another by adding a prefix or qualifying phrase to define the specific type. Cupboards fitted with doors or drawers were variously described as 'close' or 'livery' cupboards, or cupboards with a 'loker', 'aumbrie' or 'presse'; while low open cupboards consisting of two or three tiered shelves were generally known as 'court' cupboards. Contemporary spellings also began to reflect changes in function and 'cubbard', 'cubard', 'cubberd' were common contractions.

By the second half of the 16th century, the fashion for displaying plate on cupboards of various kinds had become widespread. As William Harrison remarked in his *Description of England* published in 1577 the 'furniture of our houses … is growne in manner even to passing delicacie: and herein I do not speake of the nobilitie and gentrie onelie … Certes, in noble mens houses it is not rare to see abundance of … silver vessell, and so much plate, as may furnish sundrie cupboards to the sum oftentimes of a thousand or two thousand pounds at the least… [but] even the inferiour artificers have for the most part learned to garnish their cupboards with plate.'[11] Almost every type of cupboard could be used to show off a few cups and other vessels, but as the fashion for garnishing furniture with large amounts of plate and other precious objects increased, special cupboards were developed with high backs, shelves and multiple stages, which were specifically designed for ostentatious show. These purpose-built plate cupboards were variously described as high-standing court-cupboards, a cupboard of plate, high-standing plate cupboards or buffets.[12] The French term buffet seems to have been applied specifically to those cupboards with a really elaborate superstructure incorporating a stepped arrangement of stages, and since

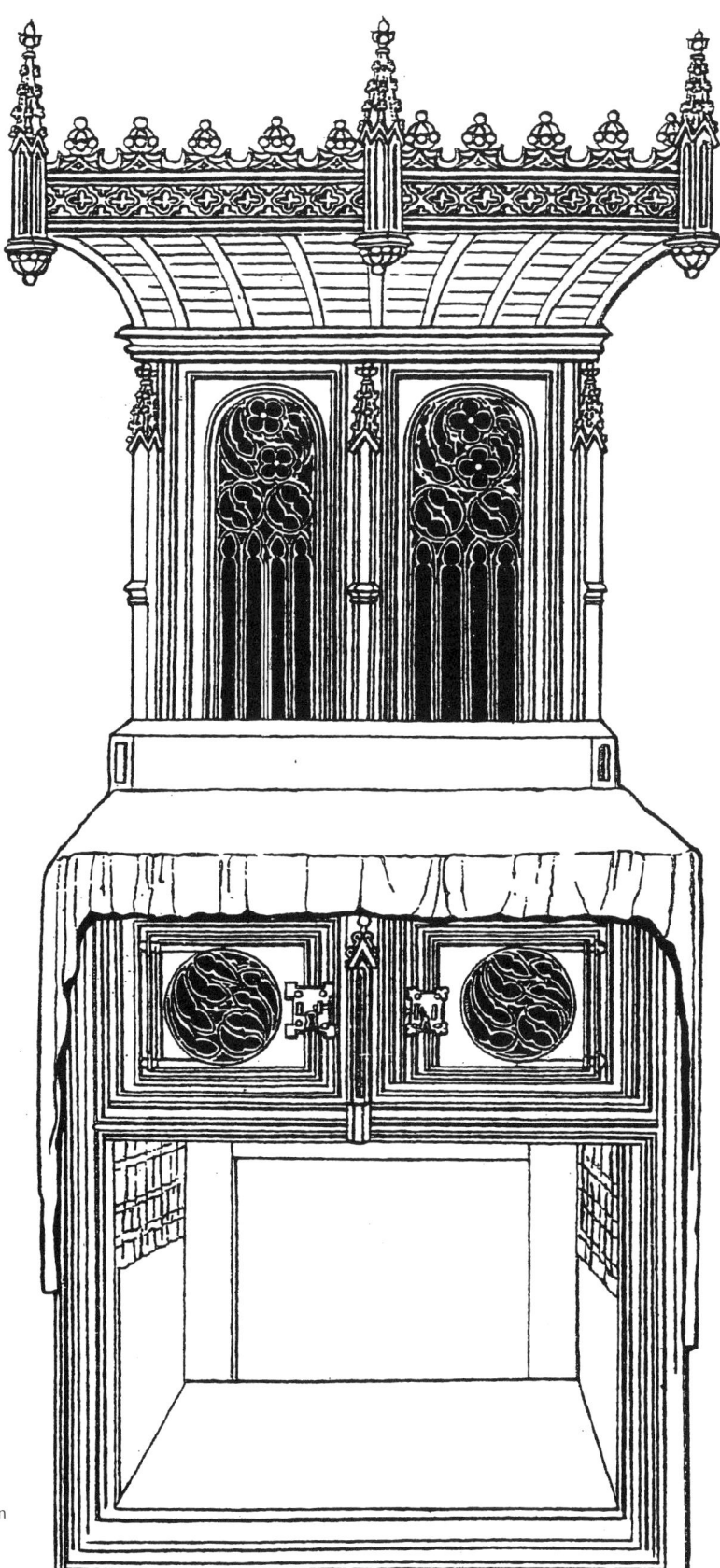

Fig. 44. French buffet with arched pediment and single stage, late 15th century
Reproduced from Kenny Shaw's drawing in *Specimens of Ancient Furniture*, 1836, plate XXV, taken from a manuscript in what was then the King's Library, Paris

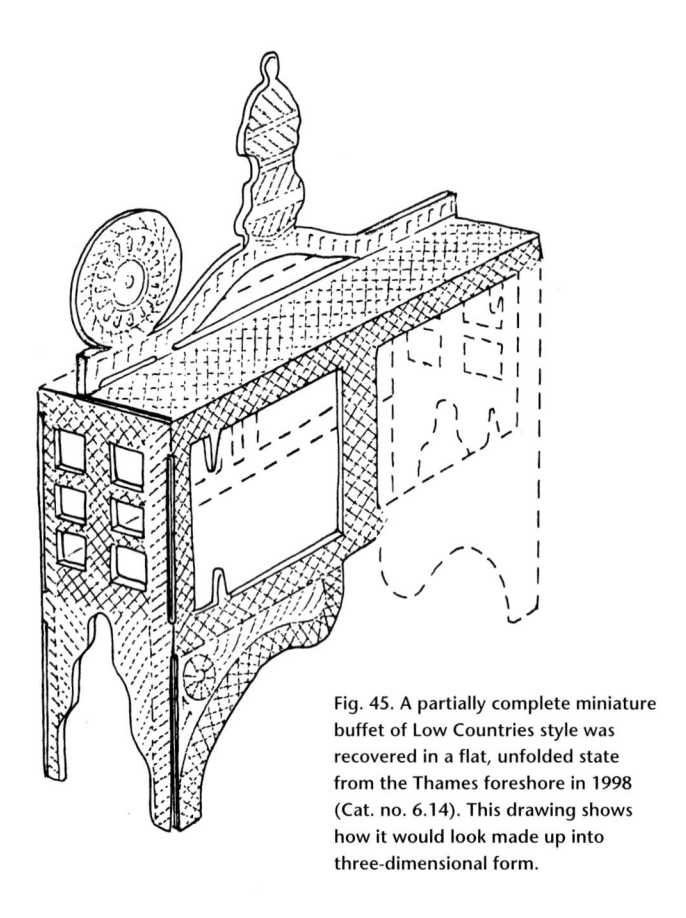

Fig. 45. A partially complete miniature buffet of Low Countries style was recovered in a flat, unfolded state from the Thames foreshore in 1998 (Cat. no. 6.14). This drawing shows how it would look made up into three-dimensional form.

the toys discussed in this section are of this type, the label buffet has been chosen in preference to other contemporary terms.[13]

Construction and design details

The 44 objects which have been identified as buffet or buffet components constitute the second largest furniture group in the collection, and although much of the material is fragmentary there seem to be three distinct types with 12 design variations.

Structural evidence suggests that the buffets were manufactured flat in a two-piece mould for subsequent assembly to three-dimensional form, and the matrix was designed in such a way that the flat casting could be bent and manipulated to produce a high-standing enclosed buffet with decorative high back, multiple stages, display board and miniature articles of plate (fig. 45).[14] To keep the structure intact and reinforce the joins, integrally cast tabs positioned at key points along the edges were bent at right angles and soldered on to an adjacent panel. When the three-dimensional form was complete, the 'storage' space was enclosed by separately cast hinged doors and although the precise method of attachment is uncertain, it seems that the hinge was dropped over a fixed pintle projecting upwards from the bottom of the frame approximately 3mm from the outer corner. This simple device held the door in place and enabled it to pivot. Once the door was vertically aligned in the frame the top of the hinge was secured; this seems to have been achieved by passing a pin through a hole in the display board.[15] The hole was then plugged with solder. This potentially hazardous procedure incurred risks to the door and its delicate hinge and to the display board and frame, and many of the display boards show signs of damage with melted edges adjacent to the 'hinge' apertures. Although these areas of damage can probably be attributed to the method of door attachment, it is possible that some of the blemishes mark the position of miniature plate which has since broken off.

Because the toys are so insubstantial only the gentlest handling would have ensured that they reached the customer in perfect condition and it stretches credulity to suppose that they were transported any distance in a made-up form. The fact that two of the buffets were recovered from the foreshore in pre-assembly condition lends some support to this supposition, and although Cat. no. 6.11 was folded by the finder before it was acquired by the museum, Cat. no. 6.14 remains as found: the tabs are undamaged, there is no evidence of solder and the surface is uniformly even. If the toys were transported flat to reduce the risk of damage, were they manufactured in one London workshop and passed to another for assembly, or were they made elsewhere?

The most complete buffets have an openwork back panel divided into two sections linked by horizontal bars. The upper half, above the display board and stage, is surmounted by a segmental arched pediment or 'canopy', but the lower section consists of two rows of paired saltires. The panels have moulded decoration on the front, but the backs are completely smooth and there are several bent tabs at various points around the edge which do not seem to serve any structural purpose. The function of these tabs is unclear but it is possible that they were designed to hold a metal or textile foil in place imitating the textile hangings behind the carved tracery backs and canopies on some of the full-scale buffets. These textiles were an essential part of the buffet display and in her treatise *Les Honneurs de la Cour,* Alienor de Poitiers provides a very vivid and detailed description of a four-stage buffet with a fringed 'dorseret' or canopy of gold and crimson cloth bordered in black velvet and worked in gold thread with the personal device of Duc Phillippe of Burgundy. The 'dorseret' was draped behind the buffet from top to bottom and the borders were trimmed with different fabrics to enhance the decorative effect.[16] Did the toy furniture makers use a textile foil to replicate this custom, and is this why the toy buffets have a flimsy openwork back rather than a solid moulding?[17] Unfortunately there is no trace of a foil on any of the buffets but one of the chests in the collection has a thin sheet of copper alloy underneath the openwork tracery of the domed lid which serves to reflect the light and accentuate the design.[18] A copper-alloy foil would have made a supportive backing and lining material but it is also possible that a paper insert or a coloured cloth was used.

Since full-sized buffets were costly and designed for conspicuous display they were usually placed in a prominent position in the parlour or hall where they could be seen to great effect. On special occasions every available surface was covered with a splendid array of plate and family treasures which enhanced the prestige of the host and complimented his guests. The standard of carving, height and grandeur of the superstructure, the number of stages, the magnificence of the plate and the quality of the textile covers and hangings all helped to emphasize wealth and status, and buffets were greatly prized. The most prestigious examples had an elaborate canopy or 'sayling hance' which provided a physical and aesthetic counterbalance to the multiple-stage display and this feature is suggested by the arched openwork pediment on the toys.[19]

Multiple-staged buffets with a high back and canopy seem to have gone out of fashion during the first half of the 17th century and because most were broken up or remodelled to suit contemporary tastes, few have survived. The best English example, made for Sir John Wynne in 1535, has elaborately carved cupboard doors with an arched and pierced canopy, and the overall shape is not unlike the buffet depicted in the Chelsea home of Sir Thomas More in a preparatory drawing by Holbein of *c.* 1527.[20] In many respects the toy buffets seem to be stylistically similar to Continental forms which were far more flamboyant than their English counterparts: they had longer legs, the cupboards only occupied the upper part of the lower stage, and the back boards were usually surmounted by an intricately pierced and carved canopy. The most complete examples represented by Type 1 are not unlike a late 15th-century oak buffet from the Lower Rhine with two carved solid cupboard doors, display board, stage and canopy, now in the collections of the Landschaftsmuseum, Burg Linn, Krefeld,[21] and the toys' moulded detail also resembles the carving on an elegant French walnut buffet of slightly later date in the Michel Dumez-Onof collection.[22] But the closest parallels come from visual sources. A buffet with a high back and several shelves is shown in a 15th-century miniature included in *L'Histoire d'Olivier de Castille et d'Artus d'Algarbe,* and there are others with elaborate canopies and stages in the 15th-century miniatures of the *Histoire du Bon Roi Alexandre* and the *Roman de Renaud de Montauban,*[23] as well as von der Heide's *The Feast of Ahaseurus and Esther, c.* 1500–10.[24]

Although the toy buffets have some 'foreign' features, it is possible that the comparative abundance of pictorial sources and surviving furniture from the Continent has presented a false and misleading picture of the types and styles available to the English market, and the toys could well represent an English form which has not survived in full scale. This might account for the absence of toy buffets in collections and excavations on the Continent and the very Englishness of the shield and chevron on the Type 1 buffets.[25] The repeated use of the City of London arms also suggests London production. A precise attribution for the buffets is very difficult, however, because whilst certain elements seem to have been drawn from full-scale furniture, many of the fragments are little more than a fanciful interpretation, reflecting rather than representing a specific type of high-status furniture, and since they seem to be an eclectic mix of styles they probably do not represent a single source.

Dating evidence

The toys appear to resemble full-scale buffets of late 15th- to mid-16th-century date and the decorative elements include a wide range of motifs commonly found on furniture in this period. The use of egg and dart, guilloche, scrolls, nulling, strapwork, spindle and linenfold mouldings, the shield shapes on the solid doors, and the absence of heavy, bulbous Renaissance designs which were so characteristic of the Elizabethan and Jacobean period might indicate production in the early to mid-16th century. While analogous comparisons can be drawn between the design motifs on the toys and full-scale buffets, however, this process can only be taken so far. The malleable nature of metal offers a wide range of decorative possibilities but the manufactured product is only as good as the mould from which it was made. Engraving a stone mould with fine detail for delicate metal casting is extremely difficult, and the metalworker undoubtedly compromised, relying on the traditions and conventions of his trade to execute a mould for the toys. This is evident in much of the decoration; for example, hatching, beading and pellets are frequently employed in the decorative scheme, and even though these designs do suggest a 'carved' surface, they were part of the metalworkers' standard repertoire, employed on a wide range of small metal artefacts from the medieval period onwards.

A certain amount of dating and production evidence can be gleaned from the tiny reproductions of plate on the display board and stages. The ewer and candlesticks have intricate detail and the degree of ornamentation suggests that the pieces were intended to represent high-status products of silver or silver gilt, rather than bronze or pewter. The style of the ewer and basin resembles Low Countries/German plate of *c.* 1550, but the candlesticks are more difficult to date, and the small scale and stylized representation compounds the problem of attribution. To some extent the shapes are suggestive of Low Countries work, although one has a straight sided socket and 'bell' base, a characteristic feature of many English candlesticks. The problem is compounded because similar forms were cast coevally in Britain and the Low Countries for much of the 16th century and national characteristics are difficult to define.[26]

Inscriptions and devices

As Table 6.2 shows (p. 204), 15 buffets are inscribed with letters and devices of various kinds. These include the letters RC; R [...], [C] R and EL[Z]; the City of London arms; motifs resembling triple crowns – possibly the arms of the Worshipful Company of Drapers; and an unknown armorial achievement of a shield and chevron.[27]

One of the most intriguing features is the prominent and repeated use of the letters RC and their inclusion on two, perhaps three differently moulded buffets. Unlike other inscribed toys in the corpus, the letters are a major feature of the design and they are not only prominently placed within the frame of the back board, but are also repeated twice on the riser of the stage. The actual significance of these inscriptions and motifs has given rise to considerable speculation. Were the letters the initials of the toymaker, or do they represent the ownership marks commonly incorporated into the design of full-scale furniture?

The inclusion of ciphers, monograms and personal devices within the design of full-scale furniture is well documented, and as Penelope Eames has argued in her analysis of buffets and dressoirs 'it is possible that most, if not all the furniture which was newly acquired for a great household in the later Middle Ages was rendered as individual to that household as was the livery worn by its servants', although she stresses that such objects were not necessarily used personally by the owner.[28] An oak buffet c. 1478–97, in the collections of the Busleyden Museum, Malines for example, carries the personal devices of Phillip the Good and Charles the Bold, as well as the monogram CM for Charles and his wife Marguerite (of York), and there is a late 15th-century oak chest inscribed 'N FARES' with NF monograms carved on the end panels in the collections of the Victoria and Albert Museum.[29] The carving of personal arms, emblems and motifs on furniture was evidently widespread, but as Victor Chinnery notes these 'were not always strictly accurate in heraldic terms' and details could be adapted or 'omitted to suit the demands of space or materials'.[30] The practice of personalizing furniture continued into the 17th century, and a drawing attributed to the architect Pierre Collot shows a richly ornamented French cabinet with repeated double M ciphers under a royal crown, presumably intended for Queen Marie de Medici before her deposition in 1630.

The personalization of furniture also extended to the textile coverings, napery and towels which were used to adorn a buffet or cupboard, and it is possible that the devices and inscriptions covering the display board and side panels on the toy buffets were meant to replicate the kind of decoration found on a highly figured 16th-century linen cupboard cloth or runner. Full-scale buffets were adorned with fine-quality cloths, towels and passementerie fringing[31] to emphasize wealth and status and enhance the aesthetic appeal of the display, and figured damask and diaper linens were imported into England from the Low Countries and France from the early 16th century.[32] Analysis of contemporary records and investigation of surviving examples shows that some of the designs were made specifically for the English market or were especially commissioned to incorporate the personal arms, emblems or portraits of wealthy consumers, and the highly decorative 'cupboard cloths' on the toy buffets seem to represent textiles of this sort and quality. If this interpretation

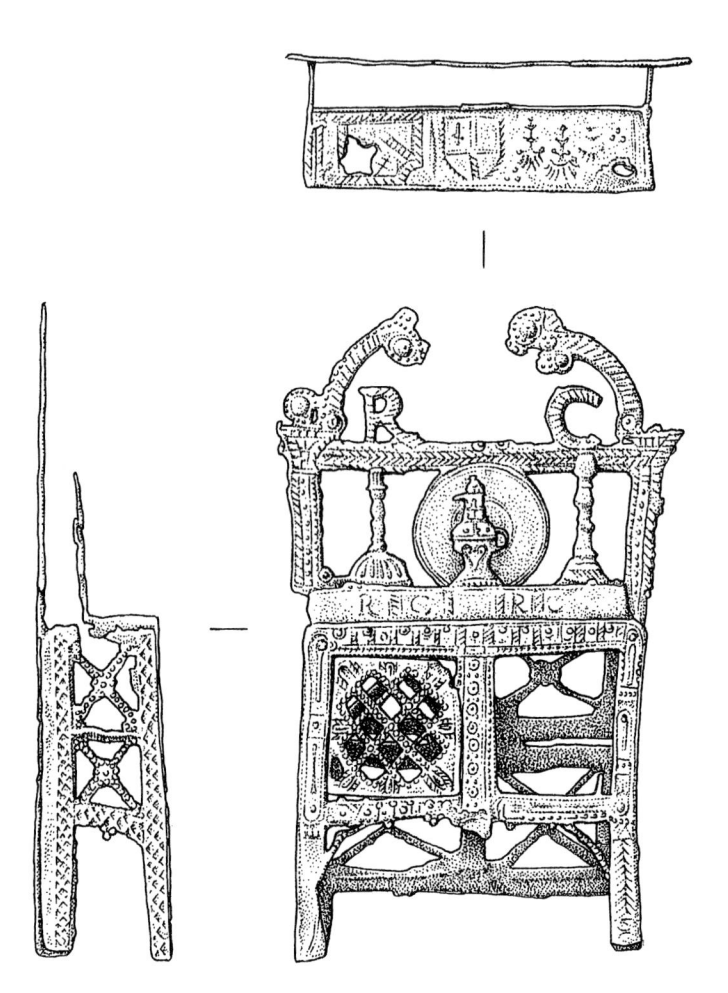

Fig. 46. Side and front of a buffet (Cat. no. 6.5), with a top view to show the 'cupboard cloth' incorporating a shield, the City of London arms and, apparently, the triple crowns of the Worshipful Company of Drapers. Possibly made as a souvenir for a mayoral banquet in the late 16th century

OPPOSITE: Fig. 47. Detail showing a late 15th-century buffet in the *Roman de Renaud de Montauban*. See plate VII, p. 167

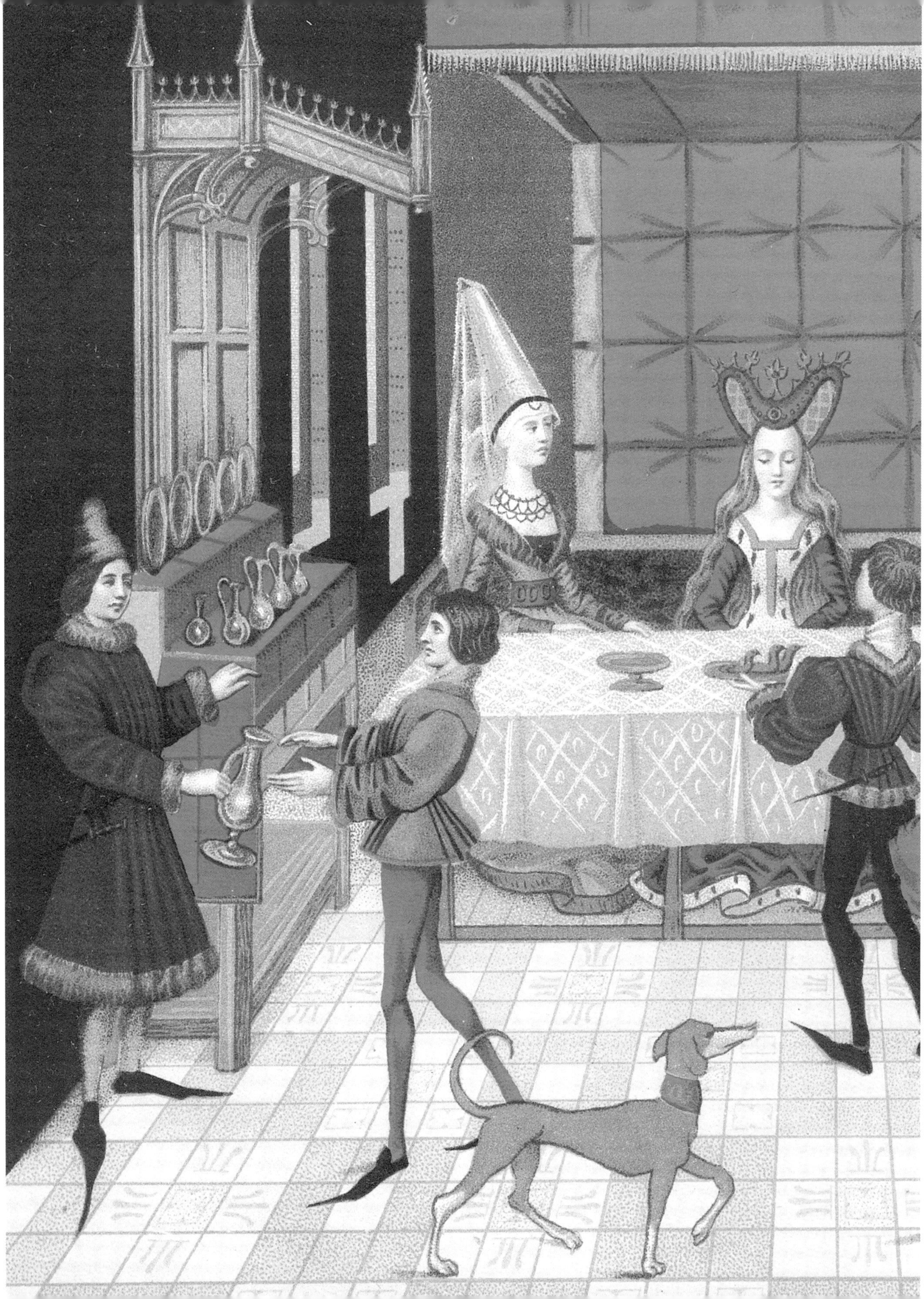

is correct, this might explain why the letters RC are repeated on the back board and again on the stage riser, and why the letters EL[Z] appear on the display board with the City of London arms and other motifs. The 'cupboard cloth' on the most complete buffet only covers the display board, but there are a number of fragments with detailed mouldings on the side panels which might represent the overhang of a runner.[33]

Although it is unclear whether the motifs and inscriptions were meant to represent carving or textile patterns, the intriguing question of their significance remains. Why are the inscriptions linked with the City of London arms, and why are those arms repeated on the display boards, doors and side panels? The buffets inscribed RC (T1, D1) are also marked with 'triple crown' motifs which appear to be a stylized version of the arms of the Worshipful Company of Drapers, namely three clouds proper, the sun beams issuing with three imperial crowns.[34] Are the inscriptions and devices a ruse on the part of the toymaker, or do they have particular meaning? The buffets are not the only articles of toy furniture marked in this way and components from three-dimensional chests or chairs also have the triple crown motifs and the arms of the City of London.[35] Although the symbolic relevance and association of these inscriptions and devices can only be guessed at today, the deliberate juxtaposition of the City of London arms, triple crowns and the letters RC clearly had some significance in the 16th century.

If the triple crown motifs have been correctly interpreted as the arms of the Worshipful Company of Drapers, it is possible that a range of toy furniture was commissioned to mark a particular Company event or commemorate a distinguished member with the initials RC. The most eminent member of the Drapers' Company in the 16th century with the initials RC was Sir Richard Champion, who was Master of the Company six times between 1557 and 1568, and Lord Mayor as well as Master in 1565–6. Sir Richard was evidently renowned for his munificence and largesse and is described by the early 17th-century historian Jaggard in somewhat eulogistic terms as a Lord Mayor 'who shewed himselfe very diligent and carefull in the discharge of the trust to him committed … at his death he left a very Christian and charitable token of remembrance to all after ages, for as in his life time he relieved the poore, so he hath ordained a weekly stipend to be bestowed upon the poore of the parish of S. Dunstans in the East, where he lyth under a very faire monument erected. In his time was purchased by the City, certain houses in Cornhill, amounting to the some of 532 poundes …'[36] After his death in 1568, Lady Barbara erected the St Dunstan's monument to her husband, and the accompanying inscription included the following phrase: '*Both rich and poor did like him well and yet do praise his Name*'.[37] Such was Sir Richard's reputation as a righteous man that he was commemorated in a heroic pageant of 1621 entitled *The Sun in Aries* commissioned and paid for by the Drapers' Company.[38]

Sir Richard seems to have been a generous man and although there is no documentary evidence to link him with the toys, it is just possible that they were used at an election feast to mark place settings in jesting allusion to the practice which entitled the Master to use

Table 6.2

Type	Design	Quantity	Inscription	Side panel	Device/s	H	W	Dpt
1	1	3	RC	Saltire lattice	City of London arms/ shield with chevron/ triple crowns	85mm	55mm	17mm
	2	1	[C] R					
	3	1	R [...]					
	4	1						
	5	1						
	6	1						
2	1	4	EL[Z]	Solid/City arms	City of London arms		51mm	17mm
	2	1		Solid/City arms	City of London arms			
	3	2		Solid/City arms	City of London arms			
3	1	1		Grid lattice			50mm	19mm
	2	1		Lattice				
	3	1						
	4	1						

Company plate during his term of office. It is also possible that they were distributed as souvenirs on Lord Mayor's Day in 1565 and the inclusion of a flaming heart 'medallion' on the buffet ewer, an emblem of charity, could be significant in this regard.[39] If these buffets were used as adult conceits, and if they were commissioned by Sir Richard Champion, one might expect to find a version of his personal arms on the display board rather than the shield and chevron.[40] It is also unlikely that several buffet designs were commissioned by one individual, and so perhaps after all, the initials are those of a toymaker as yet unidentified.

TYPE 1

Although this type is represented by a complete buffet and nine fragments produced from six different moulds, they have a number of features in common. The most complete have the letters R and C on the pediment and stage riser, and when they survive, the display boards are decorated with a shield and chevron, the City of London arms and motifs resembling the triple crowns of the Drapers' Company. Because most of the pieces are very small it is impossible to know whether the buffets had a similar shape in their original condition, but they all have elaborate mouldings and an abundance of plate, indicative of top-quality furniture. An exact parallel for these buffets is unknown, but the stylistic elements and form of the most complete example (Acc. no. 94.43) suggests an early to mid-16th-century date for the type.

TYPE 1, DESIGN 1

6.5 Buffet

Accession number: 94.43*; 98.2/2; 98.2/7
Material: Lead alloy
Condition: 94.43: almost complete; door; some plate and part of pediment missing. 98.2/2: cupboard only; two doors extant; some damage and restoration. 98.2/7: part of cupboard side panel (right side)
Inscription: RC
Dimensions: 94.43: H 85mm; H (door) 18mm; H (door aperture) 20mm; W 55mm; W (door) 18mm; W (door aperture) 17mm; Dpt 17mm
Description: A three-dimensional openwork structure with part of a possible segmental arched pediment or 'canopy', display board and enclosed 'storage' area. The central section of the pediment is missing, leaving curving hatched struts on either side with stylized crocket or volute terminals defined by beading. The pediment is supported by classical-style capitals and pilasters decorated with cross-hatching, vertical ribbing and pellets, and these are braced by two horizontal rails with herring-bone relief to imitate staging or shelves on a full-scale buffet. Rising above the top rail are the letters R and C and these are widely spaced to accommodate a vessel, now missing but indicated by a moulded scar.

There are two 'stages' above the display board separated by a gap of 5mm (missing on Acc. no. 98.2/2) (see fig. 46, p. 202). One 'stage' is integral with the back board, in effect doubling up as the lower horizontal rail, while the other rises at right angles from the display board itself. Both 'stages' are of equal height and both support plate. Spanning the space between the top of the back 'stage' and the bottom edge of the rail above, is a large basin flanked by socketed candlesticks. The basin has a rim cordon, wide flat flange, flat base and pronounced boss. The candlestick on the left has a cylindrical 'fluted' socket with bevelled rim, an inverted baluster multiple-knopped stem and fluted domed foot with beaded basal edge, while the other has a plain flaring socket, inverted baluster stem with central flattened knop and conical foot decorated with a plain cordon and diagonal cross-hatching suggestive of gadrooning.

Just in front of the basin, on the top edge of the front 'stage', is an elaborate pear-shaped ewer, with fluted domed lid, decorative cordons, medallion with heart motif, part of a curving rod handle and 'gadrooned' pedestal foot. The jagged scars with moulded decoration either side of the ewer, suggest additional plate – possibly standing cups or bowls which have broken off. On the riser of the 'stage' the letters R and C are divided by vertical bands of diagonal hatching.

The display boards are embellished from left to right (fig. 46, p. 202) with a partially formed and damaged armorial achievement, consisting of a shield and chevron within a hatched frame: in the centre, the City of London arms; and to the right, stylized triple crowns with pellets. There are two melted holes, one at each end. The whole buffet is supported on legs folded at right angles for strength, and these are longer at the front and braced at the top with open fretwork-style brackets. Above, the carcass is divided to form two enclosed spaces fronted by doors and these (one missing on Acc. no. 94.43) are decorated with beaded diaper lattice within a framework of hatched and ovolo-style mouldings. The doors have an integrally cast socket hinge which drops over a small tab projecting upwards from the bottom frame. A pin inserted through the display board secures the top of the door and this is permanently fixed by solder. Both display boards show signs of heat damage.

Viewed from the front and sides, the surface of the cupboard is covered with various types of hatched decoration representing strapwork and guilloche carving. The front is embellished with egg and dart moulding, whilst the uprights have bosses and vertical spindle ribs. Pendant trefoil mouldings run along the bottom rail of the cupboard.

The small paired side panels are structurally similar to those on the back of the buffet, but are divided horizontally to match the proportions of the enclosed cupboard front. The 'panels' of saltire latticework are embellished with beading in a cross-hatched frame, and the unobtrusive tabs extending from the outer edges are folded at right angles and fastened with blobs of solder to the back. Latticework saltire 'panels', in two pairs one above the other, provide a supporting framework for the back board. The lower panel extends below the front rail which adds strength to the structure. The upper saltires have decorative roundels at the point of intersection, but these are absent from the lower pair, possibly because this detail would be obscured by the front rail.

Date: Early to mid-16th century

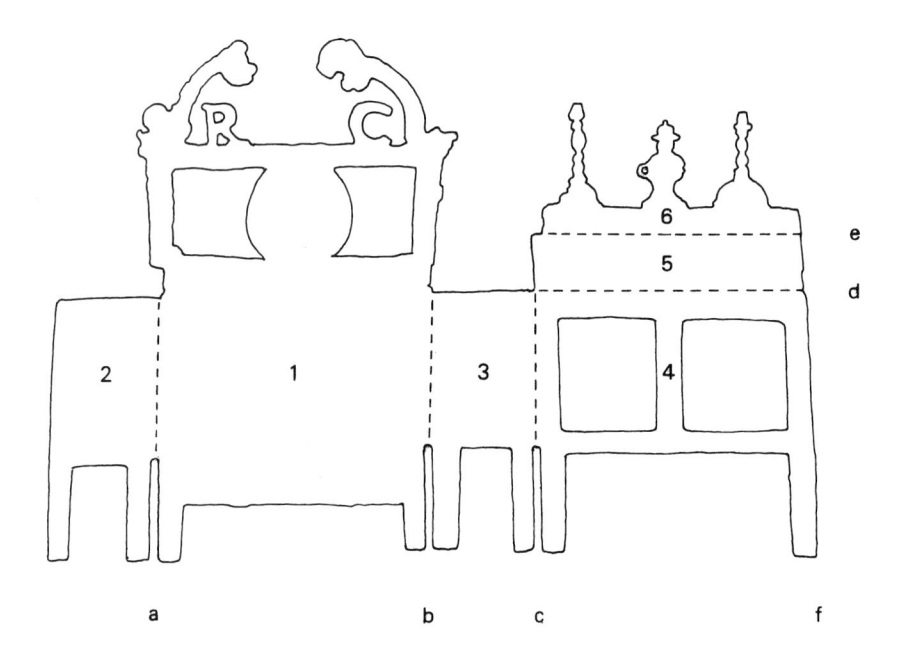

Fig. 48. Diagram showing what the Type 1 buffet would have looked like before it was assembled into a three-dimensional form. The letters indicate the folds and the numbers represent the various sections. The two doors and other items of plate were added separately.

TYPE 1, DESIGN 2

6.6 Buffet: basin and part of stage

Accession number: 98.2/19
Material: Lead alloy
Condition: Fragment
Inscription: C (backwards) and R
Dimensions: W 22mm; Diam (basin) 17mm
Description: A complete buffet basin attached to a 'stage' inscribed with a backwards C and the letter R divided by bands of diagonal hatching. The basin, with wide flange, curving wall and circle around the base, has a different profile to T1, D1 and is slightly smaller.
Date: 16th century

TYPE 1, DESIGN 3

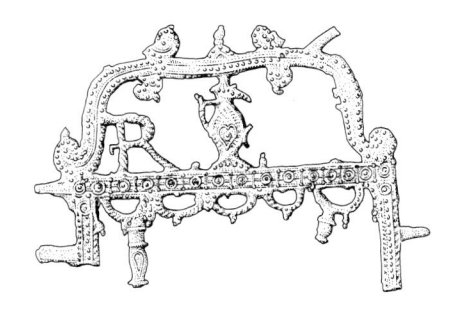

6.7 Buffet: pediment or cresting

Accession number: VAL88[2127]<236>
Material: Lead alloy
Condition: Pediment and upper part of back board
Dimensions: H 40mm; W 55mm
Inscription: R […]
Description: The upper part of a buffet back board with arched pediment or 'canopy'. The scrolled and beaded pediment has stylized crockets and volute terminals and there is one large tab (the other has broken off to leave a stub) extending outwards from the upper edge. Classical-style pilasters support the pediment and are decorated with diagonal hatching and beading. The vertical stiles are linked by a horizontal rail with stylized bead and reel moulding; hanging from the lower edge is a tracery design of hatched loops or 'swags' with acorn-shape finials. Each loop is separated by a vertical band of pellets. Joined to the bottom edge of the outer loops are two socket candlesticks. The left candlestick has pronounced rim and socket flanges, an inverted baluster stem with tear-drop motif and central cordon (the rest is missing). Only the urn-shaped socket survives from the candlestick on the right. Above the rail, occupying central place is a large ovoid-shaped lidded ewer flanked by decorative acorn-shaped knops, and, on the left, a large hatched letter R. Part of the ewer handle is missing. The vessel has a bridged spout, fluted pedestal base with decorative hatching and a heart motif on the body. There is a scar at the top edge of the rail to the right of the ewer.
Date: Stylistically 16th century, but recovered from a late 17th-century context
Provenance: Fleet Valley

TYPE 1, DESIGN 4

6.8 Buffet: fragments of cresting and plate

Accession number: 98.2/20a–b
Material: Lead alloy
Condition: Fragments
Dimensions: Cresting: H 31mm; W 16mm. Ewer: H 15mm; W 15mm
Description: Two fragments from a buffet. The larger piece seems to be part of the cresting with trellis work, pellet roundel, beading, diagonal hatching and perhaps the fluted pedestal base of a flagon or ewer. The other is part of a two-handled ewer with S-shaped handles, recurving fishtail terminals and ovoid body with a plain central band and stylized gadrooning above and below.
Date: 16th century
Comments: Found together, these two fragments may be from the same object.

TYPE 1, DESIGN 5

6.9 Buffet: part of back board

Accession number: 98.2/24a*–b
Material: Lead alloy
Condition: Fragments
Dimensions: H 32mm; W 45mm
Description: Broken central section from an openwork saltire latticework back board with decoration on one side only. The horizontal struts have diagonal hatching and the central vertical strut is cross-hatched. There is one recurving tab on the back.
Date: 16th century

TYPE 1, DESIGN 6

6.10 Buffet: part of cupboard front

Accession number: 98.2/5*; 98.2/6*
Material: Lead alloy
Condition: Complete; in two pieces
Dimensions: H 40mm; H (door aperture) 20mm; W 51mm; W (door aperture) 19mm
Description: A complete frame from a buffet cupboard front (in two pieces) divided to form two enclosed spaces fronted by doors (now missing). One of the hinge pintels has survived and this extends downwards from the top rail on the left side. The simple and crude decoration consists of beading on the outer edge and legs and diagonal hatching on the vertical spacer. There are solid cross-hatched curving 'brackets' at the top of the legs and these run along under the bottom rail and finish short of the vertical spacer.
Date: 16th century

TYPE 2

There are 11 buffets and fragments of this type, and although the basic form seems to be similar to Type 1 above, the carcass frame has egg and dart mouldings and the display board has ring and dot motifs, the letters EL[Z] and the City of London of arms. The side panels and doors incorporate designs based on, or including, the arms of the City of London, and are of solid construction. There are three different mould designs for this type.

TYPE 2, DESIGN 1

6.11 Buffet: solid side panel

Accession number: 98.2/3*; 98.2/4; 98.2/12a–b
Material: Lead alloy
Condition: 98.2/3: cupboard carcass only with part of back board. 98.2/4: left hand front of cupboard with door. 98.2/12: part of frame and door
Dimensions: H 38mm; W 51mm; Dpt 17mm
Inscription: EL[Z]
Description: Part of a three-dimensional buffet carcass and other fragments from the same mould. The most complete has a display board decorated with a repeating design which includes the City of London arms; EL[Z] above a ring and dot motif; and narrow separator bands decorated with ring and dot motifs either end of a bar. There are two melted holes at each end.

The carcass is divided to form two enclosed spaces fronted by doors. Although the doors are missing on 98.2/3, one remains on 98.2/4 and 98.2/12a, and these are matched by six identical doors in the collection (see Cat. no. 6.18 below). The doors have the City of London arms in an ornate shield, surrounded by pellets within an egg and dart border. The rounded hinge has recessed mouldings at the back and a loop at the top and bottom. The carcass frames have identical egg and dart mouldings and the vertical spacers are decorated with ring and dot motifs. The solid, left side panel bears a cross-hatched cross with devices and designs in each quarter: a dagger; stylized linenfold; a saltire with ring and dot in each segment and in the fourth quarter, the City of London arms. In effect, the City of London arms is repeated: the whole panel with cross and dagger in the first quarter; and again in reduced form in the fourth. The legs are missing.

The lower part of the back board survives on the most complete buffet, and this consists of paired panels of saltire latticework with decorative roundels at the point of intersection, and there are several tabs jutting out from the edge of the frame. The central spine is decorated with widely spaced ring and dot motifs.
Date: Possibly late 16th century
Comments: The most complete buffet of this type (Acc. no. 98.2/3) was incorrectly reconstructed before it was acquired by the Museum and has not been adjusted since. The mouldings on the frame of 98.2/4 are identical to those on 98.2/3 which is why the two are catalogued together.

TYPE 2, DESIGN 2

6.12 Buffet: side panel

Accession number: 98.2/15
Material: Lead alloy
Condition: Upper solid section only
Dimensions: H 26mm; W 16mm

Description: The solid upper section from a buffet cupboard side panel. The panel is decorated with a diagonally hatched cross with devices and designs filling each quarter: a dagger; stylized linenfold; City of London arms and a saltire with ring and dot motifs in each segment. As in T2, D1 above the City of London arms are repeated: the whole panel with cross and dagger in the first quarter and then a reduced version in the fourth quarter.

Date: 16th century

Comments: Some differences to T2, D1 above: the main cross has diagonal hatching and third and fourth quarters are reversed.

Comparandum: An identical piece found on the Vintry foreshore in August 2000 and brought in to the Museum of London (Enq. no. 1531/34) for recording (now in a private collection).

TYPE 2, DESIGN 3

6.13 Buffet: side panels

Accession number: 98.2/22*; 98.2/656

Material: Lead alloy

Condition: 98.2/22: complete. 98.2/656: upper part only

Dimensions: H 45mm; W c. 16mm

Description: Complete and partially complete side panels, with solid upper section consisting of a wide cross-hatched cross with devices and designs filling each quarter: a dagger; stylized linenfold; City of London arms and a saltire with ring and dot motifs in each segment. As with T2, D1 and D2 above, the City of London arms are repeated: the whole panel has the cross and dagger in the first quarter and then a reduced version in the third quarter. The legs on 98.2/22 are cross-hatched.

Date: 16th century

Comments: The quartering is the same as T2, D1 but the cross is cross-hatched.

TYPE 3

A rather crude and simplified version of Types 1 and 2 above, represented by a virtually complete flat-cast buffet with cross-hatched mouldings, bracket legs and tracery side panel and other leg fragments from similar buffets of similar form from different moulds.

TYPE 3, DESIGN 1

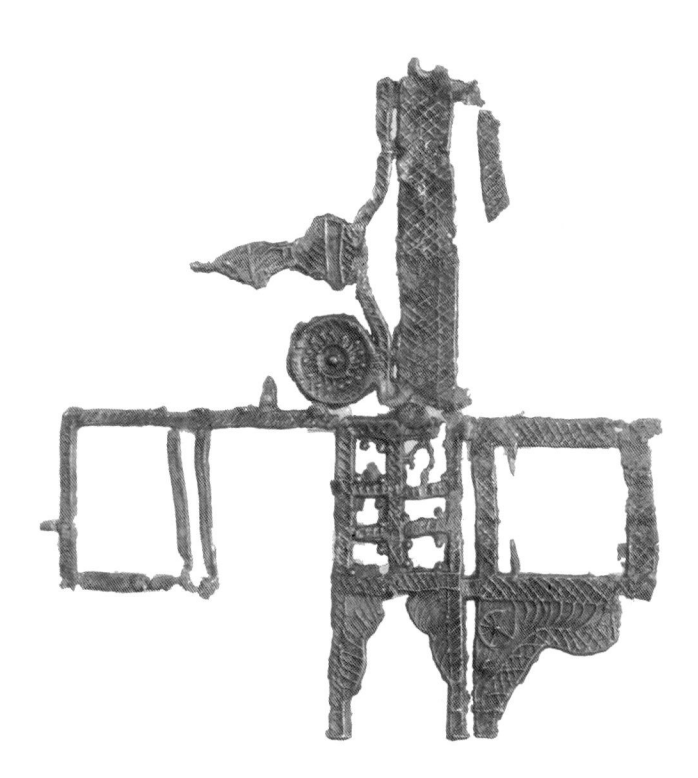

6.14 Flat buffet

Accession number: 98.2/1

Material: Lead alloy

Condition: Fairly complete

Dimensions: H (cupboard) 47mm; H (door aperture) 19mm; W c. 50mm; W (door aperture) 19mm; Dpt c. 19mm

Description: Part of a three-dimensional buffet in flat, unfolded state, consisting of the left side, left cupboard front, display board with two pieces of plate, and part of the back board. Most of the surface is cross-hatched and only the legs and brackets have crude diagonal hatching. Reposing on solid bracket legs, the cupboard side has a rectangular grid of six compartments, each with pellets in the corners and in the top right the vestiges of a circular trelliswork. There are two opposing pintels extending from the top and bottom edges of the left door aperture and the cupboard front has a very wide solid scroll bracket incorporating a spiral-hatched roundel in the top left corner representing chip-carved decoration. There are two highly stylized articles of plate loosely representing a bowl or dish decorated with a central boss, radial hatching and circle of pellets, and a lidded ewer of pear-shaped form with long narrow neck, diagonal hatching and plain central band around the body. Only part of the outer frame of the lower back board survives and this has diagonal hatching with two tabs extending from the edges (see fig. 45, p. 200).

Date: 16th century

Comments: When this buffet was examined by Peter Thornton in 1998, he thought the piece extremely crude, but still of recognizably Low Countries style.

TYPE 3, DESIGN 2

6.15 Buffet: side panel

Accession number: 98.2/23
Material: Lead alloy
Condition: Part only
Dimensions: H 38mm; Dpt *c.* 22mm
Description: Part of a buffet side panel with irregular tracery design and solid bracket legs. The entire surface is covered with diagonal hatching.
Date: 16th century
Comments: A different profile and rougher design to T3, D1 above

TYPE 3, DESIGN 3

6.16 Buffet (?): leg and bracket scroll

Accession number: 98.2/93
Material: Lead alloy
Condition: Complete
Dimensions: H 25mm; W 32mm
Description: A leg and solid bracket scroll possibly from a buffet. The bottom rail of the carcass is cross-hatched and the bracket decorated with different-sized Ss and Cs surrounded by random hatching within a diagonal hatched border. The very short leg has diagonal hatching.
Date: 16th century

TYPE 3, DESIGN 4

6.17 Buffet: leg and bracket scroll from cupboard front

Accession number: Private collection
Material: Lead alloy
Condition: Fragment
Dimensions: H 25mm; W 30mm
Description: The leg has a cross-hatched border and the bracket scroll an S-shaped moulding and random swirling lines.
Date: 16th century
Provenance: Brook's Wharf, 1 February 2000
Comments: Enq. no. 1512/12 seen by the author 23 November 2000

Buffet doors

The buffet doors have been classified by structure and design. There are three main types: solid, latticework and part-solid, part-pierced. The solid doors have decorative mouldings to suggest relief or incised carving, while the pierced doors represent those which were sometimes fitted to full-scale buffets, aumbries and livery cupboards to ventilate the storage space. Six designs have been recorded and the decoration is comparable to furniture dating from *c.* 1500 to 1550. Apart from Cat. no. 6.18, which seem to have been cast specifically for the left or right side, the other doors could be hung either side of the carcass frame.

The 'hinges' are integrally cast with the door panel and although the structures vary, they were all designed to pivot on tabs or pins extending from the frame. The cylinder hinges are either completely enclosed with horizontal bars to suggest an intricate brass or steel hinge composed of interlinking parts, or they have diagonal hatching with vertical slots around the circumference. The third type of 'hinge' consists of a recessed groove on the back with lugs at the top and bottom, and unlike the cylinder versions described above, these hinges are not visible from the front.

TYPE 1

There are five solid doors in the collection and these either have an enclosed cylinder 'hinge' or recessed groove with lugs.

TYPE 1, DESIGN 1

6.18 Buffet door

Accession number: 84.152/3; 98.2/9*; 98.2/10; 98.2/14; 98.2/16
Material: Lead alloy
Condition: Complete. 98.2/10: corner missing
Dimensions: H 17mm; W 18mm
Orientation: Left hand: 84.152/3; 98.2/9. Right hand: 98.2/10; 98.2/14; 98.2/16
Description: With ovolo-moulded border surrounding a Baroque or Tuscan shaped shield with the City of London arms. There is a recessed channel on the back of the hinge with loops at each end to accommodate the frame pintels. It is clear that different moulds were used to produce the left and right doors, because the doors with a 'hinge' on the right side are correct with the dagger in the first quarter, whereas those for the left have the dagger in the second quarter. Doors of this type seem to have been fitted to the buffet form T2, D1 (Cat. no. 6.11).
Provenance: 98.2/14: Limekiln Dock
Comments: The door described in Cat. no. 6.11 has the dagger in the second quarter, although it is clearly from the left aperture of the carcass frame.
Date: 16th century
Comparanda: Similar-shaped shields have been carved into the oak panelling of Beckingham Hall, Tolleshunt Major, Essex and these have been dated to 1546.

TYPE 2

There are just two solid doors of this type, and they are characterized by a prominent barrel 'hinge.' The symmetrical designs on these doors meant that they could be used for the left or right side of the cupboard.

TYPE 2, DESIGN 1

6.19 Buffet door

Accession number: 98.2/11; 98.2/13*
Material: Lead alloy
Condition: Complete
Dimensions: H 17mm; W 20mm
Description: These solid doors have a beaded border (apart from two ring and dot motifs on one side) which encloses a square filled with a double lozenge. The inner lozenge has a cross with pellets in each corner and diametrically opposed but matching patterns surround the outer lozenge of diagonal and cross-hatched lines and ring and dot motifs. There is an integrally cast tubular 'barrel' hinge with external horizontal ribbing.
Date: 16th century

TYPE 2, DESIGN 2

6.20 Buffet door

Accession number: 82.353/21
Material: Lead alloy
Condition: Complete
Dimensions: H 16mm; W 20mm

Description: A solid door with a border of double-lined squares each with a pellet in the centre, surrounding a diagonally hatched frame enclosing a geometric pattern of squares and rectangles decorated with Ss and pellets. There is a plain 'barrel' hinge which is slightly reeded on the external face.
Date: 16th century

TYPE 3

The most complete buffet (Acc. no. 94.43) has diaper latticework doors, but the pierced doors described below are much cruder and the 'hinges' are partially enclosed cylinders with vertical slots. All of the latticework and pierced doors seem to have been designed for use on both sides of the carcass.

TYPE 3, DESIGN 1

6.21 Buffet door

Accession number: 82.221/30
Material: Lead alloy
Condition: Complete
Dimensions: H 21mm; W 20mm
Description: The whole surface is decorated with diagonal slashing and the door has three rows of grid latticework. There is a 'barrel' hinge with longitudinal gashes possibly due to imperfect casting.
Date: 16th century

TYPE 3, DESIGN 2

6.22 Buffet door

Accession number: 21635; 98.2/17*
Material: Lead alloy
Condition: 98.2/17: complete
    21635: almost complete
Dimensions: H 20mm; W 20mm
Description: These doors have a frame of diagonal hatching with four rows of grid latticework and a narrow solid section with cross-hatched decoration. There is a 'barrel' hinge with diagonal hatching on the exterior surface and longitudinal gashes due to imperfect casting.
Date: 16th century

Buffet plates

In addition to the pieces of plate directly fixed or associated with parts of the buffet frame, the collection includes 11 detached basins which are small enough to have been part of the buffet display. The diameters range from 15mm to 26mm, and the plates are classified by design as follows.

DESIGN 1

6.23 Buffet plate

Accession number: 98.2/21*; 98.2/27*; 98.2/28; 98.2/32; 98.2/35*
Material: Lead alloy
Condition: 98.2/27, 98.2/32: complete
Dimensions: Three sizes:
    (i) Diam 15mm; (wall) 10mm; (rim) 3mm
    (ii) Diam 19mm; (wall) 11mm; (rim) 3mm
    (iii) Diam 25mm; (wall) 15mm; (rim) 5mm
Description: All plain with flat broad flange, shallow wall and flat base with central boss. Only 98.2/21 is attached to the part of the rail or 'stage' which is decorated with diagonal hatching.
Date: 16th century

DESIGN 2

6.24 Buffet plate

Accession number: 98.2/31
Material: Lead alloy
Condition: Almost complete
Dimensions: Diam c. 17mm
Description: A flanged dish with slightly curving wall, flat base and central boss. The flange is decorated with radial lines interspersed with pellets.
Date: 16th century

DESIGN 3

6.25 Buffet plate

Accession number: 98.2/29*; 98.2/30; 98.2/33; 98.2/34
Material: Lead alloy
Condition: Complete
Dimensions: Two sizes:
    i) 98.2/29; 98.2/33: Diam 17mm; Diam (wall)11mm; Diam (rim) 3mm
    ii) 98.2/30; 98.2/34: Diam 24mm; Diam (wall) 17mm; Diam (rim) 3mm
Description: These plain plates have a broad flat flange, curving wall and flat base with a cordon around the centre.
Date: 16th century

DESIGN 4

6.26 Buffet plate

Accession number: 98.2/26
Material: Lead alloy
Condition: Complete
Dimensions: Diam 18mm; Diam (wall) 11mm; Diam (rim) 3mm
Description: A flat flanged dish with vertical wall and flat base. The flange is decorated with radial hatching.
Date: 16th century

Chairs

Although the chair has been an important item of furniture for centuries, very few base-metal toy chairs are known. The 18 examples from London seem to date from the 16th to early 19th centuries and these were made from part moulds. From limited evidence, it appears that two methods of manufacture were adopted: the castings were either bent into a freestanding shape, or the constituent parts were separately cast in such a way that the various sections could be slotted, soldered or fastened together to create a three-dimensional structure. Unfortunately none of the multi-component chairs has survived intact, and until a complete example is found, the precise method of construction will remain unclear.[41] Toy chairs were evidently made in the medieval period on the Continent and several examples from 14th-century contexts have been recovered from excavations in the Netherlands.[42] But there are no chairs or identifiable chair components dating before the mid-16th century in the collection, although it is quite possible that some of the fragments consigned to the miscellaneous section are chair parts which have not been recognized.[43] The absence of medieval chairs is mirrored by the lack of later material, and only four pieces can be securely dated to the 18th century.

The chairs have been classified by design and they have been arranged as far as possible in a chronological sequence.

DESIGN 1

6.27 Armchair back and side/arm panels

Accession number: A25825
Material: Lead alloy
Condition: Almost complete
Dimensions: H 47mm; H (back panel) 37mm; H (side panel) 25mm; W 41mm; W (back panel) *c.* 26mm; W (side panel) *c.* 10mm
Description: A complete back with integrally cast side or 'arm' panels from a multi-component three-dimensional chair. Flat-cast in one piece with mouldings on one side only, the side panels are attached just below the semi-circular crest and the single scrolls at the top of each recessed 'stile'. The crest is decorated with an openwork border of S-scrolls flanking a four-pointed star and this encloses a solid, arch-topped panel divided into two zones and decorated at the top with three rosettes in triangular formation, one at the apex of the arch and the others at the bottom in the left and right corners. The zone below is finely cross-hatched. The side panels have a bevelled upper edge, with scrolled tracery to represent the turned curving arms of a chair. Both have plain saltire tracery below.
Date: Possibly representing a joined armchair of enclosed form – perhaps dating to the mid- to late 16th century

DESIGN 2

6.28 Armchair back and side panel

Accession number: 98.2/95
Material: Lead alloy
Condition: Almost complete; one side panel missing; some damage
Dimensions: H 63mm; H (back panel) 51mm; H (side panel) 36mm; W 35mm
Description: Complete back and side or 'arm' panels from a multi-component three-dimensional chair. Flat-cast in one piece with mouldings on one side only, the side panel (left side only) is attached just below the cresting 'rail' and at the top of the 'stile'. The semi-circular cresting panel has an openwork border of acanthus leaf scrolls flanking a fleur-de-lys and this encloses a semi-circular solid area decorated with three rosettes. The back panel has very faint cross-hatching and there are two square slots along the bottom edge. The side panel has a bevelled upper edge and is decorated with tracery (damaged). There is a possible slot through the base of the 'stile' and the stubs of lateral tabs remain on the outer edge of the side panel.
Date: Possibly 16th century

DESIGN 3

6.29 Armchair back and side panels

Accession number: 99.153
Material: Lead alloy; gilded
Condition: Three pieces; almost complete; some damage
Dimensions: H (back) *c.* 49mm; H (sides) 25mm; W (back) 27mm; W (sides) 11mm
Description: Crested back and side panels from a three-dimensional armchair (now detached). The back panel is divided into three zones: there is an openwork grid at the bottom, a solid panel decorated with double-scored diaper pattern in the middle and semi-circular pierced cresting enclosing the Stuart royal arms. The edges between each section are defined by prominent ridges, and the two separate openwork side or 'arm' panels are both divided into two zones of decoration with scrolling tracery at the top and a saltire/rosette in the square section below. Since the designs on the side panels are different from each other they may not come from the same object, and this supposition is supported by the fact that both seem to be for the right side with tabs on the outer edge.
Date: There are English oak joined armchairs with vaguely similar arm-rest scrolling and back panels with solid panels above openwork, dating to the mid-17th century (Chinnery 1979, figs. 3:52 & 3:53), but it is difficult to find an exact parallel. The presence of the royal arms, however, suggests that the toy was designed to replicate an armchair of authority.
Comments: Although these pieces were recovered at the same time from the same area of foreshore, they may come from two separate objects. It is unclear how the sections fit together, but Acc. nos. A25825 and 98.2/95 give a clue to their placing and fixing.
Comparandum: The carved and gilded Framework Knitters Master's chair, inscribed 'The gift of Mr Thos Cawarden June 1618' in the Museum of London (Acc. no. 21215) is surmounted by a crest incorporating the Stuart arms.

DESIGN 4

6.30 Chair back

Accession number: 79.319/10a
Material: Lead alloy
Condition: Part only
Dimensions: H 34mm; W 29mm
Inscription: 1640 and IDQ
Description: Probably the lower part of a solid rectangular chair back panel decorated with a large circle enclosing a cinquefoil double rose. The calyx points extend beyond and between the outer row of petals, and between each point are large pelleted rings flanked by ring and dot motifs. The outer edge of the circle is decorated with groups of radial lines which touch an elaborate trefoil-patterned border. The whole decoration is contained within a cross-hatched frame and there is a narrow plain zone below inversely inscribed 1640 and IDQ.
Date: 1640
Comments: This fragment was associated with the lunette-shaped panel T1, D1 with foliate/floral decoration, although they appear to be from separate objects.

DESIGN 5

6.31 Arm-chair back

Accession number: 98.2/99
Material: Lead alloy
Condition: Complete; slight damage
Dimensions: H 42mm; W 37mm
Description: A back panel from a three-dimensional arm-chair with elaborate partly pierced cresting in the form of a quatrefoil double rose surmounted by a crown and flanked by volutes, ring and dot and large double scrolls. The straight stiles have beaded edges and scrolled decoration with rectangular slots just below the ball-knop finials. The thin cresting rail and arcaded 'turned spindle' splats all have cable decoration, while the seat rail is cross-hatched.
Date: Possibly second half of the 17th century

DESIGN 6

6.32 Chair top rail

Accession number: 98.2/140
Material: Lead alloy
Condition: Complete
Dimensions: H 18mm; W 31mm
Description: A complete top rail surmounted by a pierced crest of swagged patera. The solid top rail has rounded corners and is covered with an imbricated design. Parts of the thin arcaded 'turned spindle' splats are extant below.
Date: 1680s
Comments: Possibly associated with Acc. no. 98.2/97a, although the scroll design is different
Comparandum: Chinnery 1979, p. 479, fig. 4:146

DESIGN 7

6.33 Part of a chair back

Accession number: 98.2/97a
Material: Lead alloy
Condition: Incomplete
Dimensions: H 33mm; W 30mm
Description: The upper part of a back panel from a narrow, tall-backed three-dimensional chair, with pierced diaper-work 'cane' panel flanked by pierced and elongated acanthus leaf S-scrolls. The semi-circular-shaped cresting-rail has reeded cabling and incorporates a winged putto flanked by S-scrolls.
Date: Chairs upholstered with cane are not listed in London inventories before the 1670s, and the type only really becomes common from the 1680s to the first decade or so of the 18th century. The overall shape of this chair suggests a date from 1680–90.
Comments: Possibly associated with Cat. no. 6.34 (see right) although the scroll design is a little different.

DESIGN 8

6.34 Part of a chair back

Accession number: 98.2/97b
Material: Lead alloy
Condition: Incomplete
Dimensions: H 32mm; W 34mm
Description: The lower part of a back panel from a narrow, parallel-sided, tall-backed three-dimensional chair. The pierced parallel-sided diaper-work 'cane' panel, tapers at the shoe and is flanked by pierced and elongated acanthus leaf S-scrolls (pieces missing). There is a stub of a tab below the bottom rail.
Date: 1680–1700

Cat. nos. 6.33 and 6.34

216 • TOYS, TRIFLES & TRINKETS

DESIGN 9

6.35 Chair seat

Accession number: 98.2/98
Material: Lead alloy
Condition: Almost complete; bottom right corner missing; some casting faults
Dimensions: W *c.* 40mm; W (back rail) 30mm; Dpt 23mm
Description: A trapezoidal-shaped seat from a three-dimensional chair with diaper openwork 'cane' panel surrounded by pierced and elongated acanthus leaf S-scroll borders. The back rail has two thin recurving tabs extending from the edge and the front rail has cable decoration.
Date: 1680–1700
Provenance: Queenhithe Dock
Comments: Possibly from a similar chair to Acc. no. 98.2/97a above

DESIGN 10

6.36 Chair back crest

Accession number: 82.25/8
Material: Lead alloy
Condition: Complete
Dimensions: H 22mm; W 30mm
Description: Pierced cresting with elaborate scrolling surmounted by a rosette and flanked by two cupids supporting a crown. The cupids and rosette are finely hatched.
Date: Possibly from a three-dimensional cane chair 1680–1700
Comparanda: Armchair, *c.* 1680, of pegged construction attributed to Richard Price (Temple Newsam House, Leeds). Cupid supporters were a popular motif on cane chairs. Thomas Roberts supplied similar examples to the royal household in 1697, charging for '12 cane chaires of beech carved boyes and crownes'.[44]

DESIGN 11

6.37 Chair cresting panel (?)

Accession number: 98.2/106
Material: Lead alloy
Condition: Complete; some damage
Dimensions: H *c.* 23mm; W 31mm
Description: Possibly a cresting panel from a three-dimensional chair with 'gabled' shaped, and pierced and scalloped border terminating in a loop. In the centre, enclosed by linear beading, is a hatched and beaded circle surrounded by ring and dot motifs and beading.
Date: Possibly 17th century

DESIGN 12

6.38 Chair back panel (?)

Accession number: 98.2/100; 98.2/101*
Material: Lead alloy
Condition: Complete
Dimensions: H 46mm; W 25mm
Description: Two identical back panels from three-dimensional chairs, cast in one piece from the same mould. There is a pierced and scallop-edged cresting panel composed of interlaced scrolling. The solid back panel is plain and there is a pronounced ridge around the edge with slots in each corner.
Date: Possibly late 17th century

DESIGN 13

6.39 Chair back panel (?)

Accession number: 98.2/91
Material: Lead alloy
Condition: Part only
Dimensions: H *c.* 29mm; W 29mm
Inscription: H

Description: Possibly part of a back panel from a three-dimensional chair. The solid panel is plain apart from crudely made slots in the surviving corners and the letter H in the centre.
Date: Probably 17th century

DESIGN 14

6.40 Chair

Accession number: 98.2/94
Material: Lead alloy
Condition: Almost complete; back right leg missing
Dimensions: H 57mm; W 38mm; Dpt 16mm
Description: An almost complete three-dimensional chair cast in one piece with splat back and relief-moulded front. The back stiles of semi-circular section are slightly waisted, and these curve outwards and then round towards the 'yoke-shaped' top rail. The upper part of the splat is a pierced oval and this joins a solid inverted baluster section decorated with interlacing rococo C-scrolls with a vertical line of pellets diminishing in size towards the pierced triangular-shaped base ornamented with wavy lines. The trapezoidal-shaped seat has a panel with densely packed lines running front to back within a bevelled and feathered border, suggestive of an upholstered pleated cushion. Only three hipped cabriole legs survive and these are decorated with scrolling and linked in the front by a rounded apron with relief mouldings. The feet have a flat base.
Date: 1730–60
Comparanda: English chair *c.* 1710 in the Metropolitan Museum of Art, New York, and the Arthur S. Vernay, Inc. collection

DESIGN 15

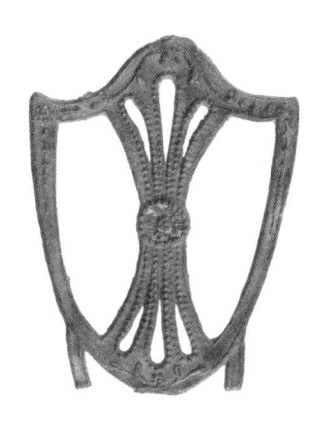

6.41 Chair back

Accession number: 98.2/103
Material: Lead alloy; red pigment
Condition: Complete
Dimensions: H 48mm; W 37mm
Description: A shield-shaped back from a three-dimensional chair with 'wheatsheaf' splats edged with beading and linked by a solid, recessed, beaded oval decorated with a rosette. The double curved top rail and the base of the ellipse have stylized rococo ornament.
Date: Reflects the fashionable style of the 1760–1800
Comparanda: Hepplewhite's *The Cabinet Maker and Upholsterer's Guide,* 1788 and new editions issued in 1789 and 1794. Shield-backed chairs were also made by Gillows, Chippendale and Sheraton.

DESIGN 16

6.42 Chair back

Accession number: 98.2/104
Material: Lead alloy; red pigment
Condition: Complete
Dimensions: H 46mm; W 38mm
Description: A shield-shaped back from a three-dimensional chair with 'wheatsheaf' splats linked by a solid oval decorated with a floret. The double curved top rail has a pointed oval in relief at the apex with a curving broken line interspersed with pellets on either side. The stiles have horizontally hatched edges.
Date: 1760–1800

DESIGN 17

6.43 Chair back

Accession number: 98.2/105
Material: Lead alloy
Condition: Upper part only
Dimensions: H 23mm; W 34mm
Description: The upper part of a ladder-backed chair, with straight tapering stiles and three rails extant. The thin semi-circular sectioned stiles and lower rail have cable decoration and the broad, parallel sided, cable-edged top rail has stylized volute or patera terminals with linear laurel leaf decoration either side of a beaded circle. The central rail is decorated with a central rosette flanked by volutes.
Date: Possibly late 18th century; probably early 19th century
Comparanda: Etruscan-influenced design and Robert Adam style armchair at Osterley Park *c.* 1776. Also comparable examples in King, T., *The Modern Style of Cabinet Work Exemplified* (London, 1829).

Chests

The high survival rate of full-sized chests compared with other forms of furniture can be partly attributed to their usefulness, popularity, size and relative low value. As Penelope Eames has argued in her comprehensive analysis of medieval furniture, chests did not suffer the fate of other types of furniture because they were 'habitually deposited in churches and abbeys for safe keeping' and were therefore largely protected from vicissitudes of fashion.[45] Because chests were so adaptable, it is not surprising that they are the most frequently listed items of furniture in household inventories, documents and literature throughout the medieval and early modern period.[46] They were needed to protect valuables and vulnerable items, to hold groups or sets of objects in different internal compartments, to travel long distances over land or water and for short- and long-term personal or general storage. Eventually different forms, structures and sizes were constructed for specific purposes, and this gave rise to a plethora of terms, such as coffer, hutch, ark, standard and casket, many of which were used interchangeably in early inventories and documents. The terminological complexities have been discussed in great detail by many furniture historians and do not need to be rehearsed here, but Penelope Eames makes a useful distinction between the flat or curved topped chest on legs and the domed topped chest which rests directly on the ground. The former were ideal receptacles for long-term storage because the raised legs protected the contents from damp penetration and allowed the air to circulate freely underneath; whereas chests resting directly on the ground were better suited for travel and their domed lids enabled splashes, precipitation or spray to run off quickly. Both types seem to be represented by the toy chest fragments.

Most of the toy chests seem to have been made from a single flat casting which was bent and manipulated into three-dimensional form, but there is at least one lid which seems to have been cast in a fully finished state, and this was presumably attached or soldered on to the other sections. The fragments are a mixture of solid and openwork panels with plain or decorative mouldings to represent the range of materials and construction methods of their full-scale counterparts. Some of the decoration seems to represent wrought-iron grisaille or scrollwork, studding, gothic tracery, relief and chip carving, and the frames and structures replicate chests of joined, boarded, panelled and bound construction.[47] One domed lid even has a copper foil which successfully imitates the difference between the carcass material and overlaying ironwork on a real chest.[48] Different kinds of fixings are also represented, including a couple of lock plate and key hole mouldings, a handle, hasp and catch, and what appear to be suspension loops at the junction of the arc and the 'stile' on the domed topped end panels. While most of the fixings are reasonably realistic,

Fig. 49. This rare chest or 'standard', c. 1427, is made from iron plates with connecting moulded ribs. There are six handles, three keyholes and three hasps for padlocks. None of the six locks survives. H 62cm; L 120cm
Corporation of London

the loops are something of an enigma since they seem to be positioned at a point of mechanical weakness and only one loop seems to have been moulded on each end.

As far as it is possible to tell, the toy chest fragments seem to be modelled on chests dating from the late 15th to late 17th century, although most represent forms and designs current from *c.* 1500 to the 1650s.[49] Two of the lunette panels are dated 1641 and 1646, and two identical end panels are inscribed with the date 1643. Since the design and shape of these fragments are stylistically similar to many of the undated pieces, the majority were probably produced at this time. A number of the end panels are also inscribed with a letter or letters R, CT, and RK or KR and R[T], and these were probably designed to represent the carved or incised owners' initials on full-scale chests during the late 16th and 17th centuries.

Most of the end panels seem to have domed tops with short legs which is something of a puzzle since none of the full-scale chests combines these features. The only vaguely comparable shape is the footed ark chest with gable ends and a canted boarded top, but since the toy chest panels have a perfect lunette-shaped top it would seem that the toymaker had a different model in mind, and until an end panel and lid are found together the precise form of these chests will remain unknown.[50] The most complete version of the domed top and footed toy chest has been recovered in a pre-assembly form from excavations in the Netherlands and it is just possible that toys of this type were made on the Continent and therefore represent a form of chest which was not used in England.[51]

Although some of the fragments seem to represent coffers, standards and other types of chest, the lack of complete examples poses problems of identification and attribution, and so to avoid the pitfalls of terminology, the generic term chest has been used instead. The material has been categorized by the various component parts, either individual panels or joined sections as appropriate, and these have been further classified by design and mould.

Lid panels

There are 35 lunette-shaped panels in the collection, and although some were definitely associated with a coffer lid (Cat. nos. 6.81, 6.82 & 6.54), it is possible that others were originally part of a chair back of 17th-century date.[52] Seven main types and 20 different moulds have been identified and the panels have been classified by design and mould variations as shown in Table 6.3. Several of the panels have lateral tabs extending outwards from the straight edge which were presumably used to attach the panel to the frame and lid, and some have a decorative finial at the apex. The purpose of the finial is unclear because this feature is neither found on full-scale chests nor lunette-topped chair backs.

Table 6.3

Type	Design	Quantity	Inscription	Motif	H	W	Assoc. chest
Foliate and floral							
1	1	8		Lobed rosette	21mm	30mm	
	2	2		Lobed rosette	20mm	30mm	
	3	1		Lobed rosette	21mm	30mm	
	4	1		Flowering plant	17mm	26mm	
	5	1		Quatrefoil double rose	18mm	33mm	
	6	1		Half of a quatrefoil double rose	14mm	24mm	
Geometric							
2	1	1		Cross-hatched	20mm	26mm	
	2	2		Plain & hatched chequer	18mm	28mm	Yes
	3	1		Pelleted diaper	26mm	33mm	
Inscribed geometric							
3	1	2	[R] [K]	Ring and dot	19mm	29mm	Yes
	2	3	R	Cross-hatched & pellets	20mm	26mm	Yes
	3	3	CT	Cross-hatched & pellets	20mm	24mm	
Triple crowns							
4	1	1		Drapers' Company arms	20mm	28mm	
	2	1		Drapers' Company arms	19mm	28mm	
Relief radial							
5	1	3		Flat & relief radial	20mm	38mm	
	2	1		Flat & relief radial	20mm	17mm*	
	3	1		Flat & relief radial	20mm	8mm	
Plain and dated							
6	1	1	1641	Plain with border	11mm	22mm	
	2	1	1646	Plain with pellet cluster	14mm	26mm	

* incomplete

TYPE 1, DESIGN 1

6.44 Chest lid: lunette-shaped panel

Accession number: 79.319/10b; 98.2/56; 98.2/58; 98.2/59; 98.2/60*; 98.2/61; 98.2/63; 98.2/64

Material: Lead alloy

Condition: Almost complete apart from 98.2/63 & 98.2/64

Dimensions: H 21mm; W 30mm; W (incl. tabs) 38mm

Description: These lunette-shaped panels have a cable edge, finial at the apex (now missing) and two lateral tabs (98.2/61) extending outwards from the straight edge, one on each side. The decoration is ranged around a centrally placed rosette with nine lobes. The rosette is enclosed within a circle which touches the straight edge, and this is surrounded by four concentric bands, each of an inverted U shape. The first contains two ring and dot motifs, one each side of the circle, the second is a simple line of nine equally spaced ring and dot motifs, the third has 17 pellets and the broad outer band has finely hatched vine-leaf scrolling.

Date: 16th–17th century

Comments: 98.2/64: has been subsequently cut down and slightly rounded.

Comparandum: ABO92[388]<892> from a 1675–1700 context: see Egan forthcoming a, no. 606

TYPE 1, DESIGN 2

6.45 Chest lid: lunette-shaped panel

Accession number: 98.2/57*; 98.2/62

Material: Lead alloy

Condition: 98.2/57: almost complete 98.2/62: damaged and large sections missing

Dimensions: H 20mm; H (incl. finial) 22mm; W 30mm

Description: Lunette-shaped panels with cable edge (98.2/57), fleur-de-lys-shaped finial and base tab (only one extant). The decoration is very similar to T1, D1, but there is an additional string of pellets within the first band enclosing the rosette, and the vine-leaf scrolling is less well defined.

Date: 16th–17th century

Provenance: 98.2/62: Custom House Quay

TYPE 1, DESIGN 3

6.46 Chest lid: lunette-shaped panel

Accession number: 98.2/686

Material: Lead alloy

Condition: Almost complete; one tab only

Dimensions: H 21mm; H (incl. finial) 24mm; W 30mm

Description: A lunette-shaped panel with cable edge, trefoil-shaped finial and base tab (only one extant). There is a ten-lobed rosette in the centre surrounded by a circle and two circumferential bands. The first is decorated with evenly spaced ring and dot motifs and the broad outer band has lily-like floral curls.

Date: 16th–17th century

Comments: Similar to D1 & D2 but with a very different outer band

TYPE 1, DESIGN 4

6.47 Chest lid: lunette-shaped panel

Accession number: 98.2/55

Material: Lead alloy

Condition: Almost complete; part of corner missing

Dimensions: H 17mm; W c. 26mm

Description: A lunette-shaped panel with diagonally hatched border enclosing a centrally placed plant with broad curling leaves, rosette-type flowers, foliate tendrils and seed pods. Attached to the apex is part of another border fragment which curves in the opposite direction.

Date: 16th–17th century

Comments: The border fragment might be part of a coffer lid.

TYPE 1, DESIGN 5

6.48 Chest lid: lunette-shaped panel

Accession number: 98.2/74
Material: Lead alloy
Condition: Complete; slight damage to right corner
Dimensions: H 18mm; W 33mm
Description: A lunette-shaped panel with cross-hatched border enclosing a centrally placed quatrefoil double rose with prominent calyx points extending beyond and between the outer row of petals. The rose is surrounded by a circle of pellets with ring and dot motifs on each side and the corners are spanned by a pair of concentric arcs with a single ring and dot in each segment.
Date: 16th–17th century

TYPE 1, DESIGN 6

6.49 Chest lid: lunette-shaped panel

Accession number: 84.276/4
Material: Lead alloy
Condition: Complete
Dimensions: H 14mm; W 24mm
Description: A lunette-shaped panel with diagonally hatched border. Positioned at mid-point along the straight edge is half a quatrefoil double rose with calyx points extending beyond and between the outer row of petals.
Date: 16th–17th century

TYPE 2, DESIGN 1

6.50 Chest lid: lunette-shaped panel

Accession number: 98.2/51
Material: Lead alloy
Condition: Almost complete; some damage
Dimensions: H 20mm; W *c.* 26mm
Description: A lunette-shaped panel with a cross-hatched surface. The spacing between the lines varies considerably and the remains of a tab are evident on the right side.
Date: 16th–17th century
Comments: This simple decoration possibly represents a studded leather covering on a coffer: see MoL Acc. no. 96.92 and Chinnery 1998, p. 126, fig. 2:128.

TYPE 2, DESIGN 2

6.51 Chest lid: lunette-shaped panel

Accession number: 98.2/50
Material: Lead alloy
Condition: Almost complete
Dimensions: H 18mm; W 28mm
Description: A lunette-shaped panel with alternating plain and diagonally hatched chequer pattern
Date: 16th–17th century
Comments: Similar to Cat. no. 6.82

TYPE 2, DESIGN 3

6.52 Chest lid: lunette-shaped panel

Accession number: 98.2/92
Material: Lead alloy
Condition: Damaged
Dimensions: H *c.* 26mm; W *c.* 33mm
Description: More or less lunette-shaped, with angular profile, uneven thickness and decorated with a pelleted diaper pattern
Date: 16th–17th century
Comments: Uncertain function – possibly not an end panel from a chest lid

TYPE 3, DESIGN 1

6.53 Chest lid: lunette-shaped panel

Accession number: 98.2/43
Material: Lead alloy
Condition: Almost complete
Dimensions: H 19mm; W 29mm
Inscription: [R] [K]
Description: Lunette-shaped panels with slightly flattened apex. The panel is decorated with a random pattern of ring and dots surrounding a backwards R and inverted K within a border of ring and dot.
Date: 16th–17th century
Comments: The end panel on Cat. no. 6.81 is identical.

TYPE 3, DESIGN 2

6.54 Chest lid: lunette-shaped panel

Accession number: 84.257/6; 98.2/44; 98.2/45*
Material: Lead alloy
Condition: 84.257/6; 98.2/45: complete
Dimensions: H 20mm; W 26mm
Inscription: R
Description: Lunette-shaped panels decorated with cross-hatching and a large letter R in relief. The surface is dotted with a random pattern of pellets and one (98.2/44) was found in association with the beaded edge and curving trellis of a coffer top.
Date: 16th–17th century
Comments: Identical mould

TYPE 3, DESIGN 3

6.55 Chest lid: lunette-shaped panel

Accession number: 98.2/46; 98.2/47*; 98.2/719
Material: Lead alloy
Condition: 98.2/46; 98.2/47: complete 98.2/719: small fragment
Dimensions: H 20mm; W 24mm
Inscription: CT
Description: Slightly asymmetrical lunette-shaped panels with slightly flattened apex and sides, decorated with cross-hatching, large relief letters C and T and pellets.
Date: 16th–17th century
Comments: Identical mould
Comparandum: Half a possible lunette-shaped panel inscribed [L]/T recovered from Abbot's Lane (ABO92[635]<976>) from a late 16th-century context: see Egan forthcoming a, no. 604

TYPE 4, DESIGN 1

6.56 Chest lid: lunette-shaped panel

Accession number: 98.2/48
Material: Lead alloy
Condition: Almost complete
Dimensions: H 20mm; W *c.* 28mm
Description: A lunette-shaped panel with a radial hatching interspersed with pellets as a border, enclosing three sunbeams surmounted by stylized triple crowns on a finely cross-hatched ground.
Date: 16th–17th century
Comments: The motif seems to be a stylized version of the Drapers' Company arms (see Type 1 buffets), namely three clouds proper, the sun beams issuing with three imperial crowns.

TYPE 4, DESIGN 2

6.57 Chest lid: lunette-shaped panel

Accession number: 98.2/49
Material: Lead alloy
Condition: Complete profile; part of central section missing
Dimensions: H 19mm; W 28mm
Description: A lunette-shaped panel with a diagonally hatched border along the straight edge and radial hatching interspersed with pellets around the curving edge. There are three very stylized triple crowns issuing from sun beams in the centre with 'rosettes' of pellets in between and in each corner.
Date: 16th–17th century

TYPE 5, DESIGN 1

6.58 Chest lid: lunette-shaped panel

Accession number: 98.2/52*; 98.2/53; 98.2/718
Material: Lead alloy
Condition: 98.2/52; 98.2/53: almost complete. 98.2/718: part of left side missing
Dimensions: H 20mm; W 38mm
Description: Lunette-shaped panels with a central pellet and alternating ridged and flat radial banding. There is a decorative border around the curved edge consisting of three concentric lines: the inner composed of pellets and the others with tiny vertical slashes.
Date: 16th–17th century
Comments: Probably from the same mould
Comparandum: For a similar design on a chair back of *c.* 1625 date, see Chinnery 1998, p. 255, fig. 3:59.

TYPE 5, DESIGN 2

6.59 Chest lid: lunette-shaped panel

Accession number: 98.2/54
Material: Lead alloy
Condition: Half only
Dimensions: H 20mm; W 17mm;
    W (incl. tab) 22mm
Description: The right half of a lunette-shaped panel with corner tab extant. Virtually identical to T5, D1, apart from the border which has two broken inner lines.
Date: 16th–17th century

TYPE 5, DESIGN 3

6.60 Chest lid: lunette-shaped panel

Accession number: Private collection
Material: Lead alloy
Condition: Complete; some damage and a hole at the apex
Dimensions: H 20mm; W 38mm
Description: Lunette-shaped panel with radial lobes emanating from the centre of the base. The lobe tips are ornamented with ring and dot surrounded by pellets and the lower lobes cross-hatched. The lobes are surrounded by a half-circle of ring and dot interspersed with pellets.
Date: 16th–17th century
Provenance: Bull Wharf, 3 November 1999
Comparandum: Similar lunette-shaped panel in Mitchiner 1986, p. 223, no. 826

TYPE 6, DESIGN 1

6.61 Chest lid: lunette-shaped panel

Accession number: 98.2/71
Material: Lead alloy
Condition: Complete
Dimensions: H 11mm; W 22mm
Inscription: 1641
Description: A plain lunette-shaped panel inscribed 1641, with a diagonally hatched border along the straight edge.
Date: 1641
Comparandum: A small lunette-shaped panel dated 1574 on an oak arm-chair in the Victoria and Albert Museum: see Ceskinsky 1922, vol. 2, fig. 215

TYPE 6, DESIGN 2

6.62 Chest lid: lunette-shaped panel

Accession number: 98.2/73
Material: Lead alloy
Condition: Almost complete
Dimensions: H *c.* 14mm; W 22mm
Inscription: 1646
Description: A plain lunette-shaped panel with cable edge. There is an inverse inscription 1646 and a cluster of pellets just below the apex which is damaged. Part of the bottom edge is missing.
Date: 1642

End panels

The 14 end panels all have the same basic shape: a domed top or lid section joined to a square box raised on two legs. Four of the domed sections are of pierced rather than solid construction. There are 12 mould variations and the decorative mouldings represent carved tracery, panelling, iron straps or ornamental metal fittings found on real chests dating from the late 15th to mid-17th century.

TYPE 1

These end panels all have solid 'lid' sections and an openwork 'box'.

TYPE 1, DESIGN 1

6.63 Chest end panel

Accession number: 75.1/37
Material: Lead alloy
Condition: Complete; one piece loose
Dimensions: H 57mm; H (lunette) 16mm;
    W 28mm
Description: End panel from a three-dimensional chest with integrally cast 'lid', box and bracket legs. A plain solid lunette or 'lid' joins a square box of cross-hatched geometric and floral/foliate tracery. The central rosette, decorated with pellets, is

now separated. The box frame and legs are defined by a hatched ridge. A large loop curves from the base of the lunette to the upper rail below. The legs have cross-hatched scrolling bracket supports.

Date: 16th–17th century

TYPE 1, DESIGN 2

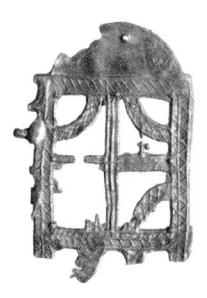

6.64 Chest end panel

Accession number: 98.2/75; 98.2/76*; 98.2/77
Material: Lead alloy
Condition: Almost complete. 98.2/77: in two halves
Dimensions: H 35mm; H (lunette) 8mm; W 24mm
Description: Almost complete end panels from a three-dimensional chest with integrally cast 'lid' and box. The plain solid lunette-shaped 'lid' is attached to a rectangular box of geometric tracery with ridged and cross-hatched decoration. The upper rail has diagonal hatching, the left stile and base rail are decorated with herringbone and the right stile is cross-hatched. All have a four 'tabs' extending from the bottom of the base rail (most evident on 98.2/76 & 98.2/77) and these may be the upper part of the legs and their openwork bracket support.
Date: 16th–17th century
Comparanda: Similar fragments in Mitchiner 1986, p. 223, no. 826 and Egan forthcoming a, no. 605, from excavations at Abbot's Lane (ABO92[388]<1192>) from a late 16th-century context. Both have tracery in the form of the City of London arms.

TYPE 1, DESIGN 3

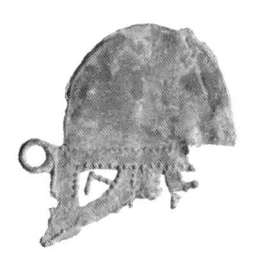

6.65 Chest end panel

Accession number: 98.2/78
Material: Lead alloy
Condition: Upper part only
Dimensions: H *c.* 30mm; H (lunette) 20mm; W 27mm
Description: Part of an end panel from a three-dimensional chest, with large, plain solid lunette or 'lid' attached to the upper rail of the box. Only the upper left side of the box is extant and this is decorated with geometric tracery embellished with beading. There is a round loop extending outwards from the left edge of the upper rail.
Date: 16th–17th century
Comments: The tracery pattern is similar to T1, D2 and T1, D4.

TYPE 1, DESIGN 4

6.66 Chest end panel

Accession number: 98.2/79
Material: Lead alloy
Condition: Upper part only
Dimensions: H *c.* 30mm; H (lunette) 20mm; W 27mm
Description: Part of an end panel from a three-dimensional chest, with large, plain solid lunette or 'lid' attached to the upper rail of the box. Only the upper part of the box is extant and this is decorated with geometric tracery embellished with cross-hatching and beading. Jutting outwards from the top of the right stile is a crushed loop.
Date: 16th–17th century
Comments: Very similar to T1, D3 and possibly associated with side panel Cat. no. 6.74

TYPE 1, DESIGN 5

6.67 Chest end panel

Accession number: 98.2/80
Material: Lead alloy
Condition: 'Lid' section only
Dimensions: H 22mm; H (lunette) 15mm; W 25mm;
Description: A plain solid lunette-shaped 'lid' from a three-dimensional chest, with top rail, loop and tip of left stile. The stile and rail are cross-hatched and the loop extends outwards from the left edge of the rail.
Date: 16th–17th century
Comments: Similar in design to T1, D3 and T1, D4

TYPE 1, DESIGN 6

6.68 Chest end panel

Accession number: 98.2/70
Material: Lead alloy
Condition: Complete
Dimensions: H 48mm; H (lunette) 15mm; W 28mm
Description: A complete end panel from a three-dimensional coffer with plain, solid lunette-shaped 'lid'. The openwork box has two outer vertical compartments of interlinking circular beaded tracery within a frame of diagonal hatching. Joined to the base rail are two solid bracket feet ornamented with scrolling. There is a small loop extending outwards from the right edge of the top rail and there are several broken tabs along the edge of the right stile which were presumably used to attach the end and side panels together.
Date: 16th–17th century

TYPE 1, DESIGN 7

6.69 Chest end panel

Accession number: 98.2/69; 2001.20/4
Material: Lead alloy
Condition: 2001.20/4: complete
Dimensions: H 32mm; H (lunette – top cut off) c. 6mm; W 22mm
Inscription: 1643
Description: End panels from a three-dimensional coffer, with integrally cast 'lid', box and legs. The solid, lunette-shaped 'lid' inscribed 1643 is joined to the top rail of the openwork box which is decorated with a quatrefoil tracery enclosing a possible stylized cross patence. The cross is embellished with 'feathered' hatching and ring and dot, and the stiles and top rail have diagonal hatching. Two short feet with curving inner profiles join the undulating lower edge of the base rail which is decorated in the centre with a stylized fleur-de-lys and pendant. Extending outwards from the edge of the right top rail is a small loop and there are two recurved tabs from the right stile.
Date: 1643
Comments: Probably produced from the same mould
Comparandum: Chest end panel recovered from excavations at Vintners' Hall (VHA89[1000]<2107>) with floral tracery, scroll brackets and diagonal hatching

TYPE 2

This type has an openwork structure with bracket legs.

TYPE 2, DESIGN 1

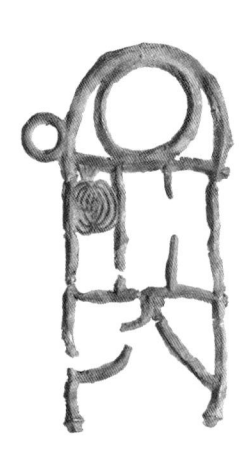

6.70 Chest end panel

Accession number: 98.2/89
Material: Lead alloy
Condition: Almost complete; some damage; left leg a separate piece
Dimensions: H 52mm; H (lunette) 16mm; W 22mm
Description: An openwork end panel from a three-dimensional coffer with integrally cast 'lid', box and legs of triangular section. The lunette-shaped 'lid' encloses a plain circle and the box is divided into three vertical compartments, plain apart from a pomegranate at the top of the left column. The legs have simple curving brackets and ridged feet. There is a large round loop extending outwards from the lunette to join the top rail on the left side.
Date: 16th–17th century

TYPE 2, DESIGN 2

6.71 Chest end panel

Accession number: 98.2/67
Material: Lead alloy
Condition: Almost complete
Dimensions: H *c.* 34mm; W: *c.* 26mm
Description: Part of an openwork end panel from a three-dimensional chest, with integrally cast box and bracket legs, curving top and straight sides of triangular section. The box is decorated with waisted lozenge tracery incorporating a central fleur-de-lys and there are trefoil pellets between each spandrel. The bracket leg mouldings take the form of an ogee-shaped arch with trefoil cusping on the underside (partially extant on the right side only). There is a round loop extending outwards from the top right corner.
Date: 16th–17th century
Comments: See Cat. no. 6.80.

TYPE 2, DESIGN 3

6.72 Chest end panel

Accession number: 98.2/68
Material: Lead alloy
Condition: Complete
Dimensions: H 39mm; W 24mm
Description: An openwork end panel from a three-dimensional chest, with integrally cast box and bracket legs, curving top and straight sides of triangular section. The box is decorated with waisted lozenge gothic-style tracery incorporating a central fleur-de-lys and there are trefoil pellets between each spandrel. The bracket leg mouldings take the form of an ogee-shaped arch with trefoil cusping on the underside. There is a round loop extending outwards from the top right corner.
Date: 16th–17th century
Comments: The same design as T2, D1, but different mould. See side and end panel Cat. no. 6.80

TYPE 3

This is a completely solid end panel with flattened 'lid' section and very small feet linked by bracket mouldings.

TYPE 3, DESIGN 1

6.73 Chest end panel

Accession number: 2001.21/25
Material: Lead alloy
Condition: Complete
Dimensions: H 29mm; W 24mm
Description: A solid panel with plain flattened 'lid' section. The box is highly decorated with foliate and floral motifs around a central flower vase. The lower body of the case has mouldings to suggest gadrooning and there are two S scroll handles. There is a tiny loop at the junction of the 'lid' and box on the right side. The end panel rests on short legs linked by scrolled bracket moulding.
Date: Probably 17th century
Comments: This panel has identical mouldings to three chest lids (Cat. no. 6.86) and was presumably made in the same workshop. The style of decoration suggests an elaborate leather- or textile-covered, or engraved, metal casket.
Provenance: Thames foreshore (?); purchased from a dealer

Side panels

TYPE 1, DESIGN 1

6.74 Chest side panel

Accession number: 98.2/18
Material: Lead alloy
Condition: Almost complete; in two halves
Dimensions: H 42mm; W 56mm
Inscription: R [T]
Description: A rectangular-framed side from a three-dimensional chest. Matching in size and decoration, the outer two square panels have geometric and possible floral/foliate tracery (see end panel T1, D4 Cat. no. 6.66). The narrow central panel is damaged. Only the right side has a complete profile and the chest reposes on solid bracket feet, inscribed on the left with the letter R and on the right with the letter T. The entire surface is cross-hatched and the rails, stiles, muntions and tracery are delineated with beading.
Date: 16th–17th century

TYPE 1, DESIGN 2

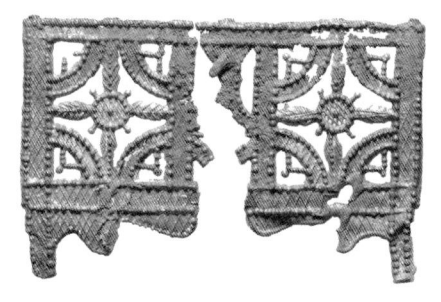

6.75 Chest side panel

Accession number: 8851*; 82.147/22; 98.2/82
Material: Lead alloy
Condition: 8851: almost complete. 98.2/82: left, central and part of right panel. 82.147/22: part of left side panel
Dimensions: H 31mm; W 56mm
Description: A rectangular-framed side from a three-dimensional chest. Matching in size and decoration, the outer two square panels have geometric and floral/foliate tracery, and the narrow central panel has a similar geometric pattern (most complete on 98.2/82). The entire surface is cross-hatched and the tracery, rails, stiles and muntions are delineated with beading. The solid brackets have semi-circular mouldings of unequal size and the right bracket on Acc. no. 8851 has a casting fault. There is a round loop on the top left corner of 82.147/22.
Date: 16th–17th century
Comments: Possibly cast from the same mould

TYPE 1, DESIGN 3

6.76 Chest side panel

Accession number: 87.175/2
Material: Lead alloy
Condition: Left side only; complete profile
Dimensions: H 41mm; W 30mm
Description: The left side from a possibly rectangular-framed three-dimensional chest. The square panel is decorated with beaded geometric tracery enclosing a floral motif decorated with diagonal hatching and pellets. There are ring and dot motifs in each corner. The rails, stile and muntion are delineated by vertical or horizontal hatching and the legs have solid scroll brackets ornamented with ring and dot and volute terminals. Only part of the central panel survives.
Date: 16th–17th century
Comments: Probably a three-panel side

TYPE 2, DESIGN 1

6.77 Chest side panel

Accession number: 98.2/87*; 98.2/88
Material: Lead alloy
Condition: 98.2/87: part only. 98.2/88: fragment
Dimensions: H 22mm; W: 34mm
Description: Side panel parts from an openwork three-dimensional chest or coffer. The panel (98.2/87) is divided horizontally creating a narrow band at the bottom. The entire frame is decorated with vertical ribbing. The ribs in the top and bottom sections are alternately positioned and the top section is further embellished with pointed gothic arcading. The entire framework is of triangular section and there are two equally spaced lateral tabs extending outwards from the edge. Fragment 98.2/ 88 is poorly cast, but probably comes from same mould as 98.2/87.
Date: 16th–17th century

TYPE 2, DESIGN 2

6.78 Chest side panel

Accession number: 98.2/86
Material: Lead alloy
Condition: Part only
Dimensions: H 23mm; W: 30mm
Description: Part of a side panel from an openwork three-dimensional chest with integral lock plate, button catch and key hole. The frame is divided horizontally and vertically with triangular-sectioned bars. The lock plate has three rows of decoration with diagonal hatching around the keyhole and cross-hatching at each end. There is a small thin tab extending upwards from the top of the frame.
Date: 16th–17th century
Comparandum: Front panel with a lock moulding recovered from Abbot's Lane (ABO92[294]<400>): see Egan forthcoming a, no. 603

TYPE 2, DESIGN 3

6.79 Chest side panel

Accession number: 98.2/118
Material: Lead alloy
Condition: Almost complete; slightly distorted
Dimensions: H 20mm; W c. 50mm
Description: The lower part of a chest side panel with plain triangular section frame and vertical ribbing interspersed with tiny pendant mouldings from the base rail. There are six tabs extending outwards from the sides and base and the panel probably formed the back of the chest.
Date: 16th–17th century
Comments: See side/lid panel (Cat. no. 6.87) which has a virtually identical back panel

End/side panels

TYPE 1, DESIGN 1

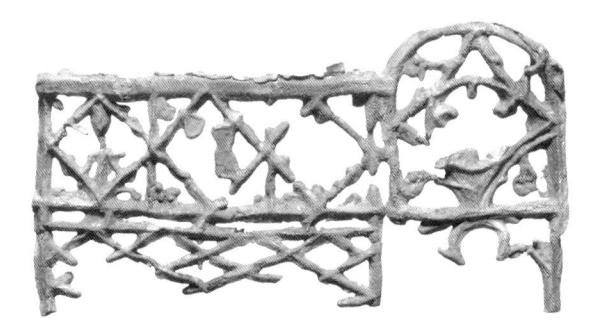

6.80 Chest end panel joined to side panel

Accession number: 81.548/12
Material: Lead alloy
Condition: Almost complete; poorly cast
Dimensions: H (end panel) 39mm; H (side) 31mm; W (end panel) 25mm; W (side) 48mm
Description: Integrally cast openwork end and side panel from a three-dimensional chest in flat, unfolded state. The end panel is joined to

the right side of the box and although extremely worn, incomplete and poorly cast, the tracery pattern is similar to the end panels of Cat. nos. 6.71 & 6.72. The end panel is also similarly supported by bracket leg mouldings in the form of an ogee-shaped arch with trefoil cusping on the underside. The framed side is divided into three compartments, each with identical mouldings of lozenge tracery enclosing a fleur-de-lys with trefoil pellets in the spandrels; a reduced version of the end panel design. Below these compartments and aligned with the height of the legs on the end panel is an incomplete panel of diaper latticework which runs the full width of the side.

Date: 16th–17th century

End/lid panels

TYPE 1

These have a solid end panel and an openwork lid.

TYPE 1, DESIGN 1

6.81 Chest end and lid panel

Accession number: 98.2/42
Material: Lead alloy
Condition: Complete end panel; part of lid only
Dimensions: H 19mm; W *c.* 25mm; Dpt *c.* 30mm
Inscription: R K or K R
Description: Part of a coffer lid with solid end panel and openwork top. The end panel is almost identical to Cat. no. 6.53 and is attached to the curved top with solder. The top panel has alternating solid and openwork bands decorated with ring and dot and interlinking circular cable twist tracery. On one side (possibly the front) there is a solid base rail decorated with ring and dots. There are tabs from the bottom edge to secure the side panels (now missing) on both sides.

Date: 16th–17th century

TYPE 1, DESIGN 2

6.82 Chest end and lid panel

Accession number: 80.152
Material: Lead alloy and copper alloy foil
Condition: Almost complete
Dimensions: H 17mm; W 57mm; Dpt *c.* 28mm
Description: An almost complete chest lid with solid end panel (one extant) and openwork top. The end panel has a chequer pattern with alternating plain and cross-hatched squares (see Cat. no. 6.51). The top panel has alternating solid and openwork transverse bands decorated with beading and circular and floral tracery. The beaded circular tracery is interrupted in the middle of the inner two bands, and replaced with a diagonally hatched lozenge incorporating a loop which is only attached with transverse and longitudinal bracing at the outer edge. Although flat, these loops could be recurved to form a handle attachment. The base rail has beading on one side and diagonal hatching on the other and there are several tabs securing a very thin sheet of copper to the underside (partly extant) which acts as a foil.

Date: 16th–17th century
Comments: It is possible that the foil was additionally secured with adhesive.

TYPE 2

These lids have a solid and pierced end panel.

TYPE 2, DESIGN 1

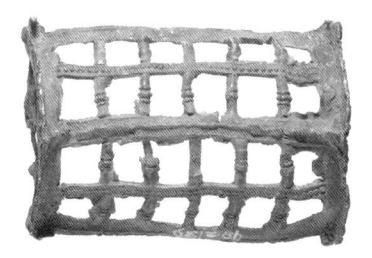

6.83 Chest lid

Accession number: 98.2/39
Material: Lead alloy
Condition: Complete; poorly cast; some damage
Dimensions: H *c.* 20mm; W 46mm; Dpt *c.* 30mm
Description: An openwork lid from a three-dimensional chest. Although the base rails align, the lunette-shaped end panels have a larger diameter so that they stick out beyond the circumference of the lid which is decorated with a grid pattern of longitudinal alternating beaded or ribbed bands linked by transverse baluster spindles. The lunettes have a beaded rail, baluster spindles and a solid arch with a cross-hatched border. Both of the lid base rails are beaded underneath. Twisted and recurving tabs extend from the panel edges.
Date: 16th–17th century

Lid panels

TYPE 1, DESIGN 1

6.84 Chest lid fragment

Accession number: 98.2/65
Material: Lead alloy
Condition: Fragment of top only; flattened
Dimensions: H 22mm; W 30mm
Description: Part of the diagonally hatched base rail and chest lid, with alternating solid and openwork transverse bands decorated with beading and beaded circles interlinked by a stylized flower head. The decoration is very similar to Cat. no. 6.82.
Date: 16th–17th century

TYPE 1, DESIGN 2

6.85 Chest lid (?) fragment

Accession number: 98.2/66
Material: Lead alloy
Condition: Fragments; now flat
Dimensions: H 10mm; W 18mm
Description: Possibly part of a chest lid with solid cross-hatched bar and interlocking plain circular tracery
Date: 16th–17th century

TYPE 2, DESIGN 1

6.86 Chest lid

Accession number: 98.2/84*; 98.2/85*; 98.2/176
Condition: 98.2/84: almost complete. 98.2/85; 98.2/176: include top and back panel only. All flat
Dimensions: H *c.* 6mm; W 43mm; Dpt 24mm
Description: These rectangular lids have been cast from the same mould and were recovered in a flat, pre-assembly condition. The lids have narrow side panels which were designed to be folded down to form a three-dimensional shape, and a separately cast handle with 'turned' mouldings was soldered on to the centre. Only one end panel from the lid survives (Acc. no. 98.2/84), and this has a deep curving edge. By contrast, the front and back panels are narrower and parallel sided and the front panel has an integrally cast clasp loop joined to ring and dot scrolling. The loop is further ornamented with pellets around the edge. The decorative motif on the front panel is used on the end panel, but the back panel is ornamented with hatched foliate scrolling. Lateral tabs extend outwards from the back panels only. The chest lids are decorated with a pair of flower-filled vases surrounded by foliage and pellets. The angular handle on Acc. no. 98.2/84 is designed to pivot.
Date: 16th–17th century
Comments: The 'flowerpotte' design was popular from 1550–1750 and the motif appears on many pieces of early modern furniture.
Comparandum: See Cat. no. 6.73 which seems to have an identical design and was probably made in the same workshop

Side/lid panels

TYPE 1, DESIGN 1

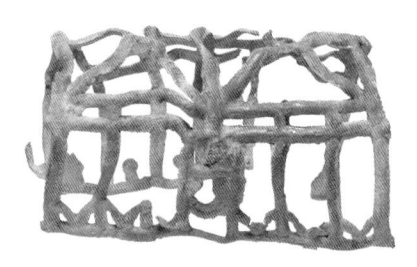

6.87 Chest sides and lid

Accession number: 81.548/11
Material: Lead alloy
Condition: Almost complete; some damage
Dimensions: H *c.* 29mm; H (side) *c.* 21mm; W (end) 25mm; W (side) 50mm
Description: The front, back and top or 'lid' of a three-dimensional openwork chest, cast in one piece with integral lock plate and key hole. Both of the sides have a narrow horizontal band at the top with vertical ribbing, but the front panel has stylized gothic arcading at the base and the back panel has pendant mouldings. The domed 'lid' is divided into two compartments decorated with saltires and an additional reinforcing rib to the outer edge aligned with the apex of the 'lid' arch. The lock plate is divided into two parts, the upper section containing a rectangular hasp aperture, and the lower with an inverted keyhole. There is a tab extending outwards from the bottom rail on the left side of the back panel.
Date: 16th–17th century

Fig. 50. Detail of children playing with their dolls in the Abbey Square in Middelburg. Various items of household equipment are scattered on the ground beside a doll-sized canopied bed and wicker cradle. Only one end of a base-metal cradle has been identified from London and this is a good deal smaller than the examples depicted by Continental artists.

Detail from an anonymous engraving after *Kinder spel ghedündet tot Sinne-beeloen ende Leere der Seden* ('Children's games expounded as symbols and moral precepts'), 1618 by Adriaen van de Venne. 21.6 x 32.2 cm
Bibliothèque royale de Belgique, Brussels

Cradle

Cradles with integral rockers were common throughout the medieval period, but although the form is well represented in art, and rocking cradles are frequently described in contemporary literature and documents, very few specimens have survived. The oldest known European rocking cradle was recovered from a 12th-century context during excavations conducted by the Archeologisches Landesmuseum in Schleswig,[53] but the earliest examples in English collections all date from the 1620s.[54]

Only one component from a three-dimensional toy rocking cradle has been recovered, and in the absence of comparable miniatures or full-scale examples the fragment is very difficult to date. Early 15th-century illustrations show cradles with pierced end panels like the toy, but the profile of the rocker and other stylistic features suggest manufacture in the post-medieval period. Seventeenth-century rocking cradles were highly decorative and robustly constructed from solid panels, and it is possible that the tracery on the toy was designed to imitate the elaborate carving and incised work on a cradle of this date.

TYPE 1, DESIGN 1

6.88 Rocking cradle

Accession number: 98.2/41
Material: Lead alloy
Condition: End panel only
Dimensions: H 38mm; W 29mm; W (rocker) 32mm
Description: An elaborate openwork end panel from a three-dimensional rocking cradle, with arched head rail, straight tapering stiles, base rail and scrolled cross bearer or rocker. The entire frame has beaded edges and there are attachment slots for additional panels at the top of the stiles and in the middle of the base rail. The head rail is decorated in the centre and corners with floral motifs and the rocker has a flower motif flanked by rings. Intricate circular interlacing with floral motifs at various interconnecting points fills the central space.
Date: Probably mid- to late 17th century
Comparanda: Cradles with pierced end panels in *Le Bain de Marie enfant*, a 15th- century engraving by Israel Van Meckenem, and a 16th-century illustration from the *Bible de Jean de Sy* (MS français 15397, fol. 32v). Both in the Bibliothèque nationale de France, Paris.

Stool

Triangular turned stools were ubiquitous in northern Europe from the early 15th to late 17th centuries. The form is also well represented in art, although no English examples in full scale have survived. As the name implies, most of the constituent parts of the stool apart from the seat were of turned construction, and the mouldings on the toy imitate the characteristic knops and rings on the genuine article. A comparable turned stool is depicted in Randle Holme of Chester's *Academy of Armory* published in 1688, but the best parallels come from Continental sources of 15th- and 16th-century date.

This is the only example known from England, although a similar stool with a decorative floral motif on the seat has been recovered from excavations in Amsterdam.[55]

TYPE 1, DESIGN 1

6.89 Stool

Accession number: 98.2/36
Material: Lead alloy
Condition: Almost complete; slightly distorted and damaged
Dimensions: H 22mm; W *c.* 20mm
Description: A three-footed 'turned' stool with a 'panelled-in' triangular seat, stretcher rail and two vertical spars or spindles (extant on one side only) connecting the seat frame to the stretcher. The legs, rail and spars are embellished with three bands of horizontal ridging to represent decorative turning, and there are rounded knops at the seat corners.
Date: Probably late 15th–16th century
Comparanda: Illustrations of turned stools in Jean Mansel, *La Fleur des histoires* (Flanders, 15th century), MS français 297, fol. 1, Bibliothèque national de France, Paris; and *Aesop's Fables* (Ghent *c.* 1490), MS 15, fol. 4, Waddesden Manor, Buckinghamshire

Fig. 51. Detail showing a triangular stool from the 15th-century manuscript *La Fleur des histoires* by Jean Mansel. The base-metal miniature is the only surviving example of what was once a very common item of furniture. See plate VI, p. 166

1. Harrison, 1577, bk 2, ch. 10.
2. Eames 1977, p. xxii.
3. It is possible that the 'Miscellaneous' section includes other furniture components which have not been recognized and there may be relevant pieces within the Museum of London's archaeological archive which have been overlooked.
4. Figdor 1913.
5. Campbell 1747, p. 245.
6. Oak bird cage with iron wires dated 1697 in Chinnery 1979, p. 408, fig. 3:508.
7. There is a turned wood bell-shaped cage dating to the first half of the 17th century in the Utrecht Museum.
8. See, for example, a 17th-century engraving by Cornelis Bloemaert after Hendrick Bloemaert. A wicker cage also hangs from the ceiling in Adriaen van Ostade's *Village Inn with Backgammon and Card Players*, 1674–5 in the Harold Samuel Collection.
9. Willemsen 1998, p. 389, B112. A number of 18th- and 19th-century versions have survived, and there is a copper-alloy bird in a cage in the Museum of Childhood in Edinburgh.
10. John Russell's *Boke of Nurture* (London, 1452), lines 231–2.
11. Harrison 1577, bk 2, ch. 10.
12. The term buffet was also used to describe multiple-stage structures erected for important corporate, ceremonial and royal feasts and dismantled afterwards. The number of stages was an indication of status and the plate exhibited for show rather than use. The entire surface of the buffet was covered in layers of linen which not only concealed the roughly made structure underneath but also helped to show the plate off to advantage.
13. Thornton 1971; Edwards 1938; Conway 1944; Hughes 1966; Chinnery 1979, pp. 332–45.
14. We are greatly indebted to Mr I. Smith who first recognized that an irregular, flat-piece casting could be folded into three-dimensional form to represent a rather crude buffet.
15. The method of pin insertion is clearly shown on Acc. no. 98.2/4.
16. *Les Honneurs de la Cour, c.* 1489–91 in Eames 1977.
17. It would have been just as easy to produce a solid back on the toy buffet: see Chinnery 1979, p. 341, fig. 3:330.
18. Cat. no. 6.82, Acc. no. 80.153.
19. Chinnery 1979, p. 344: '1504 … a standing cubbourde carven wt a sayling haunce wt ymagry gylt'.
20. The Sir John Wynne buffet is owned by the Earl of Carrington at Gwydyr Castle. The Holbein drawing is held by the Print Room in the Museum of Fine Art, Basle. See also oak buffet *c.* 1530 in the Burrell Collection, Glasgow.
21. Inv. no. M239.
22. Chinnery 1979, p. 341, fig. 3:330.
23. *Histoire du Bon Roi Alexandre*, Bibliothèque nationale de France, Paris, MS français 9342. *Roman de Renaud de Montauban*, Bibliothèque de l'Arsenal, Paris.
24. H. von der Heide in St Anne Museum, Lübeck.
25. Franklyn & Tanner 1970, entry for 'chevron'; Gwynn-Jones 1993, p. 139.
26. I am grateful to Philippa Glanville and the V&A Museum Department of Metalwork for their help with dating.
27. Gwynn-Jones 1993, p. 139. The apex of the chevron finishes in the centre of the shield, in accord with British custom. In the 16th century chevrons were often 'likened to the gable end of a house and it was declared the appropriate ordinary for a civilian', hence its adoption in the arms of many livery companies: see Franklyn & Tanner 1970, entry for 'chevron'.
28. Eames 1977, p. 69.
29. Cescinsky & Gribble 1922, vol. 2, pp. 22–4, fig. 34 and two oak chests with monograms of the late 16th century also in the V&A collection: vol. 2, figs. 83 & 84.
30. Chinnery 1979, p. 62.
31. The pediment fragment from Fleet Valley (Cat. no. 6.7) has exaggerated openwork mouldings from a rail or stage, which is suggestive of textile, metal, or leather passementerie rather than ornate wood turning.
32. Mitchell 1989, p. 63.
33. It is just possible that these mouldings are meant to imitate carving, inlays or even painted designs such as the inlaid oak panel with mastic composition *c.* 1539 depicting the arms of Lady Kingston: see Chinnery 1979, p. 193, fig. 2:220.
34. See grant by William Brugges, 10 March 1439, 17 Hen. VI '[drasure] troys Royes de soleille issantz hors de troys nues de flambe coronnez de troys corons imperialx dore …' in the possession of the Worshipful Company of Drapers.
35. Two items brought into the Museum of London for identification (PR56/48 & PR56/49) also had triple crowns and pellets, but of slightly different design.
36. Jaggard 1601.
37. Jaggard 1601.
38. The Minute Books for 1565–6 are missing, but if Sir Richard commissioned and purchased the toys himself, no record would have been kept in the Company accounts.
39. See Hall 1979, entry for 'heart', p. 146.
40. Sir Richard's arms are very distinctive: on a fess, between three trefoils, slipped ermines, an eagle displayed, with border engrailed chased with nine bezants.
41. A possible chair back panel of 17th-century date, with vertical slots for arm and seat attachments excavated from London (JAC96[207]<541>).
42. Willemsen 1998, p. 384, B94a–i. These chairs resemble a chair depicted in a 15th-century painting of St Jerome attributed to Jan van Eyck in the Naples Museum, but similar forms were also produced in the early to mid-17th century: see Cescinsky & Gribble 1922, p. 195, fig. 257, dated 1640.
43. There is one early 16th-century chair in a private collection.
44. Symonds 1934, p. 174, fig. 3. See also Cescinsky & Gribble 1922, walnut chairs from 1660–1700.
45. Eames 1977, p. xxii. The effect of the dissolution of the monasteries is not discussed, but presumably the fact that chests made perfect containers and were reasonably portable ensured their survival.
46. Eames 1977, p. 108.

47 Some of the toy chests might have been designed to represent iron chests rather than wooden chests bound with iron.

48 Acc. no. 80.152, Cat. no. 6.82.

49 This assumption is supported by comparable fragments from excavations which have been recovered from 16th- and 17th-century contexts: a bracket VHA89[1000]<1497>, chest end panel VHA89[1000]<2167> and another chest end panel from ABO92<1192>[388].

50 Acc. no. 98.2/39 seems to be the most convincing interpretation of an ark chest because the lid has the characteristic gable profile of the type.

51 An almost complete example of a domed footed chest has been recovered from excavations in the Netherlands, but the lid is missing: see Willemsen 1998, p. 390, B117.

52 Chinnery 1979, p. 451, figs 4:65 & 4:66 and MacQuoid 1988, p. 95, fig. 197.

53 Cited in Riché & Alexandre-Bidon 1994, p. 53.

54 Chinnery 1979, pp. 397–8.

55 Willemsen 1998, p. 379, B77, from a 14th-century context.

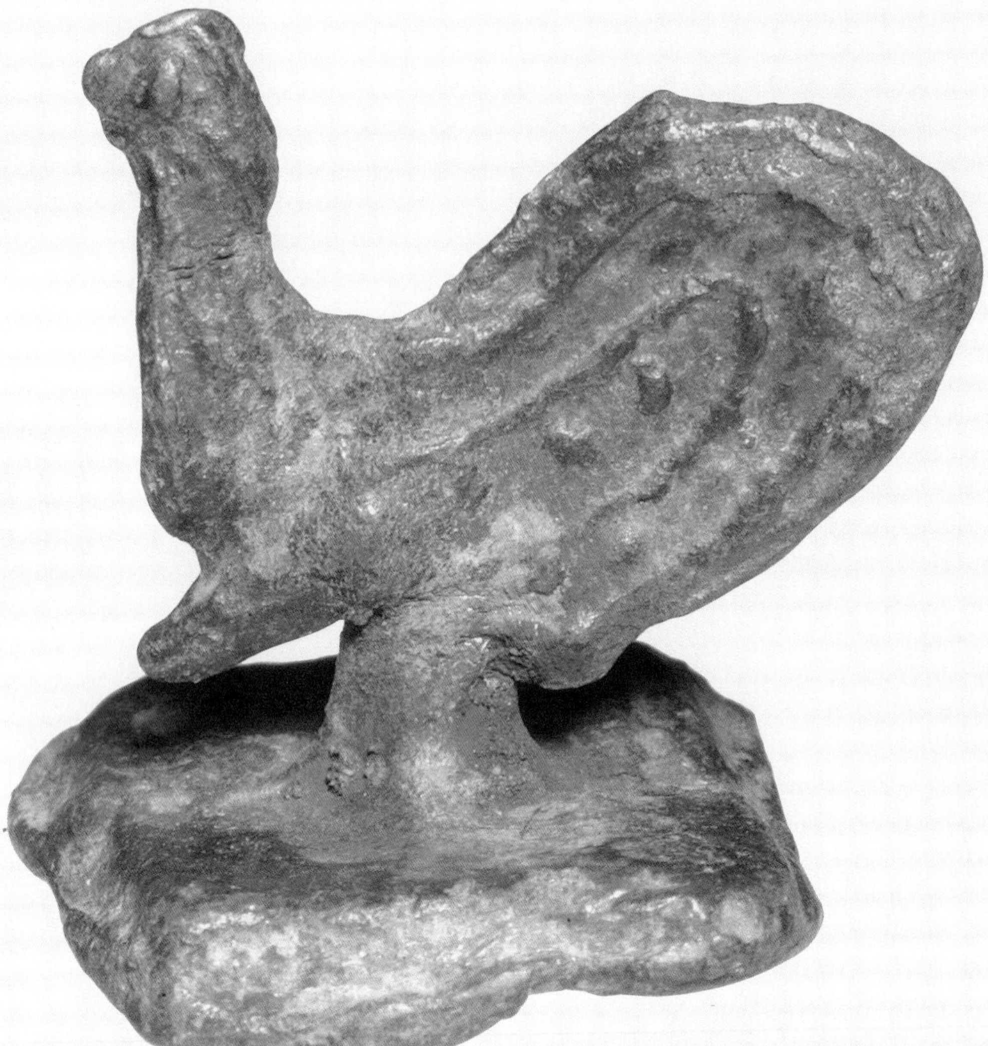

7 Shies

'There was a cocke,
For that a Priestes' sonne gave hym a knocke
Upon his legges, when he was yonge and nice,
He made him for to lose his benefice.'[1]

These curious objects may have been derived from the Shrove Tuesday pursuit of casting stones or cudgels at a live cockerel, which was either tied down or buried up to its neck in the ground.[2] This barbarous pastime was a regular feature of London life, and Sir Thomas More describes his childhood experience of hurling the 'cok-stele' with some pride.[3] An engraving of the 1683/4 Frost Fair on the Thames (fig. 52), depicting a tethered live cock, attests to the popularity of the sport in the early modern period,[4] and the practice continued in various parts of the British Isles until the early 19th century.[5]

All of the toy 'shies' are crudely cast from lead and most are detailed on one side only. The bases are flat but vary considerably in size and shape. The majority seem to represent cockerels, but two are moulded in the form of a house. One of these has obvious architectural detailing including a portico and gable, while the other, with the letters I and [T], seems to represent a rural dwelling. Some shies may have been made in the form of human figures.[6]

Although it is possible that these toys were produced in the late medieval and early modern period, the surviving examples seem to date from the 18th century. This assumption is supported by the single example from excavation, found in Narrow Street, Limehouse, and dated by ceramics to 1730–80.[7] The only possible Continental example (published as Roman) is of unknown provenance.[8]

Unlike most of the other toys in this volume, which are found in greater numbers in the capital than anywhere else, the reverse is true for the shies, which suggests that the game had a greater following in rural areas.

Fig. 52. A live cockerel is tethered to the ice in this anonymous engraving of the 1683/4 Frost Fair on the Thames.
Museum of London, Acc. no. A23101a

TYPE 1, DESIGN 1

7.1 Shy cock

Accession number: 98.2/683
Material: Lead alloy
Condition: Complete
Dimensions: H 24mm; W 24mm; L (stand) 19mm; W (stand) 19mm
Description: Cast in one piece with transverse casting seam. The crudely cast cockerel, profile to left, is placed in the centre at right angles to the plane of the stand which has bevelled edges and a chequered top.
Date: Probably 18th century

TYPE 1, DESIGN 2

7.2 Shy cock

Accession number: 98.2/684
Material: Lead alloy
Condition: Complete
Dimensions: H *c.* 26mm; W 35mm; L (stand) 15mm; W (stand) 18mm
Description: Cast in one piece with small oval-shaped stand and bird (cockerel?), profile to left.
Date: Probably 18th century

TYPE 1, DESIGN 3

7.3 Shy cock

Accession number: 98.2/680
Material: Lead alloy
Condition: Complete, some damage
Dimensions: H 35mm; W 46mm; L (stand) 32mm; W (stand) 42mm
Description: Crudely cast in one piece with a centrally placed songbird, profile to left, at right angles to the plane of the stand. There is a transverse casting seam and the edges of the stand are bevelled.
Date: Probably 18th century

TYPE 2, DESIGN 1

7.4 Shy

Accession number: 98.2/682
Material: Lead alloy
Condition: Complete
Dimensions: H 25mm; W 32mm; L (stand) 23mm; W (stand) 22mm
Inscription: [I] [T]
Description: An extremely crude shy toy, cast in one piece with centrally placed pitched roofed house at right angles to the rectangular stand. Half of the stand has a chequer pattern and on the other side are the letters [I] and [T].
Date: Probably 18th century

TYPE 2, DESIGN 2

7.5 Shy

Accession number: 2001.20/14
Material: Lead alloy
Condition: Complete
Dimensions: H 42mm; W 29mm; L (stand) 20mm; W (stand) 27mm
Description: Cast on one side only with a centrally placed house at right angles to the rough and slightly rounded flat base. The house has a steeply pitched roof, window and classical portico.
Date: Probably 18th century
Provenance: Rotherhithe

Fig. 53. Well-behaved Dutch children received presents on the Feast of St Nicholas, and in this detail of a painting of the 1660s by Jan Steen [1626–1679], the little girl is clearly delighted with her doll and shopping pail full of toys and sweets. The cockerel on a stick might have been intended for a game of 'cok-stele' and similar objects were sold by hawkers in London during the late 17th century. See plate IX, p. 361

1. Chaucer, *The Nonnes Priestes Tale*, c. 1387, lines 4503–6.
2. For further information on the game of shy cock, see Thistleton Dyer 1891, pp. 66–7.
3. More in Sylvester *et al.* 1963–97, vol. 1, pp. 3–7 & vol. 2, p. 208.
4. Cited in Egan 1996, note 98.
5. Strutt 1801, bk 3, pp. 211–12.
6. Egan 1996, fig. 51.
7. Excavated by Pre Construct Archaeology, NHU98<128>.
8. Cited in Egan 1996, note 98; Haedeke 1976, p. 56, no. 9.

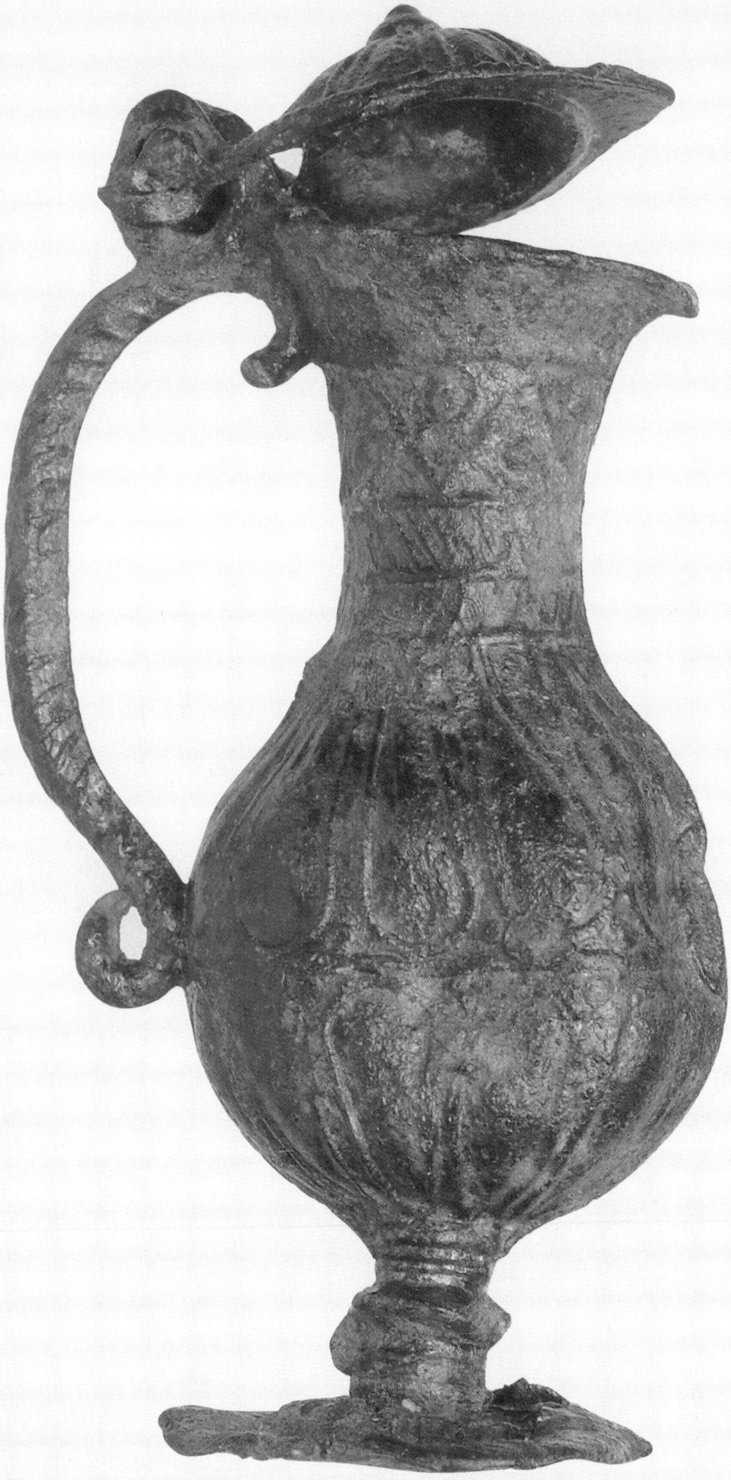

8 Tableware

'…before every trencher may stand a sallet, a Fricase, a boyled meat, a rost meat, a bak'd meat, and a carbonado which will give a most comely beauty to the Table, and a very great Contentment to the Guest'[1]

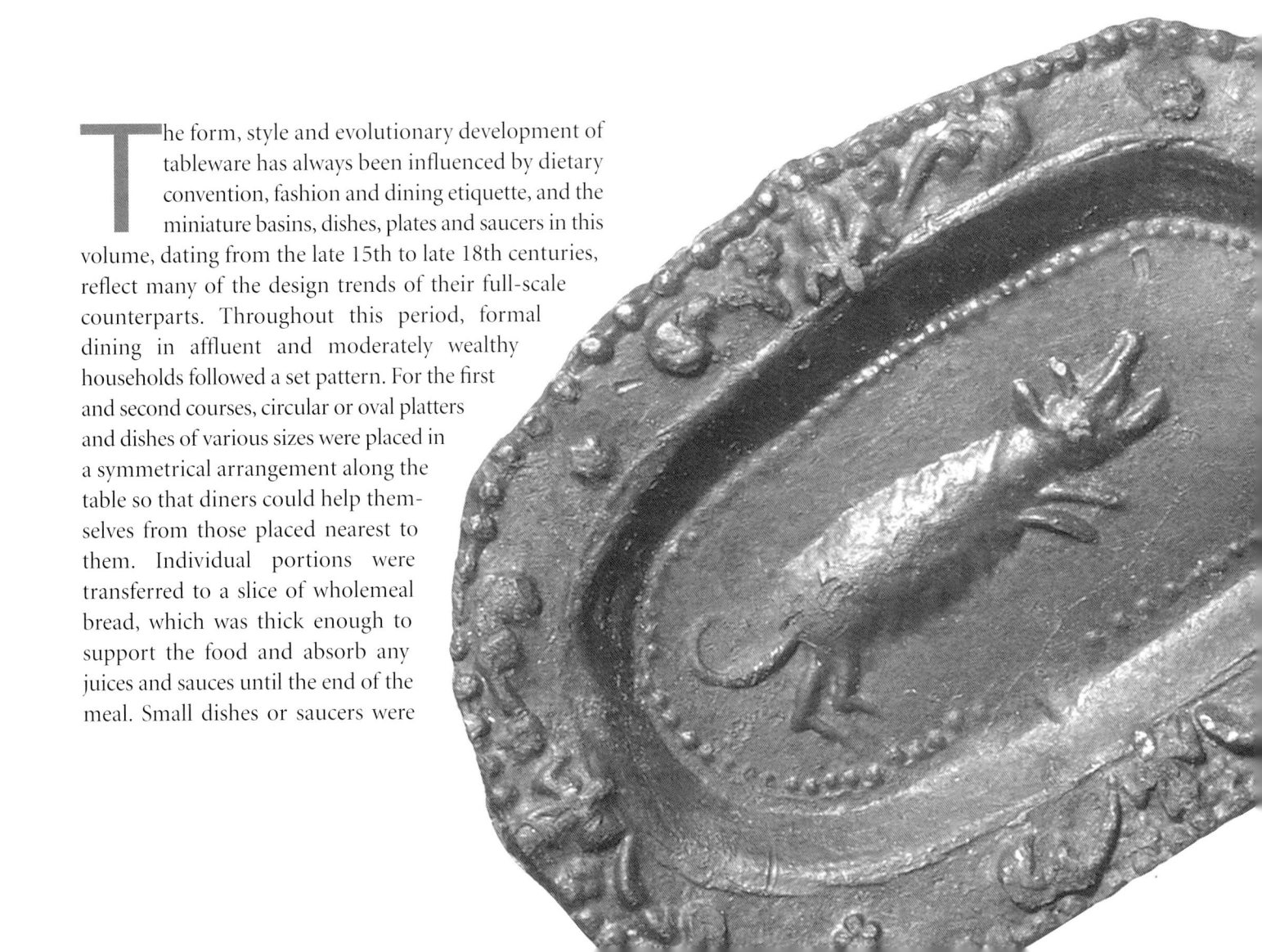

The form, style and evolutionary development of tableware has always been influenced by dietary convention, fashion and dining etiquette, and the miniature basins, dishes, plates and saucers in this volume, dating from the late 15th to late 18th centuries, reflect many of the design trends of their full-scale counterparts. Throughout this period, formal dining in affluent and moderately wealthy households followed a set pattern. For the first and second courses, circular or oval platters and dishes of various sizes were placed in a symmetrical arrangement along the table so that diners could help themselves from those placed nearest to them. Individual portions were transferred to a slice of wholemeal bread, which was thick enough to support the food and absorb any juices and sauces until the end of the meal. Small dishes or saucers were used for pulpy semi-liquid 'spoonmeats'. By the 1550s bread trenchers had been largely superseded by trenchers of wood or 'trencher plates' of pewter or silver, and by the early 17th century ceramic plates were in common use. Large flagons and serving vessels were used to replenish the cups and mazers with wine, beer or ale, and ornamental ewers with a matching basin were conveyed to the table before and after every meal and between courses for diners to wash their hands in hot, cold and scented water.

For the banquet or dessert, ornately decorated spice and sweetmeat plates 'not as broad as Trencher plates at Meat … of either silver or china'[2] were used for moist and sticky confections, succades, spiced wafers and cheese, and large decorated chargers held fruit and spiced biscuits.

Fig. 54. A servant decants wine from a large spouted pitcher into a drinking cup. Similar-shaped miniatures were made in base metals.
Reproduced from a late 12th-century English manuscript
Bodleian Library, University of Oxford, MS Gough, lit. 2, fol. 20r

Basins, dishes, plates & saucers

Although silver and pewter platters, dishes, spice plates and saucers are listed in the inventories of affluent households from the 14th century, it was not until the 16th century that pewter vessels started to feature in middle-class inventories in significant numbers.[3] Cheaper, flanged dishes and plates in lead-glazed earthenware were made on the Surrey–Hampshire borders from the late 16th century 'as a ceramic equivalent to the platters and trenchers of wood and pewter commonly used at table', and by the 1650s archaeological evidence suggests that more flanged dishes were made in Borderware than any other form.[4] Highly decorated ceramic dishes, chargers and plates of different sizes and qualities were also popular and large numbers were imported from the Continent to satisfy demand.[5] By the 1680s, most people could afford to buy significant amounts of plate, and Randle Holme noted that 'they are not looked upon to be of any great worth in personalls, that have not many dishes and much pewter, Brasse, copper and tyn wre; set round about a Hall, Parlar, and Kitchen'.[6] The 18th century saw an increase in the range of forms, and vessels of hexagonal or octagonal shape were particularly fashionable.

The miniatures represent a broad spectrum of plate of different types and qualities. Some are convincing copies of full-scale prototypes, but the majority bear little resemblance to surviving examples, which poses problems for dating and attribution. Classification is particularly difficult because contemporaries used a bewildering variety of terms to describe a particular form. For instance, a dish, 'a vessell or instrument, or what else you please to call it,' wrote Randle Holme in 1688, 'hath names proportional to its bignesse and use'. In general, the largest were known as 'platters' or 'basons', while those of moderate or small size were described as a dish or 'midleing dish'. The small dishes were commonly known as saucers. To add to the confusion, the terms used to describe a particular vessel were sometimes suggested solely by the use to which it was put. Inventories and accounts include references to 'pie', 'cheese', and 'spice' plates and to 'flesh', 'fish', 'broth', 'fruit', 'butter' and 'sallet' dishes amongst others, and while contemporaries presumably understood the relationship between use and size, the distinctions are not so obvious today. Moreover, two terms are occasionally used for one form, and in the 1699 inventory of the Pickleherring delftware factory in Southwark there are references to 'sawcer plates' and 'sawceer basons'.[7]

Contemporary accounts also suggest that the same sort and size of vessel could be used for different purposes. The large dish or platter found 'in all houses, and famileys' seems to have had a dual function 'for neccessary use (as, putting of meate into them) to serve up to tables; as also to adorne their countrey houses, and court

Plate (detail)
Acc. no. 98.2/259
Cat. no. 8.9

cuberts'. It seems that the terms basin, dish and even plate and saucer were often used interchangeably. Moreover, vessels with the same name were made in a variety of shapes, so that a basin could have a rounded or bellied profile, with a narrow or broad flange, or even 'noe brime at all', and while the shapes of some vessels evolved over time, others were made to the same basic design for years. Sometimes it is possible to make a broad chronological distinction between one form and another, but often dating is difficult because some forms were made concurrently and there is often a considerable overlap.[8]

In order to simplify and clarify nomenclature, curators, archaeologists and collectors have formulated their own classification systems to describe the various shapes and designs which are common to a particular class of material, and standard definitions have been established for specific forms. The terms used to describe a particular form are largely predicated upon the size and overall proportions. As a rule of thumb a plate is usually circular and can be anything from 127mm to 260mm in diameter. Vessels with diameters above 510mm are classified as basins or chargers, provided that their depth is greater than 38mm. Dishes can be circular, oval, oblong or any other shape as long as the depth is approximately one third to one seventh of the overall size.[9]

But while these classification systems are appropriate for full-scale vessels, the standard definitions do not work for the miniatures, and there are a number of reasons for this. Firstly, although the 131 miniature platters, basins, dishes, plates and saucers constitute the largest group of finds in the entire corpus, no one design, shape or size represents more than 10% of the total. There are no complete 'sets' or services, and yet it is evident that the toymakers were producing similar forms to different scales concurrently. What appears to be a tiny saucer within this sample, could be regarded as a moderately large dish in another context. At what point does a large decorated plate become a charger, a large dish a basin, or a small dish a saucer? Even though there are far more vessels of circular shape than any other form, the sizes are extremely variable, and the measurable diameters range from 26mm to 67mm (see Table 8.1). The flange widths also vary considerably from 1mm to 13mm, and although 48% have flanges from 5–6mm, and 22% have flanges from 3–4mm, there does not seem to be a particular correlation between the size and date, or even between the width of the flange and the overall diameter. All one can really deduce from the available evidence is that similar forms were obviously made in a range of scales, and the surviving sample is too small, with not enough examples of one maker's wares to enable comparisons to be made. The saucers, plates and round and oval dishes and platters with the maker's initials I(D)Q, which constitute the largest inscribed group in the collection, could be part of a suite or garnish, or random specimens from different sets made to different scales.

Secondly, since most of the miniatures have very shallow wells, with variable but subtly different profiles, it is very difficult to distinguish one form from another. Thirdly, a number of vessels are so crushed and distorted that potentially significant features are lost. For instance, until the 1630s and sporadically thereafter to the 1670s, full-sized English plates and dishes generally have a boss in the centre of the base.[10] One would expect the earliest miniatures to exhibit this feature, but often the flatwares are so flattened or refashioned by the finder, that it is unclear whether they originally had a boss or not.[11]

Due to the problems outlined above, the miniatures have been arranged according to their basic shape and design, and since some can be attributed to a particular maker or dated on stylistic grounds, they are listed in a broad chronological sequence. No attempt has been made to subdivide the material into arbitrary form categories, but specific terms have been applied to particular vessels. The circular vessels are listed first, followed by the single octagonal plate, and

Table 8.1

Diameter	Quantity	Diameter	Quantity	Diameter	Quantity
26mm	2	36mm	10	48mm	2
27mm	9	37mm	3	49mm	1
28mm	3	39mm	3	52mm	7
29mm	3	41mm	2	53mm	2
30mm	6	42mm	3	56mm	8
31mm	10	43mm	2	58mm	3
32mm	2	44mm	2	61mm	1
33mm	7	45mm	4	62mm	2
34mm	3	46mm	1	67mm	1
35mm	6	47mm	3	**TOTAL**	**111**

the oval and rectangular dishes and platters. The last section of the catalogue includes those of uncertain type. Nearly 100 different designs have been identified.

The vessels reflect a wide range of qualities and types. The earliest, with features suggesting a late 15th- and 16th-century date, tend to have quatrefoil or rosette mouldings on the central boss, a plain narrow flange or broader flange decorated with hatched chevrons and pellets.[12] Those of the early to mid-17th century tend to have wider flanges with foliate, floral borders and a double rose in the centre. The late 17th- and 18th-century forms have plain, flat and sometimes lathe-turned bases, with mouldings to suggest a triple-reeded or beaded rim, and the flanges are decorated with hatching, scrolling and festoons.

Sometimes the decoration is confined to the flange, but often the entire surface is ornamented. Many have mouldings to suggest engraved, hammered and cast metalwork, but others are so stylized or crudely executed that it is impossible to know whether they were modelled on metal or ceramic prototypes, or indeed ceramic copies of metal forms. The choice of motifs is partly influenced by current fashion and conventions in toy manufacture, but also by the skill and personal preferences of the toymaker. The repertoire of motifs ranges from simple linear or geometric designs to the florid styles of the 18th century, and although some makers had the necessary skills to produce elaborate patterns, no attempt seems to have been made to recreate the figurative designs or armorial devices which are often found on full-scale vessels. Foliate and floral motifs were particularly favoured, however, and over a quarter have a rosette, or a double rose in the centre of the base. Documentary evidence suggests that the double rose was used to decorate full-scale plates from at least the mid-15th century, and there are a number of slipware dishes dating between 1575 and 1625 from the Netherlands with a rosette in the centre.[13] Most of the surviving full-scale examples in silver and pewter date from the 1570s to 1660s, and the majority of the miniatures with this device were probably made during this period.[14] As the double rose seems to have been a popular and recurring motif across a range of toys and miniatures, however, it would be unwise to place too much significance on its occurrence here.[15]

None of the vessels bears a date, but 27 are inscribed with initials or maker's marks and two incorporate the sacred monogram IHS.[16] The ratio of inscribed vessels is greater than any other category of toy, and this could be due to a number of factors. The most straightforward explanation is that the basins, dishes, plates and saucers constitute the largest group in the collection, so that the relative number of inscribed vessels is accordingly greater than those in other categories. But this prosaic point does not take into account the fact that contemporaries marked full-scale vessels of pewter or silver with an identifying touch or maker's mark, and many dishes, chargers and plates were additionally inscribed with the owner's initials or a triad of initials to celebrate a particular event or more usually a betrothal or marriage.

Some of the toymakers have incorporated their initials within the design scheme, and the products inscribed DQ, IQ or IDQ are always placed in an oval cartouche on the flange like many full-scale vessels in metal and ceramic. One plate (Cat. no. 8.12) has a scratched S or 8 on the underside of the flange which might have denoted a particular marker, range or size, and several miniatures are marked on the front and back with a genuine touchmark. Notable examples are the products of John Jackson[17] and Charles Rack[18] (Cat. nos. 8.45 & 8.43), the only makers of base-metal toy flatware whose work has been identified. Both men are mentioned in the Court Minutes of the Worshipful Company of Pewterers for 1689 and both seem to have made toy flagons as well as toy dishes and saucers. Charles Rack's premises were searched by the Company on 6 May and 10 December, and on the second occasion the word 'dishes' was crossed through and replaced with the word 'saucers'. Could this be another instance of confused nomenclature, or was Rack making similar-shaped flatwares in a range of sizes?

Although the documentary and stylistic evidence is weak, most of the vessels in this collection were probably manufactured in London. Some vessels of comparable scale, shape and style have been recovered on the Continent,[19] but as their full-scale counterparts were traded extensively and imported into London, English toymakers probably drew their inspiration from several sources, and until more is known about the makers of the toy vessels and their products, issues of terminology and attribution will remain unresolved.

Circular vessels

DESIGN 1

8.1 Dish or plate

Accession number: 98.2/314
Material: Lead alloy
Condition: Almost complete; part of flange missing; other damage
Dimensions: H 2mm; Diam 27mm; Diam (base) 21mm; W (rim) 3mm
Description: A dish or plate with a narrow, flat flange, very shallow vertical wall and wide flat base. The rim is plain and the flange is decorated with large equally spaced pellets. There is a quatrefoil motif in the centre within a plain circle and chevron border.
Date: Late 15th–16th century
Comments: The vessel seems to replicate a spice or sweetmeat plate.

DESIGN 2

8.2 Dish or plate

Accession number: 98.2/266
Material: Lead alloy
Condition: Complete
Dimensions: H c. 2mm; Diam 27mm; Diam (base) 22mm; W (rim) 3mm
Inscription: IHS
Description: A dish or paten with a narrow, flat flange, very shallow vertical wall and flat base inscribed with the sacred monogram IHS in blackletter. Part of the rim is notched and the base has casting scars.
Date: Late 15th–16th century

DESIGN 3

8.3 Dish or plate

Accession number: 98.2/313
Material: Lead alloy
Condition: Complete (?); perhaps the central part of a larger vessel
Dimensions: H 1mm; Diam 27mm
Description: A flat disc with a plain border. The central motif within a raised cordon, consists of a cross of four lobes in relief with ring and dot between each lobe.
Date: Probably 16th century
Provenance: Swan Stairs
Comments: The edges are damaged, so it is difficult to tell whether the vessel is complete or the central part of a large dish or plate.

DESIGN 4

8.4 Plate

Accession number: 4106
Material: Lead alloy
Condition: Complete apart from small hole
Dimensions: H 1mm; Diam 31mm
Description: A completely flat plate with a beaded rim. The 'flange' is defined by two plain concentric circles, and is decorated with an alternating pattern of ring and dot motifs and chevrons. The central floral motif is surrounded by a waisted lozenge with fleurs-de-lys at the points, and this is surrounded by a double quatrefoil with trefoils at the intersections of each lobe. Clusters of ring and dot surround the quatrefoil. The plate has a casting seam across the back and the surface is covered with a random pattern of cross-hatching.
Date: Probably early 16th century

DESIGN 5

8.5 Dish

Accession number: 98.2/311

Material: Lead alloy

Condition: Complete

Dimensions: H *c.* 2mm; Diam 26mm; Diam (base) *c.* 9mm; W (rim) 4mm

Description: A very small circular dish with a flat flange, curving wall and pronounced boss. The vessel is plain apart from the central boss, which is decorated with a simple cross in relief. The base has a deep kick.

Date: 16th century

Comparandum: See Cat. no. 8.6 which is very similar

DESIGN 6

8.6 Dish

Accession number: 98.2/315

Material: Lead alloy

Condition: Complete; much surface damage.

Dimensions: H 3mm; Diam 31mm; Diam (base) 14mm; W (rim) *c.* 7mm

Description: A poorly moulded shallow dish with a broad, slightly curving flange, curving wall and flat base. There is a plain cross motif in the centre.

Date: Possibly 16th century

DESIGN 7

8.7 Plate

Accession number: 98.2/255

Material: Lead alloy

Condition: Complete apart from hole in centre

Dimensions: H 1mm; Diam 37mm; W (rim) 5mm

Description: This plate has a flat flange, very shallow curving wall and flat base. The rim is beaded and the flange decorated with an alternating pattern of cross-hatched and pelleted chevrons. There is a sexfoil in the centre surrounded by pellets within a plain circle. The base is a random pattern of cross-hatching underneath.

Date: 16th century

Comparanda: Plates with chevron decoration on the flange have been excavated from 14th- to 16th-century contexts in the Netherlands: see Willemsen 1998, p. 370, B55.

DESIGN 8

8.8 Dish

Accession number: 98.2/256

Material: Lead alloy

Condition: Complete

Dimensions: H 5mm; Diam 35mm; Diam (base) *c.* 20mm; W (rim) 4mm

Description: A shallow flanged dish with a deep curving wall and central boss. The rim is plain and the flange is decorated with an alternating pattern of pelleted and hatched chevrons. There is a slight boss in the centre decorated with a plain cross with trefoil terminals surrounded by ring and dot motifs. The boss is surrounded by a pair of concentric circles.

Date: 16th century

DESIGN 9

8.9 Dish or plate

Accession number: 98.2/258; 98.2/259*

Material: Lead alloy

Condition: Complete

Dimensions: H 3mm; Diam 31mm; Diam (base) 21mm; W (rim) 5.5mm

Description: Two flanged vessels from the same mould with a shallow curving wall

and central boss. The rim is plain and the flange has been decorated with an alternating pattern of hatched and pelleted chevrons. There are two concentric circles around the boss, which is otherwise plain.
Date: 16th century
Comments: 98.2/259 seems to have been flattened out.

DESIGN 10

8.10 Dish

Accession number: 98.2/257
Material: Lead alloy
Condition: Complete; casting fault
Dimensions: H 4mm; Diam 47mm; Diam (base) 17mm; W (rim) 6.5mm
Description: A flanged dish with a shallow curving wall and central boss. The rim is slightly bevelled and plain, and the flange is decorated on the upper and lower surfaces with an alternating pattern of plain and hatched chevrons. There are pellets and hatched chevrons on the lower face. There is a beaded circle at the top of the wall and the central boss is decorated with a very tiny floral motif.
Date: 16th century
Comments: There are casting scars around the rim.

DESIGN 11

8.11 Dish or plate

Accession number: 98.2/328
Material: Lead alloy
Condition: Complete; poorly cast; subsequently pierced
Dimensions: H 3mm; Diam 39mm; Diam (base) 26mm; W (rim) 6mm
Description: A flanged dish or plate of irregular shape, with a very shallow straight-sided sloping wall and flat base. The rim is beaded and the flange decorated with an alternating pattern of hatched and pelleted chevrons. This decoration is repeated on the base, although only one half of the design is clear. The central quatrefoil design is surrounded by a beaded circle and a band of alternating hatched and pelleted chevrons. There are eight holes in the base that seem to have been randomly placed.
Date: 16th century
Comments: There are a large number of casting irregularities and faults and this is particularly evident on the underside, which has large scars and a haphazard pattern of cross-hatching.

DESIGN 12

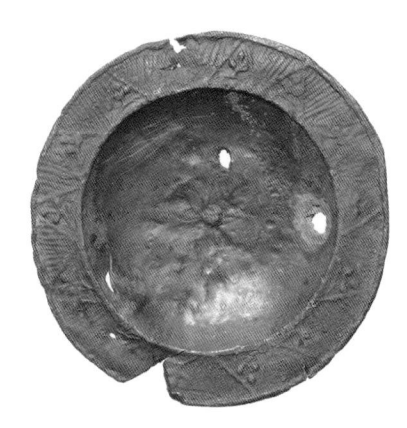

8.12 Dish or basin

Accession number: 98.2/260
Material: Lead alloy
Condition: Almost complete; part of rim missing; some damage
Dimensions: H *c.* 5mm; Diam 49mm; W (rim) 7mm
Description: A large dish or basin with a broad flange, shallow gently curving sides and rounded base. The rim is thickened and the flat flange is decorated with chevrons, alternately decorated with a floret or hatching. The base is much worn but there is a quatrefoil design in the centre. Underneath the flange is an incised S or 8 and the surface is generally scratched and abraded.
Date: 16th century

DESIGN 13

8.13 Dish

Accession number: 98.2/299
Material: Lead alloy
Condition: Almost complete; pieces of rim and base missing
Dimensions: H 2mm; Diam 36mm; Diam (base) 25mm; W (rim) 4.5mm
Description: This dish has a flat flange, shallow curving wall and flat base. The rim has a hatched edge and the flange is decorated with diametrically opposed hatched chevrons linked by debased scrolling and slashes. The central motif in high relief consists of an eight-lobed stylized rose with calyx points contained within a slashed ring.
Date: 16th century

DESIGN 14

8.14 Dish

Accession number: 98.2/364
Material: Lead alloy
Condition: Complete
Dimensions: H *c.* 4mm; Diam 30mm; Diam (base) 9mm; W (rim) 6mm
Description: A dish with a ridged rim, wide flat flange, curving wall and convex base with a central boss. Apart from the boss, which is decorated with a stylized rose, the vessel is plain.
Date: Probably 16th–early 17th century

DESIGN 15

8.15 Plate

Accession number: 98.2/288
Material: Lead alloy
Condition: Complete
Dimensions: H 2mm; Diam 28mm; Diam (base) 14mm; W (rim) 7mm
Description: A plate with a broad flange and recessed centre. The flange is decorated with foliate scrolls and there is a thick cordon around the centre containing a sexfoil. The petals curl at the tips and there are prominent calyx points. There is a radiating field around the sexfoil and a casting seam across the back.
Date: Late 16th–early 17th century
Comments: The decoration and general shape suggest a spice or sweetmeat plate of silver or pewter.

DESIGN 16

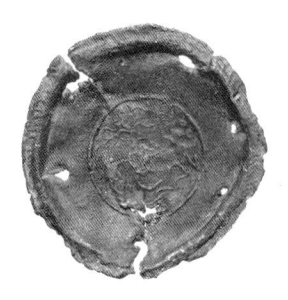

8.16 Dish

Accession number: 98.2/312
Material: Lead alloy
Condition: Complete; distorted and damaged
Dimensions: H 3mm; Diam 34mm; W (rim) 3mm
Description: A dish with a narrow flange, deep curving wall and rounded base. The edge of the rim is beaded and the flange is hatched. The central motif of a cinquefoil double rose surrounded by arabesque scrolling is contained within a plain circle. There are six holes around the wall, which were evidently added after manufacture.
Date: 16th–17th century

DESIGN 17

8.17 Dish

Accession number: 98.2/321
Material: Lead alloy
Condition: Almost complete; part of rim missing
Dimensions: H 4mm; Diam 32mm; Diam (base) 15mm; W (rim) 8mm

Description: This dish has a broad flat flange, with straight sloping wall and flattish base. The upper surface is decorated with circles of incised pellets and at one point the rim has an incised groove.
Date: 16th–early 17th century
Comments: The vessel is crudely decorated and although the irregular shape could be a casting fault, it is possible that this was caused at a later point.

DESIGN 18

8.18 Dish

Accession number: 98.2/346
Material: Lead alloy
Condition: Complete
Dimensions: H 4mm; Diam 44mm; W (rim) 6mm
Description: A dish with a ridged rim, thickened underneath, slightly bevelled broad flange, shallow curving tapering wall and slightly convex base. The centre is defined by an incised plain circle.
Date: Late 16th–early 17th century

DESIGN 19

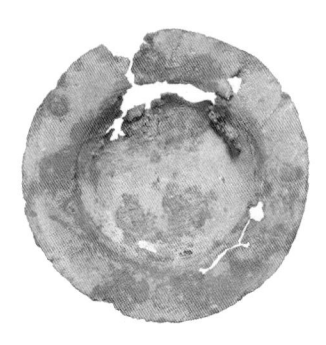

8.19 Dish

Accession number: 83.628/7
Material: Lead alloy
Condition: Almost complete; some damage; pieces missing
Dimensions: H 7mm; Diam 40mm; Diam (base) 18mm; W (rim) 8mm
Description: A plain deep broad-flanged dish with a straight sloping wall and flat base
Date: Possibly early 17th century

DESIGN 20

8.20 Dish or basin

Accession number: 98.2/211; 98.2/310*; 98.2/349
Material: Lead alloy
Condition: 98.2/211: complete; some damage. 98.2/310: almost complete. 98.2/349: part of rim missing; flattened
Dimensions: Two sizes:
i) 98.2/211 & 98.2/310: H 8mm; Diam 42mm; W (rim) 3mm
ii) 98.2/349: Diam 47mm
Description: Flanged dish or basin with gently curving sides and a rounded base. The flange is decorated with a band of ring and dot interspersed with pellets, and the central boss, ornamented with radial gadrooning, is surrounded by three widely spaced concentric bands of diagonal hatching.
Date: Probably early 17th century
Comments: 98.2/310 has a flatter profile and the rim is slightly everted. These vessels might have been made in the same workshop.

DESIGN 21

8.21 Dish

Accession number: 98.2/300
Material: Lead alloy
Condition: Complete; worn
Dimensions: H 4mm; Diam 36mm; Diam (base) 27mm; W (rim) 3mm
Description: A flanged dish with a straight, tapering wall and flat base. The narrow flange seems to be decorated with ring and dot motifs and the base has a border of arabesque scrolling surrounding a plain circle and central sexfoil double rose with very prominent feathered-edge calyx points extending beyond and between the outer row of petals. The underside shows clear evidence of manufacture.
Date: Early 17th century

DESIGN 22

8.22 Dish or basin

Accession number: 98.2/265

Material: Lead alloy

Condition: Complete apart from notch in rim

Dimensions: H 8mm; Diam 58mm; W (rim) 10mm

Description: A very large dish or basin with a broad flat flange, deep curving wall and rounded base. The flange is decorated with a double concentric band containing an invected pattern with ring and dot motifs. There is a cross composed of ring and dots in the centre, surrounded by double concentric circles of hatching. The outer circle has a border of chevrons and vertical slashes. There is a small hole at the junction of the flange and the wall.

Date: Early 17th century

DESIGN 23

8.23 Dish

Accession number: 98.2/213

Material: Lead alloy

Condition: Almost complete; some damage to rim

Dimensions: H 3mm; Diam 33mm; Diam (base) 21mm; W (rim) 2mm

Description: This dish has a wide flange, straight sloping wall and flat base. The rim has a beaded edge and the flange is decorated with rope-twist. In the centre, enclosed by a plain circle, is a sexfoil double rose with calyx points, and there are pellets either side of a ring and dot motif between each point.

Date: 17th century

DESIGN 24

8.24 Dish

Accession number: 98.2/215

Material: Lead alloy

Condition: Complete

Dimensions: H 4mm; Diam 33mm; Diam (base) 22mm; W (rim) 2mm

Inscription: AE or perhaps EA

Description: A shallow dish with a narrow flange, curved sloping sides and flattish base. The rim is beaded and the flange is decorated with densely packed fine diagonal lines between thickened diagonals in high relief. There is a finely moulded double rose of six petals in the centre and each of the calyx points is marked with a pellet. A band of foliate scrolling and pellets surrounds the central motif, and both are contained by double concentric circles. Within the foliate band are the inversely cast letters A [E] or [F]

Date: 17th century

Comments: The rim is slightly damaged and there is a possibility that this vessel was originally intended as a single-eared porringer.

DESIGN 25

8.25 Dish or basin

Accession number: 98.2/323

Material: Lead alloy

Condition: Complete; flattened; small piece of rim missing

Dimensions: H 1mm; Diam 43mm; W (rim) 5mm

Description: This completely flattened dish or basin has a rope-twist-edged rim and narrow flange decorated with foliate scrolls. The central motif consists of a quatrefoil rose with prominent calyx points. There are pellets between each point and the rose is contained within double concentric circles.

Date: 17th century

DESIGN 26

8.26 Dish

Accession number: 98.2/350
Material: Lead alloy
Condition: Complete
Dimensions: H 7mm; Diam 45mm; W (rim) 2mm
Description: A large dish with a narrow flange, gently curving sides and rounded base. The flange is decorated with fine diagonal lines and the upper part of the dish is plain. The calyx points of the sexfoil double rose extend beyond and between the outer row of petals and there are pellets between each point. A wide band of scrolling vine leaves surrounds the central motif, and both are contained by double concentric circles.
Date: 17th century

DESIGN 27

8.27 Dish

Accession number: 98.2/291
Material: Lead alloy
Condition: Complete
Dimensions: H 5mm; Diam 31mm; Diam (base) c. 13mm; W (rim) 6mm
Description: A flanged dish with a curving wall and flat base. The rim is beaded and the flange is decorated with foliate scrolls. The base decoration is worn and indistinct, but seems to incorporate a stylized double rose within a beaded circle. The central motif is enclosed by a narrow foliate band.
Date: 17th century
Provenance: Dockhead

DESIGN 28

8.28 Dish

Accession number: 98.2/289
Material: Lead alloy
Condition: Complete apart from slight damage to rim
Dimensions: H 3mm; Diam 33mm; Diam (base) 22mm; W (rim) 5mm
Description: A flanged dish with a curving wall and flat base. The rim has a rope-twist edge and the flat flange is decorated with foliate scrolling. There is a large six-petalled double rose covering the base with very prominent, hatched calyx points. The petals are of unequal size and the calyx points are interspersed with single or double ring and dot motifs.
Date: 17th century

DESIGN 29

8.29 Dish

Accession number: 98.2/282
Material: Lead alloy
Condition: Almost complete
Dimensions: H 3mm; Diam 41mm; Diam (base) 30mm; W (rim) 6mm
Description: A flanged dish with a curving wall and flat base. The rim is beaded and the flange is decorated with foliate scrolling. There is a five-petalled double rose in the centre with very prominent calyx points and there are pellets either side of a ring and dot between each point. The central motif is contained within a double concentric circle.
Date: 17th century

DESIGN 30

8.30 Plate

Accession number: 98.2/267
Material: Lead alloy
Condition: Complete
Dimensions: H. 0.5mm; Diam 29mm; Diam (base) 15mm; W (rim) 7mm
Inscription: IQ

Fig. 55. The decoration on this cast pewter saucer, c. 1600, is very similar to the toy plates and dishes produced by the maker/s I(D)Q. Although the fashion for cast decorated pewter was widespread in Europe by the late 16th century, the best-quality pieces were produced in France and Germany. Excavated at Norton Folgate, London. Diam 133mm
Museum of London, Acc. no. A2704

Description: This vessel has a very broad flat flange and small recessed centre. The rim has a rope-twist edge and the flange is decorated with foliate scrolling which encloses an oval-beaded cartouche inscribed IQ. The centre is inscribed with the sacred monogram: the hatched letters IHS surmounted by a cross.
Date: 1640s
Provenance: Custom House Quay
Comparandum: Cat. no. 8.2

DESIGN 31

8.31 Plate

Accession number: 4107; 98.2/245; 98.2/246*; 98.2/247; 98.2/248; 98.2/249
Material: Lead alloy
Condition: Complete. 98.2/248: slight damage to rim
Dimensions: H 1mm; Diam 31mm; Diam (base) 16mm; W (rim) 8mm
Inscription: IDQ
Description: Identical plates made from the same mould with a very broad flange and small recessed centre. The rim has a rope-twist edge and the flange is decorated with foliate scrolling which encloses a plain and beaded oval cartouche inscribed ID over Q. There is a five-petalled double rose in the centre and the calyx points extend beyond and between the outer row. There is a pellet between each point.
Date: 1640s
Provenance: 98.2/246: Bull Wharf

DESIGN 32

8.32 Dish

Accession number: 98.2/250; 98.2/251; 98.2/252; 98.2/254*
Material: Lead alloy
Condition: Complete. 98.2/251: part of rim missing
Dimensions: H 3mm; Diam 30mm; Diam (base) c. 20mm; W (rim) 6mm
Inscription: IQ
Description: These dishes, made from the same mould, have a flat flange, curving wall and central boss. The rim is beaded and the flange decorated with foliate scrolls enclosing a beaded oval cartouche inscribed IQ. There is a five-petalled double rose in the centre with calyx points extending beyond and between the outer row of petals. The rose is contained within a beaded circle and two plain circles.
Date: 1640s

DESIGN 33

8.33 Dish

Accession number: 98.2/269
Material: Lead alloy

Condition: Complete
Dimensions: H 5mm; Diam 37mm; Diam (base) c. 27mm; W (rim) 5mm
Inscription: IQ
Description: A flanged dish with a deep curving wall and flat base. The rim is plain and the flange decorated with floral and foliate scrolling enclosing a beaded oval cartouche inscribed IQ. The five-petalled double rose in the centre is surrounded by a beaded circle, and a decorative engrailed band with ring and dot motifs and cross-hatching.
Date: 1640s
Comparandum: An identical vessel in Gay 1887, p. 28 (wrongly attributed to the 16th century)

DESIGN 34

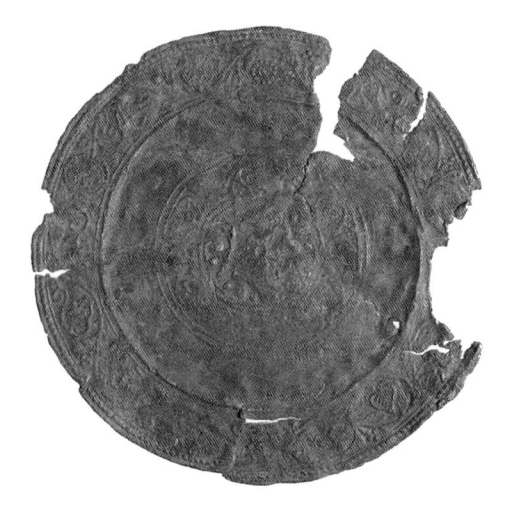

8.34 Platter

Accession number: 98.2/356
Material: Lead alloy
Condition: Almost complete; parts of rim missing or damaged; very worn
Dimensions: H 1mm; Diam 62mm; W (rim) 10mm
Inscription: DQ
Description: A platter with a broad flat flange, extremely shallow wall and flat base (now flattened and crushed). The rim is beaded and the flange decorated

with floral scrolling which encloses a beaded oval cartouche inscribed DQ. There is a five-petalled double rose in the centre and the calyx points extend beyond the outer row. Either side of the calyx point is a ring and dot between pellets. A wide band of foliate scrolling surrounds the central motif and both are contained by double concentric circles.

Date: 1640s

DESIGN 35

8.35 Plate

Accession number: 79. 302
Material: Lead alloy
Condition: Complete
Dimensions: H 1mm; Diam 36mm; W (rim) 5mm
Inscription: AB
Description: A plate with a flat flange, extremely shallow curving wall and flat base. The rim has a cable edge and the flange, inscribed AB, is decorated with foliate scrolling. There is a very large sexfoil double rose in the centre with calyx points extending beyond and between the outer row of petals. There are pellets either side of a ring and dot motif between each point, and the rose is contained within double concentric circles.

Date: 17th century

DESIGN 36

8.36 Plate

Accession number: 98.2/317*; 98.2/330
Material: Lead alloy
Condition: 98.2/317: complete, but much worn. 98.2/330: a quarter only
Dimensions: H 1mm; Diam 36mm; Diam (base) *c.* 25mm; W (rim) 5mm
Description: These plates have a flat flange, curving inner wall, bevelled underneath with a slightly convex base. The rim is beaded and the flange is decorated with ivy leaf scrolling. The central motif consists of a stylized quatrefoil with calyx points surrounded by ring and dot.

Date: 17th century

DESIGN 37

8.37 Plate

Accession number: 98.2/290*; 98.2/316
Material: Lead alloy
Condition: 98.2/290: complete. 98.2/316: almost complete; piece missing from rim and large hole; totally flattened
Dimensions: 98.2/290: H 2mm; Diam 35mm; Diam (base) 21mm; W (rim) 5mm. 98.2/316: H 1mm; Diam 36mm
Description: Probably made from the same mould, although one now damaged and flattened. 98.2/290, the better preserved, has a broad flange, straight sloping wall and flat base. The rims have a beaded edge and the flanges are decor-ated with diametrically opposed designs linked by broken scrolling. There is a four-petalled rose in the centre and the prominent calyx points extend beyond an enclosing plain circle. The edge of the wall is defined by a beaded ring.

Date: 17th century

DESIGN 38

8.38 Plate

Accession number: 98.2/293
Material: Lead alloy
Condition: Complete; pierced
Dimensions: H 0.5mm; Diam 35mm; Diam (base) *c.* 25mm; W (rim) 4mm
Description: This plate has a flat flange, extremely shallow curving wall and flat base. The rim is beaded and the flange decorated with acanthus-leaf scrolling. The central motif consists of a sexfoil double rose with calyx points extending beyond and between the outer row of petals and pellets between each calyx point. The rose is enclosed within a double concentric circle. The flange is pierced with four holes, which seem to have been done after manufacture.

Date: 17th century

DESIGN 39

8.39 Plate

Accession number: 98.2/309
Material: Lead alloy
Condition: Complete
Dimensions: H 1mm; Diam 34mm; Diam (base) 22mm; W (rim) 5mm
Description: A plate with an everted rim, curving flange and wall and flat base. The rim has rope-twist edging. The central motif consists of a cinquefoil double rose with hatched calyx points which extend beyond and between the outer row of petals. There are pellets between each point and the rose is enclosed within a narrow band of arabesque scrolling.
Date: 17th century

DESIGN 40

8.40 Dish

Accession number: O2422
Material: Lead alloy
Condition: Complete; worn surface
Dimensions: H 4mm; Diam 33mm; Diam (base) *c.* 18mm; W (rim) 4mm

Description: A circular flanged dish with a beaded rim, curving wall and central boss. The flange is decorated with a stylized scroll motif and the central boss has a sexfoil double rose with calyx points. There is a circle of beading around the boss and the base has a deep kick.
Date: 17th century

DESIGN 41

8.41 Plate

Accession number: A25669
Material: Lead alloy
Condition: Almost complete; part of rim missing; extremely worn surface
Dimensions: H 1mm; Diam 37mm; Diam (base) *c.* 27mm; W (rim) 5mm
Description: A flat plate with a flange, extremely shallow curving wall and flat base. The surface is extremely worn but the rim seems to have a cable edge and the flange is decorated with foliate scrolls. There is a sexfoil double rose in the centre.
Date: 17th century

DESIGN 42

8.42 Dish or basin

Accession number: 98.2/193
Material: Lead alloy
Condition: Complete; slight damage to rim and base
Dimensions: H 7mm; Diam 53mm; Diam (base) *c.* 28mm; W (rim) 5mm
Description: A large circular flanged dish or basin with a deep curving wall and flattish base. The flat narrow flange has a plain rim and is decorated with an alternating pattern of debased scrolls, pellets, random hatching and ring and dot. There is a large, lobed and square symmetrical design in the centre, embellished with hatching and ring and dot and surrounded by pellets. A decorative band of alternating Ss, pellets, chevrons and ring and dot encloses the central motif, and both are contained within double concentric circles.
Date: 17th century

DESIGN 43

DESIGN 44

DESIGN 45

8.43 Plate or charger

Accession number: A2529*; 98.2/270
Material: Lead alloy
Condition: A2529: complete; worn
  98.2/270: small hole in the flange
Dimensions: H *c.* 3mm; Diam 56mm;
  W (rim) 10mm
Inscription: CR
Description: These plates or chargers have a broad flat flange, very shallow curving wall and flat base. The rim is thickened and beaded and the flange is decorated with floral and foliate scrolling incorporating auriculas and tulips. Both have a beaded circular touch in the centre inscribed CR.
Date: 1680–1700
Provenance: A2529: Maze Pond
Comments: This vessel bears the touch of Charles Rack.

8.44 Dish or basin

Accession number: 98.2/359
Material: Lead alloy
Condition: Complete; some damage;
  rather worn
Dimensions: H *c.* 4mm; Diam 52mm;
  W (rim) 10mm
Description: A large dish or basin with a broad flat flange, shallow curving wall and rounded base. The cable rim is thickened and the flange decorated with floral and foliate scrolling incorporating tulips and auriculas. There is a small hole in the flange.
Date: 1680–1700
Comments: Acc. nos. 98.2/270 and A2529 have exactly the same design, but the vessel shapes are different. It is possible that these vessels formed part of a service. Although it bears no sign of a touchmark, this vessel was probably made in the same workshop as Cat no. 8.43.

8.45 Plate or charger

Accession number: A2528*; 98.2/348
Material: Lead alloy
Condition: A2528: complete
  98.2/348: five large holes in the flange
Dimensions: H 2mm; Diam 56mm;
  W (rim) 10mm
Inscription: I I
Description: Plate or charger with a broad flat flange, very shallow curving wall and flat base. The rim is thickened and beaded and the flange is decorated with floral and foliate scrolling incorporating thistles and tulips. 98.2/348 has five rough holes in the flange and the base has a faint lozenge-shaped touch with the letters I I.
Date: 1676/7–1700
Provenance: Southwark Bridge; Maze Pond
Comments: There is an indistinguishable mark on A2528, but 98.2/348 bears the touch of John Jackson (Cott. no. 2557A) and both vessels were probably made in the same workshop.

DESIGN 46

8.46 Plate

Accession number: 98.2/301
Material: Lead alloy
Condition: Complete; slight damage to rim
Dimensions: H 2mm; Diam 36mm; Diam (base) 24mm; W (rim) 5mm
Description: A plate with a very shallow straight-sided tapering wall and flat base. The rim is beaded and the flange is decorated with scrolling arabesques. There is a cinquefoil double rose in the centre and between each calyx point are pellets either side of a ring and dot-type motif. The central decoration is contained within a plain circle. There is a trilobate feather pattern around the edge.
Date: Late 17th century
Provenance: Limekiln Dock

DESIGN 47

8.47 Plate

Accession number: 98.2/294
Material: Lead alloy
Condition: Complete

Dimensions: H 1mm; Diam 35mm; Diam (base) 24mm; W (rim) 7mm
Description: A plate with a broad flange, bevelled wall and flat base. The rim is beaded and the flange decorated with diametrically opposed scrolls. The central motif consists of a stylized lobed cinquefoil within double concentric circles.
Date: Late 17th century

DESIGN 48

8.48 Dish

Accession number: 98.2/297
Material: Lead alloy
Condition: Complete
Dimensions: H 2mm; Diam 36mm; Diam (base) 21mm; W (rim) 6mm
Description: This dish has a broad flange, straight sloping sides and flat base. The rim has a beaded edge and the flange is decorated with diametrically opposed anthemions linked by foliate tendrils. There is a stylized 'flowerhead' in the centre composed of four hatched lobes interspersed with pelleted lozenges. Around the edge of the base are four diametrically opposed pellets linked by a circle of fine beading.
Date: Late 17th–early 18th century
Provenance: Queenhithe Dock

DESIGN 49

8.49 Dish

Accession number: 98.2/296
Material: Lead alloy
Condition: Complete; slight damage to rim
Dimensions: H 3mm; Diam 35mm; Diam (base) 20mm; W (rim) 5mm
Description: A shallow flanged dish with a curving wall and flat base. The rim is beaded and the slightly sloping flange has four opposing diaper panels linked by star-like motifs. The centre is decorated with a 'sunflower' head within a sharply engrailed and plain circle.
Date: 1690–1760

DESIGN 50

8.50 Dish

Accession number: 98.2/295
Material: Lead alloy
Condition: Complete; slight damage to rim
Dimensions: H 5mm; Diam 36mm; W (rim) 5mm
Description: This dish has a narrow scallop-edged flange, deep curving wall and rounded base. The edge of the rim is decorated with a contiguous pattern of large knops and the flange has a chevron pattern. There is a lobed cross in the centre surrounded by ring and dot motifs within a double concentric circle.
Date: Probably late 17th–early 18th century

DESIGN 51

8.51 Dish or plate

Accession number: 98.2/292
Material: Lead alloy
Condition: Complete; some damage to rim; very worn surface
Dimensions: H 4mm; Diam 33mm; W (rim) 3mm
Description: A shallow narrow-flanged dish or plate with a curving wall and flat base. There is a rope-twist rim and the flange is decorated with a scrolling motif. The centre is decorated with a rope-twist band enclosing a five-petalled double rose and pellets.
Date: Probably late 17th–early 18th century

DESIGN 52

8.52 Dish or basin

Accession number: 98.2/357
Material: Lead alloy
Condition: Complete; extremely worn
Dimensions: H 5mm; Diam 61mm; Diam (base) 35mm; W (rim) 10mm
Description: A large dish or basin with a broad flat flange, shallow curving wall and flat base. The rim is beaded and the flange decorated with diametrically opposed winged putti and foliate scrolling. The vessel has been lathe-turned.
Date: Probably late 17th–early 18th century

DESIGN 53

8.53 Plate

Accession number: 98.2/273
Material: Lead alloy
Condition: Complete
Dimensions: H 2mm; Diam 52mm; Diam (base) 30mm; W (rim) 11mm
Inscription: IZ
Description: A lathe-turned plate with a broad flat flange, shallow curving wall and flat base. The rim has a reeded edge underneath and the flange is stamped with the initials IZ.
Date: Late 17th–18th century

DESIGN 54

8.54 Plate

Accession number: 98.2/355
Material: Lead alloy
Condition: Complete
Dimensions: H 2mm; Diam 52mm; Diam (base) 29mm; W (rim) 10mm
Inscription: WL
Description: A lathe-turned plate with a broad flat flange, shallow curving wall and flat base. The flange has a faintly stippled rim and is stamped with the initials WL.
Date: Late 17th–18th century
Provenance: Southwark Bridge, north side

DESIGN 55

8.55 Plate

Accession number: 98.2/361
Material: Lead alloy
Condition: Complete
Dimensions: H 1mm; Diam 52mm; W (rim) 10mm
Description: A flat lathe-turned plate with a broad flange, extremely shallow wall and slightly concave base. The flange is decorated with two concentric circles of fine stippling.
Date: Late 17th–18th century

DESIGN 56

8.56 Dish

Accession number: 98.2/351
Material: Lead alloy
Condition: Complete; some damage
Dimensions: H 4mm; Diam 62mm; Diam (base) 37mm; W (rim) 13mm
Description: A plain dish with a very broad flat flange, smooth above and heavily ridged underneath, steep curving wall and flat base.
Date: Late 17th–early 18th century

DESIGN 57

8.57 Plate

Accession number: 98.2/262
Material: Lead alloy
Condition: Complete; much worn and damaged; virtually cut in two
Dimensions: H 2mm; Diam 42mm; Diam (base) 31mm; W (rim) 5mm
Description: A flat plate with a flange and flat base. The surface is much worn, but traces of a floral design can be seen in the centre contained by three, closely placed concentric circles. The plate seems to have been folded over and then straightened, thereby weakening the metal and producing a crack and scar on each side.
Date: Probably late 17th–early 18th century

DESIGN 58

8.58 Dish or charger

Accession number: 98.2/352
Material: Lead alloy
Condition: Complete; slight damage
Dimensions: H 4mm; Diam 67mm;
    Diam (base) 45mm; W (rim) 11mm
Inscription: IC
Description: A very large lathe-turned dish or charger with a very broad flat flange, bevel-edged shallow curving wall and flat base. The dish is plain apart from the edge of the flange, which is decorated with fine stippling. On the underside, in the centre, are the initials IC with a lozenge shape of four pellets below.
Date: Late 17th–early 18th century

DESIGN 59

8.59 Plate

Accession number: 98.2/344
Material: Lead alloy
Condition: Complete
Dimensions: H 1mm; Diam 39mm;
    Diam (base) 20mm; W (rim) 8mm
Description: Flat plate with very broad flange, extremely shallow curving wall and flat base with foot ring. Plain apart from two concentric circles around the rim.
Date: Late 17th–early 18th century

DESIGN 60

8.60 Plate

Accession number: 87.98/7
Material: Lead alloy
Condition: Complete
Dimensions: H 4mm; Diam 48mm; Diam (base) 31mm; W (rim) 10mm
Description: A large thick plain plate with a broad flange, slightly bevelled on the inside, straight sloping wall and flat base. The centre has a series of concentric circles produced on a lathe.
Date: 17th–18th century

DESIGN 61

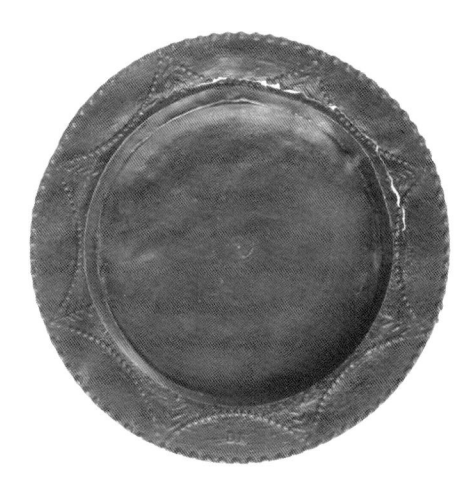

8.61 Dish or charger

Accession number: A2527; 98.2/274*
Material: Lead alloy
Condition: Complete. 98.2/274: a little squashed and damaged; large crack around the rim
Dimensions: Two sizes:
i) 98.2/274: H 2mm; Diam 58mm;
    Diam (base) c. 40mm; W (rim) 8mm
ii) A2527: H 2mm; Diam 41mm;
    Diam (base) 30mm; W (rim) 5mm
Inscription: 98.2/274: BR. A2527: [T?] F
Description: Two sizes of dish or charger with identical design, broad flat flange, curving wall and flat base. The rims are beaded and the flange has invected beading with pinnate leaf motifs between each point. The flange is marked with the letters BR (98.2/274) and the dish has been lathe-turned. A2527 has the letters F or TF on the base.
Date: Late 17th–18th century
Provenance: A2527: City Ditch

DESIGN 62

DESIGN 63

DESIGN 64

8.62 Plate

Accession number: 87.98/6
Material: Lead alloy
Condition: Complete; slightly crushed
Dimensions: H 3mm; Diam 53mm;
    Diam (base) 37mm; W (rim) 8mm
Inscription: Indistinct; seems to incorporate a crown
Description: A large plain plate with a complicated profile. The rim is rounded and recurved, the flange slightly bevelled and the wall curves down towards the flat base. There is a rounded foot ring underneath and the vessel has been lathe-turned. There are diagonal lines of pellets within a triangular 'touch' on the flange.
Date: Possibly 18th century

8.63 Plate

Accession number: 98.2/347
Material: Lead alloy
Condition: Complete; much worn and damaged
Dimensions: H 2mm; Diam 43mm;
    W (rim) 7mm
Description: A flat plate with a reeded rim, slightly concave flange and flat base. The rim has a rope-twist edge. The plate has been crushed and possibly folded, leaving a ridge and scar on both sides.
Date: 18th century

8.64 Plate

Accession number: 98.2/325
Material: Lead alloy
Condition: Complete
Dimensions: H 3mm; Diam 44mm;
    Diam (base) 30mm; W (rim) 7mm
Description: This plate has a flat flange, vertical sloping wall and flat base. The rim has pronounced beading on the front and a slightly bevelled edge. The flange is decorated with diametrically opposed stylized 'scallop shells' linked by floral and foliate scrolling.
Date: 18th century
Provenance: London Bridge, north side

DESIGN 65

8.65 Plate

Accession number: 98.2/358
Material: Lead alloy
Condition: Complete
Dimensions: H 2mm; Diam 46mm; Diam (base) 35mm; W (rim) 6mm
Description: This plate has a flat flange, curving wall and flat base. The rim has a thickened rope-twist edge and the flange is decorated with stylized sprigs.
Date: 18th century
Provenance: Limekiln Dock

DESIGN 66

8.66 Plate or charger

Accession number: 98.2/264
Material: Lead alloy; red pigment
Condition: Complete; slight damage
Dimensions: H 3mm; Diam 48mm; Diam (base) 34mm; W (rim) 9mm
Description: A large plate or charger with slightly curving flange, shallow curving wall and flat base. The rim has a 'reeded' edge and the flange is decorated with a radial pattern of 'sprigs'. There is a stylized cornucopia in the centre with a random pattern of pellets retained within a beaded circle. There are patches of red pigment on the rim flange and in the centre of the vessel.
Date: 18th century

DESIGN 67

8.67 Dish

Accession number: 98.2/207
Material: Lead alloy
Condition: Complete; greatly distorted; some damage to rim
Dimensions: H 5mm; Diam 34mm; Diam (base) 15mm; W (rim) 4mm
Description: A flanged dish with a deep vertical wall and flattish base. The dish is plain apart from a simple hatched circle at the centre. There is evidence of lathe-turning on the back.
Date: Possibly 18th century

DESIGN 68

8.68 Dish

Accession number: 98.2/209; 98.2/335; 98.2/345; 98.2/353*; 98.2/360
Material: Lead alloy
Condition: 98.2/209; 98.2/345; 98.2/353: complete. 98.2/335: half only. 98.2/360: most of rim missing
Dimensions: Four sizes:
i) 98.2/335: H (crushed); Diam 40mm; Diam (base) 22mm
ii) 98.2/209; 98.2/345: H 5mm; Diam 40mm; Diam (base) 28mm
iii) 98.2/353: H 3mm; Diam 45mm; Diam (base) 27mm
iv) 98.2/360: H (crushed); Diam c. 56mm (incomplete)
Description: Very wide, extremely shallow dishes with angular profiles. The walls are sharply carinated and taper towards the foot ring and flat base. The dishes are plain apart from a single circle of irregular incised slashes around the edge of the base. The larger dishes have two concentric circles of incised slashes (98.2/345 & 98.2/353) and another (98.2/360) has two circles of stippled ziz-zags.
Date: Probably 18th century
Comments: 98.2/345 has been pierced.

DESIGN 69

8.69 Dish

Accession number: 98.2/362
Material: Lead alloy
Condition: Incomplete; rim missing
Dimensions: Diam 43mm
Description: Part of a dish with rounded lathe-turned base. Decorated with two concentric circles of fine stippling.
Date: Probably 18th century

DESIGN 70

8.70 Dish

Accession number: 98.2/342
Material: Lead alloy
Condition: Complete; slight damage
Dimensions: H 3mm; Diam 26mm; Diam (base) 13mm
Description: This plain dish has a slightly bevelled rim and gently sloping sides. The base is flat and recessed underneath.
Date: 18th century

DESIGN 71

8.71 Dish

Accession number: 98.2/343
Material: Lead alloy
Condition: Complete; slight damage to rim
Dimensions: H 3mm; Diam 40mm; Diam (foot ring) 21mm
Description: A dish with a shallow curving profile, concave base and foot ring. The rim is beaded and there is a ring of fleur-de-lys in the centre.
Date: 18th century

DESIGN 72

8.72 Dish

Accession number: 98.2/336
Material: Lead alloy
Condition: Complete; slight damage to rim
Dimensions: H 3mm; Diam 27mm; Diam (foot ring) 17mm
Description: A small dish with a very shallow curving profile, concave base and foot ring. The rim is beaded and there is a circle of trilobate 'ball flowers' around the centre.
Date: 18th century

DESIGN 73

8.73 Dish

Accession number: 98.2/341
Material: Lead alloy
Condition: Complete
Dimensions: H 3mm; Diam 27mm; Diam (foot ring) 16mm
Description: A small dish with a very shallow curving profile, concave base and thick foot ring. The rim is beaded and there is a circular pattern of loops and pellets around the centre.
Date: 18th century
Comments: The foot ring is more pronounced than D71 & D72 above.

DESIGN 74

8.74 Dish

Accession number: 98.2/340
Material: Lead alloy
Condition: Complete
Dimensions: H c. 2mm; Diam 27mm; Diam (base) 13mm
Description: A small dish with a very shallow curving profile, concave base and underneath a circle to suggest a foot ring. The rim is beaded and there is a ring of six-pointed stars around the centre.
Date: 18th century
Provenance: Tower foreshore

DESIGN 75

8.75 Dish

Accession number: A2799; 98.2/337*
Material: Lead alloy
Condition: 98.2/337: complete. A2799: crushed; part of rim missing
Dimensions: H 3mm; Diam 29mm; Diam (foot ring) 18mm
Description: Small dish with a very shallow curving profile, concave base and foot ring. The rim is plain and there is an engrailed circle around the centre.
Date: 18th century

DESIGN 76

8.76 Dish

Accession number: 81.580/2
Material: Lead alloy
Condition: Complete; slightly crushed
Dimensions: H 3mm; Diam c. 27mm; Diam (foot ring) 18mm
Description: A shallow dish with a curving profile, flattish base and foot ring. The rim is beaded and the wall is decorated with bay-leaf foliage.
Date: 18th century

DESIGN 77

8.77 Dish

Accession number: A22899; 98.2/338*
Material: Lead alloy
Condition: Complete; slightly distorted
Dimensions: H 3mm; Diam 28mm; Diam (foot ring) 20mm
Description: This shallow dish has a curving profile, flattish base and foot ring. The rim is beaded and the entire surface has random stippling, probably due to imperfect casting rather than design.
Date: 18th century

DESIGN 78

8.78 Dish

Accession number: A859
Material: Lead alloy
Condition: Complete; flattened
Dimensions: H 2mm; Diam 27mm; Diam (foot ring) 28mm
Description: A completely flattened dish with a foot ring, beaded rim and garland around the centre.
Date: 18th century

DESIGN 79

8.79 Plate

Accession number: 98.2/298
Material: Lead alloy
Condition: Complete; damaged
Dimensions: H 3mm; Diam 39mm
Description: A plate with a slightly concave profile. The rim is beaded and the 'flange' is decorated with hatched sprigs and pellets. The central motif of eight leaves with branching flower and thistle stems is contained within a beaded circle.
Date: 18th century
Provenance: Limekiln Dock

DESIGN 80

8.80 Plate

Accession number: 98.2/261
Material: Lead alloy
Condition: Complete
Dimensions: H 1mm; Diam 33mm; Diam (base) *c.* 23mm; W (rim) *c.* 5mm
Description: A plate with a narrow flange, extremely shallow curving wall and flat base. The beaded rim is slightly ridged and thickened, and the flange is decorated with a garland of berries. There is a stylized plant in the centre with three blooms and lanceolate-shaped leaves surrounded by three concentric rings, one beaded. There is a tiny hole through the flange.
Date: 18th century
Provenance: Globe Theatre site

DESIGN 81

8.81 Plate

Accession number: 98.2/268
Material: Lead alloy
Condition: Complete
Dimensions: H 1mm; Diam 33mm; Diam (base) *c.* 23mm; W (rim) *c.* 5mm
Description: A plate with a narrow flange, extremely shallow straight tapering wall and flat base. The rim is slightly thickened and hatched. The flange design consists of pairs of leaves either side of a 'berry' or pellet and the central decoration of a stylized plant with lanceolate-shaped leaves and three blooms is contained within a broken invected ring.
Date: 18th century

DESIGN 82

8.82 Plate

Accession number: 98.2/304
Material: Lead alloy
Condition: Almost complete
Dimensions: H 2mm; Diam 36mm;
   Diam (base) 24mm; W (rim) 7mm
Description: This plate has a wide curving flange and flat base. The rim is beaded and the flange has an engrailed circle with 'bow'-shaped motifs on one side and stylized flowerheads on the other. There is a radial design of leaves with branching flowers in the centre.
Date: 18th century

DESIGN 83

8.83 Plate

Accession number: 98.2/326
Material: Lead alloy
Condition: Complete; slightly distorted and damaged
Dimensions: H 2.5mm; Diam 45mm;
   Diam (base) 33mm; W (rim) 6mm
Description: A plate with a flat flange and flat base. The rim is beaded and the flange is decorated with stylized foliate swags.
Date: 18th century

DESIGN 84

8.84 Octagonal plate

Accession number: 98.2/263
Material: Lead alloy
Condition: Complete
Dimensions: H 1mm; Diam 32mm;
   Diam (base) *c.* 24mm; W (rim) 4mm
Description: An octagonal plate with beaded rim, plain flange and extremely shallow curving wall. The wall is decorated with radial slashes, each terminating in a pellet. There is a nine-lobed star motif in the centre surrounded by a plain and invected circle.
Date: 18th century

Oval vessels

DESIGN 1

8.85 Dish

Accession number: 98.2/271*; 98.2/272
Material: Lead alloy
Condition: Complete. 98.2/272: slightly damaged
Dimensions: H 2mm; Diam 43 x 33 mm; Diam (base) 28 x 19 mm
Inscription: IQ
Description: These shallow dishes have a broad flat flange, curving wall and flat base. The dishes have a rope-twist rim, and the flat flange is decorated with foliate scrolling and incorporates an oval cartouche inscribed with the letters IQ. The centre is decorated with four lobes arranged in a cross formation surrounded by ring and dot, hatching and plain and beaded ovals.
Date: Mid-17th century

DESIGN 2

8.86 Dish

Accession number: 98.2/275
Material: Lead alloy
Condition: Complete
Dimensions: H 2mm; Diam 33 x 28 mm; Diam (base) 17 x 14 mm
Inscription: IDQ
Description: A small shallow dish with a broad flat flange, curving wall and flat base. The dish has a rope-twist rim and the flange is decorated with foliate scrolls incorporating a beaded oval cartouche inscribed ID over Q. A small hole at the top of the cartouche has been pierced from the front. The centre is ornamented with a double rose of five petals and the calyx points extend beyond and between the outer row. There is a pellet between each point. The rose is contained within a plain circle and a garland.
Date: Mid-17th century

DESIGN 3

8.87 Dish

Accession number: 98.2/306*; 98.2/307
Material: Lead alloy
Condition: 98.2/306: complete
   98.2/307: part only
Dimensions: H 2mm; Diam 33 x 28 mm; Diam (base) 19 x 15 mm
Description: This shallow dish has a flat flange, straight-sided wall and flat base. The dish has a rope-twist rim, and the flange is decorated with stylized foliate scrolls. The base has a border pattern of alternating ring and dot with pellet crosses and this surrounds a double concentric circle. There is a stylized flower surrounded by pellets in the centre.
Date: Probably 17th century

DESIGN 4

8.88 Dish

Accession number: 98.2/302
Material: Lead alloy
Condition: Complete
Dimensions: H 2mm; Diam 40 x 34 mm; Diam (base) c. 25 x c. 20 mm
Inscription: A F
Description: This shallow dish has a very broad flange, shallow curving wall and rounded base. The rim is beaded and the flange decorated with foliate scrolling incorporating stylized flowerheads and the initials A F. There is a poorly cast and stylized double rose of seven petals in the centre.
Date: Probably late 17th century

DESIGN 5

8.89 Dish

Accession number: 98.2/276
Material: Lead alloy
Condition: Complete; slight damage to rim
Dimensions: H 4mm; Diam 39 x 30 mm; Diam (base) c. 25mm x c. 15mm
Description: A shallow dish with a broad flange, curving profile and rounded base. The rim has a beaded edge and the flange is decorated with foliate scrolls. A tulip with seven leaves covers the base.
Date: Probably late 17th century

DESIGN 6

8.90 Dish

Accession number: 98.2/303
Material: Lead alloy
Condition: Complete; squashed
Dimensions: H c. 2mm; Diam 42 x 33 mm; Diam (base) c. 30mm x c. 20mm
Description: A flat dish with a broad flange and flat base. There is a rope-twist rim and the flange is decorated with foliate scrolls incorporating single stylized flowerheads. The base is decorated with longitudinally opposing radial lobes with a triad of pellets between each lobe. There is a poorly cast double rose in the centre with five petals and calyx points between the outer row.
Date: Late 17th–early 18th century

DESIGN 7

8.91 Dish

Accession number: 98.2/324
Material: Lead alloy
Condition: Complete
Dimensions: H 2mm; Diam 49 x 42 mm; Diam (base) 33 x 26 mm; W (rim) 8mm
Description: A dish with an extremely shallow wall and flat base. The rim has a rope-twist edge and the flange is decorated with an alternating pattern of conjoined scrolling crescents, pellets and a stylized flowerhead. There is a stylized double rose in the centre with eight calyx points surrounded by pellets. The central motif is contained within a beaded circle and there is an annular ring around the edge of the wall. There are four holes in the flange, suggesting that this plate may have been used as a mount.
Date: Probably 18th century
Provenance: Southwark Bridge, south side

DESIGN 8

8.92 Dish

Accession number: 84.328/2; 98.2/283*; 98.2/284
Material: Lead alloy
Condition: 98.2/283; 98.2/284: complete 84.328/2: part of rim missing
Dimensions: H 2.5mm; Diam 40 x 26 mm; Diam (base) 27 x 13 mm
Description: This dish has a flat flange, straight tapering sides and a flat base. The rim is beaded and the flange is decorated with a symmetrical pattern of swags and stars. Most of the base is covered with a large animal in high relief (possibly a suckling pig), and there is an irregular line of beading around the edge.
Date: Probably 18th century
Provenance: 98.2/283: Globe Theatre site

DESIGN 9

8.93 Dish

Accession number: 98.2/285
Material: Lead alloy; pigment
Condition: Complete
Dimensions: H 3mm; Diam 38 x 26 mm; Diam (base) 27 x 14 mm
Description: An oval dish with a flat flange, straight tapering sides and flat base. The rim is beaded and the flange decorated with an alternating pattern of debased scrolling, pellets and diaper. Most of the base is covered with a large animal in high relief (possibly a suckling pig) and traces of red pigment.
Date: 18th century

DESIGN 10

8.94 Dish

Accession number: 98.2/286
Material: Lead alloy
Condition: Complete; slight damage to rim
Dimensions: H 4mm; Diam c. 40 x c. 28mm; Diam (base) 28 x 13 mm
Description: An oval dish with a wide flange, curving profile and flat base. The decoration on the rim and flange is worn, but seems to include a plain line and stippling. A large fish, profile to right with mouth, large eye, scales and pectoral and anal fins, covers the base, and the tail curls up the side of the dish.
Date: 17th–18th century

DESIGN 11

8.95 Dish

Accession number: 98.2/287
Material: Lead alloy
Condition: Complete
Dimensions: H 2mm; Diam 42 x 25 mm; Diam (base) 30 x 15 mm
Description: An elliptical-shaped dish with a broad flange, shallow wall with curving profile and flat base. The rim is outlined by prominent beading and the flange decorated with a foliate tendril. There is a large fish in the dish, and although the details are quite convincing, the tail seems to be missing
Date: Late 18th century

DESIGN 12

8.96 Dish

Accession number: 81.231/1
Material: Lead alloy
Condition: Complete
Dimensions: H 2mm; Diam 78 x 34 mm; Diam (base) 51 x c. 18mm; W (rim) 13 & 7 mm
Description: A very large rectangular dish with rounded ends, waisted sides, vertical wall and flat base. The flange width is greatest at each end and the rim is beaded. The dish is decorated with a symmetrical pattern of stylized flowerheads linked by foliage.
Date: 18th century

Fragments

DESIGN 1

8.97 Dish or plate

Accession number: 98.2/329
Material: Lead alloy
Condition: Fragment of rim
Dimensions: L 20mm; W 11mm
Description: There is a beaded edge and the flange is decorated with floral scrolling incorporating a double rose.
Date: 17th century

DESIGN 2

8.98 Dish or plate

Accession number: 98.2/327
Material: Lead alloy
Condition: rim only
Dimensions: H 1mm; Diam 44 x 43 mm; W (rim) 7mm
Description: Beaded edge and flange decorated with invected beading and sprigs
Date: 18th century

DESIGN 3

8.99 Dish or plate

Accession number: 98.2/363
Material: Lead alloy
Condition: Part of rim
Dimensions: H 1mm; W (rim) 7mm
Description: The edge is beaded and the flange decorated with invected circles composed of jagged Vs with crosses within each loop.
Date: 18th century

Possible tablewares

TYPE 1, DESIGN 1

8.100 Dish

Accession number: 98.2/281*; 98.2/331; 98.2/332
Material: Lead alloy
Condition: 98.2/281: almost complete 98.2/331; 98.2/332: rim fragments; possibly from the same object
Dimensions: H 3mm; Diam 49 x 59 mm; Diam (base) 30 x 40 mm; W (rim) 9mm
Inscription: IDQ
Description: A very large oval dish with a broad flat flange, curving wall and concave base rising to a central well with thickened rim and internal groove. The rim is beaded and the flange decorated with floral and foliate scrolling enclosing a beaded oval cartouche inscribed ID over Q with three pellets. There is a single cordon around the edge of the flange and the base is decorated with a foliate and berry garland linked by opposing bows. There are stylized floral motifs at each end of the longitudinal axis. Two concentric circles surround the central well, which has a recurved beaded rim.
Date: Mid-17th century
Comments: Function unknown; possibly used as a basin to accompany a ewer, with the central well constituting an emplacement for the ewer[20]

274 • TOYS, TRIFLES & TRINKETS

TYPE 1, DESIGN 2

8.101 Dish

Accession number: 82.606/6
Material: Lead alloy
Condition: Almost complete; parts of rim missing; extremely worn surface; crushed
Dimensions: H 1mm; Diam 60 x c. 46mm; W (rim) 9mm
Description: A very large oval dish with a broad flat flange, curving wall and concave base rising to a central well with thickened rim and internal groove. The rim has a cable edge and the flange is decorated with radial lines, cross-hatching, scrolls and pellets. The base has diametrically opposed radial lobes linked by pellets and slashing. There are two concentric circles around the well, which has a recurved beaded rim.
Date: Mid-17th century
Comparandum: Similar to Cat. no. 8.100

TYPE 2, DESIGN 1

8.102 Dish (?)

Accession number: 98.2/277*; 98.2/278; 98.2/279; 98.2/280
Material: Lead alloy
Condition: 98.2/277: complete. 98.2/278; 98.2/279: almost complete. 98.2/280 fragment
Dimensions: H c. 3mm; Diam 42 x 35 mm; W (rim) 5mm
Inscription: IDQ
Description: Oval with fluted and scalloped rim, slightly convex profile and decorated on one side only. The rim is thickened and bevelled underneath, and the fluted flange is decorated with an alternating pattern of hatched patera interspersed with a stylized quatrefoil. Contained within a foliate garland are the letters ID over Q, a pelleted roundel, five-pointed star, pellets and ring and dot. There are four diametrically opposed slots around the edge of the base.
Date: Mid-17th century
Provenance: 98.2/278, 98.2/279 & 98.2/280: Custom House Quay.
Comments: Function unknown; clearly part of a more complex object

Drinking & serving vessels

'Of drinking cups diverse and sundry sorts we have: some of elme, some of box, some of maple, some holly; mazers, broad-mouthed dishes, noggins, whiskings, piggins ... tankards, kannes from a pottle to a pint, from a pint to a gill' [21]

The drinking and serving vessels dating from the mid-12th to early 18th century cover the widest period of any group of toys and miniatures in this volume. The earliest pieces provide the first evidence for mass-produced base-metal toys in this country, and are among the very earliest base-metal miniatures of their kind in the world. More ceramic jugs are found in medieval and early modern archaeological contexts than any other form, and the relative number of toy jugs compared to other vessel types mirrors the cultural trend. The toy jugs also seem to be the most widely distributed of all the items considered in this volume, and it is interesting that the only toy mould found outside London was used for casting jugs (fig. 9, p. 28).

All of the toys and miniatures in this section are made from lead alloy,[22] and yet the shapes and decorative styles represent full-scale vessels of different qualities and materials. Some resemble lavishly ornamented vessels of precious metal and are smothered with gadroons, guilloche, chevrons, scrolls, ring and dot and other standard motifs in the toymaker's repertoire to suggest cast and

Fig. 56. The buffet was the most important item of furniture in the dining room, supporting large ewers filled with rose-water, basins and napery for hand-washing, candlesticks and spare cups and bowls. This detail appears in the 15th-century manuscript *La Fleur des histoires* by Jean Mansel. See plate VI, p. 166

chased decoration, while others replicate base-metal, ceramic and even glass vessels. For the most part the mould-makers have done their best to recreate the characteristic textures and decorative styles of full-scale vessels, so that the miniatures imitating ceramic prototypes, for example, have mouldings to represent slip-cast, applied and stamped decoration, and some even have stylistic features which suggest that they were inspired by regional forms and styles.

Even though many of the main types of serving vessel in use from the mid-12th to early 17th century are represented in the collection, hardly any drinking vessels of equivalent date have been found. There are no cups, drinking jugs, goblets, mugs, mazers, tygs, costrels or bottles and, apart from the standing bowls of late 15th- and early 16th-century date, the only other forms of drinking vessel in the collection are a late 16th-century pot lid and a 17th-century tankard.[23] This is rather surprising because from the 15th century onwards drinking vessels were produced in an ever increasing range of forms in metal, ceramics, leather and other materials, and it is inconceivable that the toymakers were not making miniature versions to reflect contemporary tastes and fashions. Equally surprising is the lack of late 17th- and early 18th-century forms, when documentary evidence suggests that toy drinking and serving vessels were mass-produced throughout this period.[24] The Pewterers' Company records for 6 May 1689, for example, refer to the toy flagons and flagon lids made by the London pewterers Charles Rack and John Jackson,[25] and in 1717 Thomas Smith was fined for making substandard toy cups.[26] In each case, the word 'his' is inserted before the word toy, which suggests that the vessels were made by the pewterers themselves and not bought in.[27]

The scale of most of the drinking and serving vessels considered here would tend to prohibit their use in a baby house, although they could have been used with other household items as doll's toys. An engraving with a moralistic verse by Jan Luyken (1649–1712), for example, shows a doll-sized ewer and beaker which have either been dropped or thrown on to the floor by a rather peevish-looking child in a high chair, and similar-sized vessels, including a jug and tea service are depicted in the *c.* 1750s trade bill of the London pewterer Robert Peircy (fig. 33, p. 142 & fig. 81, p. 408). While tiny drinking and serving vessels were made for children, some of the better-quality miniatures may have been made as adult conceits.

The vessels have been arranged or grouped in an alphabetical sequence and where possible, each type is defined. For a few vessels, however, dating and attribution are impossible because they are a bizarre amalgam of different forms and decorative styles for which no full-scale parallels can be found.

Tripod ewer
Acc. no. 8193, Cat. no. 8.119

Coffee pots

Even though coffee was regarded by Londoners as an 'outlandish drink', within a few years of the opening of the first coffee house in the capital in 1652, coffee drinking had become widespread. By 1663 there were 83 coffee houses in the City of London alone,[28] and those who could afford them purchased roasted beans for home consumption.

The new beverage required a novel kind of serving vessel which could withstand the heat of the scalding hot liquid, and the earliest examples modelled on Turkish forms, have conical lids and long tapering spouts. By the end of the 17th century, English coffee pots in silver, pewter, copper and stoneware were made with domed lids and handles at right angles to a short straight or curving spout. This is the only miniature known.

TYPE 1, DESIGN 1

8.103 Coffee pot

Accession number: 98.2/365
Material: Lead alloy
Condition: Almost complete
Dimensions: H 38mm; Diam (rim) 18mm; Diam (base) 27mm; W (incl. handle) *c.* 49mm; L (handle) 34mm
Description: This plain conical vessel has been cast in one piece from a two-part mould. The lid is missing and the rim is thickened with a cordon, now abraded and damaged. Only the lower part of the circular spout survives, but the profile suggests a straight angle towards the rim and it is positioned at right angles to the handle. The handle of turned baluster-shape, has an annular 'ferrule' moulding around the base like a full-scale metal coffee pot, which required a non-conductive material around the tang to protect the hand from the heat. The base is slightly domed and scratched with lines that radiate from the centre in an apparently haphazard fashion.
Date: 1700–10
Provenance: Southwark bridge, north end

Ewers & jugs

The 28 ewers and jugs constitute the largest group of serving vessels in the collection. They replicate a broad spectrum of vessels of different quality, style and material in common use in England, France, Germany and the Low Countries from the mid-12th to mid-17th centuries. Some imitate earthenware jugs, which were used as serving vessels in the hall or kitchen for wine, ale or beer, or for multifarious purposes around the house. Others resemble vessels of pewter, latten, bronze and silver, which were a prominent feature of the buffet or plate cupboard and used as wine decanters or for water with 'much honor ... at all great feasts to wash withall, after eating tyme is finished'.[29]

Although serving vessels for wine, water, ale and beer are frequently mentioned in inventories, accounts and other documents throughout the medieval and early modern period, the terms used to describe these vessels are various and confused. Sometimes one term was used to cover several forms, so that, for example, the word 'ewer' could mean a vessel of 'viall fashion, with a pipe, on the side, and round bellied set on a foote' as well as a vessel 'like a cup and held like it' with a pouring lip 'by which the liquor in it is directly and evenly poured out'.[30] Ewers of the first sort are indistinguishable from the globular 'spouted jugs', 'flagons' or 'stoop pots', which were used for water, wine or beer from the 14th to early 17th centuries, and the terms 'ewer' and 'flagon' were often used interchangeably.[31] The problems of nomenclature remain unresolved, and curators and archaeologists still use different words to describe similar forms of vessel.

Since it is generally impossible to differentiate between bellied ewers with or without a spout and flagons or similar shape, for the purposes of this catalogue the term 'ewer' has been used for all of the miniatures which were modelled on contemporary metal vessels, and the term 'jug' for those which seem to be based on ceramic forms. Within each category the vessels have been arranged by form and design, and where appropriate, the terms used to define a particular form are derived from contemporary accounts or the standardized classification laid down by the Medieval Pottery Research Group. Specific definitions are noted in the catalogue.

On the whole, the miniature jugs are easier to date and attribute than the miniature ewers because a great deal is known about the medieval ceramic industry, and comparisons can be made with the thousands of earthenware jugs which have been recovered from securely dated archaeological contexts in the London area.[32] Many of the toy jugs seem to modelled on London-type wares, which were produced from local clays and distributed throughout the Home Counties and southern England from the mid-12th to late 14th century. But since some London-type wares imitated the form and decorative styles of pottery from northern France and Rouen, and ceramic jugs were also occasionally imported into London from the Continent, it is impossible to know whether the miniatures replicate English forms in the French style or imported vessels. The problem of attribution is compounded because many of the toy jugs are decorated with motifs which approximate, but do not actually replicate, ceramic schemes, and even when the mould-maker has tried to follow ceramic convention with raised mouldings to imitate incised or slip patterns, the practical difficulties of casting metal mean that the toy jugs lack the salient characteristics of their ceramic counterparts. An added complexity to the problem of identification and attribution is that the form and decoration of some ceramic jugs were inspired by contemporary metal vessels, and it is possible, although perhaps not very likely, that some of the toy jugs were modelled on ceramic copies of metal forms (see fig. 57, p. 281).[33]

Detail showing ewers: see plate VII, p. 167

Notwithstanding the difficulties described above, some of the miniatures were clearly modelled on full-scale vessels of metal, replicating lavishly decorated precious metal ewers or lavers, which were invariably used in conjunction with a basin[34] or copying base-metal vessels with plain, simple bands of ornament. Unlike many of the toy jugs, however, these miniatures often have no comparable counterpart in full-scale because very few base- and precious-metal flagons and ewers have survived the vicissitudes of centuries, and were destroyed, melted down or refashioned into other objects to suit contemporary taste and changes in dining etiquette. Those which do survive, as Hernmarck points out in his book on *The Art of the European Silversmith 1430–1830*, 'do not give us a very reliable idea of how many must once have existed ... but those which have been preserved in Spain, Portugal, Germany and England, together with those listed in other countries' inventories, show that they must have been quite common objects'.[35] In the absence of comparable examples in full scale, the dating and attribution of many of the miniatures rests largely on stylized images in illuminated manuscripts,[36] or paintings and engravings of mostly Continental origin, and as Randle Holme noted in the 17th century, since 'every countrey hath its owne forme and shape', these images may not reflect the types and forms of vessels in common use in England.

The lack of comparanda could, of course, mean that some of the miniatures were modelled on unique English forms which have not survived and are not represented in art. But it is equally possible that the toymakers took elements from full-scale vessels of metal and ceramic to create a generic type. Some of the tripod ewers (Cat. nos. 8.112 to 8.114), for example, have features which suggest that they were modelled on metal vessels, but the only comparable versions in full scale are of earthenware and these have a pouring lip instead of a spout.[37]

Although most of the miniature jugs, flagons and ewers in this country have been recovered from London, examples have been found in Salisbury, East Anglia, Sigglethorne in Humberside and as far afield as Ryton, near Malton, North Yorkshire.[38] A particularly significant find of a stone mould from a 15th-century context in Hereford, the only one of its kind so far identified in England,[39] shows that miniature jugs were widely distributed throughout the country, and probably manufactured in several locations.

Ewers

The earliest type of ewer, as Randle Holme notes in *The Academy of Armory* (1688) 'differed nothing in shape from a Jugge, save it was of a purer metle, viz., silver or pewter; haveing a Gutter side on ye further side of the mouth, by which water might be powred out it slowly and surely without scattering or flying broad.'[40] Those vessels copying metal forms with a pouring lip, spout or flaring rim have been classified as ewers in this catalogue. Four main types have been identified.

TYPE 1

These miniatures with ovoid, globular or pear-shaped bodies rest on a conical or wide-spreading foot, and resemble vessels of base and precious metals which were variously described as ewers, flagons, livery pots and stoop pots during the late 15th to early 17th century. None of the miniatures has a spout, although they all have a lid or attachments for a lid. The decorative style of some of the miniatures suggests that they were inspired by contemporaneous forms in precious metals, and although exact parallels are unknown, the gadroon and scroll mouldings are not unlike the scallop and strapwork chasing on English examples of the late 16th to early 17th century.[41]

TYPE 1, DESIGN 1

8.104 Pear-shaped lidded ewer

Accession number: 98.2/150*; 98.2/151
Material: Lead alloy
Condition: 98.2/150: lid missing
  98.2/151: lid, foot and handle missing
Dimensions: H 54mm; Diam (rim) 12mm; Diam (base) 24mm; W *c.* 31mm
Description: These pear-shaped lidded ewers were cast in three parts from the same mould. The rim is slightly thickened and the angular profile is enhanced by a beaded circle, the first of five decorative bands covering the vessel. Each band is enclosed by two circumferential ridges, and the pattern alternates between beading and hatching. The tiny stem reposes on a foot of conical form decorated with five concentric circles. The outer circle is decorated with pellets and this encloses a circle with scrolling and the numerals IXII. The S-shaped, diamond-sectioned handles (complete for 98.2/150) have a trefoil terminal. There are hinge loops (one damaged) on 98.2/150.
Date: 15th–16th century
Provenance: 98.2/150: London Bridge, August 1983
Comments: Virtually identical to T1, D2 below; probably made in the same workshop
Comparanda: *Chreitien de Hondt, Abbot of the Dunes, near Furnes,* 1499, with parcel-gilt pot on buffet, in the Royal Museum of Fine Art, Antwerp. Similar vessels are shown in 'the earliest known illustration … of this form' in the Exchequer Standard of 1496: cited in Hornsby *et. al.* 1989, p. 56, no. 25. The earliest extant example known in full size was recovered from the wreck of the *Mary Rose.*

TYPE 1, DESIGN 2

TYPE 1, DESIGN 3

TYPE 1, DESIGN 4

8.105 Pear-shaped lidded ewer

Accession number: 98.2/152
Material: Lead alloy
Condition: Lid and handle missing; worn; poorly cast
Dimensions: H 52mm; Diam (rim) 9mm; Diam (base) 26mm; W 26mm
Description: A pear-shaped lidded ewer cast in one piece in a two-part mould. The slightly everted rim is thickened and the edge abraded and damaged. The vessel is decorated with five circumferential bands consisting of three plain rings, but the lower two are poorly cast and badly aligned. The short circular stem flares out to form a conical foot decorated with three concentric circles, one beaded, and hatching around the edge. There are ridges on the underside of the foot which correspond to the decoration on the external surface. Only the base of the handle survives and this terminates in a trefoil.
Date: 15th–16th century

8.106 Pear-shaped lidded ewer

Accession number: 2001.20/1
Material: Lead alloy
Condition: Complete; lid missing; worn
Dimensions: H 47mm; Diam (rim) 14mm; Diam (base) 17 x 18 mm; W 27mm
Description: An ovoid body with a flared lip, short conical foot and scrolling handle. The corroded and blocked ring thumbpiece shows that the ewer was originally covered. The body is decorated with chevrons, vertical ribbing and scrolling, divided by cross-hatched and plain bands.
Date: Probably 1550–1600
Provenance: Billingsgate spoil, 1999
Comments: While the elegant shape and lid fixings suggest that this miniature was based on a metal ewer, the decoration is much more like that found on Surrey Whiteware 'baluster jugs' of the 13th and 14th centuries. Metal vessels of this sort were popular during the second half of the 16th century, and precious-metal examples were generally embellished with foliate and figurative chasing.
Comparandum: A silver-gilt ewer in the V&A (no. M250–1924), with London hallmarks for 1583–4, has a similar body profile, although the handles of this vessel and others of the same sort rise up above the rim.

8.107 Globular lidded ewer

Accession number: 98.2/153
Material: Lead alloy
Condition: Lid missing
Dimensions: H 50mm; Diam (rim) 13mm; Diam (base) 24 x 27 mm
Description: A globular lidded ewer with a slightly everted rim. The neck and body are decorated with horizontal bands of cross-hatched chevrons interspersed with pellets or ring and dot, and each band is defined by a pronounced circumferential ridge; these become progressively wider towards the spreading, gadrooned oval foot. The plain, S-shaped handle has two loops at the rim which form part of the lid hinge and the base is attached to the body in an upward recurving projection. This vessel is cast in three parts.
Date: Late 15th–late 16th century
Comparanda: A similar-shaped vessel is depicted on the table in a 'treatise of seven shops' of 1470, now in the Otto Schäfer Collection, and there is another in *The Family of Hans Rudolf Faesch at Table,* 1559 by Hans Hug Kluber (1535–78) in the Kunstmuseum, Basle (inv. no. 4649). Similar-shaped full-size vessels of probable English manufacture have been found in London, Oxfordshire[42] and from the wreck of the *Mary Rose*.[43]

Fig. 57. A full-sized ceramic version of a metal ewer made from Kingston-ware with a yellowish green glaze. The tubular spout ends with a conventionalized animal head. 13th century. From Whitefriars Street. H 222mm
Museum of London, Acc. no. A27544

282 • TOYS, TRIFLES & TRINKETS

TYPE 1, DESIGN 5

8.108 Pear-shaped lidded ewer

Accession number: 98.2/154
Material: Lead alloy
Condition: Complete
Dimensions: H 55mm; Diam (rim) 14 x 17 mm; Diam (base) 20mm; W 33mm
Description: A pear-shaped lidded ewer of elliptical section cast in three parts. The entire vessel is covered in low-relief decoration to replicate a vessel of high quality. The domed lid is decorated with radial ridges surmounted by a knopped finial and the close-hatched flange extends to cover the pouring lip. The lid is secured by means of a simple hinge consisting of two loops cast at right angles with a gap in the middle to accommodate a larger loop at the top of the handle. There is no 'thumbpiece' and the loops are aligned by a pin which has been fastened at each end with solder. A circular retaining ridge on the underside of the lid prevents lateral shift. The upper part of the vessel including the pouring lip is covered with a cross-hatch design, and the neck is divided into three horizontal bands each defined by a circumferential ridge. Chevrons interspersed with ring and dot decorate the top band and the lower two are hatched. Above and below a central band, the body is divided into two zones of stylized gadrooning, and the vessel is supported on a very short, slender stem with a sharp-edged annular knop. The wide, slightly domed, spreading foot has a cross-hatched edge and the decoration divides the surface into quadrants defined by radial ridges and ring and dot. The slender, hatched, S-shaped handle terminates at each end in a scroll.
Date: Late 16th–early 17th century
Comments: This object was purchased with assistance from NACF. It was found with a cherry stone.
Comparandum: A pewter vessel of similar form, but undecorated in the collections of the Worshipful Company of Pewterers (inv. no. 1/261) which has been dated to the late 16th century

TYPE 2

Cup-ewers (sometimes known as 'open-mouthed ewers') with or without a foot are known from the early 15th century.[44] The footed form seems to have gained ascendancy during the late 15th century and remained popular until the early 18th century. The three miniature cup-ewers are probably from the mid-17th century.

TYPE 2, DESIGN 1

8.109 Cup-ewer

Accession number: 98.2/178
Material: Lead alloy
Condition: Almost complete; handle and lid missing
Dimensions: H 32mm; Diam (rim) 25 x 23 mm; Diam (base) 21 x 20 mm; W 33mm
Inscription: DQ
Description: A polygonal cup-ewer with a faceted spout. The lid and handle are missing, but there is a horizontal tab inscribed DQ opposite the spout which may have formed the base for a thumbpiece or hinge. Only the terminal scroll of the handle survives. The vessel is decorated with a feather pattern which radiates from a central rope-twist band to the rim and foot. The stepped, conical faceted foot rises from a flat rope-twist border and each facet is decorated with leaves.
Date: The inscription DQ and general shape suggests manufacture between 1640–50.
Provenance: Brook's Wharf, March 1983

Comments: Randle Holme illustrates a ewer of this general shape which he describes as a cup-ewer (bk 3, ch. 14, sec. 1a, no. 8).

Comparanda: There is an earlier example of this faceted form of cup-ewer in Corpus Christi College, Cambridge with hallmarks for 1545, and there are a number of Dutch examples of this type including one by Hans Jacobsz Wesson of 1640 now in the Royal Collection, as well as those made for the inauguration of Amsterdam Town Hall by Jan Lutma, Amsterdam, 1655 in the Rijksmuseum. A similar piece is also illustrated in a painting by George Philipp Harsdoerffer (1607–58), *Vollstandiges Trincir-Buchlein Handlend*, 1640, Nuremberg, in the Folger Shakespeare Library.

TYPE 2, DESIGN 2

8.110 Cup-ewer, lidded

Accession number: 98.2/165

Material: Lead alloy

Condition: Incomplete; base, handle and lid missing; much crushed and damaged

Dimensions: H 34mm; Diam (rim) *c.* 21 x 17 mm; W *c.* 22 mm

Description: The body of a lidded cup-ewer with a triangular pouring lip (now flattened). There are two cordons around the rim and another halfway down the body which is decorated with foliate scrolling.

Date: 16th–17th century

TYPE 2, DESIGN 3

8.111 Cup-ewer

Accession number: 98.2/164

Material: Lead alloy

Condition: Incomplete; foot missing; lid possibly lost too; crushed

Dimensions: H 42mm; Diam (rim) 20 x 10 mm; Diam (base) 20 x 17 mm; W 33mm

Description: This cup-ewer seems to have been cast in two or perhaps three sections. The vessel is badly crushed, distorted and abraded and the foot has broken off to leave a circular hole at the bottom of the body. There is a thickened cordon around the rim, and the upper part of the parallel-sided body is decorated with circumferential rilling, the lower with crude gadrooning. At the top of the uneven-sectioned angular handle, there is a circular loop joining the rim, which may have formed part of the hinge attachment for a handle and thumbpiece. The lower part of the handle runs along the casting seam on the body before it curves outwards.

Date: Probably 16th–17th century

Provenance: Wapping Station, 1985

TYPE 3

Globular and pear-shaped tripod or conical-footed ewers in base and precious metals with straight, curving, angular or S-shaped bridge-spouts and curving handles were made from the 14th to the early 17th century. Several forms are represented here. Many of the full-scale vessels with sinuous spouts and handles were embellished with animal-head terminals and there are a couple of examples in the collection.

TYPE 3, DESIGN 1

8.112 Tripod ewer

Accession number: 2001.20/2

Material: Lead alloy

Condition: Complete

Dimensions: H 35mm; Diam (rim) 16 x 13 mm; Diam (base) 13 x 8 mm; W 38mm

Description: A bridged-spouted ovoid-shaped tripod ewer with a wide flaring rim. The slightly attenuated handle runs from the rim halfway down the body and terminates in a rat's tail. The vessel has three zones of decoration divided by cordons, including a diaper pattern with pellets around the rim; cross-hatching on the neck, and a patera or scale pattern in high relief on the body. The plain, tubular upward-curving spout is secured to the neck by a short thick bridge.

Date: Mid- to late 12th century

Provenance: Butler's Wharf

284 • TOYS, TRIFLES & TRINKETS

Comparanda: Very similar to Cat. nos. 8.113 and 8.114. The general shape and stump-sized feet are similar to so-called 'early style' London-type earthenware tripod pitchers of the late 12th and early 13th century, although these are without bridged spouts. A miniature vessel of similar shape and decoration has been found in Paris and dated to the 15th century (Musée au Moyen Age, 44 x 32 x 20 mm). See also Gay 1887, p. 44.

TYPE 3, DESIGN 2

8.113 Tripod ewer

Accession number: 98.2/161
Material: Lead alloy
Condition: Complete; some damage
Dimensions: H 39mm; Diam (rim) 16 x 12 mm; Diam (base) 11 x 6 mm; W 30mm
Description: An ovoid-shaped tripod ewer with a wide flaring rim and waisted neck. The curving, diamond-sectioned handle runs from the rim halfway down the body and recurves upwards at the base with a knopped terminal. The whole vessel is decorated with a patera scale pattern. The surface is abraded and worn, and there are two holes aligned with the casting seam indicating the location of the spout and bridge attachment.
Date: Mid- to late 12th century
Comparanda: Similar to T3, D1 & D3 and possibly made in the same workshop

Fig. 58. Full-sized tripod pitcher of London-type ware with applied polychrome decoration. Found in London from a mid-12th-century context. H 275mm
Museum of London, Acc. no. C676

TYPE 3, DESIGN 3

TYPE 3, DESIGN 4

TYPE 3, DESIGN 5

8.114 Tripod ewer

Accession number: 98.2/162

Material: Lead alloy

Condition: Complete; some damage

Dimensions: H 36mm; Diam (rim) 18.5mm; Diam (base) 13mm; W 27mm

Description: This ovoid-shaped tripod ewer has a wide flaring rim and waisted neck. The angular rod handle runs from the rim halfway down the body, changing from a circular to a faceted section with a diminishing diameter towards the 'rat's tail' terminal. The vessel has three zones of decoration separated by cordons around the neck: a diaper pattern with pellets around the flaring rim; cross-hatching on the neck; and, covering the body, a patera scale design in high relief. There are two holes in the seam which correspond to the location of a spout and bridge support.

Date: Mid- to late 12th century

Comparandum: Cat. no. 8.112

8.115 Bridge-spouted ewer

Accession number: 98.2/168*; 98.2/170

Material: Lead alloy

Condition: 98.2/168: complete; slight damage to rim. 98.2/170: missing foot

Dimensions: H 68mm; Diam (rim) 20 x 18 mm; Diam (base) 30 x 27 mm; W *c.* 51mm

Description: Two bridge-spouted ewers of identical form and design, probably made in the same workshop, if not the same mould. In both cases the flaring rims with pouring lips are damaged. The long necks join a pear-shaped body which reposes on a flaring, pedestal foot (98.2/168). The cross-hatched tubular bridge-spouts curve outwards and upwards, and the oblique rims incline away from the body. Curving, diamond-sectioned rod handles are attached halfway down the neck and join the body as it begins to taper to the foot. The horizontal bands of hatched chevrons and gadrooning are divided by raised cordons.

Date: Probably 15th century

Provenance: 98.2/170: Brook's Wharf, March 1987

8.116 Bridge-spouted ewer

Accession number: 98.2/167*; 98.2/171; 98.2/172; 98.2/177

Material: Lead alloy

Condition: Lids missing. 98.2/177: also missing spout and handle

Dimensions: Two sizes:
i) 98.2/167; 98.2/171; 98.2/172: H 48mm; Diam (rim) 14 x 11 mm; Diam (base) 19 x 16 mm; W *c.* 39mm
ii) 98.2/177: H 46mm; Diam (rim) 14mm; Diam (base) 20 x *c.* 17 mm

Description: These bridge-spouted and once-lidded ewers all have an everted thickened rim with a thickened cordon, pouring lip, long slender neck and biconical body reposing on a pedestal foot. The curving handles (98.2/167 & 98.2/171) join the rim with a loop for the lid hinge or thumbpiece. All except 98.2/177 have a plain, faceted tubular spout which curves sharply outwards from the body and then straightens towards the rim. The spout rims flare out to form a pouring lip and this is most evident in Acc. nos. 98.2/171 and 98.2/172. The vessels are decorated with eight horizontal bands, each defined by raised cordons and filled with vertical ribbing or gadrooning.

Date: Probably 15th century

Comparanda: These vessels are very similar to T3, D4 above. Other examples have been found on the Wapping and Greenwich foreshores.

286 • TOYS, TRIFLES & TRINKETS

TYPE 3, DESIGN 6

8.117 Bridge-spouted ewer

Accession number: 98.2/169

Material: Lead alloy

Condition: Almost complete; upper part of spout missing; rim damaged

Dimensions: H 56mm; Diam (rim) 13mm; Diam (base) 18 x 12 mm; W *c.* 41mm

Description: This bridge-spouted tripod ewer has been cast in one piece, with a tubular bridged spout (upper half missing) and rectangular-sectioned curving handle terminating in an animal's head at the neck. The neck is very long and the shoulders taper to join the pear-shaped body which in turn tapers towards the flat base. There are eight horizontal bands of decoration divided by cordons in high relief, starting with a chevron and pellet design around the neck, crudely defined chevrons around the upper body, and a band of ring and dot and foliate scrolling below.

Date: 15th century

Comments: The feet are little more than stumps of the sort found on London-type ware pitchers.

Fig. 59. Full-sized bronze bridge-spouted tripod ewer with animal-head terminal, 14th–15th century. Found in Battersea
Museum of London, Acc. no. A2752

TYPE 3, DESIGN 7

8.118 Bridge-spouted ewer

Accession number: 98.2/166
Material: Lead alloy
Condition: Complete; some damage to base
Dimensions: H *c.* 51mm; Diam (rim) 15 x 12 mm; Diam (base) 20 x 15 mm; W *c.* 45mm
Description: A bridge-spouted tripod ewer cast in one piece with a long cylindrical neck, large pear-shaped body and curving handle. The neck is decorated with cross-hatched bands and the body with cross-hatched quartered 'shields' embellished with bosses at each intersection. The 'shield' on the side illustrated above comprises: 1st quarter, a shield chequy; 2nd and 3rd quarters, overlapping scales; and in the 4th quarter a shield with a cross-hatched 'plain' cross. The 'shield' on the other side of the vessel comprises: 1st quarter, a shield barrully; 2nd and 3rd quarters, overlapping scales; and in the 4th quarter, a shield with two bendlets cross-hatched. The outer surface of the spout, which rises up from the shoulder of the body to just below the rim of the vessel, is decorated with chevrons and the bridge has diagonal hatching.
Date: 15th century
Comments: The pseudo-armorial decoration incorporates ordinary charges of a debased form. The feet are short stumps like those typically found on London-type ware pitchers. The English were particularly keen to incorporate heraldic devices, coats of arms and badges on their personal possessions throughout the 15th and 16th centuries in particular, and the 'heraldic' motif on this vessel reflects contemporary taste and fashion, albeit rather clumsily applied.

TYPE 3, DESIGN 8

8.119 Tripod ewer

Accession number: 8193
Material: Lead alloy
Condition: Complete; crushed and distorted
Dimensions: H 70mm; Diam (rim) 16 x 13 mm; Diam (base) 13mm; W 38mm
Description: This tripod, hexagonally faceted ewer has a bridge-spout and pear-shaped body. The vessel has three horizontal bands of decoration, each divided by pronounced cordons. The neck is decorated with chevrons and trefoil pellets, the shoulders and upper part of the body with quatrefoils, scrolling and bosses, and the lower body with foliate scrolling and a narrow band of ring and dot. The hexagonal spout curves upwards and is decorated with a single cordon between chevrons and pellets. Mouldings suggestive of a dragon's or serpent's head form the mouth, and the spout is linked to the neck cordon by a very thin bridge. A curving hexagonal rod handle with scroll terminal and central cordon runs from the medial band of body cordons to the lip of the vessel, and the upper part is decorated with a dragon's or serpent's head moulding. The long, thin vertically ribbed legs flare outwards towards the thickened feet.
Date: 14th–16th century
Provenance: Brook's Wharf
Comparanda: Possibly English 14th–15th century bronze ewer from Battersea, now in the Museum of London (Acc. no. A2752): see Ward Perkins 1940, p. 203 & plate 53. There is a 14th-century example in the British Museum (BM1975, 10–11) and another with an inscription from the Gower peninsula. See Lewis *et al.* 1987 and Finlay *et al.* 1996 for detailed discussion on British late medieval inscribed ewers. Faceted ewers of this type seem to have been particularly common on the Continent and Roger van der Weyden's *Verkündiging* of *c.* 1440 in the Louvre shows a ewer of this sort. Similar examples survive in the collections of the Museum Boymans-van Beuningen in Rotterdam.

TYPE 4

This vessel has no parallel in full scale, although the 'squared pots' first mentioned in the Pewterers' Company Ordinances of the 14th century were perhaps rather similar.

TYPE 4, DESIGN 1

8.120 Pedestal ewer

Accession number: A14580
Material: Lead alloy
Condition: Complete; slightly crushed; lid missing
Dimensions: H 57mm; Diam (rim) 18mm; Diam (base) 24mm; W c. 30mm
Description: A large pedestal ewer of ovoid form with an angular profile. Most of the sharply carinated angles are defined by a cordon and the upper section of the neck is roughly cross-hatched on one side. The diamond-section strap handle is slightly twisted, but aligns with the longitudinal axis of the casting seam.
Date: Probably 16th–17th century
Provenance: Hammersmith foreshore, from ballast deposits of London Bridge

Jugs

As these vessels seem to be inspired by, or modelled on, London-type ware and Surrey whiteware jugs, the Medieval Pottery Research Group standardized classification, and the various volumes which form part of *A Dated Type-Series of London Medieval Pottery* have been used to identify and define the specific types.

TYPE 1

These tall baluster jugs dating from the mid-12th to mid-14th century are characterised by their pear- or ovoid-shaped bodies on pedestal feet.[45]

TYPE 1, DESIGN 1

8.121 Baluster jug

Accession number: 98.2/157
Material: Lead alloy
Condition: Complete; distorted
Dimensions: H 49mm; Diam (rim) 20 x 14 mm; Diam (base) 15 x 11 mm; W 30mm
Description: Cast in one piece with a pouring lip and pear-shaped body which tapers to form a pedestal foot of oval section. The rim and surface are abraded and the vessel has been crushed and distorted. The upper surface of the rod handle is decorated with diagonal slashing, and the body is decorated with alternating bands of chevrons and scrolling. The pedestal foot and base are cross-hatched.
Date: Late 12th century
Comparanda: The general shape and horizontal bands of decoration are reminiscent of Kingston-type pear-shaped baluster jugs of the mid-12th to 14th century. Chevrons and scrolling decoration are not uncommon on Kingston-type wares, but the combination of motifs on the miniature is unparalleled. It is possible that the cross-hatching on the pedestal foot was included to represent knife-trimming on a full-scale jug.

TYPE 1, DESIGN 2

8.122 Baluster jug

Accession number: 98.2/158
Material: Lead alloy
Condition: Almost complete; rim damaged; handle missing
Dimensions: H 50mm; Diam (rim) 20 x 15 mm; Diam (base) 20 x 18 mm; W 34mm
Description: A large baluster jug with a wide flaring rim and pouring lip, cylindrical waisted neck and large, globular body terminating in a short, narrow, slightly conical pedestal foot. The surface is rather worn but seems to be divided into six horizontal zones of decoration composed

of cross-hatched chevrons and guilloche. The pedestal foot has vertical ribbing and the base is cross-hatched.

Date: Late 12th century

Comparanda: The form is quite similar to London-type wares with Rouen-style decoration: see Pearce *et al.* 1988, pp. 72–4, figs 30–32.

TYPE 1, DESIGN 3

8.123 Baluster jug

Accession number: 98.2/156

Material: Lead alloy

Condition: Complete

Dimensions: H 50mm; Diam (rim) 18 x 16 mm; Diam (base) 16 x 14 mm; W 33mm

Description: A baluster jug cast in one piece with a flaring rim, cylindrical neck and pear-shaped body. The plain, diamond-sectioned rod handle is attached at the base of the neck and curves round to join the body above the short, conical foot. The vessel is decorated with horizontal bands of diagonal hatching, guilloche, gadrooning and vertical ribbing, each separated by a thin milled band. The foot has vertical ribbing and the base is cross-hatched.

Date: Mid-13th–mid-14th century

Fig. 60. These early 13th-century full-sized baluster jugs were made in London, but the vessel on the left imitates pottery from northern France, and the jug on the right, pottery made in Rouen. H 292mm

Museum of London, Acc. nos. C154 & 5655

Comparanda: Apart from the handle and decoration, the basic form is similar to a Kingston-type ware cylindrical-necked baluster jug of the mid-13th to mid-14th century. Like Cat. no. 8.121, the foot decoration possibly represents thumbmarks or knife-trimming, but areas of guilloche and gadrooning must be inspired by metal vessels.

TYPE 2

Pear-shaped jugs were made in London-type wares and Surrey whitewares from the late 13th to late 14th century. Most extant examples seem to be decorated in the north French style with plain vertical ribs or roller-stamped strips on the body, and occasionally cross-hatched slip patterns on the neck. Only Acc. no. 98.2/160 has a recessed basal edge with vertical mouldings to represent the thumbed basal edge on jugs of this type.

TYPE 2, DESIGN 1

8.124 Pear-shaped jug

Accession number: 98.2/159
Material: Lead alloy
Condition: Complete; slightly damaged; very worn
Dimensions: H 39mm; Diam (rim) 20 x 15 mm; Diam (base) 19 x 16 mm; W 28mm
Description: A pear-shaped jug cast in one piece, with a wide flaring rim, pouring lip, long neck, sloping shoulders and pear-shaped body which tapers gently to the flat base. The vessel is decorated with lozenges, diagonal slashes, parallel lines, and plain and milled vertical strips. The base is cross-hatched. A plain, curving, square-sectioned rod handle is attached halfway down the neck.
Date: Mid-13th–early 14th century
Provenance: Billingsgate spoil, 1984
Comparanda: For similar forms and types of decoration, see Pearce *et al.* 1988, plate 7 and fig. 51. It is possible that this vessel originally had a tubular spout because there is some damage on the body where a spout would start and the form and decoration is extremely similar to a spouted miniature in the collections of the Musée national du Moyen Age dated to the 14th century (66 x 53 x 19 mm).

TYPE 2, DESIGN 2

8.125 Pear-shaped jug

Accession number: 98.2/163
Material: Lead alloy
Condition: Incomplete; rim and handle missing; very worn
Dimensions: H 38mm; Diam (rim) 12mm; Diam (base) 14 x 11 mm; W 18mm
Description: A crudely cast pear-shaped jug with a cylindrical neck. The vessel is damaged and worn, and the handle is missing. The rim is damaged and the decoration seems to consist of an alternating pattern of plain and milled vertical strips.
Date: Mid-13th–early 14th century
Comments: Very similar in terms of decoration to Cat. no. 8.124

TYPE 2, DESIGN 3

8.126 Pear-shaped jug

Accession number: 98.2/160
Material: Lead alloy
Condition: Complete
Dimensions: H 47mm; Diam (rim) 21 x 18 mm; Diam (base) 20 x 15mm; W 33mm
Description: This jug has a flaring rim and slightly waisted cylindrical neck decorated with four rows of chevrons, each alternately cross-hatched. The pear-shaped body has a rectangular section which tapers to an oval base and is decorated with densely packed milled vertical ribbing. There is a cordon around the recessed oval foot, decorated with vertical milling, and the base is covered with fine cross-hatching. The curving rod handle, of diamond section, is decorated on the upper surface with diagonal lines and is attached halfway down the neck.
Date: Early to mid-13th century
Provenance: Southwark Bridge, south-west side. Similarly decorated examples were found in Billingsgate spoil in 1984.
Comparanda: While the general shape and decoration is similar to north French-style London-type wares, the rectangular-sectioned body is unparalleled in either ceramic or metal vessels.

Fig. 61. An elaborately decorated, full-sized London-type ware rounded jug. Mid-12th to late 13th century. Found in Swan Street, Southwark
Museum of London, Acc. no. A11299

Fig. 62. Cheap stoneware mugs were imported into London in vast numbers during the 16th century. This vessel has been ornamented with an English-made silver-gilt lid inscribed 'The tongue that lieth, killeth the soul'. The roundel in the centre is engraved with a merchant's mark and the letters RH. The miniature pot lid (Cat. no. 8.127) seems to imitate a mount of this type.
Museum of London, Acc. no. A23406

Pots

The generic term 'pot' seems to have been used for 'any small vessel wherein wine, beer, water etc readie to be drunke is usually put',[46] and the collection includes two items in this category: one in the form of a tankard, and the other a lid of the sort usually associated with silver-gilt mounted ceramic or glass vessels which were particularly fashionable in England from 1520–90.

Tankards of various types and materials are mentioned in accounts and inventories from the 12th century, but it was not until the 1550s that the word applied to personal drinking vessels.[47]

TYPE 1, DESIGN 1

8.127 Lid

Accession number: 98.2/616
Material: Lead alloy
Condition: Complete
Dimensions: Diam 30mm
Description: A circular raised lid with radial gadrooning and a central boss decorated with a cinquefoil double rose. The gadroons are alternately decorated with a flower or patera motif. There is a cable rim and the recurving knob or clasp is matched by an opposing hole for the thumbpiece.
Date: Probably 1520–90
Comments: Mounted vessels are found in inventories of the 1620s and 30s and so it is possible that this object was made at a later date. The lid is robustly cast to withstand moderate use and the quality of the workmanship and scale suggests that it was probably made for a tiny stoneware or earthenware vessel. The central boss has a double rose motif which reflects the decorative enamelled or jewelled bosses on full-scale pots of this type.
Comparanda: Very similar in form to the silver-gilt lid on the Parr Pot in the Museum of London (Acc. no. 67.10), dated 1546, with the Parr family's coat of arms on the enamel boss; and a Raeren stoneware mug of 1540–60 also in the Museum of London (Acc. no. A23406). Another pewter miniature lid (incomplete and crushed, but with trefoil finials around the rim) was recovered from Bull Wharf (now in a private collection).

TYPE 1, DESIGN 2

8.128 Lidded tankard

Accession number: Private collection
Material: Lead alloy
Condition: Complete
Dimensions: H (incl. thumbpiece) 24mm; Diam 13mm
Description: A cylindrical hooped tankard with curving handle and ring thumbpiece. The slightly domed lid has a central knop and floral decoration and the body is decorated with a patera design. The base has a six-petalled partially cross-hatched flower.
Date: 17th century
Provenance: Dockhead, June 1988
Comments: The tiny toy tankard is highly decorated, and although no comparable example is known in full scale, the general shape and style suggests late 17th- or 18th-century manufacture. The patera decoration on the body, however, is very similar to that on a ewer (Cat. no. 8.109) which is closely datable to the 1640s.

Standing bowls or 'flat cups'

Special standing bowls or 'flat cups' in silver and other precious materials were made throughout Europe for ceremonial drinking or display from the early 15th to early 17th century. While these vessels are frequently depicted in paintings and often feature in inventories and other contemporary documents, surviving examples in full scale are rare.

The miniature drinking bowls in this collection are the only examples known in this country, and replicate full-scale vessels dating from the late 15th to late 16th century.[48] The beaded rim on Cat. no. 8.131 suggests that this toy might have had a cover like its full-scale counterpart.

TYPE 1, DESIGN 1

8.129 Standing bowl

Accession number: 98.2/180
Material: Lead alloy
Condition: Complete; slightly damaged
Dimensions: H 26mm; Diam (rim) *c.* 31mm; Diam (base) 25mm
Description: A plain curving bowl reposing on a hollow trumpet foot. There is a double cordon around the basal edge of the foot for decoration and added strength.
Date: Possibly 1480–1500
Comparandum: This vessel is very similar to an unmarked English piece of 1480–1500 in the V&A (no. M7–1964).

TYPE 1, DESIGN 2

8.130 Standing bowl

Accession number: 98.2/179
Material: Lead alloy
Condition: Complete; rim slightly damaged
Dimensions: H 23mm; Diam (rim) 26mm; Diam (base) 22mm
Description: A plain shallow bowl with straight sides tapering to a flat base and reposing on a hollow, trumpet-shaped foot.
Date: First quarter of the 16th century, perhaps 1520s
Provenance: Brook's Wharf, March 1987
Comparanda: The Campion cup, London hallmark 1500–1, in the V&A (no. M249–1924) and the Charlecote standing bowl, silver-gilt, London, 1524–5, in the private collection of Sir Edmund Fairfax-Lucy. A similar miniature found in the Netherlands has a band of decoration below the rim.

TYPE 1, DESIGN 3

8.131 Standing bowl

Accession number: 98.2/181
Material: Lead alloy
Condition: Complete
Dimensions: H 19mm; Diam (rim) *c.* 30mm; Diam (base) 16mm
Description: This vessel has a deep conical bowl reposing on a short, waisted pedestal foot with a flat base. The rim is beaded and the exterior surface of the bowl decorated with eight beaded swags, each interspersed with a pendant 'ribbon' to represent cast or chased decoration.
Date: Form reminiscent of drinking bowls of the late 16th century
Provenance: Southwark foreshore
Comparanda: This drinking bowl has a similar profile to those depicted in Anthony Claeissens, *Banquet*, 1574 (Groeninge Museum, Bruges) and to some of the prizes in the 'General Lotterie' broadsheet of 1567 (Folger Shakespeare Library, Washington).

Wine bottle

Special thick-walled green glass bottles for decanting and storing wine seem to have been made in England from the 1640s and were in common use by 1660. The shape of the glass wine bottle was adapted and altered over time to suit the needs of the product, retailer and consumer, and this miniature, the only example known, has the characteristic profile of an English or Dutch bottle of 1720–30.

TYPE 1, DESIGN 1

8.132 Wine bottle

Accession number: 98.2/366
Material: Lead alloy
Condition: Complete; slightly damaged
Dimensions: H 38mm; Diam (rim) 14mm; Diam (base) 29mm; W *c.* 31mm
Description: A complete, mallet-type bottle with wide flat rim flange and cylindrical neck which tapers out to the wide downward-sloping, angular shoulder. The circular body has straight sides which slope outwards to the base. There is a roughly incised circle at the junction of the neck and shoulder, and the flat base is incised with two concentric circles. The bottle has been cast in two parts: the body as one piece and the base as another. The edge of the base is damaged.
Date: Late 17th– early 18th century
Comments: Unlike the full-scale version in glass, this bottle has a completely flat base.
Comparanda: Similar-shaped vessels are shown in *The Quarrel of the Astronomers* by C. Troost [1697–1750], Mauritshuis, The Hague.

Porringers

'The porringers, that in a row
Hung high and made a glittering show'[49]

A potager, or porringer as it came to be known in the 16th century, is a small bowl made from metal, ceramic or wood with one or two horizontal handles aligned with, or just below, the plane of the rim. Often described by contemporaries as an 'eare disshe', the vessel was a perfect receptacle for individual portions of pulpy spoonmeats and, as the name implies, potage, the staple medieval and Tudor diet, a vegetable-based stew thickened with pulses, flavoured with herbs and occasionally augmented with scraps of meat. Porringers were also used for furmenty, a sweetened and glutinous wheat porridge, and pappy milky foods for children and invalids. Delftware and metal porringers are unlikely to have been used over a direct source of heat, but many lead-glazed earthenware porringers have sooted bases, which suggests that they were used for both warming and cooking food.[50] Small-handled bowls of pewter were used in the Roman period, but the real porringer, of the type described here, did not appear until the very end of the 15th century.[51] Ceramic porringers seem to date from the late 16th century and documentary and artefactual evidence suggests that the form remained popular in England until the 1720s.

The 35 toy porringers share certain characteristics with the full-scale vessel, but because a certain amount of post-burial 'straightening' has occurred and many are far too crushed and damaged for accurate classification, broad typological distinctions have been made on the basis of a single or double ear rather than vessel shape. Within each type, the porringers have been catalogued by mould design. Only nine porringers are complete, but missing ears are indicated by the presence of scars and residual stubs on the bowl rims. The ears are of trefoil or trilobate form, reflecting the shapes commonly found on full-scale porringers of the 16th and early 17th centuries, and they are variously decorated with an oval cartouche flanked by volutes, stylized floral patterns, radial lines and beading.

Unlike most of the surviving English examples in full scale, all of the miniature porringers have elaborate internal decoration, and as the tables show, the majority have a rose or rosette motif in the centre, which can be broken down as follows: 22 have a sexfoil rose; seven have a cinquefoil rose; two have a double rose that is too worn to be read clearly; three have a rosette; and one has a quasi-floral, radial design. Around this central motif are several concentric circles and decorative bands, and the rims are embellished with rope-twist or beading. The rose or rosette device is virtually unknown in English pewter, apart from the few late 17th-century commemorative porringers,[52] and a unique *c.* 1640 single-eared porringer of unusually small size.[53] Since it is unlikely, for the reasons outlined below, that the miniature porringers were all made during the same period, one can only conclude that the double-rose motif was used over several decades, which not only attests to the popularity of this particular design, but also to the apparent reluctance of the mould-engravers to experiment with new patterns.

Porringer (detail)
Acc. no. 98.2/219, Cat. no. 8.137

Table 8.2: Porringers with two solid ears (T1)

Design	Acc. no.	Dated	Inscribed	Central motif	Ears missing	Diameter	Depth
1	98.2/227	–	–	Rosette	Complete	33mm	5mm
2	A22301	1641	IDQ	Cinquefoil	Complete	36mm	8mm
	98.2/217	1641	?	double rose	Complete	40mm	6mm
3	98.2/225	–	–	Sexfoil d/rose	2	40mm	5mm
4	98.2/216	–	ID over Q	Sexfoil d/rose	Complete	32mm	3.5mm
5	21657	–	ID over Q	Sexfoil d/rose	Fragment	–	–
	98.2/218	–	ID over Q	Sexfoil d/rose	1	29mm	5mm
	98.2/219	–	ID over Q	Sexfoil d/rose	Complete	29mm	5mm
	98.2/220	–	ID over Q	Sexfoil d/rose	1	29mm	5mm
	98.2/221	–	ID over Q	Sexfoil d/rose	1	29mm	5mm
	98.2/223	–	ID over Q	Sexfoil d/rose	2	29mm	5mm
	98.2/224	–	ID over Q	Sexfoil d/rose	2	29mm	5mm
	90.342/4	–	ID over Q	Sexfoil d/rose	1	29mm	5mm
6	98.2/233	–	D [G]	Sexfoil d/rose	1	43mm	–
7	98.2/228	1640	AH	Cinquefoil d/rose	2	36mm	6.5mm
8	98.2/226	–	–	Other	1	35mm	3mm
9	98.2/242	–	–	Double rose	2	35mm	11mm
10	98.2/235	–	–	Sexfoil d/rose	1	30mm	1.5mm
11	98.2/318	–	–	Sexfoil d/rose	2	28mm	3mm
	98.2/319						

Table 8.3: Porringers with one pierced ear (T2)

Design	Acc. no.	Dated	Inscribed	Central motif	Ear missing	Diameter	Depth
1	98.2/222	–	ID over Q	Cinquefoil d/rose	Yes	38mm	5mm
2	98.2/234	–	–	Rosette	Yes	35mm	4.5mm

Table 8.4: Porringers with one solid ear (T3)

Design	Number	Dated	Inscribed	Central motif	Ear missing	Diameter	Depth
1	98.2/231	–	AB	Sexfoil d/rose	Yes	33mm	4.5mm
2	98.2/230	–	AB	Sexfoil d/rose	Yes	33.5mm	3.5mm
3	98.2/232	–	AB	Sexfoil d/rose	Yes	36mm	3mm
4	98.2/229	–	AF	Sexfoil d/rose	Yes	34mm	5mm
5	98.2/241	–	–	Sexfoil d/rose	Yes	28mm	6mm
6	98.2/240	–	–	Cinquefoil d/rose	Complete	22mm	3mm
7	98.2/238	–	–	Cinquefoil d/rose	Complete	38mm	–
8	98.2/237	–	–	Double rose	Complete	33mm	4.5mm
9	98.2/236	–	–	Sexfoil d/rose	Complete	33.5mm	6mm
10	98.2/244	–	–	Rosette	Complete	27mm	4.5mm
11	98.2/239	–	–	Sexfoil d/rose	Yes	47mm	8mm
12	98.2/320	–	–	Sexfoil d/rose	Yes	30mm	3mm
13	79.319/6	–	–	Cinquefoil d/rose	Yes	*c.* 43mm	4mm

Various attempts have been made to chart evolutionary changes in porringers from the early 16th to early 18th century.[54] Certain fashions and trends in vessel form and ear styles can be identified, but precise dating is extremely difficult because different shapes seem to have been made concurrently. As a general rule, however, the majority of 16th-century porringers have gently curving shallow bowls with a central boss and one or two solid ears, early 17th-century vessels usually have a narrow foot ring, and from the mid-century, a slightly deeper bowl with straightish sides and a single pierced handle becomes the norm. The central boss reappears from c. 1650 and continues to be used with flat-bottomed forms until well into the 18th century.

If the toys reflect contemporary fashions and evolutionary developments, the double-eared porringers are probably earlier than those with single ears, although both types were common in the early 17th century. It is, however, possible that many of the double-eared forms, and particularly those incorporating the initials I(D)Q were made on the Continent, where 'the double ear style persisted long after one ear become the norm in England,' and since European 'porringers were not uncommonly decorated, most if not all of the T1 miniatures could be imports'.[55] If this assumption is correct, one would expect to find equivalent items on the Continent, but so far only one of the toy porringers recovered in Europe from 16th and early 17th century contexts is decorated.[56] All of the toy porringers in this collection reflect porringer forms of the 16th and early 17th century and the tables show that some makers' were producing these toys in a range of sizes.[57] There is no evidence of either the flat based, straight sided types, or the so-called 'booged' porringers with bulging sides in vogue from c. 1675 to c. 1760, although both were probably also made in miniature form.

Five, possibly four, makers have marked their wares with initials: AB; AF; AH; D[G];[58] and IDQ. The initials are integrally cast and are either placed on the ear copying full-scale convention, or incorporated within a decorative band inside the bowl. Those inscribed with the inverted triad ID over Q are the most common, and since examples of this maker's work survive with dates ranging from 1640–46, and two other double-eared porringers in the corpus are dated 1640 and 1641, most of the Type 1 porringers were probably made during this period.[59] The large number of inscribed pieces proves that these toys were made by several makers or workshops,[60] but sadly the documentary evidence for toy porringer production is extremely scant. To date, only one maker of toy porringers, John Jackson, is recorded in archives of the Worshipful Company of Pewterers, and as yet none of his products is known.[61]

TYPE 1

There are 20 porringers of this type and they were all cast with double ears. Only four are complete, but opposing scars and stubs on the bowl rims suggest that the ears were solid rather than pierced. Dates range from the 16th to the middle of the 17th century.

TYPE 1, DESIGN 1

8.133 Porringer

Accession number: 98.2/227
Material: Lead alloy
Condition: Complete
Dimensions: Diam 33mm; W 53mm; Dpt 5mm

Description: A shallow curving bowl with two ears, and a thickened, faintly milled rim. The solid trefoil ears are decorated with beading and ring and dot. There is a crudely cast rosette in the centre of the bowl which is otherwise plain.
Date: Perhaps 16th century; probably the earliest example in the corpus

TYPE 1, DESIGN 2

TYPE 1, DESIGN 3

TYPE 1, DESIGN 4

8.134 Porringer

Accession number: A22301*; 98.2/217
Material: Lead alloy
Condition: Complete
Inscription: 1641; IDQ
Dimensions: 98.2/217: Diam 40mm; W 53mm; Dpt 6mm. A22301: Diam 36mm; W 53mm; Dpt 8mm
Description: A shallow, curving bowl with rope-twist rim. The upper part of the bowl is plain. In the centre, there is a double rose with five petals. The points of the calyx extend beyond and between the outer row of petals and between each point there is an alternating pattern of single pellets either side of a ring and dot. A wide band of foliate design surrounds the central motif, and both are contained by double concentric circles. Both of the solid, trilobate ears are decorated with pellets and volutes either side of an oval, beaded cartouche. Both cartouches are inscribed: one with the date 1641, the other with ID over Q (98.2/217 obscured by a casting fault).
Date: Probably 17th century

8.135 Porringer

Accession number: 98.2/225
Material: Lead alloy
Condition: Ears missing; some damage to bowl and rim
Dimensions: Diam 40mm; Dpt 5mm
Description: A curving bowl with a flattened base. The everted rim has a rope-twist edge and the sides are plain. In the centre there is a double rose with six petals, and the points of the calyx extend beyond and between the outer row. Pellets fill the gap between each point. A wide band of foliate design surrounds the central motif, and both are contained by double concentric circles. There is a small area of decoration on the rim indicating the position of one ear. The opposite side is damaged and part of the rim is missing.
Date: Probably 17th century
Comments: Possibly by ID or IDQ

8.136 Porringer

Accession number: 98.2/216
Material: Lead alloy
Condition: Complete
Inscription: IDQ
Dimensions: Diam 32mm; W 45mm; Dpt 3.5mm
Description: A very shallow, gently curving bowl with double ears. The rim has a rope-twist edge and most of the bowl is plain. The base is decorated with a double concentric circle, plain band, beaded circle and single ring surrounding a double rose with six petals. The points of the calyx extend beyond and between the outer row of petals. There are pellets between each point. Both of the solid, trilobate ears are decorated with volutes either side of an oval beaded cartouche identically inscribed ID above Q.
Date: Probably 17th century
Comments: Identical central design to T1, D5 below
Comparanda: Two similar porringers recovered from Queenhithe and Trig Stairs, the former with one ear extant and the latter with both missing

TYPE 1, DESIGN 5

8.137 Porringer

Accession number: 21657; 90.342/4; 98.2/218; 98.2/219*; 98.2/220; 98.2/221; 98.2/223; 98.2/224
Material: Lead alloy
Condition: 98.2/219: complete. 90.342/4; 98.2/218; 98.2/220; 98.2/221: one ear missing. 21657; 98.2/223; 98.2/224: lacking ears
Inscription: IDQ
Dimensions: Diam 29mm; W 41mm; Dpt 5mm
Description: The bowl with two ears (98.2/219) has a deeper profile to T1, D1 & D2 and the rope-twist rim is slightly everted. The central design is identical to T1, D3 above. The solid, trilobate ears are decorated with volutes either side of a cartouche, but on one side there is a beaded oval inscribed ID above Q; and on the other, the cartouche is defined by a plain line and is decorated with a stylized floral pattern composed of pellets.
Date: Probably 17th century
Comments: It is impossible to know whether Acc. nos. 98.2/ 218, 98.2/ 220, 98.2/ 221 and 98.2/224 are really the same as 98.2/219 but the overall proportions are identical. Both 98.2/218 and 98.2/220 have ID above Q; and the surviving ear on 98.2/221 is damaged. 98.2/219 was purchased with the assistance of NACF.

TYPE 1, DESIGN 6

8.138 Porringer

Accession number: 98.2/233
Material: Lead alloy
Condition: Some damage; one ear
Inscription: D[G]
Dimensions: Diam 43mm; W (one ear only) 50mm
Description: Almost completely flattened bowl, with part of one ear extant. The rope-twist rim is damaged and the area opposite the surviving ear is missing. The sides of the bowl are plain and the base is decorated with a sexfoil double rose. The points of the calyx extend beyond and between the outer petals. Between each point there is a ring and dot motif either side of a pellet. The rose is enclosed within a plain and beaded circle and there is an outer band with three pellets arranged in a trefoil pattern between ring and dots on a plain ground. The solid ear has lost the outer lobes, although part of the volute can just be seen on one side. The oval cartouche has a beaded border and is inscribed D[G].
Date: Probably 17th century
Comments: The rim opposite the ear is missing, so there may have been two ears originally. The initial D is very clear, but the second letter poses more of a problem. It does not look like a Q and may be G.

TYPE 1, DESIGN 7

8.139 Porringer

Accession number: 98.2/228
Material: Lead alloy
Condition: Almost complete; ears missing
Inscription: 1640; A H
Dimensions: Diam 36mm; Dpt 6.5mm
Description: A deep curving bowl from a double-eared porringer. The everted rim is milled and the upper part of the bowl is plain. In the centre, there is a crudely cast cinquefoil double rose. The points of the calyx extend beyond and between the outer petals, with ring and dot between each point (the ring is missing from one dot). The rose is surrounded by a decorative border inscribed 1640 and AH within an alternating pattern of a stylized sheaf of arrows, scrolling and pellets. The initials are placed so that the apex of the letters faces the rim. The rose and decorative band are both enclosed within double concentric circles. The rim bears the scars of the opposing ears, each aligned with the initials and date in the outer border.
Date: Probably 17th century

Fig. 63. Comparatively few full-scale pewter vessels have survived because many were discarded when damaged or melted down and refashioned into other objects. This battered porringer was recovered from a 17th-century rubbish dump in Finsbury. The pierced ear incorporates the initials AHL. Diam 133mm
Museum of London, Acc. no. 8126

TYPE 1, DESIGN 8

8.140 Porringer

Accession number: 98.2/226
Material: Lead alloy
Condition: Part of one ear only; one ear missing
Dimensions: Diam 35mm; W 39mm; Dpt 3mm
Description: An extremely flat porringer with part of one ear extant. The bowl has a slightly everted, beaded rim with straight, sloping sides and a flattish base. The sides of the bowl are plain and the base has three concentric circles consisting of crescents, rings and pellets. There is a swirling, quasi-floral motif in the centre. Part of the ear, decorated with radial lines and beading, is extant, and there is a scar on the edge of the rim on the opposite side.
Date: Probably 17th century

TYPE 1, DESIGN 9

8.141 Porringer

Accession number: 98.2/242
Material: Lead alloy
Condition: Poor; very worn and distorted; ears missing
Dimensions: Diam 35mm; Dpt *c.* 11mm
Description: A deep curving bowl, decorated four concentric circles, a beaded circle and a large double rose in the centre. The vessel is extremely worn and distorted. There are two stubs on the rim indicating the position of the ears.
Date: Probably 17th century

TYPE 1, DESIGN 10

8.142 Porringer

Accession number: 98.2/235
Material: Lead alloy
Condition: Worn; part of one ear extant
Dimensions: Diam 30mm; W 33mm; Dpt 1.5mm
Description: A flattened porringer with part of one ear extant. The very shallow curving bowl has a plain bevel-edged rim. There is a sexfoil double rose with calyx points in the centre, surrounded by a series of concentric circles: plain, beaded and an outer band with chevron decoration. The rounded stub of one ear survives with traces of relief decoration, and the rim on the opposite side is slightly scarred, suggesting another ear at this point. There is some damage.
Date: Probably 17th century

TYPE 1, DESIGN 11

8.143 Porringer

Accession number: 98.2/318; 98.2/319*
Material: Lead alloy
Condition: Incomplete; ears missing
Dimensions: Diam 28mm; Dpt 3mm
Description: Two very shallow bowls with plain, slightly bevelled rims. The central motif consists of a sexfoil double rose surrounded by inner beaded and outer double concentric circles. The ear stubs on one (98.2/319) have traces of decoration.
Date: Probably 17th century

TYPE 2

These porringers have a single pierced ear and were probably produced from the mid- to late 17th century.

TYPE 2, DESIGN 1

8.144 Porringer

Accession number: 98.2/222
Material: Lead alloy
Condition: Almost complete; ear missing
Inscription: IDQ
Dimensions: Diam 38mm; Dpt 5mm
Description: A gently sloping bowl with a slightly raised centre, perhaps the remains of a central boss, now flattened. The rope-twist rim is complete, and although the single ear is missing, there is an angled projection on one side with rope-twist decoration which marks its original position. The finished edges of the stub suggest a pierced handle. The centre of the bowl is decorated with a double rose of five petals, and the points of the calyx extend beyond and between the petals. There is a ring and dot motif between each point. Although the rose is surrounded by a wide foliate band of identical design to T1, D1, this band contains a plain, oval cartouche inscribed with the initials I D and Q below interspersed with pellets. The cartouche is directly aligned with the plane of the ear. The rose and foliate border are both contained within double concentric circles. The upper part of the bowl is plain.
Date: Probably 17th century
Comments: The cartouche was presumably added to the foliate border, because the ear is pierced.

TYPE 2, DESIGN 2

8.145 Porringer

Accession number: 98.2/234
Material: Lead alloy
Condition: Almost complete; ear missing
Dimensions: Diam 35mm; Dpt 4.5mm
Description: The wide, shallow bowl curves towards the flat base which has a very slight central boss, decorated with a rosette (there are six inner and four outer petals). There are eight calyx points which extend beyond the outer petals. The rosette is enclosed within double concentric circles with beading between each ring. Only the stubs of the ear remain, jutting out from the rim edge.
Date: Probably 17th century
Comments: The rim stubs suggest that this porringer had a pierced ear which has since snapped off.

TYPE 3

These porringers are distinguished by a single solid ear and they probably date from the mid-to late 17th century.

TYPE 3, DESIGN 1

8.146 Porringer

Accession number: 98.2/231
Material: Lead alloy
Condition: Almost complete; ear missing; some damage
Inscription: AB
Dimensions: Diam 33mm; Dpt 4.5mm
Description: A fairly deep bowl with a sloping profile and flat base from a one-eared porringer. The rope-twist rim is quite wide and everted. The upper part of the bowl is plain and the base is decorated in the centre with a double rose of six petals. The rose is surrounded by a wide border decorated with foliate scrolling and the initials AB, and both are contained within double concentric circles. The baseline of the letters rests on the outer edge of the foliate band, directly below a scarred area of rim which seems to be where the ear (now missing) was attached.
Date: Probably 17th century

TYPE 3, DESIGN 2

8.147 Porringer

Accession number: 98.2/230
Material: Lead alloy
Condition: Almost complete; ear missing
Inscription: AB
Dimensions: Diam 33.5mm; Dpt 3.5mm
Description: A shallow bowl with a wide everted, rope-twist rim. The single ear is missing. The upper part of the bowl is plain. In the centre there is a six-petalled double rose, and the points of the calyx extend beyond and between the outer petals. There is a ring and dot motif between each point. The rose is surrounded by a wide foliate border incorporating the initials AB with their baseline on the outer edge. There are two ring and dot motifs, one between the A and B and the other on the opposing side nearest the ear. The rose and foliate band are both contained within double concentric circles.
Date: Probably 17th century

TYPE 3, DESIGN 3

8.148 Porringer

Accession number: 98.2/232
Material: Lead alloy
Condition: Almost complete; ear missing
Inscription: AB
Dimensions: Diam 36mm; Dpt 3mm
Description: A shallow bowl with a wide flat base and wide everted rope-twist rim. The single ear is missing. The upper part of the bowl is plain. In the centre, there is a six-petalled double rose with the points of the calyx extending beyond and between the outer petals. There are pellets between each point. The rose is enclosed by a foliate band containing the initials AB, with a line of three pellets between each letter. Both letters have a partially wriggled profile, and the cap heights point to the rim. The initials are positioned opposite the ear. The rose and foliate band are both contained within double concentric circles.
Date: Probably 17th century

TYPE 3, DESIGN 4

8.149 Porringer

Accession number: 98.2/229
Material: Lead alloy
Condition: Almost complete; ear missing
Inscription: AF
Dimensions: Diam 34mm; Dpt 5mm
Description: A single-eared porringer with a wide shallow bowl and wide everted rim. The edge of the rim is beaded and the flange is decorated with relief slashing. There is a scar on one side indicating the position of the ear (now missing). The upper part of the bowl is plain. In the centre, there is a six-petalled double rose surrounded by a few pellets and a wide foliate band, inscribed AF. The decoration is extremely worn and faint. Both the rose and foliate band are enclosed within double concentric circles. There is some damage.
Date: Probably 17th century

TYPE 3, DESIGN 5

8.150 Porringer

Accession number: 98.2/241
Material: Lead alloy
Condition: Almost complete; ear missing
Dimensions: Diam 28mm; Dpt 6mm
Description: A deep curving bowl from a one-eared porringer. The rope-twist rim is slightly everted; the sides of the bowl are plain. The base is decorated with a sexfoil double rose enclosed within a sexfoil of double lines and double concentric circle.
Date: Probably 17th century

TYPE 3, DESIGN 6

8.151 Porringer

Accession number: 98.2/240
Material: Lead alloy
Condition: Poor; some damage
Dimensions: Diam 22mm; W 28mm; Dpt 3mm
Description: A single-eared porringer with a very shallow bowl with a rather angular profile. The slightly bevelled rim is defined by a circumferential ridge and the upper part of the bowl is plain. There is a cinquefoil double rose in the centre enclosed within a plain circle. Only part of the probable trilobate solid ear survives.
Date: Probably 17th century

TYPE 3, DESIGN 7

8.152 Porringer

Accession number: 98.2/238
Material: Lead alloy
Condition: Poor; part missing; one ear extant; flattened
Dimensions: Diam 38mm
Description: Part of the extremely flat, shallow bowl is missing. The wide rim has a beaded edge and the flange is decorated with oblique slashing. The centre of the bowl is decorated with a very large cinquefoil double rose. The points of the calyx extend beyond and between the outer petals and there are ring and dot motifs between each point. There is one fan-shaped solid ear with a scalloped edge.
Date: Probably 17th century
Comment: This porringer is too damaged to be certain whether it originally had one or two ears.

TYPE 3, DESIGN 8

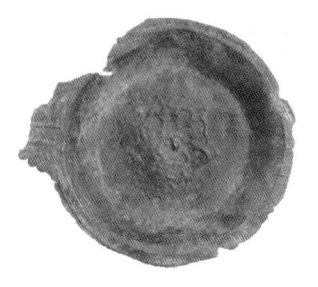

8.153 Porringer

Accession number: 98.2/237
Material: Lead alloy
Condition: Almost complete
Dimensions: Diam 33mm; W 38mm; Dpt 4.5mm
Description: A one-eared porringer with shallow, angular-profiled bowl and wide milled flange. The sides of the bowl are plain, and the flat base has a poorly cast and worn double rose in the centre. The points of the calyx extend beyond and between the outer petals of the rose. Most of the triangular, scallop-edged ear survives and there is a decorative band down the centre. There is some damage and the porringer is very worn.
Date: Probably 17th century

TYPE 3, DESIGN 9

8.154 Porringer

Accession number: 98.2/236
Material: Lead alloy
Condition: Almost complete
Dimensions: Diam 33.5 mm; W 38mm; Dpt 6mm
Description: A shallow bowl with straight, sloping sides and a slightly domed base. The rim is beaded, and the sides of the bowl are plain. The domed area of the base is defined by a milled circle, and there is a sexfoil single rose with calyx points in the centre. Part of the solid ear survives with faint traces of relief decoration.
Date: Probably 17th century
Comments: Similar profile to Acc. nos. 98.2/237 and 98.2/244.

TYPE 3, DESIGN 10

8.155 Porringer

Accession number: 98.2/244
Material: Lead alloy
Condition: Almost complete
Dimensions: Diam 27mm; W 30mm; Dpt 4.5mm
Description: A shallow bowl with straight sloping sides and a domed base. The rim is beaded and the bowl is plain apart from a stylized central rosette (there are seven 'petals') in high relief, with seven calyx points. The base is defined by a plain circle with an inner ring of eight pellets, regularly spaced around the circumference. The apex of a possible trilobate-shaped ear is missing, and the base lobes are decorated with scrolls.
Date: Probably 17th century

48 A miniature 'flat cup' similar to Acc. no. 98.2/179, but with a band of decoration below the rim and around the foot, was recovered from a late 15th-century context in the Lange Houtstraat, Amsterdam in 1972: see Baart *et al.* 1977, pp. 465–6, no. 882, now in the collections of the Amsterdams Historisch Museum (inv. no. MW 7–30).

49 Swift, J., *Baucis And Philemon, imitated from the eighth book of Ovid* (London, 1709), ch. 5.

50 Pearce 1992, p. 17.

51 An early single-eared porringer is illustrated in Hornsby *et al.* 1989, p. 32, fig. 30.

52 Lidded commemorative porringers incorporating a rose and foliate band were made during the 1680s and 90s and these have similar ornamentation to the toy porringers recorded here: see *JPS* 2 (3) (1980), pp.15 & 20. I am grateful to Ron Homer for his advice on these objects.

53 This porringer (with a diameter of 70mm and a cast pierced ear with CR in relief) is now in the collections of the Worshipful Company of Pewterers (no. S5/501.32). For similar vessels see Cotterell 1939, pp. 121–3, fig. 14; Michaelis 1971, plate 38, fig. 87 mid-17th century in author's collection, and in Bell 1906, p. 159 and plates 57 and 69.

54 Michaelis, July 1949, pp. 23–6 & September 1949, pp. 46–8.

55 Ron Homer, pers. comm.

56 Baart 1977, p. 466, no. 884 and Willemsen 1998, p. 378, B75. All of these toy porringers have two pierced trilobate ears.

57 Porringers made by I(D)Q and AB were made in two sizes.

58 Possibly DQ: see Cat no. 8.138.

59 It is possible that T1, D1, Acc. no. 98.2/217 dated 1641 is also an I(D)Q piece.

60 The earliest recorded silver miniature is a repoussé porringer, fully hallmarked for 1653 (maker's mark indistinct), diam 38mm, with two scroll ears and a central rose within a chased foliate band (Christie's, Wednesday 11 October 1972, lot 29). See also other silver porringers by Nathaniel Lock of Blackwell Hall Court, Cripplegate, dating from 1695–1712.

61 GL MS 7106, 6 May 1689. Grateful thanks to Ron Homer for this reference.

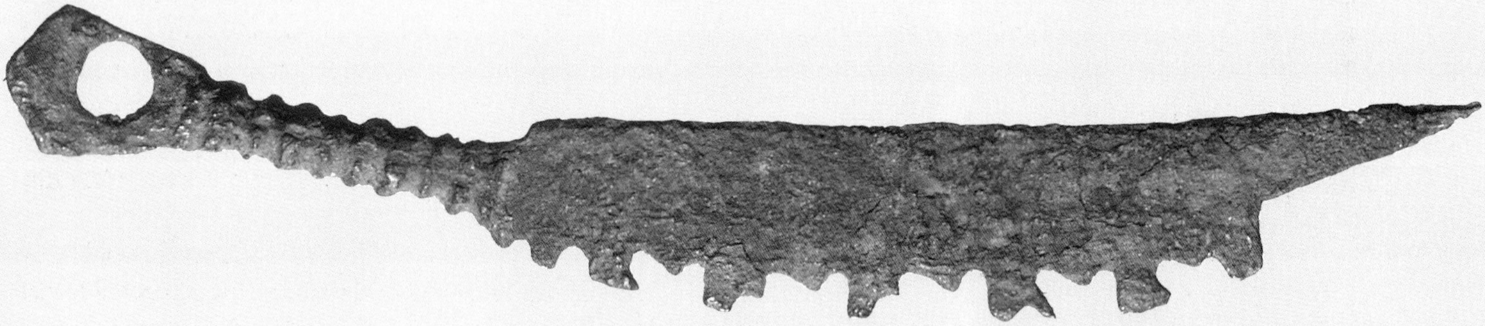

9 Tools

'All sorts of saws, for Joiner's Use, are to be sold in most Iron-monger's Shops, but especially in Foster-lane, London'[1]

Many different kinds of tool have been recovered from excavations but comparable objects in small scale are extremely scarce and the three items in this collection are the only examples known in Britain.

Despite the paucity of toy tools in the archaeological corpus and the uncertain attribution of the finds in this collection, base-metal toy and miniature tools were probably produced in some quantity from the late medieval period onwards to represent the major tools in everyday use, and their absence should not be taken as a measure of the relative importance of this category of toy in the past. After all, toy and miniature household articles, pots and pans and cooking utensils were made for little girls, so it is quite likely that a range of toy and miniature tools were made for the amusement and education of young boys.

While it would be unwise to draw any particular conclusions about this class of material from the few surviving examples, it is interesting and possibly significant that two out of the three items are made from copper alloy. This material was presumably chosen in preference to the weaker lead alloy so that the tools could withstand gentle use, and experiments show that the shears have a fine edge on the blades and a good spring action, and the saw has a very sharp point with teeth capable of scoring wood. Perhaps all of the toy tools were designed to work in a limited capacity, and even the weaker lead-alloy scissor blade has a cast pivot hole, which implies that the complete object had some sort of scissor action. If these objects saw heavy use, they might have been damaged and broken beyond repair, and any surviving fragments could be easily overlooked in the soil.

While it would be difficult to interpret the lead-alloy scissor blade as anything other than a toy, it is possible that the other objects served an entirely different purpose, and might have been made as some sort of craft trinket.[2] The copper-alloy saw and shears could have been made to adorn a hat or cloak like some of the lead-alloy tools and workaday objects which were made in miniature form as secular badges and pendants in the medieval period, which might explain the presence of the suspension loop in the saw handle.[3] But since the saw has an extremely sharp blade tip and jagged teeth, which could easily rend fabric and injure the wearer, it would have had limited appeal as an ornamental trinket. Moreover, the saw is a complete nonsense and bears little resemblance to contemporary images and surviving examples, and it is unlikely that a craftsman would choose to wear an inaccurately modelled object to reflect his trade, even as a joke. Another possibility is that the saw was made as a whimsical cosmetic implement, but it has been included here in the belief that it was made for the toy market by makers who either disregarded or misinterpreted the salient features and mechanics of the genuine article. If the finished object looked sufficiently like the real thing to appeal to a child, it would sell.

The attribution of the shear-like object is equally problematic. Geoff Egan has noted the striking similarity between this piece and silver attachment fastenings on the back of some 16th-century hat badges.[4] Unlike the fastenings, however, this object is made from copper alloy and has oblique cuts at the ends of the blades, rather than the rounded profile typically seen on a fixing loop, and there is no trace of solder. So have we misinterpreted this object? If it is not a standard fixing, was it adapted into a pair of toy shears by a resourceful toymaker, or was it simply made as a toy in the first place?

Handsaw

Small handsaws with curving blades, cross-cut teeth and straight or angled handles were widely used by shipwrights and carpenters throughout the medieval and early modern period. No examples have survived in England before the late 15th century, but pictorial evidence suggests that most had a ferrule between the blade and handle, or a circular guard to protect the hand.

The toy saw looks reasonably convincing at first glance, but closer examination shows that it is a bizarre amalgam of different styles and elements and nothing like the genuine article. The pierced terminal and the mixture of single and double teeth is unparalleled on a real saw, and the inclusion of the M-shaped tooth is anomalous. The M-shaped tooth is a particular feature of the two man cross-cut saw which was introduced in the 15th century to cut in both directions,[5] and therefore has no place on a handsaw which only works on the pushing stroke. The teeth also stop short of the tip of the blade and are disproportionately large.[6] It is possible that this object was made as an ornament because of the pierced terminal, and it is even conceivable that it was used as a fanciful toothpick which might explain the very sharp point and lack of teeth towards the tip of the blade.

TYPE 1, DESIGN 1

9.1 Handsaw

Accession number: 98.2/546
Material: Copper alloy
Condition: Complete
Dimensions: L 55mm
Description: Cast in one piece with a straight back and curving, scimitar-shaped blade. There are alternating single cross-cut teeth and double M-shaped teeth which stop abruptly 7mm from the plain, sharply pointed toe. The narrow cylindrical handle has a ribbed grip and terminates in a flat trapezoid-pieced finial.
Date: Late 15th–early 17th century

Shears

Various attempts have been made to establish a chronology and typology for the spring shear, but because the basic form has barely altered since its first appearance in the Late Bronze Age, shears are generally difficult to date. To compound the problem, subtle differences in decoration and outline, and wide variations in overall size and proportion, suggest that certain types were made for a particular purpose, and some forms were made concurrently. Recent analysis of shears from well-dated contexts in the City of London have provided additional evidence, however, and certain design trends can now be attributed more firmly to a particular period.[7]

The toy shears do not correspond exactly to any known full-scale examples, although the overall shape is reasonably convincing. Angled blade tips are common on full-scale shears during the late 14th and early 15th centuries although these, unlike the toy, have tapering blades to the tip and a curved upper edge. The toy shears still have a fairly sharp cutting edge and are robust enough to be used.

TYPE 1, DESIGN 1

9.2 Shears

Accession number: 98.2/570
Material: Copper alloy
Condition: Complete
Dimensions: L 36mm
Description: A pair of shears with a plain loop, wide blades and angled tips
Date: Very difficult to date; possibly late 14th–early 15th century

Scissors

While scissors were used in the early medieval period, they did not become widespread until the 16th century. By the 17th century the blades begin to widen, the handles generally terminate in large oval loops and the pivot point drops slightly below the junction of the blade and handle shaft.

The toy blade has a horizontal line just above the pivot point which seems to represent the ridge which is usually found at the top of scissor blades from the mid-17th century, but unlike the genuine article there is no handle shaft between the blade and finger loop, and one side of the blade is decorated with an elaborate scrolling design. It is possible, although perhaps not very likely, that the same mould was used to create a companion blade. If so, the scissors would have had ill-matched sides. Experiments with paper cut-outs suggest that the scissors would have opened and shut reasonably well, but the pivot hole on the toy shows little sign of wear.

TYPE 1, DESIGN 1

9.3 Scissors

Accession number: 98.2/571
Material: Lead alloy
Condition: One blade only
Dimensions: L 46mm
Description: One half of a pair of scissors (right side), cast in one piece with asymmetrically placed loop handle. The parallel-sided blade has an angled tip. The exterior face is decorated with scrolled moulding, and the back has fine cross-hatching. There is a small aperture or pivot point at the base of the blade.
Date: 17th–mid-18th century

---

1 Joesph Moxon, *Mechanick Exercises or the Doctrine of Handy-Works* (London, 1703).

2 Egan 1996, p. 9.

3 See references to 15th-century pewter pendants in the form of a curry comb in Spencer 1990, pp. 111–2, fig. 279 and 1998, pp. 312–3, fig. 310a.

4 See Hackenbroch 1969, p. 380, cat. nos. 327, 330 & 328.

5 Goodman 1964, pp. 143–5.

6 I am grateful to John Clark for his advice and comments on this object.

7 Cowgill *et al.* 1987.

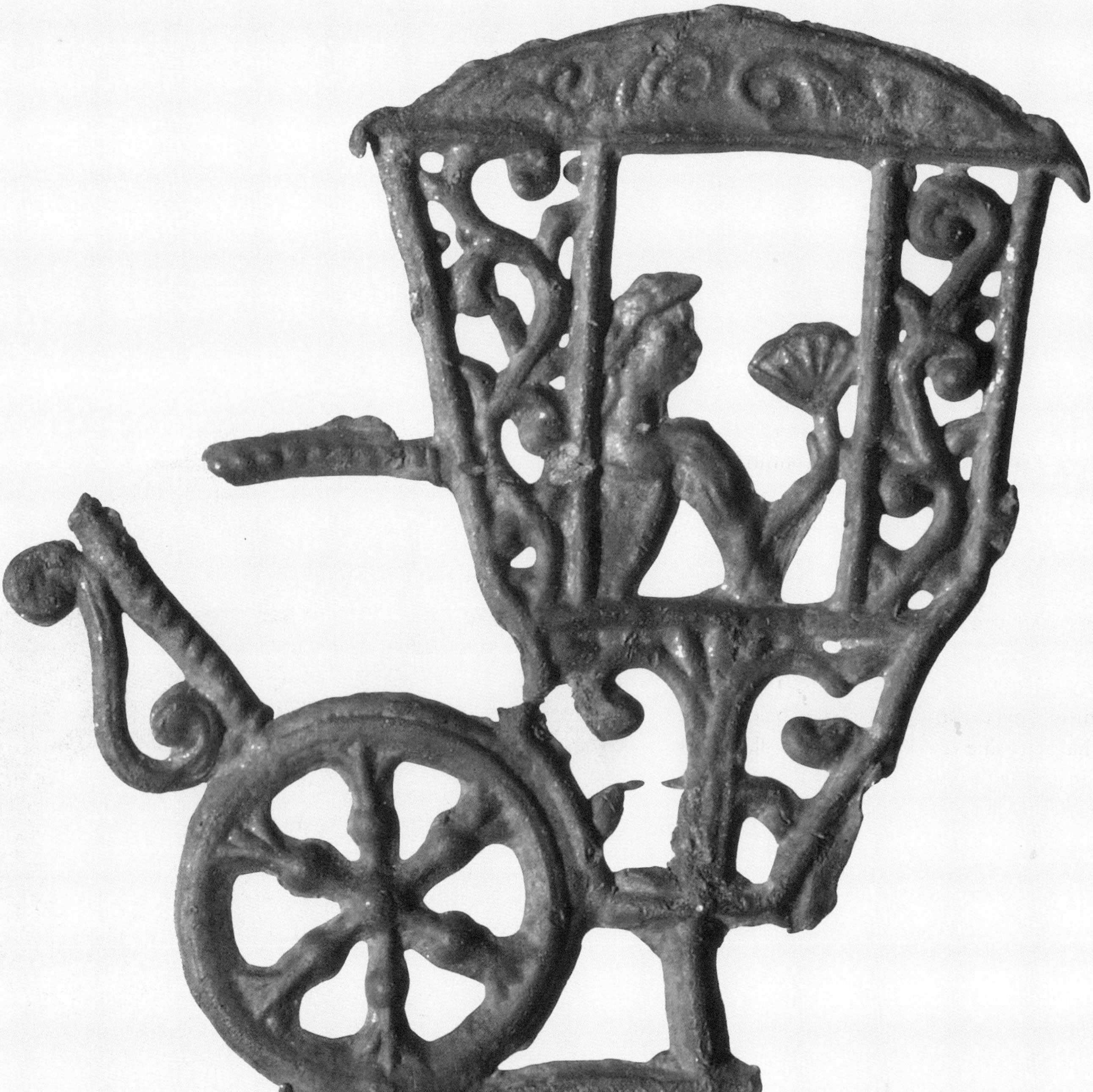

10 Transport (GE)

*'This is a rattling, rowling and rumbling age.
The world runs on wheels'*[1]

Wheeled playthings are so familiar today that it is difficult to imagine a time when they were not around. Although carriages of many forms were available to the rich in the Middle Ages, and carts for transporting goods, including rural produce, probably had an even longer history, the earliest miniature wheeled items that can be identified with certainty in England seem to be from the late 16th or very early 17th century. The remarkable three-dimensional toys or trinkets listed below seem to have become very popular. Lead-alloy ships were apparently not so common, but they appear to have spanned about the same period as the coaches.

Carriages and coaches

Coaches have a long history that is imperfectly understood prior to a period around the middle of the 16th century when they seem suddenly to have become much more plentiful and fashionable.[2] This may relate to improvements in the technology of springs and in the quality of roads. Both would make riding in these vehicles significantly more comfortable, and so the time was right for them to come to the fore as ornate, very expensive status symbols of the rich. The earliest of the toys below probably made their appearance after coaches, having gained this fresh cachet, began to become much more numerous.

As Crofts notes in his analysis of early coaches, 'the type … that set an entirely new standard in English coach-building was the Pomeranian: beautifully timbered and decorated by German craftsmen, and slung on leather braces. Metal spring shackles were also used for suspension'.[3] Although large, these coaches were light enough to be drawn quite easily by two horses. The best coaches of this kind were made in Pomerania. These could be purchased in London, with a set of spare wheels, for a princely sum. The 1576 accounts of Sir Henry Sidney's Steward of the Stillyard record: 'In primis for sending one man into the country of Pomerland by my said lordes appoyntment to provide a strong cowche with all maner of furniture therto belonging and covered with leather, and viij wheles for the same cowche: which cowche being made with furniture for iiij horse: also one manne to attend and govern the same: with the charges of conveing the same to London: cost £42.10s'.[4] By 1613 there were some 430 coaches in London and in 1636 one contemporary noted that there were upwards of 6,000.[5] The ornate openwork of many of the miniatures presumably represents the opulent carving and other embellishments of the finest coaches of the aristocracy. Lavish upholstery and elaborate trimmings often cost far more than the coach itself.[6]

The fragments of composite, two-horse coach trinkets listed below have openwork trapezoid travelling compartments tapering from the wide top to the base. These finds represent all the component parts of what was obviously a popular and long-lasting plaything. Male and female passengers look out of the opposing door windows with only

Fig. 64. A carriage pulls up outside Old Corney House in Chiswick.
Detail from *Chiswick from the River*, c. 1675–80 by Jacob Knyff [1639–1681]
Oil on canvas, 81.9cm x 159.4 cm
Museum of London, Acc. no. 62.32

their top halves visible. This raises the question of whether the frames originally had an internal sheet foil to give the impression of solidity, or the conventional openwork was readily seen as ornate decoration on a flat ground – probably the latter in view of the slightly later, two-dimensional form (Cat. no. 10.10). The horses' legs suggest movement where they survive. The three-dimensional coaches seem to have been constructed from eight (?) component parts: the sides and base of the frame in one piece (probably together with the horses); once the sides and base had been folded to make the three-dimensional frame, the separate top and front (with the liveried driver, who holds a whip) and back panels were attached with tabs; the axles (each cast integrally with one wheel) were then pushed through opposing loops at the bottom of the frame, and the other wheel was then soldered on each to retain the freely rotating axle unit in place.

There are apparently several varieties of two basic versions – Type 1, Designs 1 and 2. Some versions are slightly rougher than others and are therefore likely to have been copies. The changing clothing fashions of the passengers should provide close dating, but a range of suggestions have been made for some of them. The period represented seems to be the late 16th and 17th centuries, at its broadest perhaps lasting about a century. The sustained popularity of these complicated, attractive toys is matched by their inherent vulnerability. The survival of the many fragments recovered is remarkable in view of the flimsiness of most of the component parts, whoever owned them and whatever their function.

It can be no coincidence that very similar three-dimensional items are known on the Continent.[7] More surprisingly, the Matchbox toy Coronation coach souvenirs from 1953 are so closely comparable, with the horses even being attached to the shafts in precisely the same way, that, were it not for the intervening two and a half centuries, direct copying would be suspected.

The early 18th-century flat version listed below, with a woman passenger flexing a fan, retains the openwork tradition (Cat. no. 10.10). In contrast, the man-in-chaise flats that may be of about the same date, are much more realistically portrayed. Three versions of these are known, which can be differentiated by the vertical or angled struts of the chair, the number of spokes in the wheel, and whether the vehicle advances to the left or right (Cat. nos. 10.11–10.13). Presumably at least one version is an illicit copy (perhaps two). The curiously hunched, hatted passenger/driver adds little attraction to what was obviously a popular plaything despite his brooding presence: is it possible that a recognized character like the latter-day sullen cabbie is represented here?

TYPE 1

TYPE 1, DESIGN 1

10.1 Coach with two occupants

Accession number: 80.536/2; 2001.20/6
Material: Lead alloy
Condition: Incomplete. 80.536/2: five separated pieces plus axle
Dimensions: 80.536/2: H 38mm; W 45mm; Dpt 18mm
    2001.20/6: H 33mm; W 36mm
Description: Part of a multi-component three-dimensional coach, originally with two occupants. The flimsy base consists of a central ring retained by a bar at each pole joined to the rectangular frame, which has two pairs of holed tabs for attaching the other components to the front and back. The two passengers, integrally cast with the main side-parts of the frame, each look out of their door, one on each side (the most complete versions of similar toys suggest there was one woman and one man). The complete male figure wears a round-crowned and broad-brimmed hat with a plume, and has loose, curling shoulder-length hair and a tight-fitting buttoned doublet. The headless female wears a vertically ribbed, long-sleeved bodice with a low, curving neckline. Both have their arms bent at the elbows and

their hands rest on the door frame. The frame of the coach tapers towards the base and the symmetrical sides (one is almost complete) are filled in with openwork scrolling. The lower door panels are each decorated with an ornate, openwork quatrefoil; large, S-shaped openwork scrolls at either end of the side panels may possibly represent springs. One axle survives, minus its wheels. Acc .no. 2001.20/6 has one virtually complete side with a male passenger (voids in the openwork are from a casting bubble); although there is some perfunctory hatching, this lacks the delicacy of that on the other example.

Date: Suggestions of date range from late 16th–mid-17th century

TYPE 1, DESIGN 2

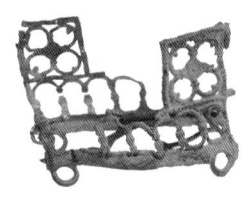

10.2 Coach

Accession number: 98.2/424
Material: Lead alloy
Condition: Incomplete
Dimensions: H 22mm; L 32mm; W 15mm
Description: The base and parts of the trapezoidal sides survive. The openwork is more delicate than in Cat. nos. 10.3 & 10.4. The rectangular base contains a structural ring that is held in place with transverse and longitudinal bars and there are opposing angular loops at each end to which the end panels were fixed. A solid band at the base of the side panels is decorated with randomly spaced wavy mouldings and in each corner there are opposing simple round lugs for the missing wheel axles. The frame sides are decorated with two registers of openwork; at the top, on either side of the window aperture, are square panels with quatrefoil grille ornament, and below, running across the entire width, is a band of arcading. The uprights separating each arcade have a central knop, which is suggestive of turned work, and the outline of the frame is embellished with diagonal hatching. A relatively delicate casting. The arcading and the mouldings of the wheels are reminiscent of the detailing on a few other items of somewhat earlier date.[8]

Date: 16th century

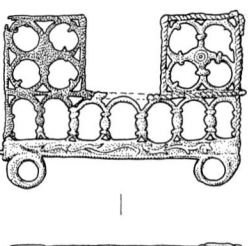

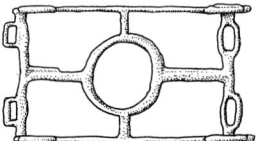

TYPE 1, DESIGN 3

10.3 Coach side with occupant

Accession number: 98.2/418
Material: Lead alloy
Condition: Almost complete side of frame
Dimensions: H 20mm; L 35mm
Description: An almost complete side from a multi-component three-dimensional coach. The basic openwork design of the trapezoidal frame is identical to Cat. no. 10.2, apart from the solid band along the base that has tendril mouldings. There is the stub of a tab, part of the axle loop and a tiny fragment of the base armature. Looking out through the door window is a female passenger with long, loose hair, an open ruff and a tight, low-cut bodice with a laced stomacher (?).

Date: Possibly late 16th century

TYPE 1, DESIGN 4

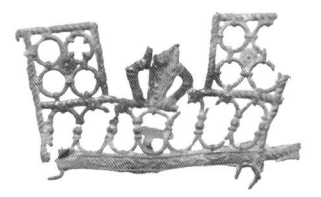

10.4 Coach side with occupant

Accession number: 98.2/419
Material: Lead alloy
Condition: Almost complete component
Dimensions: H 20mm; L *c.* 38mm
Description: An almost complete side from a multi-component three-dimensional coach. The trapezoidal frame has almost identical mouldings to Cat. nos. 10.2 and 10.3, apart from the quatrefoil grilles that have more prominent 'collars'. There is a large window aperture and a headless male (?) passenger with tight-fitting doublet and buttoned jerkin looks out. Parts of the axle loops survive and extending from the base moulding on the right side is a diagonally hatched bar, possibly part of the horse's tail (see Acc. no. 82.353/14). A fragment of the basal armature also survives.
Date: Possibly late 16th century

TYPE 1, DESIGN 5

10.5 Coach side with occupant

Accession number: 98.2/428
Material: Lead alloy
Condition: Almost complete component
Dimensions: H 18mm; L *c.* 40mm
Description: Almost complete side from a multi-component three-dimensional coach. The long, trapezoidal openwork frame has two horizontal divisions: above a solid base band of foliate mouldings is a line of arcading with knops on the uprights to suggest turning. A square panel to the left of the window contains a single ring with ring and dot 'collars'. A male passenger with a small hat, brushed-up hair, tight-fitting doublet and trunk hose (?) looks out of the door. He is in the same pose as in Cat. nos. 10.3 and 10.4. Axle loops (incomplete) extend from the lower corners.
Date: Late 16th century
Provenance: Entrance to Queenhithe Dock
Comments: Found close to, and possibly originally associated with, a front panel (Acc. no. 98.2/420) and horses (Acc. nos. 98.2/421 & 98.2/426).

TYPE 1, DESIGN 6

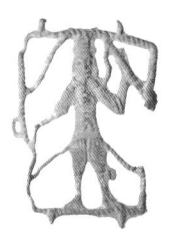

10.6 Coach front panel with driver

Accession number: 98.2/420
Material: Lead alloy
Condition: Almost complete component
Dimensions: H 27mm; W 20mm
Description: A roughly rectangular openwork panel from a multi-component three-dimensional coach. The diagonally hatched frame is slightly wider at the top and three diagonal struts support the crudely moulded standing figure of a driver. He holds a whip in his raised left hand and wears a high-crowned, conical hat, doublet, trunk hose, nether stockings and garter.
Date: Possibly 16th century
Provenance: Entrance to Queenhithe Dock
Comments: Found close to, and possibly originally associated with, a side panel (Acc. no. 98.2/428) and horses (Acc. nos. 98.2/421 & 98.2/426).

TYPE 1, DESIGN 7

10.7 Coach frame with horse
Accession number: 82.353/14
Material: Lead alloy
Condition: Slight damage; pieces missing; much worn
Dimensions: H 24mm; W 36mm; Dpt 16mm
Description: Part of the lower right side of an openwork coach frame and integrally cast horse, profile to right. The arcaded mouldings of the frame are very similar to those described in T1, D1–5. The horse's harness includes a rein hanger, loin strap, breechband and pole. Joined to the casting seam on the back are two lateral bars, one serving as a spacer and support for the other horse (now missing) and the other, probably part of the base of the frame.
Date: Possibly 16th century

TYPE 1, DESIGN 8

10.8 Coach horse
Accession number: 98.2/421; 98.2/426
Material: Lead alloy
Condition: Almost complete; front leg missing
Dimensions: H 26mm; W *c.* 30mm
Description: These horses are virtually identical to T1, D7, but the moulding is crisper. They have a bridle, engrailed reins, rein hanger, loin strap, breechband and breech tug. Their manes are tied with ribbons. Joined to the casting seam on the back is a lateral bar, which probably served as a spacer and support between them. Possibly a pair; one profile to right and the other profile to left.
Date: Possibly 16th century
Provenance: Entrance to Queenhithe Dock
Comments: Found close to, possibly originally associated with, Cat. nos. 10.5 & 10.6.

TYPE 1, DESIGN 9

10.9 Coach horse
Accession number: 98.2/425
Material: Lead alloy
Condition: Almost complete; tail missing
Dimensions: H 23mm; W 27mm
Description: A coach horse, profile to right, made from a different mould from that for T1, D7 and D8. The harness includes a headstall, bridle, reins, leading rein, rein hanger, loin strap, breechband and diagonally hatched pad cloth.
Date: Possibly 16th century

Fig. 65. From *La Chasse des Dames*, 15th century. See plate VIII, p. 168

TYPE 2

TYPE 2, DESIGN 1

10.10 Fragment of coach with passenger

Accession number: 98.2/416
Material: Lead alloy
Condition: Incomplete
Dimensions: H 50mm; W 50mm
Description: Part of a flat, one-sided, openwork coach, with shallow domed top, trapezoidal frame, S-shaped 'springs' and six-spoked wheel. The solid top and openwork sides are decorated with scrollwork and a female occupant looks out of the large rectangular window. She has long, loose hair and holds a fan in her hand. Her loose sleeve reaches only halfway along the forearm. There is a thin bar under the surviving wheel, presumably part of a stand, and a vertical structural support extends from the bottom of the door.
Date: The style of the coach and the passenger's garments suggest a late 17th- or early 18th-century date.

TYPE 3

TYPE 3, DESIGN 1

10.11 Chaise with driver

Accession number: 98.2/393; 98.2/394*; 98.2/397
Material: Lead alloy; red pigment
Condition: 98.2/394: almost complete; head of driver and horse missing
Dimensions: H 48mm; W *c.* 86mm
Inscription: H
Description: These flat, cast chaises (profile to left) have been cast from the same mould. The chair-like carriage has vertical and oblique mouldings suggestive of canework and rests on springs fitted to the axles. The large wheel has eight spokes and 98.2/394 includes the elongated stand and reins. The stand is inscribed with the letter H, presumably indicating the maker. The passenger has a front-buttoned coat with a deep collar.
Date: 18th century
Comments: These pieces conform closely to the most popular form of two-wheeled carriage in the 18th century: the lightly constructed chaise or whiskey. Such carriages generally had one horse.

TYPE 3, DESIGN 2

10.12 Chaise with driver

Accession number: 98.2/396
Material: Lead alloy; red pigment
Condition: Part only
Dimensions: H 35mm; W 27mm
Description: Part of a flat, cast chaise and driver, profile to right. The carriage has vertical ribbing with a beaded edge. The wheel has eight turned spokes and a very small nave. The driver (head missing) wears a front-buttoned coat.
Date: 18th century

TYPE 3, DESIGN 3

10.13 Chaise with driver

Accession number: 98.2/395
Material: Lead alloy
Condition: Almost complete; wheel damage; horse missing
Dimensions: H 45mm; W 75mm
Description: A flat, cast chaise with driver, profile to right. The shape of the carriage suggests a gig with S-shaped springs under the frame and this is supported by a 14-spoked wheel. Vertical ribbing on the chair probably represents a light-framed cane construction and the driver wears a broad, cocked hat and coat with turned-up cuffs. The vehicle is supported on a flat stand.
Date: Possibly late 18th century

Coach wheels

DESIGN 1

10.14 Coach wheel and part of axle

Accession number: 98.2/422
Material: Lead alloy
Condition: Complete component; some damage
Dimensions: Diam 19mm; L (axle – part missing) *c.* 22mm
Description: An ornate wheel with six turned and arched spokes and six felloes. Part of the axle remains soldered to the nave.
Date: Probably late 16th century
Comments: Probably from a T1 coach

DESIGN 2

10.15 Coach wheel

Accession number: 98.2/423
Material: Lead alloy
Condition: Complete component
Dimensions: Diam 20mm
Description: An elaborate wheel with six turned and arched spokes and a beaded or nailed hoop. The apex of each arch and the junctions between the spokes are secured by collars.
Date: Probably late 16th century
Comments: Probably from a T1 coach

Ships

TYPE 1, DESIGN 1

TYPE 1, DESIGN 2

10.16 English galleon

Accession number: 91.61/1*; 98.2/431
Material: Lead alloy
Condition: 91.61/1: one mast missing. 98.2/431: also missing mast tops, bowsprit and stern; repaired after being found broken almost in two
Dimensions: H 46mm; W 66mm
Inscription: E
Description: These two flat, one-sided ships have been made from the same mould. The vessels, shown from the port side, have three masts, a fairly high fo'castle and poop, and long, curving stempost and bowsprit.[9] There is one gun firing astern from the upper deck and six firing from the lower (three angled towards the bow and three towards the stern). The lower deck is very close to the waterline. The fore and mainmasts carry topmasts and furled sails; the mizzen mast seems to have a partially unfurled lateen sail. A pennant flag hangs from the foremast tree. A crewman or herald stands on the foredeck with a trumpet to his lips. He wears a high conical hat, doublet, trunk hose and nether stockings and the trumpet banner is inscribed with the letter E.
Date: Late 16th century
Provenance: 98.2/431: Billingsgate foreshore, 1981
Comments: The style of the seaman's clothing suggests a late 16th-century date, so the letter E presumably stands for Elizabeth I. 98.2/431 might be a souvenir of the defeat of the Spanish Armada: see Egan 1988. However, the discovery of a very similar trinket in the Netherlands (apparently with a letter L in place of E) means not all such items were connected to a single event or national cause. It now looks likely that the few such items known are the first discoveries from a distinct series of toys with international appeal.
Comparandum: A more complete version in a private collection in the Netherlands (where the banner appears to have an L inscribed on it).

10.17 Three-masted ship

Accession number: 98.2/432
Material: Lead alloy; traces of pigment
Condition: Incomplete; tops of masts missing
Dimensions: H 29mm; W 63mm
Inscription: H
Description: A flat, one-sided, three-masted warship with a single gun deck and prominent leonine figurehead.[10] The vessel is shown from the starboard side and all ten guns point astern, with conventional splayed lines indicating that they are firing. The ship is supported by a centrally placed stand with the letter H, presumably indicating the maker.
Date: Probably 1660–75

Anchors

The identification of some of the items listed in this section as miniature anchors – that is, accessories for small toy vessels – is open to doubt. Indeed, this category exemplifies in an extreme form many of the difficulties of interpretation when considering whether or not the objects catalogued in this volume were in fact children's playthings. The finders believe the present items were all recovered from 18th- or possibly late 17th-century deposits. The capability of some three-dimensional forms of anchors to get dragged down into the gravel deposits that characterize much of the foreshore, and the possibility that some might have been placed in holes especially dug to secure the miniature wooden ships they may have been attached to, means that dating is not straightforward.

In all, five distinct forms can be distinguished among the items listed. Anchors are themselves difficult to date typologically, with satisfactory forms lasting for centuries. Ones apparently similar to Types 1 and 3 are represented respectively in the Bayeux Tapestry and a 12th-century manuscript.[11] Both copper alloy and lead (apparently unalloyed in most instances) are present among the miniatures. Those of copper alloy, which certainly seem all to be post-medieval, are generally better finished than the lead or lead-alloy ones, some of which are extremely crude. Indeed, some of the latter seem very unlikely to have served as accessories for what would have been a very limited few of the most detailed model ships at the top of the range (such a level of detail is implied by the remains of wire chains in Acc. nos. 98.2/687 & 98.2/694). It is possible that 'toy' anchors might have been restricted to items of copper alloy that went with models made and used by seasoned seafarers, begging the question of what the lead-alloy items were for.

Limited comparanda discovered elsewhere are assigned to the 17th to 19th century. A lead example from Amsterdam like T3 (published as early 17th-century),[12] a copper-alloy 'pendant' very similar to Acc. no. 98.2/694 (from an early 19th-century coastal fort in Essex)[13] and another lead comparandum for T1 (excavated from an 18th-century context in America)[14] probably had nothing at all to do with playthings (see below). Mitchiner's claim that a miniature lead anchor from Greenwich is an early 16th-century 'badge of St Clement for the Guild of Bakers' should be regarded with suspicion on both counts.[15]

Fishing tackle of fanciful design may perhaps in the riverine context of the Thames account for some of the objects below. The use of lead in some fishing equipment would have distinct advantages over lighter metals. A few of the cruder items of relatively simple form (Acc. nos. 98.2/690 & 98.2/704) could be seen as analogous to a series of relatively early medieval lead weights identified among finds from Dublin (but this would go completely against the finders' perceptions of dating). Very small, flat versions of medieval date could perhaps be parts of Becket souvenir badges of ship form from the medieval period,[16] but again this does not appear to apply to any of the listed items. The symbolism of anchors as tokens of hope means there may have been a wide range of other possible roles for objects of this form – parts of jewellery or furnishings (the lead anchor found in the US near the site of an 18th-century brass foundry is probably an instance of the latter, a master form used with clay moulds for casting multiple products in copper alloy or silver).[17]

Fig. 66. In this 1833 view of new London Bridge from Billingsgate, a small boy has taken advantage of the low tide to float his wooden toy boat. Some of the anchors in the collection may have come from more elaborate miniature craft.
Etching by Edward W. Cooke [1811–1880]
Guildhall Library Print Room

Most of the items listed may, however, be the sole surviving components of what seems to have been overall perhaps the longest-lasting category of plaything through the medieval and later periods – the toy wooden boat or ship. The survival of early miniature vessels of this material in recognizable form is extremely unusual. None at all is known from London. It is perhaps not surprising that no miniature anchor is anywhere known to have been found in association with a miniature wooden vessel. The few known parallels for these accessories in England are, however, from coastal locations, where regular use of toy marine vessels might be expected: an anchor from a Napoleonic-period fort at Harwich, and an undated fluke among the many diverse finds from the site of the lost coastal settlement of Meols in Cheshire.[18]

Wooden model boats and ships, usually very accurately similar in their basic form to contemporary full-sized vessels, begin with those excavated in Viking and Norman deposits in Dublin.[19] These early finds are in marked chronological contrast to the limited archaeological finds of miniature anchors in England, and probably elsewhere, with their apparent restriction to the later post-medieval period. Like most of the subsequent examples known, the early Irish finds of model boats are basically made of one piece of wood (though some have provision for sails, which have occasionally survived as separate wooden components in some late medieval versions on the Continent).[20] The only model vessel of this sort traced in England so far is from the 17th century, from Poole in Dorset,[21] but later 17th- and 18th-century examples are known in English American colonies respectively in Maine and Virginia.[22] These at least provide a probable chronological overlap with the subject matter of this section.

It is against these sparse, scattered finds of model vessels that the series of miniature metal anchors from London are best considered. By no means all of these items would have come from miniature ships for children of whatever age. It is easier to see children's incursions to the riverside rather than those of mariner-enthusiasts of model-making as the main reason for the introduction of this repeated category of object to the waterfront among all the commercial bustle at the centre of the port of London during the 17th to 19th century. With these provisos, the riverine find spots, like the seaside ones noted above, hold a special significance.

The finds below are cast in one piece. Those made in open moulds have three-dimensional detailing on one face only (the other face being flat); those from two-part moulds are detailed on both faces. Some of those of copper alloy are prominently file-finished.

TYPE 1

This type has a stock and double arms with flukes.

TYPE 1, DESIGN 1

10.18 Anchor

Accession number: 98.2/693
Material: Lead alloy
Condition: Complete
Dimensions: L 25mm; W 22mm
Description: Flat anchor with a very large ring, thin stock and short shank, slightly recessed crown and double arms with flukes. It is possibly a pendant.
Date: 17th–19th century

TYPE 1, DESIGN 2

10.19 Anchor

Accession number: 98.2/692
Material: Lead alloy
Condition: Complete
Dimensions: L 32mm; W 22mm
Description: Detailing on both faces. Tiny ring, downwards curving stock, long thin shank and short curving double arms with long tapering flukes, which have a medial ridge. There is a solid, round moulding below the crown. Possibly a pendant.
Date: 17th–19th century

TYPE 1, DESIGN 3

10.20 Anchor

Accession number: 98.2/695
Material: Copper alloy
Condition: Complete
Dimensions: L 34mm; W 32mm
Description: From a two-part mould with a small ring, straight rectangular-section stock (much wider than the arms) and flat thin shank. The curving double arms terminate in flukes.
Date: 17th–19th century

TYPE 1, DESIGN 4

10.21 Anchor

Accession number: 98.2/694
Material: Copper alloy
Condition: Complete
Dimensions: L 36mm; W 29mm
Description: Flat ring (with piece of copper-alloy wire looped through); narrow flat stock and flat shank. The flat-section double arms terminate in flukes.
Date: 17th–19th century

TYPE 1, DESIGN 5

10.22 Anchor

Accession number: 98.2/699
Material: Lead alloy or lead
Condition: Complete
Dimensions: L 49mm; W 46mm
Description: Crudely cast; flat with expanded moulding at the top, straight triangular-section stock and short shank. Double arms have large flukes; bulge at crown.
Date: 17th–19th century
Provenance: Limekiln Dock

TYPE 1, DESIGN 6

10.23 Anchor

Accession number: 98.2/698
Material: Lead
Condition: Complete
Dimensions: L 54mm; W 38mm
Description: Small ring, thick square-sectioned stock and rounded shank. The wide double arms terminate in very small flukes. There is a bulge at the crown.
Date: 17th–19th century

TYPE 1, DESIGN 7

10.24 Anchor

Accession number: 98.2/700
Material: Lead
Condition: Complete
Dimensions: L 58mm; W 50mm
Description: The ring is at right angles to the straight, square-sectioned stock. The shank is thick and rounded and the double arms are disproportionately small with recurving flukes at each end.
Date: 17th–19th century

TYPE 1, DESIGN 8

10.25 Anchor

Accession number: 98.2/689
Material: Copper alloy
Condition: Complete
Dimensions: L 62mm; W 39mm
Description: There is low-relief detailing, a very large integral ring and a short stock. The double arms terminate in flukes.
Date: 17th–19th century

TYPE 2

Type 2 has a stock and double arms with no flukes.

TYPE 2, DESIGN 1

10.26 Anchor

Accession number: 98.2/697
Material: Lead
Condition: Complete
Dimensions: L 47mm; W 42mm
Description: Crudely made. A pin-sized hole is surrounded by a pointed moulding; straight, wide triangular-section stock; short, thick triangular-section shank; curving double arms.
Date: 17th–19th century

TYPE 2, DESIGN 2

10.27 Anchor

Accession number: 98.2/107
Material: Lead
Condition: Complete
Dimensions: L 48mm; W 36mm
Description: Distorted ring (broken); wide, downwards curving stock and thick shank. The smooth, curving double arms each terminate in a point.
Date: 17th–19th century
Provenance: Gravesend

TYPE 3

These anchors have no stock.

TYPE 3, DESIGN 1

10.28 Anchor

Accession number: 98.2/690
Material: Lead
Condition: Complete
Dimensions: L 45mm; W 25mm
Description: Grapnel form with a pin-sized hole at the top of the square-section shank, which is split at the crown to form a double arm. Possibly a fishing accessory.
Date: 17th–19th century

TYPE 3, DESIGN 2

10.29 Anchor

Accession number: 98.2/701
Material: Lead
Condition: Complete
Dimensions: L 67mm; W 31mm
Description: Rough anchor of grapnel form. The ring (crushed) was made by bending the top of the shank round to form a rough loop. The thick, uneven-sectioned shank terminates in curved double arms. There is a large bulge at the crown.
Date: 17th–19th century
Provenance: Limekiln Dock

TYPE 3, DESIGN 3

10.30 Anchor

Accession number: 98.2/706

Material: Lead

Condition: Complete

Dimensions: L 105mm; W 55mm

Description: A large anchor, made in one piece, with a tiny flattened ring hole at the top of the long rounded shank. The two curving arms terminate in small flukes.

Date: 17th–19th century

TYPE 3, DESIGN 4

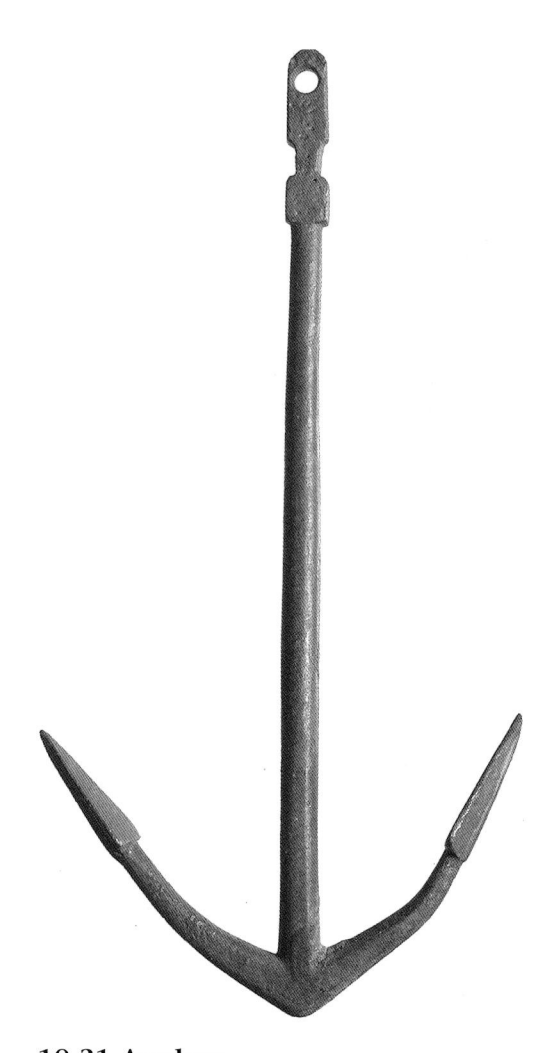

10.31 Anchor

Accession number: 98.2/705

Material: Copper alloy

Condition: Complete

Dimensions: L 130mm; W 66mm

Description: A well-made anchor from a two-part mould. The ring is part of a waisted square section at the top of the long rounded shank. The double arms curve upwards to terminate in very large flukes with prominent medial ridges.

Date: 17th–19th century

Comments: Full-sized anchors of this form appear to be of 19th- or 20th-century date.

TYPE 3, DESIGN 5

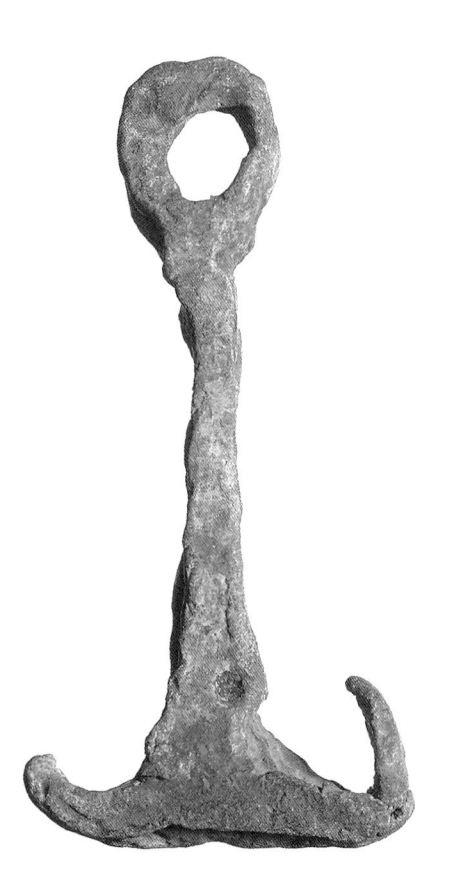

10.32 Anchor

Accession number: 98.2/704
Material: Lead
Condition: Complete (?)
Dimensions: L 106mm; W *c.* 55mm
Description: Part of an extremely crude (?) anchor with a very large distorted ring, a long shank with recessed sides and large flat double arms with upward curving flukes (?).
Date: 17th–19th century
Comments: Probably not a toy

TYPE 4

These anchors lack both stock and flukes.

TYPE 4, DESIGN 1

10.33 Anchor

Accession number: 86.238/7
Material: Lead
Condition: Almost complete
Dimensions: L 43mm; W *c.* 18mm
Description: Flat profile. The top of the ring is missing. The long shank ends in a pointed crown and double arms. Somewhat crude for a toy.
Date: 17th–19th century

TYPE 5

Cast in one piece with the arms at right angles to the stock.

TYPE 5, DESIGN 1

10.34 Anchor

Accession number: 98.2/691
Material: Copper alloy
Condition: Almost complete
Dimensions: L 29mm; W 32mm
Description: Ring broken off. Long, tapering stock and rounded shank. The small curving double arms are at right angles to the stock and terminate in flattened flukes.
Date: 17th–19th century

TYPE 5, DESIGN 2

10.35 Anchor

Accession number: 98.2/696
Material: Copper alloy
Condition: Complete
Dimensions: L 36mm; W 31mm
Description: The small ring is blocked. Straight, rounded stock and short rounded shank. Curving double arms set at right angles to the stock terminate in flattened flukes with prominent medial ridges.
Date: 17th–19th century

TYPE 5, DESIGN 3

10.36 Anchor

Accession number: 98.2/702
Material: Copper alloy
Condition: Complete
Dimensions: L 52mm; W 40mm
Description: Small ring. Short, tapering stock. The long shank ends in a pointed crown. The double arms are at right angles to the shank, and terminate in flukes with prominent medial ridges.
Date: 17th–19th century

TYPE 5, DESIGN 4

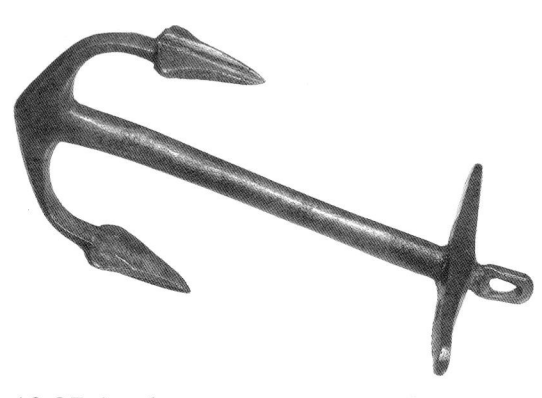

10.37 Anchor

Accession number: 98.2/703
Material: Copper alloy
Condition: Complete
Dimensions: L 71mm; W 53mm
Description: Long looped ring and flattened rectangular straight stock. The long rounded shank ends in a pointed crown. Narrow, double arms terminate in sharply pointed flukes with prominent medial ridges.
Date: 17th–19th century

TYPE 6

Anchors with the stock at a right angle to the double arms which terminate in flukes.

TYPE 6, DESIGN 1

10.38 Anchor

Accession number: 98.2/687
Material: Copper alloy
Condition: Incomplete; one arm broken off
Dimensions: L 35mm; W 22mm
Description: Small ring (with length of copper-alloy wire chain). Straight, square-sectioned stock and rounded shank. There is a leaf-shaped fluke at the end of the surviving arm.
Date: 17th–19th century

TYPE 6, DESIGN 2

10.39 Anchor

Accession number: 98.2/688
Material: Copper alloy
Condition: Complete
Dimensions: L c. 36mm; W 31mm
Description: With ring, long square-sectioned shank and rounded shaft. The double arms terminate in flukes with prominent medial ridges.
Date: 17th–19th century

---

1. Taylor 1623 in *Workes* (London, 1630; repr. 1868–70)

2. For early developments, see Bracker *et al.* 1989, vol. 1, p. 598.

3. Crofts 1967, p. 111.

4. Account of the Steward of the Stillyard for procuring a coach for Sir Henry Sidney in 1576 in the Historic Manuscript Commission, de L'Isle and Dudley Papers 1, 265.

5. Burgess 1881.

6. Crofts 1967, p. 112.

7. Willemsen 1998, p. 361, B19, with two examples from the Low Countries assigned to the 15th–16th centuries. See Willemsen 2000, p. 350, fig. 3 with photographs of two nearly complete examples of similar provenance. (The lower one, which differs from its companion and the ones found in London, seems less convincing as a vehicle).

8. Chest front excavated in Southwark (ABO92 site, Acc. no. 400 from a deposit of early 16th-century date): see Egan forthcoming a, no. 601, and Marks & Williamson 2003, p. 308, cat. no. 177. See also an openable shrine frame in Spencer 1998, pp.153–5, no.165a, again assigned to the early 16th century, and a fragment previously published as part of a late-medieval pilgrim souvenir in Ward Perkins 1940, plate 72, no. 50.

9. Egan 1996, front cover, and 1997, p. 417, fig. 7.

10. Egan 1996, front cover.

11. Stenton *et al.* 1957, plate 36 (on an English ship) and Klingender 1971, p. 385, fig. 218a.

12. Baart *et al.* 1977, p. 469, no. 898.

13. Major 1994, pp. 214 & 216, fig. 19A, no. 13.

14. Hume 1970, p. 25, fig. 19.

15. Mitchener 1986, p. 242, no. 928.

16. Spencer 1998, pp. 79–81, no. 35a, possibly early 15th century.

17. Hume 1970, p. 25, fig. 19.

18. Egan forthcoming b.

19. Lang 1988, pp. 79–80, no. DW91, fig. 94, and Christensen 1988, pp. 19–20, fig. 8 and p. 21, fig. 9 & plate 4.

20. See, for example, Gläser 1995.

21. Heal 1992.

22. Bob Bradley, Maine Historic Preservation Commission, pers. comm., and Hume 1973, p. 24, no. 1.

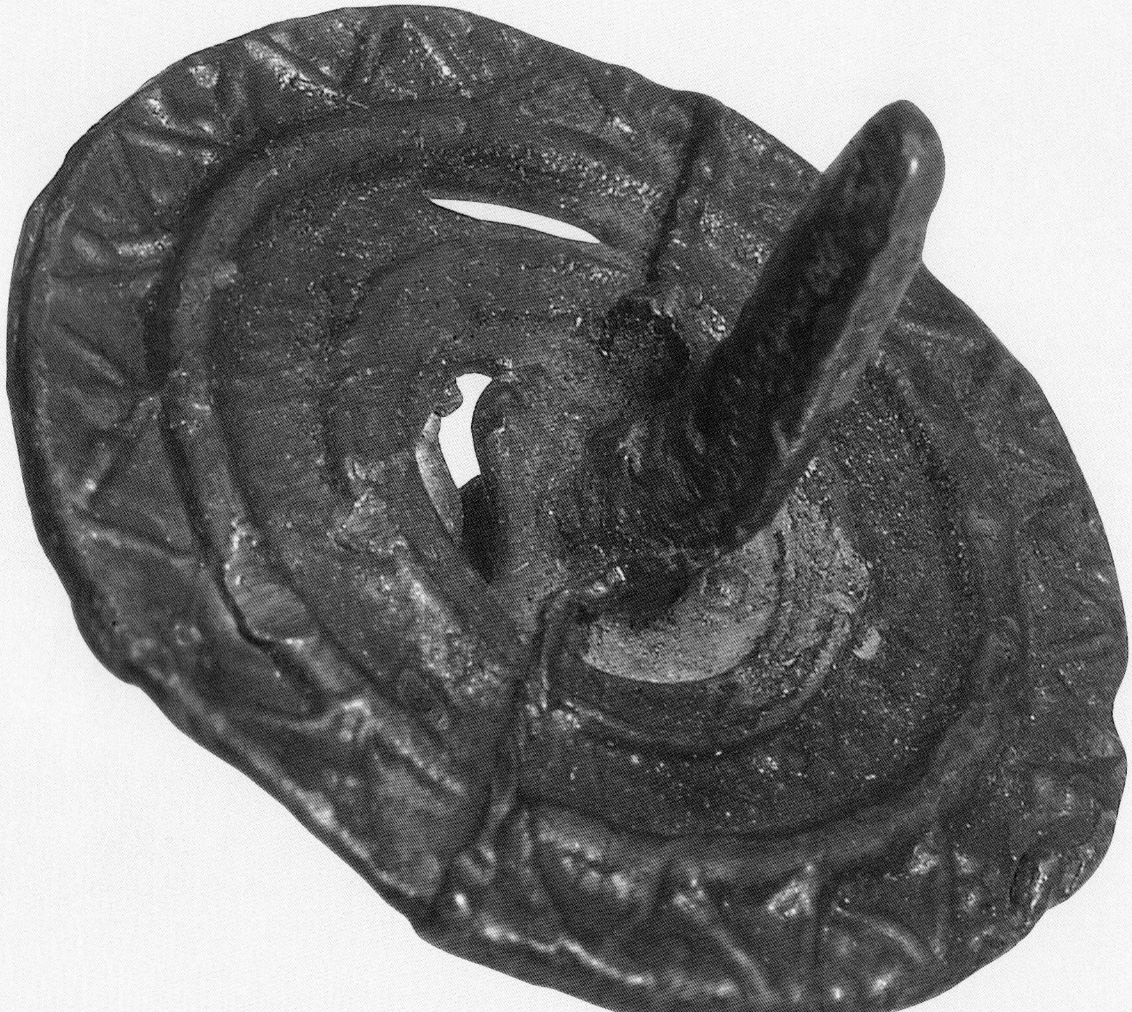

11 Twirlers

'...reels like a top, staggering to its last turnings'[1]

These cast lead-alloy toys are designed to spin on their axis by the twisting action of the fingers upon the vertical shaft. The duration and success of the spin is affected by the precision of the twist and the surface upon which the twirler rests. The basic shape is of ancient origin and these toys, which are popular today, are found throughout the world in every type of material.[2]

While many hundreds of early wood, stone, bone and ceramic whipping and spinning tops have been found,[3] base-metal twirlers are scarce, and those described below are the only ones known in this country.[4]

Fig. 67. Detail showing a boy playing with his whipping top in the abbey square of Middelburg
Detail from an anonymous engraving after *Kinderspel ghedündet tot Sinne-beeloen ende Leere der Seden* ('Children's games expounded as symbols and moral precepts'), 1618 by Adriaen van de Venne.
21.6 x 32.2 cm
Bibliothèque royale de Belgique, Brussels

334 • TOYS, TRIFLES & TRINKETS

Fig. 68. Detail from an engraving by
Experiens Silleman. See fig. 43, p. 187

DESIGN 1

11.1 Twirler

Accession number: 98.2/668*; 98.2/669
Material: Lead alloy
Condition: 98.2/669: complete
Dimensions: H 13mm; Diam 18mm
Description: Cast in one piece from an identical mould, with distorted and off-centre round-sectioned stem or axis and cone-shaped point (only the stubs remain on 98.2/668). The upper face of the disc is decorated with a cross-hatched and plain quatrefoil.
Date: Probably 17th century
Provenance: Dockhead
Comments: Bidirectional movement is normally obtained by twisting the fingers around the stem, but because this twirler is improperly cast, a smooth action is impossible, and the toy might have been discarded for this reason.

DESIGN 2

11.2 Twirler

Accession number: 98.2/667
Material: Lead alloy
Condition: Complete; some damage
Dimensions: H 22mm; Diam 23mm
Description: Cast in one piece with an oval-sectioned stem and twisted point. The disc has a transverse casting seam and the upper face has a contoured profile of three concentric bands with chevrons and pellets around the edge. The underside has a crude pattern of cross-hatched lines. There are a few holes and casting flashes.
Date: Probably 17th century

1 Homer, *Iliad*, ch. 14, line 413.
2 Gould 1975.
3 Keene 1990 and Kolchin 1989, vol. 1, p. 202 & vol. 2, p. 461, plate 215, nos. 6 & 7.
4 Willemsen 1998, p. 404, B166, from a 15th- or 16th-century context.

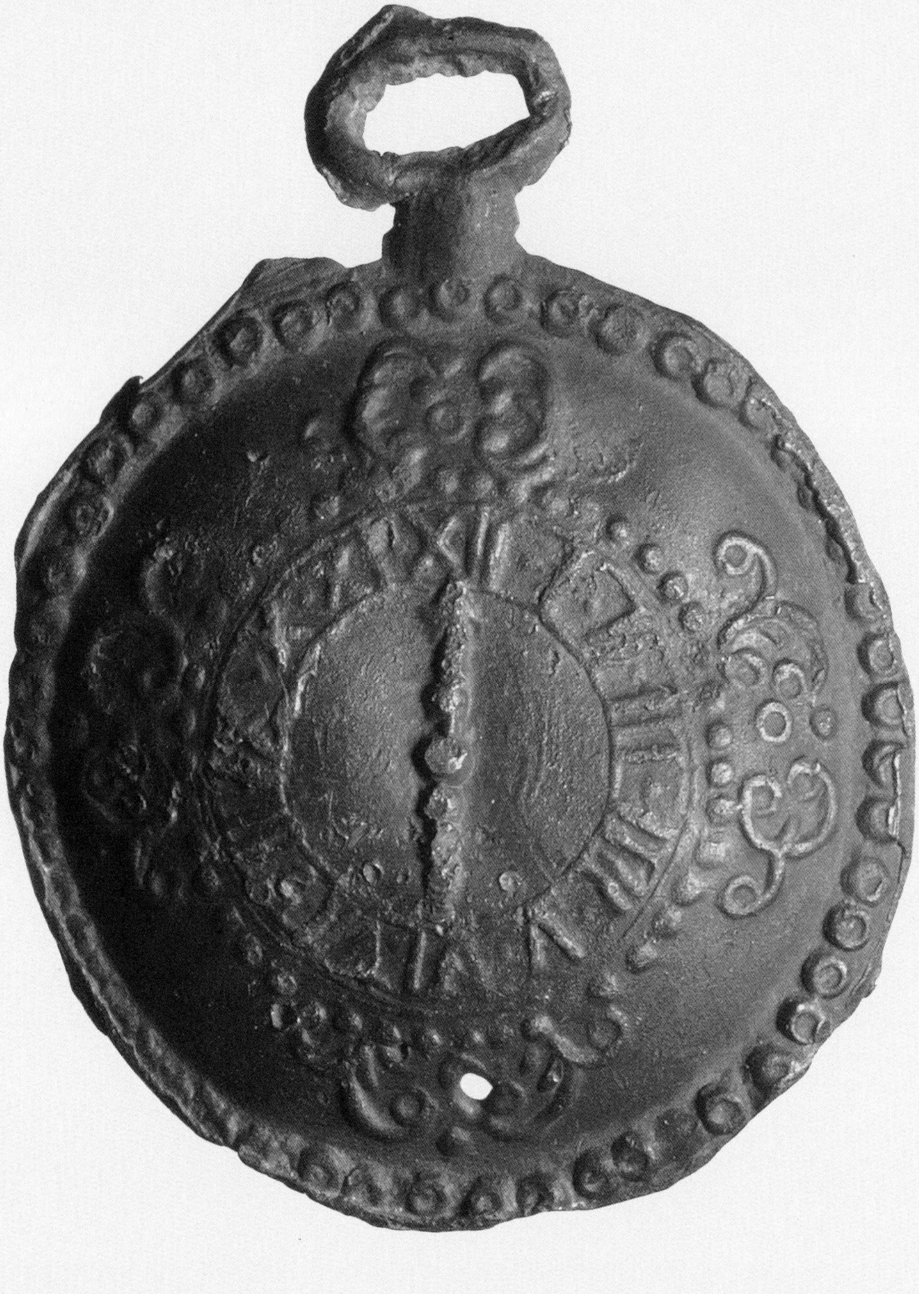

12 Watches

'The Watch-Maker's Business is but of modern Invention, and of late improved in England to the highest Perfection; we beat all Europe in Clocks and Watches of all Sorts, and export those useful Engines to all the Parts of the known world.'[1]

At the end of the 16th century London watches were largely supplied by immigrant craftsmen from Flanders and France, many of whom, to the great annoyance of those practising the trade within the control of the Blacksmiths' and Goldsmiths' Companies, had set up independent or 'illegal' workshops in the 'liberties' of the City to avoid guild controls and payments. Matters came to a head in 1622 when the 'lawful clockmakers' complained to James I that 'the multiplicitie of Forreiners usinge theire profession … offer their workes to sale, which (for the most parte) being not serviceable (the parties buying the same for the outwarde shew which comonlie is beautifull) are much deceaved in the true value, which rests in the inworke onlie'.[2] The London clock- and watchmakers had legitimate grievances because they had already established themselves as competent craftsmen, executing work to rival the very best pieces produced on the Continent, and eventually their struggle to secure control of their trade and establish a separate and autonomous Company was granted by Charles I. Notwithstanding this shaky start, English watchmaking flourished[3] and by the end of the 17th century 4,000 people were employed in the capital's watchmaking industry and London had become one of the leading horological centres in Europe.

Even though the toy watches discussed in this section are necessarily a poor cousin of the real thing, they mirror many of the major features and design trends of genuine timepieces during a particularly formative period of horological development. As Table 12.1 shows, the watches range in date from *c.* 1625 to the early 1800s and it is interesting that the earliest ones date from the period when the English watch really starts to take its place in the London market. By the late 17th century watches were commonplace and affordable to all but the poorest, significant

ABOVE: **Fig. 69. A verge watch with lobed, faceted and engraved rock crystal case. Signed Henry Ester, *c.* 1630. Diam 31 x 39 mm**
Museum of London, Acc. no. 34.181/34
W.E. Miller Collection, 1934
Miniature, Acc. no. 2001.20/9, Cat. no. 12.8

LEFT: **Fig. 70. Silver-gilt pair-cased verge watch with pierced and engraved case and champlevé dial. Signed *Rodet London*, but possibly manufactured in Switzerland, *c.* 1710. Diam 51.8mm. Shown with a toy watch of similar style and date signed HUX LONDON**
Museum of London, Acc. no. 34.181/47
Miniature, Acc. no. 98.2/442, Cat. no. 12.43

Table 12.1

Type	Design	Quantity	Date	Inscribed	Hours	Half hours	Minute circle	Quarter circle	One hand	Two hands
1	4	5	1625–40			2				
2	3	4	1630–40			2				
3	1	1	1630–40			1			1	
4	2	2	1600–50			2				
5	29*	47	1630–1750	6	3	45	3		41	7
6	1	1	1675–1700		1				1	
7	1	10	1700–25			10			10	
8	7	22	1700–50	13			15	3	2	
9	2	2	1700–50	2		2			2	
10	1	1	1700–50			1				
11	8	10	1750–50		1	9	1		1	8
12	7	9	1750–1837		1		1			
13	1	1	1800–25			1			1	
14	1	1	?		1					
15	1	1	1800–25		1			1	1	
Total	69	117		21	8	75	20	4	60	15

*Plus mould, which includes a further two different designs

advances had been made to the timekeeping qualities of the mechanism, and watch and case design was transformed, so it is hardly surprising that most of the toy watches represented by Types 3–11, have stylistic and horological details pointing to a date between c. 1650 to c. 1750, the pre-eminent period of English watchmaking.

The toy watches cannot be understood without reference to the real thing, but obviously comparisons with a genuine watch can only be taken so far. Until the 1670s the mechanical elements of a real watch hardly altered and the shape and ornamentation of the case, dial and movement are often the only guide to dating them. General trends can be identified, however, and these include the fashion for oval watches with arabesque strapwork and stylized floral motifs in the first couple of decades of the 17th century; elongated octagons and so-called 'form' watches with naturalistic ornament and glass covers in the second quarter; pierced cases from the 1640s and pair-cases from the 1650s.

Circular watches, the most common form of all, continued in use from the 16th century onwards, whereas the form watches, and strange-shaped, pendant-style watches went out of fashion by the 1670s.[4] The case and dial plate designs provide less reliable dating evidence because many were derived from pattern books which were copied by casemakers in all of the primary watchmaking centres of Europe, and since these patterns were often in circulation for long periods of time, it can be extremely difficult to attribute an early 17th-century watch to a specific place of manufacture on the basis of ornament alone. If it is sometimes difficult to date and source a real watch, the toy version presents an even greater challenge. To what extent is the shape and decoration a faithful representation of horological development? Were the toy watch moulds used over a considerable period of time? Who were the makers and for whom were they made?

Throughout the 17th century watches were prized possessions,[5] and documentary evidence suggests that watch ownership by the middle classes was rare before the 1660s. Indeed, something of the novelty, excitement and pleasure of owning a watch is expressed by Samuel Pepys in his diary entry for 13 May 1665:

> But Lord, to see how much of my folly and childishnesse hangs upon me still, that I cannot forbear carrying my watch in my hand in the coach all this afternoon, and seeing what-a-clock it is 100 times. And am apt to think with myself: how could I be so long without one …[6]

This watch had been given to Pepys as a present, and it was soon to be replaced with a 'minute' watch[7] which in turn was swapped for a cheaper 'watch with many motions', possibly an astronomical timepiece.[8] Before the invention of the balance-spring, watches were only really capable of telling the time to the nearest hour, and Pepys acquired his 'motion watch' in the hope that it would prove to be a more reliable timekeeper.

By the early 18th century, increasing numbers of Londoners could afford to buy a watch.[9] In 1720, for example, London lawyer Silvester Petyt owned four, and these are listed in an inventory of his goods appraised for the purposes of probate: 'a fashionable silver watch and chain' valued at £3; 'one flat silver watch and chain at £1.16.0'; 'one flat silver watch and chain with a studded case and chain at £1.10.0' and 'one small oval watch at 15 shillings'.[10] It is noticeable that Petyt had an expensive 'fashionable' watch as well as a small oval watch valued at 15 shillings because it was obviously old by 1719/20 and therefore cheap. This inventory is important because it shows that real watches were kept, possibly for sentimental

Table 12.2

Times	T1	T2	T3	T4	T5	T6	T7	T8	T9	T10	T11	T12	T13	T14	T15	Total
1.03											1					1
1.23					1											1
2.30					1								1			2
3.00					1											1
4.00					2											2
4.30					1											1
5.00											1					1
6.00					1											1
9.19											1					1
10.00											1					1
10.20											1					1
11.30											1					1
12.00			1	1	37	1	10				1				1	52
12.20					2											2
12.37												2				2
moving	2	2						22	2							28
n/a	3	2		1	1					1	1	9		1		19
Total	5	4	1	2	47	1	10	22	2	1	10	9	1	1	1	117

n/a = not applicable

reasons or because they were expensive, even though they were no longer fashionable or reliable as timekeepers. But it also shows that some people were keen to acquire, or were given, the very latest timepiece whether they had other watches in working order at home. For many, fashion was all, and if some owners were inclined to discard the old in favour of the new, it is possible that the toy watch also underwent a marked and rapid change in shape and design, evolving over time to imitate the innovations and developments of the genuine timepiece; and within certain limits, the surviving examples do seem to copy styles and phases of horological development. After all, an old-fashioned toy watch with out-of-date shape and decoration would hardly appeal to a child, and neither one suspects would they have found a ready market within the adult population. This is significant because even though some are extremely crude or very stylized, there are a number of reasonably convincing examples represented by Types 1 and 8 which might have been made for adults: Type 1 for their novelty value, when real watches were scarce and extremely expensive, and the best examples of Type 8 for use as imitative companion pieces worn with a real watch when it was fashionable to wear two watches, one real and one counterfeit in the late 17th and early 18th centuries.[11] Other types might have been worn by adults as a locket (see Type 9) or trinket.[12]

Horological features, design and date

The 117 watches in the corpus can be classified into three main groups: single-sided, double-sided and multi-component watches with or without moving parts. But this broad classification ignores important horological features, design and chronology, and so the watches have been categorized by form, style and decoration. By arranging the watches in this way, 15 distinct types have been identified and although the characteristics of each type are discussed in detail below, some general comments can be made here.

As Table 12.1 shows, some of the types are closely datable while others, notably Type 5, seem to have been made over a considerable period. Most of the watches are stylized but a few, notably Types 1, 7, 8 and 11, are reasonable imitations

Dial plate (Type 11), Acc. no. 98.2/462, Cat. no. 12.53

Watch (Type 8), Acc. no. 2001.15/1, Cat. no. 12.43
The dial plate has rotated out of alignment by about 45 degrees. Inscribed HUX/LONDON

of the real thing. Only a small proportion are so crude as to render precise dating and classification impossible.

For the most part, the mould-engraver has attempted to reproduce contemporary metal and enamel case-work and dial plate designs and there are 69 different mould patterns within the corpus. Some of the dial plates have realistic repoussé- and champlevé-style mouldings although the grotesques, heraldic emblems, landscapes and figurative designs found on a genuine timepieces are conspicuously absent. The case mouldings are particularly convincing, imitating shagreen, piqué, pierced and inlaid work, repoussé and engine turning, as well as naturalistic floral and foliate scrolling, geometric motifs and baroque and rococo patterns. Twelve of the 18th-century watches bear traces of red pigment which seems to have been used to highlight aspects of the design or to represent enamel, and it is possible that some of the earlier examples were also coated and buffed up to provide a contrast between, for example, the silvery appearance of the dial and 'inner case' and the 'outer case' with piqué and shagreen mouldings.

Several different designs were produced for most types of watch (Table 12.1) and since the quality of these designs is so variable, customers were presumably offered a wide choice to suit their tastes and pocket. Thus, for example, among the ten dial plates inscribed 'HUX/LONDON' there are three distinct types and three designs, and one design was produced in two sizes.[13] Most of the watches have accurately inscribed chapter rings marked with Roman hour numerals I–XII in equal divisions, and these are generally interspersed with half-hour marks which reflects contemporary dial fashions on a genuine timepiece. Pellet, star, slash, lozenge and quatrefoil half-hour marks are all represented within the corpus. But while the majority of the chapter rings are faithfully represented and well executed, there are a small group with bunched numbers, an incomplete set of half-hour marks and in the worst examples, a jumbled sequence of hours.[14] In one case it seems that the engraver just ran out of room,[15] in others the hour divisions are not only squashed and badly aligned, but missing, repeated or back-to-front.[16] The irregular sequence of numbers is not the only eccentricity: the earliest oval dial plates have XII at the 3.30 position, some have two hands and no minute circle, and there is a large group of double-sided watches with a dial on each face. Although it is difficult to believe that watches with a crazy sequence of hours, or two hands and no minutes had much to offer, perhaps the 'timekeeping' aspects of toy watch ownership was of secondary importance to the object itself.

Whether the watches were well made or not, it is highly unlikely that they were regarded as a serious educational toy, and were probably viewed in a light-hearted fashion. After all, children like to have things which make them feel grown-up, and even today, very young children wear toy wristwatches, not because they can use them to tell the time, but simply because they are 'a watch'. When the toy watches were made, children were dressed and equipped in adult attire, so ownership of a replica watch would simply enhance their 'adult' appearance. The fact that some of the toy watches had poorly cast details, irregular hours and other horological quirks was probably completely irrelevant to a small child, and slightly older children might have viewed the incongruous elements as a joke. Perhaps this is why the hour sequence on the earliest dial plates starts from the 3 o'clock position.

Apart from the single rotating hands found on Types 1, 7 and 8, all of the hands are integrally cast. The majority have arrowhead pointers in keeping with most early watches, but other contemporary styles are represented and there are hands with fleur-de-lys, trefoil and foliate pointers. General hand shapes include the half-baluster, baluster, beetle and poker, pierced swell, serpentine and crescent moon, and since the form of the real watch hand tends to vary over time, these styles provide helpful dating evidence. Towards the end of the 17th century, the counterpoise on the single hand of a genuine timepiece was removed and this fashion seems to have been copied on Type 8, Design 1.[17]

Virtually all of the fixed-hand watches have a single hand pointing to 12 o'clock, and this is shown on Table 12.2 overleaf. Why was 12 o'clock the preferred time? The reason is unclear, but it may be significant that the hands on watch dials in still-life paintings of the 17th century also invariably point to 12 o'clock.[18]

The invention of the balance spring in 1675 greatly improved the timekeeping qualities of the mechanism and for the first time it was possible to regulate a watch with great accuracy. This refinement led to the introduction of the minute circle and, eventually, to the adoption of a minute hand. Two hands do not become standard on genuine timepieces until about 1680 and within the toy watch corpus the 15 dials with two hands all have features which indicate a production date between 1700 and 1750. By c. 1700 most watches had concentric minute and hour circles, and for clarity the outer minute circle was marked in five-minute divisions in large Arabic numerals which is shown on some of the larger Type 5 and some of the Type 8 watches.

Twenty-one watches are inscribed with initials or names, as follows: AB; F Beasley; IB; IC; IG; [..]H; Richard H …; Hux and London (in upper and lower case); Randall and RR. A possible back plate from a Type 1 watch is also inscribed ID over Q and a possible cover for the same watch is dated 1646. A number of watches are just inscribed LONDON. It is significant that more watches are inscribed than any other category of toy and there are a number of reasons why this is so. The primary reason for the apparent flush of inscriptions is that the watches mostly date from the mid-17th to mid-18th century or later, when the inclusion of the maker's name and place of manufacture was standard practice on the real thing. Secondly, the watches constitute a large statistical group within the corpus and so the relative number of inscriptions is accordingly high. Thirdly, documentary evidence shows that a number of London pewterers were engaged in the manufacturing of toy watches, and so it was essential that each maker's work could be easily identified for the purposes of quality control and to protect their commercial interests.[19]

The products of two prominent toy watchmakers William Hux and Francis Beasley (or Beesley) are included in this corpus (see Appendix III). Both men are mentioned in the Court Minutes of the Worshipful Company of Pewterers and these records provide fascinating evidence for toy watch production in early 18th-century London. Hux was summoned before the Court of the Company on six occasions between 1703 and 1715 for producing toy watches of 'bad Mettle'. On his first appearance before the Quarter Court his watches were assessed and the 'case or outside [was] … 3gr. from fine' and the 'Dyall plate at 19 gr. worse than Lay'. Hux alleged that the case was sub-standard 'through some neglecte of his servant' and the dial plate 'could not be made so well of any other mettle'. The matter was considered and 'after divers debates [the Court] was of opinion that the said Dyall Plate might be made of ffine But the peice being small and inconsiderable and being informed some others make the same sort of Watches adjorned the further consideration to another time'.[20] There are no further entries until the following year, when on 22 March, Hux again appears before the Quarter Court for producing 'Dyal Plates for Watches at 12 gr worse than lay.'[21] Yet again, the matter was suspended, and it was not until 19 June 1707 that William Hux appeared to answer a complaint 'for making pewter Watch Cases at 2gr worse than fine and watch Dyall Plate at 11 gr worse than Lay'. Again Hux argued that he could not 'make the Dyall Plate of other Sort of Mettle … and hoped (the quantity being so very small) the Court would remitt it.'[22] After this submission, the Court ordered him to pay one shilling to the Poor Box and dismissed him.

After a gap of seven years, a Company search found that Hux was making toy watches '5gr wors than Lay' and when challenged, Hux argued that 'one Beasly has made the same sort of ware of lay and sometimes as Bad as pale and if he be not suffered to work as another he shall loose his Trade.' The matter was submitted to the Quarter Court and after a long debate Hux was dismissed on payment of one shilling to the Poor Box. The Court further ordered 'that for the time to come no person of the Mistery do make or cause to be made any sort of pewter watch cases of any other than ffine Mettle.'[23]

In spite of this order, Hux was again before the Quarter Court on 15 December 1714, on the charge of producing 'Toy watches and Dyall Plates at 11 gr wors than lay'. After some discussion the matter was referred for 'further consideration till another time',[24] and it was not until the 22nd March 1715 that Hux was summoned to appear to answer the charges. Yet again, 'after several debates' the problem was 'suspended until the next Court' but in the meantime Hux was asked 'to bring to the Master and Wardens an account in writing of all other persons that he shall discover that makes any Quantity of such cases.' Unfortunately this account does not survive, and since there are no more references to William Hux in the Minute Books we do not know whether the list was even compiled. In the absence of further recorded exchanges between Hux and the Court on this subject, one could infer that the Company realized that the production of poor-quality toy watches was too widespread and accordingly their standards were unenforceable. But if this was so, one would expect to find an order or modified regulation to that effect.

The debate between William Hux and the Pewterers' Company is important because the records show that two standards of metal were used to produce the Hux watches, one for the case and another for the dial plate. In his defence, Hux disclaimed responsibility for the inferior-quality case metal by blaming his servant, and further argued that it was very difficult to produce a dial plate from anything other than lay metal. The Court's equivocation and leniency suggest that they either accepted this as a truthful statement, or gave him the benefit of the doubt. And it is quite likely that the champlevé- and repoussé-style mouldings, the inscriptions, and the baroque scrolling and cartouches on the dial plates required a softer, more malleable alloy. As far as the Company was concerned, the main problem was not the combination of two kinds of alloy in one object, but rather the use of substandard material. At times Hux was making dial plates 19gr worse than the standard. Despite the fact that Hux repeatedly infringed the regulations, the lengthy debates and referrals suggest that the Court could not decide how to deal with the problem, or could not reach a unanimous decision. On the one hand, they were obliged to protect the quality of the product and the reputation of their trade, but on the other, it seems that these wares could only be produced by compromising the standard. Moreover, Hux suggests that the manufacture of 'bad Mettle' toy watches was widespread, and although he uses this argument as a major line of defence in his first submission, the matter is not addressed for another 15 years. If other pewterers were making poor-quality toy watches,

and if Hux was concerned that he would lose business to his competitors, why were they not also similarly accused? Was Hux singled out because he fell foul of the regulations and thereafter his work was kept under close scrutiny? Or did he come to particular attention because he was the principal maker of toy watches at this time? The other prominent toy watchmaker, Francis Beasley, was summoned before the Court on 19 September 1704 for making poor- metal 'new fashioned Spoons', and although these were seized by the Master and Wardens, 'in regard of his poverty' the five-shilling fine was remitted. There is no evidence that Beasley was making toy watches until Hux's accusation in 1714, and it is rather surprising that the Court did not ask Beasley to appear before them to answer similar charges.

Perhaps the most remarkable feature of the exchange between William Hux and the Company was their insistence that the toy watch cases were to be made of fine metal. Why should the Company care so much about the quality of toy watches produced by William Hux and his fellow toy watch specialists? And why fine metal rather than trifling or lay? The use of fine metal for the case was presumably due to the fact that the higher tin alloy resulted in a stronger, albeit more brittle metal, which would be more resistant to crushing and capable of taking a higher polish.[25] It is possible that the Company insisted that the cases should be made from good-quality fine metal to comply with the demands of the consumer, and if the watches attracted adult buyers they might have been more likely to complain if the product was not up to standard.

As far as the Hux watches are concerned, it is significant that there are no references in the Company records to moving parts or any other element of the watch beyond the case and dial plate, and it is possible that the multi-component Hux watches with a simple mechanism were produced after 1715. It is also worth noting that the Hux watches bear the surname only, so it is entirely possible that some of the watches in the collection were made by William's son Thomas who had a workshop at the Halfmoon and Flower de Luce in Newgate Street in 1724. Examination of two complete Hux watches and one complete Beasley watch has shown that the mechanisms were made from copper and lead alloys (fig. 71).

For the first time it has been possible to analyse a large number of Hux and Beasley watches to see whether the metallurgy conforms to the standards of the Company and moreover to see whether there are any discernible differences in the cases and dial plates. The results appear in Appendix II and, astonishingly, one of the Hux watches (Cat. no. 12.47) appears to have been silvered.

Remarkably no toy watches of the early 17th century have been recovered in Europe. The absence of I(D)Q watches is especially surprising since many examples of this maker's work have been found on the Continent and the clock and watch trade flourished in the Netherlands, France and Germany throughout the early modern period.

By the late 17th and early 18th century, English toy watches were evidently exported in considerable numbers, and several Hux watches have been found in excavations in Amsterdam.[26] Some of these watches were recovered with their winder key and several were found with fragments of glass between the rim of the case and the dial plate, which suggests that these watches were originally glazed.[27]

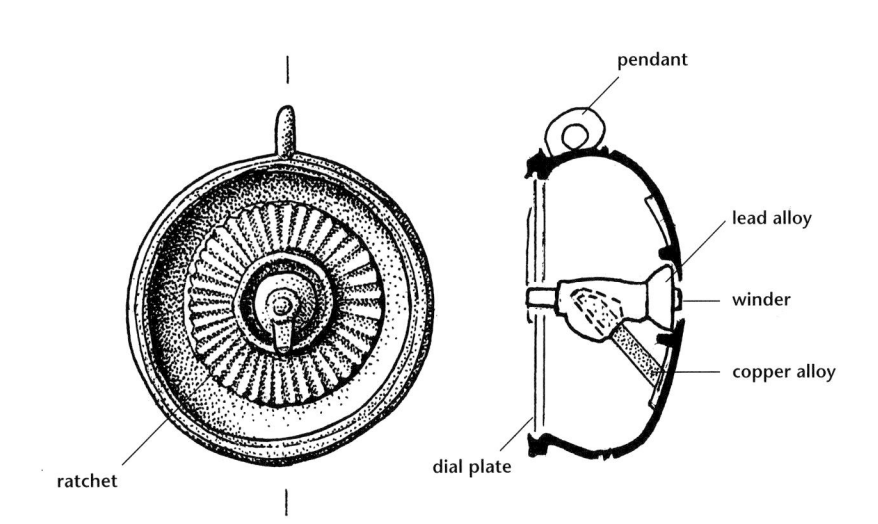

Fig. 71. Drawing to show the internal ratchet mechanism of Type 8 watches. As the winder is turned, a copper-alloy strip engages with the grooves on the base of the case to make a 'tick-tock' sound.

TYPE 1

The four dials and corresponding cover plates considered here are the only surviving elements from the earliest, and perhaps the most sophisticated, toy watches ever made. The damaged edges and lug indents around the circumference, in addition to a single surviving rotating hand (Acc. no. 98.2/475), suggest that the plates were attached to a separate case, and their shape, style and decoration resemble oval and round pendant watches made in England, France and the Low Countries during the first quarter of the 17th century (fig. 72).[28]

Even though the dial plates are a fair copy of the real thing, there are certain differences: the chapter ring is smaller and the relief cast foliate or floral decoration is not so finely delineated as the engraving on a genuine timepiece of this period. It could be argued, of course, that the mould-engraver was not trying to represent an engraved dial but rather the delicate, loose style of a cloisonné enamel decorated watch in vogue during the second quarter of the 17th century.[29] The most puzzling departure from horological convention is the bizarre placing of the Roman hour numerals on the chapter ring of the two oval dial plates. These plates seem to have been cast from the same mould, and although the normal I–XII hour sequence has been followed, XII is placed at the 3.30 position rather than the top of the long axis. The reason for this curious displacement is unclear; it is not found on any other watches in the corpus. Was it an error on the part of the mould-engraver or was it done deliberately? The round dials, however, with a foliate rather than floral border and radial lines in the centre rather than a rosette, seem to be correctly aligned, because the lug indents are equally spaced around the circumference at 10, 2, 7 and 5 which matches conventional siting on a genuine timepiece.

The strongest evidence for suggesting that these plates were attached to a case is the absence of a pendant or finial, damage to the lug indents and the amount of abrasion to the edges of the dial, which is especially marked on Acc. no. 98.2/475. The plates are extremely thin, just 0.5mm compared to 1.2mm on a genuine example and were therefore liable to snap, break loose from the case and show signs of wear. So far as is known, no complete cases have survived but there are several solid oval or round panels with four lug indents around the circumference, which might have

Fig. 72. Gilded-brass verge watch, signed Sam + Stpinwall, 1625–50. There is an engraved wreath within the lid and the dial plate has foliate designs top and bottom with an arcadian landscape in the centre. 49.8 x 39.2 mm. Shown alongside a comparable decorated lid and dial plate from a toy watch
Museum of London, Acc. no. 34.181/17
Miniature, Acc. no. 98.2/474, Cat. no. 12.1
Miniature, Acc. no. 98.2/624, Cat. no. 12.3

served as back plates for Type 1 watches.[30] Not only are these panels the same size and thickness as the dial plates, but more significantly, the lug indents correspond exactly. Other similar-sized oval panels with wreath decoration (Acc. nos. 98.2/623 & 98.2/624) have a similar style of ornament to that engraved on the outside and inside of case lids on genuine timepieces of the early to mid-17th century, and although the panels are damaged and there is no obvious method of attachment, they could be a component part of a Type 1 watch. Unlike the real watch cover, however, the decoration is on one side only. As a group, three of the panels are inscribed with the maker's initials I D over Q and one of the possible case lids also bears the date 1646. The significance of the maker I(D)Q has been discussed elsewhere (p. 67 and Appendix IV). If the panels are Type 1 components, the watches must have been made during the 1640s, even though the general design and characteristics of the dial plates suggest a date of 1625–30.

TYPE 1, DESIGN 1

12.1 Dial

Accession number: 98.2/474*; 98.2/475
Material: Lead alloy
Condition: Dial only; flat
    98.2/475: includes hand
Dimensions: Diam 34 x *c.* 22 mm; Th 0.5mm
Description: The rope-twist edge has what appear to be four fixing slots (two extant) and encloses a scrolling floral border. The chapter ring within concentric circles is marked with Roman hours I–XII interspersed with pellets to indicate the half-hours. XII is at approximately 3.31. The raised central boss decorated with a rosette is pierced to accommodate the rotating hand, which is retained by a transverse pin on the back. The hand is of half-baluster form with a fleur-de-lys pointer.
Date: 1620–30

TYPE 1, DESIGN 2

12.2 Case lid panel

Accession number: 98.2/623
Material: Lead alloy
Condition: Incomplete
Inscription: IDQ; 1646
Dimensions: Diam (across) 27mm
Description: A solid oval panel decorated on one side with a garland around the letters ID over Q and dated 1646. The plain edge is slightly raised.
Date: 1646

TYPE 1, DESIGN 3

12.3 Case lid or back panel

Accession number: 98.2/624
Material: Lead alloy
Condition: Almost complete; slight damage
Dimensions: Diam 33 x 28 mm
Description: A solid oval panel decorated on one side with a central fleur-de-lys-type motif surrounded by a foliate and hatched garland. The rim is cabled and there are three/four slots around the edge.
Date: Mid-17th century

TYPE 1, DESIGN 4

12.4 Case back panel

Accession number: 98.2/619
Material: Lead alloy
Condition: Complete
Dimensions: Diam 35 x 28 mm
Inscription: IDQ
Description: A solid oval panel with cable edge incorporating four lugs or fixing slots. In the centre there is a sexfoil double rose with prominent calyx points extending beyond and between the outer row of petals. A single ring and dot flanked by pellets fills the space between each point, and the central motif is enclosed within double concentric circles. The border of finely delineated and hatched foliate scrolling incorporates a beaded oval cartouche inscribed ID over Q.
Date: Mid-17th century

TYPE 2

These multi-component watches are round versions of Type 1 above. This style of watch eventually became popular during the period 1630–40 and miniatures were probably produced at this time.

TYPE 2, DESIGN 1

12.5 Dial

Accession number: 82.682/2; 98.2/472*
Material: Lead alloy
Condition: Dial only; flat
Dimensions: Diam 29mm; Th 0.5mm
Description: Rope-twist edge with four notches around the circumference which probably secured the dial to the case lugs (see above). A wide foliate border surrounds the chapter ring with Roman hours I–XII interspersed with pellets to indicate the half-hours. A raised central boss decorated with radial lines is pierced to accommodate the rotating hand (now missing). There is a hole in the border at the half-past-ten position which might be a further method of attachment to the case, or was added at a later date to turn the dial into a decorative mount. Even though 82.682/2 is damaged (and the central boss is missing), it was probably cast from same mould as 98.2/472.
Date: 1630–50
Comparandum: Watch by Isaac Symmes with radiating design in the centre of the dial, in Jagger 1988, plate 21

TYPE 2, DESIGN 2

12.6 Case back panel

Accession number: 98.2/620
Material: Lead alloy
Condition: Almost complete
Dimensions: Diam 29mm
Description: A solid round panel with cable edge incorporating lugs (three extant) or fixing slots. There is a quatrefoil double rose in the centre with prominent calyx points. A single ring and dot flanked by pellets fills the space between each point and the central motif is enclosed within double concentric circles. The wide border is decorated with a patera design and there are pellet clusters around the edge.
Date: Mid-17th century

TYPE 2, DESIGN 3

12.7 Case back panel

Accession number: 98.2/621
Material: Lead alloy
Condition: Complete
Dimensions: Diam 33mm
Inscription: I over DQ
Description: A solid disc with casting seam, two concentric circles, a central knob and

oval cartouche inscribed I (lower case) over DQ on the back. The edge is finely notched and the front face is decorated with, in the centre, a cinquefoil double rose with prominent calyx points between the outer row of petals. A single ring and dot flanked by pellets fills the space between each point and the central motif is enclosed within double concentric circles. There is a narrow border of hatched foliate scrolling within two more concentric circles.

Date: Mid-17th century

TYPE 3

This type is represented by just one example. Lobed watches with rock crystal, gilt-brass, silver-gilt and sometimes jewelled cases did not become common in England, France and Switzerland until the 1630s and 40s (see fig. 69, p. 338). The toy watch has been cast in a three-part mould and the heavy use of the ring and dot motif might have been used to imitate engraving.

TYPE 3, DESIGN 1

12.8 Watch

Accession number: 2001.20/9
Material: Lead alloy
Condition: Complete; slightly crushed
Dimensions: H (incl. pendant loop) c. 45mm; Diam c. 36mm; D 13mm
Description: This watch has a ten-lobe circular 'case', domed profile and integrally cast pendant loop. The two hemispheres are joined around the circumference and there is a mould seam across the back linking two vents. The dial is enclosed by a cross-hatched 'case' and each lobe is embellished with a ring and dot motif. The chapter ring is contained within concentric beaded circles and is marked with Roman hours I–XII interspersed with half-hour pellets. A border of chevrons surrounds the plain dial centre and there is a single hand with an arrowhead pointer at 12 o'clock. The back is damaged and crushed but each lobe is decorated with ring and dot and there is an inner circle of ring and dot which matches the diameter of the dial. The pendant loop is positioned at the 6 o'clock position.

Date: 1630–50
Provenance: Brooks Wharf
Comments: An almost identical example was recovered from the Tower foreshore in December 1984.
Comparanda: A Swiss watch, c. 1630, with crystal eight-lobed case in the collection of the Worshipful Company of Clockmakers (Acc. no. 18). A French watch with a 12-lobed crystal case by Aymé Noel, c. 1640, in the British Museum. A watch c. 1630 by Henry Ester with faceted oval crystal case in the Museum of London (Acc. no. 34.181/34).

TYPE 4

These watches are an extremely debased version of T2 and since they are so unconvincing, they might have been a cheaper product for less discerning customers.

TYPE 4, DESIGN 1

12.9 Watch

Accession number: 98.2/468
Material: Lead alloy
Condition: Complete; flat
Dimensions: H (incl. pendant loop) 38mm; Diam 33 x 32 mm
Description: This is a very crude imitation. Unlike T1, D1 and T2, D1, this watch never had a case. There is a debased rope-

twist edge surrounding a stylized floral border, the chapter ring is very crowded and badly spaced, and the Roman hours are numbered in an anti-clockwise direction XII–I. Most of the hours are interspersed with pellets to indicate the half-hours. It is also interesting that the 4 is delineated as IV rather than the conventional IIII, and this may have been selected because IV takes up less room. The centre of the dial is plain but disfigured by a casting flaw which obliterates part of the chapter ring between 4 and 7. The hand, half only, with arrowhead pointer at 12 o'clock, is integrally cast. There is damage to the border and a hole in the centre of the dial caused by imperfect casting. The back is plain and the pendant loop shows very little sign of wear.

Date: Early 17th century

TYPE 4, DESIGN 2

12.10 Watch

Accession number: 98.2/507
Material: Lead alloy
Condition: Fragment of dial; flat
Dimensions: Diam 27 x 26 mm; Th 0.6mm
Description: Extremely crude dial with part of leaf border and chapter ring marked with Roman hours I–XII and pellets to indicate the half-hours. There is a single, integrally cast hand with arrow pointers at both ends so that it is impossible to tell whether the time is 12 o'clock or 6 o'clock. The centre of the dial is plain.
Date: Probably early 17th century

Fig. 73. Silver verge watch with pierced case and striking mechanism. Signed Vincentius Zimmerman of Landshut, c. 1650. Diam 59.8mm. Some of the Type 5 watches, like the example shown, have decoratively pierced cases to imitate their full-scale alarm, striking or repeating counterparts.
Museum of London, Acc. no. 34.181/51
Miniature, Acc. no. 94.100, Cat. no. 12.21

TYPE 5

These double-sided circular watches have a domed profile, decorative outer 'case', recessed dial and integrally cast hands and pendant. They constitute by far the largest group in the corpus and of the 48 examples known, 31 different designs have been recorded. Whilst it could be argued that of all the watches discussed here, Type 5 are the least like genuine timepieces because they have dials on both faces, they do possess certain stylistic and horological features which reflect contemporary fashion in watch design. If these details are accepted as a genuine attempt to portray chronological development, it is possible that watches of this type were made over a considerable period from the 1630s to the late 18th century, and this may account for the relatively high incidence of finds.

Although some are far too stylized or damaged to be dated with any degree of confidence (for example, D16, D19 & D28), and others combine a minute circle with case ornament reflecting fashions of an earlier period (D4), many exhibit characteristics which seem to imitate a specific type of timepiece or an aspect of horological development. The earliest examples represented (D1–3 & D7) all seem to copy cased watches of 1630–40 and these have a single hand with arrowhead pointer, a recessed dial and a decorated border imitating piqué and inlaid case work. At this date the hinge is not particularly pronounced on genuine timepieces and does not appear on these toy examples. Several watches represented (D4, D12 & D14) have minute circles with Arabic numerals and these were probably made in the 1680s and 90s although the style of the 'cases' is very much that of the 1660s, and one watch (D12) has raised tabs for the minute numerals which seems to be a direct copy of the champlevé-style dial in vogue during the last quarter of the 17th century. Those with pierced cases (D10; D11) probably imitate alarm, striking or repeating watches (see fig. 73).[31] The latest group are represented by watches with two hands, a feature which becomes standard from the 1680s (D16, D20, D24–26) and some have 'beetle and poker' hands which were characteristic of the first quarter of the 18th century. Since the precise chronology of Type 5 is rather uncertain, the watches have been categorized by design and form rather than date. Sizes range from 27mm to 50mm, with an average diameter of 32.5mm.

Type 5 watches were made in a two-part mould (fig. 74) and the separately cast hemispheres were soldered together around the circumference. The soldered join was a potential source of weakness and as a result only six complete watches are known.

12.11 Toy watch mould

Accession number: A20772
Material: Sedimentary rock[32]
Condition: Part only
Dimensions: Block: L 108mm; W 57mm; Dpt 17mm. Matrices: 32mm
Inscription: 1746, Debr 17; Rich …d H…
Description: This is the only extant mould for toy watches so far identified. Carved into each side of the rectangular block are matrices for Type 5 watches (fig. 74: sides A & B). Adjacent funnel-shaped sprues are positioned at the top of the long axis and these divide into three channels to

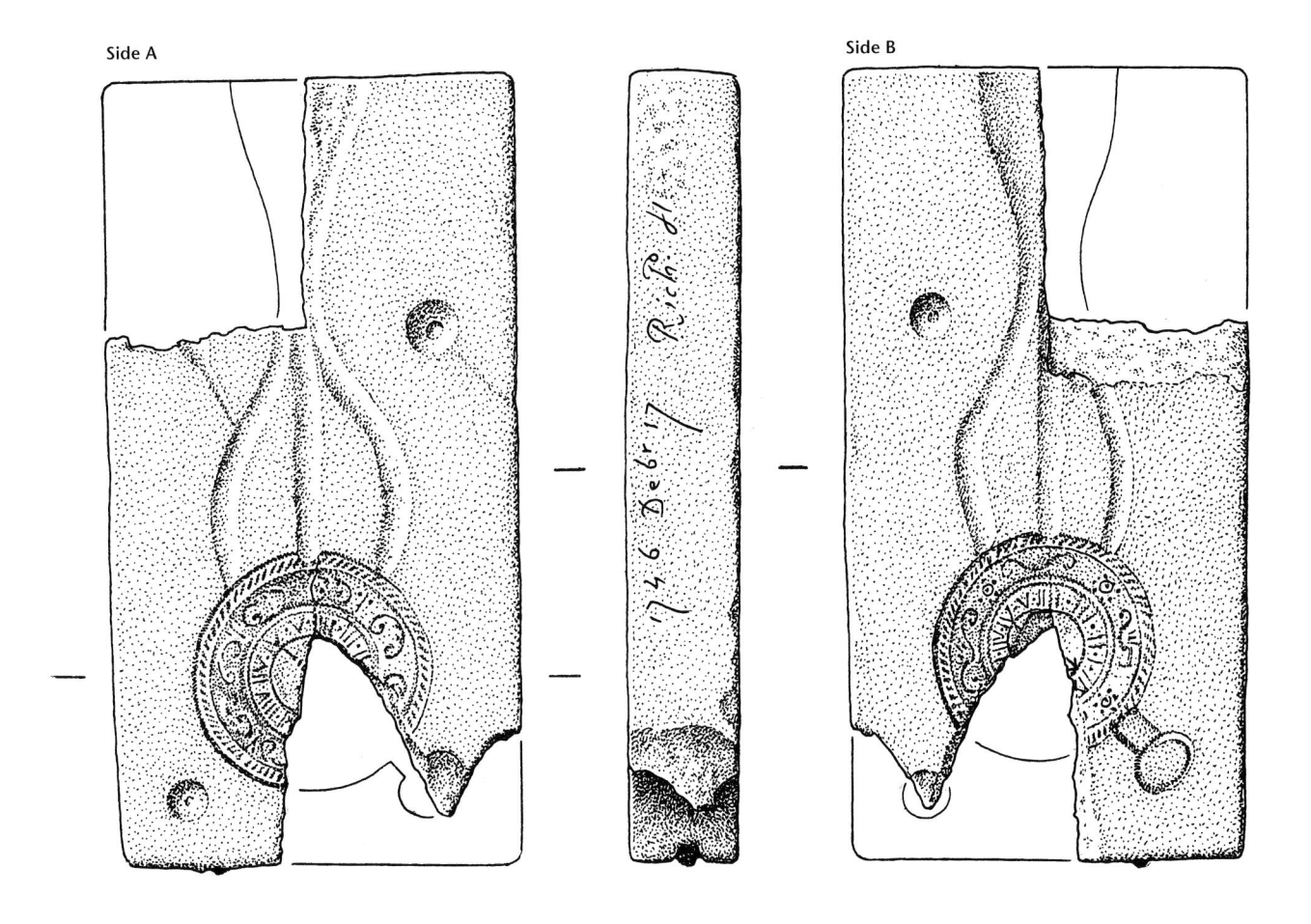

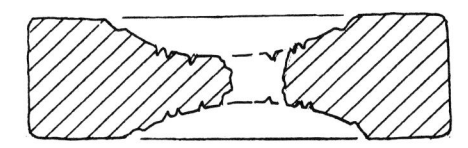

Fig. 74. A mould for toy watches with a matrix on each side, inscribed *1746 Debr 17 Rich.d ...H* (possibly Richard Heath: see Appendix III, p. 437)
Museum of London, Acc. no. A20772

Fig. 75. Silver cased verge watch with outer case of leather covered in silver-piqué floral decoration. Signed Benjamin Hill, Londini, c. 1650. Diam 45.7mm
Museum of London, 34.181/35. W.E. Miller Collection, 1934

disperse and facilitate the passage of molten metal into the watch moulds below. Side B has an additional thinly cut channel which is probably the result of damage or burial, although it could be part of a riser designed to allow air and gases to escape.

A large chunk of the mould is missing but since the matrices are directly aligned and carved as a mirror image, the overall shape and form of each can be deduced. The relative positions of the key holes, two on one side and one on the other, suggest a total of four, and both watches had a pendant loop, complete on side A and just showing on side B. Both of the watch matrices have a rope-twist edge and the chapter rings are enclosed within concentric circles marked with Roman hours I–XII interspersed with half-hour pellets. The watches both have a single hand, and side A shows an arrowhead pointer at 12 o'clock; side B, the half-baluster counterpoise. The only substantive difference between the matrices is the border decoration: side A has a symmetrical pattern of stylized flowerheads interspersed with simple scrolling, while side B has a rococo design of stylized leaf scrolls. Unfortunately neither design is represented within the surviving corpus.

From the evidence of this mould, it is clear that two toy watch hemispheres could be cast at the same time and two different patterns could be produced simultaneously, but whether the castings were ultimately joined or attached to matching hemispheres is a matter of conjecture. The shape of the mould and the alignment of the matrices also suggest that a whole series of moulds could be used side by side for batch production. It is possible that the mould maker is Richard Heath (see Appendix III).

Date: 1746
Provenance: Sumner Street, near Blackfriars, 1912

TYPE 5, DESIGN 1

12.12 Watch

Accession number: 98.2/454
Material: Lead alloy
Condition: Complete; pendant loop missing
Dimensions: Diam 30mm; Th *c.* 12mm
Description: An identically matched double-sided watch made from two hemispheres which have been soldered together around the circumference. The pendant loop which would logically be positioned at 12 o'clock is missing. A rope-twist edge surrounds a floral border, similar to that employed on T1 D2 watches. The recessed chapter ring is contained within a rope-twist band with Roman hours numbering I–XII. There are no half-hour pellets between XI–XII and IIII–X, presumably because the engraver ran out of room. The dial centre retained within a plain band is undecorated. The integrally cast hand is complete with a counterpoise and foliate pointer at 12 o'clock. There are a few areas of damage, mostly small holes.
Date: 1630–50

TYPE 5, DESIGN 2

12.13 Watch

Accession number: 98.2/498
Material: Lead alloy
Condition: One side only; pendant loop missing
Dimensions: Diam 32mm
Description: Similar to T5, D1, but not so well executed. The dial is recessed, and the Roman hours I–XII are well defined, spaced and interspersed with pellets to indicate the half-hours. The centre of the dial, defined by a rope-twist band, is otherwise plain. The integrally cast hand is complete with counterpoise and foliate pointer at 12 o'clock.
Date: 1630–50

TYPE 5, DESIGN 3

12.14 Watch

Accession number: 98.2/492
Material: Lead alloy
Condition: One side only; pendant loop missing
Dimensions: Diam 31mm
Description: Similar to T5, D1–2 above but with a slightly different floral border. The recessed chapter ring is slightly larger than either T5, D1 or D2, but is also contained within a rope-twist band. The dial is numbered with Roman hours I–XII and pellets to indicate the half-hours. The dial centre has concentric grooves but is otherwise plain, and the integrally cast hand is complete with counterpoise and trefoil pointer at 12 o'clock. Part of the edge is damaged.
Date: 1630–50

TYPE 5, DESIGN 4

12.15 Watch

Accession number: 98.2/458*; 98.2/482; 98.2/483; 98.2/484*; 98.2/485; 98.2/489; 98.2/510; 98.2/512; 98.2/518
Material: Lead alloy
Condition: One side only
Dimensions: Two sizes:
  i) 98.2/458: Diam *c.* 45mm; Th *c.* 9mm
  ii) all others: Diam *c.* 35 x *c.* 33 mm
Description: One side of a double-sided watch with domed profile. A rope-twist edge surrounds a wide border decorated with pellets and a symmetrical design of stylized pendant flowerheads stemming from and hanging alternately from a tendril. The largest version (98.2/458) shows an outer circle of minutes, numbered 5–60 in Arabic numerals and then an inner circle of Roman hours I–XII with pellet half-hour marks. None of the smaller watches has a circle of minutes. The dial centres (apart from 98.2/486) are all enclosed within a rope-twist border and decorated with an adorsed fleur-de-lys. Although the fleur-de-lys design is the same for all, the treatment of the main leaf is different: 98.2/483 has a leaf vein effect; 98.2/482, 98.2/484, 98.2/489, 98.2/512 & 98.2/518 are all cross-hatched; and 98.2/458, 98.2/485 & 98.2/510 are plain. 98.2/486 has the same border decoration, but a plain circle surrounds the dial and the dial centre. In addition the dial centre is decorated with Ss either side of the hand and the lower part of the pendant loop survives. All of the watches have an integrally cast hand with central boss, long counterpoise and trefoil pointer at 12 o'clock. 98.2/510 seems to have been repaired with solder across the dial between 1 and 7 o'clock. 98.2/518 consists only of the dial centre.
Date: 1680–1700
Comments: It was probably too difficult to include the minute circle on the smaller version.
Comparanda: The case front decoration is quite similar to that on a watch by William Snow, *c.* 1650, with a silver piqué leather case: see Camerer Cuss 1952, p. 65, plate 22. For other examples, see the Worshipful Company of Clockmakers' collection and Bendall 1994, p. 523, group 1, fig. 2.

TYPE 5, DESIGN 5

12.16 Watch

Accession number: 98.2/481

Material: Lead alloy

Condition: One side only

Dimensions: Diam 32mm

Description: Rope-twist edge surrounds a wide border, very similar to T5, D4 in overall scheme, but the stylized 'flower' heads comprise a cross with a central pellet and pellets in each quadrant. The dial is contained within a plain circle and the chapter ring is marked with Roman hours I–XII interspersed with pellets to indicate the half-hour. The dial centre has an adorsed fleur-de-lys with hand (part surviving) pointing to 12 o'clock. There are two large holes in the chapter ring and dial centre, and the general detail is unclear, suggesting either a worn mould or poor casting technique.

Date: 1630–40

TYPE 5, DESIGN 6

12.17 Watch

Accession number: 87.147/2

Material: Lead alloy

Condition: Complete

Dimensions: Diam 30 x 29 mm

Inscription: IB

Description: Double-sided watch with two matching hemispheres originally joined around the circumference with solder. Traces of the pendant loop, positioned at 6 o'clock, remain. The rope-twist edge contains a wide scrolling floral border and a rope-twist band encloses a plain circle and the chapter ring marked with Roman hours I–XII. There are no half-hour marks. The otherwise plain dial centre is inscribed I and B either side of the single hand which has a central boss, inverted baluster counterpoise and trefoil pointer at 6 o'clock.

Date: The style is very much that of 1630–50.

Comparanda: Very similar border decoration to T5, D1, but not so fine. See T5, D8 with initials on central dial. Other examples have been recorded from Wapping High Street and New Crane Stairs.

TYPE 5, DESIGN 7

12.18 Watch

Accession numbers: 98.2/471*; 98.2/508

Material: Lead alloy

Condition: One side only

Dimensions: Diam 32mm

Inscription: IG

Description: One side from a double-sided domed watch with a wide flange, beaded edge and wide decorative border consisting of a symmetrical pattern of stylized pendant flowerheads hanging either side of a beaded stem with leaves. The flowerheads are tighter and more pronounced than those on T5, D4. Concentric circles, the outer beaded, enclose the dial with Roman hours I–XII and pellets mark the half-hours between all except XI and XII. The otherwise plain dial centre is inscribed I and G either side of the single hand with has a large multi-knopped boss, short counterpoise and arrowhead pointer at 12 o'clock. 98.2/508 seems to be from the same mould as 98.2/471, but only half survives showing the hours XI–IIII and the initial G to the right of the hand. This fragment has also been flattened.

Date: Late 17th–early 18th century

TYPE 5, DESIGN 8

12.19 Watch

Accession number: 98.2/473
Material: Lead alloy
Condition: One side only
Dimensions: Diam 31.5mm
Inscription: … H
Description: One side of a double-sided domed watch. The lower stem of the pendant loop is extant and decorated with a single pellet. There is a fairly wide flange around the circumference, with two circles of beading, the outer more pronounced and more widely spaced. These enclose a decorative border with a symmetrical design of raised stars either side of a beaded swirling band. A beaded circle encloses the dial defined by an outer graduated band, and this surrounds a chapter ring with Roman hours I–XII, interspersed with pellets to indicate the half-hours. Concentric circles enclose a plain dial centre, inscribed with the initial H to the right of the hand. The initial to the left has been obliterated in casting. The single hand has a half-baluster counterpoise, central boss and arrowhead pointer at 12 o'clock.
Date: Late 17th–early 18th century

TYPE 5, DESIGN 9

12.20 Watch

Accession number: 98.2/478
Material: Lead alloy
Condition: One side only
Dimensions: Diam 40mm
Description: One side, now flattened, from a double-sided domed watch. The beaded edge contains a border with a symmetrical design of stylized flowerheads linked with foliage (now very worn). The chapter ring is marked with Roman hours I–XII, interspersed with pellets to indicate the half-hours. The dial centre is plain and there is a single hand with a central boss, counterpoise and pointer at 12 o'clock. This is a rather crude version with some damage.
Date: Late 17th–early 18th century
Comparanda: Worshipful Company of Clockmakers' collection and Bendall 1994, group 1, fig. 7

TYPE 5, DESIGN 10

12.21 Watch

Accession number: 94.100
Material: Lead alloy
Condition: Complete
Dimensions: Diam 45mm; Dpt 17mm
Description: A complete double-sided domed watch consisting of two hemispheres soldered around the circumference with a pierced front and solid back; both with matching borders and chapter ring. The rope-twist edge surrounds a wide border decorated with three different flowerheads, each contained within the loops of a twining stem with leaves. A rope-twist circle encloses the dial on both sides, marked with Roman hours I–XII interspersed with pellets to indicate the half-hours. The hours are unequally spaced, VIII and IX virtually join and the half-hour pellet is placed over the first digit of IX. On the front, the centre of the

dial is pierced and a cross bar at right angles to the single hand divides the space into quadrants. At the back, the dial centre is solid and there is a thin cross-hatched band at right angles to the hand. The areas between are filled with fine decorative scrolling. Both hands have a central boss, baluster counterpoise and trefoil pointer at 12 o'clock. There is no sign of a pendant loop.
Date: Late 17th–early 18th century
Provenance: Westminster, north side, opposite Lambeth Palace, 1994

TYPE 5, DESIGN 11

12.22 Watch

Accession number: 98.2/513
Material: Lead alloy
Condition: Fragment of one side
Dimensions: H *c.* 22; W 42 mm
Description: A flattened fragment from a double-sided domed watch with pierced decoration, similar to but cruder than T5, D10. The edge seems to be plain and the wide border is decorated with large stylized flowerheads, each enclosed within the loops of the scrolling leafy stem. The dial is enclosed within a beaded circle, with Roman hours IIII–IX (the rest are missing). Pellets indicate the half-hours. The dial centre, enclosed within a beaded circle, is damaged, but may contain the lower part of the hand counterpoise. If so, this is set at an extraordinary angle.
Date: Late 17th–early 18th century

TYPE 5, DESIGN 12

12.23 Watch

Accession number: 98.2/521
Material: Lead alloy
Condition: Fragment of one side
Dimensions: Diam 45 x 39 mm
Description: Part of one side of a domed double-sided watch (now flattened). The stub of the pendant loop remains with part of the decorative border which is now enclosed by a rope-twist edge. The decoration consists of a stylized flowerhead between stylized symmetrical scrolling. The dial is retained within a rope-twist circle and there is an outer minute circle with Arabic numerals graduated 5 to 60. Each number is marked on a tab with spaces between. The dial division is poor and the minute tabs are unequally spaced and badly aligned with the inner chapter ring which shows Roman hours I–XII interspersed with pellets to indicate the half-hours. A plain circle encloses the dial centre decorated with an adorsed fleur-de-lys in high relief. The single hand has a long counterpoise, central boss and trefoil pointer at 12 o'clock.
Date: The minute circle and champlevé-style dial suggest a date during the last quarter of the 17th century.

TYPE 5, DESIGN 13

12.24 Watch

Accession number: 98.2/443
Material: Lead alloy
Condition: One side only; some damage
Dimensions: Diam 44mm
Description: One side of a double-sided domed watch with a rope-twist edge, wide floral border consisting of a symmetrical design of double-headed roses interspersed with swirling leafy stems and tendrils. A plain circle encloses the chapter ring marked with Roman hours I–XII. There are no half-hour marks. The dial centre is decorated with a symmetrical scrolling pattern and the single hand, with central boss, baluster counterpoise and trefoil pointer is at 12 o'clock. There is no sign of a pendant loop.
Date: 1675–1700

TYPE 5, DESIGN 14

12.25 Watch

Accession number: 98.2/517
Material: Lead alloy
Condition: Fragment of one side
Dimensions: Diam *c.* 50mm
Description: Part of one side of a double-sided domed watch. A rope-twist edge contains a wide decorative border of raised flowerheads interspersed with scrolling. The dial is enclosed within a rope-twist circle and there is an outer minute circle marked in Arabic 5–60. The inner chapter ring has Roman hours I–XII with pellets to indicate the half-hours. The dial centre has symmetrical scrolling and the single hand has a central boss, baluster counterpoise and trefoil pointer at 12 o'clock.
Date: 1675–1700

TYPE 5, DESIGN 15

12.26 Watch

Accession number: 98.2/445*; 98.2/465
Material: Lead alloy
Condition: 98.2/445: complete
98.2/465: one side only
Dimensions: Diam 32mm; Dpt *c.* 9mm
Inscription: AB
Description: A complete double-sided domed watch with identical sides. Each hemisphere is joined around the circumference with solder. The pendant loop is missing, but there are two large holes through the border at approximately 4 and 8 o'clock, both showing signs of wear. The rope-twist edge contains a border decorated with a symmetrical pattern of fleur-de-lys, small and large, alternating around the circumference. A rope-twist circle encloses the chapter ring marked with Roman hours I–XII interspersed with pellets to indicate the half-hours. There is an unequal division of hours, and the numerals become more cramped from VI–XII. The plain dial centre enclosed by a circle is inscribed with the letters A and B, and these are placed either side of the single hand. The hand has a central boss, baluster counterpoise and trefoil pointer at 12 o'clock.

98.2/465 has identical decoration and inscription, and was probably made in the same mould.
Date: 1675–1700
Provenance: 98.2/445: Southwark Bridge, north end

TYPE 5, DESIGN 16

12.27 Watch

Accession number: 98.2/480
Material: Lead alloy
Condition: One side only
Dimensions: Diam 35mm
Description: One side of a double-sided domed watch. The stub of the pendant loop is extant. A rope-twist edge contains a wide border decorated with baroque-style ornament, consisting of S-scrolls, scallop shells, foliage and tiny flowerheads. The chapter ring is enclosed within a beaded circle. The Roman hour divisions, interspersed with pellets to mark the half-hours, are badly aligned, unequal and squashed and some are missing or repeated: thus there are two XIs and two VIs, instead of a XII and VII. The plain dial centre is contained within a beaded circle and there are two hands which are positioned at approximately half past two.
Date: 1720s
Comments: Having two hands suggests a date after 1675–80, although the decoration is suggestive of the 1720s.

TYPE 5, DESIGN 17

12.28 Watch

Accession number: 98.2/449*; 98.2/470
Material: Lead alloy
Condition: Complete
Dimensions: 98.2/449: Diam 47 x 45 mm; Dpt c. 7mm. 98.2/470: Diam 32mm
Description: A double-sided domed watch of flattened profile, with tiny circles around the edge. Both sides are matching and the two hemispheres are joined by solder around the circumference. The wide border has symmetrical baroque- or rococo- style ornamentation and the dial is enclosed with a plain circle surrounded by sprigs. The chapter ring has Roman hours I–XII interspersed with pellets to indicate the half-hours. The numerals are rather bunched up between IIII and IX. A plain circle surrounds the dial centre which has scrolling either side of the central boss on the hand. The single hand has a large baluster counterpoise and trefoil-style pointer at 12 o'clock. The smaller version (98.2/470: one side only) has virtually identical decoration, although the outer edge has a dot and circle pattern.
Date: Late 17th–early 18th century

TYPE 5, DESIGN 18

12.29 Watch

Accession number: 91.204/2*; 98.2/467; 98.2/479
Material: Lead alloy
Condition: One side only
Dimensions: H (incl. pendant) 41mm; Diam 33mm
Description: One side from a double-sided domed watch. 91.204/2 includes the pendant loop. The outer edge has tiny circles and a wide flange enclosing a border with rococo-style decoration. There is a beaded circle around the chapter ring which is marked with Roman hours I–XII and interspersed with pellets to indicate the half-hours. The dial centre is plain and there is a single hand with counterpoise and arrowhead pointer at 12 o'clock.
Date: Late 17th–early 18th century
Comparanda: Worshipful Company of Clockmakers' collection (Acc. no. 1209), and Bendall 1994, group 1, fig. 1

TYPE 5, DESIGN 19

12.30 Watch

Accession number: 98.2/499
Material: Lead alloy
Condition: One side only; very worn; some damage
Dimensions: Diam 32mm
Description: One side of a double-sided domed watch, very worn, with some damage. Similar to T5, D18, but of a debased form. There are tiny circles around the edge and a wide flange around the circumference. The border has a rococo-style pattern which abuts onto the outer edge of the proportionally large but narrow chapter ring. The dial has Roman hours I–XII, but there are no half-hour marks. The single hand with central boss and long, thin counterpoise, has an arrowhead pointer at 12 o'clock. There is no sign of the pendant loop.
Date: Late 17th–early 18th century
Comparanda: Worshipful Company of Clockmakers' collection (Acc. no. 1209) and Bendall 1994, group 1, fig. 4.

TYPE 5, DESIGN 20

TYPE 5, DESIGN 21

TYPE 5, DESIGN 22

12.31 Watch

Accession number: 98.2/506

Material: Lead alloy; traces of red pigment

Condition: One side only; part of pendant loop

Dimensions: Diam 32mm

Description: One side of a double-sided domed watch with the lower part of the pendant loop. There is a wide flange around the circumference and the edge, decorated with beading, encloses a border with rococo-style decoration which abuts onto the beaded circle surrounding the dial. The chapter ring has Roman hours I–XII, interspersed with pellets to indicate the half-hours. The hour divisions are a little unequal and the VI does not align with XII. There are two hands and the hour hand has an arrowhead pointer at approximately 23 minutes past 1.

Date: Probably 1690–1700. Use of two hands clearly points to a date after 1675–80, although the decoration is suggestive of the 1720s.

Comparandum: Another watch with a similar rococo-style design, but otherwise with a very different hatched rim and single hand at 12 o'clock recovered from Custom House on 3 May 1992

12.32 Watch

Accession number: 98.2/477

Material: Lead alloy

Condition: One side only; flattened

Dimensions: Diam 40mm

Description: One side, now flattened, of a double-sided domed watch. There is a semi-circular looped edge containing a wide border with a symmetrical design of four lozenges linked by scrolling. A beaded circle encloses the dial, and the chapter ring is marked with Roman hours I–XII interspersed with pellets to indicate the half-hours. The dial centre is plain and there is a single hand with central boss, long thin counterpoise and trefoil pointer at 12 o'clock.

Date: Mid- to late 17th century

Comparanda: A complete example with traces of red pigment and pendant loop (one side only; Diam 33mm; Th 3mm) recovered from the Thames foreshore at Vintry, 16 March 2000 (Enq. no. 1517/19); also example from Didcot, Oxfordshire, 11 February 1999.

12.33 Watch

Accession number: 98.2/487

Material: Lead alloy

Condition: One side only; flattened

Dimensions: Diam 33mm

Description: One side, now flattened, of a double-sided watch, with semi-circular looped edge containing a wide border with a symmetrical design of four lozenges between stylized flowerheads and ring and dot motifs. The sides of the lozenges are concave. The inner part of the border design touches the chapter ring which is marked with Roman hours I–XII, and interspersed with pellets to indicate the half-hours. The dial centre is enclosed within a slashed circle and the single hand with counterpoise and arrowhead pointer is at 12 o'clock.

Date: Probably late 17th–early 18th century

TYPE 5, DESIGN 23

12.34 Watch

Accession number: 98.2/516
Material: Lead alloy; slight trace of red pigment on the border
Condition: Part of one side only; flattened; damaged
Dimensions: Diam 42 x 24 mm
Description: Part of one side of a double-sided domed watch which is completely flattened and damaged. The thickened crescent edge contains a wide border decorated with lozenges interspersed with rococo scrolling. A beaded circle encloses the chapter ring marked with Roman hours I–V and XI–XII (the rest is missing) interspersed with pellets to indicate the half-hours. The dial centre is plain and the single hand with central boss, counterpoise and arrowhead pointer is at 12 o'clock.
Date: Probably late 17th–early 18th century

TYPE 5, DESIGN 24

12.35 Watch

Accession number: 98.2/501
Material: Lead alloy
Condition: part of one side only; some damage
Dimensions: Diam 27mm
Description: One side with some damage from a double-sided domed watch. There is a beaded edge with an inner circle of tiny beading surrounding a swirling foliate border. The dial is recessed within a thickened plain circle. The chapter ring is marked with Roman hours I–XII, interspersed with dots to indicate the half-hours. The hour spacing is unequal. Fine concentric circles enclose the plain dial centre and there are two hands with a large central boss and elaborately decorated pointer indicating half past four.
Date: Probably early to mid-18th century

TYPE 5, DESIGN 25

12.36 Watch

Accession number: 98.2/446*; 98.2/505
Material: Lead alloy. 98.2/505: red pigment
Condition: 98.2/446: complete
98.2/505: one side only
Dimensions: H (incl. pendant loop) 41mm; Diam 33mm; Dpt 7.5mm
Description: Complete double-sided domed watch with matching hemispheres which have been soldered together around the circumference. Both sides have complete pendant loops and these are cast with convincing detail. A rope-twist edge and a plain flange surrounds concentric beaded circles and a chapter ring marked with Roman hours I–XII and pellet half-hours. The four is rendered as IV rather than the conventional IIII. The dial centre is enclosed within a beaded circle and there are three beaded circles around the hand pivot for decorative effect. There are two hands, with a central boss and detail suggestive of the so-called 'beetle and poker'-style, positioned at 20 minutes past 12. 98.2/505 was probably cast from the same mould.
Date: Late 18th century

Plate IX. Jan Steen [1626–1679] has captured the delight and disappointment, reward and punishment associated with the Feast of St Nicholas, the most important family holiday in the Netherlands. Good children could expect to receive presents and the little girl and boy are clearly delighted with their toys and sweets, while their tearful older brother thinks he has been forgotten. Instead his family are teasing, and the parted bed curtains and gesture from the old woman suggest that his presents have been tucked away for him to find.

The Feast of St Nicholas, 1665–8
Oil on canvas, 82 x 70.5 cm
Rijksmuseum, Amsterdam

362 • TOYS, TRIFLES & TRINKETS

Plate X. The child is unwell and his nurse tries to amuse him with two knights on horseback.
From the autobiographical costume book of Matthäus Schwarz of Augsburg [1496–1574]
Herzog Anton Ulrich-Museum,
Kunstmuseum des landes Niedersachsen,
Braunschweig, Germany

Plate XI. With considerable verve and ingenuity, Bruegel has managed to squeeze some 80 different games into this study of children's play. He has even included an interior scene where little girls dress their dolls beside shelves loaded with miniature household furniture and goods (inset).
Der Kinderspiele, 1560 by Pieter Bruegel [*c.* 1525–1569]
Oil on panel, 118 x 161 cm
Kunsthistorisches Museum, Vienna

Plate XII. In this quiet scene the women and children seem to be completely absorbed in their respective tasks. We are left in little doubt about the activities of the women: washing and making lace, but what are the children doing? Are they playing with base-metal toys of the sort described in this volume?

Het Straatje ('The Little Street'), 1655–60
by Jan Vermeer [1632–1675]
Oil on canvas, 54.3 x 44 cm
Rijksmuseum, Amsterdam

Plate XIII. On a small patch of exposed foreshore, two mudlarks search for lumps of coal, bones, rope, pieces of iron and copper nails and other items to sell in this dramatic moonlight view of the Thames.
York Water Gate and the Adelphi, c. 1850
by Henry Pether [1828–1865]
Oil on canvas, 58.7 x 84.1 cm
Museum of London, Acc. no. 60.50

Plate XIV. Despite the hazards of her surroundings, a tiny child has been left to play on this quay on the Thames.
The City from Bankside, 1820–30, attributed to Thomas Miles Richardson [1784–1848]
Oil on canvas, 71.5 x 92 cm
Museum of London, Acc. no. 95.185

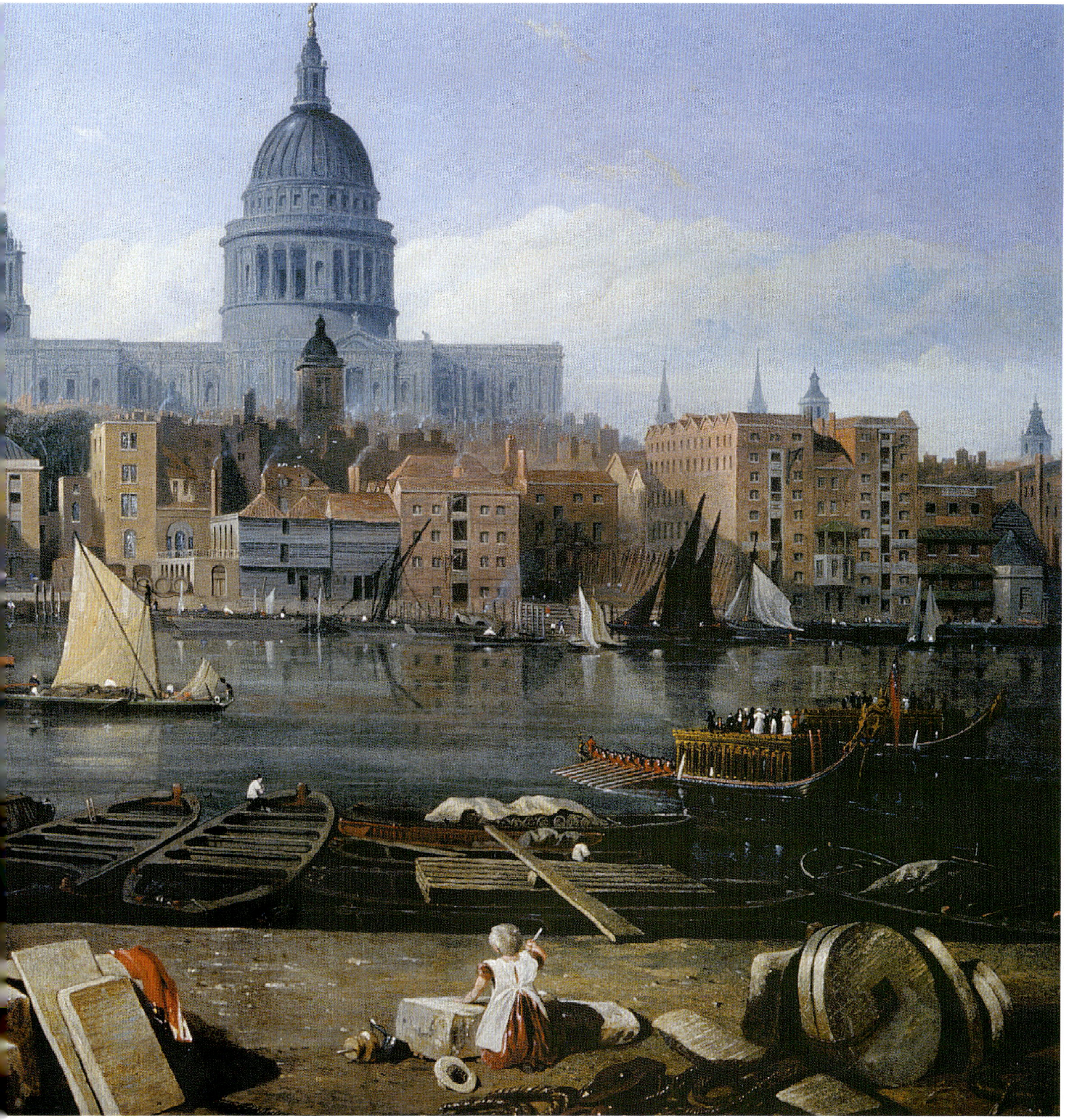

Plate XV. The main subject of the painting, the feast day procession of Abbot Antony of Egypt, has been relegated to the background, and our attention is drawn to the merrymaking, dancing, shopping and archery practice in the middle ground where pilgrims and villagers are making the most of the religious holiday. St Antony's piety and miracles were greatly venerated in the 16th century and the procession is led by members of the Crossbowmen's Guild who were dedicated to his service. The attributes of the saint are indicated by the prominent Tau-cross, a pig carried on a litter and pig skulls embedded in the path. People often travelled considerable distances to take part in Saint's Day Festivals and trinket stalls were set up to sell a range of souvenirs, knick-knacks and toys to pilgrims.

Retour d'un pèlerinage à Saint Antoine, c. 1550
by Pieter Aertsen [1508–1575]
Oil on panel, 110 x 170 cm
Musées royaux des Beaux-Arts de Belgique, Brussels

TYPE 5, DESIGN 26

TYPE 5, DESIGN 27

TYPE 5, DESIGN 28

12.37 Watch

Accession number: 98.2/491*, 98.2/503
Material: Lead alloy
Condition: One side only. 98.2/503: very damaged and worn
Dimensions: Diam 34mm
Description: Single sides from a double-sided domed watch cast from the same mould, with slight damage to the edge. The watch is decorated with a series of ridges and plain circles, a beaded circle, and narrow border of alternating stars and sprigs. The chapter ring is marked with Roman hours I–XII, interspersed with stars which indicate the half-hours. The dial centre is enclosed by a beaded circle and decorated with another. There are two beetle and poker hands at 4 o'clock.
Date: Late 17th–early 18th century

12.38 Watch

Accession number: 98.2/469*; 98.2/476
Material: Lead alloy. 98.2/469: red pigment
Condition: One side only.
    98.2/476: slightly flattened
Dimensions: Diam $c.$ 33mm
Description: These single sides from double-sided domed watches have been cast from the same mould. The ring and dot edge contains a border with a simple symmetrical pattern of ring and dot and pellets, and the chapter ring has Roman hours I–XII interspersed with pellets to indicate the half-hours. The dial centre is plain and the single hand with central boss, counterpoise and arrowhead pointer is at 12 o'clock. 98.2/476 also has a large hole at the 12 o'clock position pushed through from the front and this was possibly used as a method of suspension. There is no sign of the original pendant loop.
Date: Late 17th–early 18th century

12.39 Watch

Accession number: 98.2/466
Material: Lead alloy
Condition: One side only
Dimensions: Diam $c.$ 35mm
Description: One side of a double-sided domed watch, with ring and dot edge and a beaded circle enclosing the chapter ring. The Roman hours are a nonsense, back to front from XII–VIII; and thereafter the I and Xs are confused with the following sequence: XI, X and IX. There are half-hour pellets between the hours. The dial centre is plain and the single hand with a central boss, counterpoise and arrowhead pointer is at 12 o'clock. In addition, there are four tiny holes in the beaded circle, and these are equally spaced around the circumference which perhaps suggests an alternative use for this piece as a mount.
Date: Late 17th–early 18th century
Comparandum: A similar dial found by Southwark Bridge, south-west side, again with four holes around the circumference

TYPE 5, DESIGN 29

12.40 Watch

Accession number: 98.2/490
Material: Lead alloy
Condition: One side only
Dimensions: Diam 33mm
Description: One side of a double-sided domed watch with feather-pattern edge and fine concentric circles enclosing the chapter ring. The Roman hours are marked I–XII, interspersed with pellets to mark the half-hours. The dial centre is plain and there is a single hand with counterpoise and arrowhead pointer at 3 o'clock. The stub of the pendant loop is extant.
Date: Late 17th–early 18th century

TYPE 6

There appears to be only one example of this type. The decoration seems to represent enamel, engraved or piqué casework of the late 17th century. The watch is badly crushed and damaged, but was probably cast in one piece.

TYPE 6, DESIGN 1

12.41 Watch

Accession number: 82.606/2
Material: Lead alloy
Condition: Complete
Dimensions: H (incl. pendant loop) 45mm; Diam 37mm; Th 1.5mm
Description: This watch is crushed so that it is impossible to tell whether it had been cast in one piece. There is an integrally cast, but misshapen, pendant loop with rope-twist decoration and hatched scrolled supports and the 'case' front is decorated with a wreath which stems from a ribbon below the pendant. The raised chapter ring is surrounded by a groove, and although it is extremely worn and damaged, it is marked with Roman hours I–XII. The dial centre is plain and there is a single hand with a central boss and arrowhead pointer at 12 o'clock. The design on the back of the watch is off-centre, and consists of two stylized flowerheads with leafy stems which are joined at the base, each stem arching around the sides of the watch to form a decorative border, and a circular reserve enclosing a raised flowerhead surrounded by concentric circles.
Date: Late 17th–early 18th century

TYPE 7

From the surviving evidence, watches of this type seem to have been made in three sizes ranging from 24mm to 38mm. They were cast in one piece with a completely plain 'case', recessed dial, integral hands and pendant loop. There is a casting seam on the back aligned with the 12 and 6 o'clock positions on the dial, and two vents – one or both subsequently plugged to disguise the manufacturing process and improve the watch's appearance – which enabled the gas to escape.

These watches were probably made in the early 18th century, even though they all have a single hand – harking back to an earlier period.

WATCHES • 371

TYPE 7, DESIGN 1

which has a stylized floral motif around the central boss, and most have a plain band between the chapter ring and central plate. The integrally cast single hands have a long thin counterpoise and arrowhead pointers at 12 o'clock, apart from 98.2/452 and perhaps 98.2/450, (which is very damaged, but possibly from the same mould or workshop) which have a counterpoise with ball decoration and a trefoil pointer.

Date: 1700–50

TYPE 8

These circular watches, represented by 22 examples, are the only known type with moving parts and a simple mechanism. They are a very good imitation of English or French pair-case watches dating from about 1700 to the mid-18th century, and of all the toy watches described here, perhaps Acc. no. 2001.15/2 is most like the genuine article (see Cat. no. 12.47 and fig. 70, p. 338). The earliest examples with thick plain cases (D1–D4) probably date to about 1700, even though they have flatter tops and bases and rounded sides compared with the domed and angular profile of genuine timepieces of the period; while the thinner watches with angular bevelled case fronts and elaborately decorated case backs (represented by D5–D7) are closer in shape and proportion to watches of a slightly later date between 1730 and 1750. Five sizes are known, and the diameters range from 28–55mm, but the largest is still smaller than a genuine watch of the period.

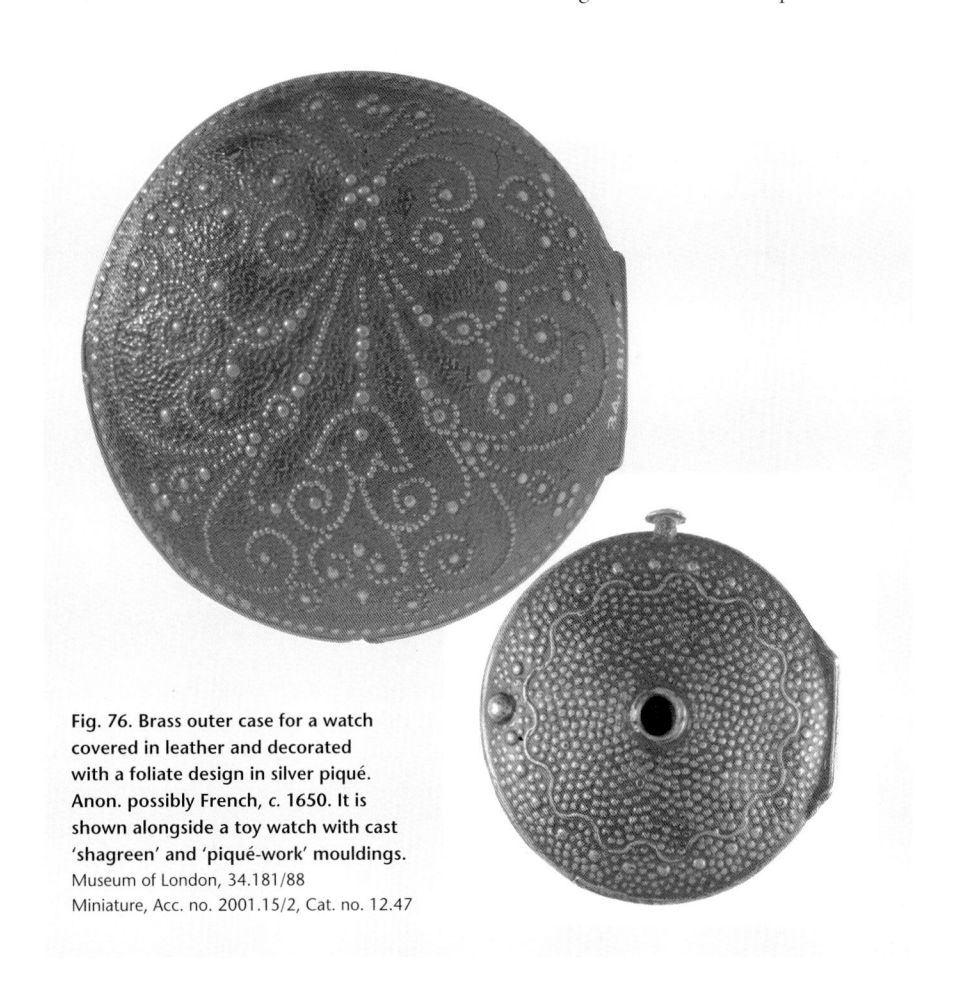

12.42 Watch

Accession number: A24849; A25822; 98.2/444; 98.2/447; 98.2/448; 98.2/450; 98.2/451; 98.2/452*; 98.2/455; 98.2/457
Material: Lead alloy
Condition: 98.2/444; 98.2/447; 98.2/452: complete
Dimensions, Three sizes:
   i) A24849; 98.2/444; 98.2/455: Diam 24mm
   ii) 98.2/457: Diam 30mm (squashed)
   iii) 98.2/447; 98.2/448; 98.2/450; 98.2/451; 98.2/452; A25822: Diam 38mm
Description: All of these watches have a plain case with a sharply carinated profile, recessed dial, Roman hours I–XII and pellet half-hours. Some have a clearly defined edge between case and dial to represent the difference between the outer and inner cases on a real watch. All of the dial centres are plain, apart from 98.2/452

Fig. 76. Brass outer case for a watch covered in leather and decorated with a foliate design in silver piqué. Anon. possibly French, c. 1650. It is shown alongside a toy watch with cast 'shagreen' and 'piqué-work' mouldings.
Museum of London, 34.181/88
Miniature, Acc. no. 2001.15/2, Cat. no. 12.47

Watches of this type have four main elements: the 'outer case' cast in one piece with integral pendant, hinge and button; the dial plate, the rotating hand and the mechanism. They all have two encircling ridges around the widest part of the case to represent the junction of the outer case rims on a real pair-case watch, and some even have mouldings to suggest a hinge (D5–D7) and button. Four of the watches have decorated cases, but only one has really convincing 'outer case' decoration, with mouldings imitating shagreen piqué and inlaid casework (fig. 76, p. 371). The other three watches represented by D6 and D7 have relief patterns on the front and back which are not unlike some of the repoussé designs favoured by case-makers during the first half of the 18th century. The pendants have stirrup or ring-shaped bows reflecting late 17th-century to mid-18th-century fashion in pendant design.

Whilst the overall shape and proportions of the watch provide useful dating evidence, the dial plates are an even better indicator of contemporary taste and horological fashion. These have a plain border, and the chapter rings engraved with Roman hour numerals I–XII have either a lozenge or slash to mark the half-hours. D1 and D3 have an additional minute circle numbered every fifth division in Arabic. The simple style of the dials, the proportions of the numerals and the shape of the half-hour marks all point to a date from the end of the 17th century to the first quarter of the 18th century, and the general appearance imitates English or French engraved champlevé dials in vogue at this time. A couple of the toy watches have traces of red pigment (D2: Acc. no. 98.2/500 and D7: Acc. no. 98.2/524) which was probably employed to highlight the numerals in much the same way as engraver's wax was used on a real champlevé dial. Efforts to portray a convincing *c.* 1700 watch also extend to the decoration of the recessed dial centres which reflect contemporary fashion by incorporating relief designs and inscribed cartouches. The relief baroque scrolling on the toy watches imitates repoussé work on a genuine timepiece and the cartouche inscriptions: HUX and LONDON or F BEESLEY and LONDON mimic the late 17th- and early 18th-century enthusiasm for putting the maker's name and sometimes the place of production on the front of a watch. Hux and Beesley (Beasley) were pewterers and their work and importance has been discussed in the introduction to this chapter (pp. 343–5) and in Appendix III.

Only one hand with an arrowhead pointer has survived (D1: Acc. no. 98.2/442) and it was probably made without a counterpoise in keeping with contemporary fashion.[33] The centre of the hand is pierced for attachment and although it is secured to the dial plate with a rivet, the fixing is sufficiently slack to enable the hand to rotate.

Unfortunately even though the most complete and promising examples have been subjected to x-radiography and mechanical investigation, none has complete 'mechanisms'. From limited evidence, however, it seems that the hand is attached to a central rod or strut of cast lead alloy which passes straight through the case to the winder hole at the back (fig. 71, p. 345). This meant that the time could be altered by turning the rod with the fingers, or possibly with a crank-winding key. On a real watch the outer case has to be removed to expose the winding hole in the back of the inner case, but this is obviously impossible with an integrally cast 'pair-case' style toy, which is why the winder hole appears through the 'outer' case. The winder hole is surrounded by a ratchet of radial grooves and ridges, and a simple leaf spring or strip of copper (now missing) was inserted into the central rod so that the lower end was held in tension against the ratchet. Each turn of the winder lifted the strip of copper out of one groove into the next so that continual rotation produced a ticking sound. Violent turns of the winder probably caused the strips to snap, which probably explains their absence here.

TYPE 8, DESIGN 1

12.43 Watch

Accession number: A10894; A11517; 80.230/4; 80.230/9; 88.36/3; 98.2/442*; 98.2/461; 98.2/464; 98.2/493; 98.2/494; 98.2/522; 98.2/523; 2001.15/1*
Material: Lead alloy
Condition: Complete: 98.2/442; 2001.15/1. Dials only: A10894; 80.230/4; 80.230/9; 98.2/461; 98.2/464; 98.2/493; 98.2/494. Cases only: A11517; 88.36/3; 98.2/522; 98.2/523

Dimensions: Two sizes:
i) A10894; 98.2/442; 2001.15/1; 98.2/464; 98.2/493; 98.2/494: Diam (dial) 38mm; Diam (case) c. 45mm; Dpt (case) c. 22mm
ii) 80.230/9; 98.2/461: Diam (dial) 44mm; Th 2mm. 98.2/522 (case only): Diam c. 55mm; Dpt c. 22mm

Inscription: HUX LONDON

Description: These multi-component watches have a plain case, angular profile and integrally cast pendant loop. There are two circumferential grooves at the widest part of the case which represent the rims of an outer case in a pair-case watch, and the dial rim is slightly thickened and everted to suggest the junction of glass and metal on a real timepiece. The dial is recessed and supported on an internal flange just below the rim of the case and the rim has been pushed over the edge of the dial. The loose dial plates have a plain outer band and a circumferential groove which encloses the chapter ring, and all are marked with engraved Roman hour numerals I–XII and slashes to indicate the half-hours. In addition, all have a thickened inner section, which is only obvious on the back, and this area corresponds to the diameter of the dial centre on the front. Two dials (80.230/9 & 98.2/461) have an outer minute ring in Arabic, graduated 5–60. A plain inner band encircles the dial centre which is decorated with raised baroque scrolling around two cartouches, the upper inscribed HUX and the lower LONDON. Only part of one hand survives (on 98.2/442); the counterpoise has broken off and the pointer has a pierced arrowhead. The centre of the hand is pierced for attachment and secured with a rivet. The centres of the dials are pierced to accommodate the single hand and the edges of the hole thickened to lift it above the decoration and facilitate rotation.

Date: 1700–50

Provenance: 98.2/442: recovered by Eric Horne, 20 June 1975 under Southwark Bridge, north end. According to his detailed notes, it was found at a depth of about 30cm in a crushed but robust state.

Comparanda: Dial only: Queenhithe, Diam 38mm; Wapping, 31 March 1999, Diam 38mm (Enq. no. 2013/2).
Case only: London Leadworks, May 1983; Worshipful Company of Clockmakers' collection and Bendall 1994, group 2, fig. 9.

TYPE 8, DESIGN 2

12.44 Watch

Accession number: NN18218*; 98.2/500
Material: Lead alloy. 98.2/500: red pigment
Condition: NN18218: nearly complete
 98.2/500: dial only
Dimensions: Diam 38mm; Dpt 20mm
Description: The plain case has an angular profile and circumferential ridge to suggest the junction of the case rims on a genuine pair-case watch. There are two bands around the rim of the case and an integrally cast pendant loop which is a reasonable imitation of the real thing. The dial plate rests on an internal flange and the edge of the case is partly pinched-over to keep it from falling out. A wide plain band around the outer edge of the dial encloses the chapter ring marked with engraved Roman hours I–XII which are interspersed with lozenges to indicate the half-hours. There is an unequal division of hours and poor alignment as a result. A plain band encloses the recessed dial centre which is decorated with relief

baroque scrolling and two plain cartouches. Both dials (probably made from the same mould) have a central hole with a thickened rim for the hand. NN18218 has a corresponding winder hole at the back of the case.
Date: 1700–50

TYPE 8, DESIGN 3

12.45 Watch

Accession number: 98.2/459
Material: Lead alloy
Condition: Dial only
Dimensions: Diam 45mm
Inscription: F BEESLEY LONDON
Description: A dial from a multiple component watch with simple mechanism. The back of the dial plate is smooth. A wide plain outer band encloses a raised minute ring with incised Arabic numerals graduated 5–60. A deep groove surrounds the raised chapter ring with engraved Roman hours I–XII interspersed with lozenges to mark the half-hours. The dial centre is recessed and the surface decorated with a raised design including a scallop shell and baroque scrolling. There are two cartouches inscribed at the top F BEESLEY and at the bottom LONDON. The dial's centre is pierced and the rim thickened to accommodate a moving hand.
Date: 1700–50
Comparandum: Dial only (damaged and possibly not Beesley) from a site in Rotherhithe, 100 yards west of the Mayflower Public House

TYPE 8, DESIGN 4

12.46 Watch

Accession number: 98.2/495*; 98.2/504
Material: Lead alloy
Condition: Dial only
Dimensions: 98.2/495: Diam 39mm
            98.2/504: Diam 30mm
Inscription: LONDON
Description: Dials only from a multi-component watch. The largest (98.2/495) has a wide plain outer band encircling the chapter ring with engraved Roman hours I–XII, interspersed with slash/lozenges to indicate the half-hours. The recessed dial centre is enclosed within a wide plain circle and decorated with raised baroque-style ornament and a cartouche at the bottom inscribed LONDON. There is a hole in the centre of the dial for the hand. The dial plate has either been punched or lathe-turned too heavily because the dial centre has parted from the chapter ring. Likewise, some of the chapter ring has also begun to separate from the outer band. 98.2/504 is identical, although smaller. The outer band and part of the chapter ring are missing and the Roman hours are marked I–VIII with slashes to indicate the half-hours.
Date: 1700–50

TYPE 8, DESIGN 5

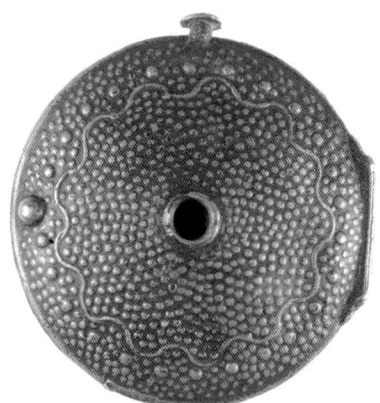

12.47 Watch

Accession number: 2001.15/2[34]
Material: Lead alloy
Condition: Complete; mechanism intact
Dimensions: Diam 50mm; Th 17mm
Inscription: Hux London
Description: This multi-component watch has an angular profile, integrally cast pendant (loop missing), separate dial and simple mechanism. There is a moulded button on the back and the circumferential groove around the widest part of the case is aligned with a hinge moulding to represent the outer case rims on a real watch. The front is decorated with a ring of large pellets and smaller randomly scattered dots. The slightly convex back has similar mouldings and an engrailed circle resembling shagreen and inlaid

casework. The dial rim is slightly thickened and everted to suggest the junction of glass and metal on a real timepiece, and the dial plate is held in place by the case rim. A wide plain band around the outer edge of the dial encloses the chapter ring which is marked with engraved Roman hours I–XII and these are interspersed with slashes to indicate the half-hours. The dial centre encircled by a plain band is decorated with relief baroque scrolling and two cartouches, inscribed at the top, Hux, and below, London. The tip of the crank shaft can be seen but the hand is missing, and there is a corresponding winder hole at the back of the case. The analysis undertaken on this watch suggests that it was silvered (see Appendix II).

Date: 1700–50

TYPE 8, DESIGN 6

12.48 Watch

Accession number: 98.2/519; 98.2/525*
Material: Lead alloy
Condition: Part of case and back of case
Dimensions: Diam *c.* 43mm; W (incl. hinge) *c.* 45mm; Dpt *c.* 8mm
Description: An almost complete case from a multiple-component watch, very similar to T8, D7 below. The case is cast in one piece and the stump of the pendant loop is extant. The profile of the watch is angular and there is a pronounced circumferential ridge aligned with the 'hinge' which marks the edges of the outer case on a real watch. The 'hinge' is correctly aligned on the left side of the case. The case front has a gently sloping profile and the decoration consists of alternating vertical lines and horizontal crescents. The case rim is recurved and there is an internal groove just below the rim to accommodate and support the dial. Inside the case, the winder hole has a thickened, protruding rim surrounded by a plain circle and outer ring marked with radial lines in relief. The back is decorated with a symmetrical design of radial lines arranged in groups of different lengths to create a starburst effect. A beaded circle encloses a central pattern of eight oak leaves with pellets at the apex of each leaf, all radiating outwards from the winder hole (compare 98.2/519 pictured below). The outer section of the case back is missing.

Date: 1730–40

TYPE 8, DESIGN 7

12.49 Watch

Accession number: 98.2/524
Material: Lead alloy; red pigment
Condition: Complete case
Dimensions: H (incl. pendant loop) 48mm; Diam: 42mm; W (incl. hinge) 44mm; Dpt 8mm
Description: A complete case from a multiple-component watch with an integrally cast bow pendant of convincing shape and design, case 'hinge' and 'button'. The watch profile is flat and there is a pronounced circumferential ridge aligned with the hinge which is correctly positioned on the left side. The ridge separates front and back and marks the edges of the two case halves on a real watch. The front has a contoured profile, with a beaded edge, inner crescent and dot circle. Traces of red pigment remain in gaps between the raised decoration. The case rim is domed and recurved with a groove around the inner edge to support the dial. There is a large winder hole in the base surrounded by a wide plain band and narrow circle with raised radial lines. The back has a zig-zag edge with a flat rim. The rest of the back is convex with a wide outer border decorated with a raised symmetrical pattern of radial lines arranged in groups of different lengths to create a starburst effect. A beaded circle surrounds the central raised design of oak leaves interspersed with ellipses which radiate from the winder hole.
Date: 1750–60

TYPE 9

This type is represented by two circular multi-component watches, each with a separate dial plate, rotating hand, plain case and pendant loop. Unlike any other watch in the corpus, the cases are made from two sections which screw together to form a hollow receptacle. The upper section has an internal flange to support the dial plate and the bottom edge is threaded to fasten on to the bowl-shaped lower section. The case profiles are slightly different, but both have a flat base and the lower sections have been turned on a lathe. The pendants have been separately cast and are poorly aligned at the 2 o'clock position. Both of the dial plates sit loosely in the frame of the case and the chapter rings are both marked with Roman hour numerals I–XII interspersed with pellet half-hours. The dial centres are decorated with baroque scrolling and an inscribed cartouche, and although the decorative motifs have been well executed on both dials, the middle letters forming the word LONDON on Cat. no. 12.51 are back-to-front. The watches have single rotating hands with arrowhead pointers and a counterpoise and these are held in place by pierced or quatrefoil-shaped fasteners which are soldered on to the pin. Particular effort has been made to decorate the fastener on D2. One of the watches is inscribed 'Hux London', and this information coupled with the shape and design of these pieces points to a date between 1700 and 1750. The Hux watch is probably the earlier of the two. Watches of this type might have served as lockets, trinkets or even pill boxes.[35]

TYPE 9, DESIGN 1

12.50 Watch

Accession number: 2001.15/3
Material: Lead alloy
Condition: Complete
Dimensions: Diam 32mm; Th 17mm
Inscription: Hux London
Description: A multi-component watch made from seven parts. The case is made in two sections which screw together around the widest part of the circumference to form a hollow receptacle. The dial plate rests loosely in the internal flange of the upper case and the chapter ring is marked with Roman hour numerals I–XII interspersed with pellets to indicate the half-hours. Some of the numerals are rather faint and the V of VIII and the X of XI are barely formed, which might be due to a worn mould or poor engraving on

the part of the mould-maker. Within concentric circles, the dial centre is decorated with baroque scrolling surrounding two cartouches inscribed Hux and London. The rotating single hand with arrowhead pointer and counterpoise is the same diameter as the dial centre and this is held in place with a pin and quatrefoil-shaped fastener. The fairly deep plain case has an angular profile and flat base and the crudely formed knob-shaped pendant has a tiny hole at right angles to the plane of the case.

Date: 1700–50

Comparanda: Worshipful Company of Clockmakers' collection (half of lower case only) and Bendall 1994, fig. 12

TYPE 9, DESIGN 2

12.51 Watch

Accession number: 2001.15/4
Material: Lead alloy
Condition: Complete
Dimensions: Diam 34mm; Th 12mm
Inscription: LONDON
Description: A multi-component watch made from seven parts. The case is made in two sections which screw together around the widest part of the circumference to form a hollow receptacle. The dial plate rests loosely in the internal flange of the upper case and the chapter ring is marked with Roman hours I–XII interspersed with pellets to indicate the half-hours. The dial centre is enclosed within concentric circles and decorated with fine baroque-style scrolling and a motto at the top inscribed LONDON, although the middle letters are back-to-front. A single rotating hand with arrowhead pointer and counterpoise is held in place by a pin and decorative pierced fastener. The plain case has straight sides and a flat base and the separately cast stirrup-shaped pendant bow has been soldered into the top of the case.

Date: 1700–50

TYPE 10

This dial is a complete puzzle because there are no hands. Lozenge half-hour marks were common in the early 18th century, so it is possible that the dial dates to this period.

TYPE 10, DESIGN 1

12.52 Watch

Accession number: A3918
Material: Lead alloy
Condition: Dial only
Dimensions: Diam 42mm
Description: Flat dial only with cast decoration. There are three, possibly four, tabs around the edge. The decoration consists of an outer beaded circle enclosing a foliate garland. The chapter ring is marked with Roman hours I–XII, interspersed with lozenges to indicate the half-hours. The dial centre is filled with an irradiated sun face. There are no hands.

Date: 1700–50

TYPE 11

The only elements known to survive from watches of this type are seven complete and three fragmentary dial plates. The plate diameters range from 27mm to 46mm and as none appears to have any means of suspension, they were probably associated with watches of two or more parts. It is difficult to see how the dial plates were secured to the case; there are no lug indents and the edges are decorated, a detail which would otherwise have been obscured by the case rim. Indeed, the absence of complete examples may indicate a weak and unsatisfactory method of attachment, and since the dials have integrally cast hands, they might have been a cheaper version of the ratchet watch represented by Type 8. The decorative style and the beetle and poker (D1) and pierced swell hands (D3) suggest a date between 1700 and 1750 for these watches.

TYPE 11, DESIGN 1

12.53 Watch

Accession number: 98.2/462*; 98.2/463
Material: Lead alloy
Condition: Dial only. 98.2/463: damaged
Dimensions: Diam 46mm
Description: These flat dial plates with integrally cast hands were almost certainly made from the same mould, and although 98.2/463 is damaged the design is crisper and it may be an earlier casting. The edges of the dials are decorated with crescents enclosing a border of harebells and leaves interspersed with pellets. A beaded circle surrounds the large chapter ring marked with Roman hours I–XII, interspersed with pellets to indicate the half-hours, and the dial centre (which is plain apart from a tiny stylized flowerhead, crescent pattern in the middle) is also encircled with beading. There are two hands with beetle and poker pointers at 12:37.
Date: 1700–50

TYPE 11, DESIGN 2

12.54 Watch

Accession number: 98.2/460*; 98.2/497
Material: Lead alloy
Condition: dial only
Dimensions: 98.2/460: Diam 42mm
  98.2/497: Diam 34mm
Description: Flat dials only with integrally cast hands. An outer circle of harebells surrounds a beaded circle and the large chapter ring is marked with Roman hours I–XII interspersed with pellets to indicate the half-hours. The plain dial centre is enclosed within a beaded circle and there are two pierced swell hands with a star in the centre to represent the rivet. The hands on one dial (98.2/460) point to approximately 19 minutes past 9 and although there is no minute circle, the minute hand points to the outer circle of beading. Both hands have arrowhead pointers. The time on 98.2/497 (which is damaged) is approximately 20 minutes past 10.
Date: 1700–50

TYPE 11, DESIGN 3

12.55 Watch

Accession number: 98.2/509
Material: Lead alloy
Condition: Half dial only
Dimensions: Diam 40mm
Description: A flat dial with an integrally cast hand. An outer minute circle graduated with slashes and circles encloses the chapter ring with Roman hours I–XII, and pellets to indicate the half-hours. However, XII and probably XI (broken at this point) are back-to-front IIX and probably IX. An inner beaded circle surrounds the dial centre which is decorated with a random pattern of fine circles. Only one pierced swell hand survives and this points to 3 minutes past 1.
Date: 1700–50

TYPE 11, DESIGN 4

12.56 Watch

Accession number: 98.2/511
Material: Lead alloy
Condition: Half dial only
Dimensions: Diam 34mm
Description: A flat dial with an integrally cast hand. An outer border of oak leaves encloses a beaded circle and chapter ring marked with Roman hour numerals I–XII, interspersed with pellets to indicate the half-hours. The plain dial centre is enclosed by a beaded circle and the single hand with arrowhead pointer is at 12 o'clock.
Date: 1700–50

TYPE 11, DESIGN 5

12.57 Watch

Accession number: 98.2/488
Material: Lead alloy
Condition: Dial only
Dimensions: Diam 35mm
Description: A flat dial with integrally cast hands. The edge is decorated with fine beading which encloses a plain border decorated with pellets which are widely, but equally spaced around a solid circle. The circle contains the chapter ring which is marked with Roman hours I–XII, interspersed with pellets to indicate the half-hours. A solid circle encloses the plain dial centre and there are two hands, both with arrowhead pointers at 11.30. The edges are damaged.
Date: 1700–50

TYPE 11, DESIGN 6

12.58 Watch

Accession number: 98.2/496
Material: Lead alloy
Condition: Dial only
Dimensions: Diam 34mm
Description: A flat dial with integrally cast hands. There is a beaded edge surrounding a crescent border and beaded circle. The chapter ring is marked with Roman hours I–XII, interspersed with quatrefoils to indicate the half-hours. The plain dial centre is enclosed within a beaded circle and there are two hands with an arrowhead pointer at 5 o'clock. There is no minute ring.
Date: 1700–50

TYPE 11, DESIGN 7

12.59 Watch

Accession number: 98.2/514
Material: Lead alloy; traces of red pigment
Condition: Fragment of dial only
Dimensions: H 29mm; W 15mm
Description: This flat dial has a rope-twist edge, a quarter circle and a chapter ring enclosed within beaded circles and Roman hours between V and V[III]. The rest is missing. The dial centre is decorated with masses of pellets.
Date: 1700–50

TYPE 11, DESIGN 8

12.60 Watch

Accession number: Private collection (no picture available)
Material: Lead alloy
Condition: Dial only
Dimensions: Diam 27 x 30 mm
Description: This slightly domed dial has a beaded edge surrounding a chapter ring with Roman hours I–XII and pellets to indicate the half-hours. There is a beaded circle around the dial centre and this seems to represent a minute circle, although there are only 39 pellets, since there are two hands at 10 o'clock.
Date: 1700–50

TYPE 12

These circular multi-component watches share certain characteristics with Type 8: the cases are cast in one piece with an integral pendant, hinge, button or catch; there are circumferential ridges around the widest point to represent the rims of an outer case on a pair-case watch; and the dial plates seem to have been secured by recurving case edges and an internal groove. But unlike Type 8, there is no evidence that these watches ever had moving parts, and the only known complete example has a paper dial protected by a glass with printed concentric rings for the minutes and hours (D2). By about 1775 simple painted enamel dials were a standard feature on genuine watches and it is possible that the toymakers began to incorporate printed paper dials to reflect current trends in horological design.

There are nine watches in this group and the general proportions, angular profile and decoration reflect the styles of English pair-case watches from the mid-18th to early 19th century. Sizes range from 25–41mm and like the Type 9 watches they appear to have been cast and turned. Most of the case fronts have a contoured profile and apart from D1 which has a hatched chevron design, all are plain with beaded or rope-twist edges suggestive of piqué work or perhaps engine-turning on a genuine timepiece. The relief moulded case backs, imitating repoussé, have floral, heraldic and figurative designs which provide a tight framework for dating. The earliest, represented by D1 and D2, have Prince of Wales plumes and these were almost certainly produced during the period 1811–20. At this time, hundreds of objects, ranging from clay pipes to thimbles as well as watch cases and watch cocks, were marked with the Prince of Wales plumes to honour the Prince Regent (later King George IV).[36]

A slightly later watch is represented by D4, which has an imperial crown with flowers above and a thistle and rose below, and was produced to celebrate the accession and coronation of either George IV in 1820 or William IV in 1830.

The shape and proportions of D5 – decorated with a crudely rendered portrait bust of a male head, laureate, profile to left with the letters W and R and a branching rose and thistle on either side – point to a date in the second quarter of the 19th century. This is supported by the inscription and appearance of the profile bust which is loosely modelled on Benedetto Pistrucci's famous portrait of William IV.[37] But while the general aspect of the bust is a fair copy of William's portrait, the other details are a curious amalgam of elements which were probably derived from the obverse and reverse sides of coins issued between 1820 and 1830. Laureate busts profile to left are only found on coins issued during the reign of George IV, and the rose, thistle and shamrock were used to garnish the shield on the reverse; whereas on the obverse side of coins issued between 1830 and 1837, William IV is shown bare-headed, profile to right, and the reverse sides have a wreath of laurel and oak leaves surmounted by a crown.

TYPE 12, DESIGN 1

12.61 Watch

Accession number: 98.2/532*; 98.2/533; 98.2/534
Material: Lead alloy. 98.2/533: red pigment
Condition: Case only
Dimensions: Two sizes:
   i) 98.2/532; 98.2/533: Diam 41mm; W (incl. hinge) 42mm; Dpt *c.* 12mm
   ii) 98.2/534: Diam *c.* 26mm (distorted and crushed)
Description: Cast in one piece with an integral hinge, button, catch and pendant loop, although only the stub on 98.2/532 and lower part of 98.2/533 have survived. The case has a slightly domed profile and there is a pronounced circumferential ridge aligned with the hinge which represents the outer case rims on a real watch. The front is decorated with raised chevrons alternately hatched, and the edge of the case is thickened and recurved with an internal groove to support the recessed dial (now missing). There is no sign of a ratchet system inside the case. On the back, the case has an identical

border to that on the front and this encircles a beaded ring and the centre motif of Prince of Wales plumes. There is a small round button at 3 o'clock.
Date: 1811–20
Comparandum: Hammersmith, 24 June 1997, slightly smaller (Enq. no. 1848/9)

TYPE 12, DESIGN 2

12.62 Watch

Accession number: 84.328/1
Material: Lead alloy with paper and glass
Condition: Almost complete
Dimensions: Diam 37mm
Inscription: ICH DIEN
Description: Almost complete watch with a case cast in one piece with integral pendant loop and hinge. The hinge is on the right side, and the pendant is just a loop with beading on the front. There is a pronounced circumferential groove around the centre of the case aligned with the hinge to represent the junction of the outer case rims on a genuine watch. The front has a beaded edge and plain contoured profile, thickened and recurved around the dial with an internal groove which supports a printed paper dial. An outer circle of minutes in Arabic numerals 5–60 encircles a graduated minute ring. The chapter ring is marked in Roman hours I–XII, but the numbers between VII and XII have been destroyed by chemical reaction which presumably resulted from damage to the glass. The dial paper has slipped in a clockwise direction, so that XII is no longer aligned with the pendant loop. The dial is protected by a glass, now cracked with parts missing, and this is held in place by the recurved case rim. The back of the case is decorated with a beaded edge, enclosing a flowerhead border, beaded circle and central design of the Prince of Wales plumes and ICH DIEN motto. There is considerable damage to the back of the case and, curiously, no evidence of hands.
Date: 1811–20
Provenance: Acquired in August 1984 from Temple Road, Richmond, Surrey. No earlier provenance is known.

TYPE 12, DESIGN 3

12.63 Watch

Accession number: 98.2/527
Material: Lead alloy; red pigment
Condition: Case only
Dimensions: H (incl. pendant loop) 43mm; Diam 36mm; Dpt c. 10mm
Description: Cast in one piece with a fairly convincing bow pendant. There is no hinge. The case is plain apart from the pronounced circumferential ridge dividing front from back, which has rope-twist decoration. The case rim recurves towards the dial and there is an internal groove for the dial which is now pinched over.
Date: Late 18th–early 19th century

TYPE 12, DESIGN 4

TYPE 12, DESIGN 5

TYPE 12, DESIGN 6

12.64 Watch

Accession number: 98.2/530
Material: Lead alloy
Condition: Case only
Dimensions: Diam *c.* 29mm
Description: Cast in one piece with an integral pendant loop, but no hinge. Only the lower part of the pendant survives. The case is flattened but was originally domed, and there is a pronounced circumferential cordon dividing front from back to represent the junction of the outer case rims on a genuine watch. The front has a contoured profile and is plain apart from a circle of beading. The case rim recurves inwards and there is an internal groove now pinched together which originally held the dial in place. The back has an outer border of hatched lines encircling an imperial crown with flowers above and a thistle and rose below.
Date: 1820–37
Comparandum: Fragment of a case back (top left quadrant) with two holes which suggest later use as a mount. Private collection, 25 October 2000, provenance unknown.

12.65 Watch

Accession number: 98.2/529
Material: Lead alloy; red pigment
Condition: Case only; some damage
Dimensions: Diam *c.* 32mm; Dpt *c.* 8mm
Inscription: WR
Description: Cast in one piece with an integral pendant loop, but no hinge. Only the lower part of the pendant survives. The case has a pronounced circumferential cordon dividing front from back to represent the junction of the outer case rims on a genuine watch. The front is plain apart from a beaded circle and the case rim is thickened and recurved. An internal groove probably supported the dial but the edges have been destroyed and the method of attachment is uncertain. There is a wide border of lines on the back radiating out from a beaded circle which encloses the male head, laureate, profile to left. Below, and branching to left and right of the head, is a rose and thistle. At the bottom the stems cross and separate the initials W and R.
Date: 1830–7

12.66 Watch

Accession number: 98.2/531
Material: Lead alloy
Condition: Case only
Dimensions: H (incl. pendant loop) 31mm; Diam *c.* 26mm; Dpt *c.* 9mm
Description: Cast in one piece with integral bow pendant, hinge and button. The pendant is fairly convincing and the hinge is positioned correctly on the left side. There is a pronounced ridge around the circumference separating front from back and representing the outer case rims on a genuine watch. The front has a contoured and sharply convex profile, and there is no decoration apart from a beaded circle. The edge of the case rim recurves and there is an internal groove which is designed to support the dial. The inside of the case is plain, but there is a central boss and clear evidence of lathe-turning. The back has a beaded edge enclosing ring and dot and zig-zag circles which surround a flower with twining stem and lanceolate-shaped leaves.
Date: Late 18th–early 19th century
Comparanda: Worshipful Company of Clockmakers' collection (Cat. no. 1209), which imitates engine-turned decoration on a real watch

TYPE 12, DESIGN 7

12.67 Watch

Accession number: 98.2/526
Material: Lead alloy
Condition: Case only
Dimensions: H (incl. pendant loop) 30mm; Diam 25mm; Dpt c. 10mm
Description: Cast in one piece with integral bow pendant, hinge and catch. The pendant loop is fairly convincing and the hinge is positioned correctly on the left side. There is a pronounced ridge around the circumference dividing front from back to represent the outer case rims on a genuine watch. The front of the case is very narrow and plain apart from slash decoration around the edge. The case rim recurves and there is an internal groove to support the dial. The inside of the case is plain but there is clear evidence of lathe-turning. The case back has an outer circle of slashed lines surrounding a cross-hatched field decorated with flowerheads and leaf tendrils.
Date: Late 18th–early 19th century

TYPE 13

This type is represented by an extremely thin dial with incuse, possibly stamped decoration. The use of the serpentine hand suggests an early 19th-century date.

TYPE 13, DESIGN 1

12.68 Watch

Accession number: 98.2/502
Material: Lead alloy; possible pigment
Condition: Fragment of dial
Dimensions: Diam c. 31mm
Description: Flat dial, half only with integral hand. Most of the decoration is incuse apart from the beaded circle. There is an outer circle and plain band enclosing a raised beaded and solid circle. The hours with Roman numerals XII–I run anti-clockwise (VI–XI are missing) and they are not contained within a separate chapter ring. Stars indicate the half-hours. There is a single serpentine hand with solid arrow tip pointer at half past two. The rest of the dial is decorated with stars, trefoils and a crescent-edged circle.
Date: Early 19th century

TYPE 14

This dial is badly damaged and may be a trial piece.

TYPE 14, DESIGN 1

12.69 Watch

Accession number: 98.2/515
Material: Lead alloy
Condition: Dial only – trial piece (?); much damaged
Dimensions: Diam 29mm
Description: A completely plain, crudely executed flat dial without hands. The chapter ring is marked with Roman hours I–XII and there is a tiny hole (off centre) in the middle. This dial plate is so crude that it might have been an experimental piece.
Date: Probably 18th–early 19th century

TYPE 15

This type was cast in one piece with an integral hand and pendant loop. Some aspects suggest an early to mid-18th-century date, but the crescent moon hands are a 19th-century feature, and the watch probably dates from this period. There is a hole through the centre of the dial.

TYPE 15, DESIGN 1

12.70 Watch

Accession number: 98.2/453
Material: Lead alloy; red pigment (?)
Condition: Complete
Dimensions: H (incl. pendant loop) *c.* 44mm; Diam 40mm; Dpt *c.* 10mm;
Description: A complete one-piece watch with integral pendant loop, plain case and flat, angular profile. The dial occupies the entire face of the watch and there is an outer chapter ring with raised Roman hours marked I–XII and a recessed centre with a raised quarter circle, defined by pellets and lines. The dial centre is enclosed within a plain circle and is decorated with a central rosette. The single hand has a counterpoise with crescent moon tail, and the D-shape extension is designed to indicate the hours and quarters.
Date: Early 19th century

1. Campbell 1747, ch. 54, sec. 1.
2. The agreevanunces of the Clockmakers Cittizens and inhabitants in London, 1622. PRO State Papers, Domestic Series 14, vol. 127.
3. The Clockmakers' Company received its Charter of Incorporation from Charles I on 22 August 1631. GL MS 6430.
4. I am most grateful to David Thompson (British Museum) for his help and comments on this section. He suggests that form watches, and those of other than circular shape, probably went out of fashion with the introduction of the pocket in clothing. Pers. comm., April 2001.
5. As a child, the future Louis XIII (1601–43) of France was given a number of silver toys, and in 1606 these included a miniature silver watch from his mother Marie de Medici. It is not known whether this watch was simply a small-scale version of the real thing or an imitation piece: see Houart, 1981.
6. *The Diary of Samuel Pepys,* Latham & Matthews, eds, vol. 6.
7. *The Diary of Samuel Pepys,* 13 September 1665, Latham & Matthews, eds, vol. 6.
8. *The Diary of Samuel Pepys,* 22 September 1666, Latham & Matthews, eds, vol. 7.
9. CLRO Mayor's Court Original Bills and Orphan's Court Inventories. It is often unclear from these inventories whether items were new or secondhand. See J. Evans' transcription of a court case in *Antiquarian Horology* 26 (July 2002) which contains details and prices of stolen watches from a London shop in 1646.
10. PRO PROB 5/2768, 19 November 1719.
11. Cited by Baillee 1928, p. 91 – although no references are supplied.
12. See T9, p. 376. It is possible that these watches were used as pill boxes. I am grateful to Ron Homer for this suggestion (pers. comm.).
13. T8, D1 & D5; T9, D1.
14. T5, D16: Acc. no. 98.2/480 and D28: Acc. no. 98.2/466; T9, D1: Acc. no. 2001.15/3. T10, D1: Acc. no. A3918 has no hands.
15. T5, D1: Acc. no. 98.2/454.
16. T5, D16: Acc. no. 98.2/480 and T5, D28: Acc. no. 98.2/466.
17. Acc. no. 98.2/442.
18. The symbolic reason for the position of the hands at 12 o'clock in a painting possibly serves to remind the viewer of the transience of life.
19. Worshipful Company of Pewterers' Court Minutes: GL MS 7090, no. 9 [1711–40], 24 March 1715, Quarter Court and 22 March 1715, Quarter Court.
20. GL MS 7090, no. 8 [1691–1711], 22 June 1703.
21. GL MS 7090, no. 8 [1691–1711], 22 March 1704.
22. GL MS 7090, no. 8 [1691–1711], 19 June 1707.
23. GL MS 7090, no. 9 [1711–40], 24 March 1714.
24. GL MS 7090, no. 9 [1711–40], 15 December 1714.
25. I am grateful to Ron Homer for making this point (pers. comm.).
26. Van der Horst 1979.
27. Van der Horst 1979, p. 30.
28. See Museum of London: watch in an oval gilded-brass and silver case by Robert Grinkin senior, London, *c.* 1615, 41.5 x 34 mm (Acc. no. 34.181/12); and an oval gilded-brass verge watch by Binet, France, *c.* 1616, 57 x 43.5 mm (Acc. no. 34.181/10).
29. A typical example of this type of cloisonné enamel dial is represented by a watch made by John Ramsay, *c.* 1625, length of case 38mm: see Clutton & Daniels 1975, p. 10, cat. no. 12.
30. Egan 1988, p. 12 & fig. 43.
31. Alarm and striking watches were made from the mid-16th century, but the repeating watch was introduced in 1687. The cases were pierced so that the bell could be heard.
32. Probably a greywacke – a sandstone with clay, quartz, feldspar and metamorphic rock fragments. I am grateful to Peter Tandy and colleagues at the Geology Museum for their efforts in trying to establish the source of this rock.
33. See a silver pair-case watch by Ignatius Huggeford, England, *c.* 1675: see Clutton & Daniels 1975, p. 16, cat. no. 45.
34. This watch was generously given to the Museum of London by Mr S. Shemmel. See Shemmel 1994, pp. 101–2 & figs 1–2.
35. Ron Homer, pers. comm.
36. There is some evidence, however, that Prince of Wales plumes continued to be worn well after the accession. Charles Dickens is wearing a cravat pin with Prince of Wales plumes in his portrait of 1839 by Daniel Maclise (National Portrait Gallery, London), so it is possible that the toy watches were worn and possibly made over a longer period.
37. Benedetto Pistrucci [1784–1855]: see Williamson 1910 and Oman 1931, pp. 372–3. Compare also an onyx cameo portrait of George IV as Prince Regent (Fitzwilliam Museum, Cambridge).

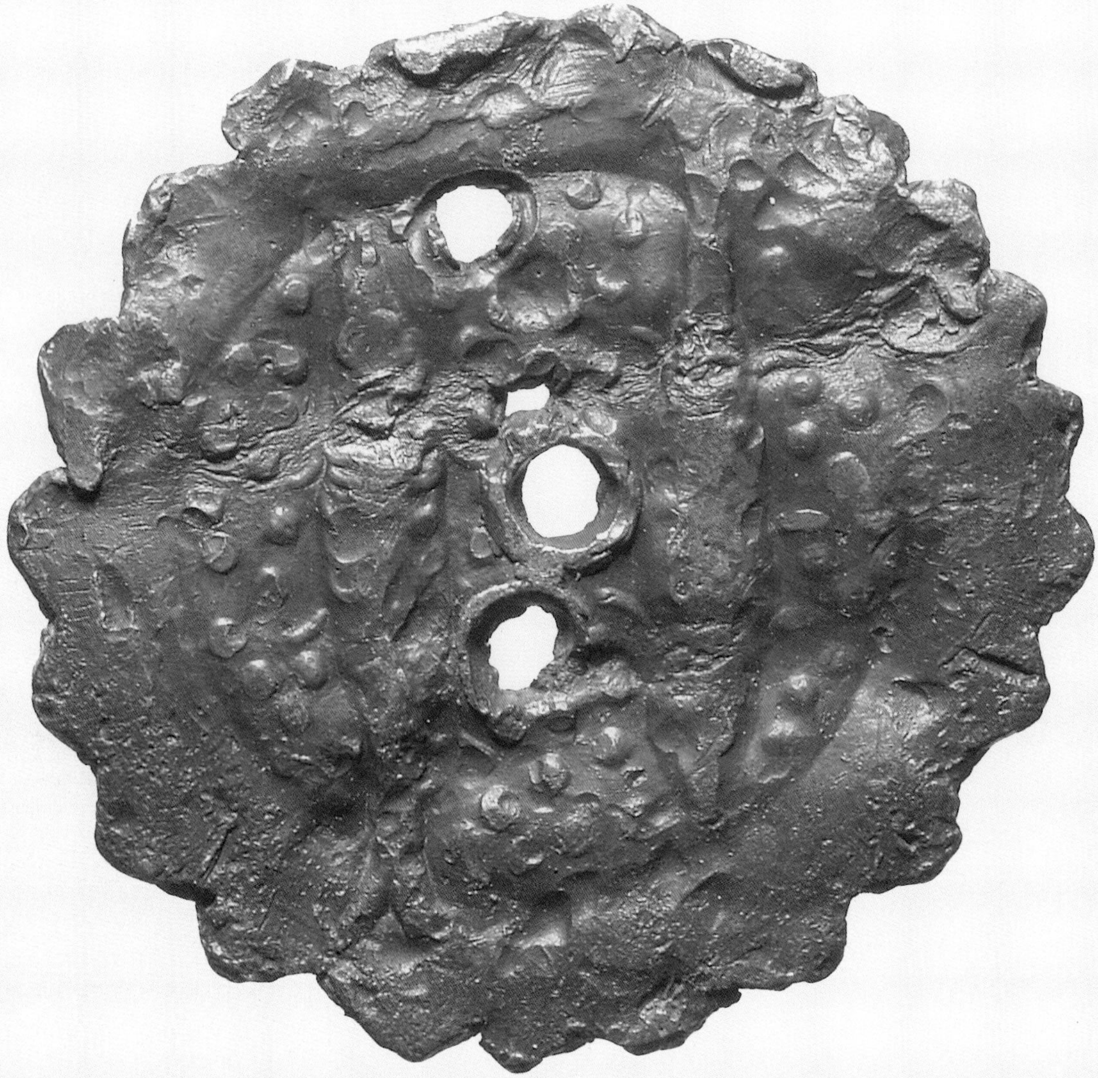

13 Whirligigs

'The intellect is a very nice whirligig toy'[1]

These perforated discs, known as whirligigs or buzz wheels, were mounted on a looped string or cord, which was held in tension at each end. Rapid rotation twisted the strings, and at a critical point, the torsion was relaxed by pulling the hands apart. With alternate pulling and relaxing the serrated edge of the spinning disc produced a whirring noise which could be maintained as long as desired. The buzzing sound was affected by the size and angle of the serrations as well as the degree of tension maintained on the strings.

In addition to producing a noise, it is possible that the whirligigs were also used for their shock effect, since within living memory cardboard versions supplied free with cereal packets were occasionally used by mischievous boys to cut through paper or across an unsuspecting victim's exposed arm, and it is possible that the whirligigs with the smallest serrations in this collection were used in a similar way in the past.[2]

The whirligigs range in size from 20mm to 106mm. Most are plain, and have been roughly cut from scrap metal sheeting, but a few have decoration (on one or both faces), which is either incised or cast. None appears to be coloured although it is possible that pigments were originally applied to enhance the decorative effect during rotation.

All of the examples in this collection have been made from other objects and these include a toy frying pan, which had probably lost its handle, as well as an adapted late Elizabethan counter and 17th-century halfpenny. The collection also includes a whirligig with an incomplete set of serrations.

It is possible that metal whirligigs of the sort described below were introduced at the end of the medieval period to replace similar whirling toys made from pig metapodial.[3] But although the term had fairly wide currency in the late Elizabethan period, the only example from a stratified assemblage which has been recognized in this country comes from a 1675–1700 context.[4] The whirligigs in the collection are impossible to date closely because they have all been made from other objects. We do not know, for example, how long the counters and coins were in circulation or kept before they were adapted. Nor do we know how long the toy frying pan (Cat. no. 13.5) was played with before its owner or a subsequent finder decided to change its function. Whirligigs seem to have been particularly popular during the 18th century, and many examples in metal and ceramics have been recovered from excavations of Colonial and Revolutionary sites in America.[5] The only published example from the Continent was excavated in Louvain, Belgium.[6]

DESIGN 1

13.1 Whirligig

Accession number: 98.2/710
Material: Lead alloy (?)
Condition: Complete
Dimensions: Diam 20mm
Inscription: CAMERE.CO.REGIORUM
Description: A cut-down counter of 1574 (?) with notched circumference and two small holes in the centre. The obverse shows a two-headed eagle, crowned, and in the field, R and K. The reverse has a shield with three fleurs-de-lys, crowned (the arms of France) and the legend: CAMERE.CO.REGIORUM [of the royal Exchequer-chamber].
Date: Possibly 17th–18th century
Provenance: Queenhithe
Comments: These counters seem to relate to Mary Queen of Scots, and all those known have been found in London: see Hawkins 1885, vol. 1, pp. 121–4, nos. 58–69, and in particular p. 122, no. 64.

DESIGN 2

13.2 Whirligig

Accession number: 98.2/713
Material: Lead alloy
Condition: Complete
Dimensions: Diam 25mm; Th 2mm
Description: A small thick disc with coarsely cut teeth and two large holes in the centre. The teeth have a rounded truncated profile.
Date: Possibly 17th–18th century
Comments: Limekiln Dock

DESIGN 3

13.3 Whirligig

Accession number: 98.2/709
Material: Lead alloy
Condition: Complete; some damage
Dimensions: Diam 28mm; Th 1mm
Description: A small disc with long, irregularly spaced teeth and two holes through the slightly indented centre.
Date: Possibly 17th–18th century

DESIGN 4

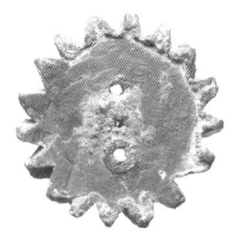

13.4 Whirligig

Accession number: 98.2/708
Material: Copper
Condition: Complete
Dimensions: Diam 29mm; Th 3mm
Description: This whirligig has been created from a regal Britannia halfpenny issued from 1672–5. The coin is extremely worn which suggests that it probably remained in circulation for some years before it was adapted into a whirligig.
Date: Possibly 17th–18th century

DESIGN 5

13.5 Whirligig

Accession number: 98.2/714
Material: Lead alloy
Condition: Complete
Dimensions: Diam 31mm; Th 1mm
Description: Made from the flattened dish of a toy frying pan with notched rim and three holes. The pan has two fish, placed head to tail across the base and surrounded by large pellets suggestive of hot bubbling fat. Both fish seem to be identical, with the suggestion of scales and pectoral, dorsal and anal fins showing on both sides. The tails cover the sides of the pan and the tips reach the rim.
Date: Possibly 17th–18th century
Comparandum: Frying pan (Cat. no. 2.20) from an identical mould

DESIGN 6

13.6 Whirligig

Accession number: 98.2/711
Material: Lead alloy
Condition: Incomplete
Dimensions: Diam 40mm; Th 1mm
Description: A partially finished whirligig (?) with plain disc, six badly cut teeth, abraded surface and casting seam
Date: Possibly 17th–18th century

DESIGN 7

13.7 Whirligig

Accession number: 98.2/712
Material: Lead alloy
Condition: Almost complete; some damage
Dimensions: Diam 44mm; Th c. 4mm
Inscription: GH
Description: A very badly cast disc with coarse radial fluting around the edge, two holes in the centre and the initials G and H on either side. The surface is extremely rough and abraded.
Date: Possibly 17th–18th century
Provenance: Billingsgate foreshore

DESIGN 8

13.8 Whirligig

Accession number: 98.2/715
Material: Lead alloy
Condition: Complete
Dimensions: Diam 55mm; Th 1mm
Description: A large, heavy disc with crudely cut teeth and two holes in the centre. Some of the teeth have a hooked profile.
Date: Possibly 17th–18th century

DESIGN 9

13.9 Whirligig

Accession number: 98.2/716
Material: Lead alloy
Condition: Complete; some damage
Dimensions: Diam *c.* 65mm; Th: 2mm
Description: A large disc with teeth around the edge and two holes in the centre. The teeth are crudely cut and irregularly spaced, with hooked profiles angled in different directions. There is a roughly incised pattern of cross-hatched bands on one side.
Date: Possibly 17th–18th century
Provenance: Queenhithe Dock

DESIGN 10

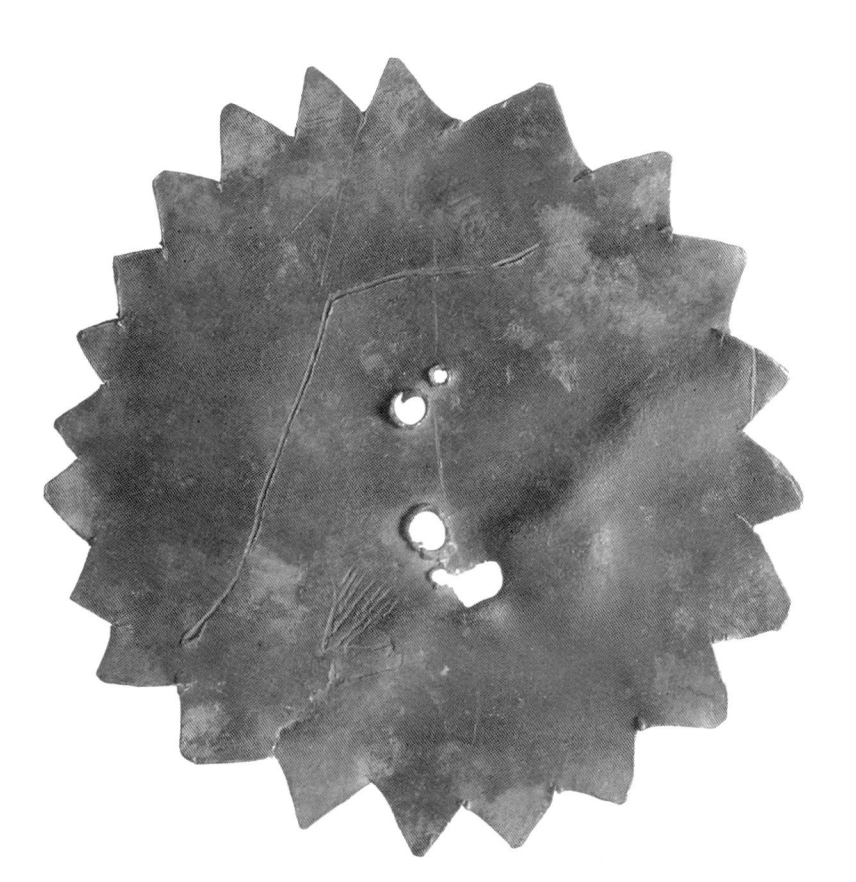

Whirligig: detail showing crowned rose
Acc. no. 98.2/717, Cat. no. 13.10

13.10 Whirligig

Accession number: 98.2/717

Material: Lead alloy

Condition: Complete; slight damage

Dimensions: Diam 105mm; Th 1mm

Inscription: LONDON

Description: A very large disc with coarse triangular teeth around the edge and four holes in the centre. This whirligig is made from another object, as evinced by the very faint straight-sided and dome-topped stamp of a crowned rose within two palm branches surmounted by a scrolling cartouche inscribed LONDON. The surface is abraded and scored and two of the holes are now joined.

Date: Possibly 17th–18th century

Comments: The touchmark is unidentified. The only stratified example so far recognized in this country was recovered from a 1675–1700 context in Abbots Lane, Southwark.[7]

1 Ezra Pound, Letter to his mother [undated]; quoted in Carpenter, H., *A Serious Character* (London, 1988), part 5, ch. 6

2 Geoff Egan, pers. comm.

3 Lawson 1995.

4 Excavated by the Museum of London from Abbot's Lane, Southwark, ABO92[388]<1992>.

5 Hume 1970, p. 321.

6 Smeyers & van Dooren 1998.

7 Egan forthcoming a, no. 599.

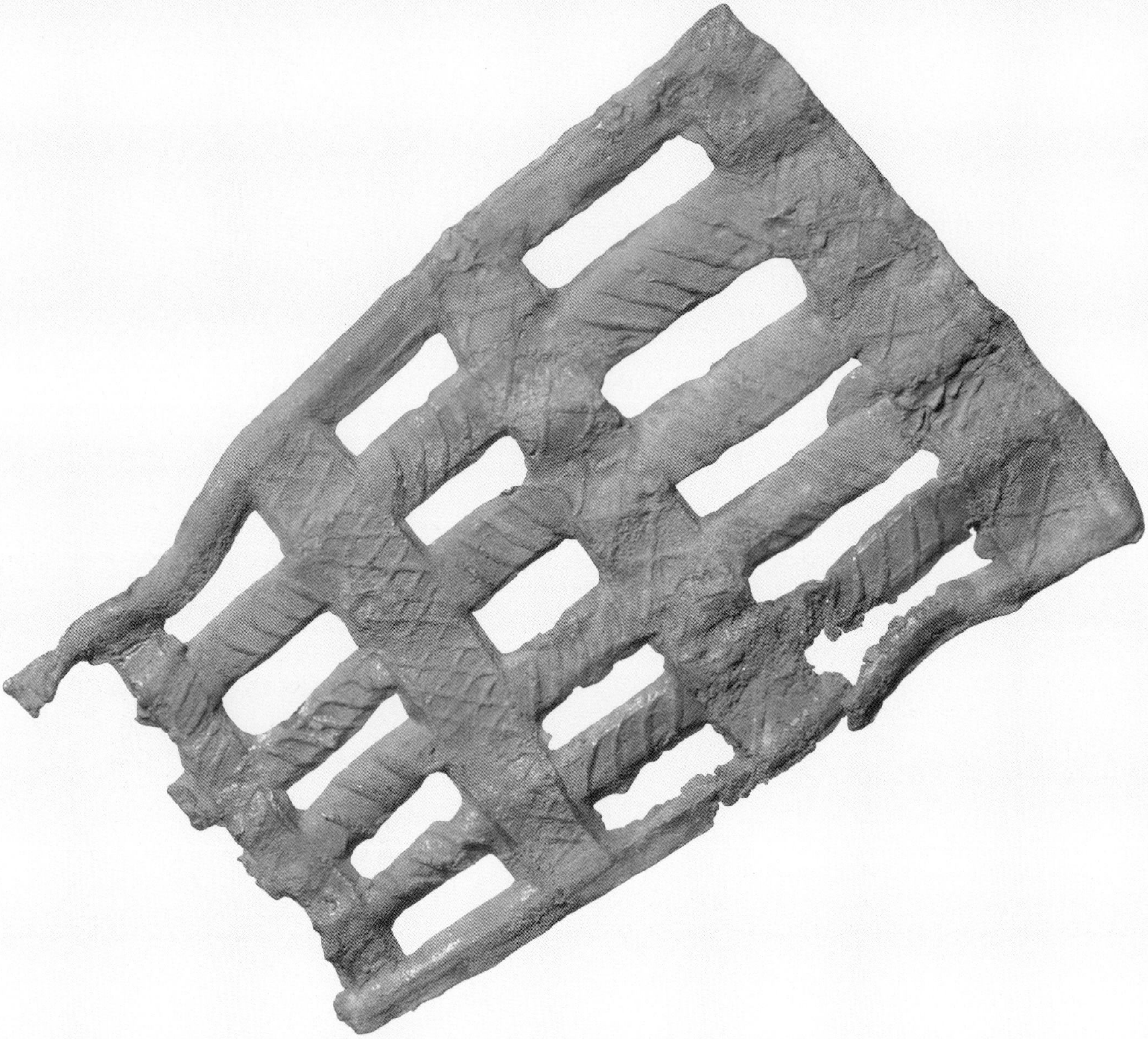

14 Windmills

'On some hill-tops there are little houses stood on poles which they turn towards the direction of the wind.'[1]

Toy windmills, made in a wide variety of shapes, materials and sizes for children and adults alike, have been popular for centuries. Some of the earliest, intended for outdoor use and comprising a wooden stick with paper sails at one end, differ little from those sold in toy and souvenir shops today. A new form appeared in the early 1500s (fig. 79, p. 396) incorporating a simple spring mechanism activated by a string which enabled the sails to rotate, and by the end of the century, toy and miniature windmills were made in silver and base metals to represent contemporary tower and post mills. Many of the silver windmills were applied to stirrup cups as a novelty feature and the drinker had to invert the vessel and blow through the post in order to turn the sails.[2] The only surviving base-metal post mill (found in the Netherlands) is freestanding and seems to be a toy.[3]

It is by no means certain that the fragments described below are windmill components but if they are, it would seem that toy windmills were made in several different forms and sizes in the early modern period.

Fig. 77. Reproduced from an illustration in the *Cris de Paris dessinés d'après Nature*, c. 1773 by M. Poisson. The image of the toy windmill-seller was accompanied by her cry:
'Pleurez, petits Enfans,
Vous aurez des Moulins à vent.'
Bibliothécaire du Roi, Paris

DESIGN 1

14.1 Windmill side panel (?)

Accession number: 98.2/83

Material: Lead alloy

Condition: Complete

Dimensions: H 32mm; W 35mm

Description: Cast in one piece with a small semi-circular top and square panel below. The domed top has a cabled edge and is decorated with ring and dot motifs and pellets. There is a large round hole in the centre of the panel and six slots around the edge; two on each side and one in the centre at the top and bottom.

Date: Possibly 17th century

Comments: Possibly from a domed roofed postmill, the round hole providing the aperture for the sails

DESIGN 2

14.2 Windmill roof and side panel (?)

Accession number: 98.2/135

Material: Lead alloy; red pigment

Condition: Complete

Dimensions: H 60mm; W 22mm

Description: A narrow rectangular panel cast in one piece and decorated on one side only. The panel is divided into two distinct areas of decoration. At the one end (probably the top) the mouldings seem to represent a stepped roof, with overhanging tiles running downwards towards the heavily ridged 'eave'. The lower section comprises a diagonally hatched border, which frames two equal-sized compartments, each decorated with tendrils and hatched leaves. The upper compartment has two large round cast holes, while the lower has one, and there is a small round hole in the centre which seems to have been punched through from the front. A number of solder blobs and melted areas can be seen around the edge and on the back.

Date: Possibly 17th century

Comments: If this panel constitutes part of the roof and side panel of a windmill, the holes are curiously placed.

Fig. 78. A child holds his windmill aloft to catch the breeze, in this detail of an engraving by Experiens Silleman. See fig. 43, p. 187

WINDMILLS • 395

DESIGN 3

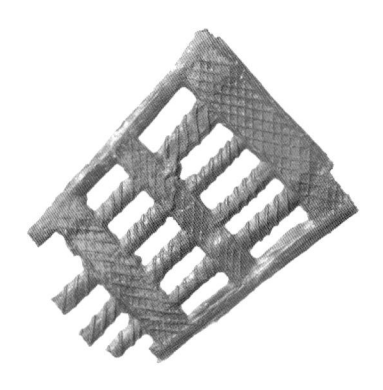

14.3 Windmill sail (?)

Accession number: 98.2/109*; 98.2/110
Material: Lead alloy
Condition: Incomplete
Dimensions: L 42mm; W 33mm
Description: Incomplete openwork panels cast in one piece from the same mould with straight, tapering sides and longitudinal struts. Both have an indented section on the widest edge and both are decorated with cross-hatched and diagonal hatching.
Date: Possibly 17th century
Provenance: 98.2/109: Queenhithe Dock
Comments: Possibly part of a windmill sail

ABOVE: **Fig. 79. Detail from Bruegel's** *Der Kinderspiele*, 1560. See plate XI, p. 363

RIGHT: **Fig. 80. Detail of a toy windmill**
Reproduced from *La très desirée et proufitable naissance du très illustre enfant Charles d'Austrice* by Jean Moulinet, 1500. Bibliothèque nationale de France, Paris, fol. 1077

DESIGN 4

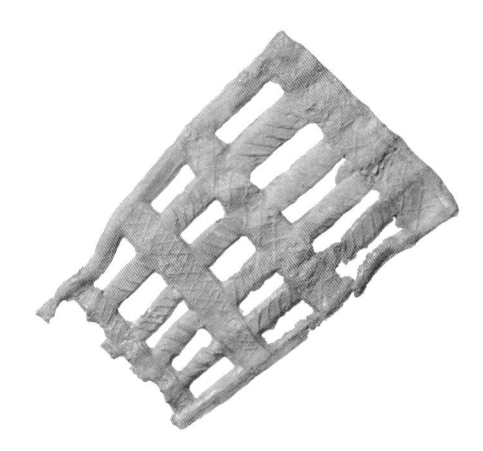

14.4 Windmill sail (?)

Accession number: 98.2/111
Material: Lead alloy
Condition: Incomplete
Dimensions: L 52mm; W 34mm
Description: Part of an openwork panel with straight, tapering sides and longitudinal struts decorated with cross-hatched and diagonal hatching.
Date: Possibly 17th century
Comparanda: Virtually identical scale and design to Acc. nos. 98.2/109 and 98.2/110, but from a different mould

DESIGN 5

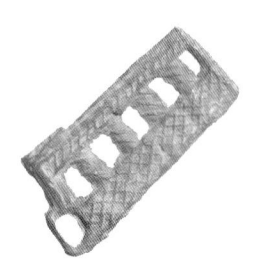

14.5 Windmill sail (?)

Accession number: 98.2/124
Material: Lead alloy
Condition: Complete
Dimensions: L 33mm; W 15mm
Description: A rectangular-shaped panel with an angular loop at one end. The diagonally hatched openwork struts are sandwiched between a broad cross-hatched band and a narrow diagonally hatched band.
Date: Possibly 17th century

1 Magno 1562.
2 Seling 1980, vol. 2, fig. 166.
3 Willemsen 1998, pp. 127–30, and 2000, fig. 3.

15 Miscellaneous

Since these fragments do not fit readily into any of the preceding categories, they have been grouped together here. In some cases a tentative interpretation of function has been suggested, but most remain enigmatic and of uncertain date. As far as possible, similar-shaped objects have been grouped together; otherwise the sequence of entries is arbitrary.

15.1 Openwork panel

Accession number: 98.2/149
Material: Lead alloy
Condition: Incomplete and damaged
Dimensions: H 16mm; L 47mm
Description: Part of an intricate openwork panel with diagonal latticework embellished with ring and dot at each intersection. The cable-edged frame also encloses a narrow band of circular and pellet tracery. There are several tabs suggesting that it was originally part of a three-dimensional object.

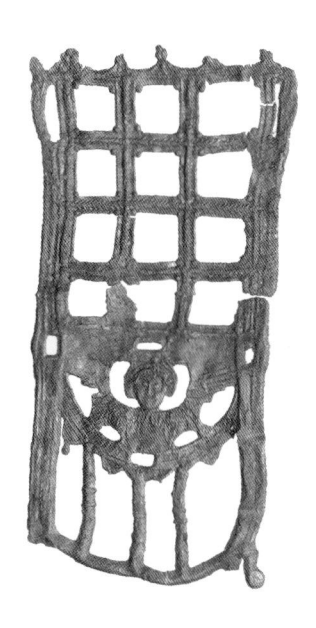

15.2 Openwork panel

Accession number: 98.2/685
Material: Lead alloy
Condition: Almost complete
Dimensions: H 73mm; W 33mm
Description: An angel with outstretched wings within a rectangular openwork panel. This object has been cast in one piece and there are four slots in the frame and one in the centre.
Comments: Probably part of an item of furniture
Comparandum: Another example (lower half only) recovered from Three Cranes Wharf in June 2003

15.3 Openwork panel, perhaps from chest

Accession number: 98.2/8a & c
Material: Lead alloy
Condition: Fragments
Dimensions: H 28mm; W 11mm. H 29mm; W 21mm
Description: Fragments from an openwork panel (possibly from two separate objects) decorated with diagonal and cross-hatching. There are pellets at each corner.
Comments: Possibly part of a chest

15.5 Openwork panel

Accession number: 98.2/629; 98.2/630*
Material: Lead alloy
Condition: Complete
Dimensions: H 30mm; W 56mm
Description: Rectangular panels (possibly cast from the same mould) with a cross-hatched frame infilled by diagonally hatched grid latticework. There is an open square at the intersection of each grid and these are surrounded by pellets. Some of the sides have tabs.

15.4 Openwork panel

Accession number: 98.2/628
Material: Lead alloy
Condition: Almost complete; slight damage
Dimensions: H 30mm; W 56mm
Description: A rectangular openwork panel with diagonally hatched latticework. The open squares at the intersection of each grid are surrounded by pellets. There are tabs on two sides and there is a plain strip at one end.
Provenance: Southwark Bridge, south side
Comparanda: Similar to Acc. nos. 98.2/629 & 98.2/630

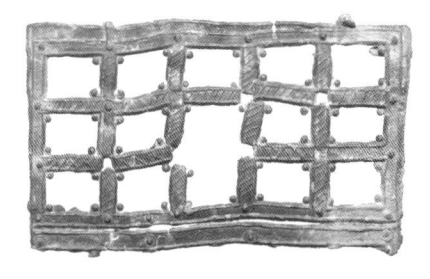

15.6 Openwork panel

Accession number: 98.2/631
Material: Lead alloy
Condition: Complete
Dimensions: H 31mm; W 53mm
Description: A rectangular openwork panel with diagonally hatched grid latticework. Some of the intersections are pierced and others are decorated with a pellet. The wide frame on three sides is plain apart from a single pellet at the base of each strut, and the fourth side has an additional band of diagonal hatching. There are tabs on two sides.

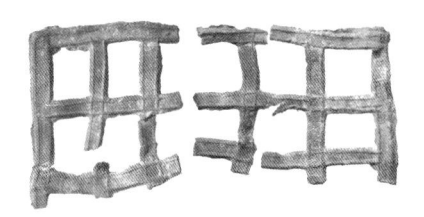

15.7 Openwork panel

Accession number: 98.2/632
Material: Lead alloy
Condition: Incomplete
Dimensions: H *c.* 30mm; W *c.* 46
Description: Part of a rectangular openwork panel with plain grid latticework. The grid pattern is enhanced by linear mouldings.

15.9 Openwork panel

Accession number: 98.2/130
Material: Lead alloy
Condition: Incomplete; damaged
Dimensions: H 20mm; W 35mm
Description: Part of an openwork panel with 'turned spindle' struts. The frame has diagonal hatching.

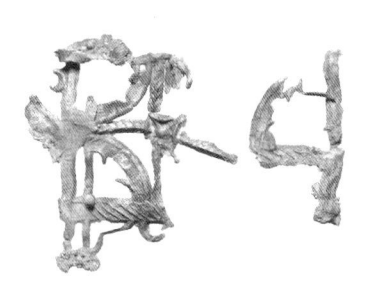

15.8 Openwork panel, perhaps from chest

Accession number: 98.2/90
Material: Lead alloy
Condition: Incomplete; much damaged
Dimensions: H *c.* 32mm; W *c.* 32mm
Description: Part of an openwork panel with diagonally hatched tracery
Comments: Possibly part of a chest

15.10 Openwork panel

Accession number: 98.2/120
Material: Lead alloy
Condition: Complete
Dimensions: H 28mm; W 48mm
Description: A rectangular frame surrounding diaper tracery interspersed with 'pine cones' or leaves. There is a solid band at one end decorated with a fleur-de-lys which is surmounted by an ogee-shaped pierced arch with beading. The top edge of the frame has a line of stylized pine cones, and there are two 'bun'-shaped feet.

15.11 Openwork panel

Accession number: 98.2/112
Material: Lead alloy
Condition: Partially complete
Dimensions: H 32mm
Description: A openwork panel of cone shape with slightly curving profile and one straight, finished edge. The decoration consists of two rows of circular tracery embellished with ring and dot and diagonal hatching. Most of the frame is diagonally hatched. There are several recurving tabs and three loops.

15.12 Openwork panel

Accession number: 98.2/127
Material: Lead alloy
Condition: Complete
Dimensions: H 23mm; W 33mm
Description: A rectangular diagonally hatched frame enclosing delicate rosette tracery embellished with trefoil cusps. The central struts have cable decoration.

15.13 Openwork panel

Accession number: 98.2/129
Material: Lead alloy
Condition: Fragment
Dimensions: H 28mm; W 24mm
Description: Part of an openwork panel with gable-shaped frame surmounted by a trefoil flanked by ring and dot motifs enclosing a hatched rosette (?) with scrolling tracery (?). The frame is diagonally hatched.

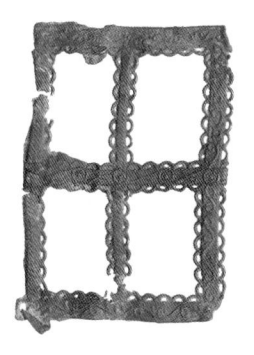

15.14 Frame

Accession number: 87.83/1
Material: Lead alloy
Condition: Complete (?)
Dimensions: H 42mm; W 31mm
Description: A rectangular frame divided by vertical and horizontal bars. The horizontal bar is decorated with an alternating pattern of crosses and ring and dot. Three sides of the frame have scrolled moulding, and the fourth side and vertical bars are diagonally hatched. The grid is embellished with openwork scallop edging and there is a folded tab on one side.

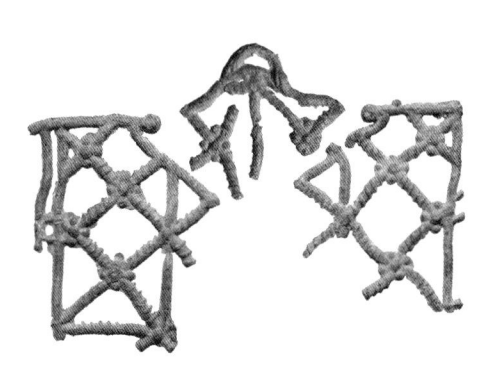

15.15 Openwork panel

Accession number: 98.2/633
Material: Lead alloy
Condition: Incomplete; three pieces
Dimensions: H *c.* 38mm; W *c.* 60mm
Description: Three fragments of hatched diaper tracery with pellets at each intersection. One of the fragments has a domed profile.
Comments: Possibly a component from a three-dimensional chest

15.16 Panel with key hole

Accession number: 86.153
Material: Lead alloy
Condition: Incomplete
Dimensions: H 15mm; W *c.* 20mm
Description: Part of a panel with circular decoration flanking a rectangular lock plate with four pellets or 'rivets' in each corner and a key hole.
Comments: Probably from a chest or coffer

15.17 Openwork panel

Accession number: 98.2/146
Material: Lead alloy
Condition: Fragment
Dimensions: H 18mm; W 10mm
Description: Part of an openwork panel with angular profile, cable edge and linear ring and dot. There is scrolled ring and dot cresting.
Comments: Possibly from a chair

15.18 Openwork panel or door

Accession number: 98.2/417
Condition: Complete component (?)
Dimensions: H 40 mm; W 14 mm
Description: Possibly a complete side panel from a multi-component, three-dimensional object. The narrow rectangular panel has a diagonally hatched border and a pierced upper half divided into four sections by vertical and horizontal bars. The solid lower section is decorated with a diagonally hatched saltire and there are ring and dot and semi-circular mouldings within each segment. There are three tab stubs on one side and opposing angular loops at the top and bottom.
Date: Possibly 17th or 18th century
Provenance: Southwark Bridge, north side
Comments: Precise identification unknown. The shape is suggestive of the door or side panel of a sedan chair, but no other part of a miniature version of one of these has yet been recognized.

15.19 Panel

Accession number: 98.2/132
Material: Lead alloy
Condition: Incomplete
Dimensions: H *c.* 19mm; W 23mm
Inscription: 1641
Description: Part of an ogee-shaped solid panel inversely inscribed 1641 with tracery below
Comments: Possibly an I(D)Q product

15.20 Solid panel

Accession number: 98.2/142
Material: Lead alloy
Condition: Complete
Dimensions: H 21mm; W 41mm
Inscription: IDQ
Description: A solid rectangular panel with two lugs at one end and cable-edged border. There is a garland in the centre enclosing the letters ID over Q with mullets, and the rest of the panel is decorated with a diaper pattern.

15.21 Disc

Accession number: 98.2/622
Material: Lead alloy
Condition: Almost complete; some damage
Dimensions: Diam 45mm
Inscription: IDQ
Description: An extremely thin solid disc with moulded decoration on one side, consisting of a small garland enclosing the letters ID over Q with mullets and a pellet cluster. The rest of the panel is decorated with a diaper pattern.
Comparanda: Acc. nos. 98.2/142, 98.2/617 & 98.2/626 with semi-circular notches around the edge

15.22 Disc

Accession number: 98.2/617
Material: Lead alloy
Condition: Part only
Dimensions: H 26mm; W 43mm
Inscription: IDQ
Description: Part of an extremely thin solid disc with moulded decoration on one side, consisting of a small garland enclosing the letters ID over Q with mullet and pellet cluster. The rest of the panel is decorated with a diaper pattern.
Comparanda: Very similar to Acc. no. 98.2/622, but from a different mould. The garland is placed in the reverse position to Acc. no. 98.2/622.

15.23 Disc

Accession number: 98.2/626
Material: Lead alloy
Condition: Half only
Inscription: AF 1668
Dimensions: Diam 45mm
Description: Part of an extremely thin solid disc with moulded decoration on one side, consisting of a circle surrounded by a garland inscribed AF and 1668. The rest of the panel is decorated with a diaper pattern.
Comparanda: Acc. nos. 98.2/617 & 98.2/622

15.24 Disc

Accession number: 98.2/618
Material: Lead alloy
Condition: Complete; flattened
Dimensions: Diam 41mm
Inscription: ID over Q
Description: A solid disc with moulding on one side only. There is a cable edge with two stubs on one side. A wide plain border encloses double concentric circles, a narrow foliate band incorporating an oval cartouche inscribed ID over Q, two further concentric circles and the central motif of a cinquefoil double rose with calyx points between the outer rows of petals. There is a single ring and dot between each point.
Comments: Possibly a flattened porringer
Provenance: Southwark Bridge, north side

15.25 Solid panel

Accession number: 98.2/148
Material: Lead alloy
Condition: Incomplete
Dimensions: H 30mm; W c. 35mm
Description: Part of a solid panel with broken side pieces from a three-dimensional object (?). The complete panel is decorated with a diaper pattern and there is a square aperture in one corner.

15.26 Solid panel

Accession number: 98.2/136
Material: Lead alloy
Condition: Complete
Dimensions: H 20mm; W 29mm
Description: A solid rectangular panel with beading around three sides and cable decoration on the fourth. There is a large square in the centre enclosing a sexfoil double rose with prominent calyx points surrounded by pellets and ring and dot motifs in each corner. On either side are borders of foliate decoration and there are two tabs aligned with the cabled edge.
Provenance: Southwark Bridge, north side

15.27 Solid panel

Accession number: 98.2/582
Material: Lead alloy
Condition: Complete
Dimensions: H 21mm; W 44mm
Description: A solid panel with triangular-shaped ends, angled sides and hatched and foliate decoration
Comparandum: Identical shape and similar decoration on Acc. no. 98.2/583

15.28 Solid panel

Accession number: 98.2/583
Material: Lead alloy
Condition: Incomplete
Dimensions: H *c.* 19mm; W 41mm
Description: A solid panel with triangular-shaped ends, angled hatched sides and hatched and stylized floral decoration
Comparandum: Acc. no. 98.2/582

15.29 Toy house front

Accession number: 98.2/625
Material: Lead alloy
Condition: Complete
Dimensions: H 48mm; W 29mm
Description: The front elevation of a gabled house with five windows (four with mouldings suggestive of a sash system). The lower windows and front door have arched pediments and the gable is embellished with a fleur-de-lys flanked by scrolling. The façade is decorated with a symmetrical pattern, which suggests a pargeted surface. There are two rectangular slots, one on each side, for attachment to other sections (now missing).
Date: Late 17th century
Provenance: Bull Wharf
Comments: The gabling on this façade is of Low Countries style. The first floor windows are larger and therefore correspond with the principal living rooms of domestic dwellings in this period.

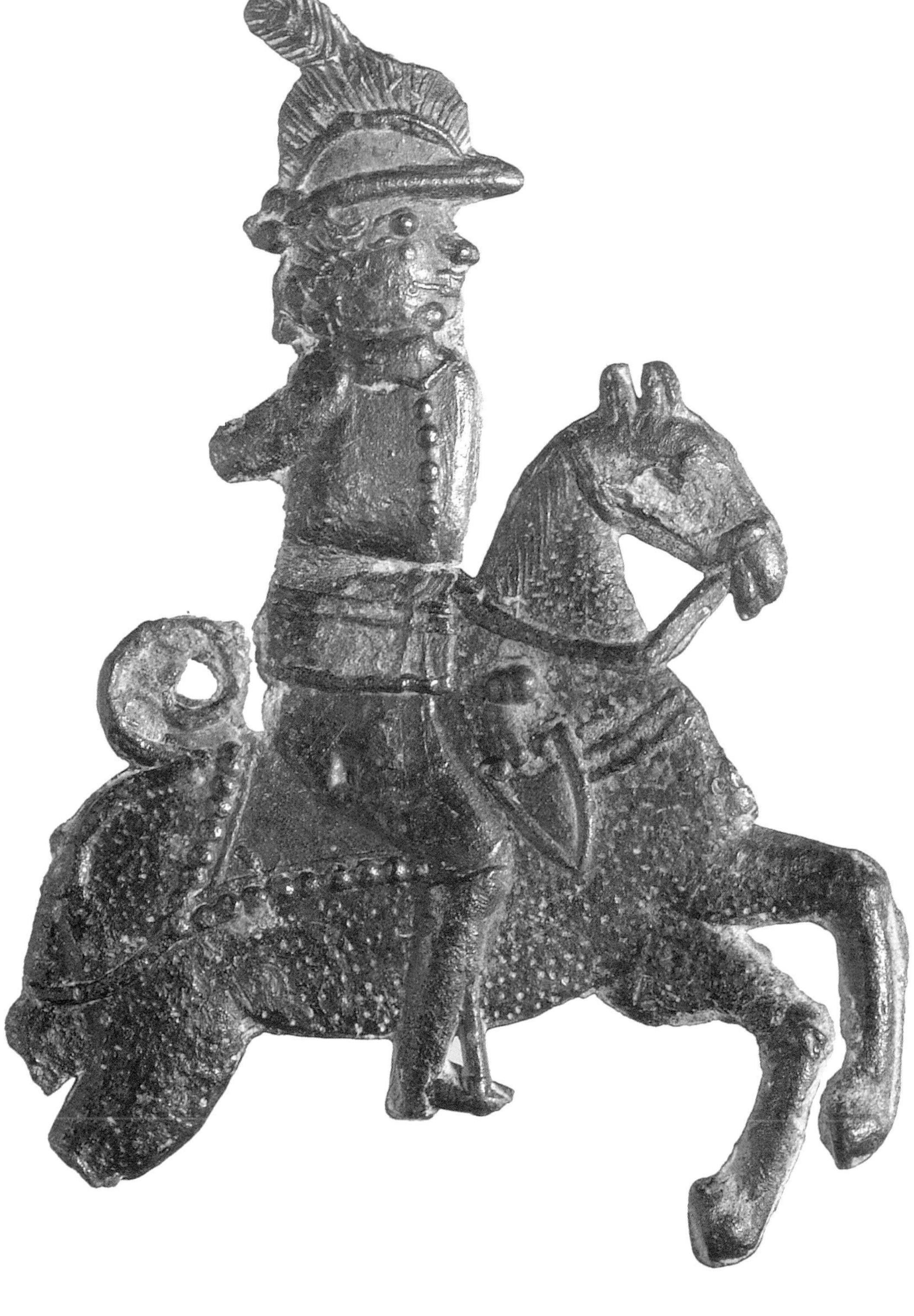

Robert Peircy

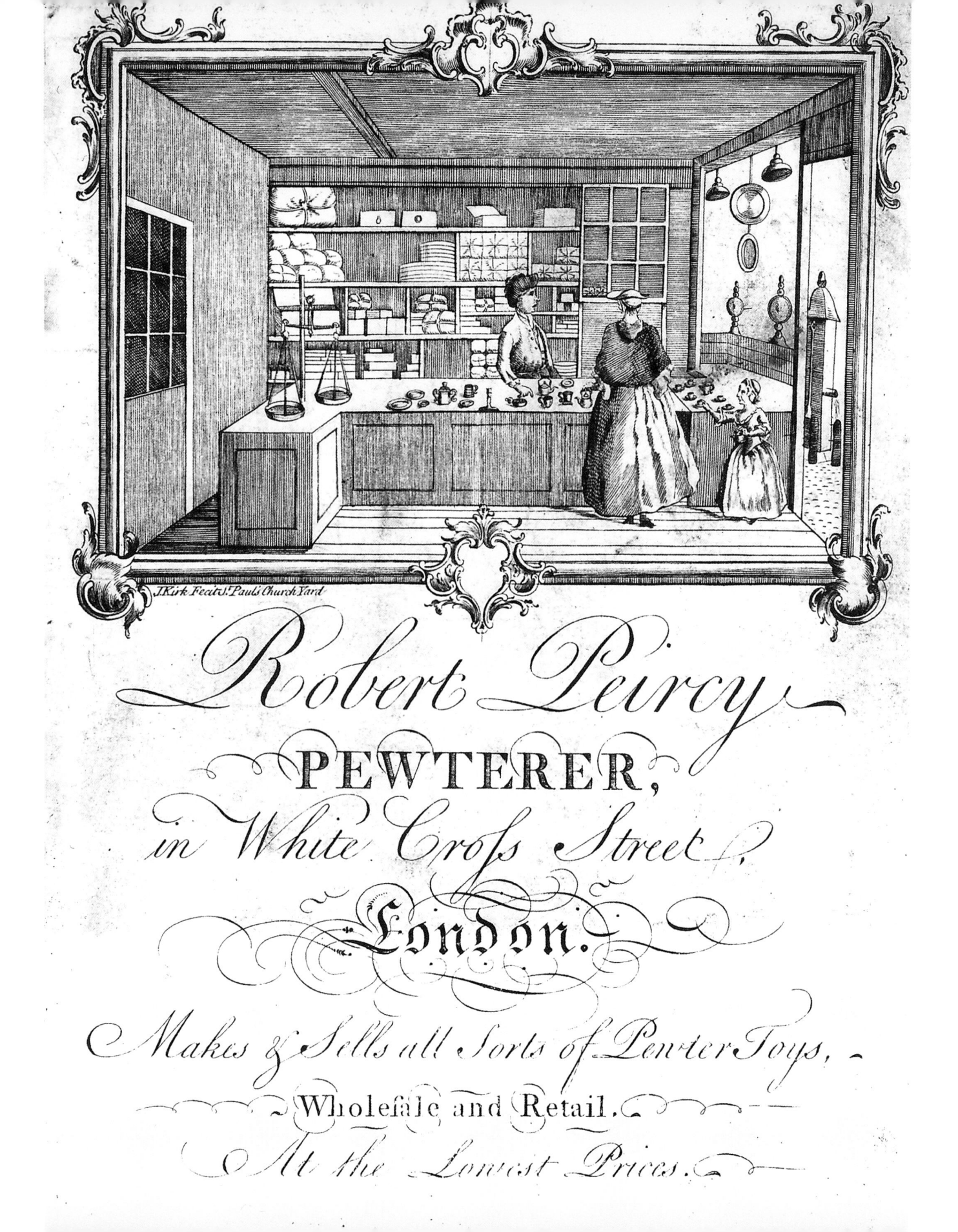

PEWTERER,

in White Cross Street,

London.

Makes & Sells all Sorts of Pewter Toys,

Wholesale and Retail.

At the Lowest Prices.

J. Kirk Fecit S.t Pauls Church Yard

PART III

Appendices

Fig. 81. The trade card of pewterer Robert Peircy, c. 1750
Trustees of the British Museum
Heal Collection

Appendix I

Microstructure and composition of pewter miniatures from medieval London

Meg Chuping Wang
Edited by Helen Ganiaris & Dafydd Griffiths

Introduction

Most of the toys or miniatures analysed for this study were made of a leaded tin alloy. The study was carried out as an item of assessed coursework (towards an MSc in Conservation) to establish whether the lead-tin alloy used for the toys was 'ley metal'. Ley metal is a lower- standard pewter, that is a tin alloy containing a more substantial proportion of lead. Fine pewter contains little lead and has a high tin content. According to a *Table of the Assays of Metal and of the Weights and Dimensions of the Several Sorts of Pewter Wares* published by the Worshipful Company of Pewterers in 1772, ley metal was the required alloy for children's toys. For this study, 17 of the lead-tin alloy toys in the collection were analysed.

There is much published historical literature on the English pewter industry[1] but few compositional investigations of ancient pewter have been published. In 1983 Pollard investigated 24 Roman pewter objects (bowls, plates and one flagon) from the Appleford Hoard; his results by X-ray fluorescence (XRF) analysis showed three compositional ranges (grouped around 50wt% tin, a 1:1 tin:lead alloy; 66.7wt% tin, a 2:1 tin:lead alloy; and 99wt% tin) were represented in the analysed samples.[2] Also using XRF, Brownsword and Pitt analysed 36 English 13th–16th-century pewter items of flatware.[3] Their results showed that most were made from high-quality tin-rich alloys (tin content in excess of 95wt% tin) with a low lead content (below 5wt%), hardened with a small amount of copper. From the Roman to the medieval periods, the use of lead in pewter seems to be reduced gradually, particularly in tableware. It is possible that it was realized that an alloy with more than 25% lead would be poisonous.[4]

In the exhibition catalogue *Playthings from the Past: Lead-alloy miniature artefacts c. 1300–1800*, Geoff Egan suggests, based on empirical observation, that the majority of the objects in this collection are of lead-tin alloy with some likely to be of fairly pure tin and others pewter of different grades.[5] The purpose of this study was to ascertain whether a different composition was used for different types of toys (such as vessels, furniture, human figures etc.) or at different times during the period from *c.* 1150 to 1800, and whether particular makers were using specific compositions. If there were correlations between date of manufacture or maker and the composition of the alloy, then analysing the chemical composition of an alloy might indicate (within a range of uncertainty) the date of manufacture or the manufacturer of the toy. In addition, by identifying impurities in the alloy, it might also be possible to provide information about the provenance of the metal used to make the alloys. For example, tin ore from Cornish mines has characteristic impurities (such as sulphur, iron, cobalt, arsenic and tungsten) which might distinguish it from imported tin ore.

Methods of analysis

Several techniques were used in order to determine the microstructure and chemical composition of the toys. The techniques employed included reflected light microscopy, scanning electron microscopy with energy dispersive X-ray spectrometry (SEM-EDS), and electron probe microanalysis (EMPA – commonly called 'microprobe' analysis) using wavelength dispersive X-ray spectrometry.

Reflected light microscopy revealed the metallographic microstructure of the samples. Scanning electron microscopy with energy dispersive X-ray spectrometry was used to determine the elemental composition of each sample by both bulk analysis and analysis of individual phases, as well as to confirm the microstructure. SEM-EDS only measures the major elements in the alloys above about 1wt% with any precision, although it can (depending on other components present) often detect elements present at levels above about 0.1wt%. Microprobe analysis (EMPA) was employed to detect chosen elements present with greater accuracy, including those present at lower levels (*c.* 0.01wt% and above).

Six elements were selected for analysis using a microprobe – tin (Sn), lead (Pb), copper (Cu), antimony (Sb), bismuth (Bi) and arsenic (As). The microprobe system was operated at an accelerating potential of 25 kV using the Sn(L?), Pb(M?), Cu(K?), Sb(L?), Bi(M?), and As(L?) X-ray peaks for the measurements, with Pb(L?) and Bi(L?) peaks also being used for calibration. For each sample four spot analyses were usually undertaken, two on the bright lead-rich phase, another two on the dark (lower backscattered electron intensity) tin-rich phase. More spots were analysed if any unusual results appeared. In total, 84 point analyses were performed.

Sample preparation

Small samples were removed from damaged or concealed areas of the objects. This allowed the uncorroded metal core of the objects to be analysed, avoiding the surface of the object which may have been altered by corrosion or depletion of certain components during burial. Traces of paint surviving on some surfaces also had to be avoided. One sample less than 1mm in size was removed from each of the 17 objects. The locations from which they were removed were recorded. Visual examination under the stereomicroscope was used to align the sample so as to obtain the desired cross-section. Each sample, being small and soft, was clamped and then embedded with cold-mounting epoxy resin (Metprep EPO-SET resin). The exposed surfaces were ground on successively finer grades of silicon carbide paper (120, 320, 600 and 1200 grit [15 micron]), polished with 6 micron and 1 micron diamond pastes, and finally polished with colloidal silica (0.06 micron).

Results

The microstructure under reflected light microscopy

Using reflected light microscopy, it was discovered that four specimens had a single-phase metal microstructure – Acc. nos. 98.2/151, 98.2/170, 98.2/195 and 98.2/372. These samples are referred to in this paper as Group 1. The polished sections are lustrous white and have a homogeneous equiaxial grain structure (see fig. 82) indicating that the metal is relatively free of impurities. Tin is the main constituent and it appears that no other metals, such as lead or antimony, were added. The other 13 specimens are two-phase metals which are tin alloys containing varying amounts of lead. Characteristic of their microstructure is a dendritic structure formed during casting (see fig. 83), a segregation phenomenon that often arises in impure metals or alloys.[6] As a lead-tin alloy cools, it tends to separate into two phases, a lead-rich phase and a tin-rich phase. The relative amounts of these two phases will depend on the overall composition of the alloy.

Fig. 82. Group 1 – High-purity tin
Bridge-spouted ewer
Acc. no. 98.2/170, Cat. no. 8.115

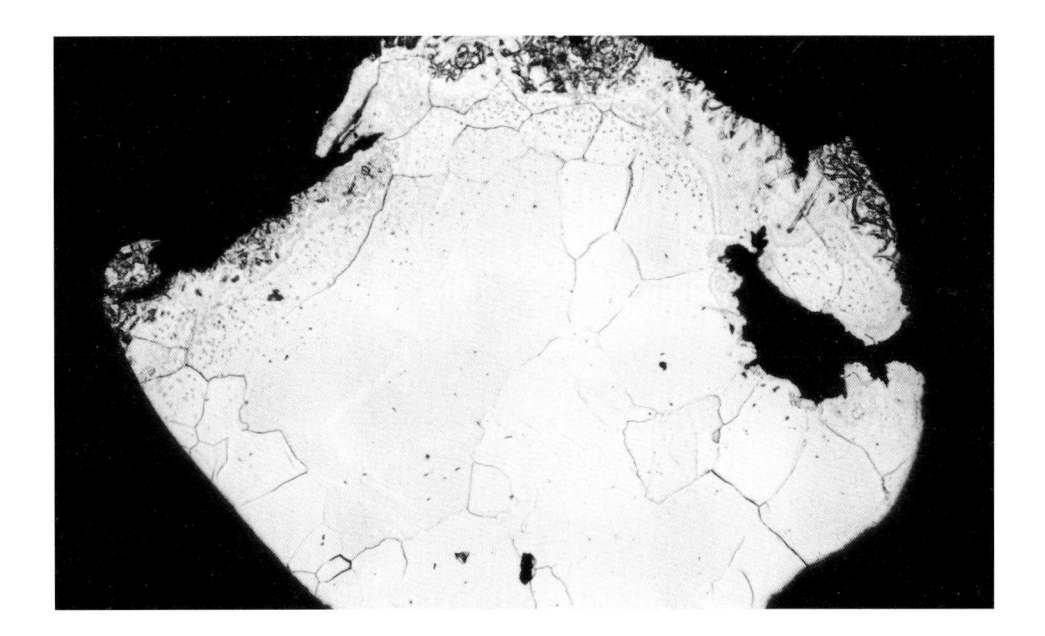

414 • TOYS, TRIFLES & TRINKETS

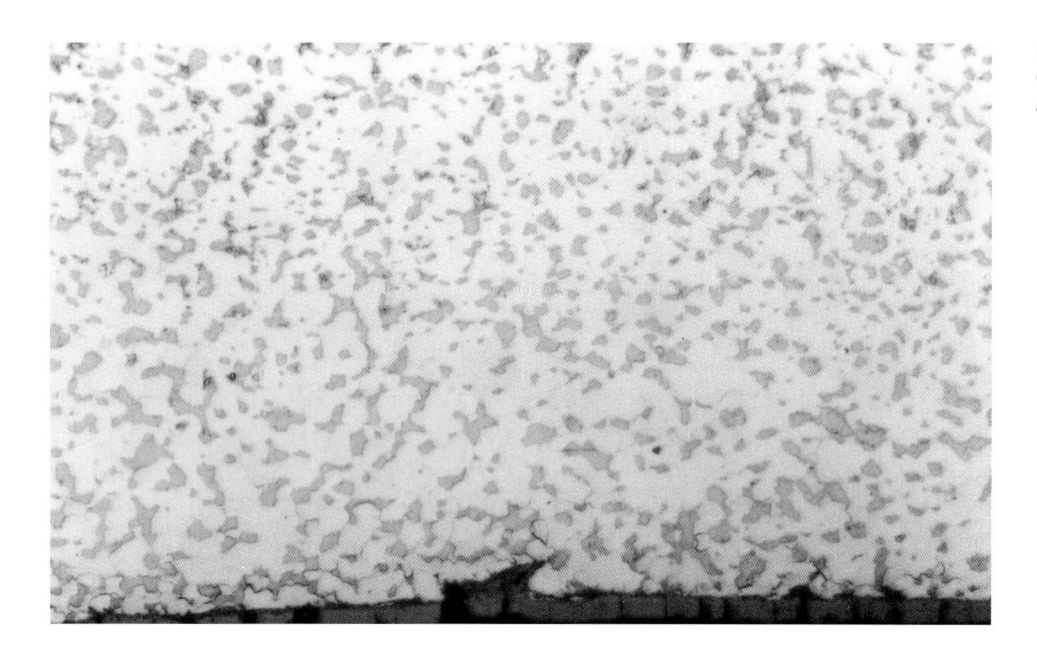

Fig. 83. Group 2 – 3:1 tin:lead
Candlestick
Acc. no. 98.2/544, Cat. no. 5.5,

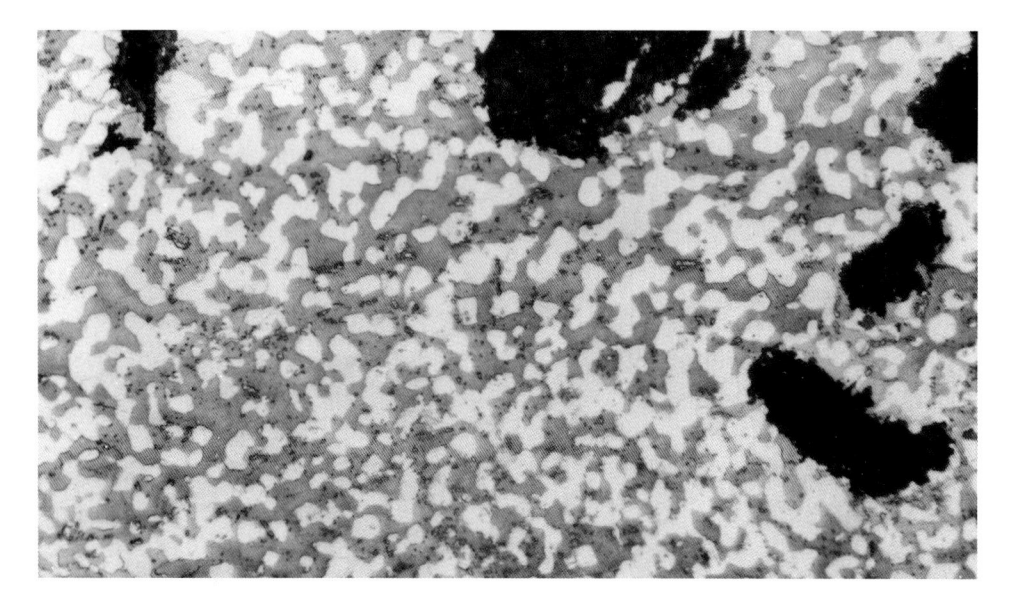

Fig. 84. Group 3 – 1:1 tin:lead
Dripping pan
Acc. no. 98.2/575, Cat. no. 2.13,

Chemical composition by SEM-EDS

The chemical compositions of the single-phase and two-phase samples were confirmed by SEM-EDS. The white metal (single-phase) specimens were confirmed to be almost pure tin (Table 1). No other alloying metals were detected. The difference between the determined tin concentration and 100% is probably due to porosity, surface imperfections or oxidation.

Table 1
Elemental composition of single-phase metals measured by SEM-EDS

Specimen	Sn	Pb	Cu	Si	Total	Description
98.2/151	95.8	n.d.	n.d.	1.6	97.4	flagon
98.2/170	94.2	n.d.	n.d.	0.2	94.4	bridged ewer
98.2/195	95.1	n.d	n.d.	0.2	95.3	skillet
98.2/372	99.3	n.d.	n.d.	0.3	99.6	male figurine

* Values are not normalised; n.d. means not detected, i.e. below detection limit

The two-phase specimens were confirmed to be lead and tin alloy (Table 2). Tiny amounts of copper were detected but are thought to be an impurity from the lead ores. The 13 two-phase specimens can be further divided into two groups according to the results of SEM-EDS bulk analysis (Table 3).

Table 2
Elemental composition of two-phase metals measured by SEM-EDS (area analysis to estimate bulk composition, 1600x, 20kV)

Specimen	Sn	Pb	Cu	Si	Description
98.2/109	76.1	23.9	n.d	n.d.	furniture leg
98.2/221	73.5	25.4	1.1	n.d.	porringer
98.2/225	75.6	23.1	1.3	n.d.	porringer
98.2/280	69.2	30.2	0.6	n.d.	fluted dish
98.2/282	70.5	28.9	0.6	n.d.	plate
98.2/286	47.1	52.9	n.d	n.d.	oval dish
98.2/299	80.7	18.8	0.5	n.d.	plate

98.2/544	77.8	21.7	0.5	n.d.	candlestick
98.2/575	51.7	48.9	n.d	n.d.	dripping pan
98.2/588	79.5	20.5	n.d	n.d.	gridiron
98.2/614	77.7	22.3	n.d	n.d.	bird cage
98.2/617	78.1	21.9	n.d	n.d.	roundel by maker/s I(D)Q
98.2/719	70.4	29.6	n.d	n.d.	chest

* Values are normalized to bring the total to 100% so as to facilitate comparison of the compositions of the alloys and to remove the effect of features such as casting porosity in reducing the analytical totals; n.d. means not detected, i.e. below detection limit.

Table 3
Composition wt%

Group 2: 11 specimens		
	69.2–80.7% Sn,	mean 75.4% Sn
	18.8–30.2% Pb,	mean 24.2% Pb
Group 3: 2 specimens		
	47.1–51.7% Sn,	mean 49.4% Sn
	48.9–52.9% Pb,	mean 50.9% Pb

Group 2 alloys contain tin with a lead content of around 20–30wt%, but Group 3 is different, containing approximately equal weights of tin and lead (Table 3), corresponding to the 1:1 recipe found in Roman pewter. The higher lead content alloy of Group 3 would have been considered an inferior-quality pewter.

Detection of trace elements by EMPA

Because SEM-EDS only identified the major elements in the alloys (tin and lead), EMPA was employed to detect trace elements, particularly antimony and bismuth. Minor and trace concentrations of impurities may be correlated with the date, place and technique of manufacture as well as poor alloy preparation. For example, in the 1760s a pewter alloy known as Britannia metal was introduced. It contained 91–93wt% tin, 6–7wt% antimony and 1–2wt% copper, with antimony replacing the lead used in earlier alloys. The detection of antimony is useful for dating these toys as genuine medieval artefacts or more recent copies or forgeries. A significant amount of antimony was detected only in sample 98.2/299 (see p. 420).

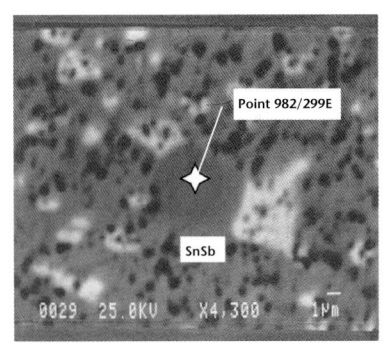

Fig. 85. Intermetallic compound SnSb is found in the metallographic section of this specimen. Plate
Acc. no. 98.2/299, Cat. no. 8.13

SnSb: intermetallic compound

On the metallographic section of specimen 98.2/299, both phases – lead and tin – are quite porous, compared with other lead-tin alloy specimens whose tin-rich (darker grey) phase is usually not as porous as the lead-rich (lighter grey) phase. In this sample a third phase, the intermetallic compound SnSb, was found (microprobe photograph, fig. 85). This intermediate phase is solid and slightly darker than the tin phase surround. Point analyses on the SnSb phase (Table 4) show a proportion of tin to antimony – 58.7 to 34.2 or 56.2 to 37.5, which is about 60:40. The antimony-tin phase diagram shows an alloy of composition between 60%Sn:40%Sb to 45%Sn:55%Sb producing the intermetallic compound while cooling down from the melt. However, as seen in Table 2, specimen 98.2/299 shows no antimony detected by SEM-EDS, which suggests that the bulk proportion of antimony is no more that a fraction of a percent, albeit that inhomogeneous distribution could make it seem lower than the true bulk value if little happened to be present in the analysed volume. The antimony should very probably be regarded as an impurity rather than a deliberate addition.

Table 4
Point analyses by EPMA on specimen 98.2/299

Composition (wt%)

Point no.	Phase	Sn	Pb	Cu	Sb	As	Bi	Total
98.2/299A	lead-rich	2.25	84.8	0.17	n.d.	n.d.	n.d.	87.2
98.2/299B	lead-rich	2.21	88.2	0.09	n.d	n.d	n.d.	90.5
98.2/299C	tin-rich	91.6	2.95	0.09	3.01	n.d	0.11	97.8
98.2/299D	tin-rich	98.1	1.35	n.d.	n.d.	n.d.	0.09	99.6
98.2/299E	SnSb	58.7	0.90	0.43	34.2	1.01	n.d.	95.2
98.2/299F	SnSb	56.2	0.64	0.56	37.5	2.30	n.d.	97.2
98.2/299G	lead-rich	1.70	88.0	n.d.	n.d.	n.d.	n.d.	89.7
98.2/299H	tin-rich	96.3	0.28	0.03	0.15	n.d.	0.07	96.8

Single-phase metals (high-purity tin)

Point analysis on Group 1 samples (single-phase high-purity tin), measured by EMPA (Table 5), gave results very similar to those obtained by SEM-EDS (Table 1). Neither the data from SEM-EDS nor those from EMPA show any copper in the four high-purity tin samples, confirming that specimens were made of high-purity tin, not tin hardened with copper. Tin hardened with copper typically contains around 0.4wt% copper. In addition to this, the microstructure of the Group 1 samples consists of large, equiaxial grains identical to that of high-purity tin, but different from the structure of hard tin which has dendritic grains of tin-rich solid solution with interdendritic Cu_6Sn_5.[7]

Table 5
Point analysis on single-phase metals measured by EMPA

Composition (wt%)

Specimen	Sn	Pb	Cu	Sb	As	Bi	Total
98.2/151	95.3	n.d.	n.d.	n.d.	n.d.	n.d.	95.3
98.2/170	99.1	n.d	n.d	n.d.	n.d.	n.d.	99.1
98.2/195	98.0	n.d.	n.d.	n.d.	n.d.	n.d.	98.0
98.2/372	98.0	0.12	n.d	n.d.	n.d.	n.d.	98.1

Two-phase metals (lead-tin alloy)

Due to the fact that only point analyses were available from EMPA, it is difficult to distinguish the various bulk compositions, such as 80% tin to 20% lead or 50% tin to 50% lead. The only trace element found in this group was antimony in specimen 98.2/299 as reported above.

Discussion

Grouping

In terms of lead content, the 17 samples can be grouped into three compositional ranges as shown in Table 6. Group 1 samples are almost pure tin, three of the four containing no detectable lead. Group 2 samples (11) are composed of a tin alloy containing around 20–30wt% lead content while Group 3 samples (2) contain approximately equal amounts of tin and lead by weight.

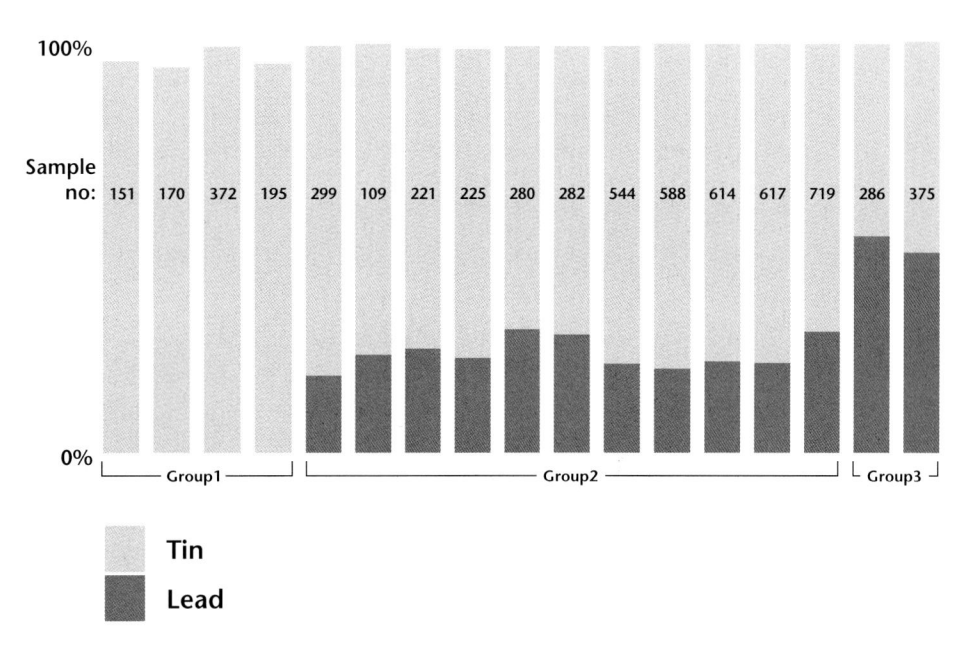

Table 6
Lead-tin concentration of 17 pewter samples

Correlation between composition, grades of pewter, and types of objects

Group 1, including samples 98.2/151, 98.2/170, 98.2/195, 98.2/372, made from high-purity tin (94–99%), is regarded as *fine pewter*, the first grade of pewter. This does not conform to the Pewterers' Company regulation that all children's pewter toys were to be made from ley metal which contains 80% tin to 20% lead or the 3:1 recipe. The four Group 1 pewter toys – flagon, bridged ewer, male figurine and skillet – are all finely decorated, indicating they might have had a higher market value requiring fine pewter to be used rather than ley metal. But as these pewter miniatures may have been made earlier than the 1772 regulation, they might conform to an earlier standard.

The compositional Group 2 contains objects that were made of alloys which contained 20–30wt% lead (25±5 wt%). The types of objects include a plate, furniture, porringer, fluted dish, candlestick, gridiron, birdcage and chest.

The samples from Group 3 – 98.2/286 and 98.2/575 – which contained about 50wt% tin and 50wt% lead (the 1:1 recipe) are thought to represent 'inferior quality' pewter toys.[8]

Table 7

Relation between microstructure, composition, grades of pewter and types of objects

Microstructure	Composition wt%	Grades of pewter	Types of objects (function)
Single phase	high-purity tin	fine pewter	toys(?)
Two phases	75% tin to 25% lead (**3:1 recipe**)	ley metal	toys
	50% tin to 50% lead (**1:1 recipe**)	inferior pewter	toys

Correlation of microstructure and production techniques

The two basic means of shaping metals – casting or coldworking and annealing – result in two different types of crystal structures in pewter. Cast metals in section often display characteristic spherical holes or porosity, due to either dissolved gases in the melt or to interdendritic holes and channels that have not been filled with metal during solidification. On the other hand, twinned grains usually occur during the recrystallization accompanying annealing after working.[9] Pewter vessels were generally made by casting in a mould.[10] Most of the metallographic sections show some porosity and no twinning, indicating that these pewter miniatures were made by casting.

Correlation between trace elements in chemical composition and date and place of manufacture

Trace elements such as antimony and bismuth were found in several samples but in such small quantities that they are likely to be impurities from ores. For example an intermetallic compound SnSb was found using EMPA in the sample 98.2/299 (a plate), but no antimony was detected by SEM-EDS which means the amount of antimony is probably low. Antimony should probably be regarded as an impurity in this sample rather than an artificial addition.

Tin for the English pewter industry was mined in Cornwall and Devon; by the end of the 17th century there were 26 smelting houses in Cornwall and two in Devon.[11] Tin was also imported from other parts of Europe. Insufficient trace metals were detected to be a guide to the geographical source of tin ore, therefore giving no direct information that would distinguish raw material from Cornish or European mines.

Correlation between chemical composition and individual manufacturer

The London guild, the Worshipful Company of Pewterers (originally designated the 'Pewterers' Company') survives to this day. In 1503 an Act of Parliament gave the Company the authority to control the pewter trade, making it compulsory for all makers to stamp their ware with a touchmark and to register their mark on the touch plates of the Company. Registration of touchmarks continued to about the year 1824, and it is by this means that the date and the maker of pewter objects can be determined.[12] Although several of the miniatures are marked, it is difficult to identify particular makers from the composition of the alloy. Although in medieval times pewter craftsmen always prepared their own metal, composition could vary from batch to batch.[13]

Conclusion

The metal from which the sampled miniatures were made can be grouped into three recipes: high-purity tin, 3:1 (tin:lead) and 1:1 (tin:lead). The few objects made from high-purity tin are classified as fine pewter, the objects grouped around the 3:1 recipe may be considered to approximate ley metal, while the 1:1 objects would have been considered inferior pewter. Several minor elements, such as copper, bismuth and arsenic, were detected in some samples but in small amounts only. These minor or trace concentrations are more likely to be impurities from lead ores, rather than deliberate additions.

Because only 17 objects were analysed, it was not possible to correlate a particular composition of pewter to a certain type of toy, to distinguish between different makers, or to date the toys by composition. The absence of significant amounts of antimony is consistent with these objects being of an early date.

Insufficient trace elements were detected to indicate the geographical source of the raw materials. Examination of the microstructure confirmed that the production technique used was casting.

Acknowledgements

I would like to thank the Museum of London for initiating the project and to thank the curator, Hazel Forsyth, for her encouragement. Hazel and conservator Rose Johnson at the Museum of London are thanked for carrying out the sampling of the objects. Thanks are also due to Prakash Dodia (sectioning), Sandra Bond and Stuart Laidlaw (photomicroscopy) and Kevin Reeves (SEM & Microprobe) for their technical help. I would particularly like to thank Prof. Thilo Rehern, Dr Dafydd Griffiths and Dr John Merkel for their help in interpretation of the data.

Bibliography

ASM, *ATLAS of Microstructures of Industrial Alloys*, Metals Handbook vol. 7, 8th edn (American Society for Metals, 1972)

Brownsword, R. & Pitt, E.E.H., 'A Note on Some Medieval Pewter Spoon Alloys', *Historical Metallurgy* 17 (2) (1983), p. 119

Brownsword, R. & Pitt, E.E.H., 'X-ray Fluorescence Analysis of English 13th–16th-century Pewter Flatware', *Archaeometry* 26 (2) (1984), pp. 237–44

Charron, S., *Modern Pewter: Design and techniques* (Newton Abbot, 1973)

Cotterell, H.H., *Old Pewter: Its makers and marks* (London, 1929)

Cronyn, J., *The Elements of Archaeological Conservation* (London, 1990)

Egan, G., *Playthings from the Past: Lead-alloy miniature artefacts* c. 1300–1800 (London, 1996)

Englefield, E., *A Short History of Pewter* (London, 1933)

Englefield, E., *A Treatise on Pewter* (London, 1934)

Evans, C.J., *Tin: Handbook* (Heidelberg, 1994)

Forsyth, H., Pers. comm. to Elizabeth Pye, 2000

Hedges, E.S., *Tin and its Alloys* (London, 1960)

ITRI, *Metallography of Tin and Tin Alloys*, International Tin Research Institute 580 (Uxbridge, 1982)

Massé, H.J.L.J., *Chats on Old Pewter*, rev. and ed. by Michaelis, R.F. (London, 1949)

Michaelis, R.F., *Antique Pewter of the British Isles* (London, 1955)

Pollard, M., 'X-ray Fluorescence Analysis of the Appleford Hoard of Romano-British Pewter', *Historical Metallurgy* 17 (2) (1983), pp. 83–90

Pollard, M., 'Investigations of Lead Objects using XRF' in Miles, G. & Pollard, S., eds, *Lead and Tin Studies in Conservation and Technology*, UKIC Occasional Papers 3 (London, 1985), pp. 27–32

Pollard, M. & Heron, C., *Archaeological Chemistry* (Royal Society of Chemistry, Letchworth, 1996)

Scott, D.A., *Metallography and Microstructure of Ancient and Historic Metals* (London, 1991)

Tylecote, R.F., *A History of Metallurgy* (London, 1976)

Wang, M.C., *Scientific Analysis of Mediaeval and Later Pewter Miniatures from the Thames,* Unpublished project, MSc Conservation: materials science (Institute of Archaeology, University College London, 2001)

Welch, C., *History of the Worshipful Company of Pewterers of the City of London*, 2 vols (London, 1902)

Worshipful Company of Pewterers, *Table of the Assays of Metal and of the Weights and Dimensions of the Several Sorts of Pewter Wares* (London, 1772)

1. Welch 1902; Cotterell 1929; Englefield 1933 & 1934; Masse 1949, Michaelis 1955.
2. Pollard 1983.
3. Brownsword & Pitt 1984.
4. Cronyn 1990, p. 210.
5. Egan 1996.
6. Scott 1991, p. 5.
7. ASM 1972, p. 318.
8. Englefield 1933.
9. Scott 1991, pp. 5–6.
10. Masse 1949, Evans 1994).
11. Tylecote 1976 .
12. Evans 1994; Englefield 1933, pp. 31, 39.
13. Hedges 1960, pp. 17–19; Evans 1994. See also Appendix II.

Appendix II

Elemental analyses of six tin-lead toy watches from London

Dafydd Griffiths
Institute of Archaeology, University College London

Background

Records show that between 1703 and 1715 a certain Mr Hux was summoned before the Court of the Worshipful Company of Pewterers on six occasions accused of using alloys of substandard composition in the manufacture of pewter toy pocketwatches (see pp. 53–4 & 343–5).

The purpose of the elemental analyses reported in this essay is to start to investigate the material evidence relating to the accusations made against Hux and the evidence relating to the comments reported to the composition of pewters used by other makers of toy watches. In a broader context, the analyses may increase understanding of the pewter trade, and understanding of the behaviour and values of its practitioners and patrons in early 18th-century society. As with many other aspects of archaeology, material remains often illuminate aspects of life that receive little or no attention in surviving documentary sources.

Having a court debate the quality of metal used to make a toy seems a little peculiar if we understand 'toy' in terms of its present-day usage as a children's plaything or a non-functional model. The level of concern about the quality of the alloy used, the scale of the fines, and the existence of related summonses, counter-arguments, debates and preserved minutes may, however, suggest that these 'toys' were a matter of some significance, importance and cost. It might be worth considering whether it would be more appropriate to consider these toys as significant, and perhaps costly, items of costume jewellery or as fashion accessories rather than as children's playthings.

However the term 'toy' should be understood in the present context, the Minutes of the Court of the Worshipful Company of Pewterers suggest that at least one London toy watchmaker, Hux, was producing toy pocketwatches of 'bad Mettle'. This may be taken to indicate that he was using alloys other than those specified by the Company for producing the watches. In 1703 the Quarter Court recorded a watchcase made by Hux as being '3gr. from fine' and a 'Dyall plate [face] at 19gr. worse than Lay' (see p. 343).

In 1772 a *Table of the Assays of Metal and of the Weights and Dimensions of the Several Sorts of Pewter Wares* was printed 'by Order of the Court of Assistants of the Worshipful Company of Pewterers, London'. The term 'pewter' was used at this time to refer to a tin alloy containing, according to to its category of fineness, various proportions of lead. Fine tin was defined in this publication as being 182 grains, fine or plate metal 1.5 grains heavier than tin or 183.5 grains, and ley metal as 16.5 grains heavier than tin or 198.5 grains. The increased density (weight per unit volume) of these different standard alloys reflected their increased lead content, pure metallic tin having a specific gravity of 7.3 (density 7.3 grammes/cc) and pure lead a specific gravity of 11.3.

Although the present writer has not discovered any documented explanation of how the pewterers' description of their standard alloys functioned, it seems reasonable to infer that 182 grains was the weight of a certain volume of pure tin. Calculation based on the specific gravities (density in grammes/cc) shows that the same volume of pure lead would weigh 282 grains, thus being 100 grains heavier than fine tin. If this interpretation is correct, then a pewter that is a certain number of grains heavier than fine tin contains that same number wt% of lead. Assuming the same definitions of 'fine metal' and 'ley metal' existed in 1703 as were documented in 1772, the above example from the court hearing of 1703 would then constitute an accusation that Hux had made a case containing 4.5wt% lead and a face containing 35.5wt% lead. (Although this would seem a good working interpretation of the pewterers' system in that it explains why pure tin should be designated 182 grains – so as to give a 100 grains weight difference between that volume of pure tin and the same volume of pure lead – it is for the present a supposition.)

Metallic tin is slightly harder than lead, but tin-lead alloys such as pewters can be notably harder than either of the constituent pure metals so this provides at least one utilitarian reason for making pewter. One may also note that lead has always been cheaper than tin in Britain, a factor which may have contributed to the wish of the Pewterers' Company to require the use of standard alloy compositions.[1]

Hux (the maker referred to above as being accused of producing toy watches out of substandard alloys) claimed to the Pewterers' Court that the fact that the case of one of his watches had a lead content greater than that stipulated for fine metal, was due to 'some neglecte of his servant'. Concerning the even higher lead content of the face of the toy watch, Hux claimed that the dial plate 'could not be made so well of any other mettle'. The Court also heard from Hux that other makers also used alloys of higher than stipulated lead content (see pp. 343).

An error on the part of an alloy-making seems plausible. Both the constituent metals (tin and lead) are volatile and might be lost by evaporation and oxidation so even if the correct proportions were weighed out initially, if not kept carefully covered the final alloy might have a different composition due to preferential loss of one component. The idea that an alloy with a higher lead content might have been better for making toy watch faces also sounds quite plausible.

As it stands, however, the above documentary evidence appears to relate primarily to a single maker on a limited number of occasions, although that maker is reported as claiming that other makers also use non-standard alloys in the making of toy watches. The purpose of this initial analytical investigation of toy watches is to begin to test and assess on a broader basis the indications given by the documentary evidence. One of the aims of analysing the watches is to get a broader view of the ranges of alloys actually being used in the manufacture of toy watches, to investigate whether makers other than Hux were using non-standard alloys and to investigate whether the use of different alloys for the cases and dials was a widespread practice. Information gained from future analytical work may be able to provide a clearer indication of the extent of the use of non-standard pewter alloys and so corroborate or amplify the concerns expressed in the documentary evidence surviving from the Pewterers' Company. It is also possible that with the benefit of future analyses, correlations will emerge between the composition of the alloy used, the maker, the place of manufacture, the style of decoration and the date of manufacture. Any such correlations might make compositional analysis useful in determining some of the other parameters which might not otherwise be known.

For this initial study, six watches were selected by curator Hazel Forsyth of the Museum of London. The cases and dials were analysed to determine their compositions. Three relatively complete watches by Hux provided analyses of both cases and dials. A fourth face by Hux provided a further example of a Hux dial composition. A fifth watch (dial only) is by Beeslee, a maker cited by Hux as also using high lead alloys for toy watches (see p. 343). The sixth watch, by an unknown maker, provides a comparative example of case and dial compositions.

Analytical technique

On the basis of previous reports, it was considered unlikely that the analysis of the tarnished surface of the watches would yield much useful information on the bulk composition of the toy watch alloys. It was expected that analyses would need to be conducted either on untarnished parts of the objects as received or on areas deliberately cleaned to remove tarnish and corrosion.

Reports on the effects of tarnish and corrosion on surface composition of tin-lead alloys have been varied, no doubt reflecting differences in composition and microstructure and differences in the microenvironment in which the corrosion took place. It has been reported that enrichment of tin often occurs in the corrosion products as the lead salts are often more soluble, although this is not always the case.[2] In 2001 Meg Wang found that corrosion layers on tin-lead alloy toys she analysed from the Thames were depleted in lead.[3] She also reported that other analyses of corrosion and deposits on lead alloys from anaerobic Thames-side waterlogged environments had detected lead, iron and copper-iron sulphides. Whatever the situation in a particular case, it is unlikely that the ratios of the metals in tarnished or corroded layers can be considered representative of the metal below. Furthermore, corrosion and surface deposits are likely to be layered to some extent, so the composition given by a surface analysis at a given point on the surface of an object may vary depending upon the extent to which such deposits and corrosion-affected layers have been removed prior to analysis, either deliberately or by natural or inadvertent processes.

It was thus necessary to choose areas for analysis where bare metal would be exposed. The need to avoid any notable change to the appearance of the objects and the vital need to avoid any loss of stylistic or manufacturing information constrained sample preparation. Initially parts of the objects that appeared tarnish-free were analysed, such as protuberances and raised features on the objects where the tarnishing was often less apparent.

Surprisingly different results were obtained from different parts of the same object when attempting this initial totally non-invasive approach. The investigation therefore moved on to very light cleaning of small areas that had suffered previous mechanical damage. This was effected with diamond paste or a very fine grinding stick. Previous optical and electron beam metallographic cross-section studies of tin-lead alloy toys from the Thames had suggested that the elemental composition of the bare metal surface would often be reasonably similar to that of the bulk,[4] although the metallographic structure seen from the surface on the small cleaned areas might well be distorted by the previous damage or by over-vigorous cleaning off of tarnish. The samples investigated by Wang often showed a fairly sharp division between metal and corrosion, although corrosion could penetrate deeper along cracks.

In practice it was found that even after cleaning to an extent that revealed what appeared to the naked eye to be bright metal, the analytical results still varied to a surprising extent from one cleaned area to another on the surface of an object. A slightly more invasive approach was thus adopted and tiny areas of previous damage were ground down with a fine diamond burr to expose metal from a greater depth. Damage was still minimal, hardly detectable with the naked eye, and restricted to areas of previous damage. Surface analyses of these ground areas yielded consistent results in different analysed areas so it is these results that are reported for each watch in Table 1 below.

The results of analyses without any surface preparation or with very light cleaning do have some interest, however, and these are reported first in the section entitled 'Superficial analyses'.

As the areas available for analysis were in all cases very small (being restricted to areas that could be cleaned of tarnish and corrosion without detriment to the information content or appearance of the object,) an analytical technique which did not require the removal of a sample and which could analyse a controllable and restricted area had to be chosen. Scanning electron microscopy with energy-dispersive X-ray analysis (SEM-EDS) was used to analyse the objects. SEM-EDS was chosen as an appropriate technique for elemental analysis as it provides images to guide the choice of area for analysis and permits the analysis of a wide range of elements (from sodium upwards) with concentrations between about 0.1% up to 100%. Under the conditions used in the present analyses, the instrument analyses the surface layer of the sample to a depth of about 2 micrometres (0.002 mm).

The SEM part of the hybrid instrument provided images showing compositional variation, limits of the area ground down by the fine burr and the presence of any surface contamination or deposits. These images were used to guide the selection of different areas to be analysed.

The accelerated electron beam, in addition to providing signals that can be used to generate images of the surface, also generates characteristic X-rays from the atoms at and near the surface of the area chosen for analysis. These X-rays are analysed by the energy-dispersive spectrometer to identify the elements present and to provide (in this case) a semi-quantitative indication of the amounts of the different elements present in the sample.

(The analysis was performed using a Hitachi S-570 SEM with secondary and backscattered electron detectors using an accelerating voltage of 20kV and an Oxford Instruments ISIS energy-dispersive X-ray spectrometer with conventional beryllium window and Si-Li detector. The metallic nature of the samples made the application of a conducting coating, the use of low accelerating voltages and the use of charge-dissipating gases unnecessary.)

Although the SEM-EDS analysis provides ample spatial resolution for analysis of a small volume (around 2 x 2 x 2 micrometres under the present conditions),[5] the microstructure of the alloys themselves makes analyses of such small samples unrepresentative of the composition of the alloy as a whole. (It is of course the bulk compositions of the alloys that are of interest in terms of studying any departures from the Pewterers' Company standards.) During cooling of the alloy from the molten state, tin-lead alloys tend to separate into different phases (areas of distinctly different composition), some tin-rich and some lead-rich. Only by combining analyses of the different phases weighted in proportion to the volume occupied by each can a bulk composition be derived from analyses of individual phases. In practice this is normally achieved by scanning the electron beam over a wide area so as to generate characteristic X-rays and analytical information from a representative sample of each phase present. Fortunately, high magnification SEM images, particularly images obtained using backscattered electrons, clearly show the phases of different composition as different levels of grey. (The backscattered electron intensity is proportional to the average atomic weight of the phase scattering the electrons). The images thus provide some guidance as to the size of area needed for a representative scan. The area required increases with the scale of inhomogeneity, needing to be larger where larger-size phases are present.

In the case of the present preliminary study of the watch compositions, the relatively small areas analysed, distortions to surface structure by previous damage or by surface preparation, possible preferential alignments of phases, possible surface contamination, and occasional porosity in the alloys are all factors that should cause the analytical results presented here to be regarded as semi-quantitative rather than wholly accurate indications of the relative amounts of different metals in the alloys analysed. The results are presented as weight percentages normalized to 100%.

Despite the above cautions, similar results from different analysed areas on single objects suggest the results are reasonably robust and provide clear and reliable indications of variations in composition between the different samples. The 'semi-quantitative' aspect refers primarily to the fact that high-quality analytical procedures of sample preparation, direct comparison with standards etc. have not been used in this study. The results are reasonably precise within a percentage point or two (the scatter in results being due to factors mentioned above) but may not necessarily be that accurate (the scatter and the average value may be displaced a little from the true value). To give a rough indication to the layman, the results presented here reliably indicate that alloys having, for example, compositions containing 20wt% lead and 25wt% lead do indeed have genuinely different compositions, and that a third alloy containing 20wt% lead is reliably similar to the first alloy and different to the second. The results are internally consistent and can be compared one to another. In comparison with other published work done with rigorous sample preparation and appropriate standards, one might find the results presented here might be displaced by a few percentage points one way or another.

Analytical results

General observations

Within the detection limits of the technique employed, all the alloys analysed in the present study have been found to be pewters comprising tin as the major element together with various amounts of lead ranging from around 8 to around 35wt%. No other significant components were seen in the bulk alloys, although copper and iron were common in surface deposits.

As noted above, tin-lead alloys tend to separate on cooling into tin-rich and lead-rich phases. Spot analyses on the individual phases show them to be close to pure tin and pure lead. As expected from previous studies, there was found to be slightly more tin in the lead-rich phase than there was lead in the tin-rich phase. (The separate phases are typically 10–30 micrometres across [0.01 – 0.03mm] in pewter toys, based on Wang's unpublished photomicrographs[6] and observations in the present study.)

The relatively large size of the phases compared with the volume analysed by a stationary focused beam of electrons means that individual 'spot analyses' will not be representative of the bulk composition but only of the restricted volume analysed which may include solely one phase or a mixture of two in any relative proportion. To get an indication of bulk composition one may analyse while scanning the beam over a large enough area to sample a representative amount of each phase – this is the approach that has been adopted for the analyses reported here.

Superficial analyses

The initial exploratory results reported in this section were made on the objects as received or after light surface cleaning. They are reported primarily to illustrate the difficulties of obtaining reliable bulk composition results from these objects in a totally non-destructive way. No firm conclusions on bulk composition can really be drawn from analyses of the uncleaned surfaces, although some tentative approximate inferences on bulk composition might be drawn from superficial analyses of similar alloys deposited in similar burial environments.

The initial exploratory spot analyses (taken in areas of the samples that appeared relatively free of corrosion) showed the expected variation in analytical results from nearly pure tin up to much higher lead content depending on the composition of the analysed volume at each point. Slightly more surprisingly some of the spot analyses showed the clear presence of significant copper and some iron. As copper and iron sulphides have been reported on the surface of lead alloy objects from the Thames, it was possible that these components might have been deposited from the burial environment. Sulphur is difficult to quantify in the presence of lead with the detector used for this preliminary investigation as the peaks overlap significantly.

Because of the variability in the spot analysis on the Hux dial (Acc. no. 2001.15/1), three larger, raised and apparently tarnish-free areas were analysed. Analyses of three different areas each gave a result of around 8wt% lead and 1–2wt% copper. This consistency might suggest that where there are raised relatively untarnished areas, they may give a representative result regarding the bulk composition of the dial. Other partly tarnished areas gave much higher and more variable levels of lead and copper. Later experience showed that the copper is only present in surface deposits and that the lead content is higher in these than in the bulk alloy.

Moving on to the case of Acc. no. 2001.15/1, analyses on four separate areas gave normalized results indicating 8–21wt% lead and 1–14wt% copper. Again these results, despite the cleanest areas being chosen, reflect compositions of surface deposits, not bulk compositions.

In order to try to reach some firmer conclusions on bulk composition, two areas of previous damage on the 2001.15/1 watch dial were very lightly cleaned down to shiny metal using a fine abrasive polishing rod. Four separate area analyses (each considerably larger than the scale of phase separation) yielded analyses showing tin and lead alone with lead contents of 3, 5, 5 and 7wt% lead (normalized). Two similar analyses on a ground area of the case both indicated a pure tin-lead alloy containing 5wt% lead. A tentative conclusion after light cleaning might be that both the case and the dial of this Hux watch were made of a metal containing about 5wt% lead.

There will perhaps be occasions in the future where only totally non-invasive, non-destructive analyses will be permitted. It is thus appropriate to ask what, if any, useful conclusions might be drawn about bulk composition from such analyses of the surface.

Further analyses on more thoroughly cleaned and ground down areas (see below) suggest that the results from the lightly cleaned areas are slightly depleted in lead compared to the bulk, even though these areas appeared clean to the naked eye and under the SEM. This result may correspond to some corrosion (or invisible effects of corrosion) still being present. Previous workers have reported that corrosion layers are often depleted in lead.[7]

In the case of analyses of totally untouched but apparently clean areas, one might conclude that the presence of copper suggests (for the Thames foreshore depositional environment at least) that the results are being coloured by surface deposits that contain copper and are generally a fair amount higher in lead than the bulk alloy.

The distortion by surface deposits is certainly less marked on the relatively bright high-points. Such points on Acc. no. 2001.15/1 gave a result of 8wt% lead and 1–2wt% copper. Here a little surface deposit (copper associated with enhanced lead but with the low copper indicating that not much of the deposit is present) is perhaps being balanced by a little corrosion (with a slightly depleted lead content) to give an overall lead content that fortuitously matches the 'true' bulk composition reported below.

Broadly similar results were obtained from superficial analyses of the other watches. Very roughly speaking, for surface analyses of apparently clean areas from the depositional environment in question, if a little copper is present the lead analysis may be approximately that of the bulk. If more than a few percent copper is found, the bulk lead content is probably less than that in the surface analysis. If no copper is found, the surface lead content may be less than that in the bulk due to corrosion. There are, however, exceptions to these very tentative observations. Despite the absence of copper, one superficial analysis gave a significantly higher lead content than the bulk, so superficial composition permits only a 'guess' at bulk composition.

Despite the apparent unreliability of surface analysis in indicating bulk alloy composition, surface analyses still have their place in looking for surface coatings. In examining the highly decorated case of a watch by Hux (Acc. no. 2001.15/2) using backscattered electron imaging under under the SEM, darker areas were apparent within what appeared to the naked eye to be naturally polished high-points of the decoration. Analysis of one of the dark areas showed that it appeared to be primarily composed of copper, iron and sulphur with a little silver and lead also present, the difference in composition accounting for its darker appearance when using the backscattered electron detector. A number of these dark areas were analysed, all of which proved to be of broadly similar normalized compositions (34–42at% Cu, 14–18at% Fe, 40–44at% S with 1–3at% silver and 1at% lead in each case). The silver (which was found only on the case of the one Hux watch) might be evidence that the watchcase was originally silvered and that the closely adhering deposit preserved some of the silvering. This aspect will need further investigation.

The fact that copper-iron sulphides have been reported as surface deposits from lead alloys from similar environments, have not been noted in metallographic sections of similar material[8] and were absent once the surfaces of the metal were ground away is consistent with their being surface deposits rather than phases in the alloy. The other watches also had surfaces with copper, iron and sulphur present at the surface but only the one watch showed any silver.

Bulk compositions

All the following compositions were obtained by grinding down small areas of previous damage with a fine diamond burr. As the pewter is quite soft it is generally possible to find suitable areas without much difficulty. Although the ground areas are shiny after being made, pewter tarnishes fairly quickly so these prepared areas will soon become dull. Even when freshly made, the prepared areas are very small and hardly noticeable. Indeed the prepared areas can be quite difficult to find under the SEM.

The areas chosen for analysis were selected under the SEM to be as free from contamination, surface irregularities, darker surface deposits and corrosion as possible, while at the same time maximizing the area analysed to include plenty of each of the two phases. Areas analysed were typically around 0.1–0.2 mm^2 compared to phases which have typical areas of around 0.0004 mm^2 so it is expected that they should be large enough to provide typical bulk compositions.

The table below presents the normalized results in terms of weight percentage of lead (the balance of the alloy being tin). The initial figures represent the analytical results from different areas within the single area that was cleaned by diamond burr on each dial and case. The lead wt% is the average of these rounded to the nearest whole number.

Table 1

This table shows the normalized lead content of the watch dials and cases analysed in wt%. In all cases the balance of the alloy is tin. The first line of figures in each cell gives the analytical results from separate areas within the region ground down to bulk metal prior to analysis. The figure in bold in the second line of each cells is the average of the analyses in the first line rounded to the nearest whole number.

Maker	Acc. no.	DIAL	Lead wt%	CASE	Lead wt%
Hux	2001.15/1	8.3, 8.4	8 wt%	7.8, 8.4	8 wt%
Hux	2001.15/2	34.1, 34.3	34 wt%	32.6, 32.0	32 wt%
Hux	2001.15/3	26.8, 29.0, 29.9	29 wt%	26.2, 24.7	25 wt%
Hux	98.2/461	9.7, 9.4, 9.9	10 wt%	n/a	
Beeslee	98.2/459	34.5, 31.5, 34.8	34 wt%	n/a	
Unknown	NN18218	30.6, 32.0	31 wt%	20.3, 23.4, 21.1	22 wt%

Table 1 shows that there is considerable variation in the pewter-alloy compositions used in the manufacture of toy pocketwatches. On the basis of this small sample we see that Hux was using both moderate (8–10wt%) and high (29–34wt%) lead-content pewters for his watches, although these watches may represent products made at different periods in his career. In the three complete Hux watches analysed, the lead content of the dial is marginally higher than that of the case in two examples but the differences are not great.

In the example cited in the first section of this chapter (assuming the suggest interpretation of the pewterers' alloy system is correct), Hux was accused of making a watchcase that contained 4.5wt% lead and a watchdial that was 35.5wt% lead. The cases analysed here all contain more lead than this but the composition of the 2001.15/2 dial is close to that cited in the court.

The analysis of the Beeslee dial corroborates Hux's contention that Beeslee also used high lead alloys for his dials. The Beeslee dial analysed has the same composition as the Hux 2001.15/2 dial, with both being similar to the analysis presented at the 1703 Pewterers' Court.

The watch by the unknown maker again illustrates the use of high-lead alloys for dial and case. This watch provides a clear example of a higher lead alloy being used for the dial than for the case, although the contrast is still not so marked as that cited against Hux in the 1703 court hearing.

Conclusion

The results presented here suggest that there was a real basis for the concerns expressed in the Minutes of the Pewterers' Courts and that a wide range of non-standard tin-lead alloy compositions were being used to make toy watches. All the alloys analysed contained (within the detection limits of the technique employed) only tin and lead. They are tin-rich alloys with quite a range of lead contents varying from 8 to 34 wt%.

This initial study has shown the need for careful and thorough removal of deposits and corrosion if a proper indication of bulk composition is to be obtained from a surface analysis. In the future, it would be well worth analysing parts of broken watch dials or cases in cross-section for the information they could yield on homogeneity of the metal and changes occurring near and at the surface in terms of corrosion and deposits. This might allow more to be deduced from totally non-destructive analyses in future.

As a range of variation in alloy composition has been detected, it is possible that analyses of further watches may reveal useful correlations between the compositions of the alloys used, makers, places of manufacture, styles of decoration and dates of manufacture. The detection of silver on the surface of the highly decorated case of one of the Hux watchcases is interesting and worthy of further investigation.

Bibliography

Potts, P.J., *A Handbook of Silicate Rock Analysis* (Glasgow, 1987)

Tylecote, R.F., *The Prehistory of Metallurgy in the British Isles* (London, 1986)

Wang, M.C., *Scientific Analysis of Mediaeval and Later Pewter Miniatures from the Thames,* Unpublished project, MSc Conservation: materials science (Institute of Archaeology, University College London, 2001)

1 Tylecote 1986, p. 47.
2 Tylecote 1986, p. 52.
3 Wang 2001, pp. 16–17.
4 Wang 2001.
5 Potts 1987, p. 337.
6 Wang 2001.
7 Tylecote 1986; Wang 2001.
8 Wang 2001.

Appendix III

Pewter toymakers from the Worshipful Company of Pewterers' records and other sources[1]

AUSTIN, Job
Freedom: 15 December 1687; apprenticed to **William Jackson**, 1680–5, with **John Jackson** and **Charles Rack**. Premises searched 26 February, 1691–2 'at Job Austin's, his toy boules [bowls]' (GL MS 7106).

BEESLEE, Francis [or Beasly]
Freedom: 14 December 1693; apprenticed to **Richard Heath**, November 1685. Summoned before the Court of Assistants on 19 September 1704, but alleged that he had not 'wrought in the Trade for above a year and a half' (GL MS 7090/8). His poor-quality spoons seized, but in view of his poverty the five shilling fine was remitted. By 1714 he was obviously engaged in making toy watches, for on 24 March 1714 the Court Minutes record an accusation by **William Hux** concerning poor-quality toy watches, 'one Beasly has made the same sort of ware of lay and sometimes as Bad as pale …' (GL MS 7090/9). His widow, Mary, applied to the Company for charity support on 17 March 1725 (GL MS 7090/9). Cott. no. 338.

DEAN, William
Freedom: 10 December 1731; apprenticed to **Thomas Hux** (son of **William Hux**), Jonathan Broadhurst and Edward Quick. Had leave to strike touch on 10 June 1736 (London Touch Plate no. 864). Entered into partnership with **Robert Peircy** by 1737. Summoned with Peircy to appear before the court on 15 December 1737 for various deficiencies, which included making 'two small Porringers 8 grains worse than lay; 2 watches cases one grain bad, 1 watch case 9 grains worse than lay, as well as poor quality sugar dish covers, tea kettle tops and tea cups' (GL MS 7090/9). They were fined 5s to the Poor Box. Cott. no. 1344.

HEATH, Richard

Freedom: 13 December 1666; apprenticed to Richard Heath (father). Obtained leave to strike touch on 11 August 1671. His premises were searched and he was summoned to appear before the court on numerous occasions between 19 June 1673 and 1699 (GL MS 7090/8). His apprentices included **Francis Beeslee** (from 1685). The toy watch mould in the collection (Cat. no. 12.11) inscribed *1736, Debr 17 Richard H[…]* is most probably his work.

HODGE(S), Robert Peircy

Freedom: 22 October 1772; apprenticed to **William Wightman**, July 1765. Obtained leave to open shop on 22 October 1772; Liveryman 20 June 1782; Renter Warden 1796; Upper Warden 1801; Master 1802. London Touch Plate struck *c.* 1773. In 1793 his business premises were at 58 & 61 Whitecross Street, Islington, and from 1822, 63 Long Lane. Took over the business of **Robert Peircy** (probably a relative by marriage). Cott. no. 2355.

HUX, Thomas

Freedom: London 10 October 1723; apprenticed to **William Hux** (father). Obtained leave to strike touch and open shop on 10 October 1723. Apprentices included **William Dean** (1724–8) and **Robert Randall**. In April 1724 he was working at the Halfmoon and Flower de Luce in Newgate Street, but had moved to the Pewter Dish in Fore Street by 1739 (Sun Insurance policies 31657 and 80170). Dead by 1760 when widow Grace carried on the business. Probably engaged in making toys like his father. Cott. no. 2497.

HUX, William Thomas

Freedom: London 24 June 1700; apprenticed to Gabriel Redhead, May 1693. Obtained leave to set up shop and strike touch on 24 June 1700 (London Touch Plate no. 574). He was summoned before the court and accused of making toy watches of bad metal on ten occasions (GL MS 7090/8 [1691–1711] and MS 7090/9 [1711–1740]): Quarter Court, 22 June 1703; Court of Assistants, 19 September 1703/4; Quarter Court, 22 March 1704; Court of Assistants, 27 September 1705; Quarter Court, 19 June 1707; Quarter Court, 17 June 1708; Quarter Court, 14 December 1710; Quarter Court, 24 March 1714 (accuses **Francis Beeslee**); Quarter Court 15 December 1714/15; Quarter Court, 22 March 1715. One of his apprentices, **Robert Peircy,** seems to have been a specialist maker of toys and other small items. Dead by 1730 when his widow Mary bound an apprentice. Cott. no. 2498.

JACKSON, John
Freedom: 23 February 1674; apprenticed to **William Jackson** of the Pewter Platter near the Kings Head Inn, Southwark. Bound with **Charles Rack** and **Job Austin**. Obtained leave to strike touch (London Touch Plate no. 282) and set up a shop on 5 April 1677. On 1 September 1685 called to the Livery, but excused because he declared that he was not worth £300. Premises searched on 6 May 1689 'at John Jackson's, toys flagon lids and a small porringer' (GL MS 7106); 9 December 1689 'at John Jackson's, his toy dishes' (GL MS 7106). Had two apprentices: Henry Brasted (1692) and his son William (1701). There is a trade card in the Heal Collection of the British Museum for John Jackson 'at the Unicorn the Corner of Woodstreet, Cheapside, London' with his touch mark and text referring to 'all sorts of Toys for Children' (see fig. 10, p. 33). By 31 July 1733, however, Jackson seems to have been working from the Golden Cock, Southwark (Sun Insurance policy 61502). Cott. no. 2557A.

JACKSON, William
Freedom: 7 August 1662; apprenticed to Simon Read, June 1655. Obtained leave to strike touch (London Touch Plate no. 166) and to open a shop on 15 June 1665. On 15 September 1669 (GL MS 7090/6) he was summoned before the court for 'his toyes at 3 gr and 6 gr and pestle and mortar at 2 gr'. He was fined 20 shillings and the matter was referred. Then on 11 August 1670 he appeared again before the Quarter Court: 'William Jackson his Toyes at 2 gr …'. Jackson gave 30 shillings to the court to settle the matter (GL MS 7090/6). By 1690 he was working 'at the Pewter Platter near the Kings Head Inn, Southwark', and his apprentices included his son **John Jackson** (1674), **Charles Rack** (1681) and **Job Austin** (1687), all of whom seem to have been engaged in making toys at some point in their careers.

LEA, Francis
Freedom: 18 March 1651; apprenticed to **William Lea** (father). Liveryman 11 August 1664. Seems to have been allowed to strike several marks, which Cotterell suggests 'may have been allowed to him as being a toymaker' (London Touch Plate nos. 18, 39 & 40, all restruck *c.* 1670 after the Great Fire). On 15 September 1668/9 (GL MS 7090/6) he was fined 10 shillings for selling 'Toy Pestell and Mortars and other toyes at five grains' (below the standard quality) and was fined 10 shillings. Cott. no. 2882.

LEA, William
Freedom: 9 October 1628; apprenticed to Francis Kimberley. Obtained leave to strike touch on 17 June 1630. Apprentices included his son **Francis** (1651) and **William White** (1661). Dead by 1661 when his widow Elizabeth continued the business. Possibly made toys.

PEIRCY, Robert

Freedom: 21 June 1722; apprenticed to **William Hux** and Robert Crosfield. Obtained leave to strike touch (London Touch Plate no. 858) on 9 October 1735. By 13 October 1737 in partnership with **William Dean**, when they were jointly summoned for various deficiencies (see **Dean** above). Business premises: Whitecross Street as advertised on his *c.* 1750 trade card (in the Heal Collection of the British Museum) which states that he 'Makes and Sells all Sorts of Pewter toys, Wholesale and Retail At the Lowest Prices' (see fig. 81, p. 408). Moved to Redcross Street a few years later. Dead by 1766 and succeeded by **Robert Peircy Hodge**. Cott. no. 3596.

PIGGOTT, Francis

Freedom: 24 March 1736. Had leave to strike touch (London Touch Plate no. 886) and to open a shop on 22 June 1738. Traded from the sign of the 'Golden Dish, in Pater Noster Row, next Cheapside London', and between 1754 and 1771 from 76 Newgate Street. Cott. plate XI and nos. 3682 & 3683.

RACK, Charles

Freedom: 18 August 1681; apprenticed to **William Jackson** in August 1674. Had leave to strike touch (London Touch Plate no. 355) on 18 August 1681 and to open a shop. His premises were searched on 6 May 1689 'at Charles Rack's, his toy flagons and his toy saucers' (GL MS 7106); on 10 December 1689 'at Charles Rack's, his toy dishes [crossed through] saucers'; and again on 1 May 1691 (GL MS 7106). Cott. no. 3810.

RANDALL [probably Robert]

Freedom: 13 October 1748; apprenticed to **Thomas Hux**, 13 October 1740. Obtained leave to strike touch (London Touch Plate no. 955) on 17 October 1751. Seems to have made toy watches. (One dial plate from the Thames foreshore at Brook's Wharf, in a private collection, was brought into the Museum of London for identification in 1983, inscribed 'RANDALL and LONDON'. The style is extremely similar to those produced by Hux. It is possible that the cheaper Type 5 watches inscribed RR are also by this maker). Cott. no. 3835.

SMITH, Thomas

Freedom: 21 March 1705; apprenticed to **John Jackson** in April 1696. Had leave to open shop and strike touch (London Touch Plate no. 632) on 15 April 1706. On 20 March 1717 (GL MS 7090/9) appeared before the Quarter Court for poor quality metal 'his … toy cups at 3:gr and the quantity very small', and fined one shilling to the Poor Box. Cott. no. 4387.

STRICKLAND, John

Freedom: 16 December 1703; apprenticed to Joseph Pickard, December 1695. Obtained leave to strike touch and open shop on 27 November 1716. On 10 April 1718 (GL MS 7090/9), Strickland appeared before the court for 'his toy porringers at 3 gr'. He claimed 'that these were made by **Mr Hux**', but because Hux was not present to affirm or refute the charge, and because the wares were 'untouched', the case was dismissed. This case does, however, suggest that if Strickland was telling the truth, he was not only probably making toys himself but also selling toys by another maker.

WHITE, William

Freedom: 28 May 1661; apprenticed to **William Lea**, February 1653. Obtained leave to strike touch on 20 March 1661. On 15 September 1669 he appeared before the court because 'his toyes at severall places at 3 gr and 4 and 5 gr and one pestle and mortar at 19[?] grs'. He was fined 30 shillings (GL MS 7090/6).

WIGHTMAN, William

Freedom: 22 June 1758; apprenticed to **Robert Peircy**, 1750. Took three apprentices, one of whom, **Robert Peircy Hodge**, obtained his freedom in 1772. On 18 October 1770 complained to 'Court that the toymakers in general made their toys of very bad metal and that as a consequence of this alone was not able to keep his wares up to the Standard and sell at the same price with the rest of the persons in that Branch and therefore praying the Directions of the Court in that respect as he was desirous of making his wares of good metal and yet could not afford to be a loser by his trade' (GL MS 7090/10). Cott. no. 5139.

1 Most of the references have been culled from the records of the Worshipful Company of Pewterers lodged in the Manuscripts Department of the Guildhall Library. A few details have been added from the Sun Insurance Registers, and other facts, notably the dates of freedom admissions, the names of apprentices, and the dates for permission to strike touch, have been taken from Cotterell, H.H., *Old Pewter its Makers and Marks* (London, 1929) and the recent work and publication by Ricketts, C. et al., *Pewterers of London 1600–1900* (Welshpool, 2001).

Appendix IV

The maker/s I(D)Q

Geoff Egan & Hazel Forsyth

Since the listing of I(D)Q products put together in 1996,[1] several new examples of this maker/s work have been recovered from excavations on the Continent. The most notable, a miniature cannon (bearing a fleur-de-lys and the earliest known date accompanying the initials) raises the possibility that the maker/s could be French (see fig. 18, p. 81).[2] At least two I(D)Q products were found in Paris in the 19th century, though the initials were not noted in the published commentaries.[3] The absence of subsequent I(D)Q toys from this city might reflect the fact that shortly after these items were found, deposits along the Seine were barred to searchers, and more recently perhaps, to a general lack of awareness that the initials exist since they are not at all easy to spot. Willemsen and others have suggested that the maker may be a Dutchman, partly because of the large number of I(D)Q products emerging in that region (see fig. 40, p. 169).[4] As Gadd notes, the medial initials 'D', 'V' and 'L' are often associated with Flemish or Walloon names, such as Pieter De Prost (PDP), Pieter Dewitte (PDW), Ioannes Van Kamp (IVK), André Lequesne (ALQ) and so on.[5] Willemsen speculates whether he was perhaps a 'Jan or Joost de Q ... toymaker of Amsterdam'.[6] This however, does not explain why some of the toys are marked IQ when others are DQ or IDQ.[7]

Initials aside, the form, style and decoration of the I(D)Q wares do point to a Low Countries or Continental source. Ron Homer notes that the 'rose motifs have radial striations in the petals which is characteristic of the roses in the touches of Netherlands pewterers (notably Antwerp and Amsterdam) which never appear on English ones'.[8] Stylistic influences of Continental origin are also evident in the spoons with twisted stems and round bowls, and the large oval 'dishes' (Cat. nos. 8.100–2) which have no counterparts in England. A bell (not included in this catalogue) and candlestick (Cat. no. 5.1) 'do not look typically English either'.[9] The polygonal ewers of the type represented by Cat. no. 8.109 were not unknown in England, but the style is 'thought to have been introduced by French goldsmiths, presumably by Huguenots who had fled France after the St Bartholomew Massacres of 1572',[10] and the shape is commonly found in Continental collections. So far, the only watches made by I(D)Q have been found in England, but since these resemble full-scale timepieces of English, French and Flemish origin, a definitive attribution is impossible. There is still no evidence for the identity and location of this prolific and innovative craftsman in the form of irrefutable documentary evidence or moulds for his products. Only when such material becomes available will it be possible to tie down this most intriguing early toymaker and see his international trade in proper perspective.

1 Egan 1996, p. 17.

2 See Willemsen 2000, fig. 5. The three initials seem an anomaly when compared with the other I(D)Q products listed here.

3 Gay 1887, p. 79 (this plate needs to be turned through a right angle to get the tiny roundel with the initials at the top); Bruna 1997, p. 265, no. 505, described as a 'clochette de pèlerinage'. This distinctive form with its tripartite suspender is well represented in the collections of the Musée de Cluny, and so it may well be specifically French – see Bruna pp. 264–5, nos. 500–1, 506–7 & 511–12 for others apparently without initials. A pilgrim souvenir or religious trinket would be more appropriate in Catholic France than England, though similar items have been found in London.

4 See Willemsen 2000, p. 348 top right – Mertens collection.

5 Jan Gadd, pers. comm.

6 Willemsen 2000, p. 353, fig. 5.

7 The bar across the D could be a contraction as Geoff Egan suggests for ID, but if so, this is included on some toys which have ample space for the full triad of initials, such as the spoons. The slash across the downstroke of a letter to indicate another initial is not conventional practice in England and the inverted triad of initials I D over Q is also a puzzling and non-English marking. I am grateful to James Mosely (former curator of St Bride's Printing Library) for his help on this point.

8 Pers. comm.

9 Ron Homer, pers. comm.

10 Hernmarck 1977, vol. 1, p. 239 & note 31.

Bibliography

MANUSCRIPT SOURCES

Bodleian Library, Oxford
Ashmole MSS 487–8

British Library
Add. MS 36785; Harley MS 3980, fol. 36.6

British Museum
Lansdowne MS 8/17, 1568/9. Digges: Lansdowne MS 105, 1568/9

Corporation of London Record Office
Alchin Papers, Box H/103/12; Common Serjeants Books: Bk 2, fol. 216, 575; fol. 252, 694; fol. 261; Bk 4, fol. 956, 1587; Bk 5, fol. 3, 2217; fol. 36, 2298; fol. 55B, 2342. Mayor's Court Original Bills: MC1/ 52B/79; MC1/56/190; MC1/145/59; MC1/91A/91; MC1/228/118; MC1/7/B/38; MC1/199A/144; MC1/205/381; MC1/160/10. Orphans Inventories: 116; 266; 276; 280; 282; 298; 309; 320; 334; 345; 347; 360; 442; 456; 461; 555; 575; 625; 631; 632; 663; 672; 694; 701; 719; 735; 742; 744; 747; 748; 759; 762; 768; 775; 791; 808; 856; 868; 889; 905; 911; 913; 927; 950; 951; 966; 968; 981; 988; 997; 1001; 1021; 1070; 1071; 1072; 1060; 1082;1089; 1200; 1284; 1308; 1322; 1353; 1419; 1465; 1564; 1612; 1651; 1662; 1685; 1763; 1786; 1794; 1836; 1846; 1904; 2034; 2054; 2069; 2105; 2119; 2139; 2197; 2217; 2226; 2237; 2243; 2286; 2288; 2298; 2304; 2342; 2352; 2390; 2440; 2449; 2501; 2543; 2558; 2561; 2611; 2756; 2955; 2965

Guildhall Library, London
Monumental Inscriptions in City Churches, MS 2480

Records of the Worshipful Company of Pewterers:
Court Minute Books, MS 7090, 26 vols: 7090/1 [155–61]; 7090/2 [1561–89]; 7090/3 [1589–1611]; 7090/4 [1611–43]; 7090/5 [1646–62]; 7090/6 [1662–75]; 7090/7 [1675–91]; 7090/8 [1691–1711]; 7090/9 [1711–40]; 7090/10 [1740–71]; 7090/11 [1771–1807]. Court Orders: 7119/2, 7120, 22213. Letters patent (search powers): 1474, 1477(c), 1548, 1556i, 1563, 1623 and 1639 MS 8696–701. Index to Court Minutes for 1691–1740: MS 7091. Livery lists: MS 7099, 22175–81; Ordinance Books for 1564 and 1572: MS 7115; for 1702: MS 7116. Parliamentary bill against the hawking of brass and pewter, *c.* 1533: MS 2212. Record Book of Complaints and Defaults: MS 7104/1–10. Rough Court Minute Books 1558–1724/5–7, vols 1–10. Searches: MSS 7106/1–4, 7125, 22196 and 22198.

Public Record Office
Enrolled Customs Accounts E.356; Petty Customs Accounts E.122/194/25; JUST 2 Records of the Justices Itinerant, Coroners' Rolls; Port Books E.190; State Papers 12/8, no 31

Worshipful Company of Drapers
Accounts: W.A.5/1 [1562–3]; W.A.5/3 [1564–5]; [1567–8]; Minute Books for 1557–1560 and 1567–77; Dinner Book for 1563–1601 D.B.I

PRINTED SOURCES

Anon, 'Giorattoli o soprammobili? Sono modelli antichi auedi perfetti in orni dettaglio', *Antiquariato* 141 (October, 1992), pp. 90–5

Alciati, A., *Emblematum Liber* (Augsburg, 1531)

Alexander, J., 'The Economic and Social Structure of the City of London, *c.* 1700', PhD thesis (University of London, 1989)

Alexandre-Bidon, D., 'Le Vêtement de la petite enfance à la fin du Moyen Age: Usages, façons, doctrines', *Ethnologie française* 16 (Paris, 1986), pp. 249–60

Alexandre-Bidon, D. & Lett, D., *Children in the Middle Ages 5th–15th centuries* (Indiana, 1999)

Allan, J.P., *Medieval and Post-Medieval Finds from Exeter 1971–80*, Exeter Archaeological Reports 3 (Exeter, 1980)

Amman, J., *Ritterliche Reutter Junst* (Frankfurt, 1584)

Amman, J., *Gynaeceum, sive Theatrum Mulierum* (Frankfurt, 1586)

Amoyt, T., 'Some Remarks on the Early Use of Carriages in England', *Archaeologia* 20 (1821), pp. 443–78

Ampzing, S., *Spigel ofte Toneel der Ydelheyd* (Haarlem (?), 1633)

Amsterdam Rijksmuseum, *All the Paintings of the Rijksmuseum* (Amsterdam & Maarssen, 1978)

Andree, R., 'Das Kreiselspielen', *Globus* 69 (1896)

Archer, M., *Delftware, the Tin-Glazed Earthenware of the British Isles: A catalogue of the collection in the Victoria and Albert Museum* (The Stationery Office, 1997)

Archer-Thomson, W., *Drapers' Company History of the Company's Properties & Trusts*, vol 1 (London, 1939–40)

Ariès, P., *L'Enfant et la vie familiale sous l'Ancien régime* (Paris, 1960); transl. as *Centuries of Childhood* (London, 1962)

Arnold, J., *Patterns of Fashion: The cut and construction of clothes for men and women c.1560–1620* (London, 1985)

Arnold, J. ed., *Elizabeth's Wardrobe Unlock'd* (London, 1988)

Ashelford, J., *The Art of Dress Clothes and Society 1500–1914* (London, 1996)

Ashton, T.S., *Economic Fluctuations in England 1700–1800* (London, 1985)

Baarren, R., *Nederlandse Meubelen 1600–1800* (Rijksmuseum, Amsterdam, 1993)

Baart, J.M. *et al.*, *Opgravingen in Amsterdam* (Amsterdam, 1977)

Baart, J.M., 'Opgravingen van het Middeleeuwse Havenfront aan het IJ' *Amstelodanum* 25 (1988), pp. 99–102

Bailey, C.T.P., *Knives and Forks* (Plymouth, 1927)

Baillee, G.H., *Watches: Their history, decoration and mechanism* (London, 1928)

Baines, M., *Spinning Wheels* (London, 1977)

Bangs, C., 'Sad Irons', *Antique Finder* (September, 1975), pp. 44–9

Barbera, M., 'I Crepundia de Terracina: Analisi e interpretatzione di un dono', *Bollettino di Archeologia* 10 (1991), pp. 11–33

Bateman, N., *Gladiators at the Guildhall* (Museum of London, 2000)

Bazin, G.E., *The Museum Age* (Brussels, 1967)

Beall, K.F., *Kaufurfe und Strassenhändler: Eine Bibliographie* (Hamburg, 1975)

Beard, C.R., 'Miniature armours', *Connoisseur* (December, 1928). pp. 208–9

Beaven, A.B., *The Aldermen of the City of London*, 2 vols (London, 1908, 1913)

Becq de Fouquières, L., *Les Jeux des Anciens* (Paris, 1869)

Beier, A.L., 'Engine of Manufacture: The trades of London' in Beier & Finlay 1986

Beier, A.L. & Finlay, R., eds, *London 1500–1700: The making of the metropolis* (London, 1986)

Bell, M., *Old Pewter* (London, 1906)

Bencard, M. & Hein, J., 'Three Cabinets on Stands from the 17th Century', *Furniture History* 21 (1985), pp. 146–55

Bendall, S., 'Notes on Toy Watches', *Antiquarian Horology* (Winter 1994), pp. 531–3

Benhamen, R., 'Imitation in the Decorative Arts of the 18th Century', *Journal of Design History* 4 (1991), pp. 1–13

Biek, L.R., 'Objects in Copper alloy, Bone, Lead alloy and Glass' in Rahtz, P.R. and Greenfield, E., *Excavations at the Chew Valley Lake, Somerset*, DOE Archaeological Report 8 (London, 1977), pp. 334–7

Blackmore, D., *Arms and Armour of the English Civil Wars* (London, 1990)

Blackmore, H.L., *Ordnance: The armouries of the Tower of London*, vol. 1 (London, 1976)

Blackmore, H.L., *English Pistols* (The Royal Armouries, London, 1985)

Blackmore, H.L., *Elizabethan Toy Guns*, Catalogue of the Sixth Park Lane Arms Fair (London, 1989)

Blair, C., *Pistols of the World* (London, 1968)

Boesch, H., *Kinderleben in der Deutschen Vergangenheit* (Leipzig, 1900)

Bolton, J., *Dutch Drawings from the Collection of Dr C. Hofstede de Groot* (Utrecht, 1967)

Bonfield L. et al., eds, *The World We Have Gained* (Oxford, 1986)

Boyd, P., *Roll of the Drapers' Company of London* (Croydon, 1934)

Bracker, J. et al., *Die Hanse Lebenswirklichkeit und Mythos: Katalog der Austellung über die Hanse in Hamburg* (Hamburg, 1989)

Brackton, H., *On the Laws and Customs of England*, Woodbine, G.E. & Thorne, S.E., eds, 4 vols (Cambridge, MA, 1968–77)

Brett, V., *Phaidon Guide to Pewter* (Oxford, 1981)

Brighton Museum, *Comedy Characters: Harlequin, Punch and Pieriot in England* (Brighton, 1985)

Brimblecombe, P., 'The Urban Climate and Atmosphere' in Hall, A. & Kenward, H., eds, *Environmental Archaeology in the Urban Context* (London, 1982), pp. 10–25

Britten, F.J., *Britten's old clocks and watches and their makers* (London, 1894); rev. by Clutton, C., (London, 1982)

Britton, F., 'The Pickleherring Potteries: An inventory' in *Post-Medieval Archaeology* 24 (1990), pp. 61–92

Brodsky, V., 'Widows in Late Elizabethan London: Remarriage, economic opportunity and family orientations' in Bonfield *et al.* 1986, pp. 122–54

Brown, K.D., *The British Toy Business: A history since 1700* (London & Rio Grande, 1996)

Brownsword, R. & Pitt, E.E.H., 'An Analytical Study of Pewter-ware from the *Mary Rose*', *JPS* 7 (4) (1990), pp. 109–25

Bruna, D., *Le Petit Journal des grandes expositions: Insignes et souvenirs de pèlerinage et insignes profanes* (Musée national du Moyen Age, Paris, 1997)

Bruton, E., *Clocks and Watches 1400–1900* (London, 1967)

BTHA, *The Toy Industry in the United Kingdom* (London, 1992)

Buchheit, H. & Oldenbourg, R., *Das Miniaturenkabinett der Munchener Residenz* (Munich, 1921)

Burchoorn, I., *Spiegel der Staten ofte't Vermaeck der Sinnen* (The Hague, 1637)

Burgess, J.W., *Practical Treatise on Coach-Building* (London, 1881)

Burke, T., *The Wind and the Rain: A book of confessions* (London, 1924)

Burt, R., 'The transformation of the non-ferrous metals industries in the 17th and 18th centuries', *Economic History Review* 48 (1) (1995), pp. 23–45

Burton, A., 'On Toy-Shops and Toy-Sellers', *The Victoria & Albert Museum Album* 3 (1984), pp. 116–27

Butler, R. & Green, C., *English Bronze Cooking Vessels and their Founders 1350–1830* (Somerset, 2003)

Camerer Cuss, T.P., *The Story of Watches* (London, 1952)

Camerer Cuss, T.P., *The Country Life Book of Watches* (London, 1967)

Campbell, M., *Decorative Ironwork* (Victoria & Albert Museum, London, 1997)

Campbell, R., *The London Tradesman* (London, 1747; repr. 1969)

Cantwell, A.M. & di Zarega Wall, D., *Unearthing Gotham: The archaeology of New York City* (London, 2001)

Carver Wees, B., *English, Irish & Scottish Silver at the Sterling and Francine Clark Art Institute* (New York, 1977)

Caspall, J., *Making Fire and Light in the Home pre-1820* (London, 1987)

Cats, J., *Maedchen-plicht ofte Ampte der ionck-vrouwen, in eerbaer liefde, aen-ghewesen door sinne-beelden* (Middelburgh, 1618)

Cats, J., *Houwelijck, dat is de gantsche gelegentheyt dest echten-staets* (Middelburgh, 1625)

Cats, J., *Spiegel Van den Ouden ende Nieuwen Tijt* (The Hague, 1632)

Cescinsky, H. & Gribble, E.R., *Early English Furniture and Woodwork*, 2 vols (London, 1922)

Chartres, J.A., *Internal Trade in England 1500–1700* (London, 1977)

Chartres, J.A., 'Trade and Shipping in the Port of London: Wiggins Key in the later 17th century', *Journal of Transport History*, 3rd series, 1 (1980), pp. 29–48

Chinnery, V., *Oak Furniture: The British tradition* (Antique Collectors Club, 1979)

Chippendale, T., *The Gentleman and Cabinet Maker's Director* (London, 1754)

Christensen, A.E., 'Ship Graffiti and Models' in Wallace, P.F., ed., *Miscellanea 1: Medieval Dublin excavations 1962–81* (Royal Irish Academy, Dublin, 1988)

Clayton, M., *The Collector's Dictionary of the Silver and Gold of Great Britain and North America* (London, 1971)

Clifford, H., 'Invention, Identity and Imitation in London and Provincial Metalworking Trades 1750–1899', *Journal of Design History* 2 (1999), pp. 241–55

Clutton, C. & Daniels, G., *Clocks and Watches: The collection of the Worshipful Company of Clockmakers* (London, 1975)

Coke, R., *A Discourse of Trade* (London, 1670)

Comenius, J., *Orbis Sensualium Pictus* (Nuremberg, 1658); trans. from German into English by Charles Hoole (London, 1689)

Conway, M., 'Old English Cupboards', *Apollo* (January, 1944), pp. 3–6

Cooper, R.G., *English Slipware Dishes 1650–1850* (London, 1968)

Coryat, T., *Crudities* (London, 1611)

Cotterell, H.H. & Heal, A., 'Pewterers' trade-cards', *Connoisseur*, (December, 1926) and 'About pewterers' trade-cards etc.', *Connoisseur* (February, 1928)

Cotterell, H.H., *Old Pewter its Makers and Marks* (London, 1929; repr. 1963)

Cotterell, H.H., 'Porringers, Caudle, Posset and Toasting Cups', *Apollo*, part 1 (August, 1938); part 2 (March, 1939); and part 3 (October, 1942)

Cotgrave, R., *A French & English Dictionary with another in English & French* (London, 1650; rev. 1673)

Cowgill, J., de Neergaard, M. & Griffiths, N., *Knives and Scabbards*, Medieval Finds from Excavations in London 1 (London, 1987)

Cowper, W., *The Poetical Works of William Cowper* (London, 1872)

Crawford, S., *Childhood in Anglo-Saxon England* (Stroud, 1999)

Cremer, W.H., *The Toys of the Little Folks of all Ages and Countries* (London, 1873)

Crofts, J., *Packhorse, Waggon and Post: Land carriage and communications under the Tudors and Stuarts* (London, 1967)

Crouch, H., *Complete View of British Customs* (London, 1725)

Crouch, H., *Complete Guide to Officers* (London, 1732)

Cunnigham, W., *Alien Immigrants to England* (London, 1897)

D'Allemagne, H.R., *Decorative Antique Ironwork* (Rouen, 1924)

D'Allemagne, H.R., *Les anciens maîtres serruriers et leurs meilleurs travaux* (Paris, 1943)

Darlington, I., ed., *London Consistory Court Wills 1492–1547*, London Record Society 3 (London, 1967)

Davies, D., *A History of Shopping* (London, 1966)

Davies, D.W., *Dutch Influences on English Culture, 1558–1625* (New York, 1964)

Davis, R., 'English foreign trade 1660–1700' in Carus-Wilson, E.M., ed., *Essays in Economic History*, 3 vols (London, 1962), vol. 2, pp. 257–72

De Brune, J., *Emblemata of Zinne-Werck* (Amsterdam, 1624)

De Bruyn, A., *Omnium pene Europae, Asiae, Aphricae atque Americae gentium habitus* (Antwerp, 1581)

De Wilde, B., *De Thuiskomst Michiel Quaetjonc: Archéologie in de Verdronken Weiden van Ieper* (Ypres, 1995)

Demaître, L., 'The Idea of Childhood and Child Care in Medical Writings of the Middle Ages', *Journal of Psychohistory* 4 (1977), pp. 461–90

Den Blaauwen, A.L., *Nederlands Zilver: 1580–1830* ('s Gravenhage, 1979)

Den Blaauwen, A.L., *Zilver op Sypesteyn* (Nieuw Loosdrecht, 1996)

Didsbury, P., 'A Miniature lead jug from Sigglesthorne', *East Riding Archaeological Society Newsletter* 31 (1989), pp. 10–2

Dietz, B., *The Port and Trade of Early Elizabethan London: Documents* (London, 1972)

Digges, L., 'Proofs of the Queen's Interest in lands set by the Sea and The Salt Shores thereof.' See manuscript sources above.

Dixon, S.C., *English Gold and Silver Trays* (London, 1964)

Dodsley, R., *The Toy-Shop; to which are added, Epistles and Poems on several occasions* (London, 1756)

Drysters, K., *'Al's werelds goed, is popple-goed': Miniaturzilver in Nederland* (Historisch Museum het Burgerweeshuis, Arnhem, 1999)

Dubbe, B., 'Arent Jan Coenen, ambachtsman in een tijd van verval Een acttiende-eeuwse tinnegieter en 'fabrikant' van tinnen speelgoed te Amsterdam', *Antiek* 4 (November, 1970), pp. 213–39

Dubbe, B., *Keur van tin uit de havensteden Amsterdam, Antwerpen en Rotterdam*, Catalogue from the Museums Willet-Holthuysen, Amsterdam; Provinciall Museum Sterckshof, Antwerp, and Museum Boymans-van Beuningen (Rotterdam, 1979)

Dubbe, B., 'British Contacts with the Pewterer's Trade in the Low Countries', *Journal of the Pewter Society* 12 (Spring, 1999), pp. 4–10

Dufour, I. in *Keur van Tin uit de Havensteden, Amsterdam, Antwerpen en Rotterdam*, Belgisch Nederlands Cultureel Verdrag exhibition catalogue (Rotterdam, 1979)

Duncan, L.L., ed. *Index of Wills Proved in the Prerogative Court of Canterbury 1558–1583*, vol. 3 (British Record Society, London, 1898)

Duncan, S.J. & Ganiaris, H., 'Some Sulphide Corrosion Products on Copper Alloys and Lead Alloys from London Waterfront Sites' in *Recent Advances in the Conservation and Analysis of Artefacts* (London, 1987), pp. 109–18

Eames, P., 'Documentary Evidence concerning the Character and Use of Domestic Furnishings in England in the 14th and 15th centuries' *Furniture History* 7 (1971), pp. 41–60

Eames, P., 'An Iron Chest at Guildhall of about 1427', *Furniture History* 10 (1974), pp. 1–5

Eames, P., 'Medieval Furniture: Furniture in England, France and the Netherlands from the 12th to the 15th century', *Furniture History* 13 (1977)

Earle, P., *The Making of the English Middle Class: Business, society and family life in London 1660–1730* (London, 1989)

Earle, P., *A City Full of People: Men and women of London 1650–1750* (London, 1994)

Early, A.K., *English Dolls, Effigies & Puppets* (London, 1955)

Earnshaw, N., *Collecting Dolls' Houses and Miniatures* (London, 1989)

Edwards, R., 'What was a court-cupboard?', *Apollo* (September, 1938), pp. 136–7

Edwards, R., *Dictionary of English Furniture from the Middle Ages to the late Georgian Period* (London, 1964)

Egan, G., 'Finds Recovery on Riverside Sites in London', *Popular Archaeology* 6 (14) (1985/6), pp. 42–50

Egan, G., 'Base Metal Toys', *Finds Research Group 700–1700 Datasheet* 10 (Oxford, 1988a)

Egan, G., 'A 16th-century Miniature Ship from London', *Post Medieval Archaeology* 22 (1988b), pp. 181–2

Egan, G., *Playthings from the Past: Lead-alloy miniature artefacts c.1300–1800* (Jonathan Horne Antiques, London, 1996)

Egan, G., 'Children's Pastimes in Past Times: Medieval toys found in the British Isles' in de Boe, G. & Verhaege, F., eds, *Material Culture in Medieval Europe* (Bruges, 1997)

Egan, G., *The Medieval Household: Daily living c. 1150–c. 1450*, Medieval Finds from Excavations in London 6 (London, 1998)

Egan, G., 'Lead/Tin Playthings' in Williams, D., 'Some Recent Finds from Surrey', *Surrey Archaeological Collections* 86 (1999), pp. 192–3

Egan, G., 'Lead/tin alloy metalwork' in Saunders, P., ed., *Salisbury and South Wiltshire Museum Medieval Catalogue 3* (Salisbury & South Wiltshire Museum, 2001), pp. 92–118

Egan, G., *Material Culture in London in an Age of Transition: Tudor and Stuart period finds from Bermondsey* (forthcoming, a)

Egan, G., 'Copper alloy finds' in Griffiths, D., *The Archaeology of Meols* (forthcoming, b)

Egan, G., 'Note on copper alloy toy candlestick' in *Records of Buckinghamshire* (forthcoming, c)

Egan, G. & Forsyth, H., 'Wound Wire and Silver Gilt: Changing fashions in dress accessories *c.* 1400–*c.* 1600' in Gaimster, D. & Stamper, P., eds, *The Age of Transition: The archaeology of English culture 1400–1600*, Society for Medieval Archaeology Monograph 15 (London, 1997), pp. 215–38

Endrei, W. & Zolnay, L., *Fun & Games in Old Europe* (Budapest, 1986)

Fairclough, G., 'Plymouth Excavations: St Andrews Street 1976', *Plymouth Museum Archaeology Series 2* (Plymouth, 1979)

Fairholt, F.W., *Dictionary of Terms in Art* (London, 1854)

Falk, A., '"...ein hölzins Rösslin, das zoch ich an eim Faden vor der Thür": Speilzeug und Spielen im Mittelalter' in Gläser 1995, pp. 24–53

Fastnedge, R., *English Furniture Styles from 1500–1830* (London, 1962)

Fearn, J., *Domestic Bygones* (Tring, 1977)

Fella, T., *A book of diverse devices* (MSS, 1585–1598, 1622, V.a.311: Shakespeare Folger Library, Washington)

Ffoulkes, C., *Decorative Ironwork from the 11th to the 18th Century* (London, 1913)

Ffoulkes, C., *The Gun-Founders of England* (Cambridge, 1937)

Field, R., *Irons in the Fire: A history of cooking equipment* (Wiltshire, 1984)

Figdor, A., 'Collection of Dolls' Furniture (Vienna)', *Connoisseur* 35 & 37 (1913), pp. 81–8, 17–25

Finlay, M., Brownsword, R. & Pitt, E., 'British Late Medieval Inscribed Bronze Jugs', *Journal of the Antique Metalware Society* 4 (June, 1996), pp. 1–13

Finlay, R.A.P., 'Population and Fertility in London 1580–1650', *Journal of Family History* 4 (1979), pp. 26–38

Finlay, R.A.P., *Population and Metropolis: The demography of London 1580–1650* (Cambridge, 1981)

Fisher, F.J., 'The Development of London as a Centre of Conspicuous Consumption in the 16th and 17th centuries', *Transactions of the Royal Historical Society*, 4th series, 30 (1948), pp. 37–50

Florio, J., *A Worlde of Wordes ...* (London, 1598)

Forgeais, A., *Collection des plombs historiés trouvés dans la Seine*, vols 1, 2 & 4 (Paris, 1858, 1863 & 1865)

Fournier, E., *Histoire des jeux, jouets et amusements* (Paris, 1889)

Fox, R. & Barton, K.J., 'Excavations at Oyster Street, Portsmouth, Hampshire 1968–71', *Post Medieval Archaeology* 20 (1986), pp. 31–255

Fox-Davies, A. C., *Heraldic Badges* (London, 1907)

Franklin, A., *La vie privée d'autrefois* (Paris, 1896)

Franklyn, J. & Tanner, J., *An Encyclopaedic Dictionary of Heraldry* (Oxford, 1970)

Fraser, A., *A History of Toys* (London, 1966)

French, G.F., ed., *A Catalogue of the Antiquities and Works of Art Exhibited at Ironmongers Hall, London in the Month of May, 1861*, vol. 2 (London, 1869)

Fritsch, K.E. & Bachmann, M., *An Illustrated History of Toys* (London, 1966)

Furnival, F.J., ed., *The Fifty Earliest Wills in the Court of Probate* (Early English Text Society, London, 1882)

Gaimster, D., *German Stoneware 1200–1900: Archaeology and Cultural History* (London, 1997)

Garau, E. & Zagari, F., 'Oggetti per il gioco nel Lazio medievale' in de Doe, G. & Verhaeghe, F., eds, *Material Culture in Medieval Europe: Papers of the Medieval Europe 1997 Brugge' Conference* (Zellik, Belgium, 1997), pp. 385–403

Garratt, J.G., *Model Soldiers: A collector's guide* (London, 1965; repr. 1971)

Garratt, J.G., *Collecting Model Soldiers* (London, 1975)

Gask, N., 'Old Base-Metal Spoons', *Connoisseur* (November, 1937), pp. 253–6

Gay, V., *Glossaire Archéologique du Moyen Age et de la Renaissance* (Paris, 1887)

Gemeentemuseum, *Een rondgang door het poppenhuis* (The Hague, 1977)

George, J.N., *English Pistols and Revolvers* (North Carolina, 1938)

Gentle, R. & Feild, R., *Domestic metalwork 1640–1820* (London, 1994)

Gerson, H. & Ter Kuike, E. H., *Art and Architecture in Belgium 1600–1800* (London, 1960)

Gilbert, C., ed., *Furniture at Temple Newsam and Lotherton Hall: A catalogue of the Leeds Collection* (Leeds, 1968)

Gilbert, C. & Wells-Cole, A., *The fashionable fireplace 1660–1840* (Leeds, 1985)

Glanville, P., *Silver in Tudor and Early Stuart England* (London, 1990)

Gläser, M. ed., *'Daz Kint Spilete und was Fro': Spielen vom Mittelalter bis heute* (Lübeck 1995)

Glass, D.V. *London Inhabitants Within the Walls* (London, 1695), repr. London Record Society Publication 2 (London, 1966)

Glissman, A.H., *The Evolution of the Sad-iron* (California, 1970)

Gloag, J., *The Englishman's Chair: Origins, design and social history of seat furniture in England* (London, 1964)

Gloag, J., *A Short Dictionary of Furniture* (London, rev. 1972)

Goodich, M.E., *From Birth to Old Age: The human life cycle in medieval European thought 1250–1350* (London & New York, 1989)

Goodman, W.L.,*The History of Woodworking Tools* (London, 1964)

Gould, D.W., *The Top, Universal Toy, Enduring Pastime* (Folkestone, 1975)

Grancsay, S.V., 'Miniature Firearms', *American Rifleman* (July, 1949), pp. 28–9

Green, V., *English Dolls' Houses of the 18th and 19th Centuries*, (London, 1955)

Gröber, K., *Children's Toys of Bygone Days* (London, 1932)

Groeneweg, G., 'Tinnen Miniaturen/Kinderspeelgoed' in Bos, H. et al., *Schatten uit de Schelde*, Exhibition catalogue (Bergen op Zoom, Netherlands, 1987), pp. 71–3

Grönke, E. & Weinlich, E., *Mode aus Modeln: Kruseler- und andere tonfiguren des 14 bis 16 Jahrhunderts aus dem Germanischen Nationalmuseum und andere Sammlungen*, Wissenschaftlich Beibände zum Anzeiger des Nationalmuseums14 (Nuremberg 1998)

Grove, J.R., *Antique Brass Candlesticks 1450–1750* (Maryland, 1967)

Gruber, A.,*Weltliches Silber* (Zurich, 1977)

Guildhall Museum Catalogue, *Catalogue of the Collection of London Antiquities in the Guildhall Museum* (Library Committee of the Corporation of the City of London, London, 1903 & 1908)

Gwynn-Jones, P., 'International Heraldry' in Bedingfeld, H. et al., *Heraldry* (New Jersey, 1993)

Hackenbroch, Y., *English & Other Silver in the Irwin Untermeyer Collection* (London, 1969)

Haedeke, H-U., *Metalwork: The social history of the decorative arts* (London & New York, 1970)

Haedeke, H-U., *Zinn: Ein Handbuch für Sammler und Liebhaber* (Brunswick, 1973)

Haedeke, H-U., *Zinn*, Kunstgewerbemuseum Catalogue 3 (Cologne, 1976)

Haley, K.H.D.,*The Dutch in the 17th Century* (London, 1972)

Hall, J., *Dictionary of Subjects and Symbols in Art* (London, 1979)

Halsbury's Laws of England, 4th edn, vols 12 (1) (London, 1998) & 49 (2) (London, 1996)

Hanawalt, B.A., *The Ties that Bound: Peasant families in medieval England* (New York & Oxford, 1986)

Hanawalt, B.A., *Growing up in Medieval London* (Oxford, 1993)

Harding, V., 'The population of London, 1550–1700: A review of the published evidence', *London Journal* 15 (1990), pp. 111–28

Harris, J., *Lexicon Technicum* (London , 1714)

Harrison, W., A *Description of Elizabethan England* (London, 1577), ed. F .J. Furnivall from first edn of *Holinshed's Chronicle* 1577–87 (New Shakespeare Society, 1876)

Harvey, Y., 'The Bronze' in Platt, C. & Coleman Smith, R., *Excavations in Southampton 1953–69* (Leicester, 1975), pp. 254–68

Hatcher, J., *English Tin Production and Trade before 1550* (Oxford, 1973)

Hatcher, J. & Barker, T.C., *A History of British Pewter* (London, 1974)

Hawkins, E., *Medallic Illustrations of the History of Great Britain and Ireland*, 2 vols, Franks., A.W. & Grueber, H.A., eds (London, 1885; repr. 1969)

Hawkins, R.N.P. & Baldwin, E., *A Dictionary of Makers of British Metallic Tickets, Checks, Medalets, Tallies and Counters 1788–1910* (A.H. Baldwin & Sons Ltd, 1989)

Hayward, J.F., *English Cutlery 16th to 18th Century* (London, 1957)

Hayward, J.F., *Virtuoso Goldsmiths and the Triumph of Mannerism 1540–1620* (London, 1976)

Heal, A., *London Tradesmen's Cards of the 18th Century* (London, 1925)

Heal, A., *The Signboards of Old London Shops* (London, 1947)

Heal, V., 'Model Boat' in Horsey, I.P., ed., *Excavations in Poole 1973–83*, Dorset Natural History & Archaeological Society Monograph 10 (Dorset, 1992)

Hearn, K., ed. *Dynasties: Painting in Tudor and Jacobean England 1530–1630* (Tate Gallery, London, 1995)

Hedges, E.S., *Tin and its Alloys* (London, 1960)

Hedges, E.S., *Tin in Social and Economic History* (London, 1964)

Henkel, A. & Schone, A., *Emblemata* (Stuttgart, 1967; supp., 1976)

Hennell, Sir R., *The History of the King's Body Guard of the Yeomen of the Guard* (London 1904)

Henry, C.T., 'Artillery in Miniature', *Royal Armouries Yearbook* 4 (1999), pp. 24–5

Hepplewhite, G., *The Cabinet Maker and Upholsterer's Guide* (London, 1788; repr. 1970)

Hernmarck, C., *The Art of the European Silversmith 1430–1830*, 2 vols (London & New York, 1977)

Heroard, J., *Le 'Journal' d'Heroard: L'enfance et la condition royale 1601–28*, Chaunn, P. & Foisil Fayard, M., eds (Paris, 1989)

Herteig, A.E., *Kongers Havn & Handels Sete* (Oslo, 1969)

Herwijer, N., et al., *Speelgoed en Blik*, Deventer Museum exhibition catalogue (Amsterdam, 1986)

Hewitt, M., *Children in English Society*, 2 vols (London, 1969)

Hexham, H., *A copious English and Netherduytch Dictionarie...*, 2 vols (Rotterdam, 1648)

Hick, D.S.A., 'Model and Miniature Small Arms', *Arms Fair* (Spring, 1977), pp. 38–41

Hills, J., *Das Kinderspielbild von Pieter Bruegel*, Oesterreichische Museum (Vienna, 1957)

Hilton Price, F. G., *Old Base-Metal Spoons* (Batsford, 1908)

Himmelheber, G., *Kleine Möbel Modell-, Andachts und Kassettenmöbel vom 13–20 Jahrhundert* (Bayerisches Nationalmuseum München, Munich, 1979)

Hinrichsen, T., *Battenberg Antiquitaten: Spielzeug* (Munich, 1980)

Hoever, O., *A Handbook of Wrought Iron from the Middle Ages to the End of the 18th century* (London & New York, 1962)

Hogg, O. F. G., trans. & ed., *The Compleat Gunner in Three Parts* (1672; repr. Wakefield, 1971)

Holme, R., *The Academy of Armory* (Chester, 1688)

Hollstein, F.W.H., *Dutch and Flemish Etchings, Engravings and Woodcuts c. 1450–1700* (Amsterdam, 1947)

Homer, R.F., *Five Centuries of Base-Metal Spoons* (London, 1975)

Hornsby, P.R.G., *Pewter of the Western World 1600–1850* (London, 1983)

Hornsby, P.R.G., et al., *Pewter A Celebration of the Craft 1200–1700* (London, 1989)

Houart, V., *Miniature Silver Toys* (New York, 1981)

Howarth, E., *Catalogue of the Bateman Collection of Antiquities in the Sheffield Public Museum* (London, 1899)

Hughes, G.B., 'A Status Symbol of Tudor Times: The English court-cupboard', *Country Life* 6 (January, 1966), pp. 16–17

Hughes, T. & B., *Collecting Miniature Antiques: A guide for collectors* (London, 1973)

Hume, I.N., *Treasure in the Thames* (London, 1955)

Hume, I.N., *A Guide to the Artifacts of Colonial America* (New York, 1970)

Hume, I.N., *James Geddy and Sons, Colonial Craftsmen*, Colonial Williamsburg Archaeological Series 5, (Virginia, 1970)

Hume, I.N., 'A Group of Artifacts Recovered from an 18th-century Well in Williamsburg' in Hume, I.N., ed., *Five Artifact Studies*, Colonial Williamsburg Occasional Papers in Archaeology 1 (Virginia, 1973), pp. 1–24

Hummel, C.F., *Ancient Carpenters' Tools* (Buckinghamshire County Historical Society, 1929)

Hurst, J.G., *et al.*, *Pottery Produced & Traded in North West Europe 1350–1650*, Rotterdam Papers 6 (Rotterdam, 1986)

Jackson, C.J., 'The Spoon and its History: Its form, material, and development, more particularly in England', *Archaeologia* 53 (2) (1890), pp. 107–46

Jackson, P.W., 'Some Main Streams and Tributaries in European Ornament 1500–1750', parts 1–3, *Bulletin [of the Victoria and Albert Museum]* 111 (2–4) (April, July, October, 1967)

Jackson-Stops, G., 'Formal splendour: The Baroque Age' in *The History of Furniture* (London, 1976)

Jacobs, F.G., *A History of Dolls' Houses* (Maryland, 1954)

Jaggard, W., *A View of all the Right Honourable the Lord Mayors of this Honourable City of London 1558–1601* (London, 1601)

Jagger, C., *The Artistry of the English Watch* (London, 1988)

Jarmuth, K., *Lichter Leuchten im abendland Zweitausend Jahre Beleuchtungskoiper* (Berlin, 1967)

Jenning, C., *Early Chests in Wood and Iron*, Public Record Office Museum Pamphlet 7 (London, 1974)

Jewell, B., *Smoothing Irons: A history and collector's guide* (Kent, 1977)

Jewers, A.J., *Monumental Inscriptions in the City of London* (Corporation of the City of London, 1919)

Johnson, A.H., *The History of the Worshipful Company of the Drapers of London*, 5 vols (Oxford, 1914, 1915 & 1922)

Jones, W., *The Grammar of Ornament* (London, 1856)

Jonson, B., *The Devil is an Ass* (London, 1616)

Karel, K., *Spel, Speelgoed en vrije tijd* (Speelgoedmuseum Mechelen, 2001)

Karskens, G., 'Small Things, Big Pictures: New perspectives from the archaeology of Sydney's Rock Neighbourhood' in Mayne, A. & Marray, T., eds, *The Archaeology of the Urban Landscape: Explorations in Slumland* (Cambridge, 2001), pp. 69–85

Kashden, M., 'Miniature medieval votive candlesticks', *Journal of the Pewter Society* 6 (2) (Autumn, 1987), pp. 46–7

Keene, D., 'Whipping Top' in Biddle, M., *Object and Economy in Medieval Winchester*, Winchester Studies 7 ii, (Oxford, 1990) pp. 706–7

Kevill Davis, S., *Yesterday's Children: The antiques and history of childcare* (Antique Collectors Club, Woodbridge, 1991)

Kiesiel, H., *Die Kunst des deutschen mobels van den Anfangen bis zum Hochbarock*, vols 1 & 2 (Munich, 1968)

King, E., *Toys and Dolls for Collectors* (London, 1973)

Klingender, F., *Animals in Art and Thought* (London, 1971)

Kolchin, B.A., *Wooden Artefacts from Medieval Novgorod*, British Archaeological Reports S495 1 & 2 (Oxford, 1989)

Koldeweij, A.M. & Willemsen, A., eds, *Helig en Profaan, Laatsmiddeleuwse Insignes in Cultuurhistorisch Perspectief* (Amsterdam, 1995)

Kurle, O., *Koper en Brons*, Staatsintegeverig, Rjksmuseum (Amsterdam, 1986)

Lamond, E., ed., *A Discourse of the Common Weal of this Realm of England* (Cambridge, 1954)

Lang, J.T., *Viking Age Decorated Wood: A study of its ornament and style*, Medieval Dublin Excavations 1962–81, series B (Royal Irish Academy, Dublin, 1988)

Lang, R.G., ed., *Two Tudor Subsidy Assessment Rolls for London 1541 and 1582*, London Record Society vol. 29 (London, 1993)

Laurioux, P., *Le Moyen Age à Table* (Paris, 1989)

Lawson, G., 'Pig Metapodial 'Toggles' and Buzz-discs: Traditional musical instruments', *Finds Research Group 700–1700 Datasheet* 18 (1995)

Leber, W., *Die Puppenstadt Mon Plaisir* (Arnstadt, 1986)

Leopold, J.H., *Zilveren Speelgoed 17e tot begin 19e* (Gronings Museum, 1972)

Levetus., A.S., 'Dr Albert Figdor's Collection of Doll's Furniture, Vienna', 2 parts, *Connoisseur* 35 (138) & 36 (145), (February & September 1913), pp. 81–8 & 17–25

Lewis, J.M. *et.al.*, 'Medieval Bronze Tripod Ewers from Wales', *Medieval Archaeology* 31 (1987), pp. 80–93

Lindsay, J. S., *Iron and Brass Implements of the English House* (London, 1927); repr. as *Iron and Brass Implements of the English and American House* (London, 1970)

Lindsay, M.K., *Miniature Arms* (London, 1970)

Lipski, L.L. & Archer, M., *Dated English Delftware* (London, 1984)

Lister, R., *Decorative Cast Ironwork in Great Britain* (London, 1960)

Lloyd, N., 'Domestic Ironwork 1: Firebacks', *Archaeological Review* 58 (1925)

Louvre des Antiquaires., *Mobilier miniature: Objets de Maitre 16–20 siècle,* Collection Vendeuvre exhibition catalogue (Paris, 1986)

MacQuoid, P., *A History of English Furniture* (London, 1988)

Magno, Alessandro, 'The London Journal of Alessandro Magno' (1562) repr. Barron, C., Coleman, C. & Gobbi, C., eds, *London Journal* 9 (2) (1983), pp. 136–52

Mainwaring-Baines, J., *Wealden firebacks* (Hastings, 1958)

Major, H., 'Miscellaneous Finds' in Godbold, S., ed., 'A Napoleonic Coastal Gun Battery at Harwich', *Essex Archaeology & History* 25 (1994), pp. 214–18

Mann, J., *Wallace Collection Catalogues: European arms and armour,* 3 vols (London, 1962)

Margeson, S., *Norwich Households: Medieval and post-medieval finds from Norwich survey excavations 1971–8*, East Anglian Archaeology 58 (Norwich, 1993)

Markham, C.A., *Pewter Marks and Old Pewter Ware: Domestic and ecclesiastical* (London, 1909)

Marks, R. & Williamson, P., eds *Gothic: Art for England 1400–1547* (V & A, London, 2003)

Marquardt, K., *Eight Centuries of European Knives, Forks and Spoons: An art collection* (Arnoldsche, Germany, 1997)

Massé, H.J.L.J., *Pewter Plate: A historical and descriptive handbook* (London, 1904)

Mayhew, H., *London Labour and the London Poor*, vol. 2 (London, 1861)

McKenzie, I., *Collecting Old Toy Soldiers* (London, 1975)

Menkes, S., *Silver Toys & Miniatures* (Victoria and Albert Museum, London, n.d.)

Michaelis, R.F., 'English Pewter Porringers', parts 1–4, *Apollo*(July, August, September, October, 1949)

Michaelis, R.F., *British Pewter* (London, 1969)

Michaelis, R.F., *Antique Pewter of the British Isles* (London, 1971)

Michaelis, R.F., *Old Domestic Base-Metal Candlesticks from 13th-19th century* (Antique Collectors Club, 1975)

Miller, D., *Material Culture and Mass Consumption* (Oxford, 1987)

Milne, G. & C., *Medieval Waterfront Development at Trig Lane, London,* London and Middlesex Archaeological Society, Special Paper 5 (London, 1982)

Milne, G., Bates, M. & Webber, M., 'Problems, Potential and Partial Solutions: An archaeological study of the tidal Thames', *World Archaeology* 29 (1) (1997), pp. 130–46

Milne, G., *The Port of Medieval London* (London, 2003)

Miniature Arms Society., *The Art of Miniature Firearms: Centuries of craftsmanship* (Wisconsin, 1999)

Mitchell, D.M., '"By your leave my Masters": British taste in table linen in the 15th and 16th centuries', *Textile History* 20 (1) (1989), pp. 49–77

Mitchiner, M, *Medieval Pilgrim and Secular Badges* (Sanderstead, 1986)

Moore, A.A., *History of the Foreshore and the Law relating thereto*, 3rd edn (London, 1888)

More, T., *The Complete Works of St. Thomas More*, Sylvester, R.S. *et al.*, eds, 15 vols (New Haven & London, 1963–97)

Morley, H., *Memoirs of Bartholomew Fair* (London, 1859)

Moscow Museum, *Moscow Museum and its Collections* (Moscow, 1995)

Neff, J.U., 'The Progress of Technology and the Growth of Large-scale Industry in Great Britain 1540–1640', in Carus-Wilson, E.M., ed., *Essays in Economic History*, 3 vols (London, 1962), vol. 1, pp. 88–107

Neufeld, C., *The Skilled Metal Workers of Nuremberg* (New Brunswick, 1989)

Neu Koch, R., 'Eine Bilderbäcker: Werkstatt des Spätmittelalters an der Goldgasse in Köln', *Zeitschrift für Archäologie des Mittelalters* 21 (Germany, 1993), pp. 3–70

Neville Jackson, F., *Toys of Other Days* (London, repr. 1975)

Nevinson, J., 'The Dress of the Citizens of London 1540–1640' in Bird, J., Chapman, H. & Clark, J., eds, *Collectanea*

Londiniensia: Studies in London archaeology and history presented to Ralph Merrifield, London and Middlesex Archaeological Society Special Paper 2 (1978), pp. 265–80

Newbury, J., *The Toy-Shop* (London, 1787)

Nickel, H., 'The Little Knights of the Living Room Table', *Metropolitan Museum of Art Bulletin* 25 (4) (1966), pp. 170–83

Norman, A.V.B., 'A Note on Miniature Armours', *Journal of the Arms and Armour Society* 9 (2) (December, 1977), pp. 61–71

Oakeshott, E., *The Knight and his Horse* (London, 1990)

Oakeshott, E., *The Sword in the Age of Chivalry* (London, 1995)

Oexle, J., 'Minne en Miniature-Kinderspiel im Mittelalterlichen Konstanz' in *Landesdenkmalamt Baden Württemberg & die Stadt Zürich, Stadtluft, Hirsebrei & Bettelmönch, die Stadt um 1300*, Exhibition catalogue (Stuttgart, 1992), pp. 392–5

Oman, C., *The Coinage of England* (Oxford, 1931)

Oman, C., *Caroline Silver 1625–88* (London, 1970)

Orme, N., *Education and Society in Medieval and Renaisance* (London, 1989)

Orme, N., *From Childhood to Chivalry: The education of the English kings and aristocracy 1066–1530* (London, 1984)

Orme, N., 'The Culture of Children in Medieval England', *Past & Present* 148 (1995), pp. 48–88

Orme, N., *Medieval Children* (London & New Haven, 2001)

Patten, J., 'Urban Occupations in Pre-Industrial England', *Transactions of the Institute of British Geographers*, new series, 2 (1977), pp. 296–313

Peal, C., *Pewter of Great Britain* (London, 1983)

Pearce, J.E., Vince, A.G. & Jenner, M.A., *A Dated Type-Series of London Medieval Pottery, Part 2: London-type ware*, London and Middlesex Archaeological Society Special Paper 6 (London, 1985)

Pearce, J.E., Vince, A.G., et al., *A Dated Type-Series of London Medieval Pottery, Part 4: Surrey whitewares* (London and Middlesex Archaeological Society, London, 1988)

Pearce, J.E., *Post-Medieval Pottery in London 1550–1700, Vol 1: Border wares* (London, 1992)

Pepys, S., *The Diary of Samuel Pepys* (1660–9), Latham R. & Mathews, W, eds, 11 vols (London, 1970–83)

Perry, J., *Spinning Tops* (London, 1929)

Petényi, S., *Games and Toys in Medieval and Early Modern Hungary* (Krems, 1994)

Peterson, H.L., ed., *Encylopaedia of Firearms* (Connoisseur, London, 1964)

Phelps Brown, E.H. & Hopkins, S.V., 'Seven Centuries of the Prices of Consumables Compared with Builders' Wage-rates', *Economica* (November, 1956)

Pijzel-Domisse, J., *De 17de-eeuwse Poppenhuizen in het Rijksmuseum* (Wormer, 1994)

Pijzel-Domisse, J., *Het poppehuis in het Frans Hals Museum De Haan* (Haarlem, 2000)

Pinchbeck, I. & Hewitt, M., *Children in English Society*, 2 vols (1969 & 1973)

Plumb, J.H., 'The New World of Children in 18th-Century England', *Past & Present* 67 (1975), pp. 286–315

Poliakoff, M., *Silver Toys & Miniatures* (Victoria & Albert Museum, 1986)

Pollock, L., *Forgotten Children: Parent-child relationships from 1500–1900* (Cambridge, 1983)

Power, E. & Postan, M.M., eds, *Studies in English Trade in the 15th Century* (London, 1933)

Praz, M., *An Illustrated History of Interior Decoration from Pompei to Art Nouveau* (London, 1964)

Rappaport, S., 'Social Structure in 16th-Century London', part 1, *London Journal* 9 (2) (Winter, 1983), pp. 107–52

Reynolds, G., *Costume of the Western World: Elizabethan and Jacobean 1558–1625* (London, 1951)

Riché, P. & Alexandre-Bidon, D., *L'Enfance au Moyen Age* (Bibliothèque nationale de France, Paris, 1994)

Ricketts, C. et al., *Pewterers of London 1600–1900* (Welshpool, 2001)

Riley, H.T., ed., *Memorials of London Life in the 13th, 14th and 15th Centuries* (London, 1868)

Robergs, J.C. & Jourdain, M., *English Furniture*, 2nd edn (London, 1961)

Roberts, H.D., *Downhearth to Bar Grate* (Bath, 1981)

Roberts, S., *Bird-Keeping and Birdcages: A history* (London, 1972)

Robertson, E.G. & J., *Cast-Iron Decoration: A world survey* (New York, 1977)

Roe, F., *Ancient Church Chests and Chairs* (London, 1929)

Rodwell Jones, L.L.,*The Geography of London River* (London, 1931)

Royalton-Kisch, M., *Adriaen van de Venne's Album* (British Museum Publications, London, 1988)

Sala, G.A., *Gaslight and Daylight* (London, 1859)

Salaman, R.A., *Dictionary of Tools used in the Woodworking and Allied Trades c. 1700–1970* (London, 1975)

Samaja, U., *Modelli di Mobili* (Milan, 1987)

Sand, M., *The History of the Harlequinade*, 2 vols (London, 1915)

Sarfatij, H., 'Dordrecht deel 2', *Spiegel Historiael* 7 (Amsterdam, 1972)

Scheffler,W., *Goldschmiede Oberfrankens daten werke zeichen* (Berlin, 1989)

Schepers, W., *Zinn* (Kunstmuseum, Dusseldorf, 1981)

Schiffer, H.R.P.B., *Miniature Antique Furniture* (Pennsylvannia, 1972)

Schofield, J. & Dyson, T., *Archaeology of the City of London* (London, 1980)

Schofield, J., *Medieval London Houses* (New Haven & London, 1995)

Schroder, T.B., *The Gilbert Collection of Gold and Silver* (Los Angeles County Museum, 1988)

Schumpeter, E.B., *English Overseas Trade Statistics 1697–1808* (Oxford, 1960)

Schutte, S., 'Spielen and Spielzeug in der Staat des Späten Mittelatlers' in Wittstock, J., ed., *Aus dem Alltag der Mittelalterlichen Stadt*, Focke Museum, Bremen Hefte 62 (Bremen, 1982), pp. 201–10

Schwarz, L.D., *London in the Age of Industrialisation: Entreprenueurs, labour force and living conditions 1700–1850* (Cambridge, 1992)

Scott, D., *Metallography of Ancient Metallic Artifacts* (Institute of Archaeology, London, 1987)

Scott, M., *The History of Dress Series: Late Gothic Europe 1400–1500* (London, 1980)

Seling, H., *Kunst der Augsburger Goldschmiede 1529–1868: Meister – Marken – Werke*, 3 vols (Munich, 1980)

Senst, O., *Die Metallspielwarenindustrie und der Spielwarenhandel von Nurnberg und Furth* (Nurnberg, 1901)

Shahar, S., *Childhood in the Middle Ages* (London & New York), 1990

Sharpe, R.R., ed., *Calendar of Letter Books*, Book A (London, 1898)

Sharpe, R.R., ed., *Calendar of Wills Proved and Enrolled in the Court of Hustings, London,* AD*1258*–AD*1688*, 2 vols (London, 1889–90)

Shemmel, S., 'William Hux: His toy watches', *Journal of the Pewter Society* 9 (3) (1994), pp. 101–2

Shesgreen, S., ed., *The Cries and Hawkers of London: Engravings and drawings by Marcellus Laroon* (Hampshire, 1990)

Shoesmith, R., *Hereford City Excavations 3: The finds*, CBA Research Report 56 (London, 1985)

Simon, J., *The Art of the Picture Frame: Artists, patrons and the framing of portraits in Britain* (National Portrait Gallery, London, 1996)

Singleton, E., *Dutch and Flemish Furniture* (London, 1907)

Smeyers, M. & van Dooren, R., *Het Leuvense Stadhius* (Louvain, 1998)

Smith, E.J.G., 'The English Silver Spoon', part 1, *The Antique Dealer & Collectors' Guide* (March, 1973), pp. 59–62

Spence, C., *London in the 1690s: A social atlas* (University of London, 2000)

Spencer, B., 'King Henry of Windsor and the London Pilgrim' in Bird, J., Chapman, H. & Clark, J.,eds, *Collectanea Londiniensia: Studies in London archaeology and history presented to Ralph Merrifield,* London and Middlesex Archaeological Society Special Paper 2 (1978), pp. 235–64

Spencer, B., *Salisbury Museum Medieval Catalogue Part 2: Pilgrim souvenirs and secular badges* (Salisbury & South Wiltshire Museum, 1990)

Spencer, B., *Pilgrim Souvenirs and Secular Badges,* Medieval Finds from Excavations in London 7 (London, 1998)

Spufford, M.,*The Great Reclothing of Rural England: Petty chapmen and their wares in the 17th century* (London, 1984)

Stadtarchiv und Stadtisches Museum, *Zu Allen theilen Inss mittel gelegen: Wesel und die Hanse an Rhein, Yssel und Lippe* (Wesel, 1991)

Stenton, F., et al., *The Bayeux Tapestry: A comprehensive survey* (London, 1957)

Stockbauer, J., ed., *Die Junstbestrebungen am Bayerischen Hof unter Herzog Albert V und seinem Nachfolger Wilhelm V* (Vienna, 1874)

Stokes, M.V., 'The Lowther Arcade in the Strand', *London Topographical Record* 23 (1972), pp. 119–28

Stone, L., 'Elizabethan Overseas Trade', *Economic History Review*, 2nd series, 2(1949), pp. 36–57

Strutt, J., The *Sports and Pastimes of the People of England* (London, 1801)

Sugden, E.H., *A Topographical Dictionary to the Works of Shakespeare and His Fellow Dramatists* (Manchester University Press, 1925)

Symonds, R.W., 'Cane chairs of the late 17th and early 18th centuries', *Connoisseur* 93 (March 1934), pp. 173–81

Symonds, R.W., 'English Looking-glass Plates and their Manufacture', *Connoisseur* 97 (May 1936), pp. 243–50

Symonds, R.W., *Furniture Making in 17th and 18th century England* (London, 1940)

Symonds, R,W., 'The Chest and the Coffer: Their difference in function and design', *Connoisseur* 107 (1941), pp. 15–21

Taylor, J., *All the Workes of Iohn Taylor the Water-Poet* (London, 1630); repr. by the Spenser Society in 5 vols (London, 1868–70)

Taylor P., *Dutch Flower Painting 1600–1720* (New Haven, 1995)

Theuerkauff-Liederwald, A.E., *Die Formen der Messingkannen im 15. und 16. Jahrhundert,* Rotterdam Papers 2 (Rotterdam, 1975)

Thistleton Dyer, T.F., *British Popular Customs, Present and Past, Illustrating the Society and Domestic Manners of the People Arranged According to the Calendar of the Yea*r (London, 1891)

Thornton, P., *The Italian Renaissance Interior 1400–1600* (London, 1991)

Thornton, P., *Authentic Decor: The domestic interior 1670–1720* (London, 1984)

Thornton, P., *Seventeenth-century interior decoration in England, France and Holland* (New Haven & London, 1978)

Thornton, P., 'Two Problems', *Furniture History* 7 (1971), pp. 61–71

Tilley, M.P., *A Dictionary of the Proverbs in England in the 16th and 17th Centuries* (University of Michigan, 1950)

Toller, J., *Antique Miniature Furniture* (London, 1966)

Tracy, C., *English Medieval Furniture and Woodwork* (Victoria & Albert Museum, London, 1988)

Tylecote, R.F., *A History of Metallurgy* (Metal Society, London, 1976)

Untracht, O., *Metal Techniques for Craftsmen* (London & New York, 1968)

Van der Horst, A.J., 'De Speelgoedhorloges van Vloienburg', *Antiek* 20 (1) (Netherlands, 1979), pp. 28–31

Van de Venne, A., *Album*, Royalton-Kisch, M., ed. (British Museum, London, 1988)

Van Fockenburgh, W.G.V., *Alle de Wercken soo Oude als Nieuwe*, 2 vols (Amsterdam & Utrecht, 1700)

Van Heemskerk, J., *Minne-Kunst, Minne-Baet* (Amsterdam, 1622)

Vermeersch, V., *Cuisines anciennes* (Bruges, 1992)

Verster, A.J.G., *Old European Pewter* (London, 1958)

Victoria & Albert Museum, *Masterpieces of Cutlery and the Art of Eating* (London, 1979)

Von Boehn, M., *Dolls and Puppets* (London, 1932)

Von der Marwitz, C., *Das Gontard'sche Puppenhaus* (Frankfurt, 1987)

Von Wilckens, L., *Das Puppenhaus Von Spiegelbild des burgerlichen Hausstandes zum Speilzeug fur Kinder* (Munich, 1978)

Von Wilckens, L., *Mansions in Miniature: Four centuries of dolls' houses* (New York, 1980)

Ward Perkins., J.B., *London Museum Medieval Catalogue* (London, 1940)

Wassenbergh-Clarys, P.C., 'Speelgoedcollecties in Nederlandse musea', *Antiek* 4 (November, 1970), pp. 253–66

Weatherill, L.M., *Consumer Behaviour and Material Culture in Britain 1660–1760* (London, 1988)

Webber, M., *Report on the Thames Archaeological Survey 1996–7* (London, 1999)

Welch, C., *History of the Worshipful Company of Pewterers of the City of London*, 2 vols (London, 1902)

Wheaten, B.K., *Savoring the Past: The French kitchen and table from 1300–1789* (Philadelphia, 1983)

White, G.S.J., *The Clockmakers of London* (London, 1998)

Wilhide, E., *The Fireplace* (Boston & London, 1994)

Wilkinson, F., *Edged Weapons* (London, 1970)

Willan, T.S., *The English Coasting Trade 1600–1750* (Manchester, 1938)

Willan, T.S., *Studies in Elizabethan Foreign Trade* (Manchester, 1959)

Willan, T.S., ed., *A Tudor Book of Rates* (Manchester, 1962)

Willemsen, A., Kinder-spel en poppe-goet. 17de-eeuwse miniatuur-gebruiksvoorwerpen en hun functie', *Antiek* 28 (1994), pp. 392–99

Willemsen, A., *Kinder delijt: Middeleeuws speelgoed in de Nederlanden* (Nijmegen, 1998)

Willemsen, A., 'Poppengoed precies bekeken Verzameling, herkomst en functie van loodtinnen miniatuurtjes' in Kicken, D., Koldeweij, J. & ter Moen, J., eds, *Lost and Found: Essays on medieval archaeology for H.J.E. van Beuningen*, Rotterdam Papers 2 (Rotterdam, 2000), pp. 347–55

Willliamson, G.C., ed., *Bryan's Dictionary of Painters & Engravers* (London, 1910)

Wills, G., *English Looking Glasses: A study of the glass, frames and makers 1670–1820* (London, 1965)

Wills, G., *English Furniture 1550–1760* (London, 1971)

Wills, G., *English Furniture 1760–1900* (London, 1971)

Winter, M., *Kindheit und Jugend im Mittelalter* (Freiburg, 1984)

Woodward, D., '"Swords into Ploughshares": Recycling in pre-industrial England' *EHR*, 2nd series 38 (2) (1985), pp. 175–191

Wooley, H., *Queen-like Closet* (London, 1675)

Woolgar, C.M., *The Great Household in Late Medieval England* (London, 1999)

Worshipful Company of Pewterers, *Catalogue of Pewter in its Possession* (London, 1968 & 1979)

Wright, L., *Home Fires Burning: The history of domestic heating and cooking* (London 1964)

Wright, T & Halliwell, J.O., eds, *Reliquiae antiquae* (London, 1841–3)

Wrigley, E.A., 'A Simple Model of London's Importance in Changing English Society and Economy 1650–1750', *Past & Present* 37 (1967), pp. 44–60

Wttewaall, B.W.G., *Nederlands Klein Zilver 1650–1880* (Amsterdam, 1983)

Wustenhoff, H., 'Dutch Excavated Pewter', *Journal of the Pewter Society* 12 (1) (Spring, 1999), pp. 11–17

Zedler, J.H., *Großes, vollständiges Universal-lexicon 23* (Leipzig, 1741)

Zingerle, I.V. & von Summersberg, E., *Das deutsche kinderspiel im mittelalter* (Innsbruck, 1873)

Concordance

Cat. no.	Acc. no.	Object	Provenance
8.78	A859	dish	Thames foreshore
1.16	A1152	cannon	unknown
1.48	A2457	pistol	Lincoln's Inn
1.32	A2459	musket	unknown
8.61	A2527	dish or charger	City Ditch, Newgate
8.45	A2528	plate or charger	Maze Pond
8.43	A2529	plate or charger	Maze Pond
8.75	A2799	dish	Thames foreshore
12.52	A3918	watch	unknown
1.28	A6479	musket	London Wall
1.31	A9454	musket	unknown
1.26	A10374	musket	City of Westminster
1.34	A10429	musket	Westminster
1.42	A10489	pistol	Millbank Street, Westminster
1.45	A10751	pistol	Kingsway
12.43	A10894	watch	unknown
12.43	A11517	watch	Southwark
1.23	A13941	musket	unknown
8.120	A14580	pedestal ewer	Hammersmith, from ballast deposits of London Bridge
1.44	A18742	pistol	Old Queen Street
12.11	A20772	toy watch mould	Sumner Street, near Blackfriars, 1912
8.134	A22301	porringer	Thames foreshore
8.77	A22899	dish	Thames foreshore
1.30	A22903	musket	Great Smith Street, Westminster
12.42	A24849	watch	Victoria Tower, Westminster, site of
8.41	A25669	plate	Thames foreshore
12.42	A25822	watch	unknown
6.27	A25825	chair back & side/arm panels	unknown
12.44	NN18218	watch	unknown
5.4	NN21169	candlestick	unknown
8.40	O2422	dish	Thames foreshore
1.40	O2455	pistol	unknown
6.7	VAL88[2127]<236>	buffet pediment or cresting	Blackfriars, Holborn Viaduct Station
6.63	75.1/37	chest end panel	unknown
1.24	78.45	musket	St Giles, north of Bastion
2.25	78.219	frying pan	unknown
1.22	79.262	musket	unknown
8.35	79.302	plate	unknown

Cat. no.	Acc. no.	Object	Provenance
2.2	79.319/4	bowl	unknown
6.30	79.319/10a	chair back	unknown
6.44	79.319/10b	lunette-shaped panel	unknown
8.158	79.319/6	porringer	unknown
6.82	80.152	chest end & lid panel	Trig Stairs River Thames
12.43	80.230/4	watch	Thames foreshore
12.43	80.230/9	watch	Thames foreshore
4.15	80.244/9	female figure	unknown
1.37	80.271/38	musket	unknown
10.1	80.536/2	coach with two occupants	Fulham foreshore
4.16	81.35/3	female figure	unknown
8.96	81.231/1	dish	unknown
4.22	81.231/2	female figure	unknown
5.15	81.302/7	fire shovel	Bankside
4.20	81.542/2	female figure	unknown
6.87	81.548/11	chest: sides & lid	Bull Wharf River Thames
6.80	81.548/12	chest end panel joined to side panel	Bull Wharf River Thames
8.76	81.580/2	dish	unknown
6.36	82.25/8	chair back crest	unknown
6.75	82.147/22	chest side panels	between London Bridge & Queenhithe River Thames
6.21	82.221/30	buffet door	unknown
4.21	82.353/1	female figure	Trig Stairs
10.7	82.353/14	coach frame with horse	unknown
6.20	82.353/21	buffet door	unknown
12.41	82.606/2	watch	Thames foreshore
8.101	82.606/6	dish	unknown
12.5	82.682/2	watch dial	Fishmongers' Hall foreshore
1.13	83.422/2	cannon	Bankside
8.19	83.628/7	dish	Trig Stairs
4.9	84.18	mounted Brit Lgt Dragoon	Wapping
6.18	84.152/3	buffet door	London Bridge River Thames
6.54	84.257/6	lunette-shaped panel	unknown
6.49	84.276/4	lunette-shaped panel	unknown
12.62	84.328/1	watch	Isleworth
8.92	84.328/2	dish	Isleworth
4.26	85.586	male figure	unknown
4.24	86.144/1	female figure	unknown
15.16	86.153	panel with key hole (chest?)	Cannon Street Railway Bridge
10.33	86.238/7	anchor	unknown
2.32	86.239/23	pot hanger	Queenhithe & Southwark Bridge, between
2.32	86.239/24	pot hanger	Queenhithe & Southwark Bridge, between
5.8	86.416/1	bellows	Cardinal Wharf, Southwark
15.14	87.83/1	frame	Butler's Wharf
8.62	87.98/6	plate	unknown
8.60	87.98/7	plate	unknown
12.17	87.147/2	watch	Thames foreshore
6.76	87.175/2	chest side panel	unknown
4.37	88.9/35	male figure, game hawker	unknown
12.43	88.36/3	watch	Thames foreshore
4.50	88.432/11	conical hat	Dockhead

Cat. no.	Acc. no.	Object	Provenance
2.5	90.245	cauldron	Thames Exchange spoil
8.137	90.342/4	porringer	Thames foreshore
10.16	91.61/1	English galleon	Bull Wharf
5.4	91.123/2	candlestick	Custom House Quay
12.29	91.204/2	watch	Thames foreshore
4.50	92.95/3	conical hat	unknown
6.5	94.43	buffet: lattice side panel	between Southwark Bridge & Cannon Street railway bridge, south side
12.21	94.100	watch	Westminster, north side opp Lambeth Palace
4.26	96.1	male figure	Blackfriars Bridge, north end
5.18	96.62/1	fire shovel	Blackfriars
5.11	96.62/2	fire shovel	Blackfriars
6.14	98.2/1	buffet – flat	Thames foreshore
6.5	98.2/2	buffet: lattice side panel	Thames foreshore
6.11	98.2/3	buffet: solid side panel	Thames foreshore
6.11	98.2/4	buffet: solid side panel	Thames foreshore
6.10	98.2/5	buffet: part of cupboard front	Thames foreshore
6.10	98.2/6	buffet: part of cupboard front	Thames foreshore
6.5	98.2/7	buffet: lattice side panel	Thames foreshore
15.3	98.2/8a & c	openwork panel (chest?)	Thames foreshore
6.18	98.2/9	buffet door	Thames foreshore
6.18	98.2/10	buffet door	Thames foreshore
6.19	98.2/11	buffet door	Thames foreshore
6.18	98.2/12	buffet door	Thames foreshore
6.11	98.2/12a	buffet: solid side panel	Thames foreshore
6.11	98.2/12b	buffet: solid side panel	Thames foreshore
6.19	98.2/13	buffet door	Thames foreshore
6.18	98.2/14	buffet door	Limekiln Dock
6.12	98.2/15	buffet side panel	Thames foreshore
6.18	98.2/16	buffet door	Thames foreshore
6.22	98.2/17	buffet door	Thames foreshore
6.74	98.2/18	chest side panel	Thames foreshore
6.6	98.2/19	buffet basin & part of stage	Thames foreshore
6.8	98.2/20a	buffet: fragments of cresting & plate	Thames foreshore
6.8	98.2/20b	buffet: fragments of cresting & plate	Thames foreshore
6.23	98.2/21	buffet plate	Thames foreshore
6.13	98.2/22	buffet side panels	Thames foreshore
6.15	98.2/23	buffet side panel	Thames foreshore
6.9	98.2/24a	buffet: part of back-board	Thames foreshore
6.9	98.2/24b	buffet: part of back-board	Thames foreshore
3.11	98.2/25	spoon	Thames foreshore
6.26	98.2/26	buffet plate	Thames foreshore
6.23	98.2/27	buffet plate	Thames foreshore
6.23	98.2/28	buffet plate	Thames foreshore
6.25	98.2/29	buffet plate	Thames foreshore
6.25	98.2/30	buffet plate	Thames foreshore
6.24	98.2/31	buffet plate	Thames foreshore
6.23	98.2/32	buffet plate	Thames foreshore
6.25	98.2/33	buffet plate	Thames foreshore
6.25	98.2/34	buffet plate	Thames foreshore

Cat. no.	Acc. no.	Object	Provenance
6.23	98.2/35	buffet plate	Thames foreshore
6.89	98.2/36	stool	Thames foreshore
6.83	98.2/39	chest lid	Thames foreshore
6.88	98.2/41	rocking cradle	Thames foreshore
6.81	98.2/42	chest end & lid panel	Thames foreshore
6.53	98.2/43	lunette-shaped panel	Thames foreshore
6.54	98.2/44	lunette-shaped panel	Thames foreshore
6.54	98.2/45	lunette-shaped panel	Thames foreshore
6.55	98.2/46	lunette-shaped panel	Thames foreshore
6.55	98.2/47	lunette-shaped panel	Thames foreshore
6.56	98.2/48	lunette-shaped panel	Thames foreshore
6.57	98.2/49	lunette-shaped panel	Thames foreshore
6.51	98.2/50	lunette-shaped panel	Thames foreshore
6.50	98.2/51	lunette-shaped panel	Thames foreshore
6.58	98.2/52	lunette-shaped panel	Thames foreshore
6.58	98.2/53	lunette-shaped panel	Thames foreshore
6.59	98.2/54	lunette-shaped panel	Thames foreshore
6.47	98.2/55	lunette-shaped panel	Three Cranes Wharf
6.44	98.2/56	lunette-shaped panel	Thames foreshore
6.45	98.2/57	lunette-shaped panel	Thames foreshore
6.44	98.2/58	lunette-shaped panel	Thames foreshore
6.44	98.2/59	lunette-shaped panel	Thames foreshore
6.44	98.2/60	lunette-shaped panel	Thames foreshore
6.44	98.2/61	lunette-shaped panel	Thames foreshore
6.45	98.2/62	lunette-shaped panel	Custom House Quay
6.44	98.2/63	lunette-shaped panel	Thames foreshore
6.44	98.2/64	lunette-shaped panel	Thames foreshore
6.84	98.2/65	chest lid fragment	Thames foreshore
6.85	98.2/66	possible chest lid fragment	Thames foreshore
6.71	98.2/67	chest end panel	Thames foreshore
6.72	98.2/68	chest end panel	Thames foreshore
6.69	98.2/69	chest end panel	Thames foreshore
6.68	98.2/70	chest end panel	Thames foreshore
6.61	98.2/71	lunette-shaped panel	Thames foreshore
4.32	98.2/72	male figure	Thames foreshore
6.62	98.2/73	lunette-shaped panel	Thames foreshore
6.48	98.2/74	lunette-shaped panel	Custom House Quay
6.64	98.2/75	chest end panel	Thames foreshore
6.64	98.2/76	chest end panel	Thames foreshore
6.64	98.2/77	chest end panel	Thames foreshore
6.65	98.2/78	chest end panel	Thames foreshore
6.66	98.2/79	chest end panel	Thames foreshore
6.67	98.2/80	chest end panel	Thames foreshore
6.75	98.2/82	chest side panels	Thames foreshore
14.1	98.2/83	windmill side panel	Thames foreshore
6.86	98.2/84	chest lid	Thames foreshore
6.86	98.2/85	chest lid	Thames foreshore
6.78	98.2/86	chest side panel	Thames foreshore
6.77	98.2/87	chest side panel	Thames foreshore
6.77	98.2/88	chest side panel	Thames foreshore

Cat. no.	Acc. no.	Object	Provenance
6.70	98.2/89	chest end panel	Thames foreshore
15.8	98.2/90	openwork panel (chest?)	Thames foreshore
6.39	98.2/91	possible chair back panel	Thames foreshore
6.52	98.2/92	lunette-shaped panel	Thames foreshore
6.16	98.2/93	buffet (?): leg & bracket scroll	Thames foreshore
6.40	98.2/94	chair	Thames foreshore
6.28	98.2/95	armchair back & side panel	Thames foreshore
6.33	98.2/97a	part of a chair back	Thames foreshore
6.34	98.2/97b	part of a chair back	Thames foreshore
6.35	98.2/98	chair seat	Queenhithe Dock
6.31	98.2/99	armchair back	Thames foreshore
6.38	98.2/100	possible chair back panels	Thames foreshore
6.38	98.2/101	possible chair back panels	Thames foreshore
6.41	98.2/103	chair back	Thames foreshore
6.42	98.2/104	chair back	Thames foreshore
6.43	98.2/105	chair back	Thames foreshore
6.37	98.2/106	chair cresting panel (?)	Thames foreshore
10.27	98.2/107	anchor	Gravesend
14.3	98.2/109	windmill sail	Queenhithe Dock
14.3	98.2/110	windmill sail	Thames foreshore
14.4	98.2/111	windmill sail	Thames foreshore
15.11	98.2/112	openwork panel	Thames foreshore
6.79	98.2/118	chest side panel	Thames foreshore
15.10	98.2/120	openwork panel	Thames foreshore
14.5	98.2/124	windmill sail	Thames foreshore
15.12	98.2/127	openwork panel?	Thames foreshore
6.3	98.2/128	bird cage	Thames foreshore
15.13	98.2/129	openwork panel	Thames foreshore
15.9	98.2/130	openwork panel	Thames foreshore
15.19	98.2/132	solid panel	Thames foreshore
14.2	98.2/135	windmill roof/side panel	Thames foreshore
15.26	98.2/136	solid panel	Southwark Bridge, north
6.32	98.2/140	chair top rail	Thames foreshore
15.20	98.2/142	solid panel	Thames foreshore
15.17	98.2/146	openwork panel (chair?)	Thames foreshore
15.25	98.2/148	solid panel	Thames foreshore
15.1	98.2/149	openwork panel	Thames foreshore
8.104	98.2/150	pear-shaped ewer	London Bridge
8.104	98.2/151	pear-shaped ewer	Thames foreshore
8.105	98.2/152	pear-shaped ewer	Thames foreshore
8.107	98.2/153	globular lidded ewer	Thames foreshore
8.108	98.2/154	pear-shaped ewer	Thames foreshore
8.123	98.2/156	baluster jug	Thames foreshore
8.121	98.2/157	baluster jug	Thames foreshore
8.122	98.2/158	baluster jug	Thames foreshore
8.124	98.2/159	pear-shaped jug	Billingsgate spoil
8.126	98.2/160	pear-shaped jug	Southwark Bridge south-west side
8.113	98.2/161	tripod ewer	Thames foreshore
8.114	98.2/162	tripod ewer	Thames foreshore
8.125	98.2/163	pear-shaped jug	Thames foreshore

Cat. no.	Acc. no.	Object	Provenance
8.111	98.2/164	cup-ewer	Wapping Station
8.110	98.2/165	cup-ewer, lidded	Tower of London
8.118	98.2/166	bridge-spouted ewer	Thames foreshore
8.116	98.2/167	bridge-spouted ewer	Thames foreshore
8.115	98.2/168	bridge-spouted ewer	Thames foreshore
8.117	98.2/169	bridge-spouted ewer	Thames foreshore
8.115	98.2/170	bridge-spouted ewer	Brook's Wharf
8.116	98.2/171	bridge-spouted ewer	Thames foreshore
8.116	98.2/172	bridge-spouted ewer	Thames foreshore
1.18	98.2/174	scabbard	Southwark Bridge, south side
6.86	98.2/176	chest lid	Thames foreshore
8.116	98.2/177	bridge-spouted ewer	Thames foreshore
8.109	98.2/178	cup-ewer	Brook's Wharf
8.130	98.2/179	standing bowl	Brook's Wharf
8.129	98.2/180	standing bowl	Thames foreshore
8.131	98.2/181	standing bowl	Southwark foreshore
2.27	98.2/182	frying pan	Thames foreshore
2.18	98.2/183	frying pan	Thames foreshore
2.19	98.2/184	frying pan	Thames foreshore
2.18	98.2/185	frying pan	Thames foreshore
2.22	98.2/186	frying pan	Thames foreshore
2.26	98.2/187	frying pan	Thames foreshore
2.21	98.2/188	frying pan	Thames foreshore
2.24	98.2/189	frying pan	Thames foreshore
2.20	98.2/190	frying pan	Thames foreshore
2.19	98.2/191	frying pan	Thames foreshore
2.10	98.2/192	cauldron	Thames foreshore
8.42	98.2/193	dish or basin	Thames foreshore
2.34	98.2/194	skillet	Thames foreshore
2.7	98.2/195	cauldron	London Bridge, north side
2.6	98.2/196	cauldron	London Bridge, south side
2.8	98.2/197	cauldron	Thames foreshore
2.11	98.2/198	cauldron	Thames foreshore
2.2	98.2/199	bowl	Thames foreshore
2.4	98.2/200	bowl	Thames foreshore
2.2	98.2/201	bowl	Thames foreshore
2.2	98.2/202	bowl	Thames foreshore
2.1	98.2/203	bowl	Thames foreshore
2.3	98.2/204	bowl	Thames foreshore
2.2	98.2/205	bowl	Thames foreshore
8.67	98.2/207	dish	Thames foreshore
2.23	98.2/208	frying pan	Thames foreshore
8.68	98.2/209	dish	Thames foreshore
8.20	98.2/211	dish or basin	Thames foreshore
8.23	98.2/213	dish	Thames foreshore
8.24	98.2/215	dish	Thames foreshore
8.136	98.2/216	porringer	Thames foreshore
8.134	98.2/217	porringer	Thames foreshore
8.137	98.2/218	porringer	Thames foreshore
8.137	98.2/219	porringer	Thames foreshore

Cat. no.	Acc. no.	Object	Provenance
8.137	98.2/220	porringer	Thames foreshore
8.137	98.2/221	porringer	Thames foreshore
8.144	98.2/222	porringer	Thames foreshore
8.137	98.2/223	porringer	Thames foreshore
8.137	98.2/224	porringer	Thames foreshore
8.135	98.2/225	porringer	Thames foreshore
8.140	98.2/226	porringer	Thames foreshore
8.133	98.2/227	porringer	Thames foreshore
8.139	98.2/228	porringer	Thames foreshore
8.149	98.2/229	porringer	Thames foreshore
8.147	98.2/230	porringer	Thames foreshore
8.146	98.2/231	porringer	Thames foreshore
8.148	98.2/232	porringer	Thames foreshore
8.138	98.2/233	porringer	Thames foreshore
8.145	98.2/234	porringer	Thames foreshore
8.142	98.2/235	porringer	Thames foreshore
8.154	98.2/236	porringer	Thames foreshore
8.153	98.2/237	porringer	Thames foreshore
8.152	98.2/238	porringer	Thames foreshore
8.156	98.2/239	porringer	Thames foreshore
8.151	98.2/240	porringer	Thames foreshore
8.150	98.2/241	porringer	Thames foreshore
8.141	98.2/242	porringer	Thames foreshore
8.155	98.2/244	porringer	Thames foreshore
8.31	98.2/245	plate	Thames foreshore
8.31	98.2/246	plate	Bull Wharf
8.31	98.2/247	plate	Thames foreshore
8.31	98.2/248	plate	Thames foreshore
8.31	98.2/249	plate	Thames foreshore
8.32	98.2/250	dish	Thames foreshore
8.32	98.2/251	dish	Thames foreshore
8.32	98.2/252	dish	Thames foreshore
8.32	98.2/254	dish	Thames foreshore
8.7	98.2/255	plate	Thames foreshore
8.8	98.2/256	dish	Thames foreshore
8.10	98.2/257	dish	Thames foreshore
8.9	98.2/258	dish or plate	Thames foreshore
8.9	98.2/259	dish or plate	Thames foreshore
8.12	98.2/260	dish or basin	Thames foreshore
8.80	98.2/261	plate	Globe Theatre site
8.57	98.2/262	plate	Thames foreshore
8.84	98.2/263	plate, octagonal	Thames foreshore
8.66	98.2/264	plate or charger	Thames foreshore
8.22	98.2/265	dish or basin	Thames foreshore
8.2	98.2/266	dish or plate	Thames foreshore
8.30	98.2/267	dish or plate	Custom House Quay
8.81	98.2/268	plate	Thames foreshore
8.33	98.2/269	dish	Thames foreshore
8.43	98.2/270	plate or charger	Thames foreshore
8.85	98.2/271	dish	Thames foreshore

Cat. no.	Acc. no.	Object	Provenance
8.85	98.2/272	dish	Thames foreshore
8.53	98.2/273	plate	Thames foreshore
8.61	98.2/274	dish or charger	Thames foreshore
8.86	98.2/275	dish	Thames foreshore
8.89	98.2/276	dish	Thames foreshore
8.102	98.2/277	dish (?)	Thames foreshore
8.102	98.2/278	dish (?)	Custom House Quay
8.102	98.2/279	dish (?)	Custom House Quay
8.102	98.2/280	dish (?)	Custom House Quay
8.100	98.2/281	dish	Thames foreshore
8.29	98.2/282	dish	Thames foreshore
8.92	98.2/283	dish	Globe Theatre site
8.92	98.2/284	dish	Thames foreshore
8.93	98.2/285	dish	Thames foreshore
8.94	98.2/286	dish	Thames foreshore
8.95	98.2/287	dish	Thames foreshore
8.15	98.2/288	plate	Thames foreshore
8.28	98.2/289	dish	Thames foreshore
8.37	98.2/290	dish or plate	Thames foreshore
8.27	98.2/291	dish	Dockhead
8.51	98.2/292	dish or plate	Thames foreshore
8.38	98.2/293	plate	Thames foreshore
8.47	98.2/294	plate	Thames foreshore
8.50	98.2/295	dish	Thames foreshore
8.49	98.2/296	dish	Thames foreshore
8.48	98.2/297	dish	Queenhithe Dock
8.79	98.2/298	plate	Limekiln Dock
8.13	98.2/299	dish	Thames foreshore
8.21	98.2/300	dish	Thames foreshore
8.46	98.2/301	plate	Limekiln Dock
8.88	98.2/302	dish	Thames foreshore
8.90	98.2/303	dish	Thames foreshore
8.82	98.2/304	plate	Thames foreshore
8.87	98.2/306	dish	Thames foreshore
8.87	98.2/307	dish	Thames foreshore
8.39	98.2/309	plate	Thames foreshore
8.20	98.2/310	dish or basin	Thames foreshore
8.5	98.2/311	dish	Thames foreshore
8.16	98.2/312	dish	Thames foreshore
8.3	98.2/313	dish or plate	Swan Stairs
8.1	98.2/314	dish or plate	Thames foreshore
8.6	98.2/315	dish	Thames foreshore
8.37	98.2/316	dish or plate	Thames foreshore
8.36	98.2/317	plate	Thames foreshore
8.143	98.2/318	porringer	Thames foreshore
8.143	98.2/319	porringer	Thames foreshore
8.157	98.2/320	porringer	Thames foreshore
8.17	98.2/321	dish	Thames foreshore
8.25	98.2/323	dish or basin	Thames foreshore
8.91	98.2/324	dish	Southwark Bridge, south side

Cat. no.	Acc. no.	Object	Provenance
8.64	98.2/325	plate	London Bridge north side
8.83	98.2/326	plate	Thames foreshore
8.98	98.2/327	dish or plate	Thames foreshore
8.11	98.2/328	dish or plate	Thames foreshore
8.97	98.2/329	dish or plate	Thames foreshore
8.36	98.2/330	plate	Thames foreshore
8.100	98.2/331	dish	Thames foreshore
8.100	98.2/332	dish	Thames foreshore
8.68	98.2/335	dish	Thames foreshore
8.72	98.2/336	dish	Thames foreshore
8.75	98.2/337	dish	Thames foreshore
8.77	98.2/338	dish	Thames foreshore
8.74	98.2/340	dish	Tower foreshore
8.73	98.2/341	dish	Thames foreshore
8.70	98.2/342	dish	Thames foreshore
8.71	98.2/343	dish	Thames foreshore
8.59	98.2/344	plate	Thames foreshore
8.68	98.2/345	dish	Thames foreshore
8.18	98.2/346	dish	Thames foreshore
8.63	98.2/347	plate	Thames foreshore
8.45	98.2/348	plate or charger	Southwark Bridge
8.20	98.2/349	dish or basin	Thames foreshore
8.26	98.2/350	dish	Thames foreshore
8.56	98.2/351	dish	Thames foreshore
8.58	98.2/352	dish or charger	Thames foreshore
8.68	98.2/353	dish	Thames foreshore
8.54	98.2/355	plate	Southwark Bridge north
8.34	98.2/356	Platter	Thames foreshore
8.52	98.2/357	dish or basin	Thames foreshore
8.65	98.2/358	plate	Limekiln Dock
8.44	98.2/359	dish or basin	Thames foreshore
8.68	98.2/360	dish	Thames foreshore
8.55	98.2/361	plate	Thames foreshore
8.69	98.2/362	dish	Thames foreshore
8.99	98.2/363	dish or plate	Thames foreshore
8.14	98.2/364	dish	Thames foreshore
8.103	98.2/365	coffee pot	Southwark bridge, north end
8.132	98.2/366	qine bottle	Thames foreshore
4.27	98.2/367	male figure	Thames foreshore
4.26	98.2/368	male figure	Thames foreshore
4.26	98.2/369	male figure	Thames foreshore
4.26	98.2/370	male figure	Thames foreshore
4.26	98.2/371	male figure	Thames foreshore
4.28	98.2/372	male figure	Thames foreshore
4.26	98.2/373	male figure	Thames foreshore
4.26	98.2/374	male figure	Thames foreshore
4.26	98.2/375	male figure	Thames foreshore
4.30	98.2/376	male figure	Thames foreshore
4.29	98.2/377	male figure	Thames foreshore
4.36	98.2/378	male figure (?)	Dockhead

Cat. no.	Acc. no.	Object	Provenance
4.41	98.2/379	male figure	Thames foreshore
4.43	98.2/380	male figure, military	Thames foreshore
4.38	98.2/381	male figure	Thames foreshore
4.47	98.2/382	male figure (pirate?)	Limekiln Dock
4.39	98.2/383	male figure	Thames foreshore
4.40	98.2/384	male figure	Thames foreshore
4.45	98.2/385	male figure, military	Thames foreshore
4.48	98.2/386	male figure, flautist	Thames foreshore
4.46	98.2/387	male figure, military	Thames foreshore
4.42	98.2/388	male figure	Thames foreshore
4.44	98.2/389	male figure, military	Thames foreshore
4.49	98.2/390	male figure, harlequin	Thames foreshore
4.19	98.2/391	female figure	by Southwark Bridge
4.37	98.2/392	male figure, game hawker	Thames foreshore
10.11	98.2/393	chaise with driver	Thames foreshore
10.11	98.2/394	chaise with driver	Thames foreshore
10.13	98.2/395	chaise with driver	Thames foreshore
10.12	98.2/396	chaise with driver	Thames foreshore
10.11	98.2/397	chaise with driver	Thames foreshore
4.34	98.2/398	male figure	Thames foreshore
4.35	98.2/399	male figure	Greenwich
4.33	98.2/400	male figure	Thames foreshore
1.1	98.2/402	morion	Thames foreshore
4.51	98.2/403	hat with brim	Bull Wharf
4.1	98.2/404	mounted knight	Billingsgate site spoil
4.2	98.2/405	mounted knight	Thames foreshore
4.4	98.2/406	mounted knight	Thames foreshore
4.3	98.2/407	mounted knight	Thames foreshore
4.5	98.2/408	mounted knight	Thames foreshore
4.5	98.2/409	mounted knight	Thames foreshore
4.10	98.2/410	mounted soldier	Thames foreshore
4.12	98.2/411	mounted figure Dragoon	Thames foreshore
4.11	98.2/412	mounted figure Dragoon	Thames foreshore
4.7	98.2/413	mounted soldier Dragoon	Thames foreshore
4.8	98.2/414	mounted figure Dragoon	Limekiln Dock
4.30	98.2/415a	male figure	Dockhead
10.10	98.2/416	coach with passenger	Thames foreshore
15.18	98.2/417	openwork panel or door	Southwark Bridge, north
10.3	98.2/418	coach side with occupant	Thames foreshore
10.4	98.2/419	coach side with occupant	Thames foreshore
10.6	98.2/420	coach front panel with driver	Queenhithe Dock, entrance to
10.8	98.2/421	coach horse	Queenhithe Dock, entrance to
10.14	98.2/422	coach wheel / part of axle	Thames foreshore
10.15	98.2/423	coach wheel	Thames foreshore
10.2	98.2/424	coach	Thames foreshore
10.9	98.2/425	coach horse	Thames foreshore
10.8	98.2/426	coach horse	Queenhithe Dock, entrance to
4.6	98.2/427	mounted figure	Thames foreshore
10.5	98.2/428	coach side with occupant	Queenhithe Dock, entrance to
10.16	98.2/431	English galleon	Billingsgate foreshore

Cat. no.	Acc. no.	Object	Provenance
10.17	98.2/432	three-masted ship	Thames foreshore
4.13	98.2/433	female figure	Thames foreshore
4.14	98.2/434	female figure	Thames foreshore
4.17	98.2/435	female figure	Thames foreshore
4.18	98.2/436	female figure	Dockhead
4.21	98.2/437	female figure	Dockhead
4.23	98.2/439	milkmaid	Thames foreshore
4.25	98.2/440	female figure	Thames foreshore
12.43	98.2/442	watch	Southwark Bridge, under north end
12.24	98.2/443	watch	Thames foreshore
12.42	98.2/444	watch	Thames foreshore
12.26	98.2/445	watch	Southwark Bridge, north end
12.36	98.2/446	watch	Thames foreshore
12.42	98.2/447	watch	Thames foreshore
12.42	98.2/448	watch	Thames foreshore
12.28	98.2/449	watch	Thames foreshore
12.42	98.2/450	watch	Thames foreshore
12.42	98.2/451	watch	Thames foreshore
12.42	98.2/452	watch	Thames foreshore
12.70	98.2/453	watch	Queenhithe
12.12	98.2/454	watch	Thames foreshore
12.42	98.2/455	watch	Thames foreshore
12.42	98.2/457	watch	Thames foreshore
12.15	98.2/458	watch	Globe Theatre site
12.45	98.2/459	watch	Thames foreshore
12.54	98.2/460	watch	Thames foreshore
12.43	98.2/461	watch	Thames foreshore
12.53	98.2/462	watch	Thames foreshore
12.53	98.2/463	watch	Thames foreshore
12.43	98.2/464	watch	Thames foreshore
12.26	98.2/465	watch	Blackfriars Bridge, south side
12.39	98.2/466	watch	London Bridge
12.29	98.2/467	watch	Thames foreshore
12.9	98.2/468	watch	Thames foreshore
12.38	98.2/469	watch	Thames foreshore
12.28	98.2/470	watch	Thames foreshore
12.18	98.2/471	watch	Thames foreshore
12.5	98.2/472	watch dial	Thames foreshore
12.19	98.2/473	watch	Thames foreshore
12.1	98.2/474	watch dial	Thames foreshore
12.1	98.2/475	watch dial	Thames foreshore
12.38	98.2/476	watch	Thames foreshore
12.32	98.2/477	watch	Thames foreshore
12.20	98.2/478	watch	Thames foreshore
12.29	98.2/479	watch	Thames foreshore
12.27	98.2/480	watch	Thames foreshore
12.16	98.2/481	watch	Bankside
12.15	98.2/482	watch	Thames foreshore
12.15	98.2/483	watch	Thames foreshore
12.15	98.2/484	watch	Thames foreshore

Cat. no.	Acc. no.	Object	Provenance
12.15	98.2/485	watch	Thames foreshore
12.33	98.2/487	watch	Thames foreshore
12.57	98.2/488	watch	Thames foreshore
12.15	98.2/489	watch	Thames foreshore
12.40	98.2/490	watch	Thames foreshore
12.37	98.2/491	watch	Thames foreshore
12.14	98.2/492	watch	Thames foreshore
12.43	98.2/493	watch	Thames foreshore
12.43	98.2/494	watch	Thames foreshore
12.46	98.2/495	watch	Thames foreshore
12.58	98.2/496	watch	Thames foreshore
12.54	98.2/497	watch	Thames foreshore
12.13	98.2/498	watch	Thames foreshore
12.30	98.2/499	watch	Thames foreshore
12.44	98.2/500	watch	Thames foreshore
12.35	98.2/501	watch	Thames foreshore
12.68	98.2/502	watch	Thames foreshore
12.37	98.2/503	watch	Thames foreshore
12.46	98.2/504	watch	Thames foreshore
12.36	98.2/505	watch	Thames foreshore
12.31	98.2/506	watch	Tower of London
12.10	98.2/507	watch	Thames foreshore
12.18	98.2/508	watch	Thames foreshore
12.55	98.2/509	watch	Thames foreshore
12.15	98.2/510	watch	Thames foreshore
12.56	98.2/511	watch	Thames foreshore
12.15	98.2/512	watch	Thames foreshore
12.22	98.2/513	watch	Thames foreshore
12.59	98.2/514	watch	Thames foreshore
12.69	98.2/515	watch	Thames foreshore
12.34	98.2/516	watch	Thames foreshore
12.25	98.2/517	watch	Thames foreshore
12.15	98.2/518	watch	Thames foreshore
12.48	98.2/519	watch	Thames foreshore
12.23	98.2/521	watch	Thames foreshore
12.43	98.2/522	watch	Thames foreshore
12.43	98.2/523	watch	Globe Theatre site
12.49	98.2/524	watch	-Thames foreshore
12.48	98.2/525	watch	Limekiln Dock
12.67	98.2/526	watch	Thames foreshore
12.63	98.2/527	watch	Thames foreshore
12.65	98.2/529	watch	Thames foreshore
12.64	98.2/530	watch	Thames foreshore
12.66	98.2/531	watch	Thames foreshore
12.61	98.2/532	watch	Custom House
12.61	98.2/533	watch	Thames foreshore
12.61	98.2/534	watch	Thames foreshore
5.1	98.2/539	candlestick	Thames foreshore
5.3	98.2/540	candlestick	Thames foreshore
5.6	98.2/541	candlestick	Southwark Bridge, north side

Cat. no.	Acc. no.	Object	Provenance
5.5	98.2/542	candlestick	West London foreshore
5.5	98.2/543	candlestick	Thames foreshore
5.5	98.2/544	candlestick	Thames foreshore
5.2	98.2/545	candlestick	Bankside
9.1	98.2/546	hand-saw	Thames foreshore
3.8	98.2/547	spoon	Thames foreshore
3.10	98.2/548	spoon, ball-knopped	Thames foreshore
3.7	98.2/549	spoon, slip top	Thames foreshore
3.9	98.2/550	spoon	Thames foreshore
3.9	98.2/551	spoon	Thames foreshore
3.11	98.2/552	spoon	Thames foreshore
3.11	98.2/553	spoon	Thames foreshore
3.11	98.2/554	spoon	Thames foreshore
3.12	98.2/555	spoon	Thames foreshore
3.12	98.2/556	spoon	Thames foreshore
3.12	98.2/557	spoon	Thames foreshore
3.15	98.2/558	spoon	Thames foreshore
3.14	98.2/559	spoon	Thames foreshore
3.13	98.2/560	spoon	Thames foreshore
3.2	98.2/561	fork	Thames foreshore
3.2	98.2/562	fork	Thames foreshore
3.3	98.2/563	fork	Thames foreshore
3.5	98.2/564	knife	Thames foreshore
3.6	98.2/565	knife	Dockhead
3.4	98.2/566	knife	Thames foreshore
3.4	98.2/568	knife	Thames foreshore
3.1	98.2/569	fork	Thames foreshore
9.2	98.2/570	shears	Thames foreshore
9.3	98.2/571	scissors	Thames foreshore
5.28	98.2/574	voider	Thames foreshore
2.13	98.2/575	dripping pan	Thames foreshore
5.26	98.2/576	picture	Thames foreshore
5.27	98.2/577	tray	Thames foreshore
2.12	98.2/578	dripping pan	Thames foreshore
2.13	98.2/579	dripping pan	Thames foreshore
2.16	98.2/580	dripping pan	Thames foreshore
2.15	98.2/581	dripping pan	Thames foreshore
15.27	98.2/582	solid panel	Thames foreshore
15.28	98.2/583	solid panel	Thames foreshore
2.28	98.2/584	gridiron	Thames foreshore
2.29	98.2/585	gridiron	Thames foreshore
2.30	98.2/586	gridiron	Thames foreshore
2.31	98.2/587	gridiron	Thames foreshore
2.31	98.2/588	gridiron	Thames foreshore
2.33	98.2/589	pot hanger	Thames foreshore
2.35	98.2/590	spit	Thames foreshore
5.24	98.2/591	mirror frame	Thames foreshore
5.22	98.2/592	probable mirror frame	Thames foreshore
5.23	98.2/593	mirror frame	Thames foreshore
5.21	98.2/594	mirror	Southwark Bridge north side

Cat. no.	Acc. no.	Object	Provenance
5.25	98.2/595	mirror frame	Thames foreshore
6.1	98.2/596	bird cage	Thames foreshore
6.2	98.2/597	bird cage	Thames foreshore
2.15	98.2/598	dripping pan	Thames foreshore
2.14	98.2/599	dripping pan	Thames foreshore
2.13	98.2/600	dripping pan	Thames foreshore
2.15	98.2/601	dripping pan	Thames foreshore
5.20	98.2/602	fire tongs	Thames foreshore
5.7	98.2/603	andiron	Southwark Bridge, north side
5.10	98.2/604	fire grate	Tower of London
5.9	98.2/606	fire grate	Thames foreshore
5.16	98.2/607	fire shovel	Southwark Bridge, culvert s-e end
5.17	98.2/608	fire shovel	Thames foreshore
5.12	98.2/609	fire shovel	Thames foreshore, Limekiln Dock
5.14	98.2/610	fire shovel	Thames foreshore
5.19	98.2/611	fire shovel	Thames foreshore
5.13	98.2/612	fire shovel	Thames foreshore
6.4	98.2/614	bird cage	Southwark Bridge, north
6.4	98.2/615	bird cage	Bull Wharf
8.127	98.2/616	lid	Thames foreshore
15.22	98.2/617	disc	Thames foreshore
15.24	98.2/618	porringer (?)	Southwark Bridge north
12.4	98.2/619	case back panel	Thames foreshore
12.6	98.2/620	case back panel	Thames foreshore
12.7	98.2/621	case back panel	Thames foreshore
15.21	98.2/622	disc	Thames foreshore
12.2	98.2/623	case lid panel	Thames foreshore
12.3	98.2/624	case lid or back panel	Thames foreshore
15.29	98.2/625	toy house front	Bull Wharf
15.23	98.2/626	disc	Thames foreshore
15.4	98.2/628	openwork panel	Southwark Bridge
15.5	98.2/629	openwork panel	Thames foreshore
15.5	98.2/630	openwork panel	Thames foreshore
15.6	98.2/631	openwork panel	Southwark Bridge, north side
15.7	98.2/632	openwork panel	Thames foreshore
15.15	98.2/633	openwork panel (chest?)	Thames foreshore
1.11	98.2/634	cannon	South Bank
1.6	98.2/636	cannon	Thames foreshore
1.7	98.2/638	cannon	Custom House Quay
1.14	98.2/639	cannon	Dockhead
1.4	98.2/640	cannon	Greenwich
1.15	98.2/641	cannon	Dockhead
1.4	98.2/642	cannon	Thames foreshore
1.5	98.2/643	cannon	Greenwich
1.10	98.2/644	cannon	Rotherhithe
1.9	98.2/645	cannon	Thames foreshore
1.12	98.2/646	cannon	Greenwich
1.9	98.2/647	cannon	Thames foreshore
1.8	98.2/648	cannon	Limekiln Dock
1.33	98.2/650	musket	Thames foreshore

CONCORDANCE

Cat. no.	Acc. no.	Object	Provenance
1.27	98.2/651	musket	Thames foreshore
1.47	98.2/652	pistol	Brook's Wharf
1.2	98.2/653	artillery rammer	Thames foreshore
1.2	98.2/654	artillery rammer	Thames foreshore
1.39	98.2/655	petronel	Thames foreshore
6.13	98.2/656	buffet side panels	Thames foreshore
1.17	98.2/659	gun carriage	Wapping
1.21	98.2/660	sword	Dockhead
1.39	98.2/661	petronel	Southwark Bridge, north
1.50	98.2/662	rammer	Custom House Quay
1.49	98.2/665	rammer	Brook's Wharf
11.2	98.2/667	twirler	Thames foreshore
11.1	98.2/668	twirler	Dockhead
11.1	98.2/669	twirler	Dockhead
7.3	98.2/680	shy cock	Thames foreshore
7.4	98.2/682	shy	Thames foreshore
7.1	98.2/683	shy cock	Thames foreshore
7.2	98.2/684	shy cock	Thames foreshore
15.2	98.2/685	openwork panel (chair?)	Greenwich
6.46	98.2/686	lunette-shaped panel	Queenhithe
10.38	98.2/687	anchor	Thames foreshore
10.39	98.2/688	anchor	Thames foreshore
10.25	98.2/689	anchor	Thames foreshore
10.28	98.2/690	anchor	Thames foreshore
10.34	98.2/691	anchor	Thames foreshore
10.19	98.2/692	anchor	Thames foreshore
10.18	98.2/693	anchor	Thames foreshore
10.21	98.2/694	anchor	Thames foreshore
10.20	98.2/695	anchor	Thames foreshore
10.35	98.2/696	anchor	Thames foreshore
10.26	98.2/697	anchor	Thames foreshore
10.23	98.2/698	anchor	Thames foreshore
10.22	98.2/699	anchor	Limekiln Dock
10.24	98.2/700	anchor	Gravesend
10.29	98.2/701	anchor	Limekiln Dock
10.36	98.2/702	anchor	Thames foreshore
10.37	98.2/703	anchor	Thames foreshore
10.32	98.2/704	anchor	Thames foreshore
10.31	98.2/705	anchor	Thames foreshore
10.30	98.2/706	anchor	Thames foreshore
13.4	98.2/708	whirligig	Brook's Wharf
13.3	98.2/709	whirligig	Thames foreshore
13.1	98.2/710	whirligig	Queenhithe
13.6	98.2/711	whirligig	Thames foreshore
13.7	98.2/712	whirligig	Billingsgate foreshore
13.2	98.2/713	whirligig	Limekiln Dock
13.5	98.2/714	whirligig	Thames foreshore
13.8	98.2/715	whirligig	Thames foreshore
13.9	98.2/716	whirligig	Queenhithe Dock
13.10	98.2/717	whirligig	Thames foreshore

Cat. no.	Acc. no.	Object	Provenance
6.58	98.2/718	lunette-shaped panel	Three Cranes Wharf
6.55	98.2/719	lunette-shaped panel	Thames foreshore
6.29	99.153	armchair back & side panels	between Blackfriars & Trig Lane
1.3	2000.59	cannon	Bull Wharf
12.43	2001.15/1	watch	Thames foreshore
12.47	2001.15/2	watch	Thames foreshore
12.50	2001.15/3	watch	Thames foreshore
12.51	2001.15/4	watch	Thames foreshore
8.106	2001.20/1	pear-shaped lidded ewer	Billingsgate site spoil
8.112	2001.20/2	tripod ewer	Butler's Wharf
3.7	2001.20/3	spoon, slip top	Bull Wharf
6.69	2001.20/4	chest end panel	Bull Wharf
10.1	2001.20/6	coach with two occupants	unknown
1.20	2001.20/7	sword guard	Queenhithe
12.8	2001.20/9	watch	Brook's Wharf
1.19	2001.20/12	sword hilt	Brook's Wharf
7.5	2001.20/14	shy	Rotherhithe
4.31	2001.21/5	male figure	Brook's Wharf
6.73	2001.21/25	chest end panel	unknown
8.4	4106	plate	unknown
8.31	4107	plate	London
1.36	7738	musket	Brook's' Wharf
1.42	7739	pistol	Bunhill Row
1.25	7740	musket	Thames
1.46	7743	pistol	London
1.43	7744	pistol	London
1.41	7745	pistol	London
1.35	7746	musket	London
2.9	7860	cauldron	London Wall
8.119	8193	tripod ewer	Brook's Wharf
6.75	8851	chest side panels	Thames near London Bridge; 1866
1.29	11697	musket	South Place Chapel, site of
6.22	21635	buffet door	unknown
1.38	21642	musket	unknown
8.137	21657	porringer	unknown
2.17	Private collection	frying pan	unknown
3.11	Private collection	spoon	Bull Wharf
6.17	Private collection	buffet: leg & bracket scroll from cupboard front	Brook's Wharf
6.60	Private collection	lunette-shaped panel	unknown
8.128	Private collection	lidded tankard	Dockhead
12.60	Private collection	watch	unknown

Index

Abbots Lane, Southwark (Bermondsey) 27, 225, 227, 391
Adam, Robert 218
Addison, Joseph 24–5
adult clientèle 47, 50
Aertsen, Pieter, *Retour d'un pèlerinage à Saint Antoine* 368
AF (maker) 44
Albrecht V, Duke of Bavaria 48
alloy terminology and analysis 52, 54–5, 410–35
America 30, 50, 77, 81, 324, 325, 388
   New York 30
      Metropolitan Museum of Art 217
   Washington, Shakespeare Folger Library 283, 294
ampullae, pilgrims' 60, 144
Amsterdam 54, 81, 146, 234, 283, 324, 345
anchors 324–31
andirons (firedogs) 184
Angetel, William 111
animal figurines 59, 64, 143
Anne, Queen 173
antimony 54, 55
antler peg-doll figure 60, 140
Antony, St, of Egypt 368
Antwerp, Royal Museum of Fine Art 279
Appleford hoard 410
archaeological contexts of toys 26–31
Ariès, Philippe 58
armour 77, 78
arms 76–105
Arnold, Janet 48
arquebuses (petronels) 97
artillery rammers (ramrods) 79
Augsburg 50
Austin, Job 436, 438
axes 64

'babies' (dolls) 42, 152

Baby Houses 48–51
baluster jugs 288–90
Bambergischen halzgerichts und rechtich Ordenung 119
Bankside 84, 182
barge beds 11, 15
barges 11
bark boat 30
Bartholomew (or St Bartholomew) Fair 36–7, 39, 148, 165
basins 245–74
  see also dishes; plates; saucers
Basle, Kunstmuseum 280
Battersea 286, 287
Bayeux Tapestry 324
Beasly, Francis *see* Beeslee
Becket, Thomas 146
Becket souvenir badges 324
Beckingham Hall, Tolleshunt Major, Essex 211
Beeslee (or Beasly), Francis 55, 343, 344, 345, 372, 436, 437
Belgium
   Antwerp, Royal Museum of Fine Art 279
   Bruges 152
      Groenige Museum 294
   Brussels, Meyers Collection 146
   Louvain 388
   Malines, Busleyden Museum 202
bellows 185
Bendall, S. 353, 355, 358, 373, 377
Bermondsey (Southwark), Abbots Lane 27, 225, 227, 391
Bible de Jean de Sy 234
Billingsgate 22, 27, 87, 91, 138, 142, 144, 280, 290, 323, 389
bird
   hollow-cast 59, 63–4, 143
   lead-sheet 60

bird cages 197–8
bird figures (shy cocks) 29, 67, 238–41
Blackfriars Bridge 17
Blackmore, Howard, *Elizabethan Toy Guns* 81, 87, 89
Blacksmiths' Company 337
Blair, Claude, *Pistols of the World* 98
boats 30, *see also* ships
Borderware 245
bottles 295
bowls 110
   (standing bowls) 58–9, 63, 294
brass, definition 52
Brasted, Henry 438
bread trenchers 243, 244
Bridall foundry, Exeter 128
Bridewell Estate foreshore, Wapping 15
bridge-spouted ewers 285–7
Bridge Wharf 11
British Museum 287, 349
Broadhurst, Jonathan 436
brooches 64, 146
Brook's Wharf 96, 103, 104, 210, 282, 285, 287, 294, 349
Bruegel, Pieter, *De Kinderspelen* 363, 396
Bruges
   Belgium 152
   Groenige Museum 294
Brune, Johan de, *Emblemata op Zinnewerck* 142
Buckinghamshire 29
buffets (cupboards) 27, 43, 195, 197–212
   doors 210–12
   plates 212
Bull Wharf 81, 123, 137, 138, 154, 176, 224, 256, 293, 406
Bunhill Row 100
Burgundy, Duc Phillippe of 200
Burke, T. 12
Burton, James 34

Busleyden Museum, Malines 202
Butler, R. and Green, C. 128
Butler's Wharf 120, 197, 283
buzz wheels (whirligigs) 67, 119, 121, 386–91

Campbell, Robert 43
Campion Cup 294
candlesticks 29, 181–3
cannon 29, 30, 55, 65, 79–84
Canterbury, Kent 146
carriages 168, 316–22
Caspall, J. 181, 182, 183
Castile, arms of 86
casting process 56–7
Catholic Church 39
Cats, Jacob
　Houwelijck: 'Kinderspel' 75, 180, 187, 334
　Schoon voor-doen is half verkocht 153
cauldrons 29, 65, 111–15
　full-size 113, 115, 163
Cawarden, Thomas 214
Cescinsky, H. 224
chairs 65, 213–18
Chasse des Dames, La 168, 320
chaises 66, 143, 321–2
　see also carriages
Chambers Journal 40
Champion, Lady Barbara 204
Champion, Sir Richard 204–5
chapmen 35
chargers 244
Charlecote standing bowl 294
Charles the Bold 202
Charles I 337
Chelmsford, Essex 86
chests 29, 43, 65, 195–6, 218–32, 401
　end/lid panels 230
　end panels 224–7
　end/side panels 229–30
　lid panels 220–4, 231–2
　side/lid panels 232
　side panels 228–9
Child, Coles 34
children, numbers of 41
children's play 20–5, 30, 31, 51, 58, 59, 179–80, 184
　views of 23, 36, 75, 108, 142, 180, 187, 233, 333, 334, 363
chimneys 184

Chinnery, Victor, *English Oak Furniture* 202, 214, 215, 222, 223
Chippendale, Thomas 217
Chiquart (French cook), *Du Fait de Cuisine* 113
chivalry 142, 144
Chretien de Hondt, Abbot of the Dunes, near Furnes 279
Christ 64
Christie's *Antique Arms and Armour* 81
Christmas present-giving 42
City Ditch 263
City of London 13, 15, 22
　arms of 43, 44, 201, 202, 204, 205, 206, 208, 209, 211, 225
Civil War 149, 150
Claeissens, Anthony, *Banquet* 294
Clement, St 324
Clockmakers' Company 337, 349, 353, 355, 358, 373, 377, 382
coaches 66, 316–22
coal 184, 185
coffee pots 277
coins, adapted to whirligigs 388, 389
Colchester, Essex 86
collecting 48–51
Collot, Pierre 202
Cologne 154
consumers 47–8
Continental fashions in toys and collecting 48–50
Cooke, Edward W. *View of new London Bridge* 21, 324
cooking vessels and utensils 106–31
Copenhagen City Museum 29
copper alloy toys, discussion of manufacture 52–7
Coronation coach souvenir (Matchbox) 317
Corpus Christi College, Cambridge 283
Coryat, Thomas 134
Cotgrave, *Dictionary of the French and English Tongues* 32
Cotterell, H.H. 259
cradles 234
'Cries of London' series (Laroon) 43, 143, 171, 172, 197
Crofts, J. 316
Crosfield, Robert 439
Crossbowman's Guild 368
Crown Estate Commissioners 15

cupboard cloths 202, 204
cupboards see buffets
cup-ewers 282–3
cups (flat cups or standing bowls) 58–9 63, 294
Cuss, T. P. Camerer, *The Story of Watches* 353
Custom House Quay 17, 104, 122, 123, 221, 256, 274, 359
cutlery 132–9

Dartford 15
dated toys 44–5, 66
dating methods 27–8
Day, Gregory 34, 191
dealers 13
Dean, William 436, 437, 439
Dee, John 20, 22
Denmark, Copenhagen City Museum 29
Didcot, Oxfordshire 359
dining habits 243–4, 296
discs 404–5
dishes 36, 45, 245–74
　see also basins; plates; saucers
Dockhead 17, 78, 135, 155, 156, 170, 254, 293
dolls ('babies') 42, 152
doll's house furniture 185, 191
Dollshouse Miniatures magazine 50
Dou, Gerrit, *A Lady Playing a Clavichord* 198
Drapers' Company, arms of 43, 44, 202, 204–5, 223
drinking and serving vessels 275–307
dripping pans 116–18
Dublin 59, 64, 324
Dulwich Picture Gallery 198
Dumez-Onof (Michel) collection 201

Eames, Penelope 196, 202, 218
East Anglia 279
eating habits 243–4, 296
edged weapons 86–7
educational toys 60
Egan, Geoff 18, 221, 223, 225, 229, 312, 323
　Playthings from the Past 19, 120, 192, 411
Elizabeth I 323
　court of 48, 152
Epitres d'Ovide 168, 320

INDEX

equestrian figures 144–51
Ester, Henry 338, 349
ewers 278–88
    full-size 62, 161, 281, 286
Exchequer Standard (1496) 279
Exeter Flying Post 35

Fairfax-Lucy, Sir Edmund 294
fairs and markets 35–9, 148, 165, 239
fashions in toys 43, 44, 48–50, 56, 60–1, 142
figurines 43, 140–60, 168–77
    female 65, 141, 152–7
    male 63, 65, 158–60, 169–76
finds, licensing arrangement for 15, 17
find spots, recording 17
Finsbury 301
Finsbury Circus 86
firearms 65, 87–104
firedogs (andirons) 184
fire grates 185
fireplaces 184
fire shovels 184, 186, 188–9
fire tongs 189
firewood 184
fish 119–20
fish griddles 65
fishing tackle 324
flagons 278, *see also* ewers
'flat cups' (or standing bowls) 58–9, 63, 294
flat or shallow toy forms 56, 57, 65–6, 142, 143, 146, 149–51, 155–7, 169–76
Fleet Valley site 27, 207
flues 184
foreign imports, law on 42
forks 134
frames 402
    mirror 189–91
Framework Knitters' Master's chair 214
France 29, 45, 61, 65, 124, 143, 189, 202, 255, 278, 289, 346, 349
    Paris 54, 146, 181
        Louvre 287
        Musée de Cluny 78, 146, 169
        Musée national du Moyen Age 124, 284, 290
Frankfurt 154
Froschauer, Johann, *Kuchenmeisterel* 112
frying pans 119–24
    adapted to whirligig 388, 389

furmenty 296
furniture 65, 194–237

game-sellers or hawkers 35, 143, 171
Gammon, Alan 27
Gask, N. 138
Gay, V. 256, 284
'General Lotterie' broadsheet 294
Geneva, Switzerland 154
genre pictures 107–8, 179–80, 184
George IV 380
Germany 29, 42, 45, 136, 137, 138, 154, 255, 278
    Augsburg 50
    Cologne 154
    Frankfurt 154
    Krefeld, Burg Linn, Landschaftsmuseum, 201
    Nuremberg 50, 65
        Germanisches Nationalmuseum 78
        toy fair 36, 39
    Schleswig, Archaeologisches Landesmuseum 234
Gillows (furniture maker) 217
glass 189, 190, 295
Globe Theatre site 268, 271
globular lidded ewers 280, 282
Goldsmiths' Company 337
Granger, William 22
grates 185
grave goods, toys as 60
Gravesend 327
Great Smith Street, Westminster 94
Greenmoor Wharf 19
Greenwich 15, 170, 285, 324
gridirons 63, 124–6
Groenige Museum, Bruges 294
Guild of Bakers 324
Guildhall Museum 9, 13, 14
Guildhall Yard 60
gun carriages 85
guns *see* cannon; muskets; petronels; pistols

haberdashers 34
Haberdashers' Company 88
Halsbury's *Laws of England* 14
Hammersmith 381
hand saws 312
'hards' (barge beds) 11, 15
harlequin 176

Harrison, William, *Description of England* 198
Harsdoerffer, George Philipp, *Vollstandiges Trincir-Buchlein Handlend* 283
Harwich, Essex 324
hat badges 312
hats 176
hawkers 35, 143, 171
hearth furniture and grates 164–86, 187–8
Heath, Richard 351, 352, 436, 437
Heide, H. von der, *The Feast of Ahaseurus and Esther* 201
helmets 146
    (morion) 78
Hepplewhite, George, *The Cabinet Maker and Upholsterer's Guide* 217
Hereford 28, 29, 56, 57, 279
Heritage Lottery Fund 19
Hernmarck, C., *The Art of the European Silversmith* 278
Herod, King 64
Hérouard (dauphin's physician) 48
Hill, Benjamin 352
Hilton Price Collection 103
Histoire d'Olivier de Castille et d'Artus d'Algarbe, L' 201
Histoire du Bon Roi Alexandre, L' 201
hob grates 185
Hodge, Robert Peircy 439, 440
Hodge(s), Robert 437
Holbein, Hans 201
hollow-cast toy forms 56, 60, 65, 66, 143, 144–7, 152, 154–5, 158–60
Holme, Randle, *The Academy of Armory* 116, 118, 127, 181, 234, 245, 279, 283
holy water containers (ampullae) 60, 146
Homer, Ron 136
Honeycomb, Will 24–5
horn books 29
Horne, Eric 373
Hornsby, P., et al. 279
horological features, design and date 341–5
horse
    ceramic 143
    wooden 59, 64
house front 406
household items 178–93
Howells, Mr 35
Hume, Ivor Nöel, *Treasure in the Thames* 14–15, 18

Hungary 59, 65, 143
hunter figures 148, 172
Hux, Thomas 344, 436, 437, 439
Hux, William Thomas 53, 55, 342, 343–5, 372, 436, 437, 439, 440
Hux (toymaker: unknown if T. or W.T.) 43, 45, 162, 338, 341

I(D)Q (maker) 27, 29, 44, 46, 47, 54–5, 57, 65, 67, 136, 247, 441–3
infantrymen 66
inscribed toys 44, 45
    see also maker's marks
inscriptions and devices 202–5
Instituto del Conde de Valencia de Don Juan 86
Ippolyta the Tartarian 48
Ireland, Dublin 59, 64, 324
Italy 29–30, 134
    Venetian glass 189

Jackson, John 34, 44, 247, 259, 276, 298, 436, 438, 439
    tradebill 33
Jackson, William 436, 438, 439
Jaggard, W. 204
Jagger, C. 348
James I 337
Jonathan Horne Antiques 19
Judas Iscariot 64, 142
jugs 28, 29, 63, 65, 278, 288–92

Kew 15
Kingston-type/Kingston wares 281, 288, 290
Kingsway 101
King, T., *The Modern Style of Cabinet Work Exemplified* 218
King William Street 91
Kluber, Hans Hug, *The Family of Hans Rudolf Faesch at Table* 280
knives 135
Knyff, Jacob, *Chiswick from the River* 316
Köferlin, Anna, Baby House 48–50

ladles 65
Lambeth 15
    view towards 11
Landsberg, Herrad von, *Hortus Deliciarum* 61
Landschaftsmuseum, Burg Linn 201

Laroon, Marcellus, 'Cries of London' 43, 143, 171, 172, 197
latten, definition 52, 136
Layton Collection 99
lead alloy toys, discussion of manufacture 52–7
lead-tin alloy analysis 410–23
Lea, Francis 53, 438
Lear Collection of Socket Candlesticks 181
Lea, William 438, 440
Lee, Luke 34
Lesney (makers of Matchbox Series) 40
Lewis, J.M., et al., *Medieval 'Bronze' tripod ewers from Wales* 287
ley metal, definition 32, 410, 419
licensing arrangement for finds 15, 17
lighters 11
Limehouse, view of dock by Two Brewers tavern 24
Limekiln Dock 17, 117, 175, 186, 211, 260, 265, 268, 326, 327
Lincoln's Inn 103
London
    City of London 13, 15, 22
        arms of 43, 44, 201, 202, 204, 205, 206, 208, 209, 211, 225
        population 41
    London Bridge 17, 20–1, 279
        (north) 113, 264
        (south) 111
    'London Cries' (Laroon's 'Cries of London') 43, 143, 171, 172, 197
    London Leadworks 373
    London Museum 9, 13, 287
    London Tradesman, The 43
    London-type wares 161, 278, 284, 286, 287, 288, 289, 290, 291
    London Wall 93, 114
looking glasses 189–91
Louis XIII, as dauphin 48
Louvain, Belgium 388
Louvre 287
Low Countries *see* Netherlands
Lowther Arcade, The 43
Lutma, Jan 283
Luyken, Jan 276
    Het Poppegoed 108

Madrid, Instituto del Conde de Valencia de Don Juan 86
maker's marks 44, 66–7, 247

table of 46–7
male figurines 63, 65, 158–60, 169–76
    see also mounted figures
Mann, J. 97
Mansel, Jean, *La Fleur des Histoires* 127, 166, 235, 275
manufacture of alloy toys 52–7
Marguerite of York 202
markets and fairs 35–9, 148, 165, 239
Mary Queen of Scots 388
Mary Rose 279, 282
Matchbox toy Coronation coach 317
Mathew, Frank 34
Mauritshuis, The Hague 295
Maximilian, Emperor 61
Mayhew, Henry 17, 22
Maze Pond 259
Meckenem, Israel van, *Le Bain de Marie enfant* 234
Medallic Illustrations 388
Medici, Marie de' 202
medieval finds 27, 29, 58–64
Medieval Pottery Research Group 278, 288
Meols, Cheshire 324
Messisburgo, Cristoforo da, *Libro novo* 126
metal detecting 13, 26–7, 28–9
Metropolitan Museum of Art, New York 217
Meyers Collection, Brussels 146
mica 189
military figures 57, 66, 143, 149–51, 172, 173–4
milkmaids 143, 157
Millbank Street 100
mirrors and mirror frames 189–91
Mitchiner, M. 111, 224, 225, 324
Moran, Mick 118
More, Sir Thomas 201
morion (helmet) 78
moulds 35, 44, 45, 56, 57
    jug 28, 29, 56, 275, 279
    watch 56, 351–2
Moulinet, Jean, *La tres desiree et prouffitable naissance du tres illustre enfant Charles d'Austrice* 396
mounted figures 149–51
    knights 43, 60, 61, 63, 65, 140, 142, 144, 146–7
mudlarks 13, 14–19, 22, 26–7
Muscovy Company 189
Musée de Cluny, Paris 78, 146, 169

Musée national du Moyen Age, Paris 124, 284, 290
Museum Boijmans van Beuningen, Rotterdam 181, 287
Museum of London
   origins 9, 13
   purchase of finds 15
musicians 66, 173, 175
muskets 89–97
   full-size 88, 164

Naples 30
Narrow Street, Limehouse 239
National Art Collections Fund 19
navvies 13
Netherlands 29, 35, 42, 45, 59, 61, 63, 152
   Amsterdam 54, 81, 146, 234, 324, 345
     Rijksmuseum 283
   buffets 200, 210
   candlesticks 181, 201
   cannon 81
   cauldrons 111
   chairs 213
   chests 220
   children at play in 36, 75, 108, 142, 179–80, 184, 187, 233, 333, 334, 363
   dishes 247
   dripping pans 117
   ewers and basins 201, 278
   forks 134
   house front (toy) 406
   jugs 278
   male figures 169
   Nieuwlande 197
   plates 249
   pot hangers 127
   Rotterdam 35, 45
     Boijmans van Beuningen Museum 181, 287
   ships 323
   spoons 136, 137, 138
   textiles 202
   The Hague, Mauritshuis 295
   trivets 124
   watches 346
   windmills 393
New Crane Stairs 354
New York 30
Nibbs, Richard Henry, *The Two Brewers Limehouse* 24
Nicholas, St, Feast of 42

Nieuwlande 197
night baskets (voiders) 192
Noel, Aymé 349
Norfolk 152
Norfolk Museums Service 120
Norman period 59
Norton Folgate 255
Norway 136, 138
Nuremberg 50, 65
   Germanisches Nationalmuseum 78
   toy fair 36, 39

Oakeshott, R. Ewart, *The Sword in the Age of Chivalry* 86
Old Queen Street 101
organic materials 31, 59, 60, 64
Osterley Park 218
ownership of foreshore finds 15

painted toys 55
paintings 191
panels 398–404, 405–6
   openwork 399–403
   solid 405–6
Paris 54, 146, 181
   Louvre 287
   Musée de Cluny 78, 146, 169
   Musée national du Moyen Age 124, 284, 290
Parr Pot 293
Pearce, J., et al. 289, 290
pear-shaped jugs 290
pear-shaped lidded ewers 279–80, 282
pedestal ewers 288
peg doll figure 60, 141
Peircy, Robert 35, 276, 436, 437, 439, 440
   trade bill 409
pendant jug 64
Pepys, Samuel 191, 340
Pether, Henry, *York Water Gate and the Adelphi by Moonlight* 365
petronels (arquebuses) 97
Petyt, Silvester 340
pewter, definition 52
Pewterers' Company 44, 55, 247, 276, 282, 288, 298, 343–4, 419
   Court cases 45, 53–4
   standards and regulations 32, 39, 53–4
pewter miniatures, microstructure and composition 54–7, 410–23
pewter toymakers 44, 436–40

Phillip the Good 202
Pickard, Joseph 440
Pickleherring delftware factory, Southwark 245
pictures (for doll's houses) 191
Piggott, Francis 35, 439
pikemen 66, 143, 169–70
pilgrim badges 56, 64, 149, 324
pilgrims' ampullae 60, 144
pilgrim trade 181
Pilson, A.G. 18, 19
pirate 175
pistols 55, 56, 98–103
Pistrucci, Benedetto 380
plates 31, 36, 45, 63, 65, 67, 245–74
   buffet plates 212
   see also basins; dishes; saucers
Poisson, M., *Cris de Paris dessinés d'après Nature* 393
Poitiers, Alienor de, *Les Honneurs de la Cour* 200
pokers 184
Pomeranian coaches 316
Poole, Dorset 325
Popish Plot 39
'poppets' (dolls) 42, 152
porringers (potagers) 45, 296–307
Port of London Authority 15
Portugal 278
post-medieval finds 27, 65–7
potagers (porringers) 45, 296–307
pot hangers 127–8
Pot, Leendert Jansz 35, 45
pots 293
Pre-Construct Archaeology 67
Price, Richard 216
private collectors 13, 18
product development 43
Puisnes Walks About London, The 37, 39
puppets' heads 64, 141, 142

quality control 44, 53–4
Queenhithe/Queenhithe Dock 17, 86, 117, 125, 183, 216, 260, 299, 319, 320, 373, 390, 396
Quick, Edward 436

Rack, Charles 44, 247, 259, 276, 436, 438, 439
Raeren stoneware 293

rammers (ramrods) 104
   artillery 79
Randall, Robert 437, 439
Read, Simon 438
Redhead, Gabriel 437
Richardson, Thomas Miles, *The City from Bankside* 25, 366–7
Richmond, Surrey 381
Rijksmuseum, Amsterdam 283
Robert of Brunne 32
Roberts, Thomas 216
rocking cradles 234
Rodet (watchmaker) 162, 338
Roman de Renaud de Montauban 167, 201, 202
Roman figure 143, 171
Roman finds 30, 239
Rotherhithe 118, 241, 374
Rotterdam 35, 45
   Boijmans van Beuningen Museum 181, 287
Rouen style 289
Royal Arms 214
Royal Collection 283
rubbish deposits 19, 20, 25
Russia 59, 143, 189
Ryton, Malton, Yorkshire 279

St Bartholomew Fair 36–7, 39, 148, 165
St Giles Churchyard 91
St Katherine's Wharf 182
Sala, George Augustus 43
Salisbury 29, 86, 279
Salisbury Museum 94
saucers 245–74
   full-size 255
   see also basins; dishes; plates
saws 312
scabbards 64, 86
Scandinavia (Norway; Sweden; Denmark) 29, 59, 136, 138, 189
Schäfer (Otto) Collection 280
Schleswig, Archaeologisches Landesmuseum 234
Schwarzburg, Prince of 78
Schwarz, Matthäus 145, 362
scissors 313
Scotsman figure 143, 171
sea coal 184, 185
secular badges 56
serving and drinking vessels 275–307

Shakespeare Folger Library, Washington 283, 294
Shaw, Kenny, *Specimens of Ancient Furniture* 199
shears 313
Sheraton, Thomas 217
shies 29, 67, 238–41
ships 43, 59, 64, 66, 323, 324
ships' anchors 324–31
shoes 64
shrines 64
sieving 27
Sigglesthorne, Yorkshire 29, 279
Silleman, Experiens 75, 180, 187, 334, 394
silver toys 30–1, 34, 50
skillets 128–9
   full-size 129
Smithfield 39, 165
Smith, Mr (mudlark) 18
Smith, Thomas 276, 439
Snow, William 353
Society of Antiquaries 111
Society of Thames Mudlarks 18, 26
soil conditions/survival 14, 29, 52, 58, 64
soldiers 57, 66, 143, 149–51, 172, 173–4
Sotro, John 34
South Place Chapel 94
Southwark 39
   (Bermondsey), Abbots Lane 27, 225, 227, 391
Southwark Bridge 155, 259
   (north) 17, 97, 184, 190, 262, 277, 357, 373, 403, 405
   (south) 118, 188, 271, 290, 369, 400
Southwark shore/waterfront 15, 22, 294
Spain 86, 278
   Madrid, Instituto del Conde de Valencia de Don Juan 86
Spanish Armada 43, 66, 323
specialization 43–4, 45
Spencer, Brian 18
spice plates 244
spindle whorls 60
spits 130
spoonmeats 244, 296
spoons 29, 136–9
standing bowls (or flat cups) 58–9, 63, 294
Steelyard 111
Steen, Jan, *The Feast of St Nicholas* 241, 361
stirrup cups 393

Stockholm City Museum 29
stoneware 292, 293
stools 65, 234
Strickland, John 45, 440
Stuart Royal Arms 214
Sturton Foundry, South Petherton, Somerset 115, 129, 163
Sumner Street, near Blackfriars 113, 352
Sun in Aries, The 204
Surrey Whiteware 280, 288, 290
Swan Lane 27
Swan Stairs 248
Swan Street, Southwark 291
Sweden 189
   Stockholm City Museum 29
sweetmeat plates 244
Switzerland 154, 349
   Basle, Kunstmuseum 280
   Geneva 154
swords 86–7
Symmes, Isaac 348

Table of the Assays of Metal 54
tablewares 30, 59, 60, 63, 242–309
tankards 293
Teddington 14, 15
Temple Newsam House, Leeds 216
textiles, personalised 202, 204
Thames Archaeological Survey 20
Thames Barrier 15
Thames foreshore
   commercial history 15, 17, 22
   definition 14
   mudlarks and 14–19, 21
   toys on 20–5
   views 11, 17, 19, 21, 22, 365, 366–7
Thames Frost Fair 239
Thornton, Peter 210
Three Cranes Wharf 90, 398
tin, sources of 411, 421
tin-lead alloy analysis 410–23
tin-lead watches, elemental analysis 424–35
tongs 189
tools 310–13
touchmarks, registration of 421
Tower of London foreshore 15, 124, 185, 267
   view of public beach 25
toy fairs 35–9, 148, 165, 239
toy house front 406

toymakers 35, 43, 44, 57, 436–43
toys
    definition 32, 34
    foreshore finds 20–5
    market/trade 35, 40–51
toysellers and toymen 34
trade bills 33, 409
transport 66, 314–31
Trautner, Johann Georg 39
trays 192
treasure hunting 14, 15, 30
tree bark boat 30
trencher plates 244
trifles, definition 32
trifling metal 32
Trig Stairs 299
Trinitie Bull 34
trinkets, definition 32
tripod ewers 283–5
    full-size 161, 286
trivets 124
Troost, C., *The Quarrel of the Astronomers* 295
twirlers 332–5

Upper Thames Street (Thames Exchange) 111, 128
USA 50, 77, 81, 324, 325, 388

New York 30
    Metropolitan Museum of Art 217
    Washington, Shakespeare Folger Library 283, 294

Vauxhall 15, 22
Vauxhall Bridge, view from 11
Vauxhall glass factory 189
Veer, Johan van der 156
Venetian glass 189
Venne, Adriaen van de 153, 172, 233, 333
Vermeer, Jan, *Het Straatje* 364
Vernay (Arthur S) Inc collection 217
Vickers engineering 40
Victoria and Albert Museum 184, 202, 224, 280, 294
Viking toy ships 59, 324
Vintners' Hall 226
Vintry 27, 182, 209, 359
voiders 192

Wales 287
Wallace Collection 78
Wapping 15, 283, 285, 354, 373
watches 37, 43, 44, 45, 53, 65, 67, 336–60, 369–85
    elemental analysis of tin-lead 55, 424–35
    features, design and date 341–5

watchmaking 337–8
watch moulds 56, 351–2
weapons *see* cannon; muskets; petronels; pistols; swords
Wesson, Hans Jacobsz 283
Westminster 15, 92, 94, 95, 356
Weyden, Roger van der, *Verkündiging* 287
wharves, view of 19, 22
wheeled toys 61
whirligigs (buzz wheels) 67, 119, 121, 386–91
Whitby, Yorkshire 155
Whitefriars Street 281
White, William 438, 440
Wightman, William 53, 54, 437, 440
Willemsen, A. 124, 249
William IV 380
Williamsburg, Virginia 30
windmills 64, 392–7
wine bottles 295
wooden toys 29, 59, 64, 141, 324
Wunderkammer 48, 50
Wynne, Sir John 201

York Cathedral 29

Zedler, Johann Heinrich 50
Zimmerman, Vincentius 350

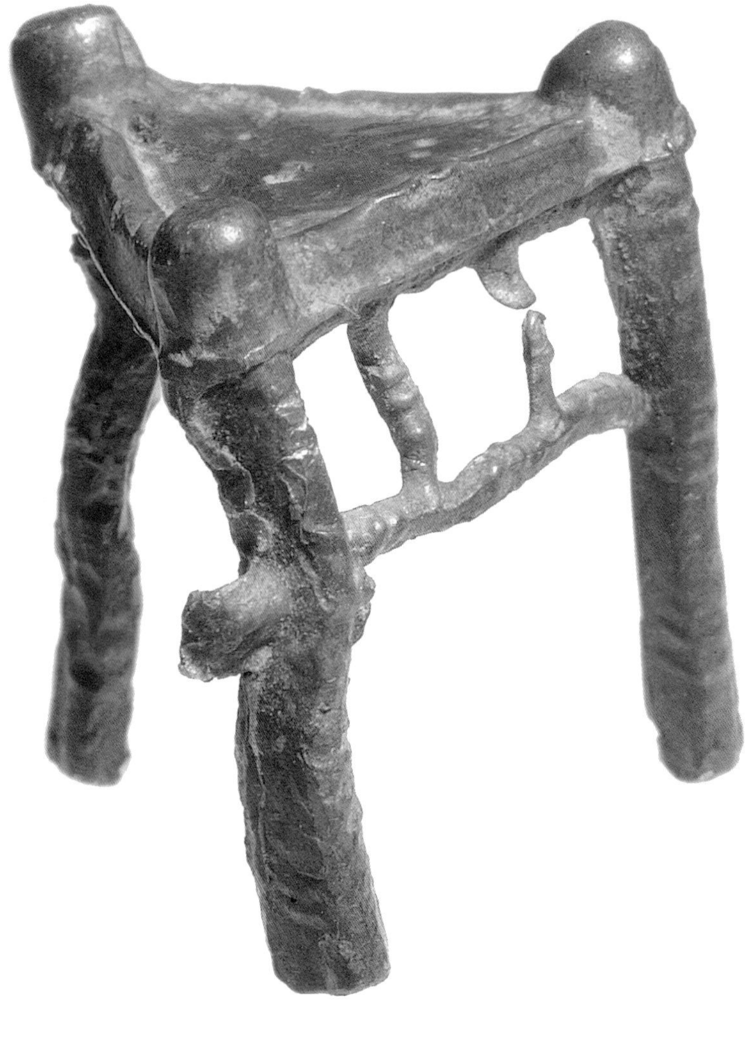

Ih möcht dau fü a' Engela.   Um dös Göld gieb ihn Korb nit Na!   Ih will d... dor...

Wen nur dös Kütschla dort mei wär.   Thout sie mir den Cauteau herlanga.   Dau hauf ers Göld für seih...

Ahn Venesseuch möcht ih Mama!    Und ih dau dös kla Trümmela.   Wos langi dau den...